Programming and Interfacing to the STMCortex-M4 Microcontroller

Han-Way Huang

innovativeink PUBLISHING
A Division of Kendall Hunt

innovativeink
PUBLISHING
A Division of Kendall Hunt

www.innovativeinkpublishing.com
Send all inquiries to:
4050 Westmark Drive
Dubuque, IA 52004-1840

Print ISBN: 979-8-3851-2702-3
Ebook ISBN: 979-8-3851-273-0

Published in the United States of America

Contents

1

Introduction to ARM Processor

1.1 Objectives

After completing this chapter, you will be able to

- Understand the history of the ARM Corporation.
- Describe the important architectural features of the ARM processors.
- Describe the business model of the ARM Corporation.
- Describe the purposes and features of three ARM processor profiles.

1.2 A Brief History of ARM Corporation

The ARM processor architecture dominates today's processor market in mobile applications. From 1985 to 2022, more than 230 billion ARM processors were produced. The share of the ARM architecture in each segment of the processor market is shown in Table 1.1.

The creator of the ARM processor is the British computer manufacturer **Acorn Computers**. In late 1970s, Acorn successfully introduced the 8-bit 6502-based BBC microcomputer. The BBC microcomputer proved to be very successful. At the beginning of 1980s, IBM introduced the IBM PC, which quickly became the dominant PC in the market. Acorn intended to stay competitive and evaluated the 16-bit Motorola 68000 and National Semiconductor 32016 microprocessors. After evaluation, Acorn engineers concluded that neither processor can enable Acorn to stay ahead. The white papers on the Berkeley RISC project inspired Acorn engineers to design their own processor. The first Acorn RISC project was started in October 1983. On April 26, 1985, the first ARM microprocessor implemented in VLSI Technology's 3-μm CMOS technology was received and worked properly. The whole processor used only about 30,000 transistors. Steve Furber and Sophie Wilson are the key designers of the first ARM microprocessor.

The first ARM microprocessor was used as the second processor in the BBC computer. In 1987, Acorn introduced the **Archimedes Computer** using the ARM processor as its central processing unit (CPU). The Archimedes Computer won significant market share in the education markets of the United Kingdom, Ireland, Australia, and New Zealand. By the early 1990s, the U.K. educational market began to turn away from the Archimedes Computer. Apple Macintosh computers and IBM compatible PCs eclipsed the Archimedes Computer in their multimedia capabilities, which led to an erosion of the Archimedes Computer market share. The Archimedes Computer was discontinued in mid-1990s.

Table 1.1 Markets for ARM: 2018 and 2028

Application	Chip Function	2018		2028
		Market share	Market value[2]	Market value[2]
Mobile	Application Processor	90%	$34 billion	$47 billion
	Other mobile chips	40%	$18 billion	$23 billion
Infrastructure	Networking	30%	$15 billion	$20 billion
	Data Center/Cloud	4%	$20 billion	$28 billion
Automotive	IVI and ADAS[1]	75%	$7 billion	$19 billion
	Other automotive chips	10%	$5 billion	$12 billion
Embedded	Controller in IoT Devices	90%	$7 billion	$20 billion
	Microcontrollers/SIM cards	25%	$18 billion	$22 billion
Other markets	Consumer Electronics	40%	$12 billion	$37 billion
	Other chips	35%	$15 billion	$21 billion
Total markets	All chips with processors (TAM)[2]	33%	$150 billion	$250 billion
	All addressable chips (future TAM)[2]	25%	$165 billion	$300 billion

Note. 1. ADAS: Advanced driver assistance system
2. TAM: total available market

VLSI Technology was the silicon foundry for the ARM processors. Apple Computer needed an alternative processor for its products. The low power consumption and good performance of the ARM processor were very attractive to Apple Computer. In the late 1980s, these three companies worked together on newer versions of the ARM processor core. In 1990, Acorn spun off the design team into a new company named **Advanced RISC Machine Ltd.**, which became **ARM Ltd** when its parent company, **ARM Holdings PLC** was listed in the stock market for stock trading. Apple computer has adopted the ARM610 processor as the CPU of its **Newton PDA**.

ARM Ltd continues to revise its processor architecture since then. Since its inception, the ARM processor architecture has gone through nine generations of revision as listed in Table 1.2. ARM processors from ARMv1 to ARMv7 are all 32 bit. However, the ARMv8 and ARMv9 are 64-bit architectures (excluding Cortex-A32, which is a 32-bit architecture), which have been used in many smart phones introduced in 2015 and later.

In the last few years, ARM Ltd also introduced additional families of CPU architectures for

- Edge computing: Neoverse
- Security computing: SecrCore
- Machine learning: Project Trillium (a heterogeneous machine learning platform)

Table 1.2 ARM architecture cores

Architecture	Family
ARMv1	ARM1
ARMv2	ARM2, ARM3
ARMv3	ARM6, ARM7
ARMv4	StrongARM, ARM7TDMI, ARM9TDMI
ARMv5	ARM7EJ, ARM9E, ARM10E, Xscale
ARMv6	ARM11, ARM Cortex-M
ARMv7	ARM Cortex-A, ARM-Cortex-M, ARM-Cortex-R
ARMv8	ARM Cortex-A78, ARM Cortex-A77, Cortex-A76, Cortex-A75, Cortex-A73, Cortex-A72, Cortex-A65AE, Cortex-A65, Cortex-A55, Cortex-A53, Cortex-A35, Cortex-A34, Cortex_A32
ARMv9	Cortex-A710, Cortex-A510

In 1990s, the accelerated adoption of the mobile devices provided an excellent growth opportunity for the ARM processor due to its low power consumption and high performance. As shown in Table 1.1, the ARM processor has become the dominant processor in many areas. On July 18, 2016, ARM Ltd agreed to be acquired by Softbank of Japan at a price of $32 billion.

1.3 ARM's Business Model

Starting as a small company without much resource, ARM decided to adopt the business model of licensing its processor architecture to any interested parties rather than manufacturing and selling its own chips. ARM Ltd collects license fees from every signed license and royalty from every chip sold (royalty is a percentage of the chip sale price).

In 2023, ARM Ltd had an annual income of 3.2 billion in U.S. dollars. More than 30.6 billion ARM processor chips were sold in 2023.

1.4 ARM Processor Profiles

ARM Ltd is creating multiple versions of the processor to target different type of applications over the years. Starting from the seventh generation, ARM Ltd classifies its processors into three different profiles to attract different applications. These three profiles are called **A-profile** (application profile), **R-profile** (real-time profile), and **M-profile** (microcontroller profile). The features of each profile are described in the following sections.

1.4.1 APPLICATION PROFILE: CORTEX-A SERIES

The Cortex-A processors are designed to run a wide variety of complex applications as those required by consumer devices like smartphones, tablets, digital TVs, set-top boxes, **Internet of Things (IoT)** devices, enterprise networking, laptop computers, server solutions, and so on.

At the moment of this writing, processors in this profile include the following:

- 32-bit processors: Cortex-A5, A7, A8, A9, A15, A17, and A32.
- 64-bit processors: Cortex-A34, A35, A53, A55, A57, A65, A65AE, A72, A73, A75, A76, A76AE, A77, A78, A78AE, A78C, A510, A710. The Cortex-A710 is the ARM application processor with the highest performance at the moment (by 2021), which is expected to be implemented using the 3 nm (or better) semiconductor technology and running at 3 GHz. The Cortex-A710 has 10% better integer performance than the Cortex-A78 at 3 GHz and consumes 30% less power.

All Cortex-A processors are designed to support operating systems (requiring a memory management unit to support virtual memory), which is indispensable for hosting complex applications. Cortex-A processors are deeply pipelined. For example, the Cortex-A8 and A77 are implemented with a 13-stage pipeline. The high-end Cortex-A processors adopt many advanced computer technologies such as **superscalar**, out-of-order instruction execution, branch prediction, register renaming, and so on to achieve higher performance. A superscalar computer issues multiple instructions in each clock cycle whenever possible.

To execute instructions out of order, the Cortex-A processor looks ahead a group of instructions to find out if they are independent of the instructions being executed and can be issued. This group of instructions being examined for possible execution is called **out-of-order window**. The out-of-order window for Cortex-A78 is 228 entries.

Cortex-A processor architecture supports:

- Multiple instruction set: 32-bit ARM, 16-bit Thumb, Thumb2 (a mix of 16-bit and 32-bit instructions), digital signal processing (DSP) instruction set, and 64-bit ARM instruction set.
- Single-precision and double-precision floating-point instruction set.
- Virtualization: this extension enables the implementation of virtual machine.
- Large physical address extension (LPAE): this enables the application to address up to 1 TB of physical memory (use 40-bit addressing).

In addition to the ARMv8-A and ARMv9-A architecture support, the Cortex-A processors support the following options to enhance the performance required by applications:

- **TrustZone**: The purpose of this extension is to improve the security of the computer system. This extension provides two virtual processors backed by hardware-based access control. This lets the application core switch between two states, referred to as **worlds** (to reduce confusion with other names for capability domains), in order to prevent information from leaking from the more trusted world to the less trusted world. This world switch is generally orthogonal to all other capabilities of the processor. Memory and peripherals are then made aware of the operating world of the processor and may use this to provide access control to secrets and code on the device.
- **NEON extension**: This extension is a combination of the 64-bit and 128-bit single-instruction-multiple-data (SIMD) instruction set to accelerate multimedia and DSP.

- **Jazelle extension**: Java language is one of the most widely used programming languages for business applications. Java programs are first compiled into bytecode and then interpreted to perform the intended operations. Bytecode interpretation is a slow process without hardware support. This extension is provided to execute bytecode directly in hardware and accelerate the execution of Java, Python, and Perl programs.
- **Multicore technology**: Multicore technology enables the simultaneous execution of multiple threads of a single application or multiple applications. This technology improves overall throughput of the application processor.

At the time of this writing, both the Cortex-A78 and Cortex-A710 can run at 3 GHz when manufactured using the 3-nm semiconductor technology.

Multicore implementation is common in Cortex-A application processors. A core is the CPU of a computer by itself. A multicore Cortex-A chip includes multiple Cortex-A CPUs in the same chip. Today, quad-core and octa-core Cortex-A chips are commonly used in smart phones and tablets. The multicore processors are often in a **big.little** configuration that consists of a few more powerful Cortex-A cores and a few less as powerful Cortex-A cores. For example, a possible combination is a Cortex-A chip to have four Cortex-A76 cores and four Cortex-A55 cores (the KIRIN-990 from HiSilicon is an example). Another possible configuration is having four Cortex-A15 (or A17) cores and four Cortex-A7 cores (the A80 from Allwinner Technology is an example).

The Apple A13 (2019) implements an Apple-designed 64-bit ARMv8.3-A six-core CPU, with two high-performance cores running at 2.65 GHz called **Lightning** and four energy-efficient cores called **Thunder**. Each of the Lightning cores implements machine-learning accelerators called **AMX** blocks. The AMX blocks are capable of up to one trillion operations per second. The A13 also integrates an Apple-designed four-core graphics processing unit. The Apple A13 is manufactured using TSMC's 7 nm semiconductor technology.

1.4.2 REAL-TIME PROFILE: CORTEX-R SERIES

The Cortex-R processors are designed to offer solutions for embedded systems that require high performance, high reliability, high availability, maintainability, and deterministic real-time responses.

High performance of the processor is the prerequisite for achieving deterministic real-time response. The Cortex-R processor implements the following technologies to achieve high performance:

- Deep pipeline: Deep pipeline enables the processor to run at higher clock rates (more than 1 GHz).
- Dual-core or quad-core multiprocessing: Dual-core or quad-core systems enable simultaneous application execution.
- SIMD instruction set: The SIMD instruction set may accelerate multimedia and DSP.

To ensure **real-time response to interrupt** requests, the Cortex-R processor is designed with

- Bounded and deterministic interrupt response,
- Tightly coupled memories (TCM) local to the processor so that interrupt service routine can be quickly executed, and
- Low-latency mode to accelerate interrupt entry.

High reliability is another important feature of the Cortex-R processor. The following measures are taken to minimize the possible errors:

- Including a memory protection unit to enforce access privilege (user mode and privileged mode);
- Implementing error correction code (ECC) to detect and correct data errors that occurred in the first-level memory system and buses (memory system closest to the CPU);
- Implementing dual-core lock-step execution of application to detect errors. The two cores run the same program and compare their results in every clock cycle. If the results differ, then one of them has an error.

Real-time performance and high reliability must be achieved at low cost. The design of the Cortex-R processors uses the following methods to achieve **cost effectiveness**:

- Circuit techniques to lower the processor power consumption.
- Configurable debug breakpoints and watch-points to facilitate product development and shorten time-to-market.

There are six devices of the Cortex-R processor at the time of this writing: Cortex-R4, R5, R8, R52, R52+, and R82. The Cortex-R82 is designed for any real-time application that requires the highest performance. The Cortex-R4, R5, and R52 are implemented in an 8-stage pipeline whereas the Cortex-R7 and R8 are implemented using an 11-stage pipeline. Cortex-R4, R5, and R7 implement dual cores whereas the Cortex-R8 and R52 are quad-core processors.

Cortex-R82 is the only 64-bit Cortex-R processor. It enables the implementation of up to eight cores. Cortex-R processors are often used as storage controller to achieve high performance and reliability. According to ARM, 85% or more of current storage solutions use Cortex-R processors.

1.4.3 MICROCONTROLLER PROFILE: CORTEX-M SERIES

The ARM Cortex-M processor family is a range of processors designed to target the widest range of applications (embedded systems) for the microcontrollers, which have been dominated by the traditional 8/16/32-bit microcontrollers. The Cortex-M family consists of ten 32-bit subfamilies of processors: Cortex-M0, M0+, M1, M3, M4, M7, M23, M33, M35P, and M55.

Cortex-M0 and M0+

These two processors are designed to be low-power (16 μW/MHz and 11.2 μW/MHz) and low-cost alternatives to the traditional 8/16 microcontrollers in a wide variety of applications. Both processors implement 56 instructions and take less than 12,000 transistors to implement their CPU core. Cortex-M0 and M0+ are designed to support low-power connectivity such as Bluetooth Low Energy (BLE), IEEE 802.15, and Z-wave. **Z-wave** is a wireless communications protocol designed for home automation, specifically to remotely control applications in residential and light commercial.

Cortex-M0 and M0+ processors are competitive in chip cost compared t0 8/16-bit microcontrollers and have advantages in performance and power consumption. Cortex-M0 and Cortex-M0+ are implemented using a three-stage and two-stage pipeline, respectively. These devices are usually running at a clock rate from 24 MHz to 50 MHz. However, there is no reason that the Cortex-M0 or M0+ devices cannot run at much higher frequency (for example, higher than 100 MHz) if they are manufactured using more advanced semiconductor process.

Cortex-M1

Cortex-M1 is designed for implementation in FPGAs. The Cortex-M1 processor enables original equipment manufacturers (OEMs) to achieve significant cost savings through rationalization of software and tools investments across multiple projects spanning FPGA, ASIC, and ASSP, plus greater vendor independence through use of an industry-standard processor. Typical applications include communications, broadcast, automotive, consumers, military/aerospace, and industrial. (**ASSP** stands for **application-specific standard product** and is an integrated circuit that implements a specific function that appeals to a wide market. As opposed to ASICs that combine a collection of functions and are designed by or for one customer, ASSPs are available as off-the-shelf components. ASSPs are used in all industries, from automotive to communications.)

However, the Cortex-M1 processor has proved to be unsuccessful due to its lower performance. Instead, the top two FPGA vendors Xilinx and Altera have chosen to introduce system-on-a-chip (SoC) products that incorporate application processors such as the 32-bit dual-core Cortex-A9 or the 64-bit quad-core Cortex-A53 onto the FPGA chip to meet the high-performance requirement. The SoC products from Xilinx and Altera consist of the processor core (either dual-core Cortex-A9 or quad-core Cortex-A53) and the reconfigurable logic cells and memory. To become more competitive, the Xilinx's Zynq UltraScale+ products also incorporate a dual-core Cortex-R5 for real-time processing and a graphic processor ARM Mali-400MP to accelerate graphics processing in addition to the quad-core Cortex-A53 processor.

Cortex-M3

The Cortex-M3 processor is designed for applications that require real-time performance and low power. Introduced in 2004, the Cortex-M3 processor is implemented using a three-stage pipeline. The Cortex-M3 processor from different vendors may run at a frequency as low as 24 MHz up to as high as 180 MHz. Of course, the Cortex-M3 processor can run at even higher frequencies when manufactured in a more advanced semiconductor process.

The Cortex-M3 implements the whole Thumb-2 instruction set. The Thumb-2 instruction set consists of 32-bit and 16-bit instructions to achieve the performance of 32-bit instructions and the code density of a 16-bit instruction set.

Like the Cortex-M0 and M0+ processors, the Cortex-M3 processor supports sleep modes to reduce power consumption.

The Cortex-M3 processor implements 32-bit multiply and divide operations directly in hardware to achieve higher performance for these two operations.

Cortex-M4

The Cortex-M4 processor can be considered as a Cortex-M3 processor adding a DSP and a single-precision floating-point instruction set. It is developed to address digital signal control market that demands an efficient, easy-to-use blend of control and signal processing capabilities. The target applications of the Cortex-M4 processor include motor control, automotive, power management, embedded audio, and industrial automation.

Cortex-M4 processor is implemented using a three-stage pipeline plus **branch speculation** to minimize the performance lost due to the branch instructions.

Dual-core implementation in the big.little and homogeneous configurations are available for the Cortex-M4 processor. NXP's dual-core products adopt the big.little configuration. The big core is a Cortex-M4 processor whereas the little core is a Cortex-M0 or M0+ processor. In normal operation, most of the computation-intensive operations (those involving floating-point and DSP) are assigned to the big core whereas those operations that involve user interface and house-keeping applications are assigned to the little core. One example is the LPC4300 series microcontrollers that consist of a Cortex-M4 and a Cortex-M0. Both processors can run at a clock rate of 204 MHz.

The dual-core devices from Atmel consist of two Cortex-M4 processors with one processor that supports floating-point instructions in hardware whereas the other does not. These devices are designed to run at 120 MHz.

Cortex-M7

The Cortex-M7 was announced in the Fall of 2014. Samples of Cortex-M7 chips became available in early 2015. Currently, Microchip, NXP, and ST are the three major licensees. ST Microelectronics introduced the most devices in Cortex-M7 family.

The Cortex-M7 processor is implemented in a six-stage pipeline with branch prediction. Both instruction and data cache memory are included to improve the memory access performance. This is a superscalar processor that issues two instructions in each clock cycle. In addition to supporting all the instruction sets supported by the Cortex-M4, the Cortex-M7 also supports double-precision floating-point instructions in hardware. The Cortex-M7 devices from ST may run at 550 MHz.

Cortex-M23

The Cortex-M23 devices include the TrustZone security feature, provide memory protection capability, and are ideal for use in energy-harvesting IoT nodes.

Cortex-M33

The Cortex-M33 devices also implement the TrustZone security feature to prevent information leaking from high-privilege zone to low-privilege zone. They also provide enhanced security services including dedicated secure user memory space for Secure Boot, symmetric and asymmetric crypto accelerations, memory and IP protection, independent read out protection between **secure/nonsecure** domains, active IO tamper detection, certified cryptolib, and embedded Secure Firmware Install loader and ecosystem.

Cortex-M35P

In addition to implementing the TrustZone security feature, this family of devices also provides a rich set of cryptographic services to mitigate possible attacks in a wide variety of operation environments.

Cortex-M55

Cortex-M55 is the most AI-capable Cortex-M processor and delivers the most efficient machine learning and DSP performance for Cortex-M. It simplifies AI implementation for endpoint.

1.5 Features of the ARM Processor Architecture

ARM processors are designed with the **Reduced Instruction Set Computer** (**RISC**) philosophy in mind and have the following features:

- General-purpose CPU registers.
  - The 32-bit ARM CPU has 16 32-bit general-purpose registers referred to as R0 to R15. All except the last three (R13, R14, and R15) can be used in every instruction. R13 to R15 are used as stack pointer (SP), link register (LR), and program counter (PC), respectively. There are 16 64-bit registers to support SIMD capability.
  - The 64-bit ARM CPU has 31 general-purpose 64-bit registers and a dedicated zero register. The program counter (PC) is no longer directly accessible as a register. There are 32 64-bit SIMD registers.
- Load/store architecture. Only the load and store instructions can access memory locations. All other instructions must use the CPU register or a value in the instruction as their operands.
- Only 32-bit instructions (referred to as **ARM instruction set** only) were initially supported by the 32-bit ARM processor. This choice simplifies the instruction decoding and pipelining at the cost of code density. The **Thumb** instruction set was introduced in 1995 to reduce the program size but it turns out to be less efficient for implementing more complex operations. The **Thumb2** instruction set introduced in 2003 provides both the 16-bit and 32-bit instructions. The Thumb2 instruction allows the application to achieve the code density of the Thumb instruction set and the performance of the ARM instruction set.
- Single cycle instruction execution. Through pipelining, most instructions are executed in one clock cycle.
- Conditional execution of most instructions (32-bit instructions only), reducing performance lost due to branch instructions and compensating for the lack of a branch predictor.
- Arithmetic instructions alter condition codes only when desired.
- 32-bit barrel shifter, which can be used without performance penalty with most arithmetic instructions and address calculations.
- Use a GPR as the **link register** to hold the **function call return address** to accelerate function calls.
- DSP and floating-point operation support in hardware. All Cortex-A, Cortex-R, and Cortex-M7 processors provide DSP and floating-point instructions to accelerate execution of applications that require them. All Cortex-M4 processors implement DSP instruction set and may optionally support single-precision floating-point instructions.

1.5.1 CONDITIONAL INSTRUCTION EXECUTION

The conditional instruction execution feature (called predication) is implemented with a **4-bit condition code selector** (the predicate) on every 32-bit instruction.

- One of the 4-bit codes is reserved as an **escape code** to specify certain unconditional instructions. Almost all common instructions are conditional.
- This feature saves the use of branch instruction and eliminates the **branch overhead**.
- Most CPU architectures only have condition codes on branch instructions.

For example, the loop:

```
while (j != k) {
        if (j > k)
                j -= k;
        else
                k -= j;
}
```

can be translated to the following ARM assembly instruction sequence; variables j and k are assigned to register Rj and Rk

```
loop:   cmp     Rj, Rk          ; set condition code NE, GT, or LT
        subgt   Rj, Rj, Rk      ; if GT, j = j – k
        sublt   Rk, Rk, Rj      ; if LT, k = k – j
        bne     loop            ; if NE, return to the loop
```

1.5.2 USE OF THE BARREL SHIFTER

Multiplying and dividing a number by the power of 2 can be implemented by shifting the given number left or right by an appropriate number of places. Left shift or right shift can be performed by using a barrel shifter. When the arithmetic or logical operation to be performed between two operands requires the second operand to be first multiplied or divided by a power of 2, then this operation (implemented by shifting left or right) can be folded into the data processing instructions (by passing the second operand through the barrel shifter), producing denser code while at the same time reducing memory accesses. For example, the operation

```
b += (k >> 2);
```

can be translated into a single-word, single-cycle instruction on the ARM:

```
ADD     Rb, Rb, Rk, LSR #2
```

1.5.3 PIPELINES AND OTHER IMPLEMENTATION ISSUES

The processor ARM7 (in ARMv3 architecture) and earlier implementations have a three-stage pipeline—the stages being fetch, decode, and execute. More stages are added to the later generations of ARM processors to achieve higher performance. For example, the Cortex-A8 has 13 pipeline stages. Additional implementation changes for higher performance include a faster adder, superscalar design, out-of-order instruction execution, and more extensive **branch prediction logic**.

1.5.4 COPROCESSORS

The ARM processor is designed to target as many applications as possible. To achieve acceptable performance and stay competitive, additional features (for example, new instructions required to perform operations specific to the new application) may be needed for certain special applications. However, the current semiconductor technology may not allow the desired additional features to be implemented on the same semiconductor die with the ARM processor.

The ARM architecture provides a nonintrusive way of extending the instruction set using "coprocessors," which can be addressed using MCR, MRC, MRRC, MCRR, and similar instructions. These instructions allow data transfer between the main ARM processor and the coprocessor. For example, the MCR instruction copies the contents of a register in the CPU to a register in the coprocessor. The MCRR instruction copies the contents of multiple CPU registers to a range of registers in the coprocessor. The MRC and MRRC instructions perform the reverse operation. The coprocessor space is divided logically into 16 coprocessors with numbers from 0 to 15, with coprocessor 15 (cp15) being reserved for some typical control functions like managing the caches and **memory management unit** (MMU) operation (on processors that have one).

In ARM-based machines, peripheral devices are usually attached to the processor by mapping their physical registers into the ARM memory space or into the coprocessor space or connecting to another device (a bus) which in turn attaches to the processor. Coprocessor accesses have lower latency, so some peripherals (for example an XScale interrupt controller) are designed to be accessible in both ways (through memory and through coprocessors).

1.5.5 DEBUGGING SUPPORT

All modern ARM processors include hardware debugging facilities. Software debuggers perform basic operations like halting, stepping, and breakpointing of code by utilizing these debugging facilities. These facilities are built using the JTAG support, though some newer cores optionally support ARM's own two-wire **SWD** protocol.

1.5.6 DIGITAL SIGNAL PROCESSING ENHANCEMENT INSTRUCTIONS

The ARM architecture adds instructions to improve the performance of DSP and multimedia applications. Instructions such as **multiply-and-accumulate**, unsigned and signed **saturate/. add and subtract**, **count leading zeros** are provided to support DSP processing.

1.5.7 THUMB INSTRUCTIONS

Processors since ARM7TDMI add a **Thumb state** to execute 16-bit Thumb instructions.

In thumb state, a compact 16-bit encodings are used to represent a subset of ARM instructions to achieve higher code density. Thumb instructions have less functionality compared with ARM instructions and hence some operations require multiple Thumb instructions to implement.

1.5.8 THUMB2 INSTRUCTIONS

The Thumb2 technology extends the original Thumb instruction set with many 32-bit instructions. The included 32-bit Thumb2 instructions permit Thumb code to achieve performance like the ARM code, with code density better than that of the earlier Thumb code.

Many common operations are most efficiently executed using 16-bit instructions. Most 16-bit instructions can only access the first eight of the ARM core registers, R0 to R7. These registers are called **low registers**. A small number of 16-bit instructions can also access high registers, R8 to R15. Many operations that would require two or more 16-bit instructions can be more efficiently executed using a single 32-bit instruction. All 32-bit instructions can access all of the ARM core registers, R0 to R15. The ARM and Thumb2 instruction sets can **interwork** freely, that is, different procedures can be compiled or assembled to different instruction sets, and still be able to call each other efficiently.

1.5.9 CHANGING BETWEEN THUMB STATE AND ARM STATE

A processor in the ARM state executes ARM instructions, and a processor in Thumb state executes Thumb instructions. A processor in the Thumb state can enter the **ARM state** by executing any of the following instructions: BX, BLX, or an LDR or LDM that loads the PC.

A processor in the ARM state can enter the Thumb state by executing any of the same instructions.

In ARMv7, a processor in the ARM state can also enter the Thumb state by executing an ADC, ADD, AND, ASR, BIC, EOR, LSL, LSR, MOV, MVN, ORR, ROR, RRX, RSB, RSC, SBC, or SUB instruction that has the PC as destination register and does not set the condition flags.

ARM recommends that new software uses the BX or BLX instruction to change from one state to another. ARM recommends that software uses the **BX LR** instruction to return from a procedure, not **MOV PC, LR**.

1.6 A Comparison of Performance of Cortex-M Processors

It would be interesting to know the performance of different versions of the Cortex-M processors. Two benchmarks are used the most to compare the relative performance of microcontrollers: one is the older **Dhrystone benchmark** and the other is the **CoreMark benchmark**. In either benchmark, the higher the score, the better the performance.

Dhrystone is a synthetic computing program developed in 1984 by Reinhold Weicker intended to be representative of system programming. Reinhold collected data from a wide range of software, including programs written in Fortran, PL/1, SAL, ALGOL 68, and Pascal. He then characterized these programs in terms of various common constructs: procedure calls, pointer indirection assignments, etc. From this he wrote the Dhrystone benchmark to correspond to a representative mix of the program constructs. Dhrystone contains no floating-point operations. Its purpose is to evaluate the general-purpose computation performance. The initial Dhrystone was written in Ada language. Later, the C version was written for Unix (by Rick Richardson). The Dhrystone benchmark result is reported in terms of **Dhrystone million instructions per second** (DMIPS) when the processor speed is 1 MHz or DMIPS/MHz.

CoreMark is a benchmark that aims to measure the performance of CPU used in embedded systems. It was developed in 2009 by Shay Gal-On at Embedded Microprocessor Benchmark Consortium (EEMBC) and is intended to become an industry standard. The code is written in C and contains implementations of the following algorithms: list processing (find and sort), matrix manipulation (common matrix operations), state machine (determine if an input stream contains valid numbers), and CRC. The benchmark result of CoreMark is reported using the value of CoreMarks/MHz or the number of iterations per second that the processor completed when the processor speed is 1 MHz.

ARM Ltd has done extensive benchmarks on all the processors that it licenses to other companies. The benchmark results of Cortex-M0, Cortex-M0+, Cortex-M3, Cortex-M4, and Cortex-M7 are listed in Table 1.3. The performance of the Cortex-M7 processor is more than twice as good as that of the Cortex-M0 and Cortex-M0+ at the same clock rate. The Cortex-M7 doesn't perform twice as well as the Cortex-M4 due to the limited parallelism contained in the program even though it can issue twice as many instructions in each clock cycle. The Dhrystone benchmarks were performed on Cortex-M4 processors with and without floating-point unit (FPU) and the results are slightly different.

Table 1.3 Benchmark scores of Cortex-M processors

Processor	Dhrystone (DMIPS/MHz)	CoreMark/MHz
Cortex-M0	0.87/1.02/1.27[(1)]	2.33
Cortex-M0+	0.95/1.11/1.36[(1)]	2.42
Cortex-M3	1.25/1.50/1.89[(1)]	3.34
Cortex-M4	1.25/1.52/1.91[(1)](No FPU) 1.27/1.55/1.95[(1)](with FPU)	3.4
Cortex-M7	2.14/2.55/3.23[(1)]	5

Note.
1. The first result abides by all of the "ground rules" laid out in the Dhrystone documentation, the second permits inlining of functions, not just the permitted C string libraries, while the third additionally permits simultaneous ("multi-file") compilation.

1.7 ST Cortex-M4 Microcontrollers

All the Cortex-M4 microcontrollers from ST implement an on-chip single-precision FPU. These Cortex-M4 devices are divided into the following subfamilies:

- STM32F3: This subfamily of Cortex-M4 microcontrollers provides from 16 to 512 KB of flash memory and can run at 72 MHz.
- STM32F4: This subfamily of Cortex-M4 microcontrollers provides from 256 KB to 2 MB of flash memory and can run at 180 MHz.
- STM32L4: This subfamily of Cortex-M4 microcontrollers provides from 64 KB to 1 MB of flash memory and can run at 80 MHz.
- STM32L4+: This subfamily of Cortex-M4 microcontrollers provides from 1 to 2 MB of flash memory and can run at 120 MHz.
- STM32G4: This subfamily of Cortex-M4 microcontrollers provides from 32 to 512 KB of flash memory and can run at 170 MHz.

1.7.1 CORTEX-M4 PROCESSOR BLOCK DIAGRAM

A Cortex-M4 microcontroller consists of a Cortex-M4 processor core licensed from ARM Ltd and many additional peripherals added by the microcontroller vendor. The block diagram of the Cortex-M4 processor is shown in Figure 1.1.

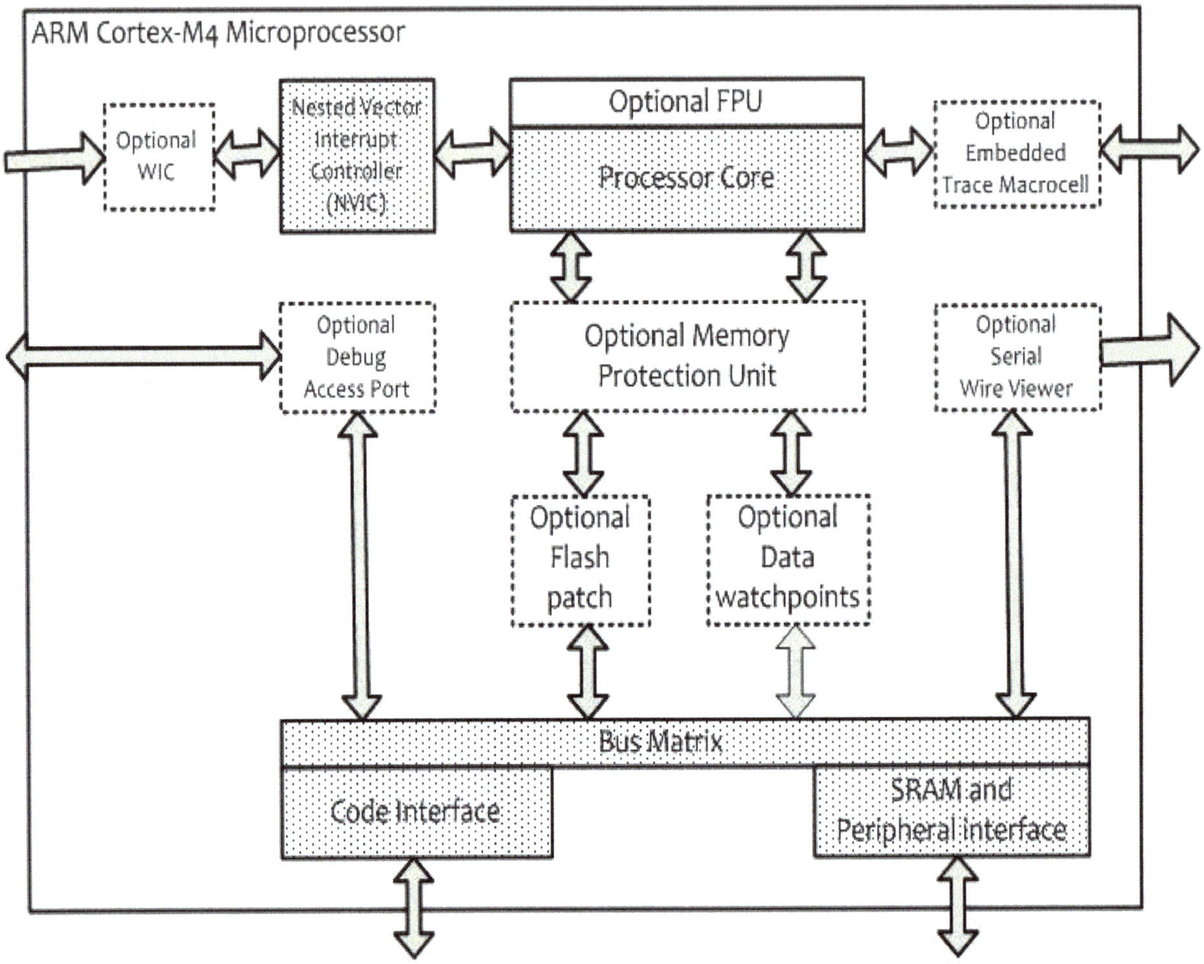

Figure 1.1 Cortex-M4 block diagram

In Figure 1.1,

- The Cortex-M4 provides Icode AHB-Lite instruction interface to access program memory (flash memory).
- The Dcode AHB-Lite Data Interface is provided for accessing data memory (SRAM).
- The Cortex-M4 supports **unaligned data accesses** and implements atomic bit manipulation for peripheral control, system spinlocks, and thread-safe Boolean data handling. If the least significant two bits of the address used to access a 32-bit data are not 00, then the access is an **unaligned access**. In the same token, if the least significant bit of the address used to access a 16-bit memory location is not 0, then the access is also an unaligned access.

- The **memory protection unit** (**MPU**) provides fine-grain memory control, enabling applications to utilize multiple privilege levels, separating and protecting code, data, and stack on a task-by-task basis.
- The **JTAG** and **SWD** ports are provided to support software debug activities.
- The **flash patch and breakpoint unit** (**FPB**) provides up to eight hardware breakpoint comparators that debuggers can use.

1.7.2 PROCESSOR MODES AND PRIVILEGE LEVELS

The Cortex-M4 processor supports two operation modes: **thread mode** and **handler mode**. The thread mode is used to execute application software whereas the handler mode is used to handle exceptions. The processor enters the thread mode (but in privileged execution) after reset.

Software execution has two privilege levels: **unprivileged** and **privileged** levels. At the privileged level, the processor can execute any instruction and access any system resources. At the unprivileged level, the processor has limited access to system registers using the MSR and MRS instructions and cannot use the CPS instruction to mask interrupts. The CPS instruction has two versions. One version (CPSIE I) is executed to enable interrupts whereas the other version (CPSID I) is used to disable interrupts. The processor cannot access the system timer, NVIC, or system control block in the unprivileged level.

In thread mode, the **CONTROL** register (in CPU) controls whether the software execution is privileged or unprivileged. In handler mode, software execution is always privileged.

Only privileged software can write to the CONTROL register to change the privilege level for software execution in the thread mode. Unprivileged software can use the **SVC** instruction to make a supervisor call to transfer control to privileged software.

1.7.3 STACKS

A stack supports push and pull operation. The Cortex-M4 stack is **descending** in the sense that it grows toward memory region with lower addresses. The stack uses a **stack pointer** to hold the address of the last stacked item. When pushing an element into the stack, the processor decrements the stack pointer first and then copies the element to the location pointed to by the stack pointer. The Cortex-M4 has two types of stacks: **main stack** and **process stack**. In the **handler mode**, the processor uses the main stack. In the thread mode, the CONTROL register controls whether the processor uses the main stack or the process stack.

1.7.4 CPU REGISTERS

Like other Cortex-M processors, the Cortex-M4 processor implements 16 registers in the CPU. These registers are referred to as **core registers** and are shown in Figure 1.2.

- **R0 to R12** are 32-bit general-purpose registers for data operations.
- **R13** is used as the stack pointer. In the thread mode, the bit 1 of the CONTROL register selects the stack pointer to use. When this bit is 0, the **main stack pointer** (**MSP**) is used. Otherwise, the **process stack pointer** (**PSP**) is used. After reset, the contents of the MSP are 0x00000000.

- **R14** holds the return address during a subroutine call or an exception.
- **R15** is used as the **program counter** (**PC**). It holds the address of the next instruction to be fetched and executed.

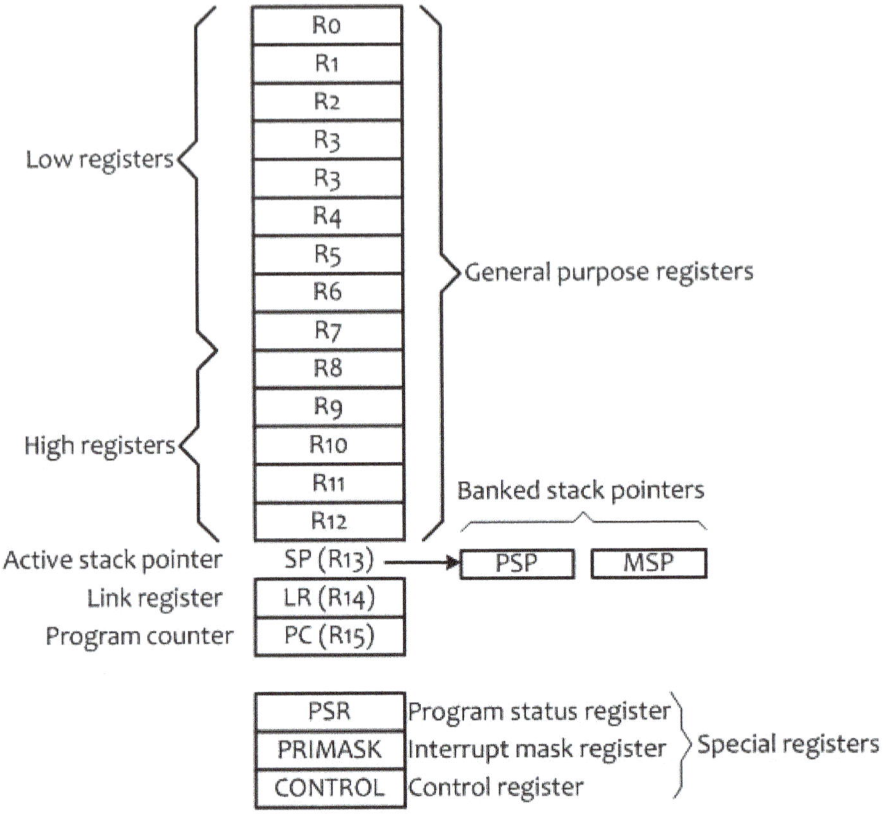

Figure 1.2 Cortex-M4 core registers

1.7.5 PROGRAM STATUS REGISTER

The **program status register** (**PSR**) combines the **application program status register** (**APSR**), **interrupt program status register** (**IPSR**), and the **execution program status register** (**EPSR**). These three registers occupy mutual exclusive bit fields in the 32-bit PSR.

These registers can be accessed individually or as a combination of two or all three registers using the register name as an argument to the MSR or MRS instructions. The MSR instruction moves the contents of a general register to a special register. For example:

(1) Use PSR to refer to all three program status registers. The instruction “MRS R1, PSR” copies the contents of all three program status registers into R1.

(2) Use APSR_nzcvq to refer to the N, Z, C, V, and Q bits in the APSR register. The instruction “MSR APSR_nzcvq R2” writes the bit 27 to 31 of R2 to the Q, V, C, Z, and N bits of the APSR register.

The PSR combinations and attributes are shown in Table 1.4.

Table 1.4 PSR register combinations

Register	Type	Combination
PSR	RW[1, 2]	APSR, EPSR, and IPSR
IEPSR	RO	EPSR and IPSR
IAPSR	RW[1]	APSR, and IPSR
EAPSR	RW[2]	APSR and EPSR

Note.
1. The processor ignores writes to the IPSR bits.
2. Reads of the EPSR bits returns zero, and the processor ignores writes to these bits.

These registers can be accessed individually or as a combination of two or all three registers using the register name as an argument to the MSR or MRS instructions. MSR moves from a general register to a special register. For example:

a) Read all of the registers using PSR with the MRS instruction.

b) Write to the APSR using APSR with the MSR instruction.

The contents of the PSR register are shown in Figure 1.3. The contents of the APSR, IPSR, and EPSR are a subset of the PSR register and are shown in Figures 1.4 to 1.6, respectively.

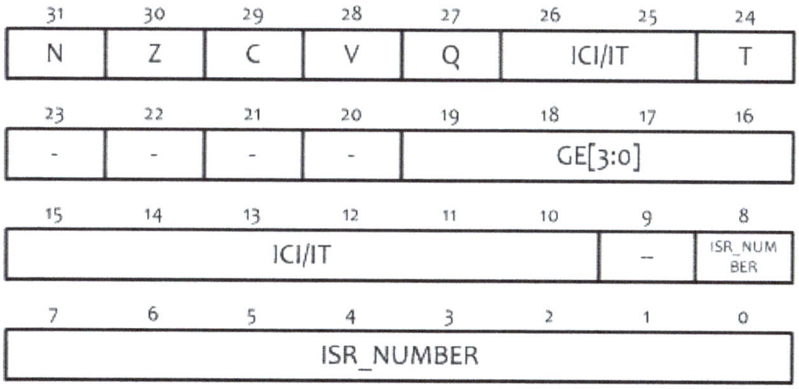

Figure 1.3 Program status register (PSR)

31	30	29	28	27	26	25	24
N	Z	C	V	Q	–		–

23	22	21	20	19	18	17	16
-	-	-	-	GE[3:0]			

15	14	13	12	11	10	9	8
–						–	–

7	6	5	4	3	2	1	0
–							

N: Negative flag
- 0: Operation result was positive, zero, greater than, or equal
- 1: Operation result was negative or less than.

Z: Zero flag
- 0: Operation result was not zero
- 1: Operation result was zero

C: Carry flag
- 0: Add operation did not result in a carry bit or subtract operation resulted in a borrow.
- 1: Add operation resulted in a carry bit or subtract operation did not result in a borrow bit.

V: Overflow flag
- 0: Operation did not result in an overflow.
- 1: Operation resulted in an overflow.

Q: DSP overflow and saturation flag
- 0: Saturation has not occurred since reset or since the bit was last cleared.
- 1: An SAT or USAT instruction results in saturation. This bit is cleared by an MRS instruction.

GE[19:16]: Greater than or equal flag
- See SEL instruction for more information.

Figure 1.4 Application Program status register (APSR)

31	30	29	28	27	26	25	24
–	–	–	–	–	–		–

23	22	21	20	19	18	17	16
-	-	-	-	–			

15	14	13	12	11	10	9	8
–						–	ISR_NUMBER

7	6	5	4	3	2	1	0
ISR_NUMBER							

ISR_NUMBER: Number of the current exception
- See chapter 5 for more information

Figure 1.5 Interrupt Program status register (IPSR)

31	30	29	28	27	26	25	24
--	--	--	--	--	ICI/IT		T
23	**22**	**21**	**20**	**19**	**18**	**17**	**16**
-	-	-	-	--			
15	**14**	**13**	**12**	**11**	**10**	**9**	**8**
ICI/T						--	--
7	**6**	**5**	**4**	**3**	**2**	**1**	**0**
--							

ICI: Interruptible-continuable instruction

When an interrupt occurs during the execution of an LDM, STM, PUSH, VLDM, VSTM, VPUSH, or VPOP instruction, the processor stops the load multiple or store multiple instruction operation temporarily and stores the next register number in the multiple operation in EPSR[15:12]. After servicing the interrupt, the processor returns to the register pointed to by bits 15:12 and resumes the execution of the multiple load or store instruction. When the EPSR holds the ICI execution state, bits[26:25, 11:10] are zero.

IT: If-then instruction

Indicates the execution state bits of the IT instruction. The if-then block contains up to four instructions following an IT instruction. Each instruction in the block is conditional. The conditions for the instructions are either all the same, or some can be inverse of others.

T: Thumb state

The Cortex-M4 processor only supports the execution of instructions in Thumb state. T bit can be cleared by:

(1) Instructions BLX, BX, and POP{PC}

(2) Restoration from stacked xPSR value on an exception return.

(3) Bits 0 of the vector value on an exception entry or reset

Attempting to execute instructions when the T bit is 0 results in a fault or lockup.

Figure 1.6 Exception Program status register (EPSR)

1.7.6 EXCEPTION MASK REGISTERS

Only the bit 0 of the **priority mask register** (**PRIMASK**) is implemented. When the bit 0 (PM bit) of the PRIMASK register is set to 1, all exceptions with configurable priority are disabled.

Only the bit 0 of the **fault mask register** (**FAULTMASK**) is implemented. When the bit 0 of the FAULTMASK register is set to 1, all exceptions except for nonmaskable interrupt (NMI) are disabled.

The **base priority mask register** (**BASEPRI**) defines the minimum priority for exception. The contents of the BASEPRI are shown in Figure 1.7. When the BASEPRI register is set to a nonzero value, it prevents the activation of all exceptions with the same or lower priority as the BASEPRI value.

31	30	29	28	27	26	25	24
--	--	--	--	--	--	--	--
23	**22**	**21**	**20**	**19**	**18**	**17**	**16**
-	-	-	-	--	--	--	--
15	**14**	**13**	**12**	**11**	**10**	**9**	**8**
-	-	-	-	--	--	--	--
7	**6**	**5**	**4**	**3**	**2**	**1**	**0**
BASEPRI							

BASEPRI: Priority mask bits
0000: no effect
Nonzero value: The base priority for exception processing. The processor does not process any exception with a priority value greater than or equal to BASEPRI. The processor implements only bit 7 to 4 of this field, bit 3 to 0 are read as 0 and ignores writes. Higher priority field values correspond to lower exception priorities.

Figure 1.7 Base priority mask register (BASEPRI)

1.7.7 CONTROL REGISTER

The CONTROL register controls the stack used and the privilege level for software execution when the processor is in the **Thread** mode. The contents of the CONTROL register are shown in Figure 1.8.

31	30	29	28	27	26	25	24
–	–	–	–	–	–	–	–
23	**22**	**21**	**20**	**19**	**18**	**17**	**16**
-	-	-	-	–	–	–	–
15	**14**	**13**	**12**	**11**	**10**	**9**	**8**
-	-	-	-	–	–	–	–
7	**6**	**5**	**4**	**3**	**2**	**1**	**0**
-	-	-	-	–	–	SPSEL	nPRIV

SPSEL: Active stack pointer
0: MSP is the current stack pointer.
1: PSP is the current stack pointer.
in handler mode, this bit reads as zero and ignores writes.
nPRIV: Thread mode privilege level
0: privileged
1: unprivileged

Figure 1.8 Control register (CONTROL)

In an OS environment, ARM recommends that **threads** running in **thread mode** use the **process stack**, and the **kernel** and **exception handlers** use the **main stack**. By default, the thread mode uses the MSP. To switch the stack pointer used in the thread mode, the user can either use the MSR instruction to set the active stack pointer bit 0 to 1 or perform an exception return to the thread mode with the appropriate EXC_RETURN value (see Chapter 5).

1.7.8 DATA TYPES

The Cortex-M4 processor supports the following data types:

- 32-bit words
- 16-bit words
- 8-bit bytes

The Cortex-M4 processor supports byte addressing. Every byte in memory has its own address. The Cortex-M4 processor manages all data memory accesses as **little-endian**. Using the little-endian style memory, the least significant byte of a 32-bit word is stored at the lowest address within a word and the most significant byte is stored at the highest address within a word.

1.7.9 CORTEX MICROCONTROLLER SOFTWARE INTERFACE STANDARD (CMSIS)

ARM Ltd provides the Cortex Microcontroller Software Interface Standard (CMSIS) for programming the Cortex-M4 microcontroller. CMSIS is an integrated part of the device driver library. For a Cortex-M4 microcontroller system, the CMSIS defines:

- A common way to access peripheral registers and define exception vectors.
- The names of the registers of the core peripherals and the core exception vectors.
- A device-independent interface for RTOS kernels, including a debug channel.

CMSIS includes **address definitions** and **data structures** for the core peripherals in the Cortex-M4 processor. It also includes optional interface for middleware components comprising a TCP/IP stack and a flash file system.

CMSIS simplifies the software development by enabling the reuse of template code and the combination of CMSIS-compliant software components from various middleware vendors. Software vendors can expand the CMSIS to include their peripheral definitions and access functions for those peripherals.

1.8 Memory Model

The Cortex-M4 has a 4 GB addressable memory as shown in Figure 1.9. The actual memory map (i.e., memory available in a specific Cortex-M4 device) can be found in the memory section of the appropriate device's reference manual or datasheet.

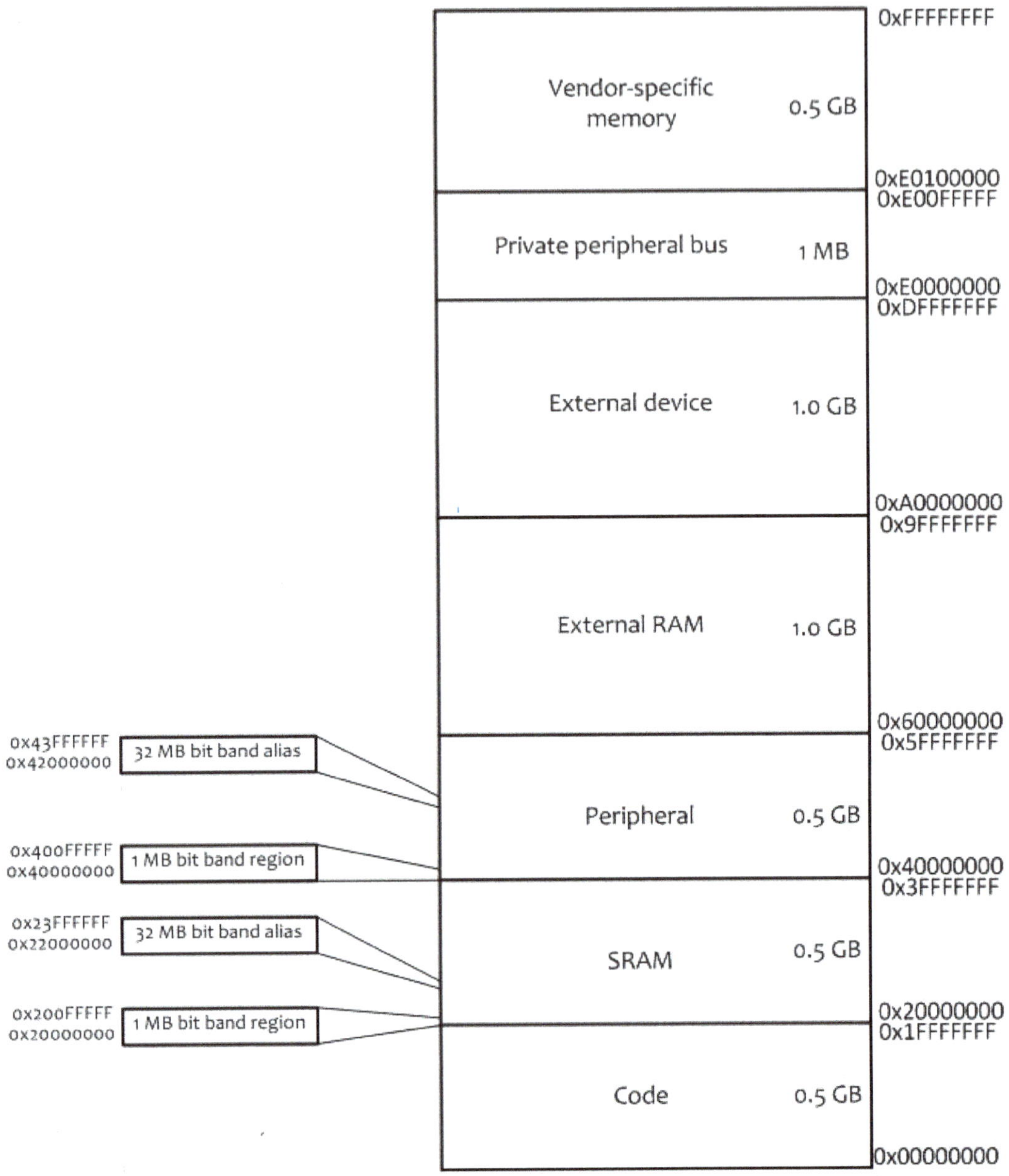

Figure 1.9 Cortex-M4 memory space

The regions for SRAM and peripherals include bit-band regions. Bit-banding provides **atomic operations** (**read-modify-write** operation without interruption) to bit data. Bit-banding is not implemented in other Cortex-M families.

The Cortex-M4 processor reserves a region of the **private peripheral bus** (**PPB**) address range for core peripheral registers.

1.8.1 MEMORY REGIONS, TYPES, AND ATTRIBUTES

The Cortex-M4 memory map is divided into regions. Each region has a defined memory type, and some regions have additional memory attributes. The memory type and attributes determine the behavior of accesses to the region.

The Cortex-M4 processor classifies memory into three types: normal, device, and strongly ordered. For a **normal type** of memory, the processor can reorder transactions for efficiency, or perform speculative reads. For a **device type** of memory, the processor preserves transaction order relative to other transactions to device or strongly ordered memory. For a **strongly ordered** type of memory, the processor preserves transaction order relative to all other transactions.

The memory system can buffer a write to device memory but must not buffer a write to strongly ordered memory.

A memory region may be **shareable**. For a shareable memory region, the memory system provides a data synchronization between bus masters in a system with multiple masters, for example, a processor with DMA controller. A strongly ordered memory is always shareable. If multiple bus masters can access a nonshareable memory region, the software must ensure data coherency among the bus masters.

Some memory regions are **execute never** (XN). Processor prevents instruction access to these regions. A fault exception is generated when the processor attempts to execute instructions fetched from these regions.

For most memory accesses caused by explicit memory access instructions, the memory system does not guarantee that the order in which the accesses complete matches the program order of the instructions; providing this does not affect the behavior of the instruction sequence. The software must insert a **memory barrier** instruction between the memory access instructions if correct program execution depends on two memory accesses completing in program order. The memory system does guarantee some ordering of accesses to device and strongly ordered memory. For two memory access instructions A1 and A2, if A1 occurs before A2 in program order, the ordering of the memory accesses is described in Table 1.5.

Table 1.5 Ordering of the memory accesses caused by two instructions

A1 \ A2	Normal access	Device access		Strongly ordered access
		Non-shareable	Shareable	
Normal access	—	—	—	—
Device access, non-shareable	—	V	—	V
Device access, shareable	—	—	V	V
Strongly ordered access	—	V	V	V

— Order of access is not guaranteed

V Access is observed in program order, access A1 will complete before A2.

By default, the Cortex-M4 processor accesses memory by following the rules given in Table 1.6. The code, SRAM, and external RAM regions can all hold program instructions. However, ARM recommends that programs always use the code region to allow instruction fetches and data accesses to occur simultaneously.

Table 1.6 Cortex-M4 memory accesses behavior

Address range	Memory region	Memory type	XN	Description
0x00000000 ~ 0x1FFFFFFF	Code	Normal	--	Executable region for program code. Data can also be put here.
0x20000000 ~ 0x3FFFFFFF	SRAM	Normal	--	Executable region for data. Code can also be put here. This region includes bit band and bit band alias areas.
0x40000000 ~ 0x5FFFFFFF	Peripheral	Device	XN	This region includes bit band and bit band alias areas.
0x60000000 ~ 0x9FFFFFFF	External RAM	Normal	--	Executable region for data
0xA0000000 ~ 0xDFFFFFFF	External device	Device	XN	External device memory
0xE0000000 ~ 0xE00FFFFF	Private peripheral bus	Strongly-ordered	XN	This region includes the NVIC, system timer, and system control block.
0xE0100000 ~ 0xFFFFFFFF	Reserved	Device	XN	Reserved

The Cortex-M4 processor prefetches instructions ahead of execution and speculatively prefetches from branch target addresses.

1.8.2 SOFTWARE ORDERING OF MEMORY ACCESSES

The order of instructions in the program flow does not always guarantee the order of the corresponding memory transactions. This is done for the following reasons:

- The processor can reorder some memory accesses to improve efficiency, provided this does not affect the behavior of the instruction sequence.
- The processor has multiple bus interfaces.
- Memory or devices in the memory map have different wait states.
- Some memory accesses are buffered or speculative.

If the order of memory accesses is critical, the software must include memory barrier instructions to force that order. The processor provides the following memory barrier instructions:

1. **DMB**: The **data memory barrier** instruction ensures that outstanding memory transactions complete before subsequent memory transactions.
2. **DSB**: The **data synchronization barrier** instruction ensures that outstanding memory transactions complete before subsequent instructions execute.
3. **ISB**: The **instruction synchronization barrier** ensures that the effect of all completed memory transactions is recognizable by subsequent instructions.

1.9 Bit-Banding

A bit-band region maps each word in a **bit-band alias region** to a single bit in the **bit-band region**. The bit-band regions occupy the lowest 1 MB of the SRAM and peripheral memory regions. The memory map has two 32 MB alias regions that map to two 1 MB bit-band regions:

- Accesses to the 32 MB SRAM alias region map to the 1 MB SRAM bit-band region, as shown in Table 1.7.
- Accesses to the 32 MB peripheral alias region map to the 1 MB peripheral bit-band region, as shown in Table 1.8.

Table 1.7 Cortex-M4 SRAM memory bit-banding regions

Address range	Memory region	Instruction and data accesses
0x20000000~0x200FFFFF	SRAM bit-band region	Direct accesses to this memory range behave as SRAM memory accesses, but this region is also bit-addressable through bit-band alias.
0x22000000~0x23FFFFFF	SRAM bit-band alias region	Data accesses to this region are remapped to bit-band region. A write operation is performed as read-modify-write. Instruction accesses are not remapped.

Table 1.8 Cortex-M4 peripheral memory bit-banding regions

Address range	Memory region	Instruction and data accesses
0x40000000~0x400FFFFF	peripheral bit-band region	Direct accesses to this memory range behave as peripheral memory accesses, but this region is also bit-addressable through bit-band alias.
0x42000000~0x43FFFFFF	Peripheral bit-band alias	Data accesses to this region are remapped to bit-band region. A write operation is performed as read-modify-write. Instruction accesses are not permitted.

A word access to the SRAM or the peripheral bit-band alias region maps to a single bit in the SRAM or peripheral bit-band region. Bit-band accesses can use byte, half-word, or word transfers. The bit-band transfer size matches the transfer size of the instruction making the bit-band region access.

1.9.1 MAPPING FROM BIT-BAND REGION ADDRESS TO BIT-BAND ALIAS REGION ADDRESS

The relationship of an address in the bit-band region and that of its corresponding word in the bit-band alias region is given by the following equation:

Bit_word_addr in bit-band alias region = bit_band_alias_base + bit_word_offset

Bit_word_offset = Byte_offset × 32 + bit_number × 4

For example, given the bit 5 of the bit_band address at 0x200FF200, it maps to

Bit_word_offset = (0x200FF200 – 0x20000000) × 32 + 5 × 4 = 0x1FE4014

Address in bit_band_alias region = 0x22000000 + 0x1FE4014 = 0x23FE4014

Given the bit 7 of the bit_band address at 0x40005840, it maps to

Bit_word_offset = (0x40005840 – 0x40000000) × 32 + 7 × 4 = 0xB081C

Address in bit_band_alias region = 0x42000000 + 0xB081C = 0x420B081C

1.9.2 MAPPING FROM BIT_BAND_ALIAS ADDRESS BACK TO BIT_BAND ADDRESS

The procedure for mapping the bit_band_alias address to bid_band address is as follows:

Step 1

Subtract the bit_band_alias base (0x22000000 or 0x42000000) from the given alias address to obtain the bit_word_offset.

Step 2

Divide the difference obtained in Step 1 by 32 to obtain **quotient** and **remainder**.

Step 3

Add the base address of the bit_band region to the quotient to obtain the word address in the bit_band region.

Step 4

Divide the remainder by 4 to obtain the **bit number**.

Example 1.1 Given the bit_band_alias address 0x23FAC018, find the corresponding word address and the bit number in the bit_band region in SRAM.

Solution: Follow the previous procedure.

Step 1

Bit_word_offset = 0x23FAC018 – 0x22000000 = 0x1FAC018.

Step 2

Divide the bit_word_offset by 32:

Quo = 0xFD600

Rem = 0x18 (or 24)

Step 3

Bit_band region address = 0x20000000 + 0xFD600 = 0x200FD600

Step 4

The bit number is 24 / 4 = 6.

Example 1.2 Given the bit_band alias address 0x42FCE018, find the corresponding word address and bit number in the peripheral bit_band region.

Solution: Follow the previous procedure.

Step 1

Bit_word_offset = 0x42FCE018 – 0x42000000 = 0xFCE018

Step 2

Divide the bit_word_offset by 32:

Quo = 0x7E700

Rem = 0x18 (or 24)

Step 3

Bit_band region word address = 0x40000000 + 0x7E700 = 0x4007E700

Step 4

The bit number is 0x18 / 4 = 6.

1.10 Cortex-M4 Core Peripherals

The Cortex-M4 processor core has several peripherals that are important to the operation of the Cortex-M4 processor. Each of these peripherals contains several registers to support its operation. These peripherals are summarized in Table 1.9. Some of these peripherals are optional. These peripherals are implemented in all ST's Cortex-M4 microcontrollers.

Table 1. 9 Cortex-M4 core peripherals

Address	Core Peripheral
0xE000E010~0xE000E01F	System timer
0xE000E100~0xE000E4EF	Nested vectored interrupt controller
0xE000ED00~0xE000ED3F	System control block
0xE000ED88~0xE000ED8B	Floating-point unit coprocessor access control
0xE000ED90~0xE000EDB8	Memory protection unit
0xE000EF00~0xE000EF03	Nested vectored interrupt controller
0xE000EF30~0xE000EF44	Floating point unit

1.11 The STM32L475 Microcontroller

The STM32L475 is a member of the STM32L4 subfamily devices. It implements all the Cortex-M4 features and has 1 MB on-chip flash memory for program code and 128 KB on-chip SRAM for dynamic data storage. This book describes the functionality, interfacing, and programming of the STM32L475 microcontroller.

This chip is chosen for introducing the Cortex-M4 programming and interfacing because it

has been used as the microcontroller of the B-L475E-IOT01A Discovery kit. This Discovery kit supports the following wireless communication protocols:

- Bluetooth 4.1
- Sub-GHz RF (868 MHz or 915 MHz)
- NFC
- Wi-Fi (802.11 b/g/n compliant)

It also includes the following sensors on the kit:

- a relative humidity and temperature sensor (HTS221)
- 3-axis magnetometer (LIS3MDL)
- 3D accelerometer and 3D gyroscope (LSM6DSL)
- 260-1260 hPa digital output barometer (LPS22HB)
- Time-of-flight and gesture-detection sensor (VL53L0X)

Wireless communication and sensors are the key components of IoT. The availability of this kit simplifies the exploration of the design ideas for IoT.

The bus structure of the STM32L475 is shown in Figure 1.10. The STM32L475 processor fetches instructions and accesses data via the bus matrix. The processor accesses peripherals via the AHB or APB1 or APB2 bus. Clock signals are distributed to most peripherals through the AHB, APB1, and APB2 buses.

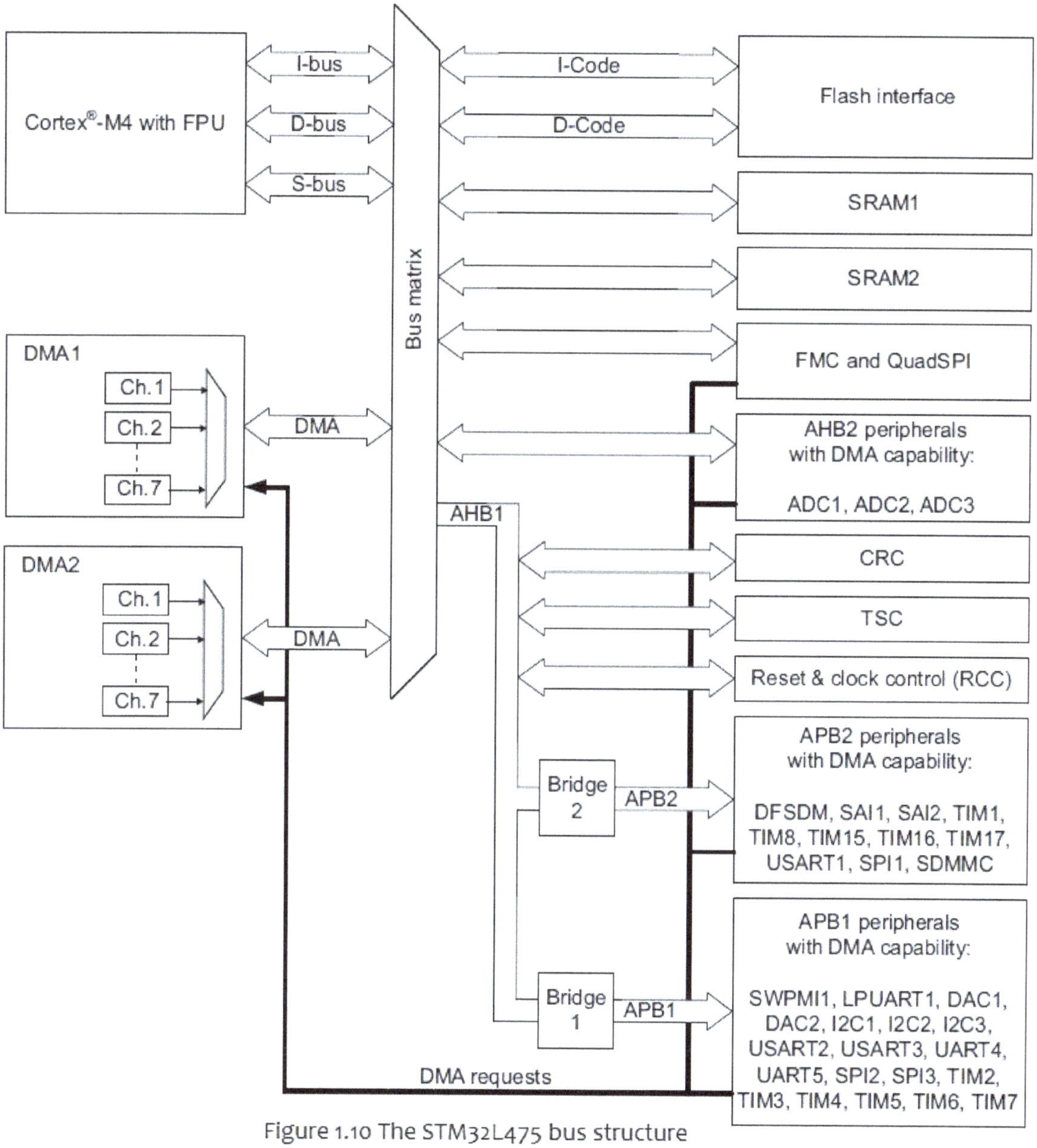

Figure 1.10 The STM32L475 bus structure

1.12 Summary

The history of computer tells us that an established software base is very critical to the success of a new computer family. When IBM introduced the 360 family computers in 1965, they made them compatible in software. Software written for the low-end members can be run by the high-end members in the same computer family. The customers can start with a small configuration and then move up to the larger configuration by upgrading to a faster CPU and adding more memory. They didn't need to rewrite software. At that time, no other computer companies had any significant software base. IBM's strategy made 360 series a big success. The successors of 360, including 370, 390, and the latest system z, all followed the same strategy. Numerous large government organizations, banks, insurance companies, and large companies in the United States and other countries developed tens of millions of lines of program code for the IBM mainframe computers. They cannot afford to throw away these software assets. The huge software base and the software compatibility made the successors of system 360 the best choice for the system 360's customers. These systems are all very successful and enable IBM to dominate the mainframe computer market until today. Today, IBM realizes that it cannot make money by selling traditional hardware, so it focuses its efforts on software and data analytics. It is the software and service around the mainframe computers that generate huge profits for IBM.

The biggest minicomputer vendor DEC followed the same strategy. It entered the minicomputer market by introducing much cheaper minicomputers than the mainframe computers. It attracted significant number of initial customers. After that, DEC continued to introduce newer, more powerful minicomputer systems and still maintain software compatibility. Even when introducing its first 32-bit minicomputer VAX 11/780 0n October 25, 1977, DEC added an emulation mode so that the 32-bit VAX computer can run the software written for the earlier 16-bit PDP-11 computers. The VAX computer family was designed with the complex instruction set computer (CISC) philosophy in mind. It implements very complex instruction set and addressing modes in hardware with the hope for better support for high-level languages. The CISC approach made VAX computer very difficult to upgrade for better performance. In late 1980s, the performance of IBM PCs improved dramatically while at the same time the price kept dropping. DEC (and all other minicomputer vendors) lost out in the price/performance war with the IBM PCs. Eventually, all of them went out of business.

Intel, the largest microprocessor vendor in the world, also adopts the same strategy—maintaining software compatibility across different generations of its microprocessor products. Intel's good luck arrived when IBM decided to use the Intel 8088 as the CPU of its first personal computer. The huge success of the IBM PCs and its compatibles drove Intel into the largest semiconductor company in the world.

The ARM processor was designed during the time that the IBM PCs were extremely popular and the minicomputers were losing steam due to their poor price performance ratio compared to PC. Mainframe computers were still doing fine due to the huge software base in large organizations in public and private sectors. Initially, it would appear that ARM does not have a good chance to succeed because it lacked the software base similar to that of mainframe computers or IBM PCs and ARM Ltd is a relatively small company that doesn't have credibility. However, by licensing the processor design to interested semiconductor companies who sell ARM processors to applications that existent software base does not matter much, ARM Ltd survives. The accelerated adoption of mobile devices such as cell phones popularizes the ARM processor. The success of the ARM processor can be attributed to four factors:

- Good performance
- Low power consumption
- Accelerated adoption of mobile devices in 1990s
- ARM Ltd's business model

High performance and low power consumption are the two most important features needed in a mobile device. With the success in mobile market, ARM Ltd started to push its processor to every possible market. To better serve the requirements of different applications, ARM Ltd divided its processor products into three profiles: application profile (A-profile), real-time profile (R-profile), and microcontroller profile (M-Profile).

Many modern computer architecture techniques have been incorporated into the ARM processors (especially in the A-profile). The most important ones are:

- Pipelining
- SIMD vector processing
- Conditional instruction execution
- Branch prediction
- Separate instruction and data cache
- Superscalar pipelining (issue multiple instructions in every clock cycle)
- Speculation instruction execution (execute instructions out-of-order but commit instructions in program order)
- Multiple core implementation

ARM processor will continue to expand toward other market segments, especially where ARM has very low market share, for example, the server and networking markets. The server market has been dominated by the Intel x86 architecture. The servers based on Intel x86 processors have good performance but consume a lot of power. The ARM processors have significant advantage in power consumption and the 64-bit version of the ARM processors also have caught up with the Intel x86 processors in performance.

1.13 Exercises

E1.1 What hardware unit is needed (by the ARM processor) in order to support the computer operating system?

E1.2 What is TrustZone?

E1.3 What is Jazelle technology?

E1.4 What is big.little technology?

E1.5 Write an ARM instruction that can compute the assignment "**a = b + 8 * c;**" assuming that variables a, b, and c are assigned to registers R1, R2, and R3, respectively.

E1.6 Why did ARM Ltd introduce the Thumb2 instruction set?

E1.7 Write an ARM instruction that can compute the assignment "**b = c/8 + a;**" assuming that variables a, b, and c are assigned to registers R1, R2, and R3, respectively.

E1.8 What is the performance of a Cortex-M0+ processing running at 50 MHz in terms of the Dhrystone and CoreMark benchmark, respectively?

E1.9 What is the performance of a Cortex-M7 processor running at 300 MHz in terms of the Dhrystone and CoreMark benchmark, respectively?

E1.10 What is the bit_band_alias address for the bit 6 of the location in bit_band region at 0x200EECC0?

E1.11 What is the bit_band_alias address for the bit 7 of the location in bit_band region at 0x200FECA6?

E1.12 What is the bit_band_alias address for the bit 3 of the location in bit_band region at 0x40022680?

E1.13 What is the bit_band_alias address for the bit 5 of the location in bit_band region at 0x400AABBC?

E1.14 Find the corresponding word address and the bit number in the SRAM bit_band region for the bit_band_alias address 0x22CD0814.

E1.15 Find the corresponding word address and the bit number in the SRAM bit_band region for the bit_band_alias address 0x23EEFFC0.

E1.16 Find the corresponding word address and bit number in the peripheral bit_band region for the bit_band_alias address 0x43EFCF60.

E1.17 Find the corresponding word address and bit number in the peripheral bit_band region for the bit_band_alias address 0x43FFAF8C.

2 Programming the STM32L475 in C

2.1 Objectives

After completing this chapter, you will be able to

- Write C programs using a good programming style.
- Use the typedef macro to assign an alternate name to a data type.
- Use alternate names of C data types to declare program variables.
- Use symbolic names to access peripheral registers.
- Use symbolic names to access bit fields of peripheral registers.
- Create projects using the Keil mVision IDE.
- Download hex files onto target hardware for execution using Keil mVision IDE.
- Perform program debugging using the Keil mVision IDE.

2.2 Good Programming Style in C

Programming style is a set of guidelines used when writing a program. By following a particular programming style, the resultant program will be more readable and easier to debug. The key issue in programming style is communication. Any program that will be used must be maintained by somebody and somebody must be able to understand the code.

A program that needs to be debugged will be easier to do if the author of the program carefully explains what's going on. Programmers have three primary tools for communicating their intentions:

- Comments
- Naming of variables, constants, and functions
- Program appearance (spacing, alignment, and indentation)

2.2.1 GENERAL GUIDELINES TO COMMENTS

There are two issues in good comment: **what to comment** and **when to comment**. The programmer should include comments explaining what every function does, what every variable does, and every tricky expression and section of code.

"**When**" is easy. The programmer should include comments before he/she writes any function, variable, and tricky expression and section of code. Obscure programming language constructs should be avoided. The programmer should rely on language-specific precedence rules. Add a comment on anything that you need to look up the rule.

2.2.2 PROGRAM DOCUMENTATION

All programs should include a comment block at or near the beginning of the program. The comment block should include the following:

- The programmer's name
- The date that the program was created
- The operating system and IDE for which the program was written
- Hardware environment (i.e., circuit connection) to run the program
- Program structure (organization)
- Algorithm and data structures of the program
- How to run the program

An example of program documentation is as follows:

```
// ------------------------------------------------------------------------------------------------------------
// Program: Multiple Seven-Segment Pattern Shifting driven by ST32L475
// Author: David Jenson
// Build environment: Keil mVision IDE under Windows 11
// Date: 02/30/2024
// Hardware connection: Port A pins 0~6 drive segment patterns g~a, Port A pins 7~10
// drives digit select through the buffer chip 74LV244.
// Operation: This program shifts seven-segment patterns of 4 consecutive BCD digits
//     by using time-multiplexing technique with each pattern lasting for 0.5 s.
```

```
//    The time-multiplexing operation is controlled by the timer interrupt that occurs once
//    every 1 ms. The patterns are
//            4 3 2 1
//            5 4 3 2
//            6 5 4 3
//            7 6 5 4
//            8 7 6 5
//            9 8 7 6
//            0 9 8 7
//            1 0 9 8
//            2 1 0 9
//            3 2 1 0
```

2.2.3 FUNCTION DOCUMENTATION

Each C function should have a clearly defined task. Writing the comment describing that task before writing the function can help to keep you straight. Functions should be short enough so that their meaning can be grasped as a unit by the reader. Every function should be preceded by a comment describing the purpose and use of that function. An example of function documentation is as follows:

```
// ------------------------------------------------------------------------------------------------------------
// Function: FindSquareRoot
// Purpose: Computes and returns the square root of a 32-bit unsigned integer
// Parameters: A 32-bit unsigned integer of which the square root is to be found
// Returned value: A 16-bit unsigned integer which is the closest approximation of the
// square root of the incoming 32-bit unsigned integer parameter
// Side effects: None
// ------------------------------------------------------------------------------------------------------------
```

One of the most common program bugs is in the interface between functions:

- Type mismatches—the types of the actual arguments for the function call are different from those of the function definition.
- Misorder of parameters—the order of actual arguments for the function call are different from those of the function definition.

- Leave some parameters out—some arguments are not passed when the function is called.

As a rule of thumb, the programmer should keep the number of parameters no more than seven to minimize the above-mentioned program bugs.

2.2.4 CODE APPEARANCE

To make the program more readable, the programmer should include proper space and indentation, and pay attention to vertical alignment.

Proper Spacing

Proper spacing of any statement makes it easier to read. An example is as follows:

Statement without proper spacing	Statement with proper spacing
for(j=0;j<100;j++)	for (j = 0; j < 100; j++)

Proper Indentation

Indentation improves the readability of the nested **if-elseif** statements and program loops. It also makes the **logical hierarchy** of **if-elseif** statements and program loops stand out. An example of program without indentation is as follows:

```
while(TRUE){
for(i = 0; i < 10; i++) {// pattern array start index
for(j = 0; j < 100; j++){ // repeat loop for each pattern sequence
for(k = 0; k < 6; k++){ // select the seven-segment display to be lighted
REG_PORT_OUT = SegPat[i+k]; // output segment pattern and digit-select values
delay_ms(1); // display one digit for 1 ms
}
}
}
}
```

This group of statements is hard to understand because it is lacking proper indentation. After adding proper indentation, the meaning of this group of statements becomes much easier to understand:

```
while (TRUE) {
    for (i = 0; i < 10; i++) { // pattern array start index
        for (j = 0; j < 100; j++) { // repeat loop for each pattern sequence
            for (k = 0; k < 6; k++) { // select the seven-segment display to be lighted
                REG_PORT_OUT = SegPar[i * 6 + k];
                delayby1ms(1); // display one digit for 1 ms
            }
        }
    }
}
```

Vertical Alignment

It is often helpful to align similar elements vertically to make typo-generated bugs more obvious. In the following, one array of constant data is not vertically aligned whereas the other is vertically aligned:

```
// values to generate 1 cycle of sine wave
uint16_t sine[60] = { 0x0800, 0x08D6, 0x09A9, 0x0A78, 0x0B40, 0x0BFF,
  0x0CB3, 0x0D5A, 0x0DF1, 0x0E78, 0x0EED, 0x0F4E, 0x0F9B, 0x0FD2,
0x0FF4, 0x0FFF, 0x0FF4, 0x0FD2, 0x0F9B, 0x0F4E, 0x0EED, 0x0E78, 0x0DF1,
  0x0D5A, 0x0CB3, 0x0BFF, 0x0B40, 0x0A78, 0x09A9, 0x08D6, 0x0800, 0x0729,
0x0656, 0x0587, 0x04BF, 0x0400, 0x034C, 0x02A5, 0x020E, 0x0187,
  0x0112, 0x00B1, 0x0064, 0x002D, 0x000B, 0x0000, 0x000B, 0x002D, 0x0064,
    0x00B1, 0x0112, 0x0187, 0x020E, 0x02A5, 0x034C, 0x0400, 0x04BF,
0x0587, 0x0656, 0x0729};
```

(a) **Nonvertically aligned array**

```
// values to generate 1 cycle of sine wave
uint16_t sine[60] = { 0x0800, 0x08D6, 0x09A9, 0x0A78, 0x0B40, 0x0BFF,
                      0x0CB3, 0x0D5A, 0x0DF1, 0x0E78, 0x0EED, 0x0F4E,
                      0x0F9B, 0x0FD2, 0x0FF4, 0x0FFF, 0x0FF4, 0x0FD2,
                      0x0F9B, 0x0F4E, 0x0EED, 0x0E78, 0x0DF1, 0x0D5A,
```

```
0x0CB3, 0x0BFF, 0x0B40, 0x0A78, 0x09A9, 0x08D6,
0x0800, 0x0729, 0x0656, 0x0587, 0x04BF, 0x0400,
0x034C, 0x02A5, 0x020E, 0x0187, 0x0112, 0x00B1,
0x0064, 0x002D, 0x000B, 0x0000, 0x000B, 0x002D,
0x0064, 0x00B1, 0x0112, 0x0187, 0x020E, 0x02A5,
0x034C, 0x0400, 0x04BF, 0x0587, 0x0656, 0x0729};
```

(b) **Vertically aligned array**

2.2.5 NAMING OF VARIABLES, CONSTANTS, AND FUNCTIONS

The naming of variables, constants, and functions should spell out their **meaning** or **purpose**. Once a set of rules for naming has been decided, the programmer should follow them consistently. A possible set of naming rules may be as follows:

- **Single-word name**: use lowercase for every character. For example, sum, limit, and average.
- **Multiword name**: use mixed case for the first character of each word with the first word starting with lowercase. For example, inBuf, outBuf, squareRoot, arrayMax.
- **Function names**: follow the same principle as variable names. For example, sevenSegShift(), putcSPI(), putsSPI(), openLCD(), and putsLCD().
- **Constant names**: use uppercase for every character and underscore to separate words. For example, HI_DELAY_COUNT, LO_DELAY_COUNT, and SONG_TOTAL_NOTES.

2.3 Providing Alternate Names to Basic and Struct Data Types

Using alternate names to replace basic data types may save typing and improve program readability. For example, many C compilers (including Keil mVision C compiler) use the **typedef** declaration to provide alternate names to basic data types:

```
typedef    unsigned long int    uint32_t    // unsigned 32-bit integer
typedef    unsigned short int   uint16_t    // unsigned 16-bit integer
typedef    unsigned char        uint8_t     // unsigned 8-bit integer
typedef    long int             int32_t     // signed 32-bit integer
typedef    short int            int16_t     // signed 16-bit integer
typedef    char                 int8_t      // signed 8-bit integer
```

With these alternate type names in place, the programmer can then define variables as follows:

```
uint32_t  ux, vx, cx[10];     // ux and vx are 32-bit nonnegative integers and cx[] is
                              // an array of 10 32-bit nonnegative integers
uint16_t  nx1, nx2;           // nx1 and nx2 are two 16-bit nonnegative integers
uint8_t   d1, d2;             // d1 and d2 are two 8-bit nonnegative integers
int32_t   x1, x2;             // x1 and x2 are 32-bit signed integers
int16_t   w1[10], w2[10];     // w1[] and w2[] are arrays of 10 16-bit signed integers
int8_t    q1, q2;             // q1 and q2 are two 8-bit signed integers
```

2.4 Use Type Names to Highlight the Read-Writability of Registers

Keil mVision IDE and several IDEs from other companies use type names to highlight the read-writability of peripheral registers. The following type names are used:

```
typedef volatile const uint32_t RoReg;    // 32-bit read-only register
typedef volatile const uint16_t RoReg16;  // 16-bit read-only register
typedef volatile const uint8_t  RoReg8;   // 8-bit read-only register
typedef volatile uint32_t WoReg;          // 32-bit write-only register
typedef volatile uint16_t WoReg16;        // 16-bit write-only register
typedef volatile uint8_t  WoReg8;         // 8-bit write-only register
typedef volatile uint32_t RwReg;          // 32-bit read-writable register
typedef volatile uint16_t RwReg16;        // 16-bit read-writable register
typedef volatile uint8_t  RwReg8;         // 8-bit read-writable register
```

2.5 Type Casting

In embedded systems programming, we often need to deal with operands of different sizes. When performing an operation on several operands with different sizes, we may lose accuracy due to truncation performed by the compiler. To avoid this problem, we can perform type casting to convert all operands to the desired type. Type casting has the following form:

```
(type_name) expression
```

For example, the expression **(uint32_t) 250** causes 250 to be represented as a 32-bit unsigned integer.

Type casting may enable the user to access the same structure in different ways. Suppose we want to access the following struct as a string:

```
struct book {
    char name[20];
    char author[20];
    char isbn[13];
    char publisher[20];
    char year[4];
    char month[2];
} ptrx;
char *cp;
```

We can use the following statement to treat the variable as a string:

```
cp = (char *)&ptrx;
```

2.6 Referencing Peripheral Registers

Peripheral registers can be accessed by using two approaches:

- Flattened approach
- Hierarchical approach

2.6.1 FLATTENED APPROACH

In this approach, the programmer is required to use the **#define** preprocessor command to assign each peripheral register address to a selected register name. For example,

```
#define    GPIOA_MODER     (*(uint32_t volatile *)0x48000000)
#define    GPIOA_OTYPER    (*(uint32_t volatile *)0x48000004)
#define    GPIOA_ODR       (*(uint32_t volatile *)0x48000014)
#define    GPIOA_IDR       (*(uint32_t volatile *)0x48000010)
...
```

Collect the above #define macros into a **header file** and include it in a program file that contains the main function. After this, the programmer can reference these registers using the symbolic names. A few examples follow:

```
GPIOA_ODR = 0xAAAA;      // GPIOA_ODR is a 32-bit register
xy        = GPIOA_IDR;   // read the PORTA pins voltage levels
```

This approach is not used in Keil mVision IDE. Instead, the hierarchical approach is followed.

2.6.2 HIERARCHICAL APPROACH

To access a peripheral register, the following three steps are taken:

Step 1

Declare one or several **struct** data types to contain all the registers of each type of peripheral using the **typedef** declaration.

Step 2

Declare one or several symbolic names to represent the pointers (starting address) to point to the struct(s) defined in Step 1 for each peripheral module. A microcontroller may have several peripheral modules of the same type.

Step 3

Each register is accessed using **ptr->reg_name**.

All microcontrollers have signal pins on the chip. These pins can be used for the following functions:

- Digital input
- Digital output
- Digital peripheral functions
- Analog peripheral functions such as analog-to-digital conversion, digital-to-analog conversion, analog comparison.

A microcontroller vendor puts multiple pins (can be 8, or 16, or 32 pins) into one group and calls it an I/O port (or general-purpose I/O (GPIO) port). To support the functioning of these signal pins, registers are needed for setting up parameters, holding data and status flags for their operations. Registers supporting the operation of the same GPIO port are assigned to a block of contiguous memory locations. A typedef declaration can be used to declare a **struct** data type, which contains all the registers that support the operation of the GPIO port. For example, the **stm32L475xx.h** header file in the Keil mVision IDE provides the following declaration:

Declaring the GPIO Struct Data Type

```
typedef     struct
{
```

```
    __IO    uint32_t    MODER;      // GPIO port mode register
    __IO    uint32_t    OTYPER;     // GPIO port output type register
    __IO    uint32_t    OSPEEDR;    // GPIO port speed register
    __IO    uint32_t    PUPDR;      // GPIO port pull-up/pull-down register
    __IO    unit32_t    IDR;        // GPIO port input data register
    __IO    uint32_t    ODR;        // GPIO port output data register
    __IO    uint32_t    BSRR;       // GPIO port bit set/reset register
    __IO    uint32_t    LCKR;       // GPIO port configuration lock register
    __IO    uint32_t    AFR[2];     // GPIO port alternate function registers
    __IO    uint32_t    BRR;        // GPIO bit reset register
    __IO    uint32_t    ASCR;       // GPIO analog switch control register
} GPIO_TypeDef;
```

Assigning Pointers to GPIO Register Blocks

The STM32L475 has eight GPIO ports: GPIOA, GPIOB, GPIOC, GPIOD, GPIOE, GPIOF, GPIOG, and GPIOH. A pointer must be assigned to each of these GPIO ports to enable users to access those registers. The pointer points to the starting address of the register block associated with each GPIO port. A straightforward method to define a pointer to each GPIO register block is as follows:

```
#define    GPIOA    ((GPIO_TypeDef *)0x48000000U)
#define    GPIOB    ((GPIO_TypeDef *)0x48000400U)
#define    GPIOC    ((GPIO_TypeDef *)0x48000800U)
#define    GPIOD    ((GPIO_TypeDef *)0x48000C00U)
#define    GPIOE    ((GPIO_TypeDef *)0x48001000U)
#define    GPIOF    ((GPIO_TypeDef *)0x48001400U)
#define    GPIOG    ((GPIO_TypeDef *)0x48001800U)
#define    GPIOH    ((GPIO_TypeDef *)0x48001C00U)
```

To allow the sharing of symbolic names, the Keil mVision IDE uses a four-step approach to define pointers to GPIO register blocks. For example, the pointer to the GPIOA block is defined as follows:

```
#define    PERIPH_BASE     ((uint32_t) 0x40000000U)
#define    AHB2PERIPH      (PERIPH_BASE + 0x08000000U)
#define    GPIOA_BASE      (AHB2PERIPH_BASE + 0x0000U)
#define    GPIOA           ((GPIO_TypeDef *)GPIOA_BASE)
```

Accessing GPIO Port Registers

Outputting a value to a GPIO port can be achieved by using a statement as follows:

```
GPIOx->ODR  = val;        // x can be A, …, H
```

To read the voltage levels from a GPIO port pins can be done as follows:

```
xyz = GPIOx->IDR;         // xyz is a variable (must be at least 16-bit variable) declared earlier
```

2.6.3 MANIPULATING BIT FIELDS OF A PERIPHERAL REGISTER

Microcontroller programming is about manipulating the peripheral registers. In this operation, the user is required to manipulate the bit fields contained in the peripheral registers. Let's take the GPIO port mode register (MODER) as an example to illustrate the process. The contents of the GPIOx->MODER register are shown in Figure 4.1 (repeated here).

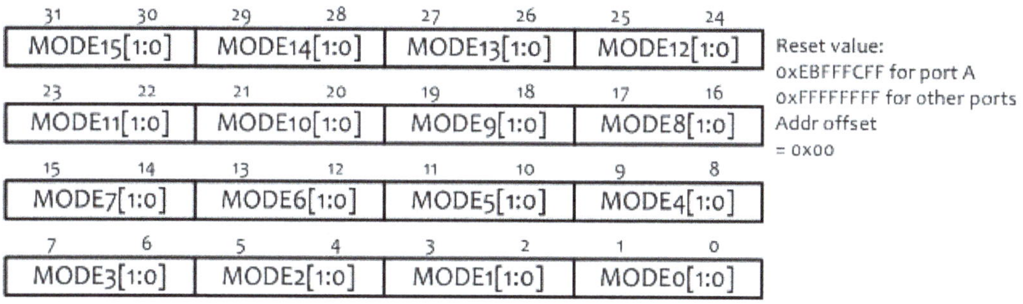

MODEy[1:0]: PORT x configuration bits (y = 0..15)
- 00: Input mode
- 01: General purpose output mode
- 10: Alternate function mode
- 11: Analog mode (reset state)

Figure 4.1 GPIO Port Mode Register (GPIOx_MODER, x = A..E, and H)

The user programs (writes an appropriate value into) this register to configure each pin for its intended use. Suppose we want to configure GPIOA pin 6 for alternate function, we can do it in two steps:

1. Clear bit 12 and bit 13 of the GPIOA->MODER register to 00.
2. Set bit 13 and 12 of the same register to 10.

Clearing bit 12 and 13 can be achieved by ANDing the GPIOA->MODER register with 0xFFFFCFFF and then ORing the GPIOA->MODER register with 0x00002000. These two operations can be achieved by the following two statements:

```
GPIOA->MODER &= ~0x00003000; // 0xFFFFCFFF = ~0x00003000

GPIOA->MODER |= 0x00002000;
```

However, using the value directly in the AND and OR operations in the above two statements makes the program much harder to understand. A better solution is providing a symbolic name for each bit field in the peripheral register that needs to be programmed. For example, the Keil mVision IDE provides the following #define macros in the **stm32L475xx.h** header file for the user to use (the letter **U** stands for **unsigned**):

```
#define   GPIO_MODER_MODE6_Pos      (12U)
#define   GPIO_MODER_MODE6_Msk      (0x3U << GPIO_MODER_MODE6_Pos)
#define   GPIO_MODER_MODE6          GPIO_MODER_MODE6_Msk
#define   GPIO_MODER_MODE6_0        (0x1U << GPIO_MODER_MODE6_Pos)
#define   GPIO_MODER_MODE6_1        (0x2U << GPIO_MODER_MODE6_Pos)
```

With these macro definitions, the user can use the symbolic names to achieve the same purpose:

```
GPIOA->MODER     &= ~GPIO_MODER_MODE6; // AND with 0xFFFFCFFF
GPIO->MODER      |= GPIO_MODER_MODE6_1; // OR with 0x00002000
```

The stm32L475xx.h header file contains similar #define macros for other bit fields in the GPIOA->MODER register.

Example 2.1 Write a sequence of C statements to configure GPIOA pins 7, 6, 5, and 4 for output.

Solution: We need to program the MODE7[1:0], MODE6[1:0], MODE5[1:0], and MODE4[1:0] fields of the GPIOA->MODER register to 01, 01, 01, and 01. This can be achieved by

- ANDing the GPIOA->MODER register with ~(GPIO_MODER_MODE7 + GPIO_MODER_MODE6 + GPIO_MODER_MODE5 + GPIO_MODER_MODE4), and then
- ORing the same register with (GPIO_MODER_MODE7_0 + GPIO_MODER6_MODE6_0 + GPIO_MODER_MODE5_0 + GPIO_MODER_MODE4_0).

The following C statements perform the specified configuration accordingly:

```
GPIOA->MODER  &= ~(GPIO_MODER_MODE7 + GPIO_MODER_MODE6 +
          GPIO_MODER_MODE5 + GPIO_MODER_MODE4);
GPIOA->MODER  |= GPIO_MODER_MODE7_0 + GPIO_MODER_MODE6_0 +
          GPIO_MODER_MODE5_0 + GPIO_MODER_MODE4_0;
```

Example 2.2 Write a sequence of C statements to configure PORTC for output and output the value of 0xAA67 to it.

Solution:

To configure the whole GPIO port for output, we can simply write a single value to the GPIOC->MODER register. The value to configure the whole port for output is 0x55555555.

The following two statements perform the specified operations:

```
GPIOC->MODER = 0x55555555;

GPIOC->ODR = 0xAA67;
```

The GPIO bit set reset register (GPIOx->BSRR) allows the user to pull a few GPIO pins high or low without affecting the remaining pins. The contents of the GPIOx->BSRR register are shown in Figure 4.3 (repeated here).

The upper 16 bits of the GPIOx->BSRR register allow the user to pull a pin to low without affecting any other pin whereas the lower 16 bits allow the user to pull a pin to high without affecting any other pin.

The stm32L475xx.h header file has three #define macros for each pin. The #define macros for the **pin 15** and **pin 0** are as follows:

```
#define    GPIO_BSRR_BS0_Pos     (0U)
#define    GPIO_BSRR_BS0_Msk     (0x1U << GPIO_BSRR_BS0_Pos)
#define    GPIO_BSRR_BS0         GPIO_BSRR_BS0_Msk
...
#define    GPIO_BSRR_BS15_Pos    (15U)
#define    GPIO_BSRR_BS15_Msk    (0x1U << GPIO_BSRR_BS15_Pos)
#define    GPIO_BSRR_BS15        GPIO_BSRR_BS15_Msk
#define    GPIO_BSRR_BR0_Pos     (16U)
#define    GPIO_BSRR_BR0_Msk     (0x1U << GPIO_BSRR_BR0_Pos)
#define    GPIO_BSRR_BR0         GPIO_BSRR_BR0_Msk
...
#define    GPIO_BSRR_BR15_Pos    (31U)
#define    GPIO_BSRR_BR15_Msk    (0x1U << GPIO_BSRR_BR15_Pos)
#define    GPIO_BSRR_BR15        GPIO_BSRR_BR15_Msk
```

31	30	29	28	27	26	25	24
BR15	BR14	BR13	BR12	BR11	BR10	BR9	BR8
23	**22**	**21**	**20**	**19**	**18**	**17**	**16**
BR7	BR6	BR5	BR4	BR3	BR2	BR1	BR0
15	**14**	**13**	**12**	**11**	**10**	**9**	**8**
BS15	BS14	BS13	BS12	BS11	BS10	BS9	BS8
7	**6**	**5**	**4**	**3**	**2**	**1**	**0**
BS7	BS6	BS5	BS4	BS3	BS2	BS1	BS0

Reset value: 0x0000 0000
Addr offset = 0x18

BRy: PORT x reset bit y (y = 0..15)
  0: No action on the ODx bit
  1: Resets the corresponding ODx bit
BSy: PORT x set bit y (y = 0..15)
  0: No action on the ODx bit
  1: Sets the corresponding ODx bit

Figure 4.3 GPIO port x bit set/reset register (GPIOx_BSRR, x = A..E, and H)

Example 2.3 Write a sequence of C statements to pull the Port A pins 15 and 8 to high and pull the pins 7 and 0 to low without affecting remaining pins.

Solution:

We need to configure the specified pins for output before we can perform the specified operations. The following statements performed the specified operations:

```
GPIOA->MODER    &= ~(GPIO_MODER_MODE15 + GPIO_MODER_MODE8 +
                     GPIO_MODER_MODE7 + GPIO_MODER_MODE0);
GPIOA->MODER    |= GPIO_MODER_MODE15_0 + GPIO_MODER_MODE8_0 +
                     GPIO_MODER_MODE7_0 + GPIO_MODER_MODE0_0;
GPIOA->BSRR       = GPIO_BSRR_BS15 + GPIO_BSRR_BS8 + GPIO_BSRR_BR7 +
                     GPIO_BSRR_BR0;
```

2.7 Microcontroller Learning Kits for STM32L475

Microcontroller boards are indispensable for the learning of the STM32L475. The only difference between the STM32L475 and STM32L476 is that the STM32L476 has an LCD controller but the STM32L475 doesn't. Therefore, any STM32L476-based demo board can be used to test the programs written for the STM32L475 MCU. The user can use either the B-L475E-IOT Discovery kit or the STM32L476G-DISCO board to test the program written for STM32L475 and STM32L476. The pictures of the **B-L475E-IOT** and the **STM-32L476G-DISCO** boards are shown in Figures 2.1 and 2.2, respectively.

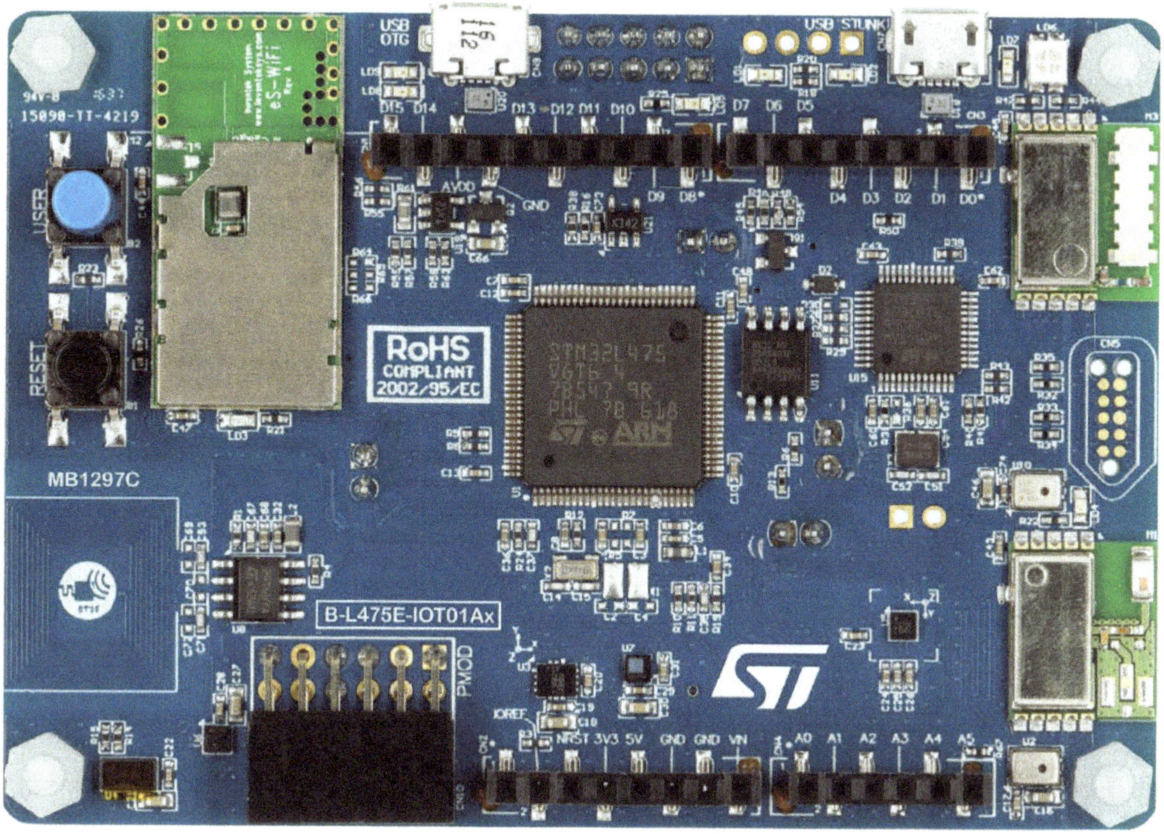

Figure 2.1 B-L475E-IOT01A Discovery kit

The B-L475E-IOT01A board provides the following resources to the user to test their applications:

- The CN1, CN2, CN3, and CN4 connectors: the signal pins A0~A7, PA15, PB0~PB2, PB4, PB8~PB9, PC0~PC5, and PD14 are made available to the user through these four connectors.
- Wireless networking protocols support: Bluetooth 4.1, Wi-Fi (802.11b/g/n), sub-Giga Hz RF, and Near Field Communication (NFC) are supported.
- Sensors: relative humidity and temperature, three-axis magnetometer, accelerometer and 3D gyroscope, absolute digital output barometer, time-of-flight and gesture-detection sensor, and two ST-MEMS audio sensors (digital microphones).
- Microphones: 2 units.
- 64-Mbit Quad-SPI NOR flash memory.
- User button for interrupt input (PC13).
- ST-LINK debugger/programmer: this USB connector provides debugging and virtual COM port support.

The STM32L476G-DISCO makes the following resources available to the user:

- ST-LINK: used as debug port and virtual COM port
- ARM mbed-enabled
- LCD: 24 segments, 4 commons

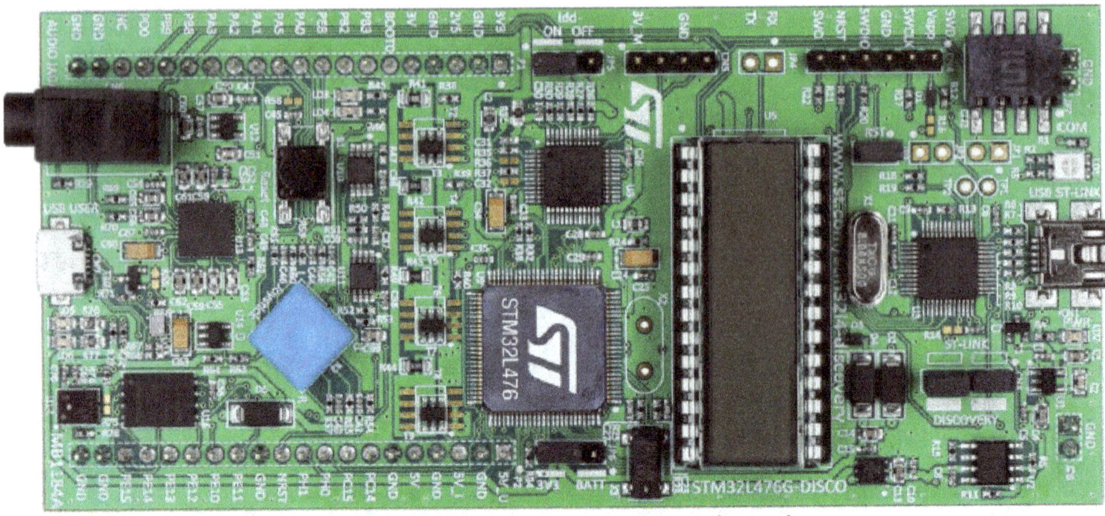

Figure 2.2 STM32L476G-DISCO board

- Two user LEDs: (red LED is connected to PB2 and green LED is connected to PE8)
- Four-direction joystick with selection
- 128-Mbit quad-SPI NOR flash memory: connected to the Quad-SPI interface
- Sensors: three-axis digital output gyroscope and a 3D accelerometer and magnetometer (using SPI interface)
- GPIO pins: PA0~PA3, PA5, PB2~PB3, PB6~PB7, PC14~PC15, PD0, PE8, PE10~PE15, PH0~PH1.
- I^2C connector: PB6 (SCL), PB7 (SDA)
- Audio stereo DAC with output jack: connected to SPI interface
- Digital microphone MEMs

Both boards are inexpensive. The B-L475E-IOT Discovery kit has two advantages over the STM32L476G-DISCO board:

1. Wireless networking capability—indispensable for Internet-of-Things (IoT) experiments.
2. More sensors—the B-L475E-IOT has eight sensors whereas the STM32L476G-DISCO has only three sensors.

2.8 The Software Development Tools

Most users will use an Integrated Development Environment (IDE) to enter and test their application programs for the STM32L475 MCU. An IDE consists of a text editor, cross-assembler, cross-compiler (mostly C compiler), linker, simulator, device drivers, debugger, and project manager.

In this text, we will use the Keil mVision IDE to compile and test all the programs. This IDE has a demo version with a 32-kB size limit. A tutorial for using this IDE is provided in this chapter.

The Keil mVision IDE (and most IDEs) uses project as the unit to manage program development task. There are five major steps in using the Keil mVision IDE to develop applications for the ARM Cortex-M MCU:

Step 1

Create a project.

Step 2

Enter the application program(s) into the project. The user may include existing programs developed earlier in this step.

Step 3

Build the project and eliminate syntax and semantic errors contained in the program.

Step 4

Start the simulator to simulate the compiled program or download the generated file to the target hardware for execution.

Step 5

Enter debug commands to debug the program.

2.8.1 CREATING A NEW PROJECT

Start the mVision IDE by clicking the icon of the Keil mVision IDE. The startup screen is shown in Figure 2.3.

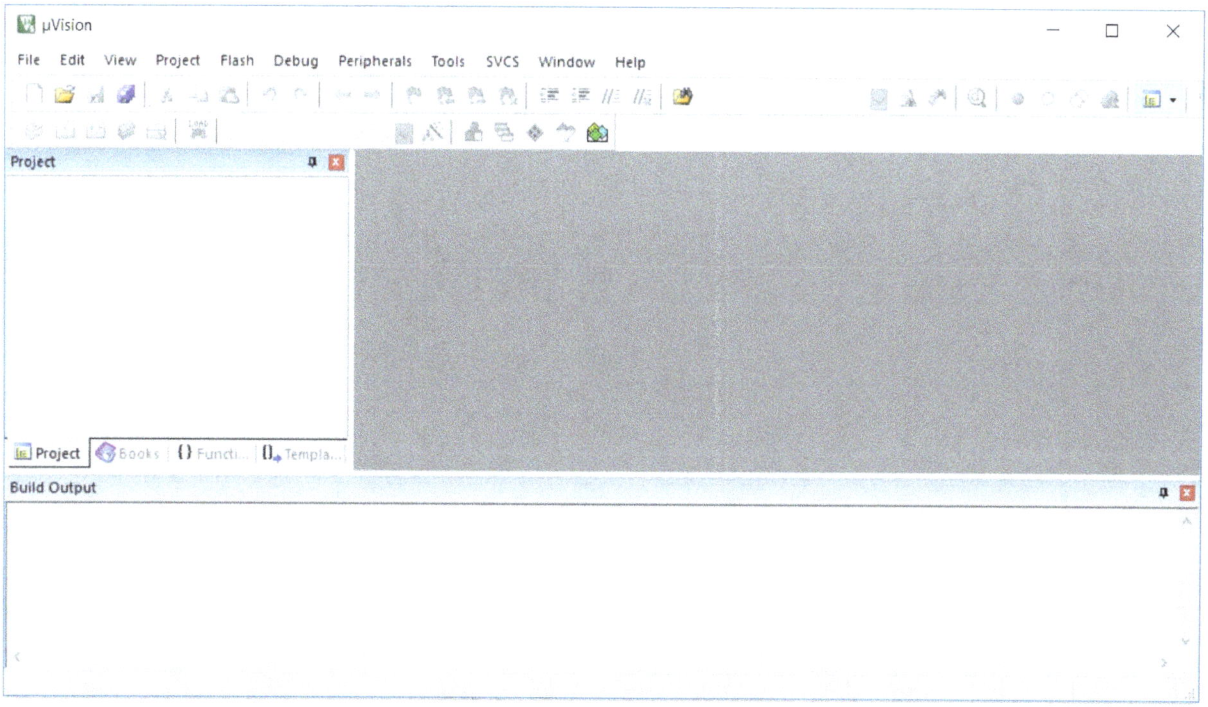

Figure 2.3 Startup screen of Keil µVision

To create a new project, press the **Project** menu and select **New mVision Project**. This step is shown in Figure 2.4. A dialog window appears in Figure 2.5 for the user to select the directory to hold the project files and enter the project name. Enter **ctutor** as the project name and click on **Save**. Another dialog window (shown in Figure 2.6) appears for the user to select the MCU device for the target project. Leave **Software Packs** the way it is. Enter the device name (STM32L475VGT) in the rectangle to the right hand side of **Search** and also click on **STM32L475VGTx**. The screen will change to that shown in Figure 2.7.

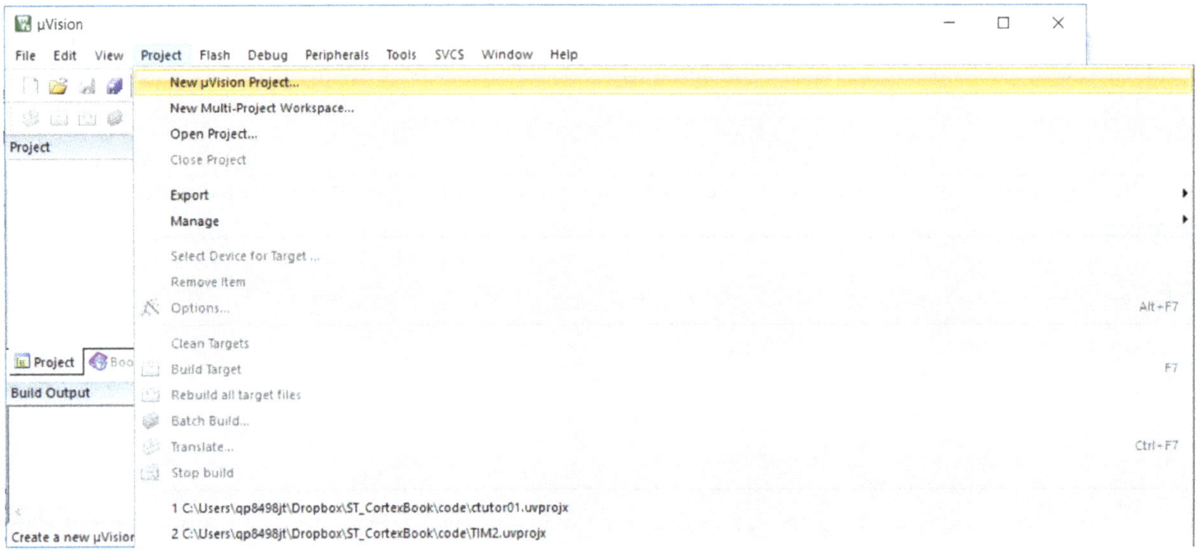

Figure 2.4 Create a new uVision project

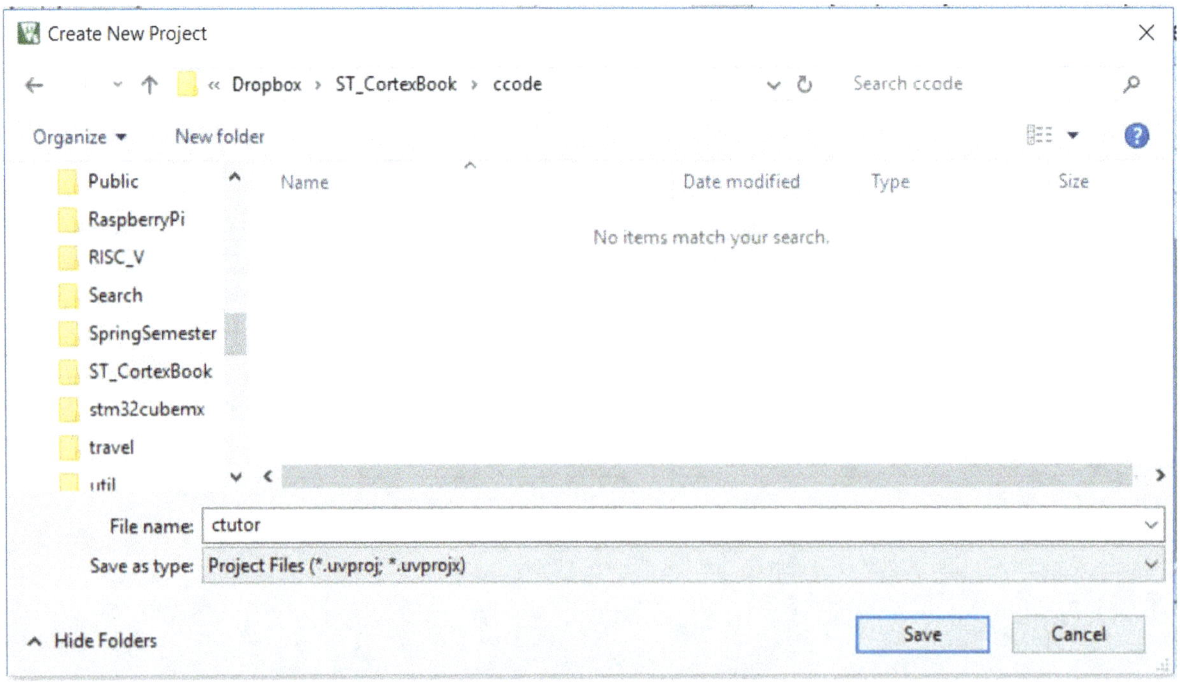

Figure 2.5 Dialog for selecting project folder and entering the project name

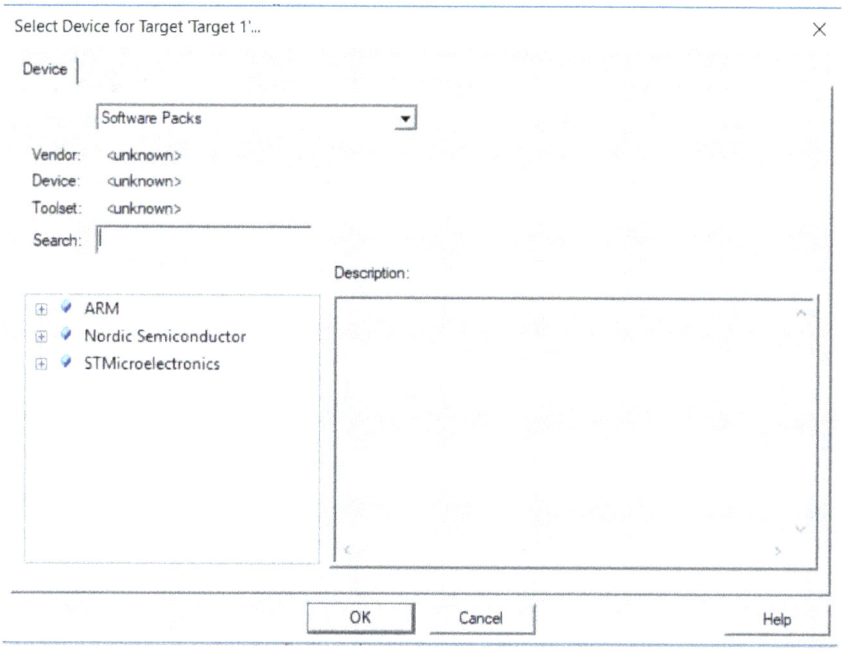

Figure 2.6 Dialog for selecting device name

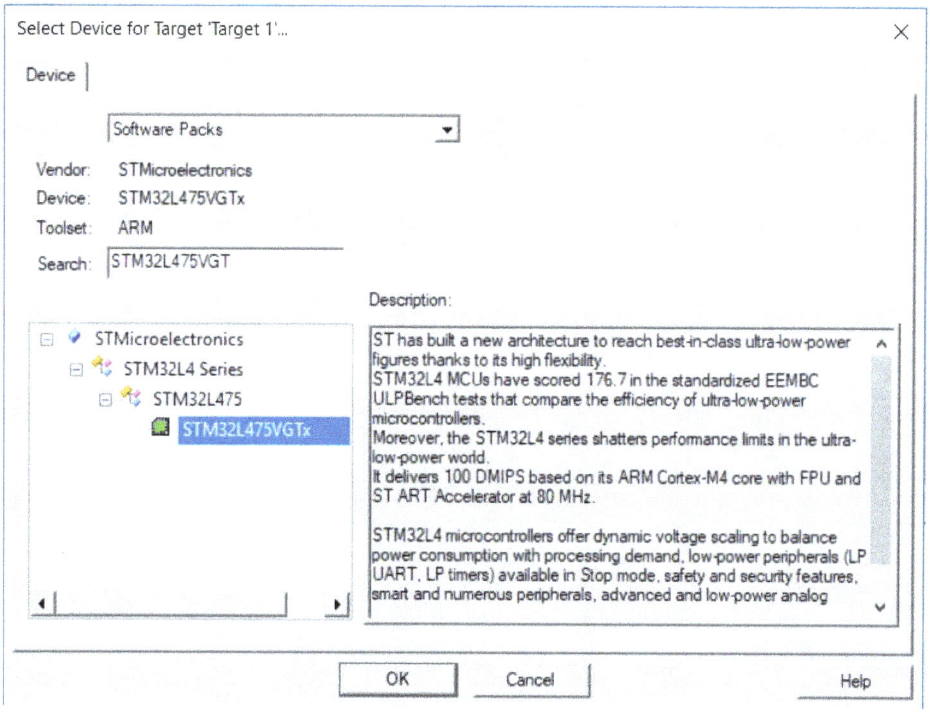

Figure 2.7 Select STM32L475VGT as the target device

Click **OK** and another dialog window (shown in Figure 2.8) will appear for the user to set up the runtime environment.

There are two things in the first column in Figure 2.8 that must be set up in this tutorial. The **first** is the **CMSIS**. Click the + symbol to the left of CMSIS to expand the options for **CMSIS**. The resultant window is shown in Figure 2.9. Click on the box to the right of **Core. Next**, expand the **Device** by clicking on the + character to the left of **Device**. Click the box to the right of **Startup** and **StartupConfig** (shown in Figure 2.10) and then click on **OK** to get rid of the dialog window. The resultant project window is shown in Figure 2.11.

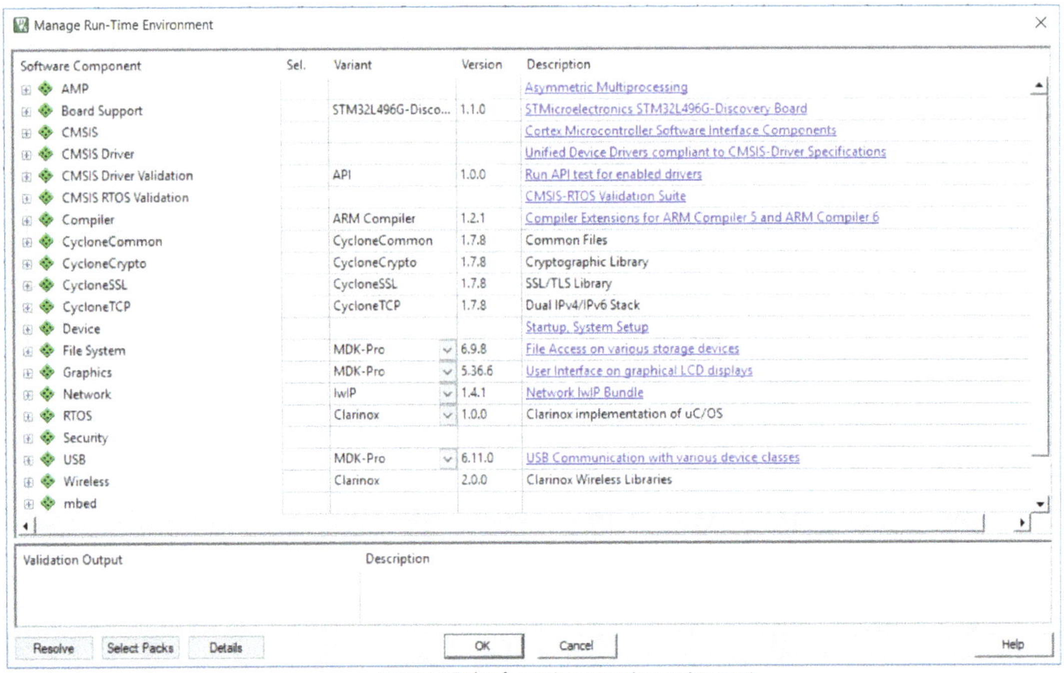

Figure 2.8 Dialog for setting up runtime environment

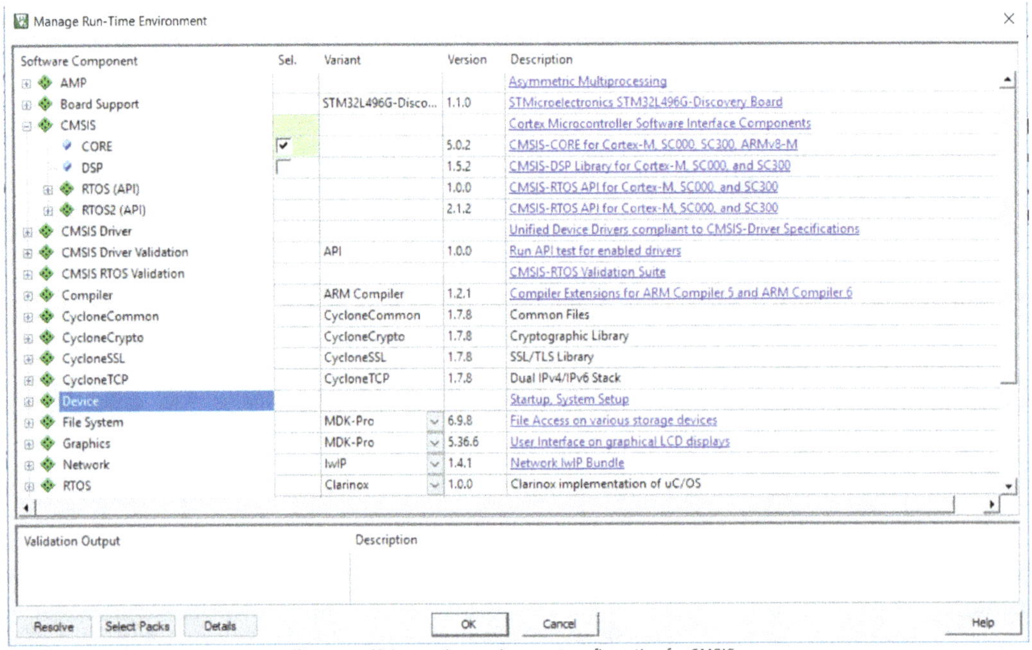

Figure 2.9 µVision runtime environment configuration for CMSIS

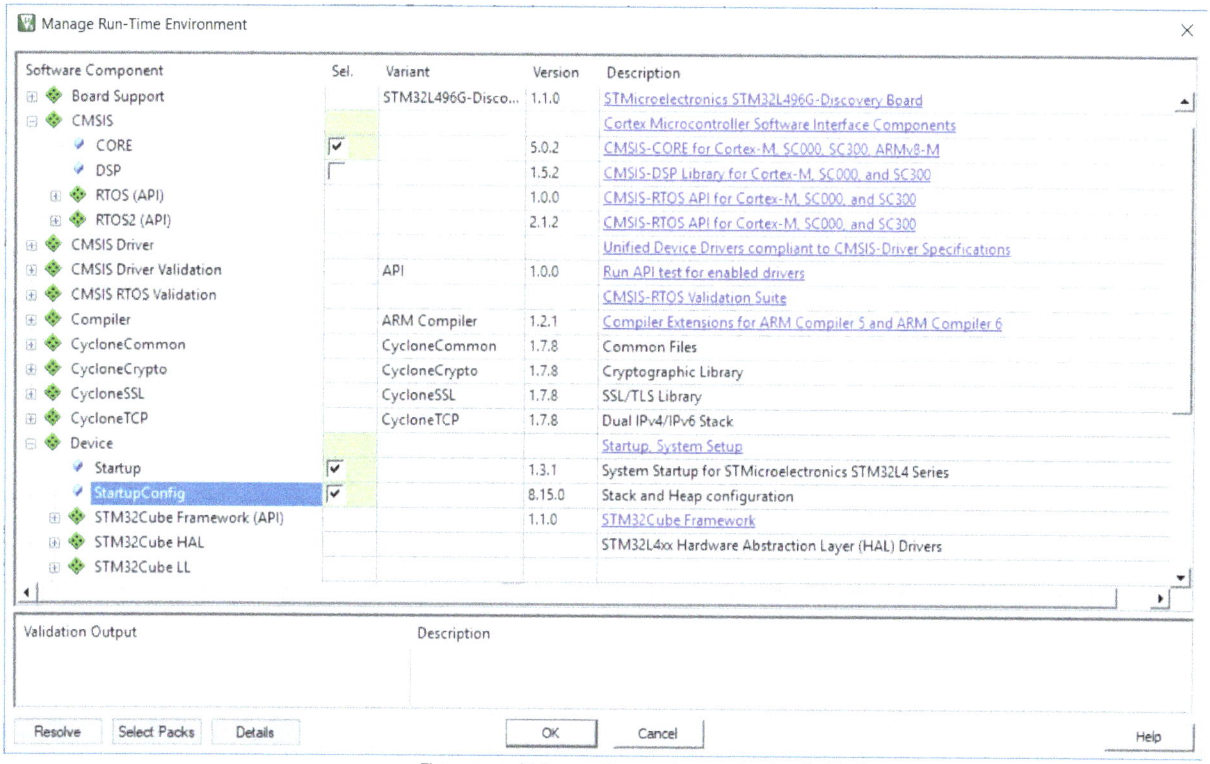

Figure 2.10 µVision runtime environment setup for **Device**

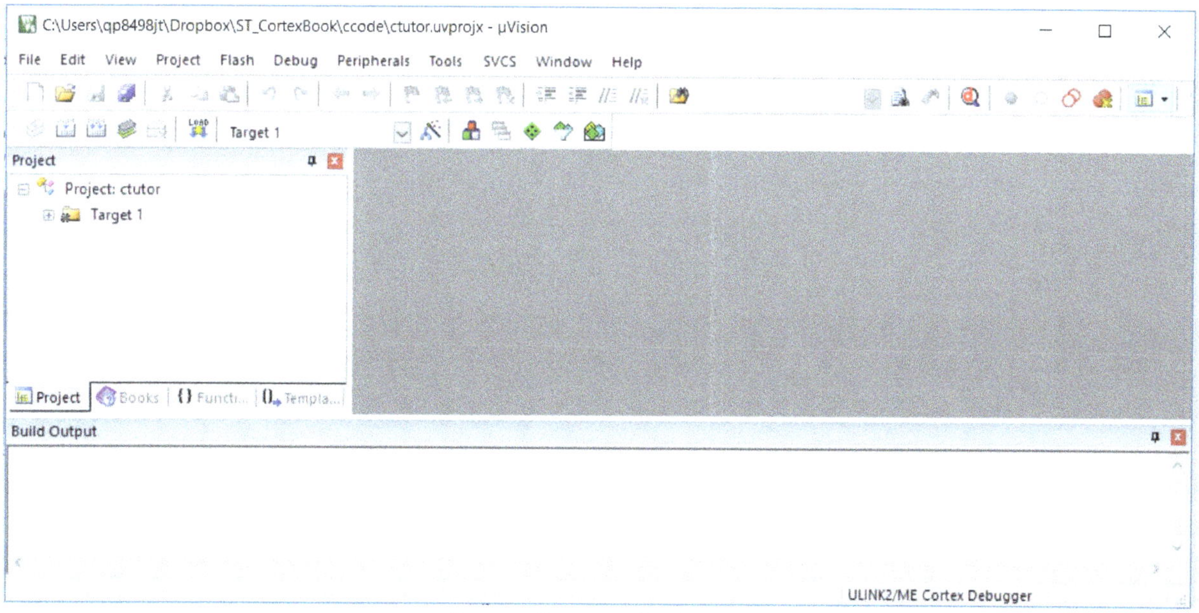

Figure 2.11 Project window for **ctutor**

2.8.2 ENTERING THE PROGRAM

The program to be used as a tutorial is to find all the four-digit decimal numbers having the property that the sum of the square of the upper half and the square of the lower half of the given number equals the original number.

The program is as follows:

```
#include <stm32L475xx.h>
uint32_t xarr[5], y1, y2, y3;
uint32_t test (uint32_t k);
int main (void)
{
    uint32_t    j, k;
    j = 0;
    for (k = 1000; k < 10000; k++){
        if (test(k) == 1) {    // does the current number has the specified property?
            xarr[j] = k;       // yes, save it
            j++;
        }
    }
    y1   = xarr[0];
    y2   = xarr[1];
    y3   = xarr[2];
    while (1);
}
uint32_t test (uint32_t k)
{
    uint32_t xa, xb, xc;
    xa   = k / 100;   // calculate the upper two digits of the number
    xb   = k % 100;   // find the lower half of the number
    xc   = (xa * xa) + (xb * xb);
    if (xc == k)
        return 1;
    else
        return 0;
}
```

To enter a new file to the project, expand **Target1** in Figure 2.11 by clicking the + character to the left of Target1 and the project window changes to that in Figure 2.12. Next, press the right mouse button on **Source Group 1** and select **Add New Item to Source Group 1** (shown in Figure 2.13) and a popup dialog appears as shown in Figure 2.14. Click on **C File (.c)**, enter the file name (for example, **ctutor** in this tutorial), and click on **Add** and the project window changes to that in Figure 2.15.

Sometimes, the user may want to enter existent programs into the project. To do this, select **Add Existing Files** to Group "Source Group 1" instead. A popup dialog will appear to allow the user to select existent files into the project.

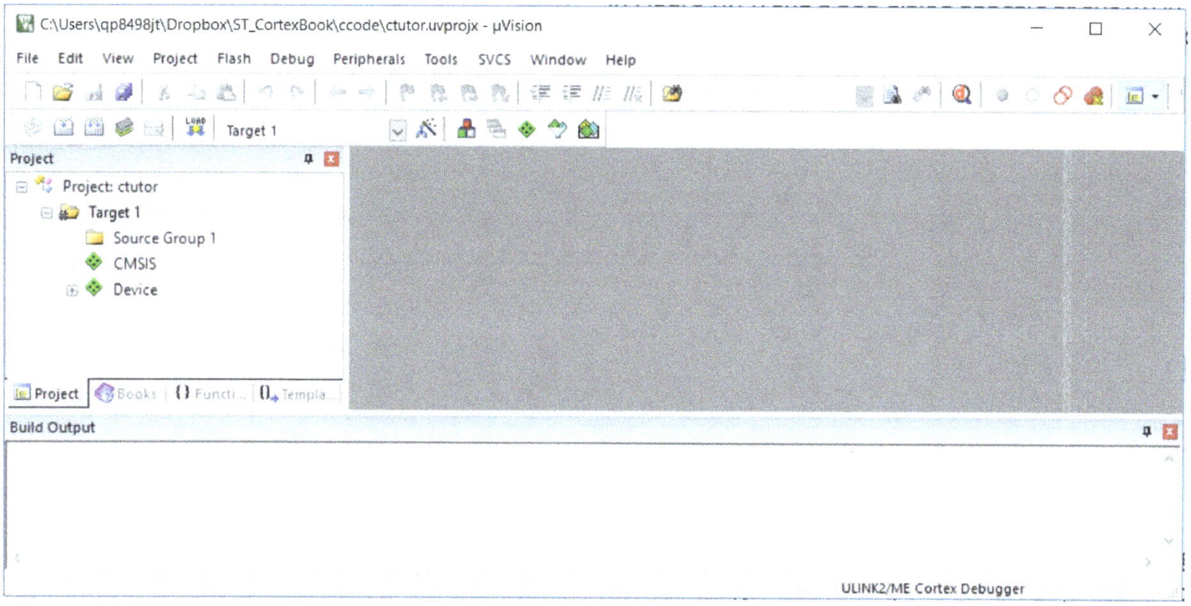

Figure 2.12 Project window after **Target 1** has been expanded

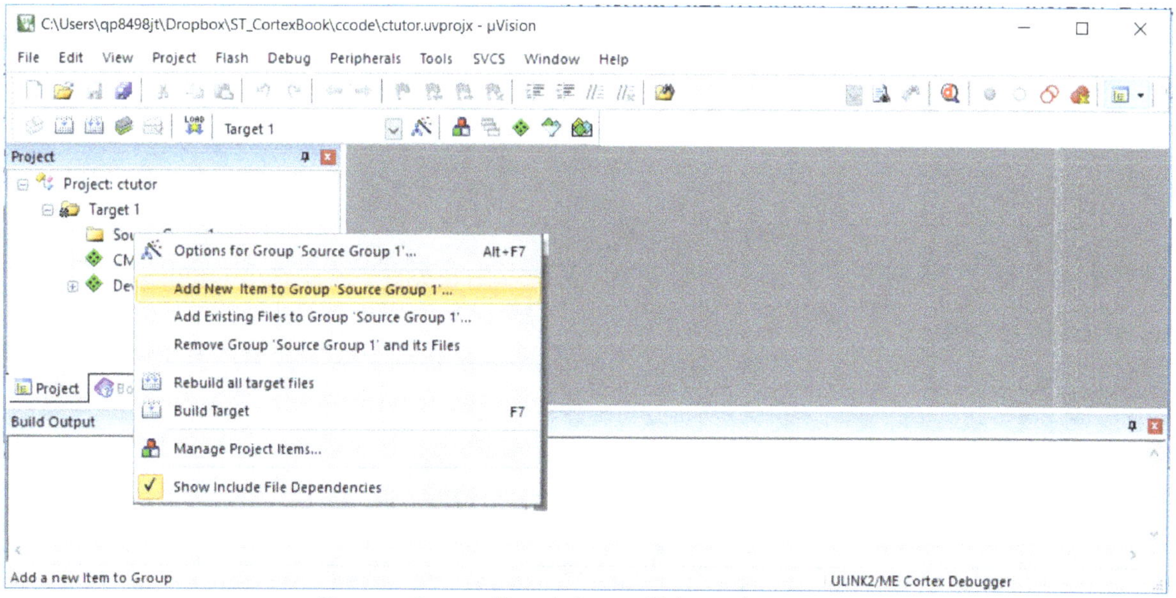

Figure 2.13 Command for entering new file into project

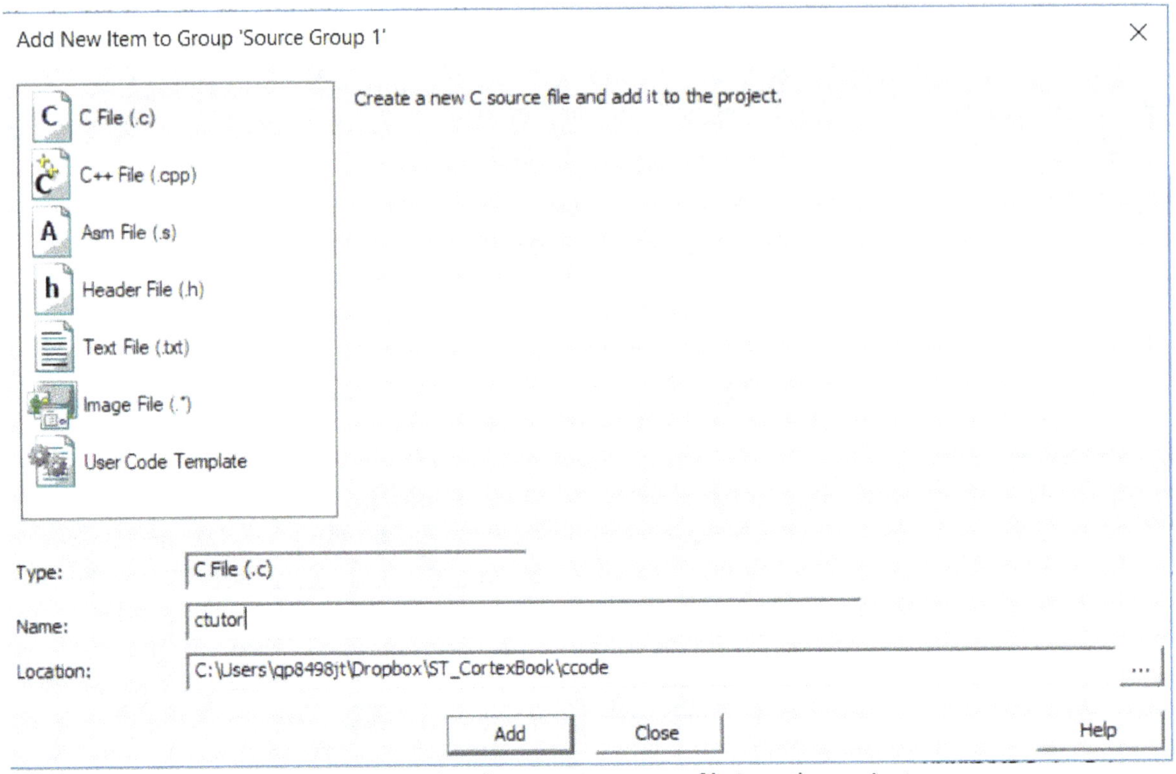

Figure 2.14 Dialog for entering a new file into the project

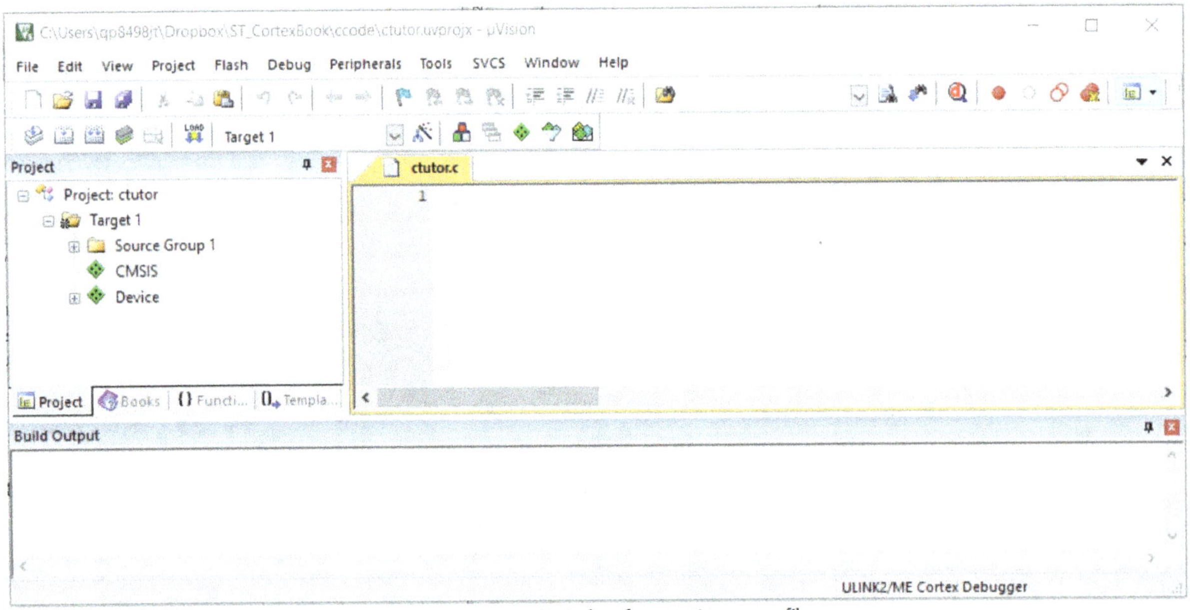

Figure 2.15 Project window for entering a new file

Enter the example program in Figure 2.15. The resultant window is shown in Figure 2.16. If the user enters any undefined variables in any statement, then the IDE will add **red waved underline** to the variable name to remind the user to fix it. For example, if we change the statement 9 to if (text(k) == 1) { // does the current number has the specified property?

then this line will be highlighted as shown in Figure 2.17. A lot of errors can be eliminated in this manner.

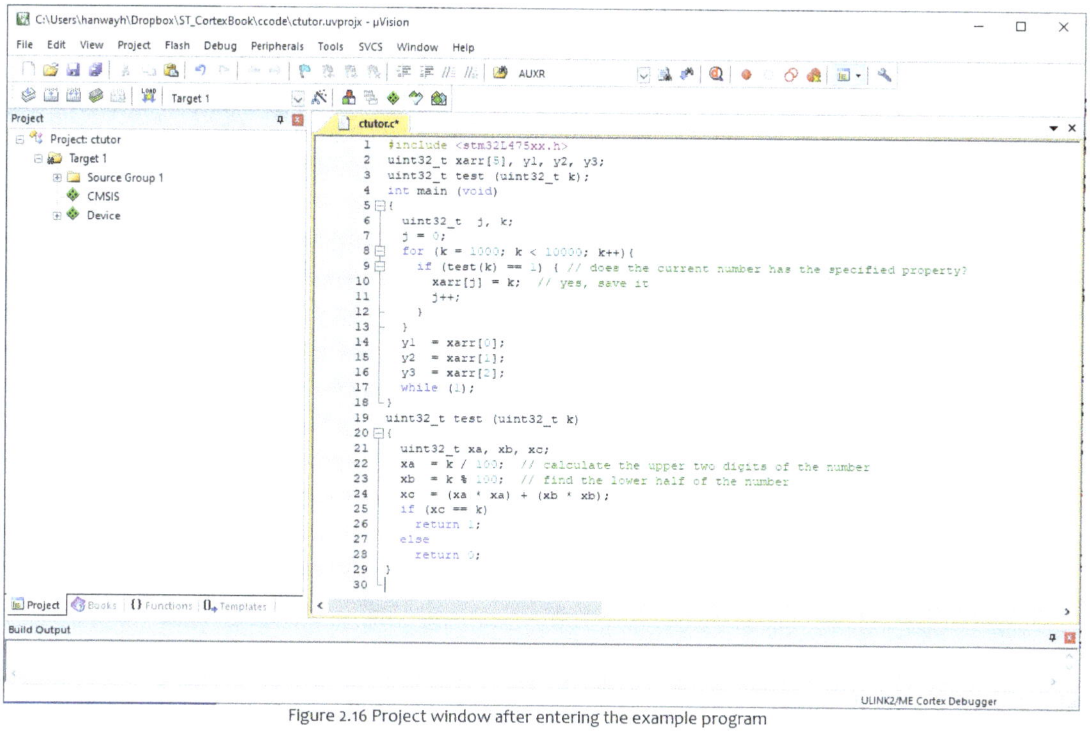

Figure 2.16 Project window after entering the example program

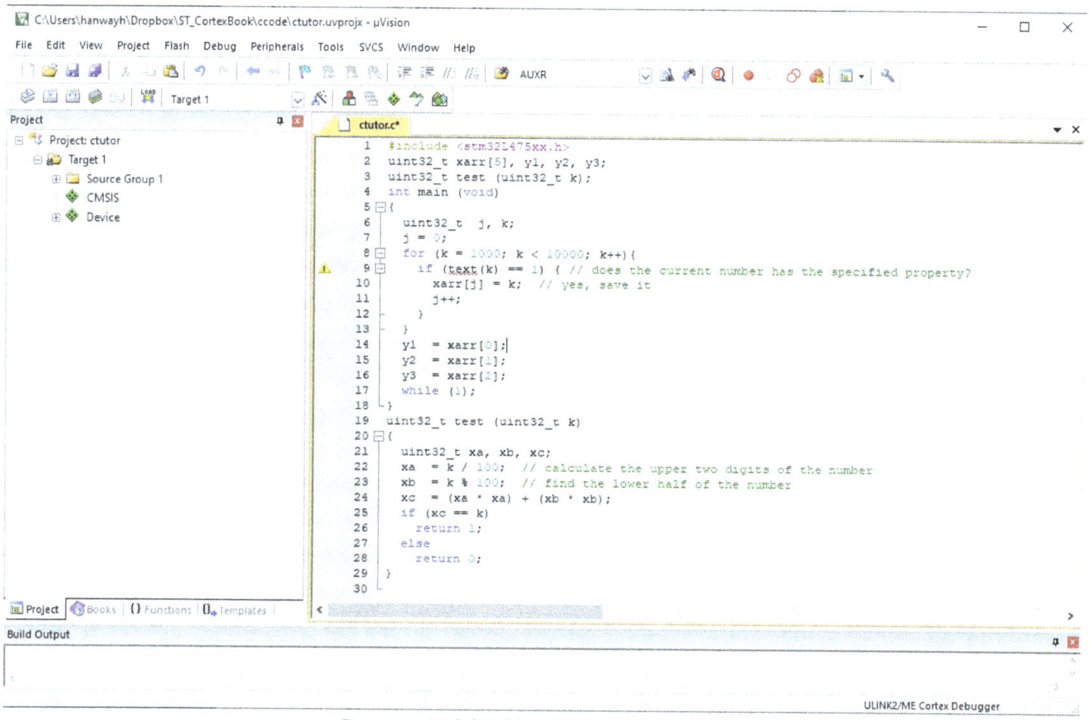

Figure 2.17 Undefined function is high-lighted in line 9

2.8.3 BUILDING THE PROJECT

To build a project is to request the IDE to compile all the source files contained in the project and link them and the involved library files together to generate a hex file that can be downloaded onto the target hardware for execution. The **Build Output** window at the bottom of the project window (see Figure 2.17) displays the build result.

By pressing the **Project** menu and selecting **Build Target** as shown in Figure 2.18, the project will be built. In the Build Output window in Figure 2.19, the Build Output shows 0 Error (s), 0 Warning (s).

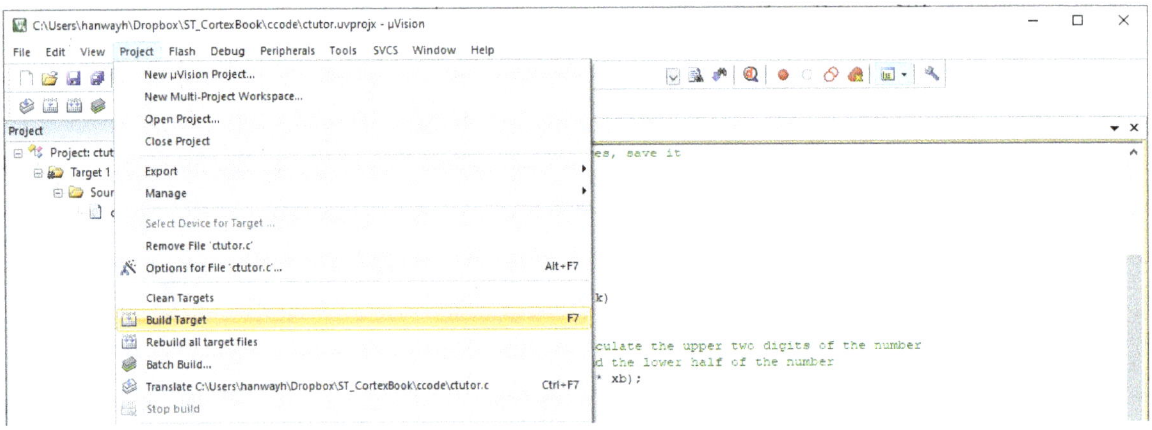

Figure 2.18 Command to build the project

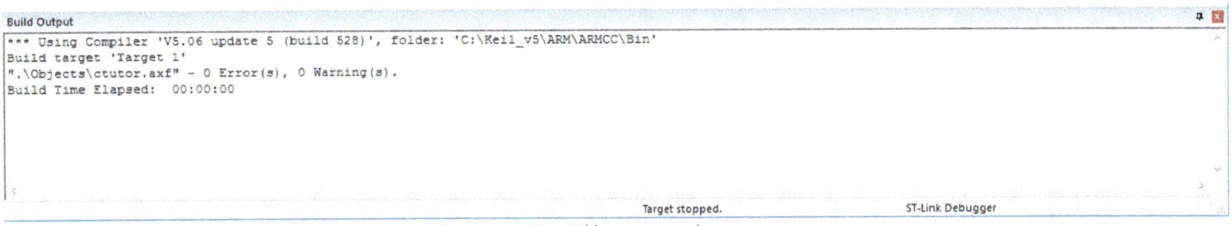

Figure 2.19 mVision Build output example

2.8.4 DOWNLOAD PROJECT ONTO THE DEMO KIT

Before we can download the compiled program onto the demo board, the user is required to configure the debug configuration properly. To do this, press the **Flash** menu and select **Configure Flash Tool...** (as shown in Figure 2.20); a dialog will appear as shown in Figure 2.21.

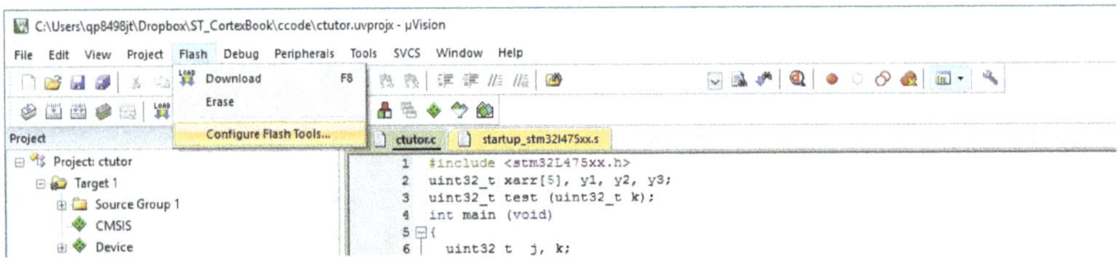

Figure 2.20 Prepare to configure flash tool

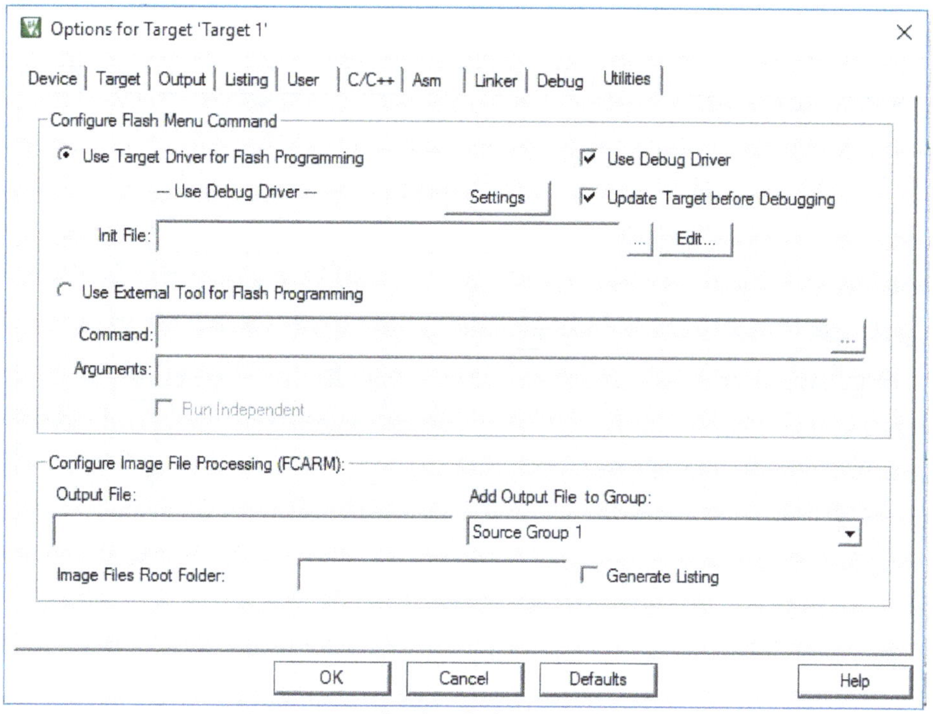

Figure 2.21 Dialog for Flash tool configuration

Click on **Debug** (second row in Figure 2.21 from the top) and make sure that **ST-Link Debugger** is selected (on the upper right corner in Figure 2.22). Click on **Setting** on Figure 2.22. A new dialogue appears as shown in Figure 2.23.

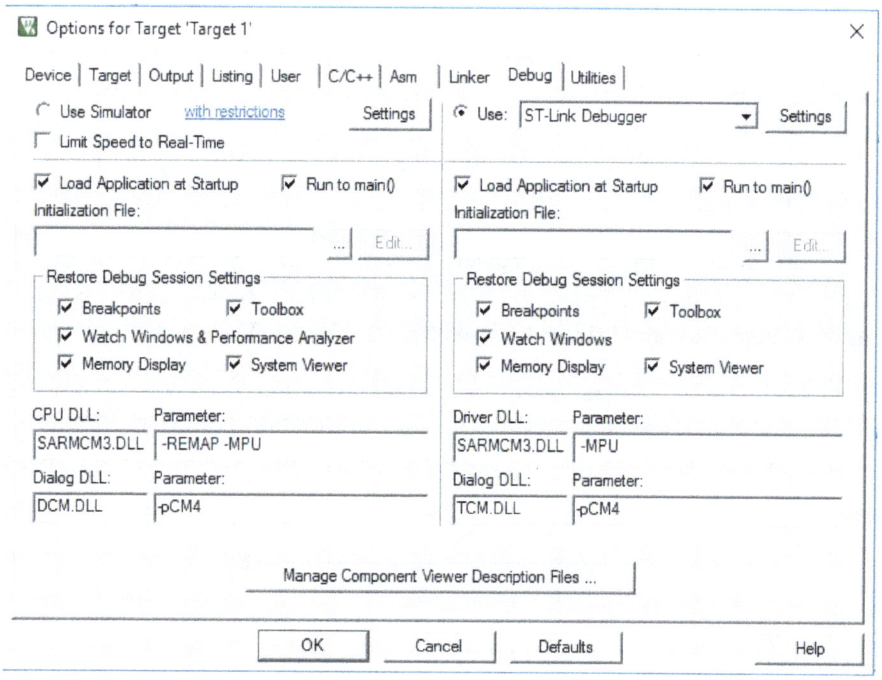

Figure 2.22 Dialog for selecting the ST-Link Debugger

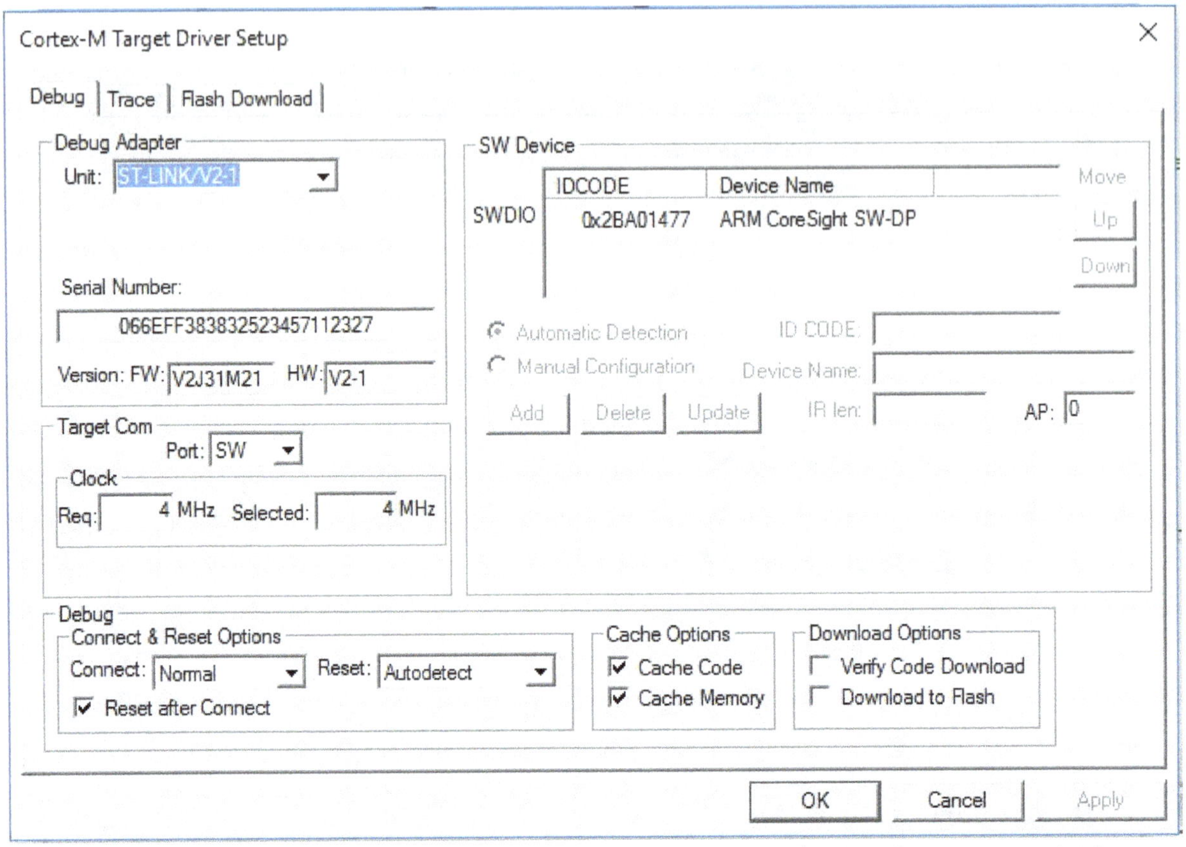

Figure 2.23 Dialogue for setting up Flash Download options (programming algorithm)

If the row to the right of the word SWDIO is empty, then there is an error. This error can be fixed most likely by swapping to different B-L475E-IOT01A1 board. If your dialog window is similar to that in Figure 2.23, click on the **Flash Download** (second row from the top) in Figure 2.23 and another dialogue appears as shown in Figure 2.24. If the space under **Programming Algorithm** is empty, press **Add**, and the programming algorithm will be added in the space. In Figure 2.24, the programming algorithm is already present. You don't need to do anything.

If the same demo board is used in the next project, then the steps described in Figures 2.20 to 2.24 need not be repeated. If you switch to different demo board (with different MCU), then you need to remove the existing programming algorithm and add new algorithm. Click on **OK**s to remove all the dialogues.

To download the program, press the **Flash** menu and select **Download** (shown in Figure 2.25). If the download is successful, the mVision IDE will output the message in the Build Output window as shown in Figure 2.26.

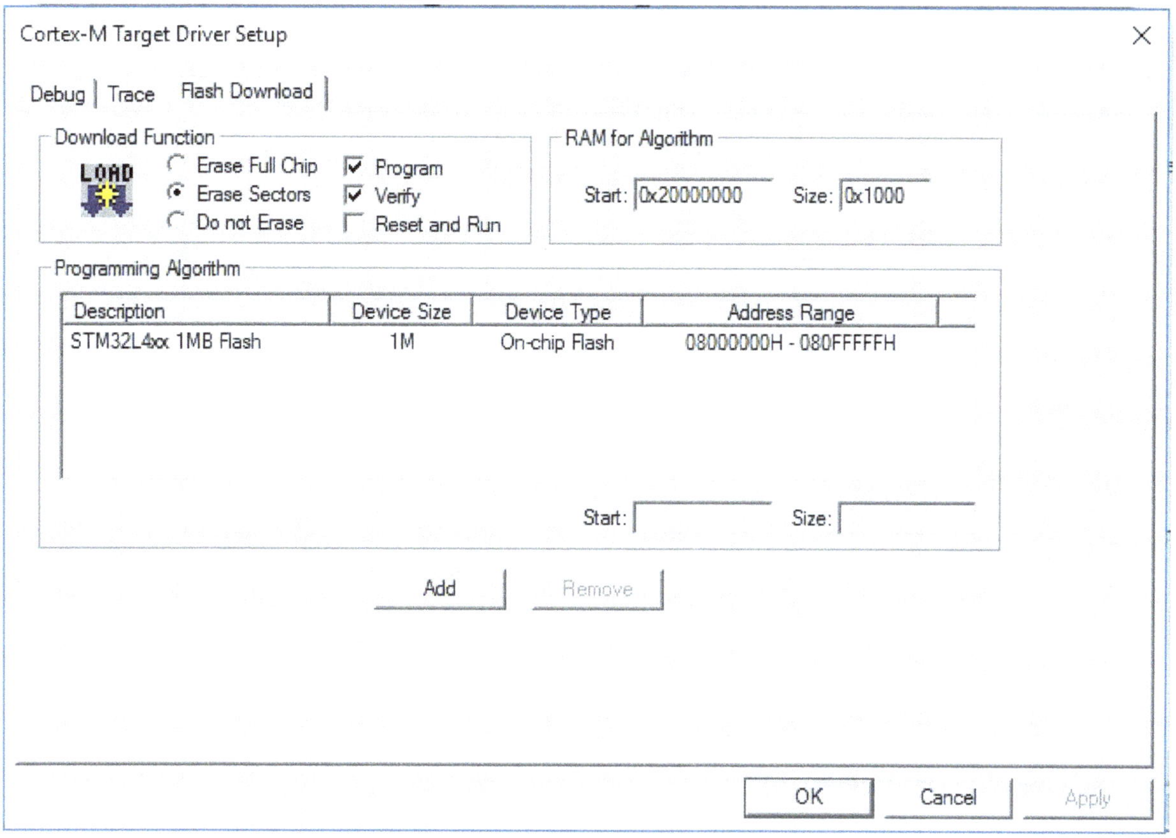

Figure 2.24 Dialogue for adding programming algorithm

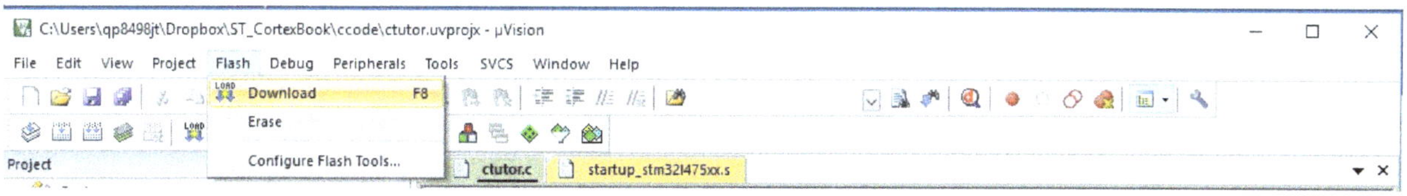

Figure 2.25 Menu for downing the program onto flash memory

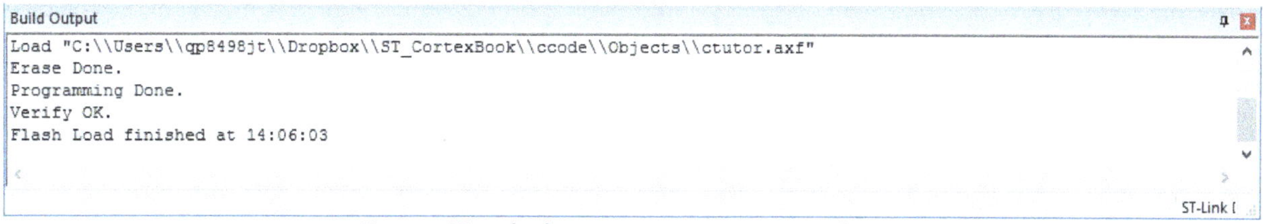

Figure 2.26 Download program output message example

2.8.5 DEBUGGING YOUR PROGRAM

To start program debugging, press the **Debug** menu and select **Start/Stop Debug Session** (**or** press **ctrl+F5**). This is a toggle command. When it is executed for the first time, it starts the debug session and sets the PC to the first executable statement (**j = 0;**) of the user program (as shown in Figure 2.27). When this command is executed during the debug session, it stops the debug session.

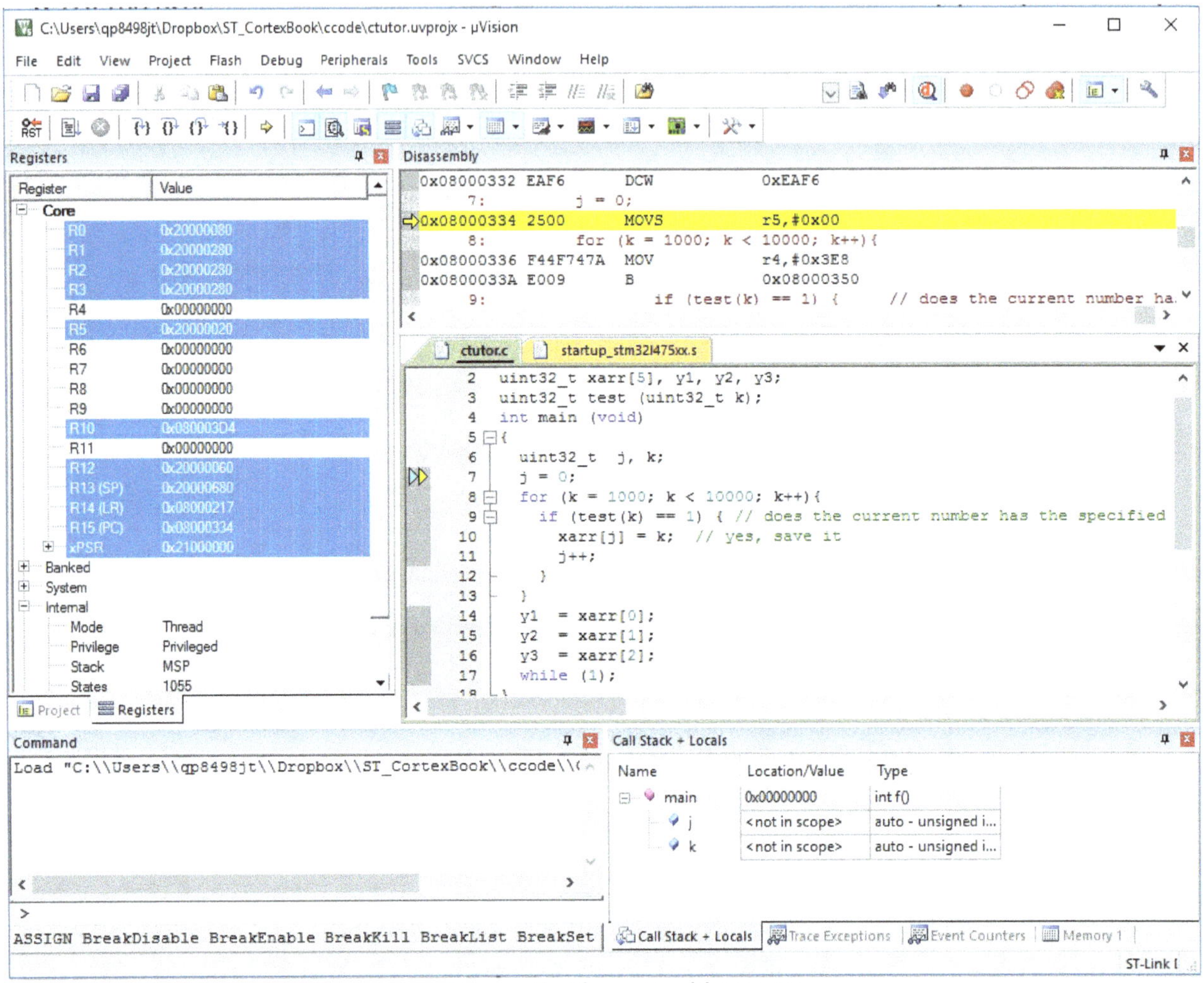

Figure 2.27 Start the program debug session

The **Registers** and **Disassembly** windows may not be useful for the debugging process. The user can get rid of them by clicking the **x** character contained in the **red square** on the upper right corner of these windows. The resultant mVision project window is shown in Figure 2.28.

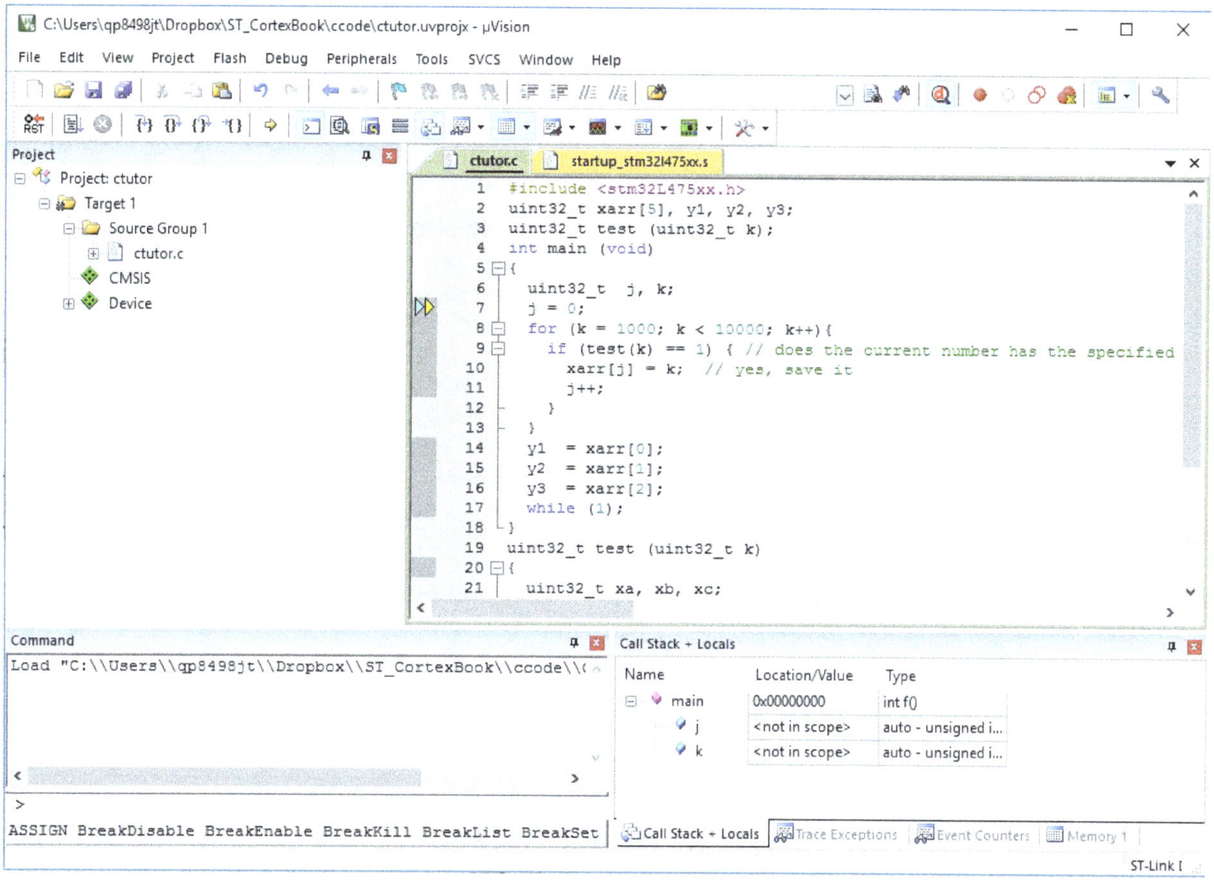

Figure 2.28 Another view of µVision debug window

Place Program Variables in a Watch Window

The example program finds all the four-digit decimal numbers (from 1000 to 9999) having the following property:

The sum of the square of the upper half and the square of the lower half of a given number is equal to itself.

In this example, we save the first three numbers that have the specified property in variables y1, y2, and y3. (We already knew there are only two numbers that have the specified property.) Therefore, these three numbers' values should be examined in order to know whether the given program runs correctly.

In this program, we only need to examine the values of these three variables after the program finishes execution. To add a variable (say, **y1**) to the watch window, press the right mouse button on the variable name (**y1**) and execute **Add 'y1' to → Watch 1** (Figure 2.29). The lower half of the mVision IDE changes to that in Figure 2.28. Follow the same procedure and add **y2** and **y3** into the **Watch 1** window. The result is shown in Figure 2.30. Before the program is executed, the values of the variables in the watch window are 0s.

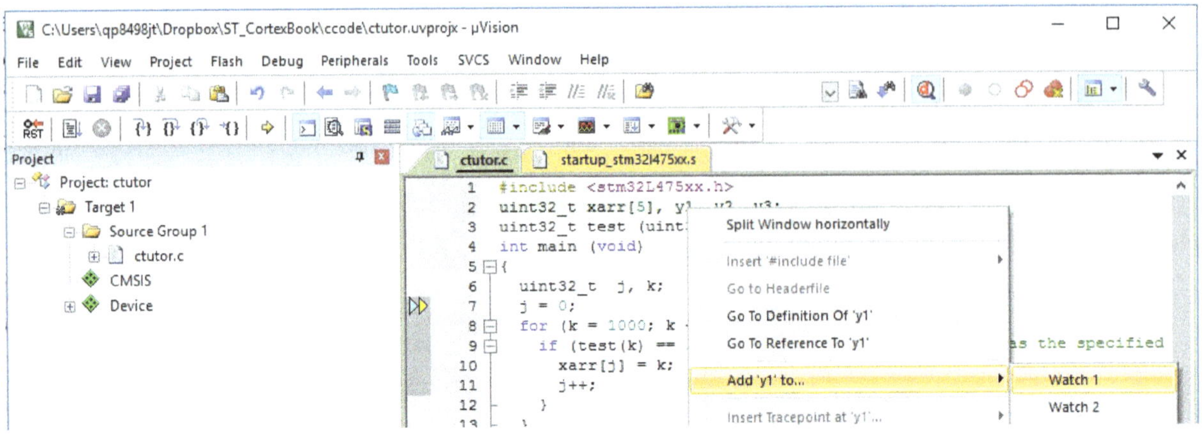

Figure 2.29 Add **y1** to watch window **Watch 1**

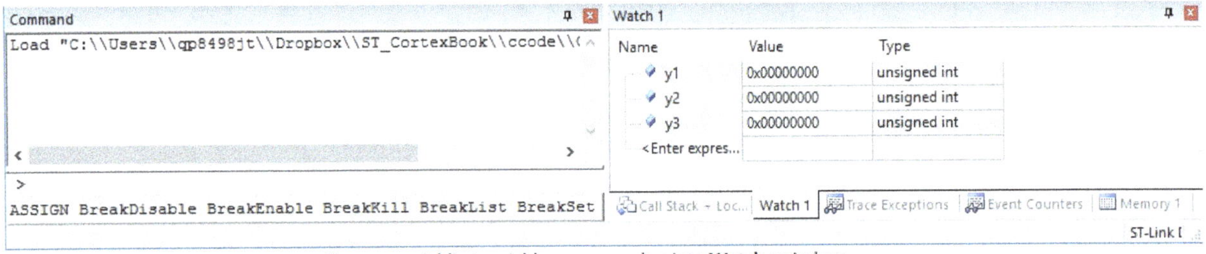

Figure 2.30 Adding variables **y1**, **y2**, and **y3** into **Watch 1** window

The value of variables in the watch window can be displayed in hexadecimal or decimal format. The default is **hexadecimal**. The display format can be changed to decimal by pressing the right mouse button on the **Value** field of the variable to be changed and unchecking the box to the left of **Hexadecimal Display** (shown in Figures 2.31 and 2.32).

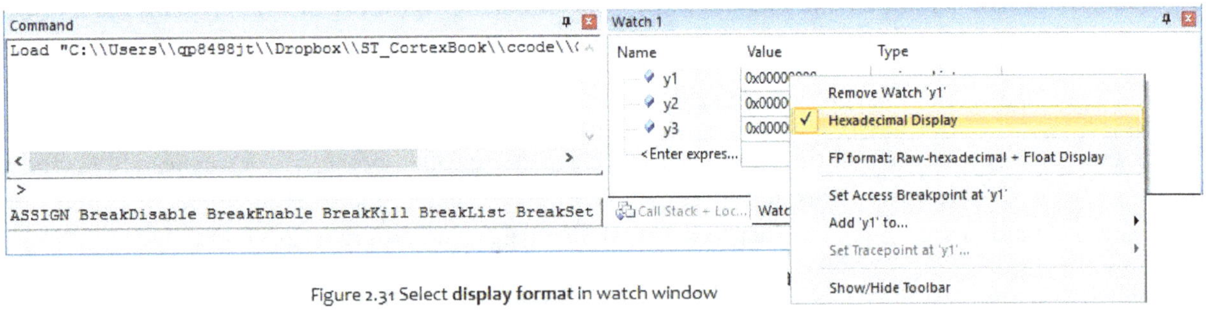

Figure 2.31 Select **display format** in watch window

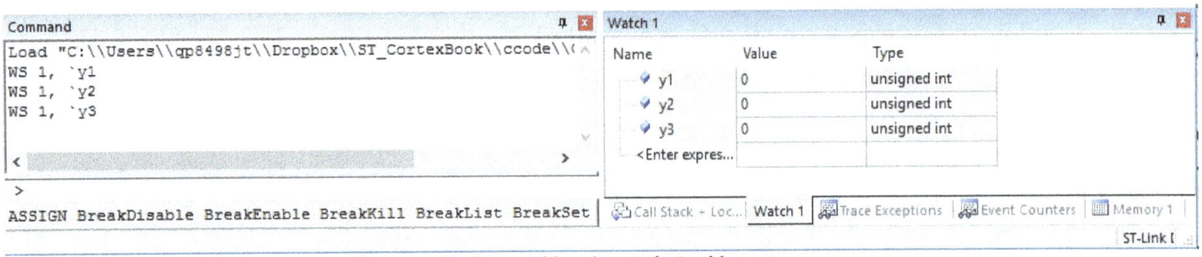

Figure 2.32 Display variable values in **decimal** format

Executing the Program

We need to have a strategy for debugging the program. If the program is not big and will not take a long time to finish the execution, then we can take the following strategy:

Step 1

Let the program executes until the last statement and examine the program variables in the watch window to find out whether the results are correct.

Step 2

If the program does not execute correctly, read the program carefully and locate the suspicious statement that may cause the error. Execute the program until the suspicious statement. You can set a breakpoint at the statement immediately after the suspicious statement and then check the execution result or execute the **Run to Cursor Line** command. The Run to Cursor Line command appears to be much easier.

Step 3

If Step 2 did not identify any error, then repeat the same process, read the program carefully and locate the next suspicious statement and execute the program until the statement immediately after that statement and check the result again.

Step 4

Repeat Step 3 until the error is located and fixed.

If the program takes a long time to execute, then we should execute the program one group of statements from the beginning at a time. Still use the Run to Cursor Line command to find out the program execution result and correct the program errors if there is any during the process.

Run to Cursor Line

To execute the program until certain statement from where the program last stopped, press the right mouse button on the statement you want to stop. For example, if we want to execute until the **while (1);** statement, then press the right mouse button on this statement (as shown in Figure 2.33) and release it. The watch window will be updated after this (shown in Figure 2.34).

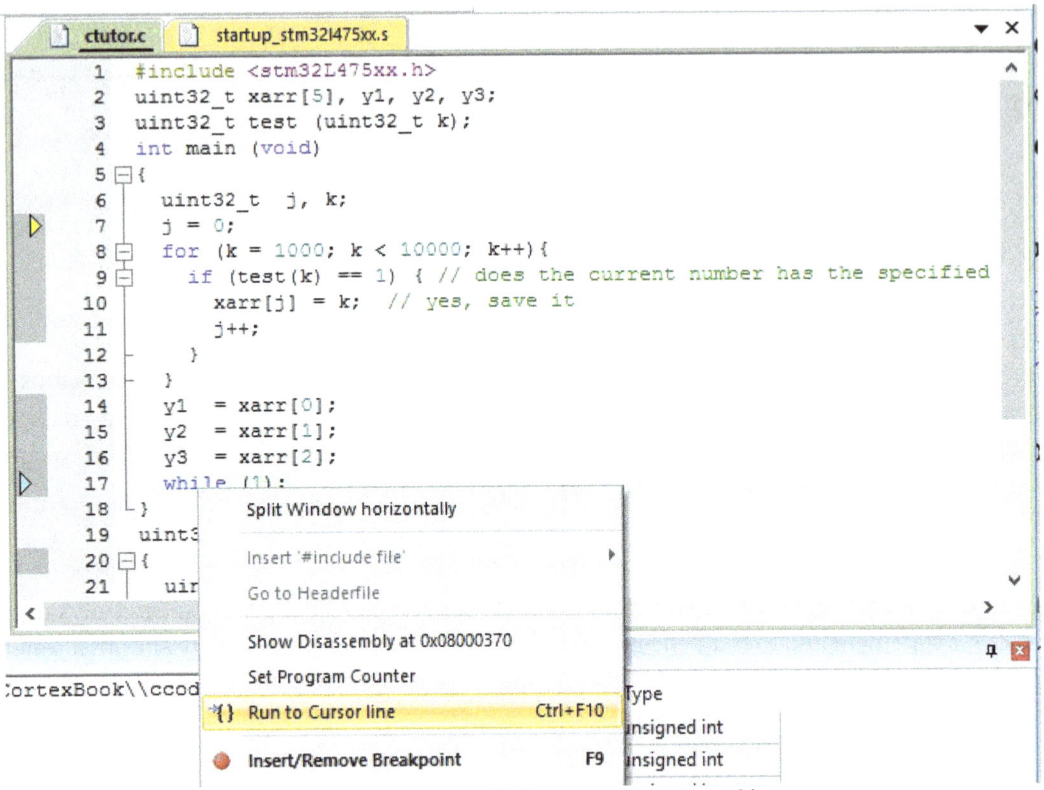

Figure 2.33 Execute until the statement **while (1);**

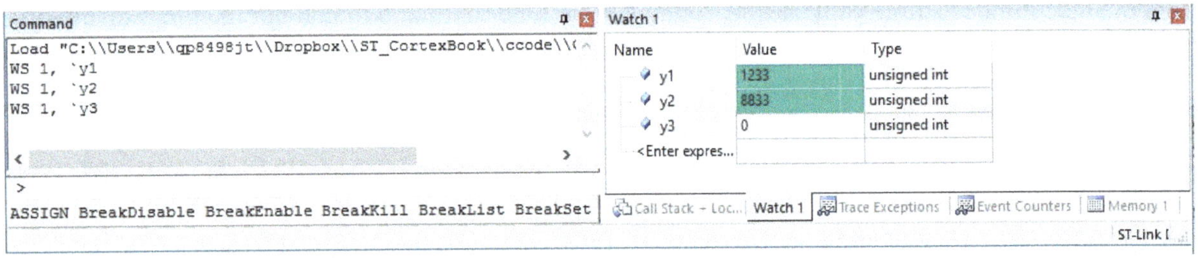

Figure 2.34 Program execution result at the **while (1)** statement

At the end of the program execution, both y1 and y2 have the specified property ($12^2 + 33^2 = 1233$; $88^2 + 33^2 = 8833$). Therefore, our example program is written correctly.

Set a Breakpoint

To set a breakpoint at a statement, press the right mouse button on that statement and execute the command **Insert/Remove Breakpoint**. This is a toggle statement, that is, when you execute this command at a certain statement, which doesn't have a breakpoint, a breakpoint is inserted at that statement. However, if you execute this command at a statement having a breakpoint, then the breakpoint is deleted.

2.9 Summary

A C program consists of one or more functions. One of the functions is the **main** function. Once compiled, built, and downloaded onto the target MCU, the main function will be the first program to execute when the microcontroller gets out of the reset. Writing a working program is not difficult. However, it takes a good discipline to write a C program that works and is easy to understand and maintain. The programming style is this discipline.

The C language provides many facilities that enable the C programmer to be more productive. C language preprocessor commands such as #define, #typedef, #include, and many others are among them. Using these commands enables the C programmer to be more productive and also makes the resultant programs easier to understand and maintain.

Microcontroller programming is about configuring and manipulating the peripheral registers. Each peripheral register is assigned to a memory location and has its own address. All IDEs use C language preprocessor commands to assign a symbolic name to each peripheral register and allows the user to use the symbolic name to access each peripheral register. The IDEs also assign symbolic names to the bit fields contained in most peripheral registers so that the programmer can also use symbolic names to manipulate the bit fields contained in the peripheral registers. This makes the resultant C programmers much more readable.

The user of the STM32L475 MCU can use many IDEs to develop applications. The following is a short list of the popular IDEs:

- Keil mVision IDE (32 KB demo version available)
- IAR Embedded Workbench (32 KB demo version available)
- STM32CubeIDE (freeware)
- SW4TM32 from AC6 (freeware)
- CXSTM32
- CrossWorks
- MULTI IDE from GreenHills
- RIDE-STM32
- SEGGER Embedded Studio

2.10 Exercises

E2.1 Write a C function to find the square root of a positive integer of 2n bits. A common method for finding the square root is the successive approximation method. An unsigned integer represented in 2n bits would have a square root of n bits. This algorithm is as follows:

Step 1

Let **x, SAR, j, mask, tmp** represent the value for which we want to find the square root, successive approximation register, loop index, the mask to guess a bit to be 1, and a temporary storage. Initialize SAR, j, and mask to 0, n, and $10\ldots0_2$.

Step 2

tmp ← SAR | mask;

Step 3

If (tmp * tmp ≤ x)

    SAR ← tmp;

Step 4

mask ← mask >> 1;

Step 5

If (j == 0) stop;

Else

    j ← j - 1;

    go to Step 2.

The successive approximation method finds the integer value which is very close to the true square root of a given positive integer but it tends to be too pessimistic. Sometimes, the value of SAR + 1 is closer to the true square root than the value of SAR. To find the better square root, you need to compare the value of $x - SAR^2$ and that of $(SAR+1)^2 - x$. If the value of $x - SAR^2$ is smaller than that of $(SAR+1)^2 - x$, then SAR is a better choice for the square root. Otherwise, SAR + 1 is a better choice for the square root. Include this consideration in your function.

E2.2 Write a main program to call the **square-root** function written in exercise **E2.1** to find the square roots of three integers such as 9090, 22810, 44599 and store them in three variables for examination.

E2.3 Write a function that performs the **prime test**. The incoming argument is a positive integer which we want to test for prime. The function returns a 1 if the number is a prime. Otherwise, it returns a 0. A natural (positive) number is a prime number if all the prime numbers from 2 to the square root of the given number cannot divide into it (i.e., the remainder of the division is nonzero). However, the prime numbers from 2 to the square root of the given natural number are not available. We are satisfied with the test that divides all the natural numbers from 2 to the square root (an integer approximation only) of the given natural number.

E2.4 Write a program to find three prime numbers that are closest to but are above 10000 and three prime numbers that are closest to but below 10000.

E2.5 Write a function to test whether a four-digit decimal number has the property that the square of the sum of the upper half and the lower half of this number equals itself. The function returns a 1 to the caller if the given number has this property. Otherwise, it returns a 0. The number to be tested is the only incoming argument to this function.

E2.6 Write a main program to find out all the four-digit decimal numbers having the property mentioned in exercise **E2.5** and store them in an array for examination.

E2.7 Write a C function that tests whether a six-digit decimal integer (from 100000 to 999999) has the property that the sum of the square of its upper half and the square of its lower half equals the original number. The function returns a 1 if the given number has the specified property. Otherwise, it returns a 0.

E2.8 Write a C program to call the C function written in **E2.7** to find out all the six-digit decimal numbers that have the property mentioned in problem **E2.7** and store these numbers in an array.

2.11 Lab Assignments

L2.1 Finding all the three-digit Armstrong numbers. A three-digit Armstrong number $d_2d_1d_0$ has the property that $d_2^3 + d_1^3 + d_0^3 = d_2d_1d_0$.

(a) Write a function to test whether a three-digit number is an Armstrong number. The number to be tested is passed to this function. The function returns a 1 to the caller if the number is a three-digit Armstrong number. Otherwise, it returns a 0.
(b) Write a main function to find all the three-digit Armstrong numbers and store them in an array.

L2.2 Finding all the four-digit Armstrong numbers. A four-digit Armstrong number $d_3d_2d_1d_0$ has the property that $d_3^4 + d_2^4 + d_1^4 + d_0^4 = d_3d_2d_1d_0$.

(a) Write a function to test whether a four-digit number is an Armstrong number. The number to be tested is passed to this function. The function returns a 1 to the caller if the number is a four-digit Armstrong number. Otherwise, it returns a 0.
(b) Write a main function to find all the four-digit Armstrong numbers and store them in an array.

L2.3 Write a program to find four prime numbers that are closest but less than 20000 and three prime numbers that are closest to but larger than 30000.

3

System Clock Generation

3.1 Objectives

After finishing this chapter, you will be able to

- Describe the STM32L475 clock sources.
- Configure every clock source of the STM32L475 MCU.
- Generate clock signals.
- Use PLL to multiply the frequency of clock signals.
- Distribute clock signals to peripheral modules.
- Selectively enable and disable clock signals during sleep and stop modes to save power.

3.2 Introduction

Clock signals are required for the proper operation of every component of the microcontroller. Because the ARM Cortex-M-based microcontroller has many on-chip peripherals, its clock system is also very complicated.

3.2.1 WHAT IS A CLOCK SIGNAL?

In a synchronous digital circuit, a **clock signal** is a special type of periodic signal that oscillates between a high and a low state in every cycle. The clock signal is used to coordinate the actions of digital circuits. The state change of flip-flops, counters, and registers are controlled by the edge of a clock signal.

3.2.2 WAVEFORM OF A CLOCK SIGNAL

A clock signal is produced by a **clock generator**. Although more complex formats have been used, the most common clock signal is in the form of a square wave with 50% duty cycle and with a fixed frequency. Circuits using the clock signal for synchronization may become active at either the rising edge, falling edge, or, in the case of double data rate, both in the rising and in the falling edges of the clock cycle.

3.2.3 CIRCUITS FOR GENERATING CLOCK SIGNALS

Every microprocessor and microcontroller has pins (usually two) to connect to an external crystal oscillator (or ceramic resonator), which generates a sinusoidal signal of certain frequency and drives one of these two pins. This sinusoidal signal will be converted into a square wave by a circuit inside the microprocessor or microcontroller and then distributed to every part of the chip. Crystal oscillators have much tighter frequency tolerance (about 0.001%) than the ceramic resonators (no better than 0.5%). Ceramic resonators should be used only for those applications for which the frequency accuracy is not critical. Modern microcontrollers also have included on-chip RC oscillators to generate clock signals. The RC oscillators have even worse frequency tolerance than the ceramic oscillator. However, microcontroller manufacturers add a calibration circuit to the RC oscillator to calibrate the RC oscillator output frequency. By doing so, microcontroller manufacturers claim that the RC oscillator can achieve a 0.1% frequency tolerance.

The operations of different parts of the microprocessor and microcontroller chip are synchronized by the clock signal. As processors become more and more complicated, the task of supplying accurate and synchronized clocks to different parts of the chip becomes increasingly more difficult.

3.2.4 GATING CLOCK SIGNALS

A clock signal might also be gated, that is, **ANDed,** with a controlling signal that enables or disables the clock signal to a certain part of the chip. This technique is often used to save power by effectively shutting down portions of a microcontroller when they are not in use.

3.2.5 PHASES OF CLOCK SIGNALS

Historically, both two-phase and four-phase clocking schemes have been used. However, these two schemes require many more wires to distribute the clock signals and hence are not suitable for today's high-density integrated circuits. Most modern synchronous circuits use only a **single phase clock**—in other words, they transmit all clock signals on one wire (i.e., one clock one wire).

3.2.6 MULTIPLYING AND SCALING CLOCK FREQUENCIES

Many modern microprocessors and microcontrollers have a **clock multiplier**, which can multiply the frequency of an external clock with a relatively low frequency to the appropriate clock rate needed by the processor. The clock signal of the higher frequency can further be scaled (divided) to several outputs of different frequencies and then distributed to peripherals that require different frequency to function. The **phase-locked loop (PLL)** is the most commonly used clock multiplier circuit.

3.3 The STM32L475 Clock System

The STM32L475 has a clock controller which distributes the clock signals coming from different oscillators to the processor core and the peripherals. The clock controller also manages clock gating for low-power modes and ensures clock robustness.

The clock controller generates a **system clock** (SYSCLK), which is used to derive clock signals used by the processor and most (not all) peripherals. Some peripherals may also obtain their clock signals directly from the clock sources in addition to the SYSCLK. This will be detailed in a later section.

3.3.1 CLOCK SOURCES

The STM32L475 has six clock sources; among them, the following four clock sources can be used as the source of the **system clock (SYSCLK)**:

- High-speed internal 16-MHz RC oscillator clock (**HSI16**)
- Multispeed internal RC oscillator clock (**MSI**), from 100 kHz to 48 MHz
- High-speed external clock (**HSE**), from 4 to 48 MHz
- PLL clock

The following two clock sources cannot be used to generate the system clock:

- 32-kHz low-speed internal RC (**LSI RC**) oscillator, which drives the independent watchdog and optionally the real-time clock (RTC) used for auto-wakeup from stop and standby modes.
- 32.768-kHz low-speed external crystal (**LSE crystal**), which optionally drives the RTC.

3.3.2 THE HSE CLOCK

The high-speed external clock signal (HSE) can be generated from two possible clock sources:

1. HSE external crystal/ceramic resonator
2. HSE external clock

The crystal oscillator or the resonator should be connected to the OSC_IN and OSC_OUT pins shown in Figure 3.1. The crystal oscillator/ceramic resonator and the load capacitors have to be placed as close as possible to the OSC_IN and OSC_OUT pins in order to minimize output distortion and startup stabilization time. The loading capacitor values must be adjusted according to the selected oscillator. The external crystal (or ceramic resonator) produces a sinusoidal wave, which will be converted into a square wave by the on-chip HSE circuit and then distributed to be used by the processor and peripherals.

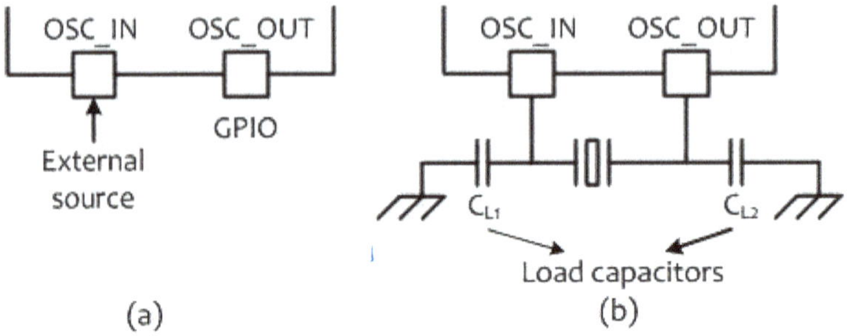

Figure 3.1 HSE clock sources

The HSE circuit must be turned on in order to function. This is achieved by setting the HSEON bit of the RCC->CR register. Before the frequency of the HSE is stabilized, it should not be selected as the source of the SYSCLK. The contents of the RCC->CR register are shown in Figure 3.2.

If the external crystal oscillator is used, its frequency can be from 4 to 48 MHz. However, we can also connect an external clock signal directly to the OSC_IN pin and leave the OSC_OUT pin in high-impedance state. The external clock signal must have a duty cycle between 40% and 60% and its waveform can be square, sinusoidal, or triangular. The frequency of the external clock signal can be up to 48 MHz. To use an external clock signal instead of a crystal oscillator, both the HSEBYP and HSEON bits in the RCC->CR register (Figure 3.2) must be set to 1.

The main advantage of the HSE is its extremely high-frequency accuracy.

31	30	29	28	27	26	25	24
--	--	PLLSAI2 RDY	PLLSAI2 ON	PLLSAI1 RDY	PLLSAI1 ON	PLLRDY	PLLON
23	**22**	**21**	**20**	**19**	**18**	**17**	**16**
--	--	--	--	CSSON	HSEBYP	HSERDY	HSEON
15	**14**	**13**	**12**	**11**	**10**	**9**	**8**
--	--	--	--	HSIASFS	HSIRDY	HSI KERON	HSION
7	**6**	**5**	**4**	**3**	**2**	**1**	**0**
MSIRANGE[3:0]				MSI RGSEL	MSI PLLEN	MSIRDY	MSION

Reset value = 0x0000 0063
Offset = 0x00
Access: no wait state

PLLSAI2RDY: SAI2 (serial audio interface) PLL clock ready flag
0: PLLSAI2 unlocked 1: PLLSAI2 locked
PLLSAI2ON: SAI2 PLL enable
0: PLLSAI2 OFF 1: PLLSAI2 enabled
PLLSAI1RDY: SAI1 PLL clock ready flag
0: PLLSAI1 unlocked 1: PLLSAI1 locked
PLLSAI1ON: SAI1 PLL enable
0: PLLSAI1 OFF 1: PLLSAI1 enabled
PLLRDY: Main PLL clock ready flag
0: PLL unlocked 1: PLL locked
PLLON: Main PLL enable
0: PLL OFF 1: PLL enabled

Figure 3.2 Clock control register (RCC->CR)

31	30	29	28	27	26	25	24
--	--	PLLSAI2 RDY	PLLSAI2 ON	PLLSAI1 RDY	PLLSAI1 ON	PLLRDY	PLLON
23	**22**	**21**	**20**	**19**	**18**	**17**	**16**
--	--	--	--	CSSON	HSEBYP	HSERDY	HSEON
15	**14**	**13**	**12**	**11**	**10**	**9**	**8**
--	--	--	--	HSIASFS	HSIRDY	HSI KERON	HSION
7	**6**	**5**	**4**	**3**	**2**	**1**	**0**
MSIRANGE[3:0]				MSI RGSEL	MSI PLLEN	MSIRDY	MSION

Reset value = 0x0000 0063
Offset = 0x00
Access: no wait state

CSSON: Clock security system enable
- 0: Clock security system OFF (clock detector OFF)
- 1: Clock security system ON (clock detector ON if the HSE oscillator is stable, OFF if not)

HSEBYP: HSE crystal oscillator bypass
- 0: HSE crystal oscillator not bypassed
- 1: HSE crystal oscillator is bypassed with external clock

HSERDY: HSE clock ready flag
- 0: HSE oscillator not ready 1: HSE oscillator ready (i.e., frequency is stable)

HSEON: HSE clock enable
- 0: HSE oscillator OFF 1: HSE oscillator ON

This bit cannot be reset if HSE oscillator is used directly or indirectly as the source of system clock.

HSIASFS: HSI16 automatic start from Stop
- 0: HSI16 oscillator is not enabled by hardware when exiting stop mode with MSI as wakeup clock.
- 1: HSI16 oscillator is enabled when exiting stop mode with MSI as wakeup clock.

HSIRDY: HSI16 clock ready flag
- 0: HSI16 oscillator not ready 1: HSI16 oscillator ready

Figure 3.2a Clock control register (RCC->CR)—(continued)

31	30	29	28	27	26	25	24
--	--	PLLSAI2 RDY	PLLSAI2 ON	PLLSAI1 RDY	PLLSAI1 ON	PLLRDY	PLLON

23	22	21	20	19	18	17	16
--	--	--	--	CSSON	HSEBYP	HSERDY	HSEON

15	14	13	12	11	10	9	8
--	--	--	--	HSIASFS	HSIRDY	HSI KERON	HSION

7	6	5	4	3	2	1	0
MSIRANGE[3:0]				MSI RGSEL	MSI PLLEN	MSIRDY	MSION

Reset value = 0x0000 0063
Offset = 0x00
Access: no wait state

HSIKERON: HSI16 always enabled for peripheral kernels
  0: No effect on HSI16 oscillator 1: HSI16 oscillator is forced ON in Stop mode.
HSION: HSI16 clock enable
  0: HSI16 oscillator OFF 1: HSI16 oscillator ON
MSIRANGE[3:0]: MSI clock ranges
  These bits choose the frequency range of MSI when MSIRGSEL is set.
  See Table 3.1.
MSIRGSEL: MSI clock range selection
  0: MSI range is provided by MSIRANGE[3:0] in RCC->CSR register.
  1: MSI range is provided by MSIRANGE[3:0] in RCC->CR register.
MSIPLLEN: MSI clock PLL enable
  This bit must be enabled after LSE is enabled. When LSEON = 0, this bit is cleared.
  0: MSI PLL OFF. 1: MSI PLL ON.
MSIRDY: MSI clock ready flag
  0: MSI oscillator not ready 1: MSI oscillator ready
MSION: MSI clock enable
  0: MSI oscillator OFF 1: MSI oscillator ON

Figure 3.2b Clock control register (RCC->CR)—(continued)

Table 3.1 MSI frequency range (RCC->CR register)

MSIRANGE[3:0]	Frequency range
0000	Range 0 around 100 kHz
0001	Range 1 around 200 kHz
0010	Range 2 around 400 kHz
0011	Range 3 around 800 kHz
0100	Range 4 around 1 MHz
0101	Range 5 around 2 MHz
0110	Range 6 around 4 MHz
0111	Range 7 around 8 MHz
1000	Range 8 around 16 MHz
1001	Range 9 around 24 MHz
1010	Range 10 around 32 MHz
1011	Range 11 around 48 MHz

Table 3.1a MSI frequency range (RCC->CSR register)

MSIRANGE[3:0]	Frequency range
0000~0011	Reserved
0100	Range 4 around 1 MHz
0101	Range 5 around 2 MHz
0110	Range 6 around 4 MHz (reset value)
0111	Range 7 around 8 MHz
1000~1111	reserved

Example 3.1 Write a sequence of C statements to (a) turn on the HSE in bypass mode, (b) enable MSI with PLL turned on, (c) set MSI frequency range to 48 MHz by programming the RCC->CR register.

Solution:

```
RCC->CR  = RCC_CR_HSEON + RCC_CR_HSEBYP + RCC_CR_MSION + RCC_CR_MSIRGSEL
           + RCC_CR_MSIRANGE_11 + RCC_CR_MSIPLLEN;
while (!((RCC->CR & RCC_CR_HSERDY) && (RCC->CR & RCC_CR_MSIRDY)));
```

3.3.3 THE HSI16 CLOCK

The HSI16 clock signal is generated from an internal 16-MHz RC oscillator. Using the HSI16 enables the user to design products at a lower cost when the accuracy of system timing is not critical. The HSI16 also has faster startup time than using the external crystal oscillator.

The HSI16 is factory calibrated by ST to achieve 1% accuracy at 25°C. After reset, the factory calibration value is loaded into the HSICAL[7:0] bits in the **internal clock sources calibration register** (**RCC->ICSCR**). The contents of the RCC->ICSCR register are shown in Figure 3.3.

If the application finds that the HSI16 frequency deviates too much from the target frequency (16 MHz), it can trim the HSI16 frequency by writing a new value into the HSITRIM[4:0] bits in the RCC->ICSCR register. When a new value is written into the HSITRIM field, the HSICAL field in the RCC->ICSCR register is updated with the sum of the HSITRIM and the HSICAL fields, which is then used to calibrate the frequency of the HSI16 clock.

The HSI16 clock source must be enabled before it can be used. It can be enabled by setting the **HSION** bit of the RCC->CR register. To make sure that the HSI16 clock is enabled, the **HSIRDY** flag in the RCC->CR register must be checked.

The HSI16 can be selected as the clock source for the I^{2}C and USART peripherals. When this is done and by keeping the HSI16 ON in stop mode (by setting the HSIKERON bit in the

RCC->CR register), the user can avoid slowing down the communication speed because of the short HSI16 startup time.

31	30	29	28	27	26	25	24
–	–	–	HSITRIM[4:0]				
23	**22**	**21**	**20**	**19**	**18**	**17**	**16**
HSICAL[7:0]							
15	**14**	**13**	**12**	**11**	**10**	**9**	**8**
MSITRIM[7:0]							
7	**6**	**5**	**4**	**3**	**2**	**1**	**0**
MSICAL[7:0]							

Reset value = 0x10xx 00xx
Offset = 0x04
Access: no wait state

HSITRIM[4:0]: HSI16 clock trimming
These bits provide an additional user-programmable trimming value that is added to the HSICAL[7:0] bits. It can be programmed to adjust to variations in voltage and temperature that influence the frequency of the HSI16.
The default value is 16, which, when added to the HSICAL value, should trim the HSI16 to 16 MHz $\pm$ 1%.

HSICAL[7:0]: HSI16 clock calibration
These bits are initialized at startup with the factory-programmed HSI16 calibration trim value. When HSITRIM is written, HSICAL is updated with the sum of HSITRIM and the factory trim value.

MSITRIM[7:0]: MSI clock trimming
These bits provide an additional user-programmable trimming value that is added to the MSICAL[7:0] bits. It can be programmed to adjust to variations in voltage and temperature that influence the frequency of the MSI.

MSICAL[7:0]: MSI clock calibration
These bits are initialized at startup with the factory-programmed calibration trim value. When MSITRIM is written, MSICAL is updated with the sum of MSITRIM and the factory trim value.

Figure 3.3 Internal clock sources calibration register (RCC->ICSCR)

3.3.4 THE MSI CLOCK

This clock is also generated from an internal RC oscillator. Its frequency can be adjusted by programming the MSIRANGE[3:0] field in the RCC->CR register. Twelve frequencies are available: 100 kHz, 200 kHz, 400 kHz, 800 kHz, 1 MHz, 2 MHz, 4 MHz, 8 MHz, 16 MHz, 32 MHz, and 48 MHz.

The MSI clock is used as the system clock after restart from reset, wakeup from standby, and shutdown low-power modes. After restart from reset, the MSI frequency is set to its default value of 4 MHz.

The MSI clock can be selected as the system clock after a wakeup from stop mode (Stop 0, Stop 1, or Stop 2). It can also be used as a **backup clock source** if the HSE crystal oscillator fails.

The MSI RC oscillator has the advantage of providing a low-cost (no external components), low-power clock source. In addition, when used in PLL mode with the LSE, it provides a very accurate clock source which can be used by the USB OTG FS device, and feed the main PLL to run the system at the maximum speed of 80 MHz.

The **MSIRDY** flag in the RCC->CR register indicates whether the MSI RC is stable or not. At startup, the MSI output is not released until this bit is set to 1 by hardware. The MSI clock can be switched on and off by setting/clearing the MSION bit in the RCC->CR register.

When a 32.768-kHz external oscillator is present in the application, it is possible to configure the MSI in the PLL mode by setting the MSIPLLEN bit in the RCC->CR register. When configured in the PLL mode, the MSI automatically calibrates itself, thanks to the LSE. This mode is available for all frequency ranges. At 48 MHz, the MSI in PLL mode can be used for the USB OTG FS device, saving the need of an external high-speed crystal.

Like the HSI16, the MSI RC oscillator output frequency may vary due to the manufacturing process variations; calibration is required to keep the variation as small as possible. A calibration process has been applied during the manufacturing process to reduce the MSI frequency deviation to no more than 1% at 25°C. After reset, the factory calibration value is loaded in the MSICAL[7:0] field in the RCC->ICSCR register. However, if the processor operates at a temperature higher than 25°C or outside the specified voltage range, the MSI output frequency may deviate from the target frequency. In this situation, the user can trim the MSI frequency by writing a value into the MSITRIM[7:0] field in the RCC->ICSCR register.

3.3.5 PHASE-LOCKED LOOP (PLL)

A PLL is often used to generate a clock signal with a frequency that is a multiple of that of the input clock signal for a computer system.

The STM32L475 has three PLLs: PLL, PLLSAI1, and PLLSAI2. The block diagram of the PLL is shown in Figure 3.4. These three PLLs share a common input reference signal, which can be one of the following three clock sources:

- MSI
- HSI16
- HSE

The input clock source must have a frequency between 4 MHz and 16 MHz. If the chosen clock source has a frequency higher than 16 MHz, it must be divided down (by the factor M) to between 4 MHz and 16 MHz.

The highest PLL output frequency is 80 MHz. All PLL parameters are configured via the **PLL configuration registers** (**RCC->PLLCFGR, RCC->PLLSAI1CFGR,** and **RCC->PLLSAI2CFGR**). The contents of RCC->PLLCFGR, RCC->PLLSAI1CFGR, and RCC->PLLSAI2CFGR are shown in Figures 3.5, 3.6, and 3.7, respectively.

The PLL module in Figure 3.4 first produces an intermediate output **VCO** of which the frequency is $\mathbf{f}_{VCO}$ = f(PLL clock input) × (PLLN ÷ PLLM), where PLLN and PLLM are defined in the RCC->PLLCFGR register.

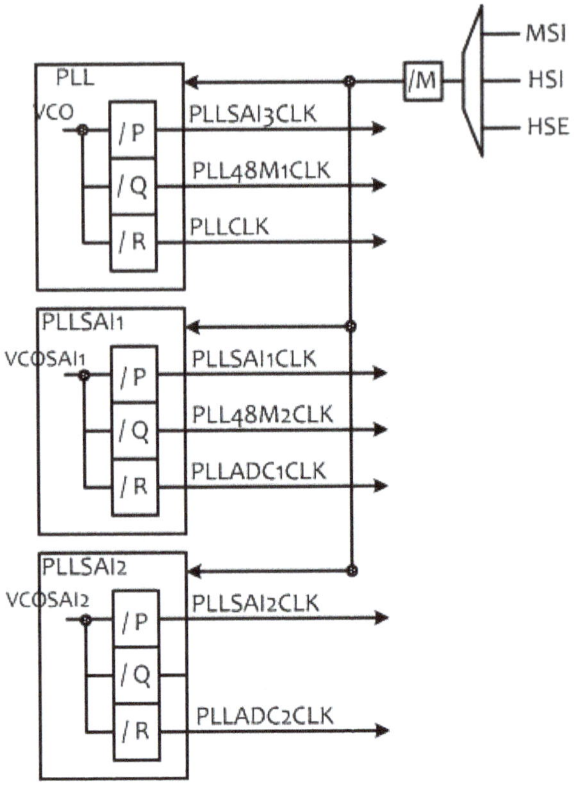

Figure 3.4 STM32L475 PLL circuit block diagram

The frequencies of the three PLL outputs are derived by dividing the intermediate output frequency f_{VCO} by the three factors PLLR, PLLQ, and PLLP (defined in the RCC→PLLCFGR register) as follows:

- f(PLLCLK) $= f_{VCO} \div$ PLLR
- f(PLL48M1CLK) $= f_{VCO} \div$ PLLQ
- f(PLLSAI3CLK) $= f_{VCO} \div$ PLLP

31	30	29	28	27	26	25	24
--	--	--	--	--	PLLR[1:0]		PLLREN
23	**22**	**21**	**20**	**19**	**18**	**17**	**16**
--	PLLQ[1:0]		PLLQEN	--	--	PLLP	PLLPEN
15	**14**	**13**	**12**	**11**	**10**	**9**	**8**
--	PLLN[6:0]						
7	**6**	**5**	**4**	**3**	**2**	**1**	**0**
	PLLM[2:0]			--	--	PLLSRC[1:0]	

Reset value = 0x0000 1000
Offset = 0x0C
Access: no wait state

PLLR[1:0]: Main PLL division factor for PLLCLK (system clock)
  PLLCLK output frequency = VCO frequency ÷ PLLR with PLLR = 2, 4, 6, or 8
  00: PLLR = 2 01: PLLR = 4 10: PLLR = 6 11: PLLR = 8
PLLREN: Main PLL PLLCLK output enable
  0: PLLCLK output disable
  1: PLLCLK output enable
PLLQ[1:0]: Main PLL division factor for PLL48M1CLK (48 MHz clk)
  PLL48M1CLK output frequency = VCO frequency ÷ PLLQ with PLLQ = 2, 4, 6, or 8
  00: PLLQ = 2 01: PLLQ = 4 10: PLLQ = 6 11: PLLQ = 8
PLLQEN: Main PLL PLL48M1CLK output enable
  0: PLL48M1CLK output disable
  1: PLL48M1CLK output enable
PLLP: Main PLL division factor for PLLSAI3CLK (SAI1 and SAI2 clock)
  PLLSAI3CLK output frequency = VCO frequency ÷ PLLP with PLLP = 7 or 17
  0: PLLP = 7 1: PLLP = 17
PLLPEN: Main PLL PLLSAI3CLK output enable
  0: PLLSAI3CLK output disable
  1: PLLSAI3CLK output enable
PLLN[6:0]: Main PLL multiplication factor for VCO
  VCO output frequency = VCO input frequency × PLLN with 8 ≤ PLLN ≤ 86
PLLM[2:0]: Division factor for the main PLL and audio PLL (PLLSAI1 and PLLSAI2) input clock (000..111 correspond to 1 to 8)
  VCO input frequency = PLL input clock frequency / PLLM with 1 ≤ PLLM ≤ 8.
PLLSRC[1:0]: Main PLL, PLLSAI1 and PLLSAI2 entry clock source
  00: No clock selected 01: MSI clock selected as the PLL source
  10: HSI16 selected as the PLL source 11: HSE clock selected as the PLL source

Figure 3.5 PLL configuration register (RCC->PLLCFGR)

31	30	29	28	27	26	25	24
--	--	--	--	--	PLLSAI1R[1:0]		PLLSAI1REN
23	**22**	**21**	**20**	**19**	**18**	**17**	**16**
--	PLLSAI1Q[1:0]		PLLSAI1QEN	--	--	PLLSAI1P	PLLSAI1PEN
15	**14**	**13**	**12**	**11**	**10**	**9**	**8**
--	PLLSAI1N[6:0]						
7	**6**	**5**	**4**	**3**	**2**	**1**	**0**
--	--	--	--	--	--	--	--

Reset value = 0x0000 1000
Offset = 0x10
Access: no wait state

PLLSAI1R[1:0]: PLLSAI1 division factor for PLLADC1CLK (ADC clock)
PLLADC1CLK output frequency = VCOSAI1 frequency ÷ PLLSAI1R
00: PLLSAI1R = 2 01: PLLSAI1R = 4 10: PLLSAI1R = 6 11: PLLSAI1R = 8
PLLSAI1REN: PLLSAI1 PLLADC1CLK output enable
0: PLLADC1CLK output disable
1: PLLADC1CLK output enable
PLLSAI1Q[1:0]: Main PLL division factor for PLL48M1CLK (48 MHz clk)
PLL48M2CLK output frequency = VCOSAI1 frequency ÷ PLLQ with PLLQ = 2, 4, 6, or 8
00: PLLQ = 2 01: PLLQ = 4 10: PLLQ = 6 11: PLLQ = 8
PLLSAI1QEN: SAI1PLL PLL48M2CLK output enable
0: PLL48M2CLK output disable
1: PLL48M2CLK output enable
PLLSAI1P: SAI1PLL division factor for PLLSAI1CLK (SAI1 and SAI2 clock)
PLLSAI1CLK output frequency = VCOSAI1 frequency ÷ PLLSAI1P
0: PLLSAI1P = 7 1: PLLSAI1P = 17
PLLSAI1PEN: Main PLL PLLSAI3CLK output enable
0: PLLSAI1CLK output disable
1: PLLSAI1CLK output enable
PLLSAI1N[6:0]: SAI1PLL multiplication factor for VCO
VCOSAI1 output frequency = VCOSAI1 input frequency × PLLSAI1N with 8 ≤ PLLN ≤ 86
0000000~0000111: wrong configuration
0001000~1010110: PLLSAI1N = 8 ~ 86
1010111~1111111: wrong configuration

Figure 3.6 PLLSAI1 configuration register (RCC->PLLSAI1CFGR)

The PLLSAI1 module produces an intermediate output **VCOSAI1** of which the frequency is $f_{VCOSAI1}$ = f(PLL clock input) × (PLLSAI1N ÷ PLLM), where PLLSAI1N and PLLM are defined in the RCC->PLLSAI1CFGR and RCC->PLLCFGR registers, respectively.

The PLLSAI1 module also produces three outputs. The frequencies of these three outputs are as follows:

- f(PLLADC1CLK) = $f_{VCOSAI1}$ ÷ PLLSAI1R
- f(PLL48M2CLK) = $f_{VCOSAI1}$ ÷ PLLSAI1Q
- f(PLLSAI1CLK) = $f_{VCOSAI1}$ ÷ PLLSAI1P

31	30	29	28	27	26	25	24	
–	–	–	–	–	PLLSAI2R[1:0]		PLLSAI2REN	Reset value = 0x0000 1000
23	**22**	**21**	**20**	**19**	**18**	**17**	**16**	Offset = 0x14
–	–	–	–	–	–	PLLSAI2P	PLLSAI2PEN	Access: no wait state
15	**14**	**13**	**12**	**11**	**10**	**9**	**8**	
–	PLLSAI2N[6:0]							
7	**6**	**5**	**4**	**3**	**2**	**1**	**0**	
–	–	–	–	–	–	–	–	

PLLSAI2R[1:0]: PLLSAI2 division factor for PLLADC2CLK (ADC clock)
PLLADC2CLK output frequency = VCOSAI2 frequency ÷ PLLSAI2R
00: PLLSAI2R = 2 01: PLLSAI2R = 4 10: PLLSAI2R = 6 11: PLLSAI2R = 8
PLLSAI2REN: PLLSAI2 PLLADC2CLK output enable
0: PLLADC2CLK output disable
1: PLLADC2CLK output enable
PLLSAI2P: SAI2PLL division factor for PLLSAI2CLK (SAI1 and SAI2 clock)
PLLSAI2CLK output frequency = VCOSAI2 frequency ÷ PLLSAI2P
0: PLLSAI2P = 7 1: PLLSAI2P = 17
PLLSAI2PEN: Main PLL PLLSAI3CLK output enable
0: PLLSAI2CLK output disable
1: PLLSAI2CLK output enable
PLLSAI2N[6:0]: SAI2PLL multiplication factor for VCO
VCOSAI2 output frequency = VCOSAI2 input frequency × PLLSAI2N with 8 ≤ PLLSAI2N ≤ 86
0000000~0000111: wrong configuration
0001000~1010110: PLLSAI2N = 8 ~ 86
1010111~1111111: wrong configuration

Figure 3.7 PLLSAI2 configuration register (RCC->PLLSAI2CFGR)

The PLLSAI2 module produces an intermediate output **VCOSAI2** of which the frequency is $f_{VCOSAI2}$ = f(PLL clock input) × (PLLSAI2N ÷ PLLM), where PLLSAI2N and PLLM are defined in the RCC->PLLSAI2CFGR and RCC->PLLCFGR registers, respectively.

The PLLSAI2 modules produce two outputs. The frequencies of these two outputs are:

- f(PLLADC2CLK) = $f_{VCOSAI2}$ ÷ PLLSAI2R
- f(PLLSAI2CLK) = $f_{VCOSAI2}$ ÷ PLLSAI2P

Example 3.2 Write a C statement to

- Select MSI (48 MHz) as the source of PLL
- Set PLLM to 3 (÷4)
- Set PLLN to 10
- Set PLLP to 7
- Set PLLQ and PLLR to 2
- Enable PLLCLK, PLL48M1CLK, and PLLSAI3CLK outputs

Solution: The following C statements will configure the PLL module accordingly:

```
RCC->PLLCFGR = RCC_PLLCFGR_PLLM_0 + RCC_PLLCFGR_PLLM_1 +
          RCC_PLLCFGR_PLLN_1 + RCC_PLLCFGR_PLLN_3 +
          RCC_PLLCFGR_PLLSRC_MSI +
```

```
RCC_PLLCFGR_PLLREN +RCC_PLLCFGR_PLLQEN + RCC_PLLCFGR_PLLPEN;
```

Example 3.3 Write a sequence of C statements to configure the PLLSAI1 to

- Select the 8-MHz HSE as input
- Set R and Q to 2
- Set P to 7
- Set M to 1
- Enable P, Q, and R output
- Set N to 20

Solution:

Refer to Figure 3.6, we need to set the PLLSAI1R, PLLSAI1Q fields in the RCC_PLLSAI1CFGR register to 0 and also force the PLLM field in the RCC_PLLCFGR register to 0. The following C statements will configure the PLLSAI1 and PLL modules accordingly:

```
RCC->PLLCFGR &= ~(RCC_PLLCFGR_PLLM + RCC_PLLCFGR_PLLSRC); // clear the PLLM
                                       // and PLLSRC fields to 0 (set M to 1)
RCC->PLLCFGR |= RCC_PLLCFGR_PLLSRC_HSE; // select HSE as PLL source
RCC->PLLSAI1CFGR = RCC_PLLSAI1CFGR_PLLSAI1N_4 + RCC_PLLSAI1CFGR_PLLSAI1N_2 +
    RCC_PLLSAI1CFGR_PLLSAI1QEN + RCC_PLLSAI1CFGR_PLLSAI1PEN +
    RCC_PLLSAI1CFGR_PLLSAI1REN;
```

Example 3.4 Assuming that the reference clock input to the PLLSAI2 is an 8-MHz HSE, write a C statement to configure the RCC_PLLSAI2CFGR register to:

- Set R to 2
- Set P to 7
- Set N to 20
- Enable P and R outputs

Solution:

Both the PLLSAI2R and PLLSAI2P fields in the RCC_PLLSAI2CFGR register must be set to 0.

```
RCC->PLLSAI2CFGR = RCC_PLLSAI2CFGR_PLLSAI2N_4 + RCC_PLLSAI2CFGR_PLLSAI2N_2 +
                   RCC_PLLSAI2CFGR_PLLSAI2REN + RCC_PLLSAI2CFGR_PLLSAI2PEN;
```

Example 3.5 Write a sequence of C statements to turn on all three PLLs and wait until the three PLLs are ready (frequency stabilized) for use.

Solution:

```
// turn on PLL, PLLSAI1, and PLLSAI2
    RCC->CR |= RCC_CR_PLLON + RCC_CR_PLLSAI1ON + RCC_CR_PLLSAI2ON;
    while(!(RCC->CR & RCC_CR_PLLRDY));
```

```
while(!(RCC->CR & RCC_CR _PLLSAI1RDY));
while(!(RCC->CR & RCC_CR_PLLSAI2RDY));
```

3.3.6 THE LSE CLOCK SOURCE

The low-speed external clock (LSE) is derived from a 32.768-kHz external crystal or ceramic resonator. Due to its frequency accuracy, an LSE is often used as the clock source of the RTC for clock/calendar or other timing functions.

The LSE clock can be turned on/off by setting/clearing the LSEON bit in the backup domain control register (RCC->BDCR). When needed, the drive strength of the LSE can be controlled by programming the LSE-DRV[1:0] field of the RCC->BDCR register. The drive strength can be set to the lowest level (LSEDRV=00) when the LSE is turned on. Once LSEDRV is selected, the drive capability cannot be increased if LSEON bit is 1.

In the bypass mode, an external clock with 50% duty cycle should be connected to the OSC32_IN pin. The bypass mode is selected by setting both the LSEBYP and LSEON bits in the RCC->BDCR register. The contents of the RCC->BDCR register are shown in Figure 3.8.

31	30	29	28	27	26	25	24
--	--	--	--	--	--	LSCOSEL	LSCOEN
23	22	21	20	19	18	17	16
--	--	--	--	--	--	--	BDRST
15	14	13	12	11	10	9	8
RTCEN	--	--	--	--	--	RTCSEL[1:0]	
7	6	5	4	3	2	1	0
--	LSECSSD	LSECSSON	LSEDRV[1:0]		LSEBYP	LSERDY	LSEON

Reset value = 0x0000 0000
Offset = 0x90
Access: no wait state

LSCOSEL: Low speed clock output selection
0: LSI clock selected 1: LSE clock selected
LSCOEN: Low speed clock output enable
0: Low speed clock output (LSCO) disable
1: Low speed clock output (LSCO) enable
BDRST: Backup domain software reset
0: Reset not activated 1: Reset the entire backup domain
RTCEN: RTC clock enable
0: RTC clock disabled 1: RTC clock enabled
RTCSEL[1:0]: RTC clock source selection
00: No clock 01: LSE oscillator used as RTC clock
10: LSI oscillator used as RTC clock 11: HSE oscillator clock divided by 32 used as RTC clock
LSECSSD: CSS on LSE failure detection
0: No failure detected on LSE (32 kHz oscillator)
1: Failure detected on LSE (32 kHz oscillator)
LSECSSON: Clock security system (CSS) on LSE enable
0: CSS on LSE (32 kHz external oscillator) OFF
1: CSS on LSE (32 kHz external oscillator) ON

Figure 3.8 Backup domain control register (RCC->BDCR)

31	30	29	28	27	26	25	24
--	--	--	--	--	--	LSCOSEL	LSCOEN
23	**22**	**21**	**20**	**19**	**18**	**17**	**16**
--	--	--	--	--	--	--	BDRST
15	**14**	**13**	**12**	**11**	**10**	**9**	**8**
RTCEN	--	--	--	--	--	RTCSEL[1:0]	
7	**6**	**5**	**4**	**3**	**2**	**1**	**0**
--	LSECSSD	LSECSSON	LSEDRV[1:0]		LSEBYP	LSERDY	LSEON

Reset value = 0x0000 0000
Offset = 0x90
Access: no wait state

LSEDRV[1:0]: LSE oscillator drive capability
00: 'Xtal mode' lower driving capability
01: 'Xtal mode' medium low driving capability
10: 'Xtal mode' medium high driving capability
11: 'Xtal mode' higher driving capability
LSEBYP: LSE oscillator bypass
0: LSE oscillator not bypassed 1: LSE oscillator bypassed
LSERDY: LSE oscillator ready
0: LSE oscillator not ready 1: LSE oscillator ready
LSEON: LSE oscillator enable
0: LSE oscillator OFF 1: LSE oscillator ON

Figure 3.8a Backup domain control register (RCC->BDCR)—(continued)

3.3.7 BACKUP DOMAIN ACCESS

After system reset, the backup domain (including RTC registers and backup registers) is protected against unwanted write access. Since the LSE clock source is in the backup domain, the user is required to enable access to the backup domain before he/she can configure the LSE clock source.

To enable access to the backup domain, proceed as follows:

- Enable the power interface clock by setting the PWREN bit in the RCC->APB1ENR register.
- Enable access to the backup domain by setting the DBP bit in the PWR->CR1 register.
- Optionally enable the LSE clock source, set its drive capability, and wait until it is ready for use.
- Select the RTC clock source in the RCC->BDCR register.
- Enable the RTC clock by setting the RTCEN bit in the RCC->BDCR register.

3.3.8 LSI CLOCK

The LSI clock is a low-power, low-frequency (32 kHz) clock source, which is mainly used as the clock source of the independent watchdog timer (IWDG) and RTC. The LSI clock can be turned on/off by setting/clearing the LSION bit in the control/status register (RCC->CSR). The contents of the RCC->CSR register are shown in Figure 3.9.

The LSI must be used when it is ready, which is indicated by the LSIRDY bit in the RCC->CSR register.

31	30	29	28	27	26	25	24
LPWR RSTF	WWDG RSTF	IWWG RSTF	SFT RSTF	BOR RSTF	PIN RSTF	OBL RSTF	FWRSTF
23	22	21	20	19	18	17	16
RMVF	–	–	–	–	–	–	–
15	14	13	12	11	10	9	8
–	–	–	–	MSISRANGE[3:0]			
7	6	5	4	3	2	1	0
–	–	–	–	–	–	LSIRDY	LSION

Reset value = 0x0C00 0600
Offset = 0x94
Access: 0~3 wait states. Wait states are inserted in case of successive access to this register.

LPWRRSTF: Low-power reset flag
 0: No illegal mode reset occurred 1: Illegal mode reset occurred
WWDGRSTF: Window watchdog reset flag
 0: No window watchdog reset occurred 1: Window watchdog reset occurred
IWWGRSTF: Independent window watchdog reset flag
 0: No independent watchdog reset occurred
 1: Independent watchdog reset occurred
SFTRSTF: Software reset flag
 0: No software reset occurred 1: Software reset occurred
BORRSTF: BOR flag
 0: No BOR occurred 1: BOR occurred
PINRSTF: Pin reset flag
 0: No reset from NRST pin occurred 1: Reset from NRST pin occurred
OBLRSTF: Option byte loader reset flag
 0: No reset from option byte loading occurred
 1: Reset from option byte loading occurred
FWRSTF: Firewall reset flag
 0: No reset from the firewall occurred 1: Reset from the firewall occurred

Figure 3.9 Control/status register (RCC->CSR)

31	30	29	28	27	26	25	24
LPWR RSTF	WWDG RSTF	IWWG RSTF	SFT RSTF	BOR RSTF	PIN RSTF	OBL RSTF	FWRSTF
23	22	21	20	19	18	17	16
RMVF	–	–	–	–	–	–	–
15	14	13	12	11	10	9	8
–	–	–	–	MSISRANGE[3:0]			
7	6	5	4	3	2	1	0
–	–	–	–	–	–	LSIRDY	LSION

Reset value = 0x0C00 0600
Offset = 0x94
Access: 0~3 wait states. Wait states are inserted in case of successive access to this register.

RMVF: Remove reset flag (all other reset flags are cleared when this bit is set)
 0: No effect 1: Clear the reset flags
MSISRANGE[3:0]: MSI range after standby mode
 This field can be written only when MSIRGSEL = 1. After a power on reset, the range is 4 MHz.
 0100: Range 4 around 1 MHz 0101: Range 5 around 2 MHz
 0110: Range 6 around 4 MHz (reset value) 0111: Range 7 around 8 MHz
 Others: reserved
LSIRDY: LSI oscillator ready
 0: LSI oscillator not ready 1: LSI oscillator ready
LSION: LSI oscillator enable
 0: LSI oscillator OFF 1: LSI oscillator ON

Figure 3.9a Control/status register (RCC->CSR)—(continued)

3.3.9 CLOCK SECURITY SYSTEM (CSS)

The clock security system is implemented to detect the failure of the HSE and the LSE clock. When a failure of the HSE is detected, the **CSSF flag** in the **clock interrupt flag register**

(**RCC->CIFR**) is set to 1. A clock failure event will be sent to the break input of the advanced-control timers (TIM1/TIM8 and TIM15/16/17) and an **NMI interrupt is generated**, allowing the MCU to take rescue actions. The contents of the RCC->CIFR register are shown in Figure 3.10. For every bit in the RCC->CIFR register, there is a corresponding bit in the

RCC->CIER register. When both bits are set, an interrupt is generated. The contents of the RCC->CIER register are shown in Figure 3.11.

The NMI service routine must clear the CSS interrupt pending flag by setting the CSSC bit in the clock interrupt clear register (RCC->CICR) to prevent this NMI interrupt from occurring indefinitely. The contents of the RCC->CICR register are shown in Figure 3.12.

If the HSE clock is used as the system clock directly or indirectly (via PLL), the detected failure causes a switch of the SYSCLK to the MSI or the HSI16 oscillator depending on the **STOPWUCK** bit (0: MSI; 1: HSI16) setting in the RCC->CFGR register.

The clock security system for the LSE must be enabled by setting the **LSECSSON** bit in the **RCC->BDCR** register (in Figure 3.8). This bit must be set after LSE and LSI are enabled and ready (LSERDY and LSIRDY set), and after the RTC clock has been selected by the **RTCSEL** field in the RCC->BDCR register.

If a failure is detected on the LSE, the LSE clock is no longer supplied to the RTC but no hardware action is made to the registers. If the MSI oscillator is in PLL mode, this mode is disabled.

In standby mode a wakeup is generated. In other modes an interrupt can be generated to request the processor to resume the software execution. The LSE failure interrupt service routine must then clear the LSECSSON bit, stop the defective 32-kHz oscillator (by clearing the LSEON bit), and change the RTC clock source, or take any required action to secure the application.

31	30	29	28	27	26	25	24
--	--	--	--	--	--	--	--
23	22	21	20	19	18	17	16
--	--	--	--	--	--	--	--
15	14	13	12	11	10	9	8
--	--	--	--	--	--	LSECSSF	CSSF
7	6	5	4	3	2	1	0
PLLSAI2 RDYF	PLLSAI1 RDYF	PLL RDYF	HSE RDYF	HSI RDYF	MSI RDYF	LSE RDYF	LSI RDYF

Reset value = 0x0000 0000
Offset = 0x1C
Access: no wait state

LSECSSIE: LSE clock security system interrupt flag
  0: No clock security interrupt caused by LSE clock failure
  1: Clock security interrupt caused by LSE clock failure
CSSF: HSE clock security system interrupt flag
  0: No clock security interrupt caused by HSE oscillator
  1: Clock security interrupt caused by HSE clock failure
PLLSAI2RDYF: PLLSAI2 ready interrupt flag
  0: No clock ready interrupt caused by PLLSAI2 lock
  1: Clock ready interrupt caused by PLLSAI2 lock
PLLSAI1RDYF: PLLSAI1 ready interrupt flag
  0: No clock ready interrupt caused by PLLSAI1 lock
  1: Clock ready interrupt caused by PLLSAI1 lock
PLLRDYF: PLL ready interrupt flag
  0: No lock ready interrupt caused by PLL lock
  1: Clock ready interrupt caused by PLL lock
HSERDYF: HSE ready interrupt flag
  0: No clock ready interrupt caused by the HSE oscillator
  1: Clock ready interrupt caused by the HSE oscillator

Figure 3.10 Clock interrupt flag register (RCC->CIFR)

31	30	29	28	27	26	25	24
--	--	--	--	--	--	--	--
23	22	21	20	19	18	17	16
--	--	--	--	--	--	--	--
15	14	13	12	11	10	9	8
--	--	--	--	--	--	LSECSSF	CSSF
7	6	5	4	3	2	1	0
PLLSAI2 RDYF	PLLSAI1 RDYIE	PLL RDYF	HSE RDYF	HSI RDYF	MSI RDYF	LSE RDYF	LSI RDYF

Reset value = 0x0000 0000
Offset = 0x1C
Access: no wait state

HSIRDYF: HSI16 ready interrupt flag
  0: No clock ready interrupt caused by the HSI16 oscillator
  1: Clock ready interrupt caused by the HSI16 oscillator
MSIRDYF: MSI ready interrupt flag
  0: No clock ready interrupt caused by MSI oscillator
  1: Clock ready interrupt caused by MSI oscillator
LSERDYF: LSE ready interrupt flag
  0: No clock ready interrupt caused by the LSE oscillator
  1: Clock ready interrupt caused by the LSE oscillator
LSIRDYF: LSI ready interrupt flag
  0: No clock ready interrupt caused by the LSI oscillator
  1: Clock ready interrupt caused by the LSI oscillator

Figure 3.10a Clock interrupt flag register (RCC->CIFR)—(continued)

31	30	29	28	27	26	25	24
--	--	--	--	--	--	--	--
23	22	21	20	19	18	17	16
--	--	--	--	--	--	--	--
15	14	13	12	11	10	9	8
--	--	--	--	--	--	LSECSSIE	--
7	6	5	4	3	2	1	0
PLLSAI2 RDYIE	PLLSAI1 RDYIE	PLL RDYIE	HSE RDYIE	HSI RDYIE	MSI RDYIE	LSE RDYIE	LSI RDYIE

Reset value = 0x0000 0000
Offset = 0x18
Access: no wait state

LSECSSIE: LSE clock security system interrupt enable
0: Clock security interrupt caused by LSE clock failure disabled
1: Clock security interrupt caused by LSE clock failure enabled
PLLSAI2RDYIE: PLLSAI2 ready interrupt enable
0: PLLSAI2 lock interrupt disabled 1: PLLSAI2 lock interrupt enabled
PLLSAI1RDYIE: PLLSAI1 ready interrupt enable
0: PLLSAI1 lock interrupt disabled 1: PLLSAI1 lock interrupt enabled
PLLRDYIE: PLL ready interrupt enable
0: PLL lock interrupt disabled 1: PLL lock interrupt enabled
HSERDYIE: HSE ready interrupt enable
0: HSE ready interrupt disabled 1: HSE ready interrupt enabled
HSIRDYIE: HSI16 ready interrupt enable
0: HSI16 ready interrupt disabled 1: HSI16 ready interrupt enabled
MSIRDYIE: MSI ready interrupt enable
0: MSI ready interrupt disabled 1: MSI ready interrupt enabled
LSERDYIE: LSE ready interrupt enable
0: LSE ready interrupt disabled 1: LSE ready interrupt enabled
LSIRDYIE: LSI ready interrupt enable
0: LSI ready interrupt disabled 1: LSI ready interrupt enabled

Figure 3.11 Clock interrupt enable register (RCC->CIER)

31	30	29	28	27	26	25	24
--	--	--	--	--	--	--	--
23	22	21	20	19	18	17	16
--	--	--	--	--	--	--	--
15	14	13	12	11	10	9	8
--	--	--	--	--	--	LSECSSC	CSSC
7	6	5	4	3	2	1	0
PLLSAI2 RDYC	PLLSAI1 RDYC	PLL RDYC	HSE RDYC	HSI RDYC	MSI RDYC	LSE RDYC	LSI RDYC

Reset value = 0x0000 0000
Offset = 0x20
Access: no wait state

LSECSSC: LSE clock security system interrupt clear
0: No effect 1: Clear the LSECSSF flag
CSSC: Clock security system interrupt flag clear
0: No effect 1: Clear the CSSF flag
PLLSAI2RDYC: PLLSAI2 ready interrupt flag clear
0: No effect 1: Clear the PLLSAI2RDYF flag
PLLSAI1RDYC: PLLSAI1 ready interrupt flag clear
0: No effect 1: Clear the PLLSAI1RDYF flag
PLLRDYC: PLL ready interrupt flag clear
0: No effect 1: Clear the PLLRDYF flag
HSERDYC: HSE ready interrupt flag clear
0: No effect 1: Clear the HSIRDYF flag
HSIRDYC: HSI16 ready interrupt flag clear
0: No effect 1: Clear the HSIRDRF flag
MSIRDYC: MSI ready interrupt flag clear
0: No effect 1: Clear the MSIRDY flag
LSERDYC: LSE ready interrupt flag clear
0: No effect 1: Clear the LSERDY flag
LSIRDYC: LSI ready interrupt flag clear
0: No effect 1: Clear the LSI RDY flag

Figure 3.12 Clock interrupt clear register (RCC->CICR)

3.3.10 SYSTEM CLOCK (SYSCLK) SELECTION

One of the following sources can be selected as the system clock:

- MSI oscillator
- HSI16 oscillator
- HSE oscillator
- PLL

The maximum frequency of the SYSCLK is 80 MHz. This frequency is possible only when the PLL is selected as the source of the SYSCLK.

After a system reset, the 4-MHz MSI oscillator is selected as the system clock. When a clock source is used directly or through PLL as the system clock, it cannot be stopped. A switch from one clock source to another is possible but can occur only when it is ready.

As shown in Figure 3.13, the SYSCLK is used to derive the **HCLK** clock. The **HCLK** clock is further used to derive the APB1 and APB2 bus clocks. Most peripherals receive their clock signals from these three bus clocks. The prescale factors for generating the HCLK, PCLK1, and PCLK2 are programmed into the RCC->CFGR register. The source clock of SYSCLK is selected by the SW field in the RCC->CFGR register. The contents of the RCC->CFGR register are shown in Figure 3.14.

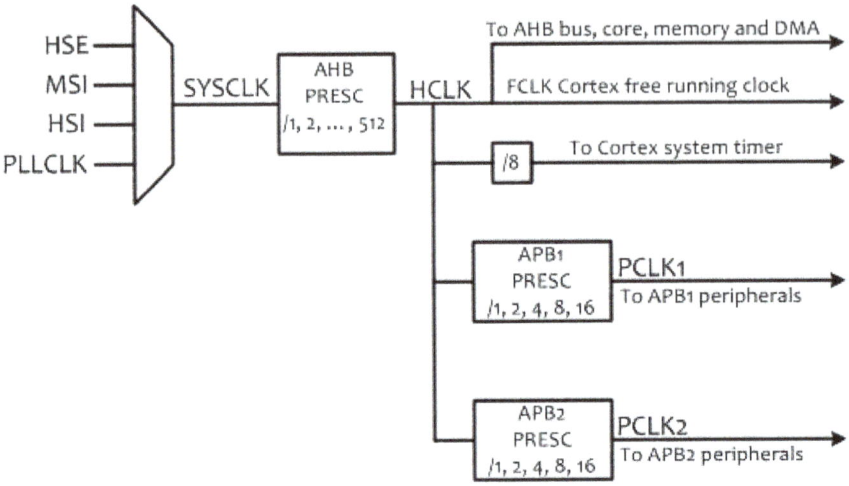

Figure 3.13 SYSCLK and bus clock generation diagram

31	30	29	28	27	26	25	24
--	MCOPRE[2:0]			--	MCOSEL[2:0]		

23	22	21	20	19	18	17	16
--	--	--	--	--	--	--	--

15	14	13	12	11	10	9	8
STOPWUCK	--	PPRE2[2:0]			PPRE1[2:0]		

7	6	5	4	3	2	1	0
HPRE[3:0]				SWS[3:0]		SW[1:0]	

Reset value = 0x0000 0000
Offset = 0x08
Access: 0~2 wait states. 1 or 2 Wait states inserted if the access occurs during clock source switch.

MCOPRE[2:0]: Microcontroller clock output prescaler
It is highly recommended to change this prescaler before MCO output is enabled.
000: MCO is divided by 1 001: MCO is divided by 2
010: MCO is divided by 4 011: MCO is divided by 8
100: MCO is divided by 16 Others: not allowed

MCOSEL: Microcontroller clock output selection
000: MCO output disabled 001: SYSCLK is selected
010: MSI clock selected 011: HSI16 clock selected
100: HSE clock selected 101: Main PLL clock selected
110: LSI clock selected 111: LSE clock selected

STOPWUCK: Wakeup from stop and CSS backup clock selection
0: MSI oscillator selected as wakeup from stop clock and CSS backup clock
1: HSI16 oscillator selected as wakeup from stop clock and CSS backup clock

PPRE2[2:0]: APB high-speed prescaler (APB2)
0xx: HCLK not divided 100: HCLK divided by 2
101: HCLK divided by 4 110: HCLK divided by 8
111: HCLK divided by 16

PPRE1[2:0]: APB low speed prescaler (APB1)
0xx: HCLK not divided 100: HCLK divided by 2
101: HCLK divided by 4 110: HCLK divided by 8
111: HCLK divided by 16

Figure 3.14 Clock configuration register (RCC->CFGR)

31	30	29	28	27	26	25	24
--	MCOPRE[2:0]			--	MCOSEL[2:0]		
23	22	21	20	19	18	17	16
--	--	--	--	--	--	--	--
15	14	13	12	11	10	9	8
STOPWUCK	--	PPRE2[2:0]			PPRE1[2:0]		
7	6	5	4	3	2	1	0
HPRE[3:0]				SWS[1:0]		SW[1:0]	

Reset value = 0x0000 0000
Offset = 0x08
Access: 0~2 wait states. 1 or 2 Wait states inserted if the access occurs during clock source switch.

HPRE[3:0]: AHB prescaler
The software must not set the system frequency exceeding the range allowed in the device voltage range.
0xxx: SYSCLK not divided
1000: SYSCLK divided by 2
1001: SYSCLK divided by 4
1010: SYSCLK divided by 8
1011: SYSCLK divided by 16
1100: SYSCLK divided by 64
1101: SYSCLK divided by 128
1110: SYSCLK divided by 256
1111: SYSCLK divided by 512

SWS[1:0]: System clock switch status (read only)
00: MSI oscillator used as system clock
01: HSI16 oscillator used as system clock
10: HSE used as system clock
11: PLL used as system clock

SW[1:0]: System clock switch (read/writeable)
00: MSI selected as system clock
01: HSI16 selected as system clock
10: HSE selected as system clock
11: PLL selected as system clock

Figure 3.14a Clock configuration register (RCC->CFGR)—(continued)

3.3.11 CLOCK OUT CAPABILITY

The STM32L475 has the capability to output both its main clock and low-speed clock to the MCO and LSCO pins. Other STM microcontroller can then use the MCO clock to generate its SYSCLK whereas the LSCO clock can be used as the clock source for the LSE clock of other MCUs to save the use of external crystal oscillators. When configured as **alternate function 0** (AF0), the **PA08** pin is used as the MCO signal.

The clock signals that can be selected as the source of the MCO clock are LSI, LSE, SYSCLK, HSI16, HSE, PLLCLK, and MSI. The selection is controlled by the MCOSEL field of the

RCC->CFGR register shown in Figure 3.14.

Either the LSI or LSE clock can be selected as the source of LSCO. The selection of LSI or LSE is controlled by the LSCOSEL field in the RCC->BDCR register. The LSCOEN bit in the

RCC->BDCR register must also be set to enable the LSCO output. When the LSCOEN bit is set, the **PA2 pin** is used as the LSCO output automatically because the LSCO is an additional function for the PA02 pin. The "additional function" has the highest priority on the use of the related pin.

Example 3.6 Write a sequence of C statements to perform the following configuration:

- Select **PLL** as the source of the MCO output
- Divide the selected source of MCO by 8
- Select **MSI** oscillator as the SYSCLK to wake up from stop mode and the backup clock when the HSE failure is detected (i.e., used as the CSS backup clock)

- Divide SYSCLK by 1 to derive HCLK
- Divide HCLK by 1 to derive APB1 clock
- Divide HCLK by 1 to derive APB2 clock
- Select PLL as SYSCLK.

Solution:

The STOPUPCK bit in the RCC->CFGR register must be set t0 0 to select MSI oscillator as the SYSCLK for wakeup from the stop mode. The following sequence of C statements will configure the RCC->CFGR register and the PA08 pin accordingly:

```
RCC->CFGR       = RCC_CFGR_MCOPRE_DIV8 + RCC_CFGR_MCOSEL_0 +
                  RCC_CFGR_MCOSEL_2 + RCC_CFGR_SW_PLL;
GPIOA->MODER    &= ~(GPIO_MODER_MODE8); // configure PA8 pin for
GPIOA->MODER    |= GPIO_MODER_MODE8_1; // alternate function
GPIOA->AFR[1]   &= ~GPIO_AFRH_AFSEL8; // Configure PA8 pin for alternate function 0
```

3.4 Distributing Clock Signals to Peripherals

As shown in Figure 3.13, majority of peripherals receive their clock signals from the AHB, APB1, and APB2 buses. Other peripherals do not receive clock signals from these buses and have multiple choices for their clock sources.

3.4.1 PERIPHERALS THAT RECEIVE CLOCK SIGNALS FROM SYSTEM BUSES

For these peripherals, the clock signal is enabled to the peripheral by setting the xxxxEN bit in the RCC->AHBxENR or RCC->APBxENRy register. The contents of the RCC->AHB1ENR, RCC->AHB2ENR, RCC->AHB3ENR, RCC->APB1ENR1, RCC->APB1ENR2, and RCC->APB2ENR register are shown in Figures 3.15 to 3.20, respectively.

When the peripheral clock is not active, the processor cannot read from or write into peripheral registers. The enable bit has a synchronization mechanism to create a glitch-free clock for the peripheral. Just after enabling the clock for a peripheral, software must wait for a delay (2 clock cycles) before accessing the peripheral registers.

31	30	29	28	27	26	25	24
--	--	--	--	--	--	--	--
23	22	21	20	19	18	17	16
--	--	--	--	--	--	--	TSCEN
15	14	13	12	11	10	9	8
--	--	--	CRCEN	--	--	--	FLASHEN
7	6	5	4	3	2	1	0
--	--	--	--	--	--	DMA2EN	DMA1EN

Reset value = 0x0000 0100
Offset = 0x48
Access: No wait states.

TSCEN: Touch sensing controller clock enable
  0: TSC clock disable 1: TSC clock enable
CRCEN: CRC clock enable
  0: CRC clock disable 1: CRC clock enable
FLASHEN: Flash memory interface clock enable
  0: Flash memory interface clock disable
  1: Flash memory interface clock enable
DMA2EN: DMA2 clock enable
  0: DMA2 clock disable 1: DMA2 clock enable
DMA1EN: DMA1 clock enable
  0: DMA1 clock disable 1: DMA1 clock enable

Figure 3.15 AHB1 peripheral clock enable register (RCC->AHB1ENR)

31	30	29	28	27	26	25	24
--	--	--	--	--	--	--	--
23	22	21	20	19	18	17	16
--	--	--	--	--	RNGEN	--	--
15	14	13	12	11	10	9	8
--	--	ADCEN	OTGFSEN	--	--	--	--
7	6	5	4	3	2	1	0
GPIOHEN	GPIOGEN	GPIOFEN	GPIOEEN	GPIODEN	GPIOCEN	GPIOBEN	GPIOAEN

Reset value = 0x0000 0000
Offset = 0x4C
Access: No wait states.

RNGEN: random number generator clock enable
  0: Random number generator clock disabled
  1: Random number generator clock enabled
ADCEN: ADC clock enable
  0: ADC clock disabled 1: ADC clock enabled
OTGFSEN: OTG full speed clock enable
  0: USB OTG full speed clock disabled 1: USB OTG full speed clock enabled
GPIOxEN: IO port x clock enable (x = A, B, C, D, E, F, G, H)
  0: IO port x clock disabled 1: IO port x clock enabled

Figure 3.16 AHB2 peripheral clock enable register (RCC->AHB2ENR)

31	30	29	28	27	26	25	24
--	--	--	--	--	--	--	--
23	**22**	**21**	**20**	**19**	**18**	**17**	**16**
--	--	--	--	--	--	--	--
15	**14**	**13**	**12**	**11**	**10**	**9**	**8**
--	--	--	--	--	--	--	QSPIEN
7	**6**	**5**	**4**	**3**	**2**	**1**	**0**
--	--	--	--	--	--	--	FMCEN

Reset value = 0x0000 0000
Offset = 0x50
Access: No wait states.

QSPIEN: Quad SPI memory interface clock enable
 0: QUADSPI clock disabled
 1: QUADSPI clock enabled
FMCEN: Flexible memory controller clock enable
 0: FMC clock disabled
 1: FMC clock enabled

Figure 3.17 AHB3 peripheral clock enable register (RCC->AHB3ENR)

31	30	29	28	27	26	25	24
LPTIM1EN	OPAMPEN	DAC1EN	PWREN	--	--	CAN1EN	--
23	**22**	**21**	**20**	**19**	**18**	**17**	**16**
I2C3EN	I2C2EN	I2C1EN	UART5EN	UART4EN	USART3EN	USART2EN	--
15	**14**	**13**	**12**	**11**	**10**	**9**	**8**
SPI3EN	SPI2EN	--	--	WWDGEN	--	--	--
7	**6**	**5**	**4**	**3**	**2**	**1**	**0**
--	--	TIM7EN	TIM6EN	TIM5EN	TIM4EN	TIM3EN	TIM2EN

Reset value = 0x0000 0000
Offset = 0x58
Access: No wait states.

LPTIM1EN: Low power timer 1 clock enable
 0: LPTIM1 clock disabled 1: LPTIM1 clock enabled
OPAMPEN: OPAMP interface clock enable
 0: OPAMP interface clock disabled 1: OPAMP interface clock enabled
DAC1EN: DAC1 interface clock enable
 0: DAC1 interface clock disabled 1: DAC1 interface clock enabled
PWREN: Power interface clock enable
 0: Power interface clock disabled 1: Power interface clock enabled
CAN1EN: CAN1 clock enable
 0: CAN1 clock disabled 1: CAN1 clock enabled
I2CxEN: I2Cx clock enable (x = 1, 2, or 3)
 0: I2Cx clock disabled 1: I2Cx clock enabled

Figure 3.18 APB1 peripheral clock enable register 1 (RCC->APB1ENR1)

31	30	29	28	27	26	25	24
LPTIM1EN	OPAMPEN	DAC1EN	PWREN	–	–	CAN1EN	–
23	**22**	**21**	**20**	**19**	**18**	**17**	**16**
I2C3EN	I2C2EN	I2C1EN	UART5EN	UART4EN	USART3EN	USART2EN	–
15	**14**	**13**	**12**	**11**	**10**	**9**	**8**
SPI3EN	SPI2EN	–	–	WWDGEN	–	–	–
7	**6**	**5**	**4**	**3**	**2**	**1**	**0**
–	–	TIM7EN	TIM6EN	TIM5EN	TIM4EN	TIM3EN	TIM2EN

Reset value = 0x0000 0000
Offset = 0x58
Access: No wait states.

UARTxEN: UARTx clock enable (x = 4 or 5)
 0: UARTx clock disabled 1: UARTx clock enabled
USARTxEN: USARTx interface clock enable (x = 2 or 3)
 0: USARTx interface clock disabled 1: USARTx interface clock enabled
SPIxEN: SPIx clock enable (x = 2 or 3)
 0: SPIx clock disabled 1: SPIx clock enabled
WWDGEN: Window watchdog clock enable
 0: Window watchdog clock disabled 1: Window watchdog clock enabled
TIMxEN: TIMx clock enable (x = 7..2)
 0: TIMx clock disabled 1: TIMx clock enabled

Figure 3.18a APB1 peripheral clock enable register 1 (RCC->APB1ENR1)—(continued)

31	30	29	28	27	26	25	24
–	–	–	–	–	–	–	–
23	**22**	**21**	**20**	**19**	**18**	**17**	**16**
–	–	–	–	–	–	–	–
15	**14**	**13**	**12**	**11**	**10**	**9**	**8**
–	–	–	–	–	–	–	–
7	**6**	**5**	**4**	**3**	**2**	**1**	**0**
–	–	LPTIM2EN	–	–	SWPMI1EN	–	LPUART1EN

Reset value = 0x0000 0000
Offset = 0x5C
Access: No wait states.

LPTIM2EN: Low power timer 2 clock enable
 0: LPTIM2 clock disable 1: LPTIM2 clock enable
SWPMI1EN: Single wire protocol clock enable
 0: SWPMI1 clock disable 1: SWPMI1 clock enable
LPUART1EN: Low power UART1 clock enable
 0: LPUART1 clock disable 1: LPUART1 clock enable

Figure 3.19 APB1 peripheral clock enable register 1 (RCC->APB1ENR2)

31	30	29	28	27	26	25	24
–	–	–	–	–	–	–	DFSDMEN
23	**22**	**21**	**20**	**19**	**18**	**17**	**16**
–	SAI2EN	SAI1EN	–	–	TIM17EN	TIM16EN	TIM15EN
15	**14**	**13**	**12**	**11**	**10**	**9**	**8**
–	USART1EN	TIM8EN	SPI1EN	TIM1EN	SDMMC1EN	–	–
7	**6**	**5**	**4**	**3**	**2**	**1**	**0**
FWEN	–	–	–	–	–	–	SYSCFGEN

Reset value = 0x0000 0000
Offset = 0x60
Access: No wait states.

DFSDMEN: Digital filter for sigma delta modulator (DFSDM) timer clock enable
 0: DFSDM clock disabled 1: DFSDM clock enabled
SAI_nEN: SAI_n clock enable (n = 1 or 2)
 0: SAIn clock disabled 1: SAIn clock enabled
TIM_kEN: TIM_k timer clock enable (k = 17, 16, 15, 8, 1)
 0: TIM_k timer clock disabled 1: TIM_k timer clock enabled
USART1EN: USART1 clock enable
 0: USART1 clock disabled 1: USART1 clock enabled
SPI1EN: SPI1 clock enable
 0: SPI1 clock disabled 1: SPI1 clock enabled
SDMMC1EN: SDMMC clock enable
 0: SDMMC clock disabled 1: SDMMC clock enabled
FWEN: Firewall clock enable
 0: Firewall clock disabled 1: Firewall clock enabled
SYSCFGEN: SYSCFG + COMP + VREFBUF clock enable
 0: SYSCFG + COMP + VREFBUF clock disabled
 1: SYSCFG + COMP + VREFBUF clock enabled

Figure 3.20 APB2 peripheral clock enable register 1 (RCC->APB2ENR)

Example 3.7 Write a sequence of C statements to enable the clock source to the following peripherals:

- Touch sensing controller, flash memory interface, DMA1 and DMA2
- Random number generator, ADC, OTG USB, all GPIO ports (A..H)
- Flexible memory controller
- DAC1, power interface, I2C1, I2C2, CAN, UART4, UART5, TIM3~TIM5
- SAI1, USART1, SPI1, SDMMC1, Firewall, SYSCFG

Solution:

```
RCC->AHB1ENR = RCC_AHB1ENR_TSCEN + RCC_AHB1ENR_FLASHEN +
               RCC_AHB1ENR_DMA2EN + RCC_AHB1ENR_DMA1EN;
RCC->AHB2ENR = RCC_AHB2ENR_RNGEN + RCC_AHB2ENR_ADCEN +
               RCC_AHB2ENR_OTGFSEN + RCC_AHB2ENR_GPIOHEN +
               RCC_AHB2ENR_GPIOGEN + RCC_AHB2ENR_GPIOFEN +
               RCC_AHB2ENR_GPIOEEN + RCC_AHB2ENR_GPIODEN +
               RCC_AHB2ENR_GPIOCEN + RCC_AHB2ENR_GPIOBEN +
               RCC_AHB2ENR_GPIOAEN;
RCC->AHB3ENR = RCC_AHB3ENR_FMCEN;
```

```
RCC->APB1ENR1 = RCC_APB1ENR1_DAC1EN + RCC_APB1ENR1_PWREN +
                RCC_APB1ENR1_I2C1EN + RCC_APB1ENR1_I2C2EN +
                RCC_APB1ENR1_CAN1EN + RCC_APB1ENR1_UART5EN +
                RCC_APB1ENR1_UART4EN + RCC_APB1ENR1_TIM3EN +
                RCC_APB1ENR1_TIM4EN + RCC_APB1ENR1_TIM5EN;
RCC->APB2ENR = RCC_APB2ENR_SAI1EN + RCC_APB2ENR_USART1EN +
                RCC_APB2ENR_SPI1EN + RCC_APB2ENR_SDMMC1EN +
                RCC_APB2ENR_FWEN + RCC_APB2ENR_SYSCFGEN;
```

3.4.2 PERIPHERALS HAVING MULTIPLE CHOICES OF THEIR CLOCK SOURCES

The user is required to program the RCC->CCIPR register to assign clock signals to those peripherals that do not obtain their clock signals from system buses. The contents of the RCC->CCIPR register are shown in Figure 3.21. As shown in Figure 3.22, seventeen STM32L475 peripherals receive their clock signals via the RCC->CCIPR register.

31	30	29	28	27	26	25	24
DFSDM SEL	SWPMI1 SEL	ADCSEL[1:0]		CLK48SEL[1:0]		SAI2SEL[1:0]	
23	22	21	20	19	18	17	16
SAI1SEL[1:0]		LPTIM2SEL[1:0]		LPTIM1SEL[1:0]		I2C3SEL[1:0]	
15	14	13	12	11	10	9	8
I2C2SEL[1:0]		I2C1SEL[1:0]		LPUART1SEL[1:0]		UART5SEL[1:0]	
7	6	5	4	3	2	1	0
USART4SEL[1:0]		USART3SEL[1:0]		USART2SEL[1:0]		USART1SEL[1:0]	

Reset value = 0x0000 0000
Offset = 0x88
Access: No wait states.

DFSDMSEL: DFSDM clock source selection
- 0: PCLK selected as DFSDM clock
- 1: System clock (SYSCLK) used as DFSDM clock

SWPMI1SEL: SWPMI1 clock source selection
- 0: PCLK selected as SWPMI1 clock
- 1: HSI16 clock selected as SWPMI1 clock

ADCSEL[10]: ADCs clock source selection
- 00: No clock selected
- 01: PLLSAI1 "R" clock (PLLADC1CLK) selected as ADCs clock
- 10: PLLSAI2 "R" clock (PLLADC2CLK) selected as ADCs clock
- 11: System clock selected as ADCs clock

CLK48SEL[1:0]: 48 MHz clock source selection
- 00: No clock selected
- 01: PLLSAI1 "Q" clock (PLL48M2CLK) selected as 48 MHz clock
- 10: PLL "Q" clock (PLL48M1CLK) selected as 48 MHz clock
- 11: MSI clock selected as 48 MHz clock

SAI2SEL[1:0]: SAI2 clock source selection
- 00: PLLSAI1 "P" clock (PLLSAI1CLK) selected as SAI2 clock
- 01: PLLSAI2 "P" clock (PLLSAI2CLK) selected as SAI2 clock
- 10: PLL "P" clock (PLLSAI3CLK) selected as SAI2 clock
- 11: External input SAI2_EXTCLK selected as SAI2 clock. If external clock is selected, it is not possible to switch to another clock if the external clock is not present.

Figure 3.21 Peripherals independent clock configuration register (RCC->CCIPR)

31	30	29 28	27 26	25 24
DFSDM SEL	SWPMI1 SEL	ADCSEL[1:0]	CLK48SEL[1:0]	SAI2SEL[1:0]

23 22	21 20	19 18	17 16
SAI1SEL[1:0]	LPTIM2SEL[1:0]	LPTIM1SEL[1:0]	I2C3SEL[1:0]

15 14	13 12	11 10	9 8
I2C2SEL[1:0]	I2C1SEL[1:0]	LPUART1SEL[1:0]	UART5SEL[1:0]

7 6	5 4	3 2	1 0
USART4SEL[1:0]	USART3SEL[1:0]	USART2SEL[1:0]	USART1SEL[1:0]

Reset value = 0x0000 0000
Offset = 0x88
Access: No wait states.

SAI1SEL[1:0]: SAI1 clock source selection
- 00: PLLSAI1 "P" clock (PLLSAI1CLK) selected as SAI1 clock
- 01: PLLSAI2 "P" clock (PLLSAI2CLK) selected as SAI1 clock
- 10: PLL "P" clock (PLLSAI3CLK) selected as SAI1 clock
- 11: External input SAI1_EXTCLK selected as SAI1 clock. If the external clock is selected, it is not possible to switch to another clock if the external clock is not present

LPTIMxSEL[1:0]: Low power timer x clock source selection (x = 1 or 2)
- 00: PCLK selected as LPTIMx clock
- 01: LSI clock selected as LPTIMx clock
- 10: HSI16 clock selected as LPTIMx clock
- 11: LSE clock selected as LPTIMx clock

I2CxSEL[1:0]: I2Cx clock source selection (x = 1..3)
- 00: PCLK selected as I2Cx clock
- 01: SYSCLK selected as I2Cx clock
- 10: HSI16 clock selected as I2Cx clock
- 11: Reserved

Figure 3.21a Peripherals independent clock configuration register (RCC->CCIPR)—(continued)

31	30	29	28	27	26	25	24
DFSDM SEL	SWPMI1 SEL	ADCSEL[1:0]		CLK48SEL[1:0]		SAI2SEL[1:0]	
23	**22**	**21**	**20**	**19**	**18**	**17**	**16**
SAI1SEL[1:0]		LPTIM2SEL[1:0]		LPTIM1SEL[1:0]		I2C3SEL[1:0]	
15	**14**	**13**	**12**	**11**	**10**	**9**	**8**
I2C2SEL[1:0]		I2C1SEL[1:0]		LPUART1SEL[1:0]		UART5SEL[1:0]	
7	**6**	**5**	**4**	**3**	**2**	**1**	**0**
UART4SEL[1:0]		USART3SEL[1:0]		USART2SEL[1:0]		USART1SEL[1:0]	

Reset value = 0x0000 0000
Offset = 0x88
Access: No wait states.

LPUART1SEL[1:0]: LPUART1 clock source selection
- 00: PCLK clock selected as LPUART1 clock
- 01: SYSCLK selected as LPUART1 clock
- 10: HSI16 clock selected as LPUART1 clock
- 11: LSE clock selected as LPUART1 clock.

UARTxSEL[1:0]: UARTx clock source selection (x = 4 or 5)
- 00: PCLK selected as UARTx clock
- 01: SYSCLK clock selected as UARTx clock
- 10: HSI16 clock selected as UARTx clock
- 11: LSE clock selected as UARTx clock

USARTxSEL[1:0]: USARTx clock source selection (x = 1..3)
- 00: PCLK selected as UARTx clock
- 01: SYSCLK clock selected as UARTx clock
- 10: HSI16 selected as UARTx clock
- 11: LSE clock selected as UARTx clock

Figure 3.21b Peripherals independent clock configuration register (RCC->CCIPR)—(continued)

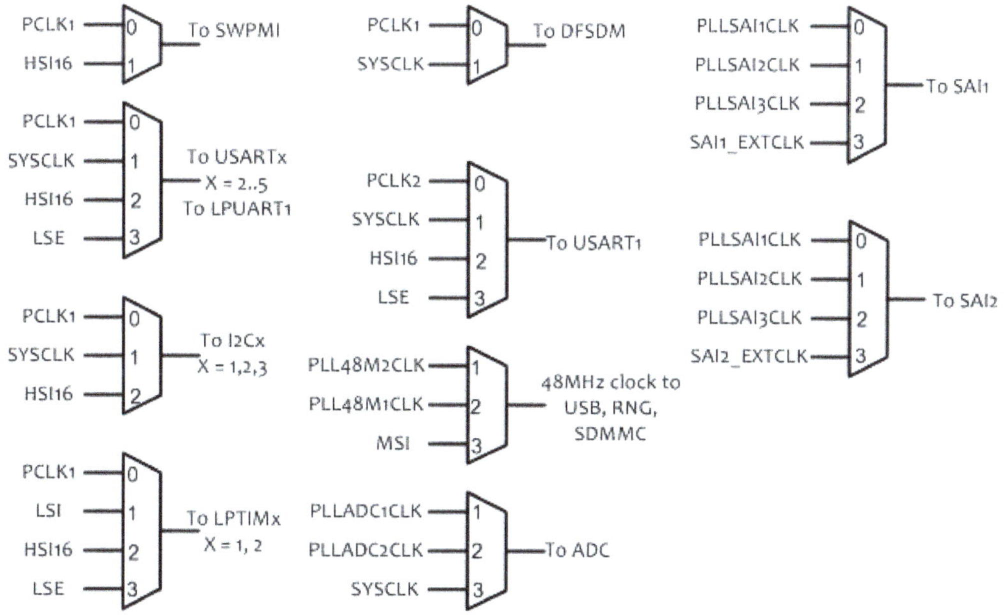

Figure 3.22 Miscellaneous clock assignment

Example 3.8 Write a sequence of C statements to make the choice of clock source for the following peripherals:

- Use SYSCLK as DFSDM clock source
- Use PCLK as SWPM1 clock source
- Use SYSCLK as ADC clock source
- Use MSI clock as 48 MHz clock
- Use PLLSAI2 P clock as SAI2 and SAI1 clock
- Use PCLK as the clock of LPTIM1, LPTIM2, I2C3, I2C2, I2C1, LPUART1, UART5, UART4, USART3, USART2, and USART1

Solution:

The following C statement performs the desired clock assignment accordingly:

```
RCC->CCIPR = RCC_CCIPR_DFSDM1SEL + RCC_CCIPR_ADCSEL + RCC_CCIPR_CLK48SEL +
             RCC_CCIPR_SAI2SEL_0 + RCC_CCIPR_SAI1SEL_0;
```

3.5 Clock Signals in Low-Power Modes

Power consumption in microcontroller is caused by the transistor switching, which is controlled by the clock signals. The STM32L475 offers low-power modes to save power consumption. Low-power modes are implemented by disabling clock signals to those peripherals that are not being used.

All peripheral clocks, including DMA clocks, distributed via the AHB and APB buses can be disabled by software. The CPU clock stops during the sleep and low-power modes. The memory interface (flash, SRAM1, and SRAM2 interfaces) clocks can be stopped by software during the sleep mode.

The AHB to APB bridge clocks are disabled by hardware during sleep mode when all the clocks of the peripheral connected to them are disabled. Stop modes (Stop 0, Stop 1, and Stop 2) stop all the clocks in the V_{CORE} domain and disable all three PLLs, the HSI16, the MSI, and the HSE16 oscillators.

All USARTs, LPUSARTs, and I^2Cs have the capability to enable the HSI16 oscillator even when the MCU is in the stop mode (if HSI16 is selected as the clock source for that peripheral).

All USARTs and LPUARTs can also be driven by the LSE oscillator when the system is in a stop mode (if LSE is selected as the clock source for that peripheral) and the LSE oscillator is enabled (LSEON is set to 1). In that case, the LSE remains ON in the stop mode.

Standby and shutdown modes stop all the clocks in the V_{CORE} domain and disable the PLL, HSI16, MSI, and HSE oscillators. When leaving the stop modes (Stop 0, Stop 1, or Stop 2), the system clock is either the MSI or the HSI16, depending on the setting of the STOPWUCK bit in the RCC->CFGR register.

The frequency of the MSI oscillator is the one configured before entering the stop mode. The user trim (the HSITRIM field of the RCC->ICSCR register) of the HSI16 is kept. If the MSI was in PLL mode before entering the stop mode, the PLL mode stabilization time must be waited for after wakeup even if the LSE was kept on during the stop mode.

When leaving the standby and shutdown modes, the system clock is MSI. The MSI frequency at wakeup from standby mode is configured with the MSISRANGE field in the RCC->CSR register (shown in Figure 3.9a), from 1 to 8 MHz. The MSI frequency at wakeup from shutdown mode is 4 MHz. The user trim (the MSITRIM field in the RCC->ICSCR register) is lost.

If the processor is performing a flash memory programming operation, it will be delayed from entering the stop, standby, and shutdown modes until the flash memory interface access is finished. If the processor is accessing the APB domain, it will be delayed from entering the stop, standby, or shutdown mode until the APB access is finished.

Peripheral clocks can be kept enabled during the sleep or stop mode by programming the appropriate peripheral clock enable bits in the AHB and APB clock enable in sleep and stop mode registers (RCC->AHB1SMENR, RCC->AHB2SMENR, RCC->AHB3SMENR,

RCC->APB1SMENR1, RCC->APB1SMENR2, RCC->APB2SMENR). The contents of these registers are shown in Figures 3.23 to 3.28, respectively.

31	30	29	28	27	26	25	24
--	--	--	--	--	--	--	--
23	**22**	**21**	**20**	**19**	**18**	**17**	**16**
--	--	--	--	--	--	--	TSCSMEN
15	**14**	**13**	**12**	**11**	**10**	**9**	**8**
--	--	--	CRCSMEN	--	--	SRAM1SM EN	FLASHSM EN
7	**6**	**5**	**4**	**3**	**2**	**1**	**0**
--	--	--	--	--	--	DMA2SM EN	DMA1SM EN

Reset value = 0x0001 1303
Address offset = 0x68

TSCSMEN: Touch sensing controller clocks enable during sleep and stop modes
- 0: TSC clocks disabled during sleep and stop modes
- 1: TSC clocks enabled during sleep and stop modes

CRCSMEN: CRC clocks enable during sleep and stop modes
- 0: CRC clocks disabled during sleep and stop modes
- 1: CRC clocks enabled during sleep and stop modes

SRAM1SMEN: SRAM1 interface clocks enable during sleep and stop modes
- 0: SRAM1 interface clocks disabled during sleep and stop modes
- 1: SRAM1 interface clocks enabled during sleep and stop modes

FLASHSMEN: Flash memory interface clocks enable during sleep and stop modes
- 0: flash memory interface clocks disabled during sleep and stop modes
- 1: flash memory interface clocks enabled during sleep and stop modes

DMAxSMEN: DMAx clocks enable during sleep and stop modes (x = 1 or 2)
- 0: DMAx clocks disabled during sleep and stop modes
- 1: DMAx clocks enabled during sleep and stop modes

Figure 3.23 AHB1 peripheral clocks enable in sleep & stop modes register (RCC->AHB1SMENR)

31	30	29	28	27	26	25	24
--	--	--	--	--	--	--	--
23	**22**	**21**	**20**	**19**	**18**	**17**	**16**
--	--	--	--	--	RNGSMEN	--	--
15	**14**	**13**	**12**	**11**	**10**	**9**	**8**
--	--	ADCSMEN	OTGFSSM EN	--	--	SRAM2SMEN	--
7	**6**	**5**	**4**	**3**	**2**	**1**	**0**
GPIOH SMEN	GPIOG SMEN	GPIOF SMEN	GPIOE SMEN	GPIOD SMEN	GPIOC SMEN	GPIOB SMEN	GPIOA SMEN

Reset value = 0x0005 32FF
Address offset = 0x6C

RNGSMEN: Random number generator clocks enable during sleep and stop modes
0: Random number generator clocks disabled during sleep and stop modes
1: Random number generator clocks enabled during sleep and stop modes
ADCSMEN: ADC clocks enable during sleep and stop modes
0: ADC clocks disabled during sleep and stop modes
1: ADC clocks enabled during sleep and stop modes
OTGFSSMEN: OTG full speed clocks enable during sleep and stop modes
0: USB OTG full speed clocks disabled during sleep and stop modes
1: USB OTG full speed clocks enabled during sleep and stop modes
SRAM2SMEN: SRAM2 interface clocks enable during sleep and stop modes
0: SRAM2 interface clocks disabled during sleep and stop modes
1: SRAM2 interface clocks enabled during sleep and stop modes
GPIOxSMEN: IO port x clocks enable during sleep and stop modes (x = A..H)
0: GPIO port x clocks disabled during sleep and stop modes
1: GPIO port x clocks enabled during sleep and stop modes

Figure 3.24 AHB2 peripheral clocks enable in sleep & stop modes register (RCC->AHB2SMENR)

31	30	29	28	27	26	25	24
--	--	--	--	--	--	--	--
23	**22**	**21**	**20**	**19**	**18**	**17**	**16**
--	--	--	--	--	--	--	--
15	**14**	**13**	**12**	**11**	**10**	**9**	**8**
--	--	--	--	--	--	--	QSPI SMEN
7	**6**	**5**	**4**	**3**	**2**	**1**	**0**
--	--	--	--	--	--	--	FMCSMEN

Reset value = 0x0000 0101
Address offset = 0x70

QSPISMEN: Quad SPI memory interface clocks enable during sleep and stop modes
0: QUADSPI clocks disabled during sleep and stop modes
1: QUADSPI clocks enabled during sleep and stop modes
FMCSMEN: Flexible memory controller clocks during sleep and stop modes
0: FMC clocks disabled during sleep and stop modes
1: FMC clocks enabled during sleep and stop modes

Figure 3.25 AHB3 peripheral clocks enable sleep & stop modes register (RCC->AHB3SMENR)

31	30	29	28	27	26	25	24
LPTIM1 SMEN	OPAMP SMEN	DAC1 SMEN	PWR SMEN	--	--	CAN1 SMEN	--
23	**22**	**21**	**20**	**19**	**18**	**17**	**16**
I2C3 SMEN	I2C2 SMEN	I2C1 SMEN	UART5 SMEN	UART4 SMEN	USART3 SMEN	USART2 SMEN	--
15	**14**	**13**	**12**	**11**	**10**	**9**	**8**
SPI3 SMEN	SPI2 SMEN	--	--	WWDG SMEN	--	--	--
7	**6**	**5**	**4**	**3**	**2**	**1**	**0**
--	--	TIM7 SMEN	TIM6 SMEN	TIM5 SMEN	TIM4 SMEN	TIM3 SMEN	TIM2 SMEN

Reset value = 0xF2FE C83F
Address offset = 0x78

LPTIM1SMEN: Low power timer 1 clocks enable during sleep and stop modes
0: LPTIM1 clocks disabled during sleep and stop modes
1: LPTIM1 clocks enabled during sleep and stop modes
OPAMPSMEN: OPAMP interface clocks enable during sleep and stop modes
0: OPAMP interface clocks disabled during sleep and stop modes
1: OPAMP interface clocks enabled during sleep and stop modes
DAC1SMEN: DAC1 interface clocks enable during sleep and stop modes
0: DAC1 interface clocks disabled during sleep and stop modes
1: DAC1 interface clocks enabled during sleep and stop modes
PWRSMEN: Power interface clocks enable during sleep and stop modes
0: Power interface clocks disabled during sleep and stop modes
1: Power interface clocks enabled during sleep and stop modes
CAN1SMEN: CAN1 clocks enable during sleep and stop modes
0: CAN1 clocks disabled during sleep and stop modes
1: CAN1 clocks enabled during sleep and stop modes
I2CxSMEN: I2Cx clocks enable during sleep and stop modes (x = 1, 2, or 3)
0: I2Cx clocks disabled during sleep and stop modes
1: I2Cx clocks enabled during sleep and stop modes
UARTxSMEN: UARTxSMEN: UARTx clocks enable during sleep and stop modes (x = 4 or 5)
0: UARTx clocks disabled during sleep and stop modes
1: UARTx clocks enabled during sleep and stop modes
USARTxSMEN: USARTx clocks enable during sleep and stop modes (x = 2 or 3)
0: USARTx clocks disabled during sleep and stop modes
1: USARTx clocks enabled during sleep and stop modes

Figure 3.26 APB1 peripheral clocks enable in sleep & stop modes register 1 (RCC->APB1SMENR)

31	30	29	28	27	26	25	24
LPTIM1 SMEN	OPAMP SMEN	DAC1 SMEN	PWR SMEN	--	--	CAN1 SMEN	--
23	22	21	20	19	18	17	16
I2C3 SMEN	I2C2 SMEN	I2C1 SMEN	UART5 SMEN	UART4 SMEN	USART3 SMEN	USART2 SMEN	--
15	14	13	12	11	10	9	8
SPI3 SMEN	SPI2 SMEN	--	--	WWDG SMEN	--	--	--
7	6	5	4	3	2	1	0
--	--	TIM7 SMEN	TIM6 SMEN	TIM5 SMEN	TIM4 SMEN	TIM3 SMEN	TIM2 SMEN

Reset value = 0xF2FE C83F
Address offset = 0x78

SPIxSMEN: SPIx clocks enable during sleep and stop modes (x = 2 or 3)
0: SPIx clocks disabled during sleep and stop modes
1: SPIx clocks enabled during sleep and stop modes
WWDGSMEN: Window watchdog clocks enable during sleep and stop modes
0: Window watchdog clocks disabled during sleep and stop modes
1: Window watchdog clocks enabled during sleep and stop modes
TIMxSMEN: TIMx timer clocks enable during sleep and stop modes
0: TIMx timer clocks disabled during sleep and stop modes
1: TIMx timer clocks enabled during sleep and stop modes

Figure 3.26a APB1 peripheral clocks enable in sleep & stop modes register 1 (RCC->APB1SMENR)—(continued)

31	30	29	28	27	26	25	24
--	--	--	--	--	--	--	--
23	22	21	20	19	18	17	16
--	--	--	--	--	--	--	--
15	14	13	12	11	10	9	8
--	--	--	--	--	--	--	--
7	6	5	4	3	2	1	0
--	--	LPTIM2 SMEN	--	--	SWPMI1 SMEN	--	LPUART1 SMEN

Reset value = 0x0000 0025
Address offset = 0x7C

LPTIM2SMEN: Low power timer 2 clocks enable during sleep and stop modes
0: LPTIM2 clocks disabled during sleep and stop modes
1: LPTIM2 clocks enabled during sleep and stop modes
SWPMI1SMEN: Single wire protocol clocks enable during sleep and stop modes
0: SWPMI1 clocks disabled during sleep and stop modes
1: SMPMI1 clocks enabled during sleep and stop modes
LPUART1SMEN: low power UART 1 clocks enable during sleep and stop modes
0: LPUART1 clocks disabled during sleep and stop modes
1: LPUART1 clocks enabled during sleep and stop modes

Figure 3.27 APB1 peripheral clocks enable in sleep & stop modes register 2 (RCC->APB1SMENR2)

31	30	29	28	27	26	25	24
--	--	--	--	--	--	--	DFSDM SMEN
23	**22**	**21**	**20**	**19**	**18**	**17**	**16**
--	SAI2 SMEN	SAI1 SMEN	--	--	TIM17 SMEN	TIM16 SMEN	TIM15 SMEN
15	**14**	**13**	**12**	**11**	**10**	**9**	**8**
--	USART1 SMEN	TIM8 SMEN	SPI1 SMEN	TIM1 SMEN	SDMMC1 SMEN	--	--
7	**6**	**5**	**4**	**3**	**2**	**1**	**0**
--	--	--	--	--	--	--	SYSCFG SMEN

Reset value = 0x0167 7C01
Address offset = 0x80

DFSDMSMEN: DFSDM timer clocks enable during sleep and stop modes
 0: DFSDM clocks disabled during sleep and stop modes
 1: DFSDM clocks enabled during sleep and stop modes
SAIxSMEN: SAIx clocks enable during sleep and stop modes (x = 1 or 2)
 0: SAIx clocks disabled during sleep and stop modes
 1: SAIx clocks enabled during sleep and stop modes
TIMxSMEN: TIMx timer clocks enable during sleep and stop modes (x = 1, 8, 15, 16, or 17)
 0: TIMx clocks disabled during sleep and stop modes
 1: TIMx clocks enabled during sleep and stop modes
USART1SMEN: USART1 clocks enable during sleep and stop modes
 0: USART1 clocks disabled during sleep and stop modes
 1: USART1 clocks enabled during sleep and stop modes
SPI1SMEN: SPI1 clocks enable during sleep and stop modes
 0: SPI1 clocks disabled during sleep and stop modes
 1: SPI1 clocks enabled during sleep and stop modes
SDMMC1SMEN: SDMMC1 clocks enable during sleep and stop modes
 0: SDMMC clocks disabled during sleep and stop modes
 1: SDMMC clocks enabled during sleep and stop modes
SYSCFGSMEN: SYSCFG + COMP + VREFBUF clocks enable during sleep and stop modes
 0: SYSCFG + COMP + VREFBUF clocks disabled during sleep and stop modes
 1: SYSCFG + COMP + VREFBUF clocks enabled during sleep and stop modes

Figure 3.28 APB2 peripheral clocks enable in sleep & stop modes register (RCC->APB2SMENR)

Example 3.9 Write a C statement to enable clock input to all the peripherals attached to the AHB1 bus during the sleep mode.

Solution: The following statement will enable clock input to all peripherals attached to the AHB1 bus during the sleep mode:

```
RCC->AHB1SMENR = RCC_AHB1SMENR_TSCSMEN + RCC_AHB1SMENR_CRCSMEN +
                 RCC_AHB1SMENR_SRAM1SMEN + RCC_AHB1SMENR_FLASHSMEN
                 + RCC_AHB1SMENR_DMA2SMEN + RCC_AHB1SMENR_DMA1SMEN;
```

3.6 Flash Memory Read Access Latency

To execute the application code, which is stored in the flash memory, the processor is required to access the flash memory. The flash memory has an access time that allows the processor to get back the contents of a memory location in **one clock cycle** up to certain frequency (f_{TH}). When the clock frequency for the processor is higher than f_{TH}, wait states must be inserted to the access cycle in order for the processor to get back the contents of the flash memory correctly.

The number of wait states that are needed at different clock frequencies is also a function of the processor core power supply (V_{CORE}). The V_{CORE} has two ranges: **range 1** and **range 2**. The number of wait states to be inserted at different processor clock frequencies is listed in Table 3.3.

The number of wait states for the flash memory at different processor clock frequencies is programmed via the FLASH->ACR register. The contents of this register are shown in Figure 3.29. After reset, the CPU clock frequency is 4 MHz and 0 wait state (WS) is configured in the FLASH->ACR register.

Table 3.3 Number of wait states according to CPU clock (HCLK) frequency

Wait states (WS) (Latency)	HCLK (MHz)	
	V_{CORE} Range 1	V_{CORE} Range 2
0 WS (1 CPU cycle)	≤ 16	≤ 6
1 WS (2 CPU cycles)	≤ 32	≤ 12
2 WS (3 CPU cycles)	≤ 48	≤ 18
3 WS (4 CPU cycles)	≤ 64	≤ 26
4 WS (5 CPU cycle)	≤ 80	≤ 26

3.6.1 ADAPTIVE REAL-TIME MEMORY ACCELERATOR (ART ACCELERATOR)

The STM32L475 processor fetches instruction via the ICode bus and the constant/data via the DCode bus. Each flash memory fetch reads 64 bits. The 64 bits of instruction may be the combination of two 32-bit instructions, one 32-bit instruction and two 16-bit instructions, or four 16-bit instructions. Therefore, each flash memory access returns from 2 to 4 instructions to the processor.

When wait states are inserted, the STM32L475 cannot achieve the theoretical highest performance, that is, one clock cycle per access. The STM32L475 implements a proprietary Adaptive Real-Time (ART) memory accelerator to minimize the wait states that are inserted.

The ART includes a 1-kB instruction cache (I_Cache) and a 256-byte data cache memory (D-Cache) and also a prefetch unit for instruction access. Whenever the processor needs to fetch instruction or data, it always starts with the I_Cache or D_Cache. The access time is one clock cycle if there is a hit in the cache memory. If there is a miss in the cache memory, the processor is required to access the flash memory. Wait states must be inserted if the processor is running with a clock at a frequency higher than f_{TH}. Whenever the processor is not accessing flash memory, the prefetch unit performs instruction prefetch sequentially. By adding cache memory and the prefetch unit, the required wait states during program execution are minimized. Cache memory is enabled by default.

31	30	29	28	27	26	25	24
--	--	--	--	--	--	--	--
23	**22**	**21**	**20**	**19**	**18**	**17**	**16**
--	--	--	--	--	--	--	--
15	**14**	**13**	**12**	**11**	**10**	**9**	**8**
--	SLEEP_PD	RUN_PD	DCRST	ICRST	DCEN	ICEN	PRFTEN
7	**6**	**5**	**4**	**3**	**2**	**1**	**0**
--	--	--	--	--	LATENCY[2:0]		

Reset value = 0x0000 0600
Address offset = 0x00

SLEEP_PD: Flash power-down mode during sleep or low-power sleep mode
 0: Flash is in idle mode during sleep or low-power sleep modes
 1: Flash is in power-down mode during sleep or low-power sleep modes
RUN_PD: Flash power-down mode during run or low-power run mode
 0: Flash in idle mode 1: Flash in power-down mode
RCRST: Data cache reset (can be written only when data cache is disabled)
 0: Data cache is not reset 1: Data cache is reset
ICRST: Instruction cache reset
 0: Instruction cache is not reset 1: instruction cache is reset
DCEN: Data cache enable
 0: Data cache is disabled 1: Data cache is enabled
ICEN: Instruction cache enable
 0: Instruction cache is disabled 1: Instruction cache is enabled
PRFTEN: Prefetch enable
 0: prefetch disabled 1: prefetch enable
LATENCY: latency (ration of SYSCLK period to the flash access time)
 000: Zero wait state 001: One wait state 010: two wait states
 011: Three wait states 100: Four wait states Others: reserved

Figure 3.29 Flash access control register (FLASH->ACR)

Example 3.10 Assuming that the STM32L475 is running at 80 MHz, write a C statement to configure the FLASH->ACR register properly and also enable instruction and data cache.

Solution: At 80 MHz, four wait states must be inserted to each flash memory access. We also need to enable instruction prefetch. The following statement will configure the flash memory properly:

```
FLASH->ACR = FLASH_ACR_DCEN + FLASH_ACR_ICEN + FLASH_ACR_PRFTEN +
             FLASH_ACR_LATENCY_4WS;
```

Example 3.11 Write a C function to generate clock signals for the STM32L475 according to the following requirements:

- Use 32.768-kHz LSE crystal.
- Enable RTC and use LSE as its clock source.
- Turn on MSI to run at 48 MHz and enable PLL mode and then use it as the clock input of all three PLLs.
- Enable the main clock output (MCO-PA8 pin, alternate function 0) and the low-frequency clock output (LSCO—PA2 pin, additional function). Set f_{MCO} to 10 MHz. Select SYSCLK as the source for the MCO.

- Configure PLL, PLLSAI1, PLLSAI2 to output 80 MHz clock.
- Select PLL output as the SYSCLK.
- Configure HCLK, PCLK1, PCLK2 to 80 MHz.
- Enable clock input to all peripherals.
- Use 48 MHz MSI as the clock input to USB.
- Enable instruction and data cache and also set the number of wait states to 4.

Solution:

```
void sysClkInit (void)
{
// enable I_Cache & D_Cache & insert 4 wait states
    RCC->AHB1ENR |= RCC_AHB1ENR_FLASHEN; // enable clock to flash memory
    FLASH->ACR = FLASH_ACR_DCEN + FLASH_ACR_ICEN + FLASH_ACR_PRFTEN +
                 FLASH_ACR_LATENCY_4WS;
// turn on 32.768 kHz external crystal oscillator, enable RTC and LSCO output
    RCC->APB1ENR1  |= RCC_APB1ENR1_PWREN; // enable clock to power interface
    PWR->CR1       |= PWR_CR1_DBP; // enable access to backup domain
    RCC->BDCR      = RCC_BDCR_LSEON + RCC_BDCR_LSEDRV_1; // turn on LSE
    while(!(RCC->BDCR & RCC_BDCR_LSERDY)); // wait until LSE is ready
    RCC->BDCR      |= RCC_BDCR_RTCSEL_0; // select LSE as the clock source of RTC
    RCC->BDCR      |= RCC_BDCR_RTCEN; // enable RTC
    RCC->BDCR      |= RCC_BDCR_LSCOSEL + RCC_BDCR_LSCOEN;
// turn on MSI, enable MSI PLL, and set MSI output to 48 MHz
    RCC->CR        =  RCC_CR_MSION + RCC_CR_MSIRGSEL + RCC_CR_MSIPLLEN +
                      RCC_CR_MSIRANGE_11;
    while(!(RCC->CR & RCC_CR_MSIRDY));
// configure PLL -- (N = 10, M = 3, P = 7, Q = R = 2)
    RCC->PLLCFGR = RCC_PLLCFGR_PLLREN + RCC_PLLCFGR_PLLQEN +
                   RCC_PLLCFGR_PLLPEN + RCC_PLLCFGR_PLLN_1 +
                   RCC_PLLCFGR_PLLN_3 + RCC_PLLCFGR_PLLM_1 +
                   RCC_PLLCFGR_PLLSRC_MSI;
    RCC->PLLSAI1CFGR = RCC_PLLSAI1CFGR_PLLSAI1N_3 + RCC_PLLSAI1CFGR_PLLSAI1N_1 +
                   RCC_PLLSAI1CFGR_PLLSAI1QEN + RCC_PLLSAI1CFGR_PLLSAI1PEN +
```

```
                    RCC_PLLSAI1CFGR_PLLSAI1REN;
    RCC->PLLSAI2CFGR = RCC_PLLSAI2CFGR_PLLSAI2N_3 + RCC_PLLSAI2CFGR_PLLSAI2N_1 +
                RCC_PLLSAI2CFGR_PLLSAI2REN + RCC_PLLSAI2CFGR_PLLSAI2PEN;
// turn on PLL, PLLSAI1, & PLLSAI2
    RCC->CR |= RCC_CR_PLLON + RCC_CR_PLLSAI1ON + RCC_CR_PLLSAI2ON;
// wait for PLLs to be ready
    while(!(RCC->CR & RCC_CR_PLLRDY));
    while(!(RCC->CR & RCC_CR_PLLSAI1RDY));
    while(!(RCC->CR & RCC_CR_PLLSAI2RDY));
// Select SYSCLK/8 as MCO & select PLL as SYSCLK (need to configure PA8 pin for AF0)
    GPIOA->MODER   &= ~(GPIO_MODER_MODE8); // configure PA8 pin for
    GPIOA->MODER   |= GPIO_MODER_MODE8_1;  // alternate function
    GPIOA->AFR[1]  &= ~GPIO_AFRH_AFSEL8; // configure PA8 pin for alternate function 0
    RCC->CFGR = RCC_CFGR_MCOPRE_DIV8 + RCC_CFGR_MCOSEL_0 + RCC_CFGR_SW_PLL;
// Enable clock signals to all peripherals connected to system buses
    RCC->AHB1ENR =   RCC_AHB1ENR_TSCEN + RCC_AHB1ENR_CRCEN +
                     RCC_AHB1ENR_FLASHEN + RCC_AHB1ENR_DMA2EN +
                     RCC_AHB1ENR_DMA1EN;
    RCC->AHB2ENR =   RCC_AHB2ENR_RNGEN + RCC_AHB2ENR_ADCEN +
                     RCC_AHB2ENR_OTGFSEN + RCC_AHB2ENR_GPIOHEN +
                     RCC_AHB2ENR_GPIOGEN + RCC_AHB2ENR_GPIOFEN +
                     RCC_AHB2ENR_GPIOEEN + RCC_AHB2ENR_GPIODEN +
                     RCC_AHB2ENR_GPIOCEN + RCC_AHB2ENR_GPIOBEN +
                     RCC_AHB2ENR_GPIOAEN;
    RCC->AHB3ENR =   RCC_AHB3ENR_QSPIEN + RCC_AHB3ENR_FMCEN;
    RCC->APB1ENR1 =  RCC_APB1ENR1_LPTIM1EN + RCC_APB1ENR1_OPAMPEN +
                     RCC_APB1ENR1_DAC1EN + RCC_APB1ENR1_PWREN +
                     RCC_APB1ENR1_CAN1EN + RCC_APB1ENR1_I2C3EN +
                     RCC_APB1ENR1_I2C2EN + RCC_APB1ENR1_I2C1EN +
                     RCC_APB1ENR1_UART5EN + RCC_APB1ENR1_UART4EN +
```

```
                    RCC_APB1ENR1_USART3EN + RCC_APB1ENR1_USART2EN +
                    RCC_APB1ENR1_SPI3EN + RCC_APB1ENR1_SPI2EN +
                    RCC_APB1ENR1_WWDGEN + RCC_APB1ENR1_TIM7EN +
                    RCC_APB1ENR1_TIM6EN + RCC_APB1ENR1_TIM5EN +
                    RCC_APB1ENR1_TIM4EN + RCC_APB1ENR1_TIM3EN +
                    RCC_APB1ENR1_TIM2EN;
    RCC->APB1ENR2 = RCC_APB1ENR2_LPTIM2EN + RCC_APB1ENR2_SWPMI1EN +
                    RCC_APB1ENR2_LPUART1EN;
    RCC->APB2ENR  = RCC_APB2ENR_DFSDM1EN + RCC_APB2ENR_SAI2EN +
                    RCC_APB2ENR_SAI1EN + RCC_APB2ENR_TIM17EN +
                    RCC_APB2ENR_TIM16EN + RCC_APB2ENR_TIM15EN +
                    RCC_APB2ENR_USART1EN + RCC_APB2ENR_TIM8EN +
                    RCC_APB2ENR_SPI1EN + RCC_APB2ENR_TIM1EN +
                    RCC_APB2ENR_SDMMC1EN + RCC_APB2ENR_FWEN +
                    RCC_APB2ENR_SYSCFGEN;
    RCC->CCIPR    = RCC_CCIPR_DFSDM1SEL + RCC_CCIPR_ADCSEL +
                    RCC_CCIPR_SWPMI1SEL + RCC_CCIPR_CLK48SEL +
                    RCC_CCIPR_SAI2SEL_0 + RCC_CCIPR_SAI1SEL_0;
              // LPTIM2..USART1 use PCLK as clock
// enable some peripherals (SRAM2, SYSCFG, COMP, & VREFBUF) during sleep mode
    RCC->AHB1SMENR = RCC_AHB1SMENR_TSCSMEN + RCC_AHB1SMENR_CRCSMEN +
                 RCC_AHB1SMENR_SRAM1SMEN + RCC_AHB1SMENR_FLASHSMEN +
                 RCC_AHB1SMENR_DMA2SMEN + RCC_AHB1SMENR_DMA1SMEN;
    RCC->AHB2SMENR   = RCC_AHB2SMENR_SRAM2SMEN;
    RCC->AHB3SMENR   = 0; // disable clock input during sleep mode
    RCC->APB1SMENR1  = RCC_APB1SMENR1_PWRSMEN;
    RCC->APB1SMENR2  = 0; // disable clock input during sleep mode
    RCC->APB2SMENR   = RCC_APB2SMENR_SYSCFGSMEN;
}
```

3.7 Summary

The STM32L475 (and all STM32 devices) has six clock sources

1. HSE oscillator clock: from 4 to 48 MHz
2. HSI16 (high-speed internal): 16-MHz RC oscillator clock
3. MSI (multispeed internal) RC oscillator clock: 12 frequencies from 100 kHz to 48 MHz
4. PLL: maximum speed is 80 MHz (use HSE, HSI16, or MSI as its reference clock)
5. LSE (low-speed external crystal): 32.768-kHz crystal
6. LSI (low-speed internal): 32-kHz RC oscillator

Any one of the first four clock sources can be selected as the source of SYSCLK and generate clock signals to be used by the CPU and peripherals.

Although many peripherals obtain their clock signals from system buses (AHB, APB1, or APB2), a few peripherals may select their clock signals from other sources (up to four—see Figure 3.22).

After reset, the MSI clock frequency is set to 4 MHz and used as the SYSCLK. The STM32L475 processor will be running at this frequency until it is changed by the software. A clock can be used only when its frequency is stable (indicated by one of the ready flag in the RCC->CR register). The source of the SYSCLK clock can be changed during the normal operation of the processor.

When timing accuracy is critical, the HSE oscillator should be chosen to generate most of the clock signals. If the application requires the processor to run at a frequency higher than 48 MHz, then the user should choose the HSE oscillator as the reference clock for the PLL and select appropriate values for the M, N, and R factors to generate the clock for the processor.

In an embedded system with multiple STM32 microcontrollers, the user can use an external crystal oscillator to generate clock signals for one device and enable its MCO output and then connect this MCO signal to the OSC_IN pin of other STM32 devices to reduce the cost of external crystal oscillator while at the same time achieving high timing accuracy.

To enable/disable the clock signal to a peripheral, the user sets/clears the corresponding enable bit in one of the peripheral clock enable registers (RCC->AHB1ENR, RCC->AHB2ENR, RCC->AHB3ENR, RCC->APB1ENR1, RCC->APB1ENR2, or RCC->APB2ENR).

The user can put the STM32L475 processor in the sleep or stop mode and also disable the clock input to most of the peripherals in order to save battery energy. The clock input to a peripheral is enabled by default in the sleep and stop mode. However, the user can disable the clock input to any peripheral during the sleep or stop mode by clearing the corresponding enable bit in one of the peripheral clock enable in sleep and stop modes registers (RCC->AHB1SMENR, RCC->AHB2SMENR, RCC->AHB3SMENR, RCC->APB1SMENR1, RCC->APB1SMENR2, or RCC->APB2SMENR).

The STM32L475 can read instructions from program flash memory in one clock cycle at up to 16 MHz (V_{CORE} range 1) or 6 MHz (V_{CORE} range 2). Wait states must be inserted if the processor is running at a frequency above these values. To achieve better performance, the designer of the STM32L475 implements an **Adaptive Real-Time Memory** (ART) Accelerator to minimize the number of wait states inserted during normal program execution. The number of wait states to be inserted is programmed via the FLASH->ACR register.

3.8 Exercises

E3.1 Write a sequence of C statements to perform the following configuration:

(a) Enable the 32,768-Hz external crystal and wait for it to become ready for use.

(b) Enable MSI and set its frequency to 48 MHz and also enable its PLL and wait for it to become ready.

(c) Enable the 16-MHz external crystal oscillator connected to the OSC_IN and OSC_OUT pins and wait for it to become ready.

E3.2 Write a sequence of C statements to configure PLL, PLLSAI1, and PLLSAI2 in the following manner:

- Select the 16-MHz HSE as their common clock source.
- Enable the R output (PLLCLK) of the PLL and set its frequency to 80 MHz.
- Enable the Q output of PLLSAI1 and set its frequency to 48 MHz.
- Enable the PLLSAI3CLK output of PLL and set its frequency to 80/7 MHz.
- Enable the R output (PLLADC2CLK) from PLLSAI2 and set its frequency to 24 MHz.
- Make sure these output are ready for use.

E3.3 Write a sequence of C statements to

- Use a 16-MHz external crystal oscillator as the source of PLL.
- Configure PLL output to 80 MHz.
- Choose PLL as the clock source of SYSCLK.
- Configure HCLK to 80 MHz, PCLK1 and PCLK2 to be 40 MHz and 20 MHz, respectively.
- Select the HSE as MCO and set its frequency to 8 MHz.

E3.4 Assuming that a 6-MHz crystal oscillator is connected to OSC_IN and OSC_OUT pins, find a combination of M, N, and R values to generate a PLLCLK output so that f_{PLLCLK} = 80 MHz.

E3.5 Assuming that a 12-MHz crystal oscillator is connected to OSC_IN and OSC_OUT pins and is used as the PLL clock source, find a combination of M, N, and R values to generate a PLLCLK output so that f_{PLLCLK} = 80 MHz.

E3.6 Assume that a 15-MHz crystal oscillator is connected to OSC_IN and OSC_OUT pins and is selected as the clock source of the PLL. Find a combination of M, N, and R values to generate a PLLCLK output so that f_{PLLCLK} = 80 MHz.

E3.7 A 24-MHz crystal is connected to OSC_IN and OSC_OUT pins. Write a sequence of C statements that perform the following operations:

(a) Enable the HSE oscillator and wait until it becomes ready.
(b) Configure the PLL and select the HSE as the reference clock of PLL and configure the M, N, and R values so that the PLLCLK output is 80 MHz and the PLLSAI3CLK output is 160/7 MHz.
(c) Configure PLLSAI1 so that its PLL48M2CLK output is 48 MHz and PLLAD1CLK output is also 48 MHz. If the value of N selected in (b) does not allow you to set the frequency of PLL48M2CLK to 48 MHz, change it to a different value to achieve this goal.

(d) Ignore the PLLSAI2.
(e) Configure the RCC->CFGR register to select PLL as the source of the SYSCLK clock, select HSE as the source for MCO output and set its frequency to 12 MHz, configure the frequency of HCLK, PCLK1, and PCLK2 to 80 MHz, 40 MHz, and 40 MHz, respectively.

E3.8 A 48-MHz external clock is connected to the OSC_IN pin. Write a sequence of C statements that perform the following operations:

(a) Enable HSE oscillator and bypass it; wait until it becomes ready.

(b) Configure the PLL and select the HSE as its reference clock and configure the M, N, Q, and R values so that the PLLCLK output is 80 MHz, PLL48M1CLK output is 40 MHz, and PLLSAI3CLK output is 160/7 MHz.

(c) Configure PLLSAI1 so that its PLL48M2CLK output is 48 MHz and PLLAD1CLK output is also 48 MHz. Use the same M divide factor as in (b).

(d) Ignore the PLLSAI2.

(e) Configure the RCC->CFGR register to select HSE as the source for MCO output and set its frequency to 12 MHz, configure the frequency of HCLK, PCLK1, and PCLK2 to 80 MHz, 40 MHz, and 20 MHz, respectively.

E3.9 Suppose a 24-MHz crystal oscillator is connected to the OSC_IN and OSC_OUT pins.

(a) Select an M value and the corresponding N and R values to make f_{PLLCLK} = 80 MHz.

(b) Select an M value and the corresponding N and Q values to make $f_{PLL48M2CLK}$ = 48 MHz.

Note: the N value for PLL and the N value for the PLLSAI1 module are independent.

E3.10 Suppose a 40-MHz crystal oscillator is connected to the OSC_IN and OSC_OUT pins.

Select an M value so that

(a) You can choose an N and R value to make f_{PLLCLK} = 80 MHz.

(b) You can choose an N and Q value to make $f_{PLL48M2CLK}$ = 48 MHz.

Note: the N value for PLL and the N value for the PLLSAI1 module are independent.

4

Parallel I/O Ports

4.1 Objectives

After completing this chapter, you will be able to

- Configure I/O pins for input.
- Configure I/O pins for output.
- Configure I/O pins for peripheral use (also called alternate function).
- Interface with DIP switches.
- Interface with LEDs and seven-segment displays.
- Use I/O pin to generate waveforms.
- Use I/O pin to make sound.
- Use I/O pins to drive a stepper motor.
- Interface with keypads and keyboards.
- Use LCD to display messages.

4.2 Introduction to I/O Port

Signal pins (pads on a silicon die) of a microcontroller can be used as **general-purpose input/output** (GPIO) to drive input/output devices or support peripheral functions. Light-emitting devices (LEDs), seven-segment displays, liquid crystal displays (LCD), stepper motors, digital-to-analog converters (with parallel data inputs), switches, keypads, keyboards, digital image sensors, and so on are examples of input/output devices. Timer/counter, Serial Peripheral Interface (SPI), Inter-Integrated Circuit (I^2C), Controller Area Network

(CAN), Universal Synchronous Asynchronous Receiver and Transmitter (USART), Analog-to-Digital converters (ADC), Digital-to-Analog converters (DAC), and so on are examples of peripheral functions.

To simplify programming, signal pins are put into groups with each group consisting of 8, 16, or 32 pins. A group of signal pins is referred to as an **I/O port**. Registers are needed to carry out I/O functions. Therefore, an I/O port actually consists of a group of signal pins and a set of related registers. An I/O port of the ST Cortex-M device has 16 pins.

An I/O pin, in general, can be configured to several possible modes. An I/O pin of an ST Cortex-M device (including Cortex-M0+, M3, M4, M7, and M33 subfamilies) can be configured into the following modes:

- Input floating or pull-up/down, or analog
- Output push-pull or open-drain with pull-up or pull-down
- Output data from output data register (GPIOx->ODR) or peripheral (alternate function output)
- Alternate function push-pull with pull-up or pull-down capability
- Alternate function open-drain with pull-up or pull-down capability

Some users may prefer to assign a name to an I/O **port,** for example, PORTA, PORTB, and so on. We will use PORTx and GPIOx interchangeably in this book, where **x** is A, B, C, etc.

The STM32L475 has 64-pin and 100-pin packages at the time of this writing. In the 100-pin version, each of the PORTA ~ PORTE port has 16 pins whereas the PORTH has 2 pins only. The remaining 18 pins are used for system functions (such as power supply, ground, reset, reference voltage, etc.). Two pairs of pins can also be used to connect crystal oscillators. Pins PC14 and PC15 can also be used as the OSC32_IN and OSC32_OUT signal, respectively. A 32,768-Hz crystal can be connected to this pair of pins. Pins PH0 and PH1 can also be used as OSC_IN and OSC_OUT signal, respectively. A high-frequency crystal oscillator or a ceramic resonator ranging from 4 to 48 MHz can be connected to these two pins.

The STM32L476 has 64-pin, 100-pin, and 144-pin packages. The 144-pin package allows the STM32L476 to add two additional ports: PORTF and PORTG.

4.3 STM32L475 GPIO Registers

Because a GPIO port can be used as general-purpose input, output, and peripheral signals, the first step in using a GPIO port is to configure the involved GPIO port or a few GPIO pins to appropriate modes. This is achieved by programming the **GPIO port mode register** (**GPIOx->MODER**, x = A..E, and H). The contents of this register are shown in Figure 4.1.

31 30	29 28	27 26	25 24
MODE15[1:0]	MODE14[1:0]	MODE13[1:0]	MODE12[1:0]
23 22	**21 20**	**19 18**	**17 16**
MODE11[1:0]	MODE10[1:0]	MODE9[1:0]	MODE8[1:0]
15 14	**13 12**	**11 10**	**9 8**
MODE7[1:0]	MODE6[1:0]	MODE5[1:0]	MODE4[1:0]
7 6	**5 4**	**3 2**	**1 0**
MODE3[1:0]	MODE2[1:0]	MODE1[1:0]	MODE0[1:0]

Reset value:
0xEBFFFCFF for port A
0xFFFFFFFF for other ports
Addr offset
= 0x00

MODEy[1:0]: PORT x configuration bits (y = 0..15)
- 00: Input mode
- 01: General purpose output mode
- 10: Alternate function mode
- 11: Analog mode (reset state)

Figure 4.1 GPIO Port Mode Register (GPIOx_MODER, x = A..E, and H)

To facilitate the programming of mode bit field, the **stm32L475xx.h** header file provides the following bit field definitions (only the first few lines are shown):

```
/****************** Bits definition for GPIO_MODER register *****************/
#define GPIO_MODER_MODE0_Pos        (0U)
#define GPIO_MODER_MODE0_Msk        (0x3U << GPIO_MODER_MODE0_Pos
#define GPIO_MODER_MODE0            GPIO_MODER_MODE0_Msk
#define GPIO_MODER_MODE0_0          (0x1U << GPIO_MODER_MODE0_Pos
#define GPIO_MODER_MODE0_1          (0x2U << GPIO_MODER_MODE0_Pos)
#define GPIO_MODER_MODE1_Pos        (2U)
#define GPIO_MODER_MODE1_Msk        (0x3U << GPIO_MODER_MODE1_Pos)
#define GPIO_MODER_MODE1            GPIO_MODER_MODE1_Msk
#define GPIO_MODER_MODE1_0          (0x1U << GPIO_MODER_MODE1_Pos)
#define GPIO_MODER_MODE1_1          (0x2U << GPIO_MODER_MODE1_Pos)
#define GPIO_MODER_MODE2_Pos        (4U)
#define GPIO_MODER_MODE2_Msk        (0x3U << GPIO_MODER_MODE2_Pos)
#define GPIO_MODER_MODE2            GPIO_MODER_MODE2_Msk
#define GPIO_MODER_MODE2_0          (0x1U << GPIO_MODER_MODE2_Pos)
#define GPIO_MODER_MODE2_1          (0x2U << GPIO_MODER_MODE2_Pos
```

Example 4.1 Write a sequence of C statements to configure PORTA as an output port and PORTB as an input port.

Solution: To configure a pin for output, set the 2-bit mode field associated with that pin to **01**. To configure a pin for input, set the 2-bit mode field associated with that pin to **00**. The following C statements will configure PORTA for output and PORTB for input:

```
GPIOA->MODER = 0x55555555;

GPIOB->MODER = 0;
```

Example 4.2 Write a sequence of C statements to configure PORTA pins 15, 9, and 3 for output and pins 12, 8, and 2 for alternate functions.

Solution: To configure these two groups of pins to different setting, we need to clear these fields first. After that, we can set these two sets of pins to different values. The mode field of an output pin should be set to 01 whereas that of an alternate function pin must be set to 10. The mode fields of pins 15, 12, 9, 8, 3, and 2 can be cleared by the following statement:

```
GPIOA->MODER &= ~(GPIO_MODER_MODE15 + GPIO_MODER_MODE12 +
                  GPIO_MODER_MODE9 + GPIO_MODER_MODE8 +
                  GPIO_MODER_MODE3 + GPIO_MODER_MODE2);
```

Where, GPIO_MODER_MODE$_k$ (k = 0…15) is defined in **stm32L475xx.h**.

After this, we can configure pins 15, 9, and 3 for output and pins 12, 8, and 2 for alternate function accordingly:

```
GPIOA->MODER |= GPIO_MODER_MODE15_0 + GPIO_MODER_MODE9_0 +
                GPIO_MODER_MODE3_0 + GPIO_MODER_MODE12_1 +
                GPIO_MODER_MODE8_1 + GPIO_MODER_MODE2_1;
```

The data to be output should be written into the GPIO port output data register

(GPIOx->ODR, x is the port name). The contents of the GPIOx->ODR register are shown in Figure 4.2.

31	30	29	28	27	26	25	24
--	--	--	--	--	--	--	--
23	**22**	**21**	**20**	**19**	**18**	**17**	**16**
--	--	--	--	--	--	--	--
15	**14**	**13**	**12**	**11**	**10**	**9**	**8**
OD15	OD14	OD13	OD12	OD11	OD10	OD9	OD8
7	**6**	**5**	**4**	**3**	**2**	**1**	**0**
OD7	OD6	OD5	OD4	OD3	OD2	OD1	OD0

Reset value: 0x0000 0000
Addr offset = 0x14

ODy: PORT output data bit (y = 0..15)
These bits can be read and written by software

Figure 4.2 GPIO Port x Output Data Register (GPIOx_ODR, x = A..E, and H)

Example 4.3 Write a sequence of C statements to configure PORTC for output and output the value 0xAA55 to it.

Solution:

```
GPIOC->MODER  = 0x55555555;   // configure PORTC for output
GPIOC->ODR    = 0xAA55;       // output the value 0xAA55 to PORTC
```

Sometimes the user has the need to pull a few pins to high or pull a few pins to low without affecting other port pins. This requirement can be achieved by writing a bit mask into the **GPIO port bit set/reset register** (**GPIOx->BSRR**, x = A..I). The contents of the GPIO->BSRR register are shown in Figure 4.3. Writing a bit in the upper half (bit 16 to 31) of the GPIOx->BSRR register to 1 clears the corresponding bit (in bit 0 to 15) of the GPIO_ODR register, whereas writing a bit in the lower half (bit 0 to 15) of the GPIOx->BSRR register to 1 sets the corresponding bit of the GPIOx->ODR register.

31	30	29	28	27	26	25	24
BR15	BR14	BR13	BR12	BR11	BR10	BR9	BR8
23	**22**	**21**	**20**	**19**	**18**	**17**	**16**
BR7	BR6	BR5	BR4	BR3	BR2	BR1	BR0
15	**14**	**13**	**12**	**11**	**10**	**9**	**8**
BS15	BS14	BS13	BS12	BS11	BS10	BS9	BS8
7	**6**	**5**	**4**	**3**	**2**	**1**	**0**
BS7	BS6	BS5	BS4	BS3	BS2	BS1	BS0

Reset value: 0x0000 0000
Addr offset = 0x18

BRy: PORT x reset bit y (y = 0..15)
  0: No action on the ODx bit
  1: Resets the corresponding ODx bit
BSy: PORT x set bit y (y = 0..15)
  0: No action on the ODx bit
  1: Sets the corresponding ODx bit

Figure 4.3 GPIO port x bit set/reset register (GPIOx_BSRR, x = A..E, and H)

Example 4.4 Write a sequence of C statements to pull the PA15 pin to high and pull the pin PA0 to low.

Solution: The stm32L475xx.h file provides bit definitions to set or reset the voltage level for each pin. For example, for PA6, the following definitions are provided:

```
#define  GPIO_BSRR_BS6_POS    (6U)
#define  GPIO_BSRR_BS6_Msk    (0x1U << GPIO_BSRR_BS6_POS)
#define  GPIO_BSRR_BS6        GPIO_BSRR_BS6_Msk
#define  GPIO_BSRR_BR6_POS    (22U)
#define  GPIO_BSRR_BR6_Msk    (0x1U << GPIO_BSRR_BR6_POS)
#define  GPIO_BSRR_BR6        GPIO_BSRR_BR6_Msk
```

Therefore, the symbols GPIO_BSRR_BS6 and GPIO_BSRR_BR6 represent two 32-bit values that have a 1 in bit 6 and bit 22 and 0 in all other bit positions.

The following statement pulls the PA15 pin to high and pulls the PA0 pin to low:

```
GPIOA->BSRR = GPIO_BSRR_BS15 + GPIO_BSRR_BR0;
```

The STM32L475 MCU also has a **GPIO port bit reset register** (**GPIOx->BRR**, x = A..E and H) that allows the user to clear a few bits in the GPIOx->ODR register without affecting other bits. This is achieved by writing a bit mask which has a 1 in those bit positions that will be reset to 0 in the GPIOx->ODR register. Bit positions in the bit mask corresponding to those bits that are not affected are cleared to 0. The contents of the GPIOx->BRR register are shown in Figure 4.4. The ST Cortex-M0 and Cortex-M7 devices do not have the BRR register. Avoid using the BRR register if the user expects to port applications to Cortex-M0 or Cortex-M7 devices.

31	30	29	28	27	26	25	24
--	--	--	--	--	--	--	--
23	22	21	20	19	18	17	16
--	--	--	--	--	--	--	--
15	14	13	12	11	10	9	8
BR15	BR14	BR13	BR12	BR11	BR10	BR9	BR8
7	6	5	4	3	2	1	0
BR7	BR6	BR5	BR4	BR3	BR2	BR1	BR0

Reset value: 0x0000 0000
Addr offset = 0x28

BRy: PORT x reset bit y (y = 0..15)
0: No action on the ODx bit
1: Resets the corresponding ODx bit

Figure 4.4 GPIO port bit reset register (GPIOx_BRR, x = A..E, and H)

An I/O pin configured for general-purpose output can further be configured to be push-pull or open-drain. This is achieved by programming the **GPIO port output type register**

(**GPIOx->OTYPER**, x = A..E, and H). The contents of this register are shown in Figure 4.5.

31	30	29	28	27	26	25	24
--	--	--	--	--	--	--	--
23	22	21	20	19	18	17	16
--	--	--	--	--	--	--	--
15	14	13	12	11	10	9	8
OT15	OT14	OT13	OT12	OT11	OT10	OT9	OT8
7	6	5	4	3	2	1	0
OT7	OT6	OT5	OT4	OT3	OT2	OT1	OT0

Reset value: 0x0000 0000
Addr offset = 0x04

OTy: PORT x configuration bit y (y = 0..15)
0: Output push-pull (reset state)
1: Output open-drain

Figure 4.5 GPIO port output type register (GPIOx_OTYPER, x = A..E, and H)

Example 4.5 Write a sequence of C statements to configure PORTB to open-drain output.

Solution: The following statements will configure PORTB accordingly:

```
GPIOB->MODER = 0x55555555;    // configure PORTB for output
GPIOB->OTYPER = 0xFFFF;       // configure PORTB for open-drain output
```

The rise and fall times (or slew ate) of GPIO pins can be programmed. A short rise and fall times allow the output pin to drive external device quickly to high or low. The output pin speeds are configured by the **GPIO port output speed register (GPIOx->OSPEEDR)**. The contents of the GPIOx->OSPEEDR register are shown in Figure 4.6.

31 30	29 28	27 26	25 24
OSPEED15[1:0]	OSPEED14[1:0]	OSPEED13[1:0]	OSPEED12[1:0]
23 22	21 20	19 18	17 16
OSPEED11[1:0]	OSPEED10[1:0]	OSPEED9[1:0]	OSPEED8[1:0]
15 14	13 12	11 10	9 8
OSPEED7[1:0]	OSPEED6[1:0]	OSPEED5[1:0]	OSPEED4[1:0]
7 6	5 4	3 2	1 0
OSPEED3[1:0]	OSPEED2[1:0]	OSPEED1[1:0]	OSPEED0[1:0]

Reset value:
0x0C00 0000 for PORTA
0x0000 0000 for other ports
Addr offset
= 0x08

OSPEEDy: PORT x configuration bit y (y = 0..15)
00: Low speed
01: Medium speed
10: High speed
11: Very high speed
The actual speed of the output can be found in the device datasheet.

Figure 4.6 GPIO port output speed register (GPIOx_OSPEEDR, x = A..E, and H)

Example 4.6 Write a sequence of C statements to configure PORTB pin 15 to pin 8 to operate at push-pull, high-speed mode and pin 7 to pin 0 to operate at open-drain, medium-speed mode.

Solution: The following statements configure the specified PORTB pins accordingly:

```
GPIOB->MODER = 0x55555555; // configure PORTB pins for output
GPIOB->OTYPER = 0x00FF; // configure PB15..PB8 to push-pull & PB7..OB0 to open-drain
GPIOB->OSPEEDR = GPIO_OSPEEDR_OSPEED15_1 + GPIO_OSPEEDR_OSPEED14_1 +
                 GPIO_OSPEEDR_OSPEED13_1 + GPIO_OSPEEDR_OSPEED12_1 +
                 GPIO_OSPEEDR_OSPEED11_1 + GPIO_OSPEEDR_OSPEED10_1 +
                 GPIO_OSPEEDR_OSPEED9_1 + GPIO_OSPEEDR_OSPEED8_1 +
                 GPIO_OSPEEDR_OSPEED7_0 + GPIO_OSPEEDR_OSPEED6_0 +
                 GPIO_OSPEEDR_OSPEED5_0 + GPIO_OSPEEDR_OSPEED4_0 +
```

```
GPIO_OSPEEDR_OSPEED3_0 + GPIO_OSPEEDR_OSPEED2_0 +
GPIO_OSPEEDR_OSPEED1_0 + GPIO_OSPEEDR_OSPEED0_0;
```

A GPIO pin can be programmed to have pull-up, pull-down, or no pull-up and no pull-down. This is achieved by programming the **GPIO port pull-up/pull-down register** (**GPIOx->PUPDR, x = A..E and H**). The contents of this register are shown in Figure 4.7.

31 30	29 28	27 26	25 24
PUPD15[1:0]	PUPD14[1:0]	PUPD13[1:0]	PUPD12[1:0]
23 22	21 20	19 18	17 16
PUPD11[1:0]	PUPD10[1:0]	PUPD9[1:0]	PUPD8[1:0]
15 14	13 12	11 10	9 8
PUPD7[1:0]	PUPD6[1:0]	PUPD5[1:0]	PUPD4[1:0]
7 6	5 4	3 2	1 0
PUPD3[1:0]	PUPD2[1:0]	PUPD1[1:0]	PUPD0[1:0]

Reset value = 0x2400 0000 for Port A
0x0000 0000 for other ports
Offset = 0x0C

PUPDy[1:0]: Port x configuration bits (y = 0..15)
- 00: No pull-up, no pull-down
- 01: pull-up
- 10: pull-down
- 11: reserved

Figure 4.7 GPIO port pull-up/pull-down register (GPIOx_PUPDR, x = A..E and H)

Example 4.7 Write a sequence of C statements to configure PORTC pin 3 to pin 0 for input with **pull-down** capability.

Solution:

```
GPIOC->MODER  &= ~(GPIO_MODER_MODE3 + GPIO_MODER_MODE2 +
                   GPIO_MODER_MODE1 + GPIO_MODER_MODE0);
GPIOC->PUPDR  &= ~(GPIO_PUPDR_PUPD3 + GPIO_PUPDR_PUPD2 +
                   GPIO_PUPDR_PUPD1 + GPIO_PUPDR_PUPD0);
GPIOC->PUPDR  |=   GPIO_PUPDR_PUPD3_1 + GPIO_PUPDR_PUPD2_1 +
                   GPIO_PUPDR_PUPD1_1 + GPIO_PUPDR_PUPD0_1;
```

The I/O pins are connected to on-chip peripherals/modules through a multiplexer that allows only one peripheral **alternate function** (**AF**) to be connected to an I/O pin at a time. In this way, there can be no conflict between peripherals available on the same I/O pin.

Each I/O pin has a multiplexer with up to 16 alternate function inputs (AF0 to AF15) that can be configured through the GPIOx->AFRL (for pin 0 to 7) and GPIOx->AFRH (for pin 8 to 15) registers. After reset, the multiplexer selection is alternate function 0 (AF0). The specific alternate function assignments for each pin are detailed in the device datasheet. The contents of the GPIOx->AFRL and GPIOx->AFRH are shown in Figures 4.8 and 4.9, respectively. The readers should refer to the device datasheet to find out which functions are multiplexed on each GPIO pin.

31	30	29	28	27	26	25	24	23	22	21	20	19	18	17	16
AFSEL7[3:0]				AFSEL6[3:0]				AFSEL5[1:0]				AFSEL4[1:0]			
15	14	13	12	11	10	9	8	7	6	5	4	3	2	1	0
AFSEL3[3:0]				AFSEL2[3:0]				AFSEL1[3:0]				AFSEL0[3:0]			

Reset value = 0x0000 0000
Offset = 0x20

AFSELy[3:0]: Alternate function selection for port x pin y (y = 0..7)

0000: AF0	1000: AF8
0001: AF1	1001: AF9
0010: AF2	1010: AF10
0011: AF3	1011: AF11
0100: AF4	1100: AF12
0101: AF5	1101: AF13
0110: AF6	1110: AF14
0111: AF7	1111: AF15

Figure 4.8 GPIO alternate function low register (GPIOx_AFRL, x = A..E and H)

31	30	29	28	27	26	25	24	23	22	21	20	19	18	17	16
AFSEL15[3:0]				AFSEL14[3:0]				AFSEL13[1:0]				AFSEL12[1:0]			
15	14	13	12	11	10	9	8	7	6	5	4	3	2	1	0
AFSEL11[3:0]				AFSEL10[3:0]				AFSEL9[3:0]				AFSEL8[3:0]			

Reset value = 0x0000 0000
Offset = 0x24

AFSELy[3:0]: Alternate function selection for port x pin y (y = 8..15)

0000: AF0	1000: AF8
0001: AF1	1001: AF9
0010: AF2	1010: AF10
0011: AF3	1011: AF11
0100: AF4	1100: AF12
0101: AF5	1101: AF13
0110: AF6	1110: AF14
0111: AF7	1111: AF15

Figure 4.9 GPIO alternate function high register (GPIOx_AFRH, x = A..E and H)

It is possible to freeze the setting of GPIO control registers by applying a specific write sequence to the GPIOx->LCKR register. The registers that will be frozen are GPIOx->MODER, GPIOx->OTYPER, GPIOx->OSPEEDR, GPIOx->PUPDR, GPIOx->AFRL, and GPIOx->AFRH.

To write the GPIOx->LCKR register, a specific **write/read sequence** has to be applied. When the right LOCK sequence is applied to the bit 16 of this register, the value of LCKR[15:0] is used to lock the configuration of the I/Os (during the write sequence the LCKR[15:0] value must be the same). When the LOCK sequence has been applied to a port bit, the value of the port bit can no longer be modified until the next MCU reset or peripheral reset. Each GPIOx->LCKR bit freezes the corresponding bit in the control registers (GPIOx->MODER, GPIOx->OTYPER, GPIOx->OSPEEDR, GPIOx->PUPDR, GPIOx->AFRL and GPIOx->AFRH). The LOCK sequence can only be performed using a word (32-bit) access to the GPIOx->LCKR register due to the fact that GPIOx->LCKR bit 16 has to be set at the same time as the lower 16 bits of the GPIOx->LCKR register. The contents of the GPIOx->LCKR register are shown in Figure 4.10. The LOCK sequence is explained in Figure 4.10.

31	30	29	28	27	26	25	24	
--	--	--	--	--	--	--	--	Reset value = 0x0000 0000
23	22	21	20	19	18	17	16	Offset = 0x1C
--	--	--	--	--	--	--	LCKK	
15	14	13	12	11	10	9	8	
LCK15	LCK14	LCK13	LCK12	LCK11	LCK10	LCK9	LCK8	
7	6	5	4	3	2	1	0	
LCK7	LCK6	LCK5	LCK4	LCK3	LCK2	LCK1	LCK0	

LCKK: Lock key
This bit can only be modified using the lock key write sequence.
0: Port configuration lock key not active
1: Port configuration lock key active. The GPIOx_LCKR register is locked until the next MCU reset or peripheral reset.
LCKn: Pin n lock bit
0: Pin n configuration is not to be locked
1: Pin n configuration will be locked
To lock the pin configuration, perform the following sequence:
(1) Write 1 to LCKK bit, and 1 to those bits corresponding to port pins to be locked.
(2) Write 0 to LCKK bit, and the same value (as in step 1) to bit 15~0 of the LCKR register.
(3) Write 1 to LCKK bit, and the same value (as in step 1) to bit 15~0 of the LCKR register.
(4) Read the LCKR register.
(5) Read the LCKR register to make sure that the LCKK bit is 1 (this is optional)

Figure 4.10 GPIO port configuration lock register (GPIOx_LCKR, x = A..E and H)

When a GPIO port is configured for general-purpose input, the voltage level of port pins can be read via the GPIO **input data register** (**GPIOx->IDR**). The contents of the GPIOx->IDR register are shown in Figure 4.11.

31	30	29	28	27	26	25	24	
--	--	--	--	--	--	--	--	Reset value = 0x0000 xxxx
23	22	21	20	19	18	17	16	Offset = 0x10
--	--	--	--	--	--	--	--	
15	14	13	12	11	10	9	8	
ID15	ID14	ID13	ID12	ID11	ID10	ID9	ID8	
7	6	5	4	3	2	1	0	
ID7	ID6	ID5	ID4	ID3	ID2	ID1	ID0	

IDy: Port input data bit (y = 0..15)
These bits are read-only. They contain the input value of the corresponding I/O pin.

Figure 4.11 GPIO port input data register (GPIOx_IDR, x = A..E and H)

The STM32L475 also has a register that controls the connection of the analog switch to the ADC input. The contents of this register are shown in Figure 4.12.

31	30	29	28	27	26	25	24
--	--	--	--	--	--	--	--
23	22	21	20	19	18	17	16
--	--	--	--	--	--	--	--
15	14	13	12	11	10	9	8
ASC15	ASC14	ASC13	ASC12	ASC11	ASC10	ASC9	ASC8
7	6	5	4	3	2	1	0
ASC7	ASC6	ASC5	ASC4	ASC3	ASC2	ASC1	ASC0

Reset value = 0x00000000
Addr. Offset = 0x28

ASCy: Port X analog switch control y (y = 0..15)
  0: Disconnect analog switch to the ADC input (reset state)
  1: Connect analog switch to the ADC input
Note: This bit must be set prior to the ADC conversion. Only the IO switch which is connected to the ADC input are effective. Other I/O must be kept in reset value.

Figure 4.12 GPIO port analog switch control register (GPIOx_ASCR) (x = A..E & H)

4.4 The STM32L475 GPIO Pin Configurations

The basic structure of a GPIO pin is shown in Figure 4.13. Some of the port pins are 5-V tolerant and their circuit is shown in Figure 4.14. A subset of this structure may be enabled or disabled when the pin is configured for different purpose. This structure is also used by all other STM32Lxxx devices.

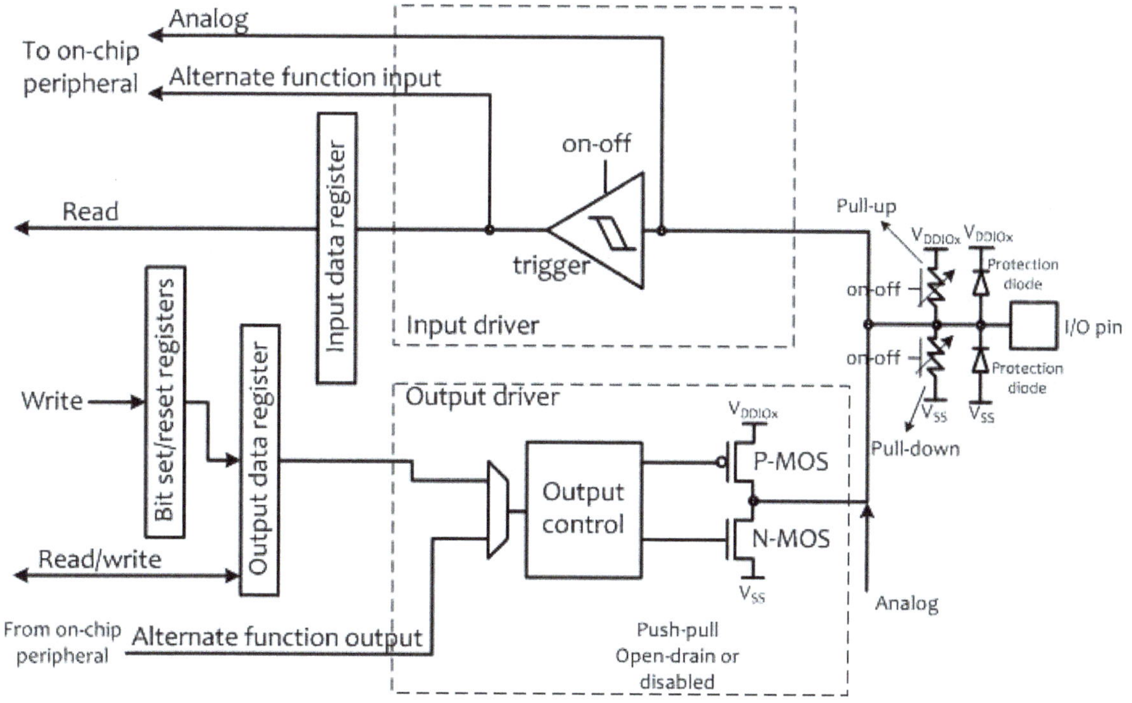

Figure 4.13 Basic structure of an I/O port pin

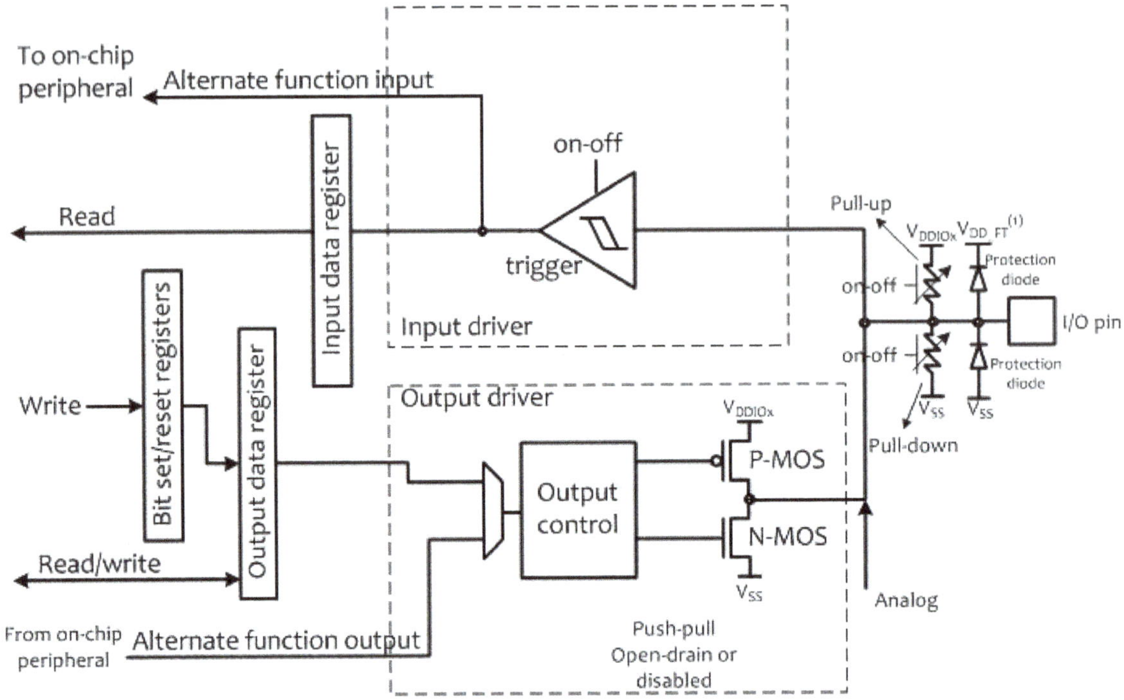

Note 1. V_{DD_FT} is a potential specific to 5-V tolerant I/Os and different from V_{DD}.

Figure 4.14 Basic structure of a 5-V tolerant I/O port pin

4.4.1 INPUT CONFIGURATION

When an I/O pin is programmed as an input,

- The output driver (in Figures 4.13 and 4.14) is disabled.
- The Schmitt trigger input is activated.
- The pull-up and pull-down resistors are activated depending on the value in the GPIOx->PUPDR register.
- The data present on the I/O pin are sampled into the input data register in every AHB clock cycle.
- A read access to the input data register returns the I/O state of all pins of the port.

4.4.2 OUTPUT CONFIGURATION

When an I/O pin is configured as an output,

- The output driver (in Figures 4.13 and 4.14) is enabled:
  - o Open-drain mode: A "0" in the output data register activates the N-MOS transistor whereas a "1" in the output data register leaves the port pin in high-impedance state (P-MOS transistor never activated).
  - o Push-pull mode: A "0" in the output data register activates the N-MOS transistor whereas a "1" in the output data register activates the P-MOS transistor.
- The Schmitt trigger input is activated.

- The pull-up and pull-down resistors are activated depending on the value in the GPIOx->PUPDR register.
- The data present on the I/O pin are sampled into the input data register in every AHB clock cycle.
- A read access to the input data register returns the I/O state of all pins of the port.
- A read access to the output data register returns the last written value.

4.4.3 ALTERNATE FUNCTION CONFIGURATION

When an I/O pin is programmed for alternate function:

- The output driver (in Figures 4.13 and 4.14) can be configured in open-drain or push-pull mode.
- The output driver (in Figures 4.13 and 4.14) is driven by the signals coming from the peripheral (transmitter enable and data).
- The Schmitt trigger input is activated.
- The activation of the weak pull-up and pull-down resistors are controlled by the GPIOx->PUPDR register.
- The data present on the I/O pin are sampled into the input data register in every AHB clock cycle.
- A read access to the input data register returns the I/O state of all pins of the port.

To configure an I/O pin to be used in an alternate function, follow these steps:

Step 1

Connect the I/O to the desired AFx in one of the GPIOx->AFRL or GPIOx->AFRH register.

Step 2

Select the type, pull-up/pull-down, and output speed via the GPIOx->OTYPER, GPIOx->PUPDR, and GPIOx->OSPEEDER registers, respectively.

Step 3

Configure the desired I/O as an alternate function in the GPIOx->MODER register.

This description does not apply to the LCD alternate function. Instead, the analog configuration in the next subsection applies.

In the header file **stm32L475xx.h**, the GPIO structure is defined as follows:

```
typedef struct
{
    __IO uint32_t MODER;
    __IO uint32_t OTYPER;
    __IO uint32_t OSPEEDR;
    __IO uint32_t PUPDR;
```

```
    __IO uint32_t IDR;
    __IO uint32_t ODR;
    __IO uint32_t BSRR;
    __IO uint32_t LCKR;
    __IO uint32_t AFR[2];
    __IO uint32_t BRR;
    __IO uint32_t ASCR;
} GPIO_TypeDef;
```

To access the register AFRL and AFRH of PORTx, the user should refer to them as **GPIOx->AFR[0]** and **GPIOx->AFR[1]**, respectively.

The bit field definitions of alternate functions in the AFRL register are as follows (pins 0 to 7):

```
#define  GPIO_AFRL_AFSELn_Pos   ((n × 4)U) // n is from 0 to 7
#define  GPIO_AFRL_AFSELn_Msk   (0xFU << GPIO_AFRL_AFSELn_Pos)
#define  GPIO_AFRL_AFSELn       GPIO_AFRL_AFSELn_Msk
#define  GPIO_AFRL_AFSELn_0     (0x1U << GPIO_AFRL_AFSELn_Pos)
#define  GPIO_AFRL_AFSELn_1     (0x2U << GPIO_AFRL_AFSELn_Pos)
#define  GPIO_AFRL_AFSELn_2     (0x4U << GPIO_AFRL_AFSELn_Pos)
#define  GPIO_AFRL_AFSELn_3     (0x8U << GPIO_AFRL_AFSELn_Pos)
```

The bit field definitions of alternate functions in the AFRH register are as follows (pins 8 to 15):

```
#define  GPIO_AFRH_AFSELn_Pos   (((n – 8) × 4)U) // n is from 8 to 15
#define  GPIO_AFRH_AFSELn_Msk   (0xFU << GPIO_AFRL_AFSELn_Pos)
#define  GPIO_AFRH_AFSELn       GPIO_AFRL_AFSELn_Msk
#define  GPIO_AFRH_AFSELn_0     (0x1U << GPIO_AFRL_AFSELn_Pos)
#define  GPIO_AFRH_AFSELn_1     (0x2U << GPIO_AFRL_AFSELn_Pos)
#define  GPIO_AFRH_AFSELn_2     (0x4U << GPIO_AFRL_AFSELn_Pos)
#define  GPIO_AFRH_AFSELn_3     (0x8U << GPIO_AFRL_AFSELn_Pos)
```

Example 4.8 Write a sequence of C statements to configure GPIOB pins PB0~PB1 for alternate function 2, GPIO pins PB9~PB11 for alternate function 5.

Solution:

```
// configure PB0~PB1 and PB9~PB11 pins for alternate function
    GPIOB->MODER &= ~(GPIO_MODER_MODE0 + GPIO_MODER_MODE1 +
                      GPIO_MODER_MODE9 + GPIO_MODER_MODE10 +
                      GPIO_MODER_MODE11);
    GPIOB->MODER |=   GPIO_MODER_MODE0_1 + GPIO_MODER_MODE1_1 +
                      GPIO_MODER_MODE9_1 + GPIO_MODER_MODE10_1 +
                      GPIO_MODER_MODE11_1;

    GPIOB->AFR[0] &=  ~(GPIO_AFRL_AFSEL1 + GPIO_AFRL_AFSEL0);
    GPIOB->AFR[1] &=  ~(GPIO_AFRH_AFSEL9 + GPIO_AFRH_AFSEL10 +
                      GPIO_AFRH_AFSEL11); // clear the AFSEL fields
// configure PB1 and PB0 pins for alternate function 2
    GPIOB->AFR[0] |=  GPIO_AFRL_AFSEL1_1 + GPIO_AFRL_AFSEL0_1;
// configure PB9~PB11 pins for alternate function 5
    GPIOB->AFR[1] |=  GPIO_AFRH_AFSEL9_0 + GPIO_AFRH_AFSEL9_2 +
                      GPIO_AFRH_AFSEL10_0 + GPIO_AFRH_AFSEL10_2 +
                      GPIO_AFRH_AFSEL11_0 + GPIO_AFRH_AFSEL11_2;
```

4.4.4 ANALOG CONFIGURATION

For the ADC, DAC, and COMP (comparator), the associated I/O pins must be configured in analog mode. When an I/O pin is programmed for analog function:

- The output buffer is disabled.
- The Schmitt trigger input is deactivated, providing zero consumption for every analog value of the I/O pin. The output of the Schmitt trigger is forced to a constant value (0).
- The weak pull-up and pull-down resistors are disabled by hardware.
- Read access to the input data register gets the value "0."

Example 4.9 Write a sequence of C statements to configure PA3~PA0 pins for analog inputs to be converted by the A/D function.

Solution: We need to program both the MODER and ASCR register for this problem. The following C statements will configure the PA3~PA0 pins accordingly:

```
// configure PA3~PA0 pins for analog mode
    GPIOA->MODER  |= GPIO_MODER_MODE3 + GPIO_MODER_MODE2 +
                     GPIO_MODER_MODE1 + GPIO_MODER_MODE0;
    GPIOA->ASCR   |= GPIO_ASCR_ASC3 + GPIO_ASCR_ASC2 + GPIO_ASCR_ASC1 +
                     GPIO_ASCR_ASC0;
```

Example 4.10 Write a sequence of C statements to toggle the PB15 pin.

Solution: To toggle a pin, we need to read back the pin's voltage and set it to the opposite level. The following statements **toggle** the PB15 pin:

```
if(GPIOB->IDR & GPIO_IDR_ID15)
    GPIOB->BSRR = GPIO_BSRR_BR15;
else
    GPIOB->BSRR = GPIO_BSRR_BS15;
```

4.4.5 ADDITIONAL FUNCTIONS

For pins used by analog functions DAC, OPAMP, and COMP, the user is required to configure the associated pins for analog function using the GPIOx->MODER register. For pins used by the ADC, the user is required to configure both the GPIOx->MODER and the GPIOx->ASCR registers.

For the additional functions like RTC, WKUPx and oscillators, configure the required function in the related RTC, PWR, and RCC registers. These functions have priority over the configuration in the standard GPIO registers. Once these functions are enabled, the associated GPIO pins will be used by these functions.

4.5 Interfacing with Simple I/O Devices

Many embedded systems only require the use of simple input/output devices such as switches, light-emitting diodes (LEDs), keypads, and seven-segment displays to interface with the user. A time delay is often needed to achieve certain special effect during an I/O operation. A time delay can be created by using a timer function or simply a dummy for-loop which performs no operation. In ARM's assembly language, the following dummy for-loop

```
for (k = 0; k < n; k++);
```

can be translated into the following ARM's instruction sequence:

```
        mov   r4, #0        // assign k to r4, k is initialized to 0
loop:   cmp   r4, #n        // check loop termination
```

```
        bge     done            // branch if k ≥ n to terminate the loop
        add     r4, r4, #1      // increment k by 1
        b       loop
done:   ...
```

Because ARM Cortex-M processor is pipelined, each of the following instructions takes one clock cycle to finish execution when the loop is not finished yet:

```
        cmp     r4, n
        bge     done            // takes one clock cycle if branch is not taken
        add     r4, r4, #1
```

Because Cortex-M4 is implemented using a three-stage pipeline, the unconditional instruction (**b loop**) will take three clock cycles to execute. The conditional branch instruction (**bge done**) will take three clock cycles to execute if the branch is taken. Therefore, an iteration of the dummy for-loop takes six clock cycles to execute. Knowing the desired delay and the processor clock rate, it is easy to figure out the number of times of the for-loop to be repeated.

Using the timer function to create time delays is discussed in Chapter 6. In Chapter 6, delay functions generate a delay, which is a multiple of a certain basic delay. For example, **delayby1ms (k)** and **delayby100ms (k)** create time delays that are a multiple of 1 and 100 ms, respectively.

Example 4.11 Assuming that the STM32L475 is running at 4 MHz and 80 MHz, respectively, how many times should the previous dummy for-loop be repeated in order to create a delay of 10 ms?

Solution: The clock period is 250 ns and 12.5 ns, respectively. One iteration of the previous for-loop takes 1.5 μs and 75 ns to execute. Therefore, the for-loop must be repeated 6,667 and 133,334 times, respectively.

4.5.1 DRIVING THE LEDS

The LED is often used to indicate the system operation status—whether power is turned on, whether the system operation is normal, and so on. An LED can illuminate when it is forward biased and has sufficient current flowing through it. The current required to light an LED may range from a few mA to more than 10 mA. The forward voltage drop across the LED can range from 1.6 V to more than 2.3 V.

Figure 4.15 suggests three methods for interfacing with LEDs. Methods (a) and (b) are recommended for use with LEDs that need only 1 or 2 mA to produce enough brightness. The circuit (c) is recommended for use with LEDs that need larger current to light or when the microcontroller needs to drive many peripheral devices. The resistors R1, R2, and R3 are called **current-limiting resistors** because they set the amount of current flowing through the LEDs. They prevent LEDs from drawing too much current from the microcontroller. A circuit that drives eight LEDs using GPIOB pins is shown in Figure 4.16.

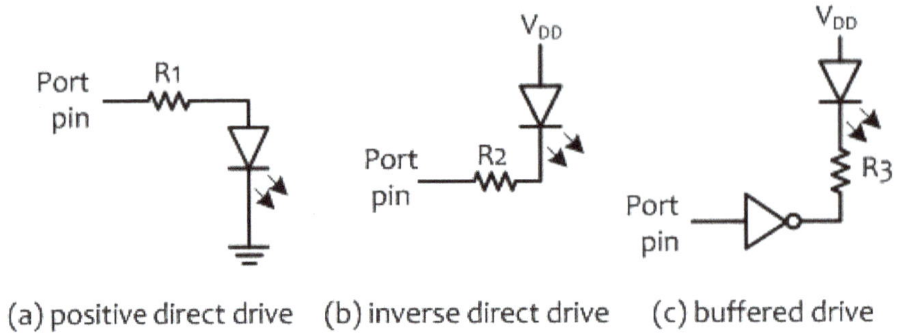

Figure 4.15 Circuit for driving an LED

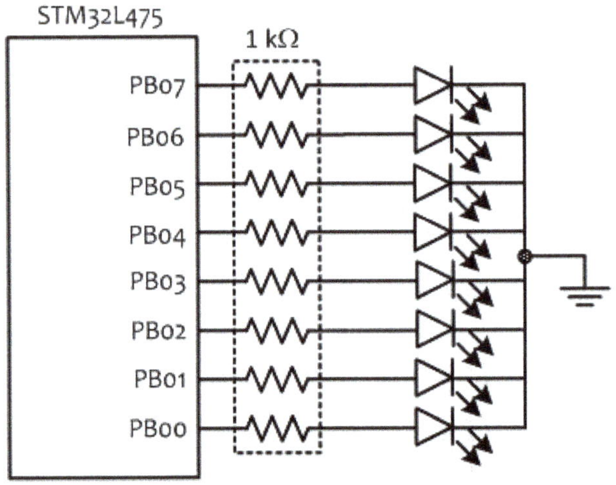

Figure 4.16 STM32L475 drives 8 LEDs

Example 4.12 Write a program to turn on one LED (shown in Figure 4.16) at a time from top to bottom and then from bottom to top and repeat forever with each LED turned on for 200 ms. Assume that the **delayby100ms (k)** function, which creates a delay of **k** × **100 ms**, is available for your use.

Solution: By using the table lookup approach, the following program displays the specified LED patterns forever:

```
#include <stm32L475xx.h>

uint32_t ledArr[16] = {0x80,0x40,0x20,0x10,0x08,0x04,0x02,0x01,
                       0x01,0x02,0x04,0x08,0x10,0x20,0x40,0x80};

void sysClkInit(void);

void delayby100ms(uint32_t k);

int main (void)

{
```

```
        uint32_t k;
        sysClkInit();
        GPIOB->MODER &= 0xFFFF0000; // clear lower 16 bits
        GPIOB->MODER |= 0x00005555; // configure PB0~PB7 pins for general output
        while(1) {
            for(k = 0; k < 16; k++){
                    GPIOB->ODR = ledArr[k];
                    delayby100ms(2);
            }
        }
}
void sysClkInit(void)
{
    ...
}
void delayby100ms(uint32_t k)
{
    ...
}
```

Example 4.13 Modify the program in the previous example and use the default 4-MHz system clock to generate all the peripheral clocks and also use the dummy for-loop to generate the required delay to drive all eight LEDs.

Solution: After system reset, the 4-MHz MSI clock is selected as the SYSCLK and the prescaler for HCLK is set to 1. All GPIO ports obtain their clocks from the AHB bus, which is HCLK. We need to enable GPIOB port to obtain its clock from AHB bus. The modified program is as follows:

```
#include <stm32L475xx.h>
uint32_t ledArr[16] = {0x80,0x40,0x20,0x10,0x08,0x04,0x02,0x01,
                        0x01,0x02,0x04,0x08,0x10,0x20,0x40,0x80};
int main (void)
{
```

```
    uint32_t j, k;
    // use the default 4-MHz MSI to generate SYSCLK, HCLK, PCLK1, and PCLK2
    RCC->AHB2ENR |= RCC_AHB2ENR_GPIOBEN; // enable clock to GPIOB
    GPIOB->MODER &= 0xFFFF0000; // clear lower 16 bits
    GPIOB->MODER |= 0x00005555; // configure PB0~PB7 pins for general output
    while(1) {
        for(k = 0; k < 16; k++){
                GPIOB->ODR = ledArr[k];
                for(j = 0; j < 133334; j ++); // wait for about 200 ms
        }
    }
}
```

4.5.2 DRIVING THE SEVEN-SEGMENT DISPLAYS

Seven-segment displays are often used when the embedded system needs to display only a few digits. Seven-segment displays are mainly used to display decimal digits and a small subset of letters.

Although a microcontroller has enough current to drive a seven-segment display, it is not advisable to do so because the microcontroller often needs to drive many other peripheral devices. In Figure 4.17, PORTB pins drive a common cathode seven-segment display through the buffer chip SN74LV244 from TI. The SN74LV244 can operate with a power supply ranging from 2 to 5.5 V. Assume that both the STM32L475 and SN74LV244 use a 3.3-V power supply. Both are implemented in CMOS technology and hence are compatible in voltage levels. The high output voltage of the SN74LV244 is 3.3 V. The segment current is **1.6 mA** (= (3.3 – 1.7 V) / 1 kΩ), assuming that the voltage drop of the seven-segment display is **1.7 V**.

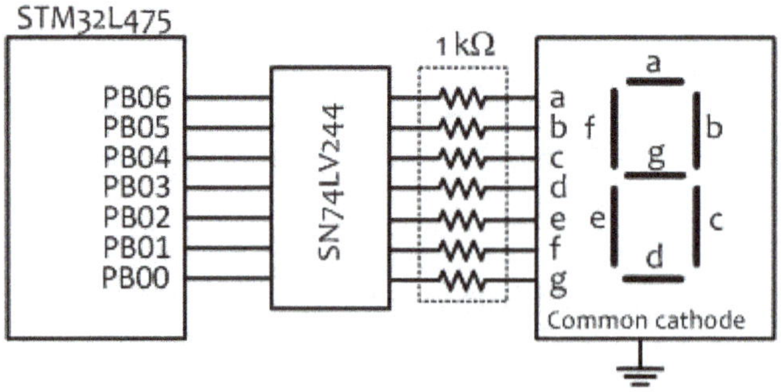

Figure 4.17 Driving a single seven-segment display

To display decimal digits 0 to 9, appropriate values must be sent to GPIOB in Figure 4.17. The segment patterns corresponding to 10 decimal digits are shown in Table 4.1. The numbers in Table 4.1 require that segments **a..g** be connected to pins PB6~PB0 in that order. The SN74LV244 can source and sink up to 35 mA continuously. The maximum current that needs to be sourced in Figure 4.17 by the SN74LV244 is 11.2 mA (= 1.6 mA × 7) and is within its capacity.

Table 4.1 Decimal to seven-segment decoder

Decimal digit	Segments							Corresponding Hex Number
	a	b	c	d	e	f	g	
0	1	1	1	1	1	1	0	0x7E
1	0	1	1	0	0	0	0	0x30
2	1	1	0	1	1	0	1	0x6D
3	1	1	1	1	0	0	1	0x79
4	0	1	1	0	0	1	1	0x33
5	1	0	1	1	0	1	1	0x5B
6	1	0	1	1	1	1	1	0x5F
7	1	1	1	0	0	0	0	0x70
8	1	1	1	1	1	1	1	0x7F
9	1	1	1	1	0	1	1	0x7B

Note. Segments **a** through **g** are connected to PB6 to PB0 pins.

When displaying multiple decimal digits is required in an application, the **time-multiplexing technique** is often used. An example of the circuit that displays six decimal digits is shown in Figure 4.18. GPIOB drives both the digit-select signals and the segment patterns. Whenever one digit-select pin is driven low, the driven display is lighted because its common cathode pin has been driven low.

In the **time-multiplexing technique**, each display is lighted in turn briefly (for example, 1 ms) and then turned off. When one display is lighted, all other displays are turned off. Within 1 second, each seven-segment display is lighted and then turned off many times. Because of the **persistence of vision**, all six displays appear to be lighted simultaneously.

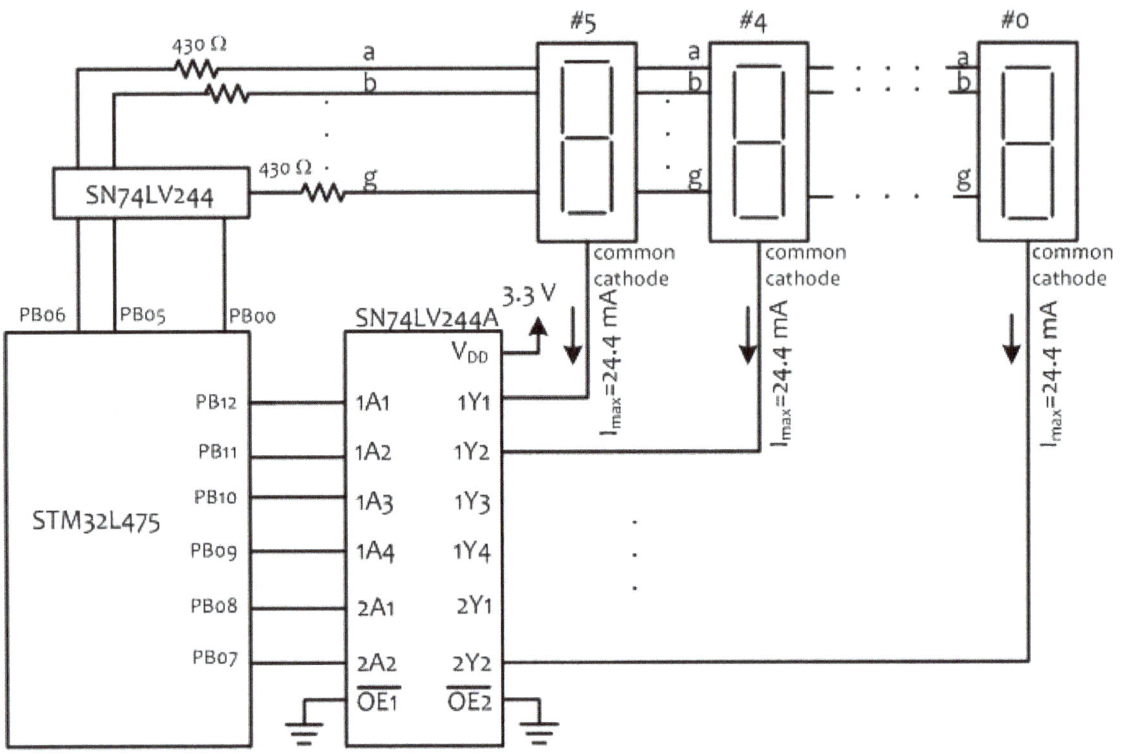

Figure 4.18 Port B of STM32L475 drives six seven-segment displays

Example 4.14 Write a program to display 123456 on the six seven-segment displays shown in Figure 4.18 assuming that the STM32L475 is running with an 80-MHz processor clock. Assume that the **delayby1ms (k)** function, which creates a delay of k ms, is available to you to call.

Solution: The digits 1, 2, 3, 4, 5, 6 are displayed on seven-segment displays #5, . . ., #0, respectively. The values to be output to the GPIOB->ODR register are shown in Table 4.2.

Table 4.2 Table of display patterns for example 4.12

Seven-Segment display	Displayed BCD digit	Value to be sent to GPIOB->ODR
#5	1	0x0FB0
#4	2	0x17ED
#3	3	0x1BF9
#2	4	0x1DB3
#1	5	0x1EDB
#0	6	0x1F5F

```
#include <stm32L475xx.h>

uint32_t seg7Pat[6] = {0x0FB0,0x17ED,0x1BF9,0x1DB3,0x1EDB,0x1F5F};

void sysClkInit(void);
```

```
void delayby1ms(uint32_t k);
int main (void)
{
    uint32_t k;
    sysClkInit();
    GPIOB->MODER &= 0xFC000000; // clear lower 26 bits
    GPIOB->MODER |= 0x01555555; // configure PB0~PB12 pins for general output
    while(1){
        for(k = 0; k < 6; k++) {
            GPIOB->ODR = seg7Pat[k]; // output segment pattern and digit select
            delayby1ms(1);
        }
    }
}
void sysClkInit(void)
{
    ...
}
void delayby1ms(uint32_t k)
{
    ...
}
```

4.5.3 GENERATING DIGITAL WAVEFORMS USING I/O PINS

A periodic waveform can be generated by manipulating I/O pin voltage level and inserting an appropriate delay (equal to half of the waveform period) between two voltage levels. For example, a 500-Hz periodic square wave can be generated from the PA15 pin, using the following algorithm:

Step 1

Configure the PA15 pin for general-purpose output.

Step 2

Pull the PA15 pin high.

Step 3

Wait for 1 ms.

Step 4

Pull the PA15 pin low.

Step 5

Wait for 1 ms.

Step 6

Go to Step 2.

Example 4.15 Write a sequence of C statements to generate a 500-Hz periodic square wave using the PA15 pin assuming that the STM32L475 is running at 80 MHz. Assume that the **delayby1ms (k)** function, which creates a delay of k ms, is available to you to call.

Solution:

```
GPIOA->MODER &= ~GPIO_MODER_MODE15; // clear bits 30~31
GPIOA->MODER |= GPIO_MODER_MODE15_0; // configure PA15 pin for general output
while (1) {
        GPIOA->BSRR = GPIO_BSRR_BS15; // pull PA15 pin high
        delayby1ms(1); // wait for 1 ms
        GPIOA->BSRR  = GPIO_BSRR_BR15; // pull PA15 low
        delayby1ms(1);
}
```

A digital waveform of any other duty cycle can easily be created by changing the delay time after pulling a pin high and low.

4.5.4 MAKING A SOUND USING AN I/O PIN

By connecting the PA15 pin in Example 4.13 to a buzzer (or a speaker as shown in Figure 4.19) and setting the frequency in the audible range, a sound can be made. The audible frequency range is from 20 to 20,000 Hz.

By alternating the frequency of the generated waveform from the I/O pin between two different values, a two-tone siren can be generated. The duration of the siren tone is variable. The siren would sound more urgent if the tone duration is shorter. The following example generates a two-tone siren that alternates between 250 and 500 Hz, with each tone lasting for half of a second. The period of a 250-Hz square wave is 4 ms. Therefore, we need to repeat this waveform 125 times (or toggle the pin voltage 250 times). Similarly, the 500-Hz square wave needs to be repeated 250 times (or toggled 500 times).

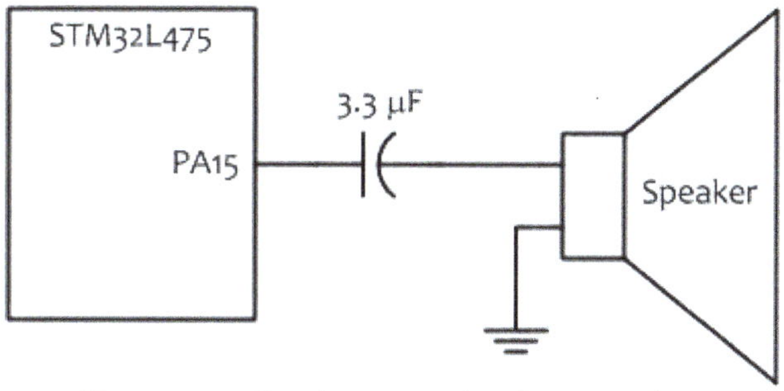

Figure 4.19 Circuit connection for a speaker

Example 4.16 Write a program to generate a two-tone siren that alternates between 250 and 500 Hz, with each tone lasting for half of a second, using the PA15 pin driving a buzzer or speaker, assuming that the frequency of the processor clock is 80 MHz. Assume that the delayby1ms(k) function, which creates a delay of k ms, is available to you to call.

Solution: The following program generates the specified two-tone siren:

```
#include <stm32L475xx.h>
void sysClkInit(void);
void delayby1ms(uint32_t k);
int main (void)
{
    uint32_t k;
    sysClkInit();
    GPIOA->MODER &= ~(GPIO_MODER_MODE15); // clear bits 31 and 30
    GPIOA->MODER |= GPIO_MODER_MODE15_0; // configure PA15 pin for general output
    while(1) {
        for (k = 0; k < 125; k++) { // generate 250-Hz tone
            GPIOA->BSRR = GPIO_BSRR_BS15; // pull PA15 pin high
            delayby1ms (2); // wait for 2 ms
            GPIOA->BSRR = GPIO_BSRR_BR15; // pull PA15 pin low
            delayby1ms (2); // wait for 2 ms
        }
```

```
            for (k = 0; k < 250; k++) {// generate 500-Hz tone
                GPIOA->BSRR = GPIO_BSRR_BS15; // pull PA15 pin high
                delayby1ms (1); // wait for 1 ms
                GPIOA->BSRR = GPIO_BSRR_BR15; // pull PA15 pin low
                delayby1ms (1); // wait for 1 ms
            }
        }
}
void sysClkInit(void)
{
    ...
}
void delayby1ms(uint32_t k)
{
    ...
}
```

4.5.5 INTERFACING WITH DIP SWITCHES

A switch is probably the simplest input device we can find. To make input more efficient, a set of eight switches organized as a **dual inline package (DIP)** is often used. A DIP package can be connected to any input PORT with at least eight pins. An example of the circuit connection for a DIP package is shown in Figure 4.20.

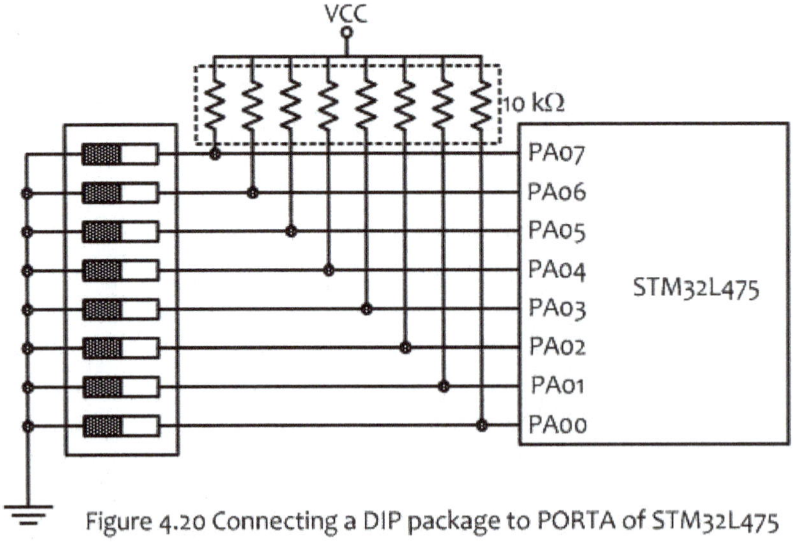

Figure 4.20 Connecting a DIP package to PORTA of STM32L475

Example 4.17 Write a sequence of C statements to configure PA07...PA00 pins for input and read the value input from the DIP switches and save it in the variable **dipVal**.

Solution:

```
unit32_t  dipVal;
GPIOA->MODER &= 0xFFFF0000; // configure PA0~PA7 for input
dipVal = GPIOA->IDR;
```

4.6 Interfacing a Parallel Port to a Keypad

A keypad is also a very commonly used input device. Like a keyboard, a keypad is arranged as an array of switches, which can be **mechanical**, **membrane**, **capacitive**, or **Hall-effect** in construction. In **mechanical switches**, two metal contacts are brought together to complete an electric circuit. In membrane switches, a plastic or rubber membrane presses one conductor onto another; this type of switches can be made very thin. **Capacitive switches** comprise two plates of a parallel plate capacitor; pressing the key cap effectively increases the capacitance between two plates. A special circuit is needed to detect this change in capacitance. In the **Hall-effect key switches**, the motion of the magnetic flux lines of a permanent magnet perpendicular to a crystal is detected as a voltage appearing between the two faces of the crystal; it is this voltage that **registers** a switch closure.

Mechanical keypads and keyboards are most popular due to their low cost and strength of construction. However, mechanical switches have a common problem called **contact bounce.** Instead of producing a single, clean pulse output, pressing a mechanical switch generates a series of pulses because the switch contacts do not come to rest immediately. This phenomenon is illustrated in Figure 4.21.

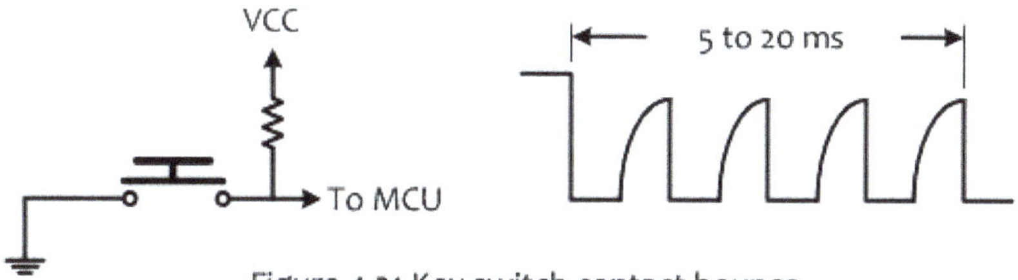

Figure 4.21 Key switch contact bounce

When the key is not pressed, the voltage output to the computer is at VCC. To detect which key has been pressed, the microcontroller has to scan every key switch of the keypad. A human being cannot press and release a key switch in less than 20 ms. During this interval, the microcontroller can scan the same key switch closure tens or even hundreds of thousand times, interpreting each low signal a new input when in fact only one input should be sent.

Because of the contact bounce and the disparity in speed between the microcontroller and human key pressing, a debouncing process is needed. A keypad input program can be divided into three stages:

1. **Keypad scanning**. This step finds out which key was pressed.
2. **Key switch debouncing**. This step ensures a key is indeed pressed.
3. **Table lookup**. This step looks up the ASCII code of the pressed key.

4.6.1 KEYPAD SCANNING

Keypad scanning is performed row by row and column by column. A 16-key keypad can easily be interfaced with any available I/O port. Figure 4.22 shows a 16-key keypad organized into four rows with each row consisting of four switches. The rows and columns are simply conductors. Pins PA03~PA00 are pulled up to high using resistors. Whenever a key is pressed, the corresponding row and column are shorted together. To distinguish the row being scanned from those not being scanned, the row being scanned is driven low, whereas the other rows are driven high. In Figure 4.22, each of the pins PA07~PA04 drives a row.

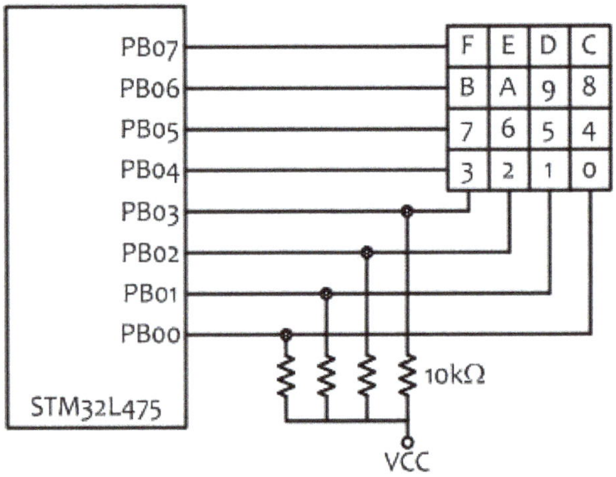

Figure 4.22 Sixteen-key keypad connected to the STM32L475

4.6.2 KEYBOARD DEBOUNCING

Contact bounce is due to the dynamics of a closing contact. The signal falls and rises a few times within a period of about 5 ms as a contact bounces. Because a human being cannot press and release a switch in less than 20 ms, a debouncer recognizes that the switch is closed after the voltage is low for about 10 ms and recognizes that the switch is open after the voltage is high for about 10 ms.

Both hardware and software solutions to the key bounce problem are available. Hardware solutions to contact bounce include an analog circuit that uses a resistor and a capacitor to smooth the voltage, and two digital solutions that use set-reset latches or CMOS buffers and double-throw switches. A dedicated keyboard (or keypad) scanning and debouncing circuitry may be incorporated into the microcontroller (one example is the Atmel SAM V71, which implements an on-chip keypad controller).

Hardware Debouncing Techniques

The following are hardware debouncing techniques:

- **Set-reset latches**. A key switch is debounced by using a set-reset latch shown in Figure 4.23a. Before being pressed, the key is touching the set input, and the Q voltage is high. When pressed, the key moves toward the reset position. When the key touches the reset position, the Q voltage goes low. When the key is bouncing and touching neither the set or the reset input, both set and reset inputs are pulled low by the pull-down resistors. Because both set and reset are low, the Q voltage remains low and the key is recognized as pressed.

- **Noninverting CMOS buffer with high input impedance.** The CMOS buffer output is identical to its input. When the switch is pressed, the input of the buffer chip 4050 is grounded and hence V_{OUT} is forced to low. When the key switch is bouncing (not touching the input), the resistor R keeps the output voltage low. This is due to the high input impedance of 4050, which causes a negligible voltage drop on the feedback resistor. Thus the output is debounced. This solution is shown in Figure 4.23b.
- **Integrated debouncer.** The RC constant of the integrator determines the rate at which the capacitor charges up toward the supply voltage once the ground connection via the switch has been removed. As long as the capacitor voltage does not exceed the logic 0 threshold value, the V_{OUT} signal continues to be recognized as a logic 0. This solution is shown in Figure 4.23c.

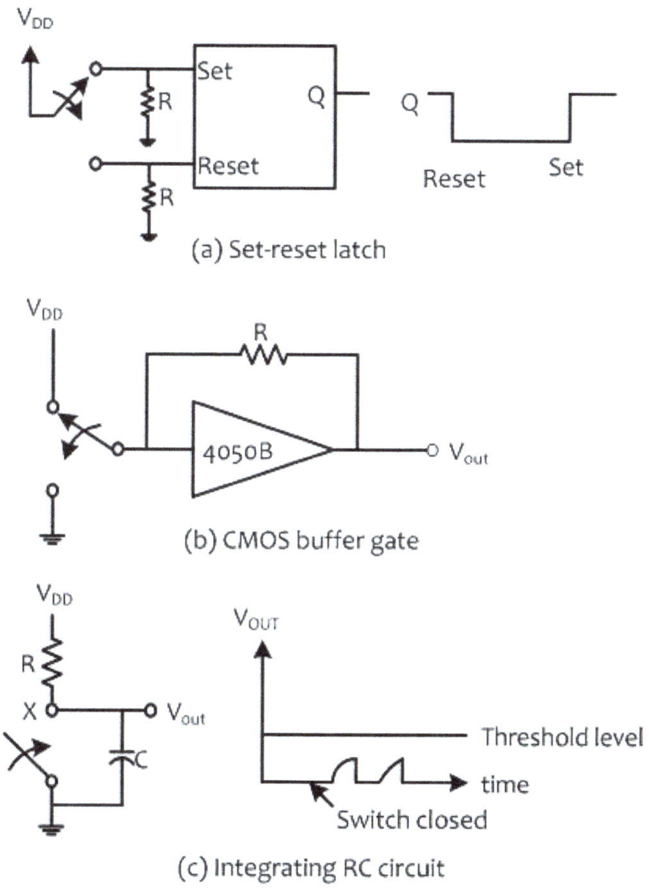

Figure 4.23 Hardware debouncing techniques

Software Debouncing Techniques

A simple software debouncing method is **wait-and-see**; that is, wait for 10 ms and reexamine the same key to see whether it is still pressed.

A key is considered pressed if its output voltage is still low 10 ms after it is detected low. If the output voltage is high, the program considers the signal as noise or the key still bouncing. In either case, the program continues to perform keypad scanning. For most applications, this simple wait-and-see method is adequate.

4.6.3 ASCII CODE LOOKUP

For an application that needs a keyboard, the easiest way to find out the ASCII code of the pressed key is to perform a table lookup. However, table lookup is not necessary for the keypad because ASCII code lookup can be embedded in the program that performs the scanning and debouncing.

Example 4.18 Write a function to perform keypad scanning and debouncing and return the ASCII code of the pressed key to the caller. Assume that the **delayby10ms (k)** function, which creates a delay of **k** × **10 ms**, is available for your use.

Solution:

```
#define keypadi GPIOB->IDR
#define keypado GPIOB->ODR
uint32_t getkey (void)
{
    uint32_t rmask, cmask, row, col;
    uint32_t keycode;
// configure PB4~PB7 pins for output and PB0~PB3 for input
    GPIOB->MODER = 0x00005500;
    while(1) {
        rmask = 0xEF; // select row 0
        for (row = 0; row < 4; row++) {
            cmask = 0x01; // select column 0
            keypado = rmask; // select current row
            for(col = 0; col < 4; col++){
                if(!(keypadi & cmask)) { // key switch detected pressed
                    delayby10ms(1);          // wait for 10 ms
                    if(!(keypadi & cmask)) { // check the same key again
                        keycode = row * 4 + col;
                        if(keycode < 10)
```

```
                    return (0x30 + keycode);
                else
                    return (0x37 + keycode);
            }
        }
        cmask = cmask << 1;
    }
    rmask = (rmask << 1) | 0x0F;
  }
 }
}
```

4.7 Interfacing with Text-Based LCD

LCDs are based on passive display technology: they control the passage of light rather than emitting the light. This contributes to the low power consumption. For this reason, use of LCDs in battery-powered embedded systems is particularly popular.

Although many types of LCDs are available, they can be divided into two basic categories: graphic displays and text displays. Notebooks and PCs use sophisticated graphic LCD displays, which are made up of millions of individual **picture elements** (pixels). Such displays are expensive in their own right and generally require large amount of memory and powerful processors for efficient processing. Many embedded systems cannot justify this level of expense. We will be concerned here with small displays intended primarily to display text.

Various types of character-based LCD displays are available. They are typically arranged as one, two, or four lines of between 16 and 40 characters. A character-based LCD usually consists of 5 × 8 or 5 × 10 dots. The task of generating characters on the LCDs is normally handled by a dedicated controller, which is referred to as the **LCD controller**. The Hitachi HD44780 is the most popular text-based LCD controller. Because of its popularity, many other semiconductor companies also introduced their own LCD controllers that are compatible to the HD44780.

The LCD is often sold as a kit, which consists of the LCD panel, the LCD controller, and other supporting logic chips.

4.7.1 THE STRUCTURE OF THE HD44780 LCD CONTROLLER

A simplified block diagram of the HD44780 is shown in Figure 4.24. The block diagram of an LCD kit incorporating an HD44780 controller is shown in Figure 4.25. The function of each component of the HD44780 LCD controller is described as follows:

DDRAM

At the heart of the HD44780 is the **display data RAM** (DDRAM). Display data represented in ASCII code is stored in the DDRAM. Its capacity is 80 characters; as a result, the maximum display sizes are 20 characters × 4 lines or 40 characters × 2 lines.

The data (represented in ASCII codes) to be displayed is sent to the LCD controller via the DB7~DB0 bus lines and stored in the DDRAM. The HD44780 will then refresh the display as required using these data. Every character displayed on the LCD screen has a corresponding location in the DDRAM. The correspondence of the LCD screen character and the DDRAM locations is shown in Table 4.3.

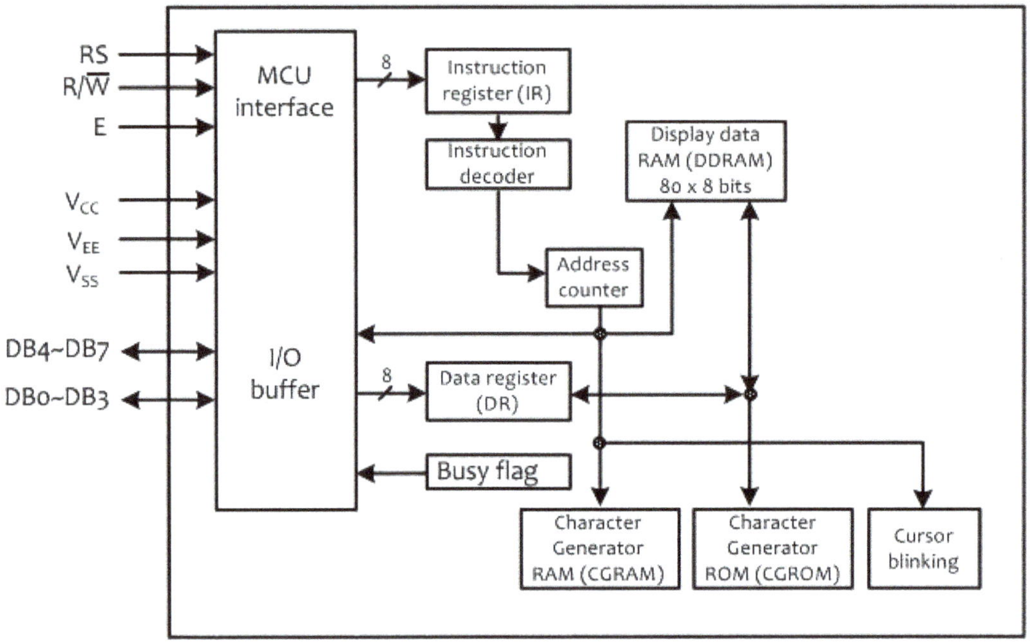

Figure 4.24 Key components of the HD44780

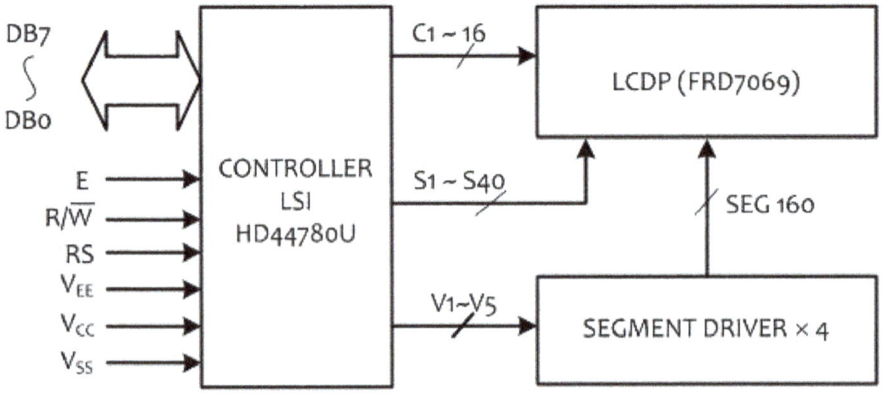

Figure 4.25 Block diagram of an HD44780-based LCD kit

Table 4.3 Memory locations for the start of each line in various LCD displays

# of characters	# of lines	First line	Second line	Third line	Fourth line
8	1	0x00 ~ 0x07	--	--	--
16	1	0x00 ~ 0x0F	--	--	--
16	2	0x00 ~ 0x0F	0x40 ~ 0x4F	--	--
16	4	0x00 ~ 0x0F	0x40 ~ 0x4F	0x10 ~ 0x1F	0x50 ~ 0x5F
20	2	0x00 ~ 0x13	0x40 ~ 0x53	--	--
20	4	0x00 ~ 0x13	0x40 ~ 0x53	0x14 ~ 0x27	0x54 ~ 0x67
24	1	0x00 ~ 0x17	--	--	--
24	2	0x00 ~ 0x17	0x40 ~ 0x57	--	--
40	1	0x00 ~ 0x27	--	--	--
40	2	0x00 ~ 0x27	0x40 ~ 0x67	--	--

CGROM

The character generator ROM generates 5 × 8 dot or 5 × 10 dot character patterns from 8-bit character codes. It can generate 208 5 × 8 dot character patterns and 32 5 × 10 dot character patterns for a total of 240 different character patterns. User-defined character patterns are also available by mask-programmed ROM.

CGRAM

The CGRAM is the character generator RAM, which is used to allow the creation and display of user-defined characters. This facility is useful if you wish to display characters not available in the CGROM. Since the CGRAM is volatile, it must be written into each time the LCD controller is powered on.

Registers

The HD44780 has two 8-bit registers, an instruction (IR), and a data register (DR). When the RS signal is high, the data register is selected. Otherwise, the instruction register is selected. The user program writes LCD instruction into the IR register. The DR register temporarily stores data to be written into DDRAM or CGRAM. Data written into the DR register by the microcontroller are automatically written into DDRAM or CGRAM by an internal operation.

Busy Flag

When the busy flag (BF) is 1, the HD44780 is performing an internal operation and further instructions or data will not be accepted.

Cursor/Blink Control Circuit

This circuit generates cursor or character blinking. The cursor or the blinking will appear with the character located at the DDRAM address set in the address counter (AC). For example, when the AC is 0x10, the cursor position is displayed at the DDRAM address 0x10.

Address Counter (AC)

The HD44780 uses a 7-bit AC to keep track of the address of the next DDRAM or CGRAM location to be accessed. When an instruction is written into the IR register, the address information contained in the instruction is transferred to the AC register. The selection of DDRAM or CGRAM is determined by the instruction. After writing into (or reading from) the DDRAM or the CGRAM, the contents of the AC register are automatically incremented (decremented) by 1. The contents of the AC register are output to the DB6~DB0 pins when the RS signal is low and the R/W signal is high.

4.7.2 LCD INSTRUCTIONS

The LCD instructions are used to set up LCD operation parameters. The supported instructions are listed in Table 4.4. The meanings of the programmable bits in Table 4.3 are listed in Table 4.5.

Table 4.4 HD44780 LCD controller instruction set

Instruction	Code										Description	Execution Time
	RS	R/$\overline{W}$	B7	B6	B5	B4	B3	B2	B1	B0		
Clear display	0	0	0	0	0	0	0	0	0	1	Clears display and set DDRAM address to 0x00 from address counter AC.	1.52 ms
Cursor home	0	0	0	0	0	0	0	0	1	*	Returns cursor to home position without changing DDRAM contents. Also returns display being shifted to the original position.	1.52 ms
Entry mode set	0	0	0	0	0	0	0	1	I/D	S	Sets cursor move direction (I/D); specifies to shift the display (S). These operations are performed during data read/write.	37 µs
Display on/off control	0	0	0	0	0	0	1	D	C	B	Turns on/off of display(D), cursor on/off (c), and blink of cursor position character (B).	37 µs
Cursor/display shift	0	0	0	0	0	1	S/C	R/L	*	*	Sets cursor-move or display-shift (S/C), shift direction (R/L) without changing DDRAM data.	37 µs
Function set	0	0	0	0	1	DL	N	F	*	*	Sets interface data length (DL), number of display line (N), and character font (F).	37 µs
Set CGRAM address	0	0	0	1	CGRAM address						Sets the CGRAM address. CGRAM data are sent and received after this setting.	37 µs
Set DDRAM address	0	0	1	DDRAM address							Sets the DDRAM address. DDRAM data are sent and received after this setting.	37 µs
Read busy flag and address counter	0	1	BF	CGRAM/DDRAM address							Reads busy flag (BF) indicating internal operation being performed and reads CGRAM or DDRAM address counter contents (depending on previous operation).	0 µs
Write CGRAM or DDRAM	1	0	write data								Writes data to CGRAM or DDRAM	37 µs
Read from CGRAM or DDRAM	1	1	read data								Reads data from CGRAM or DDRAM	37 µs

Table 4.5 LCD instruction bit names

Bit Name	Settings	
I/D	0 = decrement cursor position.	1 = increment cursor position
S	0 = no display shift.	1 = display shift
D	0 = display off	1 = display on
C	0 = cursor off	1 = cursor on
B	0 = cursor blink off	1 = cursor blink on
S/C	0 = move cursor	1 = shift display
R/L	0 = shift left	1 = shift right
DL	0 = 4-bit interface	1 = 8-bit interface
N	0 = 1/8 or 1/11 duty (1 line)	1 = 1/16 duty (2 lines)
F	0 = 5 × 8 dots	1 = 5 × 10 dots
BF	0 = can accept instruction	1 = internal operation in progress

4.7.3 LCD INSTRUCTION DESCRIPTIONS

The user sends instructions to the LCD controller to set up operation parameters. The functions of these instructions are as follows:

Clear Display

This instruction writes the space code (0x20) into all DDRAM locations. It then sets 0 into the AC and returns the display to its original status if it was shifted. In other words, the display disappears, and the cursor or blinking goes to the upper left corner of the display. It also sets the I/D bit to 1 (increment mode) in entry mode.

Return Home

This instruction sets the AC to 0 and returns the display to its original status if it was shifted. The DDRAM contents are not changed. The cursor or blinking goes to the upper left corner of the display.

Entry Mode Set

The I/D bit of this instruction controls the incrementing (I/D = 1) or decrementing (I/D = 0) of the DDRAM address. The **cursor** or **blinking** is moved to the right or left, depending on whether this bit is set to 1 or 0. The same applies to writing and reading of the CGRAM.

The S bit of this instruction controls the shifting of the LCD display. The display shifts if S = 1. Otherwise, the display does not shift. If S = 1, it will seem as if the cursor does not move but the display does. The display does not shift when reading from DDRAM. Also, writing into or reading from CGRAM does not shift the display.

Display On/Off Control

This instruction has three bit parameters: **D**, **C**, and **B**. When the D bit is set to 1, the display is turned on; otherwise, it is turned off. The cursor is turned on when the C bit is set to 1. The character indicated by the cursor blinks when the B bit is set to 1.

Cursor or Display Shift

This instruction shifts the cursor to the right or left without writing or reading display data. The shifting is controlled by 2 bits, as shown in Table 4.6. This function is used to correct or search the display. When the cursor has been moved to the end of a line, it is moved to the beginning of the next line.

When the displayed data is shifted repeatedly, each line moves only horizontally. The second line of the display does not shift into the first row. The contents of the AC do not change if the only action performed is a display shift.

Table 4.6 LCD Shift function

S/C	R/L	Operation
0	0	Shifts the cursor position to the left. (AC is decremented by 1)
0	1	Shifts the cursor position to the right. (AC is incremented by 1)
1	0	Shifts the entire display to the left. The cursor follows the display shift.
1	1	Shifts the entire display to the right. The cursor follows the display shift.

Function Set

This instruction allows the user to set the interface data length, select the number of display lines, and select the character fonts. There are three bit variables in this instruction:

- **DL**: Data are sent or received in 8-bit length (DB7~DB0) when DL is set to 1, and in 4-bit length (DB7~DB4) when DL is set to 0. When the pin count is at a premium for the application, the 4-bit data length should be chosen.
- **N**: This bit sets the number of display lines. When set to 0, one-line display is selected. When set to 1, two-line display is selected.
- **F**: When set to 0, the 5 × 8 font is selected. When set to 1, the 5 × 10 font is selected.

Set CGRAM Address

This instruction contains the CGRAM address to be set into the AC. This instruction is useful when the user needs to define his/her custom fonts.

Set DDRAM Address

This allows the user to set the address of the DDRAM in AC. This instruction is used whenever user wants to set the cursor to a certain position on the LCD screen. This command allows the user to select the first location on the LCD screen to display the information. For example, to display a message starting from the fourth column of row 1 (**address is 0x04**), write the command **0x84** into the instruction register (IR). To display a message starting from the fourth column of the second row (**address is 0x44**), write the command **0xC4** into the instruction register. Here, we assume that the column number starts from 0.

Read Busy Flag and Address

This instruction reads BF and the AC. The BF flag indicates whether the LCD controller is still executing the previously received instruction.

4.7.4 INTERFACING THE HD44780 TO THE STM32L475 MICROCONTROLLER

The microcontroller/microprocessor interface to the HD44780 LCD modules is almost always 14 pins. Table 4.7 shows the basic pin out. You may find that some displays have additional pins for backlighting or other purposes, but the first 14 pins still serve as the interface.

The first three pins provide power to the LCD module. Pin 1 is GND and should be grounded to the power supply. Pin 2 is VCC and should be connected to a 5-V power supply. Pin 3 is the LCD contrast control (or display bias). By adjusting the voltage or duty cycle of pin 3, the contrast (or brightness) of the display can be adjusted.

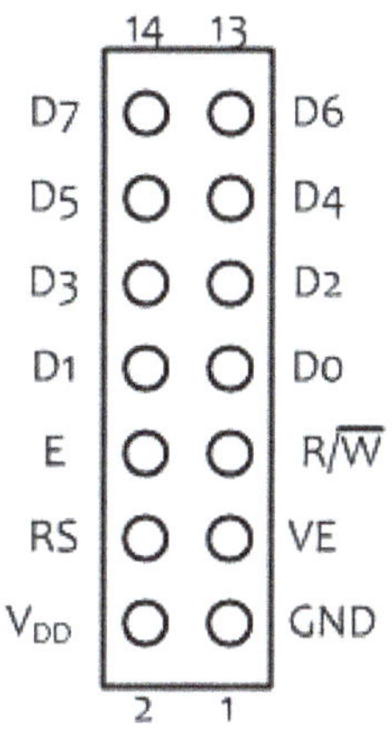

Table 4.7 Character LCD pin out

Pin #	Name	I/O	Description
1	GND	--	Ground
2	VCC	--	LCD controller power supply
3	VE	--	Contrast adjust
4	RS	I	Register select (1 = data, 0 = instruction
5	$R/\overline{W}$	I	Read/write (1 = read, 0 = write)
6	E	I	Enable (data strobe)
7	DB0	I/O	Data bus line 0
8	DB1	I/O	Data bus line 1
9	DB2	I/O	Data bus line 2
10	DB3	I/O	Data bus line 3
11	DB4	I/O	Data bus line 4
12	DB5	I/O	Data bus line 5
13	DB6	I/O	Data bus line 6
14	DB7	I/O	Data bus line 7
15	A	Power	LED backlight anode (optional)
16	K	power	LED backlight cathode (optional)

An example of circuit connection between the STM32L475 and the HD44780 is shown in Figure 4.26. This circuit connection uses 8-bit mode to transfer data. The STM32L475 and HD44780 use different power supply. If the user never wants to read anything from the LCD, the R/pin can be grounded.

Certain timing parameters must be satisfied in order to access the LCD successfully. The read and write timing diagrams for the HD44780 are shown in Figures 4.27 and 4.28, respectively. The values of timing parameters are shown in Table 4.8.

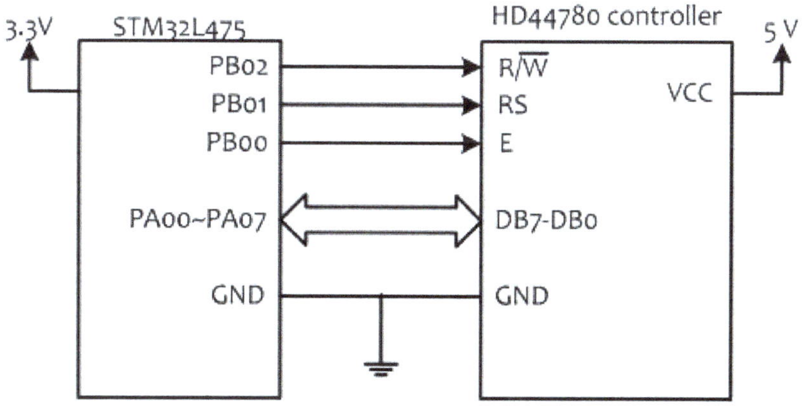

Figure 4.26 Circuit connection between STM32L475 and HD44780

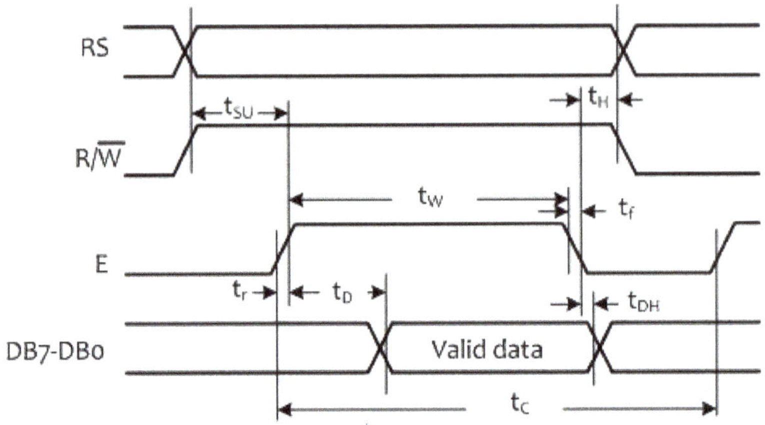

Figure 4.27 LCD HD44780 LCD controller read timing diagram

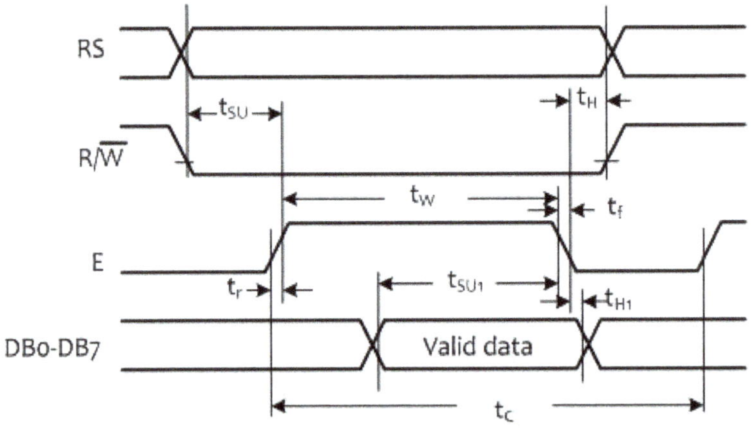

Figure 4.28 HD44780 LCD controller write timing diagram

Table 4.8 HD44780 LCD controller timing parameters

Parameter	Symbol	Min	Max	Unit
Enable cycle time	t_C	500	--	ns
Enable high pulse width	t_W	230	--	ns
Enable rise/fall time	t_r/t_f	--	20	ns
RS, R/W set up time	t_{SU}	40	--	ns
RS, R/W hold time	t_H	10	--	ns
Read data output delay	t_D	--	160	ns
Read data hold time	t_{DH}	5	--	ns
Write data setup time	t_{SU1}	80	--	ns
Write data hold time	t_{H1}	10	--	ns

Example 4.19 Write a function that sends a command to the LCD controller. Assume that the function delay50us(), which creates a delay of 50 µs, is available to you to call.

Solution: The procedure for sending a command to the LCD controller should follow the timing diagram shown in Figure 4.28 and satisfy the timing requirements:

Step 1

Pull the RS and E signal to low.

Step 2

Pull the R/W signal to low.

Step 3

Pull the E signal to high.

Step 4

Output the LCD instruction to the I/O port (PORTB in Figure 4.26) that drives the LCD controller.

Step 5

Pull the E signal to low, and make sure that the LCD internal operation is completed.

The C function that sends a command to the HD44780 controller is as follows:

```
#define LCDE         0x01            // mask for E signal of LCD
#define LCDRS     (0x01 << 1)        // mask for RS signal of LCD
#define LCDRW     (0x01 << 2)        // mask for R/W signal of LCD
#define LCDPort   GPIOA->ODR         // I/O port that drives HD44780
#define LCDPortS  GPIOB->BSRR        // use this register to set LCD signals to high
#define LCDPortC  GPIOB->BRR         // use this register to reset LCD signals to low
void cmd2LCD(uint32_t cmd)
{
    uint32 k;
    LCDPortC    = LCDRW + LCDRS; // select IR register and pull R/W low
    LCDPortS    = LCDE;          // pull E signal high
    LCDPort     = cmd;           // output command to LCD and keep E high
    for (k = 0; k < 7; k++);     // lengthen E pulse so that it is at least 230 ns long
    LCDPortC    = LCDE;          // pull E signal low
    delay50us(); // wait for 50 µs
}
```

4.7.5 LCD STARTUP SEQUENCE

A startup sequence with specific timings is required to ensure proper LCD operation. The startup sequence is shown in Figure 4.29.

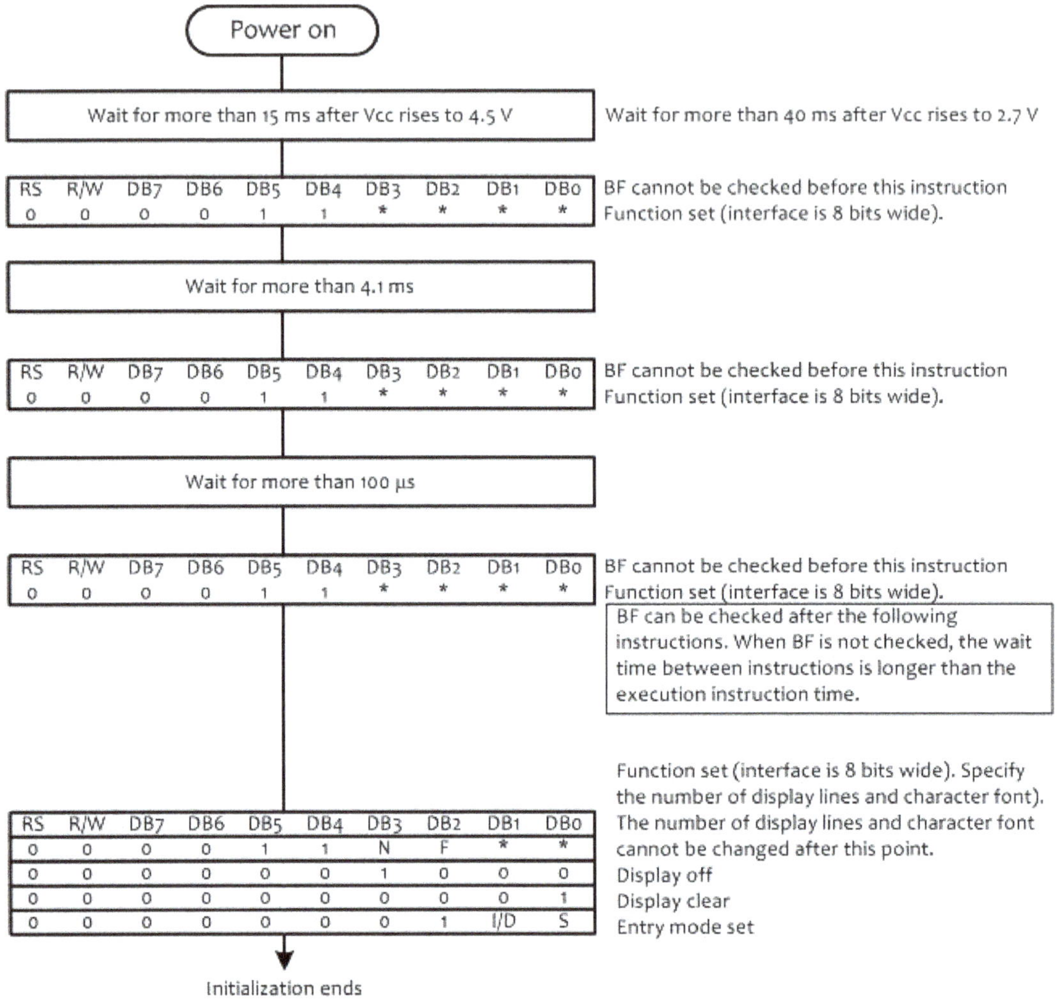

Figure 4.29 HD44780 8-bit interface initialization procedure

Example 4.20 Write a C function to configure the LCD controller to operate with 8-bit data bus, use 5 × 8 font, select two-line display, and enable display, cursor, and blinking. Assume that the STM32L475 processor is running at 80 MHz and the delay functions *delayby1ms (k)* and *delayby100ms (k)* are available to you to call.

Solution: The function to configure the LCD controller as specified is as follows:

```
void openLCD (void)

{

    GPIOA->MODER     &= 0xFFFF0000;          // clear bits 0 to 15
```

```
    GPIOA->MODER    |= 0x00005555;      // configure PA00~PA07 pins for output
    GPIOB->MODER    &= 0xFFFFFFC0;      // clear bits 0 to 5
    GPIOB->MODER    |= 0x00000015;      // configure PB00~PB02 pins for output
    delayby100ms (1);   // wait for 100 ms
    cmd2LCD (0x30);
    delayby1ms (5); // wait for 5 ms
    cmd2LCD (0x30);
    delayby1ms (1);
    cmd2LCD (0x30);
    cmd2LCD (0x38);     // 8-bit data bus, 2-line display, 5 × 8 font
    cmd2LCD (0x08);     // turn off display
    cmd2LCD (0x01);     // clear screen, move cursor to upper left corner
    delayby1ms (2); // wait until "clear display" command is completed
    cmd2LCD (0x06);     // entry mode set (move cursor right)
    cmd2LCD (0x0F);     // turn on display, cursor, cursor blinking
}
```

Example 4.21 Write a C function that sends a data byte to the LCD controller. Assume that the STM32L475 is running at 80 MHz and the function delay50µs (), which creates a delay of 50 µs, is available to you to call.

Solution: By emulating the timing diagram shown in Figure 4.28, the user can send a data byte to the LCD controller. The function that sends a data byte to the LCD controller is as follows:

```
void putc2LCD(uint32_t data)
{
    uint32_t  k;    // used as loop index
    LCDPortS    = LCDRS;        // select data register
    LCDPortC    = LCDRW;        // pull R/W low
    LCDPortS    = LCDE;         // pull E signal high
    LCDPort     = data;         // output data
    for (k = 0; k < 7; k++); // lengthen E pulse and keep it high for at least 230 ns
    LCDPortC    = LCDE; // pull E signal low
```

```
    delay50us();      // wait for most commands to complete execution
}
```

Example 4.22 Write a C function that outputs a string on the LCD screen. The pointer to the string is passed to this function.

Solution: This function can be implemented by calling the putc2LCD function repeatedly until the whole string has been displayed:

```
void puts2LCD(uint8_t *ptr)
{
    while(*ptr) {
        putc2LCD((uint32_t)(*ptr));
        ptr++;
    }
}
```

Example 4.23 Write a sequence of C statements to display the following messages on the LCD:

"STM32L475 is M4."

"LCD is bright!"

Solution:

```
uint8_t *msg1 = "STM32L475 is M4.";
uint8_t *msg2 = "LCD is bright!";
openLCD();
cmd2LCD(0x80); // set cursor to row 1, column 1
puts2LCD(msg1);
cmd2LCD(0xC0); // set cursor to row 2, column 1
puts2LCD(msg2);
```

4.8 Summary

All microcontrollers allow the user to use signal pins to drive input/output devices directly. A microcontroller may use 8, 16, or 32 signal pins to form a **port**. ST groups 16 pins into a port. An I/O port is also called **GPIO port**. Registers are needed to perform I/O operations. Some registers are used to hold configuration information. Others are used to hold data to be output or data that represent the voltage levels of the signal pins.

In addition to being used as a general-purpose I/O pin, a pin may also be used for alternate functions associated with other on-chip peripherals such as timer, serial peripheral interface (SPI), inter-integrated circuit (I^2C), analog-to-digital converter (ADC), digital-to-analog converter (DAC), etc.

After reset, an I/O pin is used as a general-purpose input. To configure a signal pin for other purpose, the user is required to program the MODER register. To configure an I/O pin for an alternate function, the user is required to program an alternate function register (AFRL or AFRH) in addition to the MODER register.

Sometimes the user may want to pull the voltage level of a few output pins to high without affecting other output pins. This can be achieved by programming the corresponding bits of the BSRR register. At other times, the user may want to pull the voltage levels of a few output pins to low without affecting the other pins. This can be achieved by programming the corresponding bits of the BRR register or the corresponding bits in the upper half of the BSRR register.

The ST Cortex-M4 device allows the user to configure each signal pin to the following modes:

- Input floating
- Input pull-up
- Input pull-down
- Analog
- Output open-drain with pull-up or pull-down capability
- Output push-pull with pull-up or pull-down capability
- Alternate function push-pull with pull-up or pull-down capability
- Alternate function open-drain with pull-up or pull-down capability

Simple I/O devices include light-emitting diodes (LEDs), seven-segment displays (SSDs), liquid crystal displays (LCDs), speakers, DIP switches, keypads, keyboards, stepping motors, and so on. Time delays are often needed to achieve the desired I/O effect. Time delays can be created by using a dummy for-loop or timer function.

4.9 Exercises

E4.1 Write a sequence of C statements to configure GPIOA pins PA00~PA07 for push-pull output with pull-up capability and also configure PA08~PA15 for input.

E4.2 Write a sequence of C statements to configure port C pins PC1, PC3, PC5, and PC11 for open-drain output with pull-up, and very high-speed output and lock this configuration.

E4.3 Write a sequence of C statements to configure port D pins PD03~PD05 to alternate function AF3 and configure PD07~PD09 pins for alternate function AF6.

E4.4 Write a sequence of C statements to configure port E pins PE0~PE1 for alternate function AF2 push-pull with pull-down and PE8 and PE9 for alternate function AF4 open-drain with pull-up.

E4.5 Write a sequence of C statements to configure port B pins PB15~PB11 and PB03~PB00 for input and then read the values of these eight pins, compact them (i.e., concatenate them according to the order of the pin number, high pin number is more significant), and then assign the resultant value to the variable **ax**.

E4.6 Assuming that the STM32L475 is running at a clock rate of 4 MHz, how many times should the dummy for-loop described in section 4.5 be repeated in order to generate a delay of 50 ms?

E4.7 Write a C program using the port B pins PB05~PB00 to drive a simulated traffic green, yellow, and red lights for the east–west bound and south–north bound direction. The duration of each light is shown in Table E4.7. Assume that the delay function delayby100ms (k) is available for your call. The created delay is a multiple of 100 ms. The multiple is passed in **k.**

Table E4.6 Traffic light pattern and duration

East-West			South-North			Duration (sec)
Green	Yellow	Red	Green	Yellow	Red	
PB05	PB04	PB03	PB02	PB01	PB00	
1	0	0	0	0	1	25
0	1	0	0	0	1	5
0	0	1	1	0	0	20
0	0	1	0	1	0	4

E4.8 Assume that port C pins PC15~PC10 are driving green, yellow, red, blue, white, and purple LEDs. The circuit connection is similar to Figure 4.16 and the LED is lighted when the pin is driven high. Write a C program to light the green, yellow, red, blue, white, and purple in turn for 0.1, 0.2, 0.3, 0.4, 0.5, and 0.6 seconds forever.

E4.9 Write a C program to flash the LEDs driven by PA15~PA00 pins in the following patterns with each pattern lasting for 200 ms:

(a) Turn on all LEDs.
(b) Turn off all LEDs.

(c) Repeat (a) and (b) three times.
(d) Turn on one LED at a time from the one driven by PA15 until the one driven by PA00 pin with each LED turned on for 200 ms.
(e) Repeat (d) three more times.
(f) Turn on one LED at a time from the one driven by PA00 until the one driven by PA15 pin with each LED turned on for 200 ms.
(g) Repeat (f) three more times.
(h) Turn on LEDs driven by PA15 and PA00 pins for 200 ms.
(i) Turn on LEDs driven by PA14 and PA01 pins for 200 ms.
(j) Turn on LEDs driven by PA13 and PA02 pins for 200 ms.
(k) Turn on LEDs driven by PA12 and PA03 pins for 200 ms.
(l) Turn on LEDs driven by PA11 and PA04 pins for 200 ms.
(m) Turn on LEDs driven by PA10 and PA05 pins for 200 ms.
(n) Turn on LEDs driven by PA09 and PA06 pins for 200 ms.
(o) Turn on LEDs driven by PA08 and PA07 pins for 200 ms.
(p) Turn on LEDs driven by PA08 and PA07 pins for 200 ms.
(q) Turn on LEDs driven by PA09 and PA06 pins for 200 ms.
(r) Turn on LEDs driven by PA10 and PA05 pins for 200 ms.
(s) Turn on LEDs driven by PA11 and PA04 pins for 200 ms.
(t) Turn on LEDs driven by PA12 and PA03 pins for 200 ms.
(u) Turn on LEDs driven by PA13 and PA02 pins for 200 ms.
(v) Turn on LEDs driven by PA14 and PA01 pins for 200 ms.
(w) Turn on LEDs driven by PA15 and PA00 pins for 200 ms.
(x) Repeat (h)~(w) three more times.
(y) Repeat (a) to (x) forever.

E4.10 For the circuit shown in Figure 4.18, write a C program to display 1, 2, 3, 4, 5, and 6 from left to right, one digit at a time, with each digit lasting for 100 ms.

E4.11 Write a C program to display the following patterns from the seven-segment displays in Figure 4.17 from display #5 to #0, and repeat with each row lasting for 600 ms:

654321

765432

876543

987654

098765

109876

210987

321098

432109

543210

E4.12 Write a C function that can use a time-multiplexing technique to display one to six digits simultaneously with the circuit shown in Figure 4.18. These digits are to be displayed for 600 ms.

E4.13 Write a C program to display the following patterns using the seven-segment display circuit shown in Figure 4.18 from display #5 to #0 and repeat with each row lasting for 600 ms:

1

21

321

4321

54321

654321

765432

876543

987654

098765

109876

210987

321098

432109

543210

E4.14 Write a sequence of C statements to display the following messages on the LCD:

"STM32L475 runs at"

"80 MHz."

E4.15 Write a C program to generate the following periodic waveforms from PB15 and PB0 pins shown in Figure E4.15 and display it using the oscilloscope:

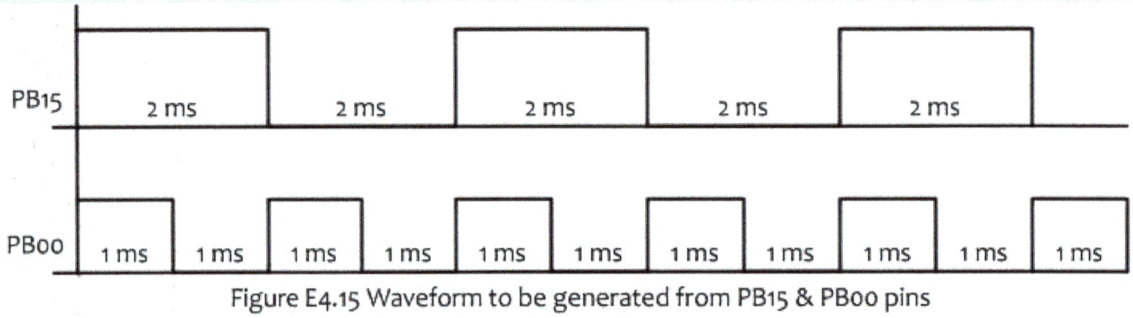

Figure E4.15 Waveform to be generated from PB15 & PB00 pins

4.10 Lab Assignments

Use the STM32 Discovery kit for IoT node (B-L475E-IOT01A) to perform the following lab experiments:

L4.1 Three-Tone Siren Generation. Connect the PA15 pin to a speaker. Write a program to generate a three-tone siren with frequency set to 125, 250, and 500 Hz, respectively. Each tone lasts for half of a second.

L4.2 LED Flashing. Write a program to flash the LEDs driven by port D pins PD7~PD0 (CN3 connector of Arduino) in the following manner:

1. Turn on all LEDs for 200 ms and then turn off for 200 ms. Perform this operation three times.
2. Turn on one LED at a time, from left (driven by PD07) to right (driven by PD00), with each LED turned on for 200 ms. Perform this operation four times.
3. Turn on one LED at a time, from right (driven by PD00) to left (driven by PD07), with each LED turned on for 200 ms. Perform this operation four times.
4. Turn LEDs driven by PD07 and PD00 pins on and off four times. The on and off durations are 200 ms.
5. Turn LEDs driven by PD06 and PD01 pins on and off four times. The on and off durations are 200 ms.
6. Turn LEDs driven by PD05 and PD02 pins on and off four times. The on and off durations are 200 ms.
7. Turn LEDs driven by PD04 and PD03 pins on and off four times. The on and off durations are 200 ms.
8. Turn LEDs driven by PD04 and PD03 pins on and off four times. The on and off durations are 200 ms.
9. Turn LEDs driven by PD05 and PD02 pins on and off four times. The on and off durations are 200 ms.
10. Turn LEDs driven by PD06 and PD01 pins on and off four times. The on and off durations are 200 ms.
11. Turn LEDs driven by PD07 and PD00 pins on and off four times. The on and off durations are 200 ms.
12. Turn on the LED driven by PD07 for 200 ms, then turn on LEDs driven by PD07~PD06 for 200 ms, then turn on LEDs driven by PD07~PD05 for 200 ms, . . ., turn on all LEDs for 200 ms.
13. Turn on LEDs driven by PD07~PD00 for 200 ms, then turn on LEDs driven by PD07~PD01 for 200 ms, . . ., turn on the LED driven by PD07 for 200 ms, and turn off all LEDs for 200 ms.
14. Go to Step 1.

L4.3 Use PD07~PD04 pins (Arduino CN3 connector) to drive one 74HC48 seven-segment decoder and PD03~PD00 pins to drive another 74HC48. The 74HC48 accepts a 4-bit decimal digit and decodes it into corresponding seven-segment pattern. Write a C program to implement a two-digit decimal counter that increments at the rate of 5 Hz. Output these two-digit decimal counter to pins PD07~PD00. The counter should increment from 00 to 99 and then repeat. Connect the segment pins (a ~ g) of 74HC48s to seven-segment displays to display the values of the two-digit decimal counter.

L4.4 Write a C program to display the following patterns from the seven-segment display circuit shown in Figure 4.15 from display #5 to #0, and repeat with each row lasting for 600 ms:

123456

234567

345678

456789

567890

678901

789012

890123

901234

012345

5

Interrupt, Exception, and Reset Handling

5.1 Objectives

After completing this chapter, you will be able to

- Explain the general concepts of interrupts and resets.
- Describe the STM32L475 and other STM32 devices' exception model.
- Enable and disable the STM32L475 peripheral interrupts.
- Set up STM32L475 interrupt priorities.
- Configure I/O pins as external interrupt sources.
- Write interrupt (or exception) handler to handle all STM32L475 interrupts and exceptions.

5.2 Basic Concepts of Interrupts and Exceptions

An **interrupt** (or **exception**) is a signal to the processor indicating the need for attention or a need to change program flow. An interrupt can be generated by hardware or software. A hardware interrupt causes the processor to save its **state of execution** and begin the execution of an **interrupt service routine** (also called **interrupt handler**). The state of execution consists of the program counter and at least a handful of CPU registers. After the interrupt handler finishes, the processor resumes normal activities (i.e., re-executes the interrupted program).

Hardware interrupts are used by devices to indicate that they need attention from the processor. Hardware interrupts are implemented as a signal, which may use its rising edge, falling edge, low level, or high level to alert the processor. Hardware events that can generate an interrupt include timer overflow, I/O pin being pressed, A/D or D/A conversion completion, real-time clock alarm, data transfer completion in a serial communication module, and so on.

A **software interrupt** is caused either by an exceptional condition in the processor itself or a special instruction in the instruction set that causes an interrupt when it is executed. The former is often called a **trap** or **exception** and is used for errors or events occurring during program execution that are exceptional enough that they cannot be handled within the program itself. For example, the processor's arithmetic logic unit is commanded to divide a number by zero; this impossible demand will cause a divide-by-0 exception, perhaps causing the computer to abandon the calculation or display an error message. **Software interrupt instructions** operate similarly to subroutine calls and are used for a variety of purposes, such as to request services from low-level system software such as device drivers. For example, computers often use software interrupt instructions to communicate with the disk controller to request data be read from or written into the disk.

5.3 Benefits of Interrupts

Interrupts provide many benefits to the computer system:

- **Improve I/O performance**. The processor should read from an input device only when it has new data. Input device often uses a flag to indicate the condition that new data are available. Without the interrupt mechanism, the processor will need to poll the flag continuously in order to find out whether there are new data to be read. The processor should send data to an output device only when the output device can handle additional data. Output device also uses a flag to indicate the condition that it is ready for new data. Without the interrupt mechanism, the processor will need to poll the flag continuously until the output device is ready for more data.
- **Enable processor to perform routine work**. Many embedded systems are designed to perform routine works such as checking the pressure, temperature, humidity, and other parameters in a process control plant; update and display time-of-day; checking and informing the users with their appointment times; and so on. Routine works are usually initiated by timer interrupts. Timers are set up to interrupt regularly, and the processor can check into the routine works that need to be done at the moment and take the appropriate actions. It is difficult to imagine how the processor can perform routine works without timer interrupts.
- **Response to emergent events**. Some embedded systems are designed to monitor emergent events such as fire alarm, overheat, power failure, and so on. Whenever one of these events occurs, the processor is interrupted and appropriate actions can be taken immediately to fix the problem.

5.4 Enabling and Disabling Interrupts

An interrupt may be useful in some conditions but not needed in other situations. Modern microprocessors and microcontrollers are designed to have the capability to pay attention to interrupts whenever they are useful and ignore them when they are not needed. That is, the processor can **enable an interrupt** whenever it is useful and **disable** it whenever it is undesirable or not useful. An interrupt that can be enabled and disabled is called a **maskable interrupt**. There are interrupts that the processor cannot ignore and must take immediate actions. These interrupts are called **non-maskable interrupts**.

A program can request the CPU to service or ignore an interrupt by setting or clearing an **enable bit**. An interrupt is said to be **pending** when it is requesting the attention of the processor but has not received the service yet. A pending interrupt may or may not receive the service from the processor depending upon whether it is enabled.

To make the interrupt enabling and disabling easier to handle, the interrupt enabling and disabling mechanism is designed to have the **global** and **local enabling capability**. The processor includes a global enable bit (or mask bit). Whenever none of the interrupts are needed, the user can simply clear the global enable bit to disable all interrupts. If some interrupts are needed and others are not, then the user needs to set the global enable bit and clear the local enable bits of those interrupts that are not needed. Today, almost all commercial microcontrollers are designed to have a two- or three-level interrupt enabling capability.

5.5 Prioritizing Multiple Pending Interrupts

A microcontroller or microprocessor usually has many interrupt sources. It is absolutely possible that many interrupt sources could be pending at about the same time. The CPU has to decide which interrupt to receive service first. The common solution is to prioritize all interrupt sources. In this approach, the processor provides service to the interrupt with the highest priority among all pending interrupts. Interrupt priority is implemented in hardware. If hardware does not prioritize interrupts, software can be written to poll interrupts in certain order and service the interrupt being recognized first. This essentially prioritizes interrupts.

5.6 Servicing Interrupts

When an enabled interrupt occurs, the processor is forced to provide service to it by executing an **interrupt service routine**, after which it must resume the execution of the interrupted program. To be able to do so, the processor saves the program counter and a few important registers before executing the interrupt service routine. After saving the program counter and the required registers, the processor identifies the interrupt source and locates the starting address of the interrupt service routine before it begins to execute the interrupt service routine. When the processor finishes the execution of the interrupt service routine, it restores the saved program counter and the saved registers and returns to the interrupted program for execution.

An interrupt service routine is quite like a subroutine, except for the last instruction. Different processors use different instructions as the last instruction of the interrupt service routine. However, the execution of the last instruction in the interrupt service routine must make sure that the processor resumes execution of the interrupted program at the same processor state. Unlike a subroutine, the execution of an interrupt service routine is triggered by the occurrence of the associated interrupt.

5.7 Interrupt Vector

The starting address of the interrupt service routine is called the **interrupt vector**. The processor is required to locate the starting address of the service routine for the interrupt to be serviced. For some microcontrollers, each interrupt source has its own predefined interrupt vector (i.e., at a fixed location), whereas others store all the interrupt vectors in a table.

When the first approach is used, the processor jumps to a predefined location to service the pending interrupt. In the second approach, the processor is required to fetch the interrupt vector from the interrupt vector table. The STM32L475 and all Cortex-M processors use the second approach.

5.8 Resets

When a computer is first powered up, the initial values of the program counter, CPU registers, flip-flops, and I/O control registers are unknown. The computer cannot execute programs correctly under this condition. To execute a program correctly after it is powered up, the computer is designed to have a reset mechanism. All critical registers, the program counter, and flip-flops are forced to a default value after a power-on reset so that the computer can start to execute a program correctly. The default value for program counter is 0 for some microcontrollers. Others may simply load the program counter from a fixed location such as 0.

In addition to the power-on reset, a computer may provide several resets to improve the performance and flexibility of the computer system. These resets include manual reset (applied to a pin), brown-out reset (detecting power supply dropping below normal operating level), watchdog reset, clock monitor reset, software reset, and so on. A manual reset without power-down has the same effect as power-on reset; it can force the program counter and critical registers to default values and allow the computer to reboot itself after a reset.

5.9 Exception Model of the ARM Cortex-M4 Processor

In ARM Cortex-M4 processors, **resets**, **interrupts**, **traps**, and **faults** are referred to as **exceptions**. The exception model of the Cortex-M4 processor is described in this section.

5.9.1 EXCEPTION STATES

An exception source may be in one of the following states:

- **Inactive**. The exception source is neither active nor pending.
- **Pending**. The exception is waiting to be serviced by the processor. The ARM Cortex-M4 processor can force an exception source to the pending state by setting an appropriate bit to 1.
- **Active**. An exception that is being serviced by the processor. When an exception is in the active state and another exception with a higher priority arrives, the current active exception will be preempted,

and the processor will switch to execute the service routine of the newly arrived exception. In this case, both exceptions are in the active state.

- **Active and pending**. The exception is being serviced by the processor and there is another exception from the same source.

5.9.2 EXCEPTION TYPES OF CORTEX-M4

The ARM Cortex-M4 processor supports the following types of exceptions:

- **Reset**. Reset is a special form of exception. It is invoked on power-up or several other causes to be discussed later. When reset is asserted, the operation of the processor stops, potentially at any point in an instruction. When the reset signal is de-asserted, instruction execution restarts from the address provided by the reset entry in the vector table.
- **NMI**. NMI stands for non-maskable interrupt. NMI can be triggered by a peripheral or software. This is the highest priority exception other than reset. It is permanently enabled and has a fixed priority of -2. NMIs cannot be masked or prevented from activation by any other exception or preempted by any exception other than reset. The HSE failure is an NMI.
- **Hard fault**. A hard fault is an exception that occurs because of an error during normal or exception processing. Hard faults have a fixed priority of -1, meaning that they have higher priority than any exception with configurable priority.
- **Memory management fault**. Memory management fault is an exception that occurs because of a memory protection–related fault. For example, instruction accesses to *Execute Never* (XN) memory regions.
- **Bus fault**. This is an exception that occurs because of a memory-related fault for an instruction or data memory transaction. This might be from an error detected on a bus in the memory system.
- **Usage fault**. Usage fault occurs because of an instruction execution fault. This includes (a) an undefined instruction, (b) an illegal unaligned address on word and half-word memory access, (c) invalid state on instruction execution, (d) an error on exception return, and (e) division by zero
- **Supervisor call (SVC)**. SVC is an exception triggered by the execution of the SVC instruction. In an operating system (OS) environment, applications can use SVC instructions to invoke OS kernel functions and device drivers. A **device driver** performs basic functions such as configuring peripheral operating parameters, sending a byte, receiving a byte, and so on.
- **PendSV**. PendSV is an interrupt-driven request for system-level service. In an OS environment, PendSV is used to perform context-switching when no other exception is active (when no active SysTick interrupt).
- **SysTick**. A SysTick exception is an exception generated by the system timer when it decrements to zero. Software can also generate a SysTick exception. In an OS environment, the processor can use this exception as system tick to perform task switching.
- **Interrupt (IRQ)**. An interrupt is an exception signaled by a peripheral or software request. In an embedded system, peripherals use interrupts to communicate with the processor.

Each exception is assigned an exception number, an IRQ number, a priority, and a memory location (in the vector table) from where its interrupt vector can be fetched. A summary of all this information for Cortex-M4 devices is given in Table 5.1. Exceptions with configurable priority can be disabled by privileged software.

Table 5.1 Properties of the different types of Cortex-M4 exception types

Exception number	IRQ number	Exception types	Priority	Vector address Or offset	Activation
1	-	Reset	-3, the highest	0x00000004	asynchronous
2	-14	NMI	-2	0x00000008	asynchronous
3	-13	Hard fault	-1	0x0000000C	–
4	-12	Memory Management fault	Configurable	0x00000010	synchronous
5	-11	Bus fault	Configurable	0x00000014	Synchronous when precise asynchronous when imprecise
6	-10	Usage fault	Configurable	0x00000018	synchronous
7-10	-	-	-	reserved	–
11	-5	SVCall	Configurable	0x0000002C	synchronous
12-13	-	-	-	reserved	–
14	-2	PendSV	Configurable	0x00000038	asynchronous
15	-1	SysTick	Configurable	0x0000003C	asynchronous
16 and above	0 and above	Interrupt (IRQ)	Configurable	0x00000040 and above	asynchronous

Note. To simplify the software layer, the CMSIS only use IRQ numbers. It uses negative value for exceptions other than interrupts.

5.9.3 EXCEPTION HANDLERS

Cortex-M4 processors use three types of handlers to handle exceptions:

- **Interrupt service routine (ISRs).** Interrupts IRQ0 to IRQ81 are handled by ISRs.
- **Fault handlers.** Hard fault, memory management fault, usage fault, and bus fault are all exceptions handled by fault handlers.
- **System handlers.** NMI, SVC, and SysTick are system exceptions to be handled by the system handlers.

5.9.4 VECTOR TABLE

The exception vector table contains the reset value of the stack pointer and the starting address of all exception handlers. The complete vector table is shown in Figure 5.1. The least significant bit of each vector must be 1, indicating that the exception handler is written in Thumb Code.

On a system reset, the vector table is fixed at address 0x00000000. Privileged software can write to the **vector table offset register (VTOR)** to relocate the vector table starting address to a different memory location, in the range from 0x00000000 to 0xFFFFFF80 in multiples of 256 bytes.

Exception number	IRQ number	Offset	Vector
255	239	0x03FC	IRQ239
		0x004C	
18	2	0x0048	IRQ2
17	1	0x0044	IRQ1
16	0	0x0040	IRQ0
15	-1	0x003C	Systick
14	-2	0x0038	PendSV
13			Reserved
12			Reserved for Debug
11	-5	0x002C	SVCall
10			Reserved
9			
8			
7			
6	-10	0x0018	Usage fault
5	-11	0x0014	Bus fault
4	-12	0x0010	Memory management fault
3	-13	0x000C	Hard fault
2	-14	0x0008	NMI
1		0x0004	Reset
		0x0000	Initial SP value

Figure 5.1 Vector Table

5.9.5 EXCEPTION PRIORITIES

All exceptions have an associated priority with lower-priority value indicating a higher priority. All exceptions except reset, hard fault, and NMI have configurable priorities. If the software does not configure their priorities, then exceptions with configurable priority have a priority of 0.

Configurable priority values are in the range from 0 to 15. When multiple exceptions have the same priority, the pending exception with the lowest exception number takes precedence.

The priorities of system exceptions are configured by system handler priority registers (SHPRx, x = 1, 2, or 3). The contents of them are shown in Figures 5.2 to 5.4, respectively.

31	30	29	28	27	26	25	24
23	**22**	**21**	**20**	**19**	**18**	**17**	**16**
PRI_6[7:4]				PRI_6[3:0]			
15	**14**	**13**	**12**	**11**	**10**	**9**	**8**
PRI_5[7:4]				PRI_5[3:0]			
7	**6**	**5**	**4**	**3**	**2**	**1**	**0**
PRI_4[7:4]				PRI_4[3:0]			

Reset value = 0x0000 0000
Offset = 0x18

PRI_6[7:0]: Priority of system handler 6, usage fault
Only the upper 4 bits are writeable. The lower 4 bits are 0000 by default.
PRI_5[7:0]: Priority of system handler 5, bus fault
Only the upper 4 bits are writeable. The lower 4 bits are 0000 by default.
PRI_4[7:0]: Priority of system handler 4, memory management fault
Only the upper 4 bits are writeable. The lower 4 bits are 0000 by default.

Figure 5.2 System handler priority register 1 (SHPR1)

31	30	29	28	27	26	25	24
PRI_11[7:4]				PRI_11[3:0]			
23	**22**	**21**	**20**	**19**	**18**	**17**	**16**
--	--	--	--	--	--	--	--
15	**14**	**13**	**12**	**11**	**10**	**9**	**8**
--	--	--	--	--	--	--	--
7	**6**	**5**	**4**	**3**	**2**	**1**	**0**
--	--	--	--	--	--	--	--

Reset value = 0x0000 0000
Offset = 0x1C

PRI_11[7:4]: Priority of system handler 11, SVCall (read-writeable)
0000~1111: priority of SVCall
PRI_11[3:0]: Priority of system handler 11, SVCall
0000: read-only field

Figure 5.3 System handler priority register 2 (SHPR2)

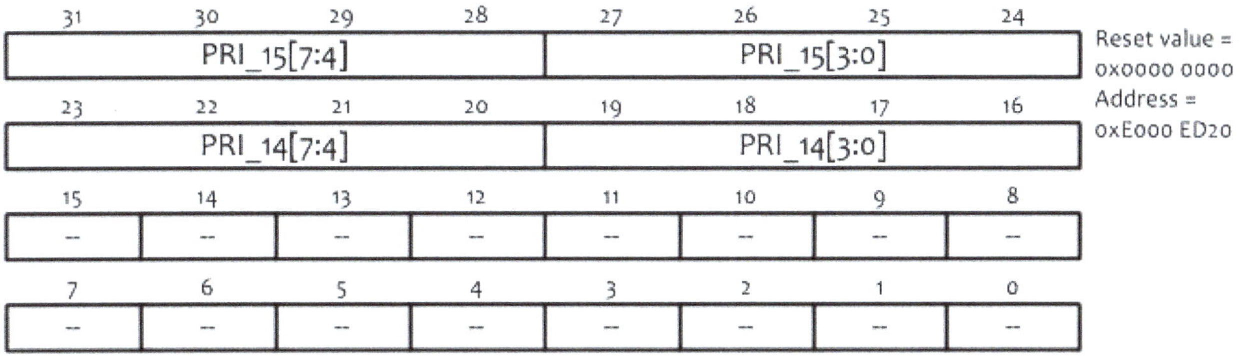

PRI_15[7:0]: Priority of system handler 15, SysTick exception
Only the upper 4 bits are writeable. The lower 4 bits are 0000 by default.
PRI_14[7:0]: Priority of system handler 14, PendSV
Only the upper 4 bits are writeable. The lower 4 bits are 0000 by default.

Figure 5.4 System handler priority register 3 (SHPR3)

The priorities of interrupts IRQ0~IRQ80 are configured by programming the NVIC interrupt priority registers NVIC_IPRx, x = 0..20. Each register configures the priority of 4 interrupts. For the 8 bits used to configure the priority of an interrupt, only the upper 4 bits (bit 7 to bit 4) are implemented, and lower 4 bits are 0000. The contents of registers NVIC_IPRx, x = 0..20 are shown in Figure 5.5.

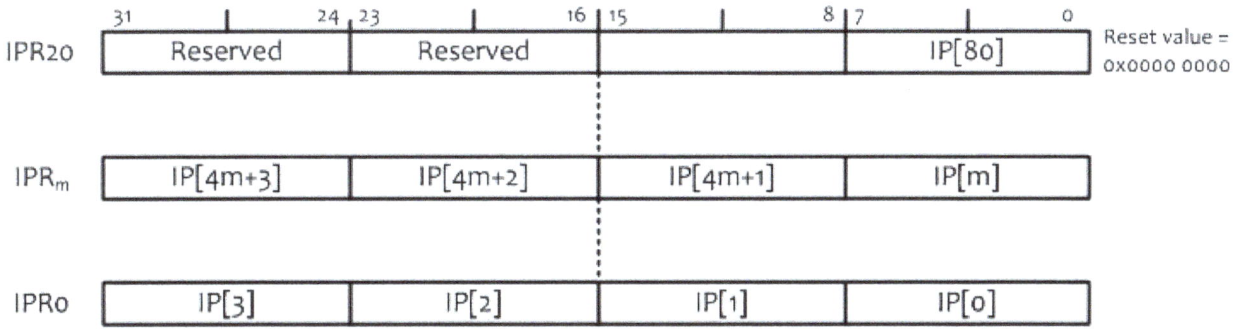

Bits[31:24]: Priority, byte offset 3
Bits[23:16]: Priority, byte offset 2
Bits[15:8]: Priority, byte offset 1
Bits[7:0]: Priority, byte offset 0
Only the upper 4 bits of each byte are implemented. The lower 4 bits are zero.

Figure 5.5 Interrupt priority register (NVIC_IPRx, x = 0..20)

5.9.6 INTERRUPT PRIORITY GROUPING

The Cortex-M4 provides the option for users to divide each interrupt priority register entry into two fields: upper field and lower field. The upper field defines the **group priority**, and the lower field defines a **subpriority** within the group.

Only group priority determines preemption of interrupt exceptions. When the processor is executing an interrupt service routine, another interrupt with the same group priority as the interrupt being serviced does not preempt the handler. If multiple pending interrupts have the same group priority, the subpriority field determines the order in which they are processed. The interrupt with the lowest IRQ number is serviced first.

The **application interrupt and reset control register (AIRCR)** determines the setting of group priority. The contents of the AIRCR register are shown in Figure 5.6.

31	30	29	28	27	26	25	24
VECTKEYSTAT[15:8](read)/VECTKEY[15:8](write)							

23	22	21	20	19	18	17	16
VECTKEYSTAT[7:0](read)/VECTKEY[7:0](write)							

15	14	13	12	11	10	9	8
ENDIAN NESS	--	--	--	--	PRIGROUP		

7	6	5	4	3	2	1	0
--	--	--	--	--	SYSRESET REQ	VECTCLR ACTIVE	VECT RESET

Reset value = 0xFA05 0000
Address offset = 0x0C

VECTKEYSTAT/VECTKEY[15:0]: register key
On writes, write **0x5FA** to **VECTKEY**, otherwise, the write is ignored.
ENDIANNESS: Data endianness bit
0: Little-endian 1: Big-endian
PRIGROUP: Interrupt priority grouping field
This field determines the split of group priority from subpriority. This field indicates the binary point that splits the PRI_n fields in the interrupt priority registers into separate group priority and subpriority fields. The split is shown in Table 5.2.
SYSRESETREQ: System reset request
This is intended to force a large system reset of all major components except the debug.
0: No system reset request
1: Asserts a signal to the outer system that requests a reset.
VECTCLRACTIVE: Reserved for debug use. Write a 0 to this bit. Othewise, behavior is unpredictable.
VECTRESET: Reserved for debug use. When write, write a 0 this bit.

Figure 5.6 Application interrupt and reset control register (AIRCR)

Table 5.2 STM32L475 Interrupt priority grouping

PRIGROUP [2:0]	Interrupt priority level value, PRI_N[7:4]			Number of	
	Binary point	Group Priority bits	Subpriority bits	Group priorities	Sub priorities
0b0xx	0bxxxx	[7:4]	None	16	None
0b100	0bxxx.y	[7:5]	[4]	8	2
0b101	0bxx.yy	[7:6]	[5:4]	4	4
0b110	0bx.yyy	[7]	[6:4]	2	8
0b111	0b.yyyy	None	[7:4]	None	16

5.10 Exception Entry and Return

Exception entry refers to the action that the processor starts to execute the service routine of a pending exception. **Exception return** refers to the action that the processor starts to finish up the exception service routine and returns to the interrupted program.

During the exception entry and return, the following events may occur:

Preemption. When the processor is executing an exception handler and another exception with a higher priority arrives, the processor will suspend the current exception handler and switch to execute the service routine of the new exception. This action is called **preemption**.

Return. When finishing the execution of an exception handler, the processor will return to the interrupted program if the following two conditions are satisfied:

1. There is no pending exception with enough priority to be serviced.
2. The completed exception handler was not handling a late-arriving exception. The processor pops the stack and restores the processor state to the state it had before the interrupt occurred.

Tail-chaining. On completion of an exception handler, if there is a pending exception that meets the requirements for exception entry (to be discussed later), the stack pop is skipped, and the processor starts to execute the new exception handler.

Late-arriving. If an exception with higher priority occurs during state-saving for a previous exception, the processor switches to handle the exception with higher priority and initiates the vector fetch for that exception. State-saving is not affected by late arrival because the state saved is the same for both exceptions. Therefore, the state-saving continues uninterrupted. The processor can accept a late-arriving exception until the first instruction of the exception handler of the original exception enters the execution stage of the processor. On return from the exception handler of the late-arriving exception, the normal tail-chaining rules apply.

5.10.1 EXCEPTION ENTRY

For the processor to start executing the service routine of a pending exception, the following conditions must hold:

- The pending exception has a priority higher than the limit set by the **BASEPRI** register (lowest 8 bits).
- One of the following two conditions is true:
  - ❖ The processor is in the Thread mode (not executing any exception handler).
  - ❖ The pending exception has higher priority than the exception being serviced—exception pre-emption occurs in this case.

When one exception preempts another, the exceptions are **nested**. When the processor takes an exception, unless the exception is **tail-chained** or **late-arriving**, the processor pushes information onto the current stack (this is also done when exception preemption occurs). This operation is called **stacking**. In this case, 8 (without floating-point storage) or 25 data words (with floating-point storage) are pushed into the stack. This data structure is called **stack frame**. A stack frame is *aligned* to a *double-word address*, i.e., the lowest three address bits are 000. The contents of a Cortex-M4 stack frame are shown in Figure 5.7.

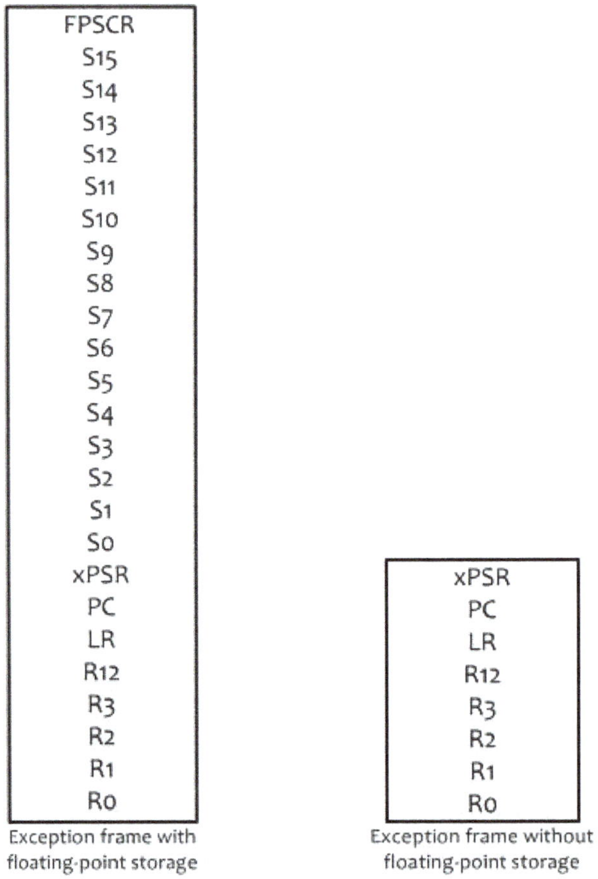

Figure 5.7 Cortex-M4 Stack frame layout

In parallel to the stacking operation, the processor performs a **vector fetch** that reads the starting address of the exception handler from the vector table. At the same time, the processor writes an **EXC_RETURN** value to **LR**. This value indicates which stack pointer corresponds to the stack frame and what operation mode the processor was in before the entry occurred. This enables the processor to recognize, when it finishes the execution of the exception handler, that it is time to return to the interrupted program and, hence, the previous process state must be restored.

If there is no occurrence of exception with higher priority during exception entry, the processor starts executing the exception handler and changes the pending interrupt (or exception) to active state.

If another exception with higher priority occurs during exception entry, the processor starts executing the exception handler for this exception and does not change the pending status of the earlier exception. This is the **late arrival** case.

5.10.2 EXCEPTION RETURN

Exception return occurs when the processor is in the **handler mode** and executes one of the following instructions to load **EXC_RETURN** value into the PC:

- An LDM or POP instruction that loads the PC
- An LDR instruction with PC as the destination
- A BX instruction using any register

EXC_RETURN is the value loaded into the LR register on exception entry. The processor relies on this value to detect when it has completed an exception handler. The lowest 5 bits of this value provide information on the return stack and processor mode. The possible values of EXC_RETURN are listed in Table 5.3.

Table 5.3 STM32L475 Exception return behavior

EXC_RETURN[31:0]	Description
0xFFFFFFF1	Return to Handler mode, exception return uses non-floating-point state from the MSP and execution uses MSP after return.
0xFFFFFFF9	Return to Thread mode, exception return uses non-floating-point state from the MSP and execution uses MSP after return.
0xFFFFFFFD	Return to Thread mode, exception return uses non-floating-point state from the PSP and execution uses PSP after return.
0xFFFFFFE1	Return to Handler mode, exception return uses floating-point state from MSP and execution uses MSP after return.
0xFFFFFFE9	Return to Thread mode, exception return uses floating-point state from MSP and execution uses MSP after return.
0xFFFFFFED	Return to Thread mode, exception return uses floating-point state from PSP and execution uses PSP after return.

5.11 Software-Triggered Interrupts

The Cortex-M4 allows the user to use software to trigger an interrupt by programming the STIR register. The contents of the STIR register are shown in Figure 5.8.

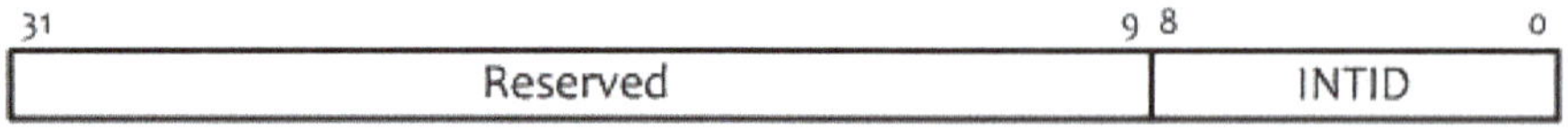

INTID: Interrupt ID of the interrupt to be triggered
  0-239: Interrupt ID to be triggered.
  others: Reserved

Figure 5.8 Software trigger interrupt register (STIR)

When the USERSETMPEND bit in the Configure and Control register (CCR) is set to 1, unprivileged software can access the STIR register. The contents of the CCR register are shown in Figure 5.9.

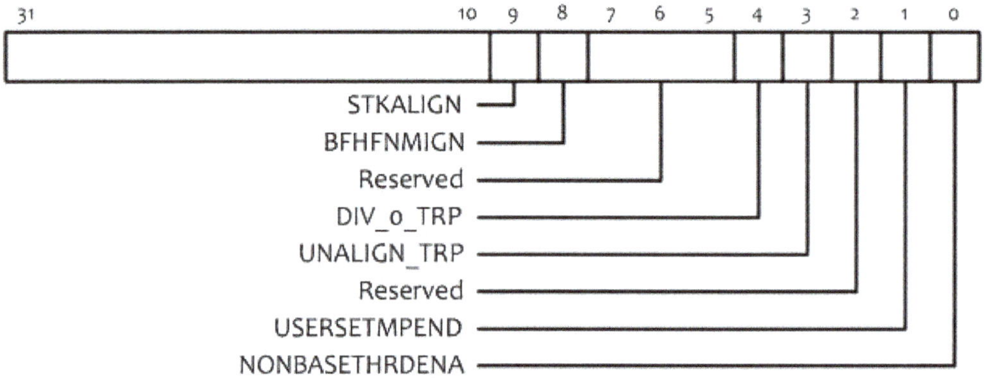

STKALIGN: stack alignment on exception entry
  0: 4-byte aligned   1: 8-byte aligned
BFHFNMIGN: Enables handlers with priority -1 or -2 to ignore data Bus faults caused by load & store
  0: data bus faults caused by load & store instructions cause a lock-up
  1: handlers running at priority -1 and -2 ignore data bus faults caused by load and store instructions
DIV_0_TRP: Enables faulting or halting when divide by 0 occurs during the SDIV or UDIV instruction execution.
  0: do not trap divide by 0   1: trap divide by 0
UNALIGN_TRP: Enables unaligned access traps (UsageFault)
  0: do not trap unaligned halfword and word access
  1: trap unaligned halfword and word access
  Unaligned LDM, STM, LDRD, and STRD instructions always fault irrespective of whether UNALIGN_TRP bit is set to 1.
USERSETMPEND: Enables unprivileged software access to the STIR register
  0: disable   1: enable
NONBASETHRDENA: Indicates how the processor enters Thread mode
  0: processor can enter Thread mode only when no exception is active.
  1: processor can enter Thread mode from any level under the control of an EXC_RETURN value.

Figure 5.9 Configuration and control register (CCR)

5.12 Fault Handling

A fault can be generated by the following causes:

- A bus error on (1) an instruction fetch or vector table load, or (2) a data access.
- An internally detected error such as an undefined instruction.
- Attempting to execute an instruction from a memory region marked as Non-Executable (XN).
- A privilege violation or an attempt to access an unmanaged region causing an MPU fault.

Faults that can be detected by the Cortex-M4 processor are listed in Table 5.4.

Table 5.4 Cortex-M4 Faults

Fault	Handler	Bit Name	Fault Status Register
Bus error on a vector read	Hard fault	VECTTBL	Hard fault status register (HFSR)
Fault escalated to a hard fault		FORCED	
MPU or default memory map mismatch:	MemManage	–	Memory management fault address register (MMFAR)
• on instruction access		IACCVIOL	
• on data access		DACCVIOL	
• during exception stacking		MSTKERR	
• during exception unstacking		MUNSTKERR	
• during lazy floating-point state preservation		MLSPERR	
Bus error:	Bus fault	–	Bus fault address register (BFAR)
• During exception stacking		STKERR	
• During exception unstacking		UNSTKERR	
• During instruction prefetch		IBUSERR	
• during lazy floating-point state preservation		LSPERR	
Precise data bus error		PRECISERR	
Imprecise data bus error		IMPRECISERR	
Attempt to access a coprocessor	Usage fault	NOCP	Configurable fault status register (CFSR; UFSR+BFSR+MMFSR)
Undefined instruction		UNDEFINSTR	
Attempt to enter an invalid instruction set state		INVSTATE	
Invalid EXC_RETURN value		INVPC	
Illegal unaligned load or store		UNALIGNED	
Divide by 0		DIVBYZERO	

5.12.1 FAULT ESCALATION AND HARD FAULTS

Faults with configurable priority can be disabled by programming the system handler control and state register (SHCSR). The contents of the SHCSR register are shown in Figure 5.10. The exception priority together with the values of the exception mask register determines whether the processor enters the fault handler and whether a fault handler can preempt another fault handler.

31	30	29	28	27	26	25	24
--	--	--	--	--	--	--	--
23	**22**	**21**	**20**	**19**	**18**	**17**	**16**
--	--	--	--	--	USG FAULTENA	BUS FAULTENA	MEM FAULTENA
15	**14**	**13**	**12**	**11**	**10**	**9**	**8**
SVCALL PENDED	BUSFAULT PENDED	MEMFAULT PENDED	USGFAULT PENDED	SYSTICK ACT	PENDSV ACT	--	MONITOR ACT
7	**6**	**5**	**4**	**3**	**2**	**1**	**0**
SVCALL ACT	--	--	--	USG FAULTACT	--	BUSFAULT ACT	MEMFAULT ACT

Reset value = 0x0000 0000
Address offset = 0x24

USGFAULTENA: Usage fault enable bit, set to 1 to enable
BUSFAULTENA: Bus fault enable bit, set to 1 to enable
MEMFAULTENA: Memory management fault enable bit, set to 1 to enable
SVCALLPENDED: SVC call pending bit, reads as 1 if exception is pending
BUSFAULTPENDED: Bus fault exception pending bit, reads as 1 if exception is pending
MEMFAULTPENDED: Memory management fault exception pending bit, read as 1 if exception is pending
USGFAULTPENDED: Usage fault exception pending bit, reads as 1 if exception is pending
SYSTICKACT: SysTick exception active bit, reads as 1 if exception is active
PENDSVACT: PendSV exception active bit, reads as 1 if exception is active
MONITORACT: Debug monitor active bit, reads as 1 is Debug monitor is active
SVCALLACT: SVC call active bit, reads as 1 if SVC call is active
USGFAULTACT: Usage fault exception active bit, reads as 1 if exception is active
BUSFAULTACT: Bus fault exception active bit, reads as 1 if exception is active
MEMFAULTACT: Memory management fault exception active bit, reads as 1 if exception is active

Figure 5.10 System handler control and state register (SHCSR)

In some situations, a fault with configurable priority is treated as a hard fault. This is called **priority escalation**. The fault is called **escalated to hard fault**. A fault is escalated to a hard fault when:

- A fault handler causes the same kind of fault as the one it is servicing. This escalation to hard fault occurs because a fault handler cannot preempt itself because it must have the same priority as the current priority level.
- A fault handler causes a fault with the same or lower priority as the fault it is servicing. This is because the handler for the new fault cannot preempt the currently executing fault handler.
- An exception handler causes a fault for which the priority is the same as or lower than the currently executing exception.
- A fault occurs and the handler for that fault is not enabled.

If a bus fault occurs during a stack push when entering a bus fault handler, the bus fault does not escalate to a hard fault. This means that if a corrupted stack causes a fault, the fault handler executes even though the stack push for the handler failed. The fault handler operates, but the stack contents are corrupted.

Only reset and NMI can preempt the fixed-priority hard fault. A hard fault can preempt any exception other than reset, NMI, or another hard fault.

5.12.2 FAULT STATUS REGISTERS AND FAULT ADDRESS REGISTERS

The fault status registers indicate the cause of a fault. For BusFaults and MemManage faults, the fault address register indicates the address accessed by the operation that caused the fault. Fault status registers and fault address registers are listed in Table 5.5.

Table 5.5 Fault status registers and fault address registers

Handler	Status register name	Address register name	Register Description
HardRFault	HFSR	--	Hard fault status register
MemManage	MMFSR		MemManage fault status register
		MMFAR	MemManage fault address register
BusFault	BFSR		Bus fault status register
		BSAR	Bus fault address register
UsageFault	UFSR	--	UsageFault status register

The contents of the HFSR, MMFSR, MMFAR, BFSR, BSAR, and UFSR registers are shown in Figure 5.11 to 5.16, respectively.

31	30	29	28	27	26	25	24
DEBUG_VT	FORCED	--	--	--	--	--	--
23	**22**	**21**	**20**	**19**	**18**	**17**	**16**
--	--	--	--	--	--	--	--
15	**14**	**13**	**12**	**11**	**10**	**9**	**8**
--	--	--	--	--	--	--	--
7	**6**	**5**	**4**	**3**	**2**	**1**	**0**
--	--	--	--	--	--	VECTTBL	--

Reset value = 0x0000 0000
Address offset = 0x2C

DEBUG_VT: Reserved for Debug use
When writing to the register you must write 0 to this bit to avoid causing problem.
FORCED: Forced hard fault
When this bit is 1, the hard fault handler must read the other fault status registers to find the cause of the hard fault.
0: No forced hard fault
1: Forced hard fault has occurred
VECTBL: Vector table hard fault
Indicates a bus fault on a vector table read during exception handling. This error is always handled by hard fault handler. When this bit is set to 1, the PC value stacked for the exception return points to the instruction that was preempted by the exception.
0: No bus fault on vector table read
1: Bus fault on vector table read

Figure 5.11 Hard fault status register (HFSR)

31	30	29	28	27	26	25	24
--	--	--	--	--	--	--	--
23	**22**	**21**	**20**	**19**	**18**	**17**	**16**
--	--	--	--	--	--	--	--
15	**14**	**13**	**12**	**11**	**10**	**9**	**8**
--	--	--	--	--	--	--	--
7	**6**	**5**	**4**	**3**	**2**	**1**	**0**
MMAR VALID	--	MLSP ERR	MSTK ERR	MUNSTK ERR	--	DACC VIOL	IACC VIOL

MMARVALID: Memory management fault address register (MMAR) valid flag. If a memory management fault occurs and is escalated to a hard fault because of priority, the hard fault handler must set this bit to 0 to prevent problems on returning to a stacked active memory management fault handler whose MMAR value is overwritten.
0: Value in MMAR is not a valid fault address
1: MMAR holds a valid fault address

MLSPERR: Memory fault on floating-point lazy state preservation
0: No management fault occurred during floating-point lazy state preservation
1: A MemManage fault occurred during floating-point lazy state preservation

MSTKERR: Memory manager fault on stacking for exception entry. When this bit is 1, the SP is still adjusted but the values in the context area on the stack might be incorrect. The processor has not written a fault address to the MMAR.
0: No stacking fault
1: Stacking for an exception entry has caused one or more access violations.

MUNSTKERR: Memory manager fault on unstacking for a return from exception.
0: No unstacking fault
1: Unstack for an exception return has caused one or more access violation

DACCVIOL: Data access violation flag.
0: No data access violation fault
1: The processor attempted a load or store at a location that does not permit the operation

IACCVIOL: Instruction access violation flag
0: No instruction access violation fault
1: The processor attempted an instruction fetch from a location that does not permit execution.

Figure 5.12 Memory management fault status register (MMFSR)

31	30	29	28	27	26	25	24
MMFAR[31:24]							
23	**22**	**21**	**20**	**19**	**18**	**17**	**16**
MMFAR[23:16]							
15	**14**	**13**	**12**	**11**	**10**	**9**	**8**
MMFAR[15:8]							
7	**6**	**5**	**4**	**3**	**2**	**1**	**0**
MMFAR[7:0]							

Reset value = undefined
Address offset = 0x34

MMFAR: Memory management fault address
When MMARVALID bit of the MMFSR register is set to 1, this field holds the address of the location that generated the memory management fault.
When an unaligned access faults, the address is the actual address that faulted. Because a single read or write instruction can be split into multiple aligned accesses, the fault address can be any address in the range of the requested access size.
Flags in MMFSR register indicate the cause of the fault, and whether the value in the MMFAR is valid.

Figure 5.13 Memory management fault address register (MMFAR)

31	30	29	28	27	26	25	24
--	--	--	--	--	--	--	--
23	22	21	20	19	18	17	16
--	--	--	--	--	--	--	--
15	14	13	12	11	10	9	8
BFARVALID	--	LSPERR	STKERR	UNSTKERR	IMPRECISERR	PRECISERR	IBUSERR
7	6	5	4	3	2	1	0
--	--	--	--	--	--	--	--

BFARVALID: Bus fault address register (BFAR) valid flag. The processor sets this flag to 1 after a bus fault where the address is known.
0: Value in BFAR value is not a valid fault address
1: BFAR holds a valid fault address
LSPERR: Bus fault on floating-point lazy state preservation
0: No bus fault occurred during floating-point lazy state preservation
1: A bus fault occurred during floating-point lazy state preservation
STKERR: Bus fault on stacking for exception entry. When the processor sets this bit to 1, the SP is still adjusted but the values in the context area on the stack might be incorrect. The processor does not write a fault address to the BFAR in this situation.
0: No stacking fault
1: Stacking for an exception entry has caused one or more bus fault.
UNSTKERR: Bus fault on unstacking for a return from exception.
0: No unstacking fault
1: Unstacking for an exception return has caused one or more bus faults.

Figure 5.14 Bus fault status register (BFSR)

31	30	29	28	27	26	25	24
--	--	--	--	--	--	--	--
23	22	21	20	19	18	17	16
--	--	--	--	--	--	--	--
15	14	13	12	11	10	9	8
BFARVALID	--	LSPERR	STKERR	UNSTKERR	IMPRECISERR	PRECISERR	IBUSERR
7	6	5	4	3	2	1	0
--	--	--	--	--	--	--	--

IMPRECISERR: Imprecise data bus error. When the processor sets this bit to 1, it does not write a fault address to the BFAR.
0: No precise data bus error
1: A data bus error has occurred, but the return address in the stack frame is not related to the instruction that caused the error.
PRECISERR: Precise data bus error. When the processor sets this bit to 1, it writes the faulting address to the BFAR.
0: No precise data bus error
1: A data bus error has occurred, and the PC value stacked for the exception return points to the instruction that caused the fault.
IBUSERR: Instruction bus error. The processor detects the instruction bus error on prefetching an instruction, but it sets the IBUSERR flag to 1 only if it attempts to issue the faulting instruction. When the processor sets this bit to 1, it does not write a fault address to the BFAR.
0: No instruction bus error
1: Instruction bus error

Figure 5.14a Bus fault status register (BFSR)—(continued)

31	30	29	28	27	26	25	24
BFAR[31:24]							
23	22	21	20	19	18	17	16
BFAR[23:16]							
15	14	13	12	11	10	9	8
BFAR[15:8]							
7	6	5	4	3	2	1	0
BFAR[7:0]							

BFAR: Bus fault address

When BFARVALID bit of the BFSR register is set to 1, this field holds the address of the location that generated the BusFault.

Flags in the BFSR register indicate the cause of the fault, and whether the value in the BFAR register is valid.

Figure 5.15 BusFault address register (BFAR)

31	30	29	28	27	26	25	24
--	--	--	--	--	--	DIVBYZERO	UNALIGNED
23	22	21	20	19	18	17	16
--	--	--	--	NOCP	INVPC	INVSTATE	UNDEFINSTR
15	14	13	12	11	10	9	8
--	--	--	--	--	--	--	--
7	6	5	4	3	2	1	0
--	--	--	--	--	--	--	--

DIVBYZERO: divide by zero usage fault

When this bit is 1, the stacked PC points to the instruction that perform divide by 0.

0: No divide by 0 fault, or divide by zero fault is disabled

1: The processor has executed an SDIV or UDIV instruction with a divisor of 0.

UNALIGNED: Unaligned access usage fault.

0: No unaligned access fault, or unaligned access trapping not enabled

1: The processor has made an unaligned memory access.

Unaligned access fault is enabled by setting the UNALIGN_TRP bit in the CCR register

NOCP: No coprocessor usage fault

0: No usage fault caused by attempting to access a coprocessor

1: The processor has attempted to access a coprocessor.

INVPC: Invalid PC load usage fault, caused by an invalid PC load by EXC_RETURN

When this bit is set to 1, the PC value stacked for the exception return points to the instruction that tried to perform the illegal load of the PC.

0: No invalid PC load usage fault

1: The processor has attempted an illegal load of EXC_RETURN to the PC, as a result of an invalid context, or an invalid EXC_RETURN value.

INVSTATE: Invalid state usage fault. When this bit is set to 1, the PC value stacked for the exception return points to the instruction that attempted the illegal use of EPSR.

0: No invalid state usage fault

1: Processor has attempted to execute an instruction that makes illegal use of EPSR.

UNDEFINSTR: Undefined instruction usage fault. When this bit is set to 1, the PC value stacked for the exception return points to an undefined instruction

0: No undefined instruction usage fault

1: The processor has attempted to execute an undefined instruction

Figure 5.16 Usage fault status register (UFSR)

The combination of UFSR, BFSR, and MMFSR is referred to as **configurable fault status register** (**CFSR**). The layout of CFSR is shown in Figure 5.17. The bit 31 to 13 contains the contents of the UFSR register. The bits 15 to 8 hold the contents of the BFSR register and the bits 7 to 0 hold the contents of the MMFSR register.

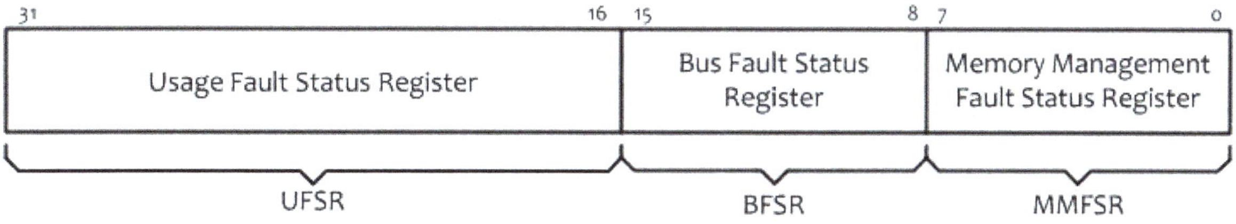

Figure 5.17 Configurable fault status register (CFSR; UFSR+BFSR+MMFSR)

5.12.3 LOCKUP

The processor enters a lockup state if a hard fault occurs when executing the NMI or hard-fault handler. In the lockup state, the processor does not execute any instructions. The processor remains in lockup state until either

- It is reset.
- An NMI occurs.
- It is halted by a debugger.

However, if a lockup state occurs from the NMI handler, a subsequent NMI does not cause the processor to leave the lockup state.

5.13 Interrupt Enabling and Disabling

In the Cortex-M4 processor, the interrupt enabling and disabling are done at three levels: global level, peripheral module level, and the individual interrupt source level.

5.13.1 GLOBAL-LEVEL INTERRUPT ENABLING/DISABLING

An interrupt is enabled only when the following three conditions are satisfied:

- Global-level interrupt is enabled.
- Peripheral module–level interrupt is enabled.
- Individual interrupt source is enabled.

If global interrupt is disabled, all interrupts are disabled. Executing the **CPSIE I** instruction enables interrupt globally. Executing the **CPSID I** instruction disables interrupt globally.

The ARM CMSIS library provides the following two functions to enable/disable interrupt globally (there are two underscore characters before **enable** and **disable**.):

```
void __disable_irq(void)        // disable interrupt globally
void __enable_irq(void)         // enable interrupt globally
```

5.13.2 PERIPHERAL MODULE-LEVEL INTERRUPT ENABLING AND DISABLING

The Cortex-M4 uses the **Nested Vectored Interrupt Controller** (**NVIC**) to handle all the interrupts. The NVIC uses registers NVIC->ISER0, NVIC->ISER1, and the bits 0 to 16 of the

NVIC->ISER2 to enable the interrupt from all peripherals. Setting a bit in these registers enables the interrupts from the corresponding peripheral.

The NVIC registers NVIC->ICER0, NVIC->ICER1, and the bits 0 to bit 16 of NVIC->ICER2 are used to disable the interrupts from all peripherals. Setting a bit in these registers disables the interrupts from the corresponding peripheral.

The NVIC registers NVIC->ISPR0, NVIC->ISPR1, and bits 0 to 16 of the NVIC->ISPR2 are used to set interrupt pending from all peripherals. Setting a bit in these registers places the interrupt from the corresponding peripheral at pending state.

The NVIC registers NVIC->ICPR0, NVIC->ICPR1, and bits 0 to 16 of NVIC->_ICPR2 are used to clear interrupt pending from all peripherals. Setting a bit in these registers clears the interrupt-pending state from the corresponding peripheral.

The NVIC registers NVIC->IABR0, NVIC->IABR1, and bits 0 to 16 of NVIC->IABR2 are used to indicate whether the interrupt of a certain peripheral is being serviced by the CPU (i.e., being in active state). A bit in these registers setting to 1 indicates that the interrupt of the corresponding peripheral is being serviced.

The NVIC registers NVIC->IPR0 to NVIC->IPR25 are used to set the interrupt priority of all peripherals. Every peripheral uses 8 bits in one of these registers to define its interrupt priority. The lower 4 bits of the priority value are all 0s. Therefore, the interrupt priority can only be 0, 16, 32, 48, 64, 80, 96, 112, 128, 144, 160, 176, 192, 208, 224, and 240.

The lowest 8 bits of the **NVIC->STIR** register indicate the interrupt identifier of the interrupt being serviced.

To simplify the task of enabling/disabling interrupts at the peripheral level and defining their priority levels, the **CMSIS library** provides **a set of functions** for the NVIC control. These functions are listed in Table 5.6.

Table 5.6 CMSIS functions for NVIC control

CMSIS interrupt control function	Description
void NVIC_SetPriorityGrouping (uint32_t priority_grouping)	Set priority grouping
void NVIC_EnableIRQ (IRQn_t IRQn)	Enable IRQn
void NVIC_DisableIRQ (IRQn_t IRQn)	Disable IRQn
uint32_t NVIC_GetPendingIRQ (IRQn_t IRQn)	Return true if IRQn is pending
void NVIC_SetPendingIRQ (IRQn_t IRQn)	Set IRQn pending
void NVIC_ClearPendingIRQ (IRQn_t IRQn)	Clear IRQn pending status
uint32_t NVIC_GetActive (IRQn_t IRQn)	Reads the pending status of interrupt or exception. This function returns a non-zero value if the pending status is set to 1.
void NVIC_SetPriority (IRQn_t IRQn, uint32_t priority)	Set priority for IRQn
uint32_t NVIC_GetPriority (IRQn_t IRQn)	Read priority of IRQn
void NVIC_SystemReset (void)	Reset the system

All except the first and last functions in Table 5.6 require the use of the IRQn number. The CMSIS library and the STM32L475xx.h header file together define all the IRQn numbers listed in Table 5.7.

Table 5.7 STM32L475xx IRQn interrupt numbers

IRQ name	IRQ number	IRQ name	IRQ number
NonMaskableInt_IRQn	-14	DMA_Channel5_IRQn	15
HardFault_IRQn	-13	DMA_Channel6_IRQn	16
MemoryManagement_IRQn	-12	DMA_Channel7_IRQn	17
BusFault_IRQn	-11	ADC1_2_IRQn	18
UsageFault_IRQn	-10	CAN1_TX_IRQn	19
SVCall_IRQn	-5	CAN1_RX0_IRQn	20
DebugMonitor_IRQn	-4	CAN1_RX1_IRQn	21
PendSV_IRQn	-2	CAN_SCE_IRQn	22
SysTick_IRQn	-1	EXTI9_5_IRQn	23
WWDG_IRQn	0	TIM1_BRK_TIM15_IRQn	24
PVD_PVM_IRQn	1	TIM1_UP_TIM16_IRQn	25
TAMP_STAMP_IRQn	2	TIM1_TRG_COM_TIM17_IRQn	26
RTC_WKUP_IRQn	3	TIM1_CC__IRQn	27
FLASH_IRQn	4	TIM2_IRQn	28
RCC_IRQn	5	TIM3_IRQn	29
EXTI0_IRQn	6	TIM4_IRQn	30
EXTI1_IRQn	7	I2C1_EV_IRQn	31
EXTI2_IRQn	8	I2C1_ER_IRQn	32
EXTI3_IRQn	9	I2C2_EV_IRQn	33
EXTI4_IRQn	10	I2C2_ER_IRQn	34
DMA1_Channel1_IRQn	11	SPI1_IRQn	35
DMA1_Channel2_IRQn	12	SPI2_IRQn	36
DMA1_Channel3_IRQn	13	USART1_IRQn	37
DMA1_Channel4_IRQn	14	USART2_IRQn	38

Table 5.7a STM32L475xx IRQn interrupt numbers—(continued)

IRQ name	IRQ number	IRQ name	IRQ number
USART3_IRQn	39	DMA2_Channel5_IRQn	60
EXTI15_10_IRQn	40	DFSDM1_FLT0_IRQn	61
RTC_Alarm_IRQn	41	DFSDM1_FLT1_IRQn	62
DFSD1_FLT3_IRQn	42	DFSDM1_FLT2_IRQn	63
TIM8_BRK_IRQn	43	COMP_IRQn	64
TIM8_UP_IRQn	44	LPTIM1_IRQn	65
TIM8_TRG_COM_IRQn	45	LPTIM2_IRQn	66
TIM8_CC_IRQn	46	OTG_FS_IRQn	67
ADC3_IRQn	47	DMA2_Channel6_IRQn	68
FMC_IRQn	48	DMA2_Channel7_IRQn	69
SDMMC1_IRQn	49	LPUART1_IRQn	70
TIM5_IRQn	50	QUADSPI_IRQn	71
SPI3_IRQn	51	I2C3_EV_IRQn	72
UART4_IRQn	52	I2C3_ER_IRQn	73
UART5_IRQn	53	SAI1_IRQn	74
TIM6_DAC_IRQn	54	SAI2_IRQn	75
TIM7_IRQn	55	SWPMI1_IRQn	76
DMA2_Channel1_IRQn	56	TSC_IRQn	77
DMA2_Channel2_IRQn	57	RNG_IRQn	80
DMA2_Channel3_IRQn	58	FPU_IRQn	81
DMA2_Channel4_IRQn	59		

5.13.3 INDIVIDUAL INTERRUPT SOURCE ENABLING

For most microcontrollers, each interrupt source has an associated status flag. The value of the status flag indicates whether the interrupt condition has occurred (become pending). ST is not consistent in dealing with interrupt status flags and enabling. Some peripherals (those with many interrupt sources) have a dedicated register to hold interrupt status flags and a dedicated register to hold interrupt enable bits. For other peripherals, interrupt flags and other status flags are stored in the same register, and the interrupt enable bits and other control bits are stored in the same control register.

To enable the interrupt at the source level, simply set the individual interrupt enable bit of interest. There is no dedicated CMSIS function to enable/disable individual interrupt source.

Example 5.1 Write a sequence of C statements to enable capture/compare 4 interrupt for timer 2 (TIM2) of the STM32L475. Setting the CC4IE4 bit in the TIM2->DIER register enables this interrupt at the source level.

Solution:

The following C statements enable the CC4 interrupt for timer 2:

```
TIM2->DIER |= TIM_DIER_CC4IE;        // enable CC4 interrupt—source level
```

```
NVIC_EnableIRQ(TIM2_IRQn);        // enable TIM2 interrupt—peripheral
__enable_irq();                   // enable interrupt globally
```

5.14 Writing Interrupt Service Routines

Keil µVision IDE provides an empty handling routine for each exception. The names of the STM32L475 exception service routines are defined in the startup file **startup_stm32l475xx.s**. The pointers to these service routines are stored in the vector table when the program is downloaded into the flash memory of the STM32L475 device. The user needs only to add the name of the handler to their program and enter the appropriate C statements into the empty service routine. These service handlers are listed in Table 5.8.

Table 5.8 STM32L475xx interrupt service routines

Name of Exception service routine	Name of exception service routine
void WWDG_IRQHandler (void);	void TIM1_UP_TIM16_IRQHandler (void);
void PVD_PVM_IRQHandler (void);	void TIM1_TRG_COM_TIM17_IRQHandler (void);
void TAMP_STAMP_IRQHandler (void);	void TIM1_CC_IRQHandler (void);
void RTC_WKUP_IRQHandler (void);	void TIM2_IRQHandler (void);
void FLASH_IRQHandler (void);	void TIM3_IRQHandler (void);
void RCC_IRQHandler (void);	void TIM4_IRQHandler (void);
void EXTI0_IRQHandler (void);	void I2C1_EV_IRQHandler (void);
void EXTI1_IRQHandler (void);	void I2C1_ER_IRQHandler (void);
void EXTI2_IRQHandler (void);	void I2C2_EV_IRQHandler (void);
void EXTI3_IRQHandler (void);	void I2C2_ER_IRQHandler (void);
void EXTI4_IRQHandler (void);	void SPI1_IRQHandler (void);
void DMA1_Channel1_IRQHandler (void);	void SPI2_IRQHandler (void);
void DMA1_Channel2_IRQHandler (void);	void USART1_IRQHandler (void);
void DMA1_Channel3_IRQHandler (void);	void USART2_IRQHandler (void);
void DMA1_Channel4_IRQHandler (void);	void USART3_IRQHandler (void);
void DMA1_Channel5_IRQHandler (void);	void EXT15_10_IRQHandler (void);
void DMA1_Channel6_IRQHandler (void);	void RTC_Alarm_IRQHandler (void);
void DMA1_Channel7_IRQHandler (void);	void DFSDM1_FLT3_IRQHandler (void);
void ADC1_2_IRQHandler (void);	void TIM8_BRK_IRQHandler (void);
void CAN1_TX_Channel2_IRQHandler (void);	void TIM8_UP_IRQHandler (void);
void CAN1_RX0_IRQHandler (void);	void TIM8_TRK_COM_IRQHandler (void);
void CAN1_RX1_IRQHandler (void);	void TIM8_CC_IRQHandler (void);
void CAN1_SCE_IRQHandler (void);	void ADC3_IRQHandler (void);
void EXTI9_5_IRQHandler (void);	void FMC_IRQHandler (void);
void TIM1_BRK_TIM15_IRQHandler (void);	void SDMMC1_IRQHandler (void);

Table 5.8a STM32L475xx interrupt service routines—(continued)

Name of Exception service routine	Name of exception service routine
void TIM5_IRQHandler (void);	void LPTIM1_IRQHandler (void);
void SPI3_IRQHandler (void);	void LPTIM2_IRQHandler (void);
void UART4_IRQHandler (void);	void OTG_FS_IRQHandler (void);
void UART5_IRQHandler (void);	void DMA2_Channel6_IRQHandler (void);
void TIM6_DAC_IRQHandler (void);	void DMA2_Channel7_IRQHandler (void);
void TIM7_IRQHandler (void);	void LPUART1_IRQHandler (void);
void DMA2_Channel1_IRQHandler (void);	void QUADSPI_IRQHandler (void);
void DMA2_Channel2_IRQHandler (void);	void I2C3_EV_IRQHandler (void);
void DMA2_Channel3_IRQHandler (void);	void I2C3_ER_IRQHandler (void);
void DMA2_Channel4_IRQHandler (void);	void SAI1_IRQHandler (void);
void DMA2_Channel5_IRQHandler (void);	void SAI2_IRQHandler (void);
void DFSDM1_FLT0_IRQHandler (void);	void SWPMI1_IRQHandler (void);
void DFSDM1_FLT1_IRQHandler (void);	void TSC_IRQHandler (void);
void DFSDM1_FLT2_IRQHandler (void);	void RNG_IRQHandler (void);
void COMP_IRQHandler (void);	void FPU_IRQHandler (void);

Example 5.2 Write an interrupt service routine for the TIM2 interrupt, which simply increments the global variable **count** by 1 and outputs it to PORTB pins. If count is 10, then resets it to 0.

Solution:

```
void TIM2_IRQHandler (void)
{
    count++;
    GPIO->ODR = count;
    if (count == 10)
        count = 0;
}
```

5.15 Power Management

The sleep modes of the Cortex-M4 and the STM32L475 processors reduce power consumption. There are two sleep modes:

- Sleep mode. The processor clock stops. All other system and peripheral clocks may still be running.
- Deep sleep mode. This mode stops most of the STM32 system and peripheral clocks. At product level, this corresponds to either the Stop or the Standby mode.

5.15.1 ENTERING THE SLEEP MODE

Software can put the processor into sleep mode by executing one of the two instructions:

- **Wait for interrupt** (WFI). When the processor executes this instruction, it stops executing instructions and enters sleep mode immediately.
- **Wait for event** (WFE). When the processor executes this instruction, it checks the value of the event register and takes different actions depending on the value of the event register:
  - 0: The processor stops executing instructions and enters sleep mode.
  - 1: The processor clears the register to 0 and continues executing instructions without entering sleep mode. This is because an external event signal is asserted or a processor in the system has executed an SEV instruction.

5.15.2 SLEEP ON EXIT

When completing the execution of an exception handler and the SLEEPONEXIT bit of the system control register (SCB->SCR) is set to 1, the processor returns to the Thread mode immediately and enters sleep mode. The contents of the SCB->SCR register are shown in Figure 5.18.

31	30	29	28	27	26	25	24
–	–	–	–	–	–	–	–
23	**22**	**21**	**20**	**19**	**18**	**17**	**16**
–	–	–	–	–	–	–	–
15	**14**	**13**	**12**	**11**	**10**	**9**	**8**
–	–	–	–	–	–	–	–
7	**6**	**5**	**4**	**3**	**2**	**1**	**0**
–	–	–	SEVON PEND	–	SLEEP DEEP	SLEEP ON EXIT	–

Offset = 0x10
Reset value = 0x0000 0000

SEVONPEND: Send event on pending bit

When an event or interrupt enters pending state, the event signal wakes up the processor from WFE. If the processor is not waiting for an event, the event is registered and affects the next WFE. Processor also wakes up on execution of an SEV instruction or an external event

0: Only enabled interrupts or events can wakeup the processor, disabled interrupts are excluded.

1: Enabled events and all interrupts, including disabled interrupts, can wakeup the processor.

SLEEPDEEP:

0: Sleep 1: Deep sleep

SLEEPONEXIT:

Setting this bit to 1 enables an interrupt-driven application to avoid returning to an empty main application.

0: Do not sleep when returning to Thread mode

1: Enter sleep, or deep sleep mode, on returning from interrupt service routine.

Figure 5.18 System control register (SCR)

The CMSIS provides the following two library functions for invoking the WFE and WFI instructions:

void __WFE (void) // wait for exception

void __WFI (void) // wait for interrupt

5.16 Extended Interrupts and Events Controller (EXTI)

The extended interrupts and events controller (EXTI) manages 40 lines that can be programmed to generate interrupts to the processor or generate events to wake up the processor from Sleep/Stop mode. Among these 40 lines, 26 of them are configurable and the other 16 are direct lines. GPIOs are connected to 16 configurable interrupt/event lines. The other lines are connected to internal peripherals. The EXTI lines connections are shown in Table 5.9.

Table 5.9 EXTI lines connections

EXTI line	Line source(1)	Line type
0 -- 15	GPIO(1)	configurable
16	PVD(1)	configurable
17	OTG_FS wakeup event(2)	direct
18	RTC alarms(1)	configurable
19	RTC tamper or timestamp or CSS_LSE(1)	configurable
20	RTC wakeup timer(1)	configurable
21	COMP1 output(1)	configurable
22	COMP2 output(1)	configurable
23	I2C1 wakeup(2)	direct
24	I2C2 wakeup(2)	direct
25	I2C3 wakeup(1)	direct
26	USART1 wakeup(2)	direct
27	USART2 wakeup(2)	direct
28	USART3 wakeup(2)	direct
29	UART4 wakeup(2)	direct
30	UART5 wakeup(2)	direct
31	LPUART1 wakeup(1)	direct
32	LPTIM1(1)	direct
33	LPTIM2(2)	direct
34	SWPMI1 wakeup(2)	direct
35	PVM1 wakeup(1)	configurable
36	PVM2 wakeup(1)	configurable
37	PVM3 wakeup(1)	configurable
38	PVM4 wakeup(1)	configurable
39	--	--

Note. 1. This line can wake up the processor from Stop 0, Stop 1, and Stop 2 mode.
2. This line cannot wake up the processor from Stop 2 mode

5.16.1 TYPES OF EXTI LINES

There are two types of EXTI lines:

- **Configurable EXTI line**. A configurable EXTI line's active edge can be chosen independently, and a status flag indicates the source of the interrupt. Configurable lines are used by the GPIO external interrupts and by a few peripherals.
- **Direct EXTI line**. A direct EXTI line is used by some peripherals to generate a wakeup from Stop event or interrupt. The status flag is provided by the peripheral.

Each line can be enabled/disabled independently for an interrupt or an event generation. A **configurable interrupt line** should be configured and enabled to generate an interrupt. This is done by programming the two trigger selection registers with the desired edge detection and by enabling the interrupt request by setting the corresponding bit in the interrupt mask register. When the selected edge occurs on the interrupt line, an interrupt request is generated. The pending bit corresponding to the interrupt is also set.

5.16.2 CONFIGURING EXTI LINES FOR INTERRUPT REQUESTS

To use an EXTI line to generate interrupts, the user is required to perform the following operations:

- Configure the active edge of the EXTI line. Setting a bit in one of the rising edge trigger registers (EXTI->RTSR1 or EXTI->RTSR2 register) allows the rising edge of the corresponding EXTI line to generate an interrupt. Setting a bit in one of the falling edge trigger registers (EXTI->FTSR1 or EXTI->FTSR2 register) allows the falling edge of the corresponding EXTI line to generate an interrupt.
- Set the corresponding bit in the interrupt mask register 1 (EXTI->IMR1) or interrupt mask register 2 (EXTI->IMR2).
- Set the enable bit of the corresponding EXTI line in one of the NVIC->ISERx (x = 0, 1, or 2) registers or call the NVIC_EnableIRQ () function to enable interrupt. From Table 5.7, we know that only 16 EXTI lines can generate interrupts. Only 7 interrupt vectors are assigned to the EXTI interrupts. Only GPIO pins can generate interrupts.
- Enable interrupt globally by calling the **__enable_irq()** function.

When the selected edge occurs on the EXTI line, the pending bit (in EXTI_PR1 & EXTI_PR2) corresponding to the interrupt line is also set. The pending bit can be cleared by writing a 1 to it. The contents of the EXTI->RTSR1, EXTI->RTSR2, EXTI->FTSR1, EXTI->FTSR2, EXTI->IMR1, EXTI->IMR2, EXTI->PR1, and EXTI->PR2 registers are shown in Figures 5.19 to 5.26.

31	30	29	28	27	26	25	24
--	--	--	--	--	--	--	--
23	22	21	20	19	18	17	16
--	RT22	RT21	RT20	RT19	RT18	--	RT16
15	14	13	12	11	10	9	8
RT15	RT14	RT13	Rt12	RT11	RT10	RT9	RT8
7	6	5	4	3	2	1	0
RT7	RT6	RT5	RT4	RT3	RT2	RT1	RT0

Offset = 0x08
Reset value = 0x0000 0000

RTx: Rising trigger event configuration bit of line x (x = 22 to 18 or x = 16 to 0)
0: Rising trigger disabled (for event and interrupt) for input line x
1: Rising trigger enabled (for event and interrupt) for input line x
Rising and falling edge triggers can be set for the same interrupt line. In this case, both generate a trigger condition.

Figure 5.19 Rising trigger selection register 1 (EXTI->RTSR1)

31	30	29	28	27	26	25	24
--	--	--	--	--	--	--	--
23	22	21	20	19	18	17	16
--	--	--	--	--	--	--	--
15	14	13	12	11	10	9	8
--	--	--	--	--	--	--	--
7	6	5	4	3	2	1	0
--	RT38	RT37	RT36	RT35	--	--	--

Offset = 0x28
Reset value = 0x0000 0000

RTx: Rising trigger event configuration bit of line x (x = 38 to 35)
0: Rising trigger disabled (for event and interrupt) for input line x
1: Rising trigger enabled (for event and interrupt) for input line x
Rising and falling edge triggers can be set for the same interrupt line. In this case, both generate a trigger condition.

Figure 5.20 Rising trigger selection register 2 (EXTI->RTSR2)

31	30	29	28	27	26	25	24
--	--	--	--	--	--	--	--
23	22	21	20	19	18	17	16
--	FT22	FT21	FT20	FT19	FT18	--	FT16
15	14	13	12	11	10	9	8
FT15	FT14	FT13	FT12	FT11	FT10	FT9	FT8
7	6	5	4	3	2	1	0
FT7	FT6	FT5	FT4	FT3	FT2	FT1	FT0

Offset = 0x0C
Reset value = 0x0000 0000

FTx: Falling trigger event configuration bit of line x (x = 22 to 18 or x = 16 to 0)
0: Falling trigger disabled (for event and interrupt) for input line x
1: Falling trigger enabled (for event and interrupt) for input line x
Rising and falling edge triggers can be set for the same interrupt line. In this case, both generate a trigger condition.

Figure 5.21 Falling trigger selection register 1 (EXTI->FTSR1)

31	30	29	28	27	26	25	24
–	–	–	–	–	–	–	–
23	22	21	20	19	18	17	16
–	–	–	–	–	–	–	–
15	14	13	12	11	10	9	8
–	–	–	–	–	–	–	–
7	6	5	4	3	2	1	0
–	FT38	FT37	FT36	FT35	–	–	–

Offset = 0x2C
Reset value = 0x0000 0000

FTx: Falling trigger event configuration bit of line x (x = 35 to 38)
0: Falling trigger disabled (for event and interrupt) for input line x
1: Falling trigger enabled (for event and interrupt) for input line x
Rising and falling edge triggers can be set for the same interrupt line. In this case, both generate a trigger condition.

Figure 5.22 Rising trigger selection register 2 (EXTI->FTSR2)

31	30	29	28	27	26	25	24
IM31	IM30	IM29	IM28	IM27	IM26	IM25	IM24
23	22	21	20	19	18	17	16
IM23	IM22	IM21	IM20	IM19	IM18	IM17	IM16
15	14	13	12	11	10	9	8
IM15	IM14	IM13	IM12	IM11	IM10	IM9	IM8
7	6	5	4	3	2	1	0
IM7	IM6	IM5	IM4	IM3	IM2	IM1	IM0

Offset = 0x00
Reset value = 0xFF82 0000

IMx: Interrupt mask on line x (x = 31 to 0)
0: Interrupt request from line x is masked
1: Interrupt request from line x is not masked
The reset value for direct lines (line 17, lines from 23 to 34, line 39) is set to '1' in order to enable the interrupt by default

Figure 5.23 Interrupt mask register 1 (EXTI->IMR1)

31	30	29	28	27	26	25	24
–	–	–	–	–	–	–	–
23	22	21	20	19	18	17	16
–	–	–	–	–	–	–	–
15	14	13	12	11	10	9	8
–	–	–	–	–	–	–	IM40
7	6	5	4	3	2	1	0
IM39	IM38	IM37	IM36	IM35	IM34	IM33	IM32

Offset = 0x20
Reset value = 0x0000 0087

IMx: Interrupt mask on line x (x = 40 to 32)
0: Interrupt request from line x is masked
1: Interrupt request from line x is not masked
The reset value for direct lines (line 17, lines from 23 to 34, line 39) is set to '1' in order to enable the interrupt by default. IM40 is only available in STM32L496xx/4A6xx devices.

Figure 5.24 Interrupt mask register 2 (EXTI->IMR2)

31	30	29	28	27	26	25	24
--	--	--	--	--	--	--	--
23	**22**	**21**	**20**	**19**	**18**	**17**	**16**
--	PIF22	PIF21	PIF20	PIF19	PIF18	--	PIF16
15	**14**	**13**	**12**	**11**	**10**	**9**	**8**
PIF15	PIF14	PIF13	PIF12	PIF11	PIF10	PIF9	PIF8
7	**6**	**5**	**4**	**3**	**2**	**1**	**0**
PIF7	PIF6	PIF5	PIF4	PIF3	PIF2	PIF1	PIF0

Offset = 0x14
Reset value = undefined

PIFx: Pending interrupt flag on line x (x = 22 to 18 or x = 16 to 0)
0: No trigger request occurred on input line x
1: Selected trigger request occurred on input line x
This bit is set to 1 when the selected edge event arrives on the interrupt line. This bit is cleared by writing a '1' to it.

Figure 5.25 Pending register 1 (EXTI->PR1)

31	30	29	28	27	26	25	24
--	--	--	--	--	--	--	--
23	**22**	**21**	**20**	**19**	**18**	**17**	**16**
--	--	--	--	--	--	--	--
15	**14**	**13**	**12**	**11**	**10**	**9**	**8**
--	--	--	--	--	--	--	--
7	**6**	**5**	**4**	**3**	**2**	**1**	**0**
--	PIF38	PIF37	PIF36	PIF35	--	--	--

Offset = 0x34
Reset value = undefined

PIFx: Pending interrupt flag on line x (x = 38 to 35)
0: No trigger request occurred on input line x
1: Selected trigger request occurred on input line x
This bit is set when the selected edge event arrives on the interrupt line. This bit is cleared by writing a '1' to it.

Figure 5.26 Pending register 2 (EXTI->PR2)

5.16.3 CONFIGURE EXTI LINES FOR EVENT GENERATION

To generate events using the EXTI line, the user is required to take the following actions:

- Program the EXTI->RTSR1 (or EXTI->RTSR2) register to select the rising edge or program the EXTI->FTSR1 (or EXTI->FTSR2) register to select the falling edge.
- Program the corresponding event mask bit in the EXTI->EMR1 (or EXTI->EMR2) register to enable event generation.

The pending bit corresponding to the EXTI line won't be set. The events associated with the direct lines are triggered only when the system is in Stop mode. If the system is still running, no event is generated by the EXTI.

The contents of the EXTI->EMR1 and EXTI->EMR2 registers are shown in Figure 5.27 and 5.28.

31	30	29	28	27	26	25	24
EM31	EM30	EM29	EM28	EM27	EM26	EM25	EM24
23	**22**	**21**	**20**	**19**	**18**	**17**	**16**
EM23	EM22	EM21	EM20	EM19	EM18	EM17	EM16
15	**14**	**13**	**12**	**11**	**10**	**9**	**8**
EM15	EM14	EM13	EM12	EM11	EM10	EM9	EM8
7	**6**	**5**	**4**	**3**	**2**	**1**	**0**
EM7	EM6	EM5	EM4	EM3	EM2	EM1	EM0

Offset = 0x04
Reset value = 0x0000 0000

EMx: Event mask on line x (x = 31 to 0)
0: Event request from line x is masked
1: Event request from line x is not masked

Figure 5.27 Event mask register 1 (EXTI->EMR1)

31	30	29	28	27	26	25	24
--	--	--	--	--	--	--	--
23	**22**	**21**	**20**	**19**	**18**	**17**	**16**
--	--	--	--	--	--	--	--
15	**14**	**13**	**12**	**11**	**10**	**9**	**8**
--	--	--	--	--	--	--	EM40
7	**6**	**5**	**4**	**3**	**2**	**1**	**0**
EM39	EM38	EM37	EM36	EM35	EM34	EM33	EM32

Offset = 0x24
Reset value = 0x0000 0000

EMx: Event mask on line x (x = 40 to 32)
0: Event request from line x is masked
1: Event request from line x is not masked

Figure 5.28 Event mask register 2 (EXTI->EMR2)

5.16.4 GENERATING EXTI LINES INTERRUPT/EVENT USING SOFTWARE

An EXTI line interrupt or event can also be triggered using the software. To use the software to trigger an interrupt or event via an EXTI line, the user is required to take the following actions:

- Program the appropriate mask register (EXTI->IMR1 & EXTI->IMR2 for interrupt request and EXTI->EMR1 & EXTI->EMR2 for event generation).
- Enable the EXTI line interrupt by calling the **NVIC_EnableIRQ** () function.
- Enable interrupt globally by calling **__enable_irq** ().
- Set the corresponding enable bit in the EXTI->SWIER1 or EXTI->SWIER2 register.

The contents of the EXTI->SWIER1 and EXTI->SWIER2 registers are shown in Figure 5.29 and 5.30, respectively.

31	30	29	28	27	26	25	24
--	--	--	--	--	--	--	--
23	**22**	**21**	**20**	**19**	**18**	**17**	**16**
--	SWI22	SWI21	SWI20	SWI19	SWI18	--	SWI16
15	**14**	**13**	**12**	**11**	**10**	**9**	**8**
SWI15	SWI14	SWI13	SWI12	SWI11	SWI10	SWI9	SWI8
7	**6**	**5**	**4**	**3**	**2**	**1**	**0**
SWI7	SWI6	SWI5	SWI4	SWI3	SWI2	SWI1	SWI0

Offset = 0x10
Reset value =
0x0000 0000

SWIx: Software interrupt on line x (x = 22 to 18 or x = 16 to 0)
If the interrupt is enabled on this line in the EXTI_IMR register, writing a '1' to this bit when it is '0' sets the corresponding pending bit in the EXTI_PR register resulting in an interrupt request generation.
This bit is cleared by writing a '1' to the corresponding bit in the EXTI_PR register.

Figure 5.29 Software interrupt event register 1 (EXTI->SWIER1)

31	30	29	28	27	26	25	24
--	--	--	--	--	--	--	--
23	**22**	**21**	**20**	**19**	**18**	**17**	**16**
--	--	--	--	--	--	--	--
15	**14**	**13**	**12**	**11**	**10**	**9**	**8**
--	--	--	--	--	--	--	--
7	**6**	**5**	**4**	**3**	**2**	**1**	**0**
--	SWI38	SWI37	SWI36	SWI35	--	--	--

Offset = 0x30
Reset value =
0x0000 0000

SWIx: Software interrupt on line x (x = 35 to 38)
If the interrupt is enabled on this line in EXTI_IMR, writing a '1' to this bit when it is '0' sets the corresponding pending bit of EXTI_PR resulting in an interrupt request generation. This bit is cleared by writing a '1' to the corresponding bit in the EXTI_PR register.

Figure 5.30 Software interrupt event register 2 (EXTI->SWIER2)

5.16.5 GPIO PINS AND EXTI INTERRUPT/EVENT LINE MAPPING

The GPIO pins are connected to the first 16 EXTI lines (all are configurable). The same numbered GPIO port pins share the same EXTI line. They are selected via the **SYSCFG external interrupt configuration register** 1 to 4 (**SYSCFG->EXTICR1** to **SYSCFG->EXTICR4**). The mapping from GPIO pins to EXTI lines is illustrated in Figure 5.31. The contents of SYSCFG->EXTICR1 and SYSCFG->EXTICR4 are shown in Figures 5.32 to 5.35, respectively.

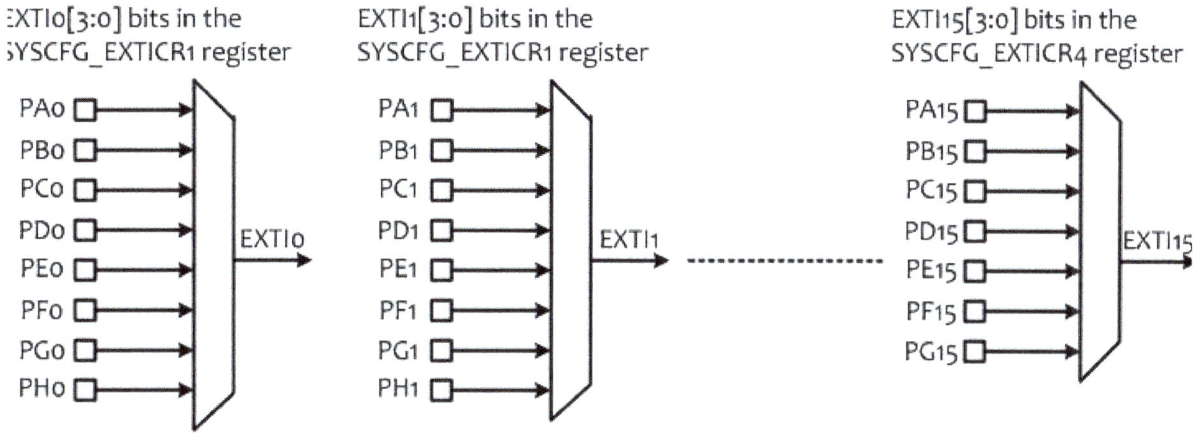

Figure 5.31 STM32L475 external Interrupt/Event GPIO Mapping

31	30	29	28	27	26	25	24
--	--	--	--	--	--	--	--
23	**22**	**21**	**20**	**19**	**18**	**17**	**16**
--	--	--	--	--	--	--	--
15	**14**	**13**	**12**	**11**	**10**	**9**	**8**
--	EXTI3[2:0]			--	EXTI2[2:0]		
7	**6**	**5**	**4**	**3**	**2**	**1**	**0**
--	EXTI1[2:0]			--	EXTI0[2:0]		

Offset = 0x08
Reset value = 0x0000 0000

EXTI3[2:0]: EXTI3 configuration bits
000: PA[3] pin; 001: PB[3] pin
010: PC[3] pin; 011: PD[3] pin
100: PE[3] pin; 101: PF[3] pin
110: PG[3] pin; 111: reserved

EXTI2[2:0]: EXTI2 configuration bits
000: PA[2] pin; 001: PB[2] pin
010: PC[2] pin; 011: PD[2] pin
100: PE[2] pin; 101: PF[2] pin
110: PG[2] pin; 111: reserved

EXTI1[2:0]: EXTI1 configuration bits
000: PA[1] pin; 001: PB[1] pin
010: PC[1] pin; 011: PD[1] pin
100: PE[1] pin; 101: PF[1] pin
110: PG[1] pin; 111: PH[0]

EXTI0[2:0]: EXTI0 configuration bits
000: PA[0] pin; 001: PB[0] pin
010: PC[0] pin; 011: PD[0] pin
100: PE[0] pin; 101: PF[0] pin
110: PG[0] pin; 111: PH[0]

Figure 5.32 SYSCFG external interrupt configuration register 1 (SYSCFG->EXTICR1)

31	30	29	28	27	26	25	24
--	--	--	--	--	--	--	--
23	**22**	**21**	**20**	**19**	**18**	**17**	**16**
--	--	--	--	--	--	--	--
15	**14**	**13**	**12**	**11**	**10**	**9**	**8**
--	EXTI7[2:0]			--	EXTI6[2:0]		
7	**6**	**5**	**4**	**3**	**2**	**1**	**0**
--	EXTI5[2:0]			--	EXTI4[2:0]		

Offset = 0x0C
Reset value = 0x0000 0000

EXTI7[2:0]: EXTI7 configuration bits
000: PA[7] pin; 001: PB[7] pin
010: PC[7] pin; 011: PD[7] pin
100: PE[7] pin; 101: PF[7] pin
110: PG[7] pin; 111: reserved

EXTI6[2:0]: EXTI6 configuration bits
000: PA[6] pin; 001: PB[6] pin
010: PC[6] pin; 011: PD[6] pin
100: PE[6] pin; 101: PF[6] pin
110: PG[6] pin; 111: reserved

EXTI5[2:0]: EXTI5 configuration bits
000: PA[5] pin; 001: PB[5] pin
010: PC[5] pin; 011: PD[5] pin
100: PE[5] pin; 101: PF[5] pin
110: PG[5] pin; 111: reserved

EXTI4[2:0]: EXTI4 configuration bits
000: PA[4] pin; 001: PB[4] pin
010: PC[4] pin; 011: PD[4] pin
100: PE[4] pin; 101: PF[4] pin
110: PG[4] pin; 111: reserved

Figure 5.33 SYSCFG external interrupt configuration register 2 (SYSCFG->EXTICR2)

31	30	29	28	27	26	25	24
--	--	--	--	--	--	--	--
23	**22**	**21**	**20**	**19**	**18**	**17**	**16**
--	--	--	--	--	--	--	--
15	**14**	**13**	**12**	**11**	**10**	**9**	**8**
--	EXTI11[2:0]			--	EXTI10[2:0]		
7	**6**	**5**	**4**	**3**	**2**	**1**	**0**
--	EXTI9[2:0]			--	EXTI8[2:0]		

Offset = 0x10
Reset value = 0x0000 0000

EXTI11[2:0]: EXTI11 configuration bits
000: PA[11] pin; 001: PB[11] pin
010: PC[11] pin; 011: PD[11] pin
100: PE[11] pin; 101: PF[11] pin
110: PG[11] pin; 111: reserved

EXTI10[2:0]: EXTI10 configuration bits
000: PA[10] pin; 001: PB[10] pin
010: PC[10] pin; 011: PD[10] pin
100: PE[10] pin; 101: PF[10] pin
110: PG[10] pin; 111: reserved

EXTI9[2:0]: EXTI9 configuration bits
000: PA[9] pin; 001: PB[9] pin
010: PC[9] pin; 011: PD[9] pin
100: PE[9] pin; 101: PF[9] pin
110: PG[9] pin; 111: reserved

EXTI8[2:0]: EXTI8 configuration bits
000: PA[8] pin; 001: PB[8] pin
010: PC[8] pin; 011: PD[8] pin
100: PE[8] pin; 101: PF[8] pin
110: PG[8] pin; 111: reserved

Figure 5.34 SYSCFG external interrupt configuration register 3 (SYSCFG->EXTICR3)

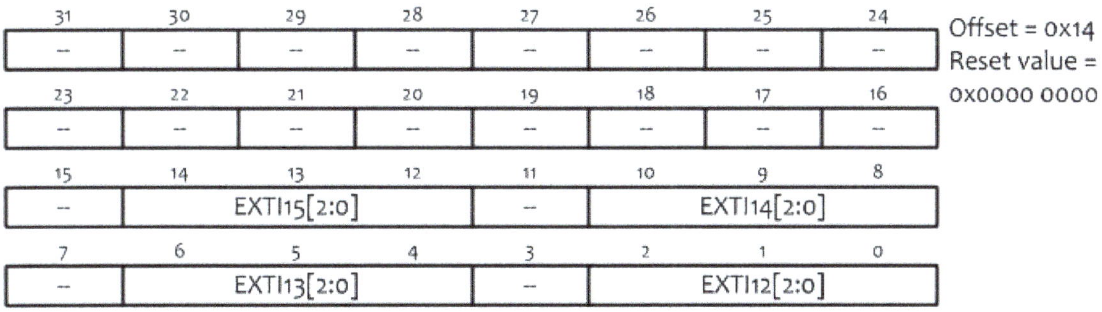

EXTI15[2:0]: EXTI15 configuration bits
000: PA[15] pin; 001: PB[15] pin
010: PC[15] pin; 011: PD[15] pin
100: PE[15] pin; 101: PF[15] pin
110: PG[15] pin; 111: reserved

EXTI14[2:0]: EXTI14 configuration bits
000: PA[14] pin; 001: PB[14] pin
010: PC[14] pin; 011: PD[14] pin
100: PE[14] pin; 101: PF[14] pin
110: PG[14] pin; 111: reserved

EXTI13[2:0]: EXTI13 configuration bits
000: PA[13] pin; 001: PB[13] pin
010: PC[13] pin; 011: PD[13] pin
100: PE[13] pin; 101: PF[13] pin
110: PG[13] pin; 111: reserved

EXTI12[2:0]: EXTI12 configuration bits
000: PA[12] pin; 001: PB[12] pin
010: PC[12] pin; 011: PD[12] pin
100: PE[12] pin; 101: PF[12] pin
110: PG[12] pin; 111: reserved

Figure 5.35 SYSCFG external interrupt configuration register 4 (SYSCFG->EXTICR4)

In the STM32L475xx.h header file, the EXTICR1 to EXTICR4 registers are assigned to the array elements SYSCFG->EXTICR[0] to SYSCFG->EXTICR[3].

Example 5.3 Write a C function to configure PB2 pin to interrupt the STM32L475 on the rising edge and also enable the interrupt.

Solution:

```
void initPB2Interrupt (void)
{
    GPIOB->MODER          &= ~ (GPIO_MODER_MODE2); // configure PB2 for input
    SYSCFG->EXTICR[0]     = SYSCFG_EXTICR1_EXTI2_PB; // configure PB2 pin for EXTI2
    EXTI->RTSR1           |= EXTI_RTSR1_RT2; // set EXTI2 line for rising edge triggered
    EXTI->IMR1            |= EXTI_IMR1_IM2; // enable interrupt from EXTI line 2
    NVIC_EnableIRQ(EXTI2_IRQn); // enable EXTI2 interrupt
    __enable_irq();           // enable interrupt globally
}
```

Example 5.4 Write a C function to configure PA4 pin to generate events on the falling edge.

Solution:

```
void initPA4forEvent(void)
```

```
{
    GPIOA->MODER        &= ~GPIO_MODER_MODE4; // Configure PA4 pin for input
    SYSCFG->EXTICR[1]   = SYSCFG_EXTICR2_EXTI4_PA;
    EXTI->FTSR1         |= EXTI_FTSR1_FT4; // EXTI4 line falling edge triggered
    EXTI->EMR1          |= EXTI_EMR1_EM4; // unmask event from EXTI line 4
}
```

Example 5.5 Write a sequence of C statements to trigger an interrupt request from the PC13 pin.

Solution:

```
GPIOC->MODER        &= ~GPIO_MODER_MODE13; // configure PC13 for input
SYSCFG->EXTICR[3]   = SYSCFG_EXTICR4_EXTI13_PC; // assign PC13 pin to EXTI13
EXTI->EMR1          |= EXTI_EMR1_EM13; // unmask EXTI13 line interrupt
NVIC_EnableIRQ(EXTI15_10_IRQn); // enable EXTI15_10 interrupt
__enable_irq(); // enable interrupt globally
EXTI->SWIER1        |= EXTI_SWIER1_SWI13; // trigger interrupt from EXTI9 line
```

Example 5.6 You are given a circuit shown in Figure 5.36. Use the EXTI interrupt 13 (pin PC13 is connected to the blue button on the STM32L475 discovery kit) to increment a two-digit decimal counter that can count from 00 to 99 and repeat. The main function performs the required initialization, and then stays in a while loop and use time-multiplexing technique to display the value of the two-digit counter using two seven-segment displays.

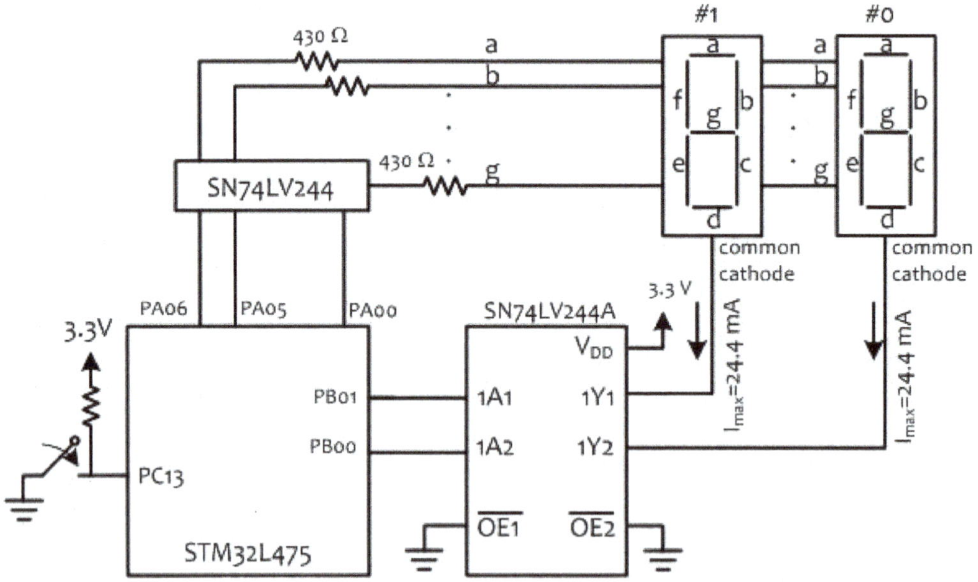

Figure 5.36 Port A & Port B of STM32L475 drives two seven-segment displays

Solution:

The following program performs the desired operation accordingly:

```
#include <stm32L475xx.h>
uint16_t  d1, d0; // tens and ones digit of two-digit decimal counter
uint16_t  disp1, disp0; // ten's and one's digit patterns to be sent to PA00~PA06
uint16_t  seg7[10] = {0x7E,0x03,0x6D,0x79,0x33,0x5B,0x5F,0x70,0x7F,0x7B};
void sysclkInit(void);
void setPINsDir(void);
void initEXTI_PC13(void);
void delayby1ms(uint16_t k);
int main (void)
{
    sysclkInit();
    setPINsDir(); // configure PA0~PA6, PB0~PB1, & PC13 directions
    d0 = d1 = 0; // initialize counter value to 00
    disp1 = disp0 = 0;
    initEXTI_PC13();   //   initialize   EXTI13/PC13   characteristics   and   enable   interrupt
    __enable_irq();
    while(1){
        GPIOA->ODR = disp1; // output ten's digit pattern
        GPIOB->BSRR = GPIO_BSRR_BR1 + GPIO_BSRR_BS0; // turn on ten's digit
        delayby1ms(1);
        GPIOA->ODR = disp0; // output one's digit pattern
        GPIOB->BSRR = GPIO_BSRR_BR0 + GPIO_BSRR_BS1; // turns on one's digit
        delayby1ms(1);
    }
}
void setPINsDir(void)
{
```

```
    GPIOA->MODER    &=  0xFFFFC000;    // clear lowest 14 bits
    GPIOA->MODER    |=  0x00001555;    // configure PA0~PA6 pins for output
    GPIOB->MODER    &=  0xFFFFFFF0;    // clear lowest MODE1 & MODE0 fields
    GPIOB->MODER    |=  0x00000005;    // configure PB0~PB1 for output
    GPIOC->MODER    &=  0xF3FFFFFF;    // clear bit 26~27 and configure PC13 for input
}
void initEXTI_PC13(void)
{
    SYSCFG->EXTICR[3] &= ~SYSCFG_EXTICR4_EXTI13;     // clear bits 4~7
    SYSCFG->EXTICR[3] |=  SYSCFG_EXTICR4_EXTI13_PC;  // configure PC13 pin for EXTI13
    EXTI->RTSR1       |=  EXTI_RTSR1_RT13;  // configure EXTI13 to sense the rising edge
    EXTI->IMR1        |=  EXTI_IMR1_IM13;   // unmask interrupt from EXTI line 13
    NVIC_SetPriority(EXTI15_10_IRQn, 0);    // set to highest priority
    NVIC_EnableIRQ(EXTI15_10_IRQn);
}
void EXTI15_10_IRQHandler(void)
{
    if(EXTI->PR1 & EXTI_PR1_PIF13) {
        EXTI->PR1 = EXTI_PR1_PIF13; // clear the EXTI13 pending flag
        if(d0 >= 9) {
            d0 = 0;
            if(d1 >= 9)
                d1 = 0;
            else
                d1 += 1;
        }
        else
            d0 += 1;
    disp1 = seg7[d1]; // find segment pattern for ten's digit
```

```
        disp0 = seg7[d0]; // find segment pattern for one's digit
    }
}
```

5.17 Summary

In ARM Cortex-M microcontroller's terminology, any event that can change program flow unexpectedly is called an **exception**. Exceptions consist of resets, interrupts, traps, and faults. In addition to providing program counter, on-chip peripheral registers, and flip-flops with default values so that the processor can start program execution, the reset mechanism is also used to getting the processor out of errors. The causes of reset include power-on reset, manual reset, software reset, **watchdog** reset, and brown-out reset.

The **watchdog timer** (WDT) is a special circuit for detecting runaway or deadlocked code. The WDT is configured to a predefined time-out period and is constantly running when enabled. The time-out period is set to slightly longer than the required time for executing the application. The condition that the application takes much longer than it should implies an error. The user can add a statement in the application to clear the WDT timer periodically (within its time-out period). If the WDT is not cleared within the time-out period, it will issue a system reset. An early-warning interrupt is available to indicate an upcoming watchdog time-out condition. The **window mode** makes it possible to define a time slot (or window) inside the total time-out period during which the WDT must be cleared. If the WDT is cleared outside this window, either too early or too late, a system reset will be issued. Compared to the normal mode, this can also catch situations where a code error causes the WDT to be cleared frequently. When enabled, the WDT will run in the active mode and all sleep modes. The WDT is often clocked by a clock source, which is independent of the CPU clock. The WDT will continue operation and issue a system reset or interrupt even if the main clocks fail.

The peripheral hardware may request the attention from the processor by asserting an interrupt signal. I/O operation can be made more efficient by using the interrupt. Routine works can be performed by using the timer interrupts. Emergent events can be handled in time by the processor using the non-maskable interrupt.

The processor executes a short program called interrupt service routine (also called exception handler) to handle the interrupt. Multiple interrupt can be pending at about the same time. The processor assigns priority to each interrupt source and provides service to the one with the highest priority. Although the STM32L475 (and other Cortex-M4 devices) uses 8 bits to encode the interrupt priority, only the highest 4 bits are used. Therefore, the STM32L475 has only 16 different priorities for interrupts.

When a program is being executed, errors or events might occur that are exceptional enough that they cannot be handled within the program itself and require a special routine to handle them. These types of errors are called **faults** or **traps**. Some microcontrollers may implement one or more special instructions in the instruction set that can cause an interrupt when they are executed. These types of exceptions are called **software interrupt**. Software interrupts can be used to facilitate the debugging of hardware interrupt service routines.

The STM32L475 uses a nested vectored interrupt controller (NVIC) to handle all the configurable exceptions and interrupts. The STM32L475 NVIC may assign one or multiple interrupt vectors to one peripheral module.

The CMSIS provides library functions to help users with interrupt handling:

- Enable and disable interrupt globally
- Enable and disable interrupt from each interrupt line (an IRQ number is assigned to each interrupt line)
- Set and read back interrupt priority of every interrupt line
- Set and clear interrupt line to pending/not pending

The CMSIS also allows the user to use symbolic names to refer to each interrupt source and its handling routine. It is simple to write the service routine for any interrupt source:

- Write down the handler name for the interrupt source.
- Enter appropriate statements required to handle the interrupt from the peripheral of interest.

5.18 Exercises

E5.1 What is an interrupt? What is a fault?

E5.2 The touch sensing controller (TSC) has two interrupt sources. One is Max Count Error (MCE) and the other is End of Acquisition (EOA). The interrupt enable bit for these two interrupt sources are MCEIE (bit 1) and EOAIE (bit 0) in the TSC interrupt enable register (TSC->IER). Write a sequence of C statements to enable the interrupt from TSC. Set the TSC interrupt priority to 0.

E5.3 Each I^2C module has seven interrupt sources and their interrupt enable bits are bits 7 to 1 of the I^2Cx->CR1 register (x = 1, 2, or 3): ERRIE (bit 7), TCIE (bit 6), STOPIE (bit 5), NACKIE (bit 4), ADDRIE (bit 3), RXIE (bit 2), and TXIE (bit 1). Write a sequence of C statements to enable the TCIE, NACKIE, RXIE, and TXIE interrupts of the I^2C1 module. The interrupt vector number of these interrupt sources is I2C1_EV_IRQn. Set the I^2C1 interrupt priority to 64.

E5.4 Write a sequence of C statements to configure the PA0 and PA3 pins to interrupt the STM32L475 on the rising edge and falling edge and set their interrupts to the highest priority.

E5.5 For the two interrupts (EXTI0 and EXTI3) mentioned in Problem E5.4, write the interrupt handling routines for them. Both handling routines have access to the global variable **count**. The EXTI0 interrupt handling routine clears the PIF0 flag in the EXTI->PR1 register, increments count by 1, and outputs it to GPIOB port. The EXTI3 interrupt handling routine clears the PIF3 flag in the EXTI->PR1 register, decrements count by 1, and outputs it to GPIOB port.

E5.6 Write a sequence of C statements to configure PC0 and PA4 pin to generate events on the rising edge and the falling edge, respectively.

E5.7 Write an interrupt handling routine for the EXTI4 interrupt, which clears the PIF4 flag in the EXTI->PR1 register and reads the PC0 pin value. If the PC0 pin voltage is high, it increments the global variable **upDown** by 1 and outputs it to the GPIOA->ODR register. If the PC0 pin voltage is low, it decrements the **upDown** variable by 1 and outputs it to the GPIOA->ODR register.

5.19 Lab Assignments

L5.1 Use the **B-L475E-IOT01A** demo kit to do this assignment. Configure the rising edge of the PC13 pin as the EXTI13 interrupt source. Connect the PA0~PA7 to LEDs. Configure PB0 pin for input and connect it to a wire so that it can be used to touch VCC or GND to change the pin voltage. Declare a global 8-bit variable **count**. Write a main function to carry out the necessary configuration and enable the EXTI13 interrupt and then stay in a while loop to wait for the interrupt to occur. Write a handling routine for the EXTI13 interrupt. The handling routine performs the following operations:

- Clears the PIF13 flag.
- Checks the voltage level of the PB0 pin. Increments the variable **count** if the PB0 pin is high. Otherwise, decrements the variable **count**.

- Outputs counts to PA0~PA7 pins.

Create the project, enter the program, build the project, eliminate syntax and semantics errors, and download the program onto the demo board. Set the PB0 pin to high voltage. Push the button connected to PC13 pin a few times and check the value represented by LED lights. Set the PB0 pin to ground. Push the button connected to PC13 a few more times and check to see if the LEDs show the variable **count** is decrementing.

6

Timers/ Counters

6.1 Objectives

After completing this chapter, you will be able to

- Describe the timer applications.
- Use timer function to generate time delays.
- Use timer input capture function to measure signal parameters.
- Use timer output compare function to create time delays and generate waveforms.
- Use timer output compare and PWM function to generate waveforms.
- Generate a PWM waveform to drive a DC motor.

6.2 Introduction to Timer/Counter Function

Every microcontroller provides timer/counter modules to meet the requirements of applications. A timer/counter needs a clock input to count. When the clock signal is a periodic signal, the module is referred to as a **timer**. However, when the clock signal is not periodic, it is called a **counter**.

Most of today's timer/counter modules consist of a **counter**, **input capture** (**IC**), **output compare** (**OC**), and **pulse width modulation** (**PWM**) circuit. Counter alone can be used to create time delays. The input capture function can be used to measure signal parameters such as pulse width, period, duty cycle, and frequency. The input capture function can also be used as a time reference for triggering other operations. The output compare function can be used to create time delays and generate waveforms. The PWM circuit is mainly used to generate a periodic waveform with a specified frequency and duty cycle and is often used to control the speed of DC motors or fans and the brightness of LEDs or light bulbs.

6.2.1 USING A TIMER TO CREATE TIME DELAYS

The **first step** in using a timer to create a time delay is to calculate the **timer count** required to create the desired time delay. The required timer count is equal to the product of the time delay to be created and the frequency of the timer clock input:

$$\text{TimerCount} = t_D \times f_{TC} \qquad \text{--- (6.1)}$$

where, t_D is the time delay to be created and f_{TC} is the frequency of the timer clock input.

The **second step** is to let the timer/counter to count up from **2^n – TimerCount** until it overflows or let the timer/counter to count down from **TimerCount** until it counts down to 0. Either way, the desired delay is created.

6.2.2 INPUT CAPTURE FUNCTION

An input capture circuit is designed to detect the arrival of a signal edge. The edge to be detected can be a rising or a falling edge. When the selected signal edge is detected, the circuit makes a copy of the timer count value and saves it in a register called the **input capture register** (**ICR**).

The period of a periodic signal can be measured by capturing two consecutive rising or falling edges as shown in Figure 6.1 and then compute the difference of these two edges. The width of a pulse can be measured by capturing a rising edge and then the following falling edge and computing the difference of these two edges as shown in Figure 6.2. The measurement of the duty cycle of a periodic square wave is illustrated in Figure 6.3. The design of many modern microcontrollers has improved on this idea by forcing the counter to count up from 0 when the first edge is detected and then capturing the counter value of the second edge. By doing that, the captured second edge is the period or pulse width of the unknown signal.

Figure 6.1a Capture two rising edges to measure signal period

Figure 6.1b Capture two falling edges to measure signal period

Figure 6.2 Capture one rising and the following falling edge to measure pulse width

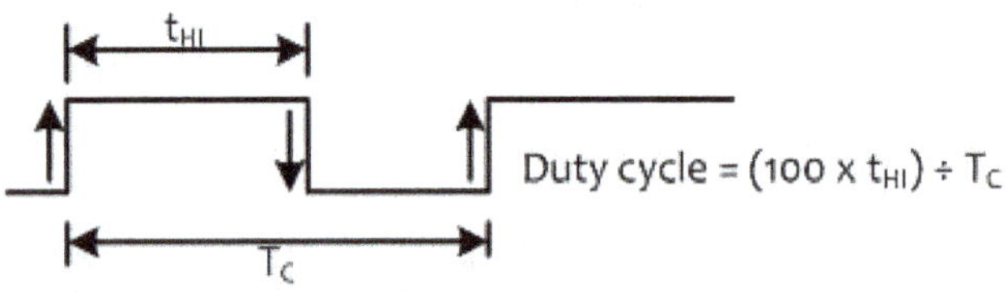

Figure 6.3 Duty cycle measurement

6.2.3 OUTPUT COMPARE

An output compare module consists of a comparator, an output compare register (OCR), a timer, several other control or status registers, and a signal pin (often called OC pin). The comparator compares the timer value with the value in the OCR register in every clock cycle. When the value of the timer equals that of the OCR, the output compare module takes the following actions:

- Sets a flag to 1.
- Optionally changes the OC pin voltage level (can be pull high, pull low, or toggle).

To use the output compare function, the processor performs the following three operations:

- Makes a copy of the current timer value.
- Adds a delay count to this copy.
- Stores the sum in the OCR register.

Of course, the implementation of the OC function of a microcontroller can be very different from this description.

6.2.4 PULSE-WIDTH MODULATION (PWM)

Waveform generation using the output compare function requires the CPU to restart the output compare function after each compare match. This requires frequent CPU involvement during the waveform generation process.

For many applications, the frequency and duty cycle do not need to be changed frequently. For this reason, a special circuitry is added to the timer system so that the CPU only needs to set up the duty cycle and period once, and the waveform continues by itself until the duty cycle or period needs to be changed. This waveform is called **pulse-width modulation** (**PWM**). A PWM module consists of an output pin, a timer/counter, a period register, a duty register, and other control circuitry.

There are two types of PWM: **single slope** and **dual slope**. In a single-slope PWM, the counter counts from 0 to a top value, rolls over to 0, and then repeats. When the counter starts from 0, the waveform is pulled high. When the counter value equals that stored in the associated **duty** register, the waveform output is pulled low. The counter continues to count to the top value and then rolls over to 0. The whole process repeats. An example of the single-slope PWM is shown in Figure 6.4. In a dual-slope PWM, the counter counts up from zero until it reaches the top value. After that, it starts to count down until it reaches zero. The counting process repeats. When the counter counts up from 0, the waveform output is pulled high until the counter value equals that of the duty register. At that point, the waveform output is pulled low. The counter continues to count up until it reaches the top value and starts to count down. When it counts down to the value stored in the duty register, the waveform output is pulled high again and stays high until the counter counts down to zero. The whole process repeats. A dual-slope PWM is shown in Figure 6.5.

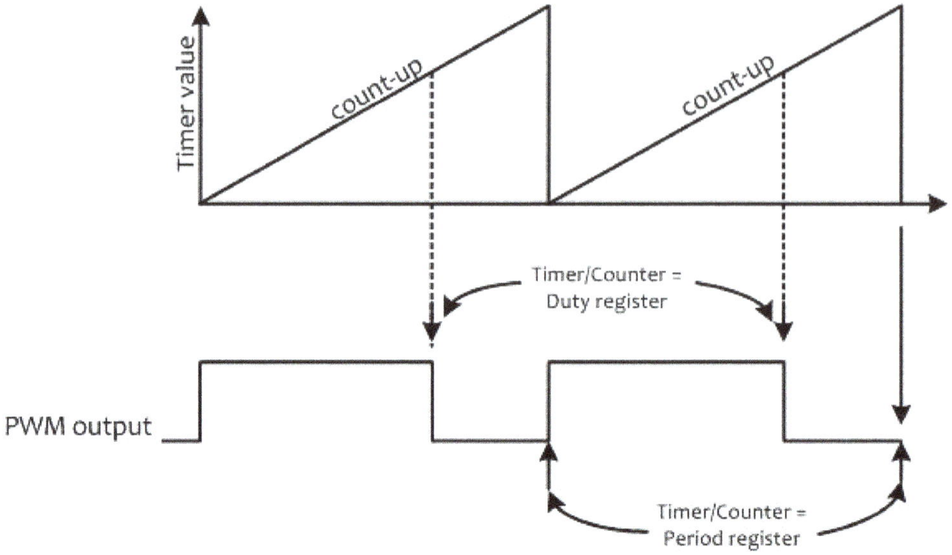

Figure 6.4 Single-slope PWM operation

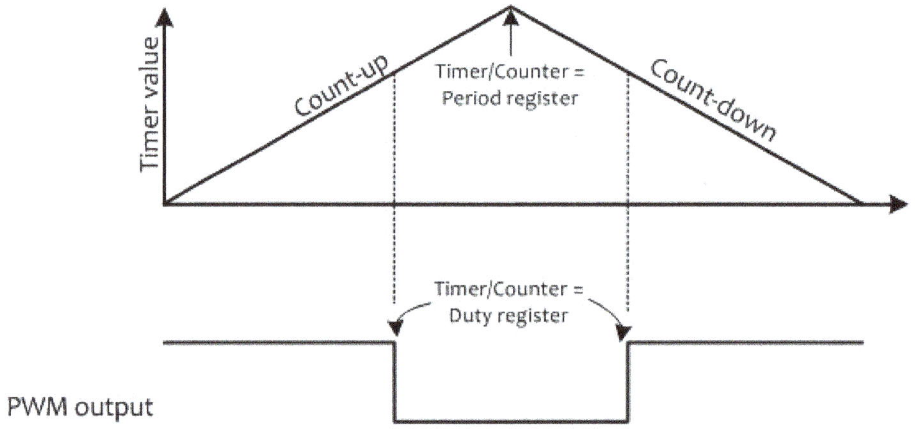

Figure 6.5 Dual-slope PWM operation (one cycle)

In ST's terminology, the single-slope mode is called **edge-aligned mode**, whereas the dual-slope mode is called **center-aligned mode**.

6.3 Overview of the STM32L475 Timer System

The STM32L475 provides the following timers:

- Basic timers: TIM6 and TIM7
- General-purpose timers: TIM2/TIM3/TIM4/TIM5
- General-purpose timers: TIM15/TIM16/TIM17

- Advanced control timers: TIM1/TIM8
- Low-power timer: LPTIM

The features of these timers are summarized in Table 6.1.

Table 6.1 STM32L475 Timer feature comparison

Timer type	Timer	Counter resolution	Counting direction	Prescaler factor	DMA request	Capture/ compare channels	Complementary outputs
Advanced control	TIM1, TIM8	16-bit	Up, down, Up/down	Integer between 1 and 65536	yes	4	3
General-purpose	TIM2, TIM5	32-bit	Up, down, Up/down	Integer between 1 and 65536	yes	4	No
General-purpose	TIM3, TIM4	16-bit	Up, down, Up/down	Integer between 1 and 65536	yes	4	No
General-purpose	TIM15	16-bit	Up	Integer between 1 and 65536	yes	2	1
General-purpose	TIM16, TIM17	16-bit	Up	Integer between 1 and 65536	yes	1	1
Basic	TIM6, TIM7	16-bit	Up	Integer between 1 and 65536	yes	0	No

All timers have a register that holds the **top value** for the timer to count up to (or count down from). This register has a **shadow register** to which the timer compares in every clock cycle. In the **count-up** mode, the timer rolls over to 0 when it counts up to the TOP value. In the **count-down** mode, the timer is reloaded with the value from the shadow register and continues to count down. The register that holds the TOP value of the counting process is referred to as **auto-reload register** (**ARR**) for the STM32 microcontrollers. Because of this double-buffer arrangement, the timer will finish a counting sequence before a TOP value can be changed.

To change the TOP value for the counting process, the user writes a new value to the ARR register. The new value will be loaded into the shadow register (a process called auto reload) when the upcounting timer counts to the TOP value or when the downcounting timer counts down t0 0.

An STM32L475 timer supports the **master mode** and/or **slave mode.** When the master mode is enabled, the microcontroller can select a signal to be used as the TRGO output to control the behavior of other timer(s). When the **slave mode** is enabled, the timer can be controlled by the **TRGI** input signal. The master mode and the slave mode can be enabled at the same time. The basic timers (TIM6/TIM7) do not support the slave mode.

6.3.1 FEATURES OF BASIC TIMERS TIM6/TIM7

These basic timers have a 16-bit ARR to hold the TOP value for the counting process. The clock inputs of both timers are derived by dividing the clock input from the system clock module by a 16-bit prescaler. Both timers have an output that can be used to trigger the D/A conversion. When either timer overflows, DMA transfer and interrupt request can be generated.

6.3.2 FEATURES OF THE GENERAL-PURPOSE TIMERS TIM2/TIM3/TIM4/TIM5

TIM2 and TIM5 are 32-bit timers, whereas TIM3 and TIM4 are 16-bit timers. All 4 timers can count up and count down. An ARR is associated with each of these 4 timers. Like basic timers, each of these timers has a 16-bit prescaler to its clock input.

Each timer has four channels with each channel configurable for (1) input capture, (2) output compare, (3) PWM generation (edge- and center-aligned modes), and (4) one-pulse output. A synchronization circuit is available for interconnecting several of these timers together using an external signal.

Interrupt and DMA transfer may be requested under four situations:

- Counter overflow/underflow and counter initialization
- Trigger event (such as counter start, stop, initialization, or count by internal/external trigger)
- Input capture
- Output compare match

These four timers include an incremental (quadrature) encoder and Hall sensor circuitry for motor positioning applications.

6.3.3 FEATURES OF THE GENERAL-PURPOSE TIMERS TIM15/TIM16/TIM17

These are 16-bit upcounting timers with auto-reload capability. TIM15 has two channels, and TIM16/TIM17 have one channel. Each timer channel can be configured for (1) input capture, (2) output compare, (3) PWM generation (edge-aligned mode), and (4) one-pulse mode output. Channel 1 has complementary output with dead-time insertion capability.

The PWM has complementary outputs with programmable dead-time. A synchronization circuit is available for interconnecting these timers together using an external signal.

A **repetition counter** is included to allow timer registers to be updated only after a given number of cycles of the counter.

A **break** input is available to put the timer's output signals in the reset state or a known state. Interrupt/DMA can be requested on the following events:

- Update: Counter overflow, counter initialization.
- Trigger event: An internal or external trigger can be used to start the counter, stop the counter, initialize the counter, or allow the counter to count.
- Input capture
- Output compare
- Break input (interrupt request)

6.3.4 FEATURES OF ADVANCED CONTROL TIMERS TIM1/TIM8

TIM1/TIM8 consists of a 16-bit up, down, up/down auto-reload counter. The clock input is the APB2 clock divided by a 16-bit programmable prescaler. Each timer has up to 6 independent channels for (a) input capture (excluding channels 5 and 6), (b) output compare, (c) PWM generation (edge- and center-aligned mode), and (d) one-pulse mode output.

PWM also includes complementary outputs with programmable dead-time. Synchronization circuit is included to allow external signal to take control of the timer and interconnect several timers together.

TIM1 and TIM8 also include a repetition counter that enables the user to set the number of cycles that the counter has gone through before the timer registers can be updated.

Two break inputs are available that can put the timer's output signals in a user-selectable configuration.

Interrupts and DMA requests can be generated on these events:

- Update: Counter overflow/underflow and counter initialization (by software or internal/external trigger)
- Trigger event (count start, stop, initialization or count by internal/external trigger)
- Input capture
- Output compare

TIM1 and TIM8 also include incremental (quadrature) encoder and Hall-sensor circuitry that can be used in motor positioning application.

6.3.5 LOW-POWER TIMER (LPTIM)

The LPTIM is a 16-bit upcounter. It has a 3-bit clock input prescaler with 8 possible dividing factors—1, 2, 4, 8, 16, 32, 64, and 128.

The clock input can be chosen between internal and external clock source. The external clock source is obtained from the ULPTIM input pin. Internal clock source can be chosen from LSE, LSI, HSI16, or APB clock.

The LPTIM has a 16-bit **auto-reload** register (ARR) and a 16-bit **compare** register. The LPTIM can be triggered using software or hardware input and can operate in either one-shot or continuous mode.

The LPTIM output can be a single pulse or a PWM waveform. The polarity of its output is configurable.

This chapter describes the programming and applications of basic timers TIM6/TIM7 and general-purpose timers TIM2/TIM3/TIM4/TIM5 only and leaves the programming and applications of other timers for the reader to self-study.

6.4 Basic Timers TIM6/TIM7

The block diagram of TIM6/TIM7 is shown in Figure 6.6. The main block of TIM6/TIM7 is a 16-bit upcounter that consists of three registers: **count register** (TIMx->CNT, x = 6 or 7), **prescaler register** (TIMx->PSC, x = 6 or 7), and **auto-reload register** (TIMx->ARR, x = 6 or 7). Both the TIMx->ARR and TIMx->PSC are double-buffered. Double-buffering ensures that the same clock prescaler and top value are used in a complete counting sequence before they are changed.

The **buffer** (or **shadow** register, also called **preload** register) of the TIM->ARR register is not user-directly-accessible. The counter counts up to the value in the preload register, rolls over to 0, and repeats. The buffers of both TIMx->PSC and TIMx->ARR are updated when an update event (UEV) occurs.

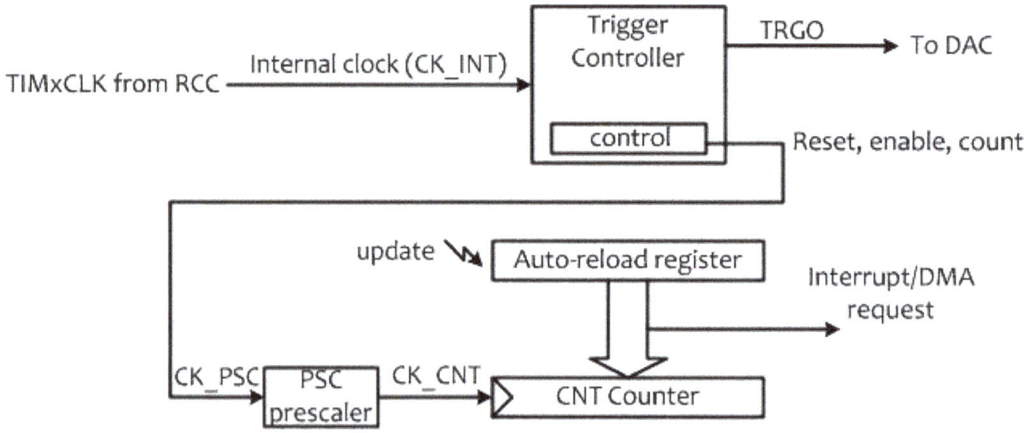

Figure 6.6 Basic timers (TIM6/TIM7) block diagram

6.4.1 TIM6/TIM7 UPDATE EVENT

The buffers of both TIMx->PSC and TIMx->ARR (x = 6 or 7) are updated when an update event (UEV) occurs. There are two possible UEVs for TIM6/TIM7: (1) timer counts up to the TIM->ARR value and (2) setting the UG bit in the TIMx->EGR register. UEV events can be disabled by setting the UDIS bit in the TIMx->CR1 register.

On an update event (UEV), the UIF flag in the status register (TIMx->SR) is set to 1. An interrupt may be generated if enabled. This flag is cleared by writing a 0 to it. The UIF flag may be copied (or remapped) to the bit 31 of the CNT register.

6.4.2 TIM6/TIM7 REGISTERS

Registers related to the operation of TIM6/TIM7 include:

- Control register 1 (TIMx->CR1, x = 6 or 7)
- Control register 2 (TIMx->CR2, x = 6 or 7)
- DMA/interrupt enable register (TIMx->DIER, x = 6 or 7)
- Status register (TIMx->SR, x = 6 or 7)
- Event generation register (TIMx->EGR, x = 6 or 7)

- Counter register (TIMx->CNT, x = 6 or 7)
- Prescaler register (TIMx->PSC,+ x = 6 or 7)
- Auto-reload register (TIMx->ARR, x = 6 or 7)

The contents of these registers are shown in Figures 6.7–6.14, respectively.

15	14	13	12	11	10	9	8
–	–	–	–	UIF REMAP	–	–	–
7	**6**	**5**	**4**	**3**	**2**	**1**	**0**
ARPE	–	–	–	OPM	URS	UDIS	CEN

Reset value = 0x0000
Offset = 0x00

UIFREMAP: UIF status bit remapping
 0: No remapping. UIF status bit is not copied to TIMx_CNT register bit 31.
 1: Remapping enabled. UIF status bit is copied to TIMx_CNT register bit 31.
ARPE: Auto-reload preload enable
 0: TIMx_ARR register is not buffered.
 1: TIMx_ARR register is buffered.
OPM: One pulse mode
 0: Counter is not stopped at update event
 1: Counter stops counting at the next update event (clearing CEN bit)
URS: Update request source
 0: Allow the following events to generate an update interrupt or DMA request if enabled (1) counter overflow/underflow (2) setting the UG bit (3) Update generation through slave mode controller
 1: Only counter overflow/underflow generates an update interrupt or DMA request if enabled.
UDIS: Update disable
 0: UEV enabled. The update event can be generated by (1) counter overflow/underflow (2) setting the UG bit (3) Update generation through the slave mode controller
 1: UEV disabled. Shadow registers keep their values (ARR, PSC).
CEN; Counter enable
 0: Counter disabled 1: Counter enabled

Figure 6.7 TIM6/TIM7 control register 1 (TIMx_CR1)

15	14	13	12	11	10	9	8
–	–	–	–	–	–	–	–
7	**6**	**5**	**4**	**3**	**2**	**1**	**0**
–	MMS[2:0]			–	–	–	–

Reset value = 0x0000
Offset = 0x04

MMS: Master mode selection
 These bits are used to select the information to be sent in master mode to slave timers for synchronization (TRGO).
 000: Reset – The UG bit from the TIMx_EGR register is used as a trigger output (TRGO)
 001: Enable – The counter enable signal, CNT_EN, is used as a trigger output.
 010: Update – The update event is selected as a trigger output. For instance, a master timer can then be used as a prescaler for a slave timer.
Note: The clock of the slave timer or ADC must be enabled prior to receive events from the master timer, and must not be changed on-the-fly while triggers are received from the master timer.

Figure 6.8 TIM6/TIM7 control register 2 (TIMx_CR2), x = 6 or 7

15	14	13	12	11	10	9	8
--	--	--	--	--	--	--	UDE
7	**6**	**5**	**4**	**3**	**2**	**1**	**0**
--	--			--	--	--	UIE

Reset value = 0x0000
Offset = 0x0C

UDE: Update DMA request enable
  0: Update DMA request disabled
  1: Update DMA request enabled
UIE: Update interrupt enable
  0: Update interrupt disabled
  1: Update interrupt enabled

Figure 6.9 TIM6/TIM7 DMA/Interrupt enable register (TIMx_DIER), x = 6 or 7

15	14	13	12	11	10	9	8
--	--	--	--	--	--	--	--
7	**6**	**5**	**4**	**3**	**2**	**1**	**0**
--	--			--	--	--	UIF

Reset value = 0x0000
Offset = 0x10

UIF: Update interrupt flag
  0: No update occurred
  1: Update interrupt pending. This bit is set by hardware when the registers are updated.

Figure 6.10 TIM6/TIM7 status register (TIMx_SR), x = 6 or 7

15	14	13	12	11	10	9	8
--	--	--	--	--	--	--	--
7	**6**	**5**	**4**	**3**	**2**	**1**	**0**
--	--			--	--	--	UG

Reset value = 0x0000
Offset = 0x14

UG: Update generation
  0: No action
  1: Reinitialize the timer counter and generates an update of the registers. The prescaler is also cleared. But the prescaler ratio is not affected

Figure 6.11 TIM6/TIM7 event generation register (TIMx_EGR), x = 6 or 7

31	30	29	28	27	26	25	24
UIFCPY	--	--	--	--	--	--	--
23	**22**	**21**	**20**	**19**	**18**	**17**	**16**
--	--	--	--	--	--	--	--
15	**14**	**13**	**12**	**11**	**10**	**9**	**8**
CNT[15:8]							
7	**6**	**5**	**4**	**3**	**2**	**1**	**0**
CNT[7:0]							

Reset value = 0x0000
Offset = 0x24

UIFCPY: UIF copy.
  This bit is the read-only copy of the UIF bit of the TIMx_ISR register
CNT[15:0]: Counter value

Figure 6.12 TIM6/TIM7 counter register (TIMx_CNT), x = 6 or 7

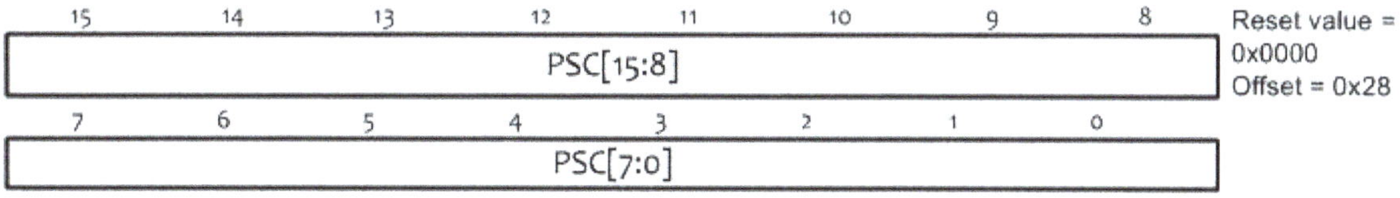

PSC[15:0]: Prescaler value
The counter clock frequency CK_CNT is equal to f_{CK_PSC} / (PSC[15:0] + 1). PSC contains the value to be loaded into the active prescaler register at each update event.

Figure 6.13 TIM6/TIM7 Prescaler register (TIMx_PSC), x = 6 or 7

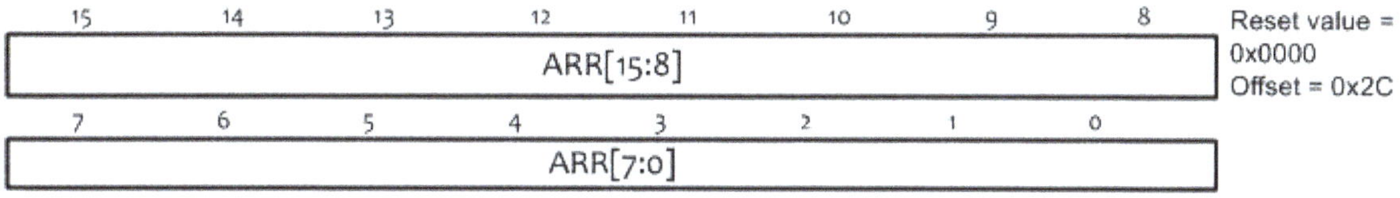

ARR[15:0]: Auto reload value
ARR is the value to be loaded into the actual auto-reload register. The counter is blocked while the auto-reload value is null.

Figure 6.14 TIM6/TIM7 Auto-reload register (TIMx_ARR), x = 6 or 7

6.4.3 APPLICATIONS OF TIM6/TIM7

TIM6/TIM7 can be used to create time delays or trigger other STM32L475 timers to perform periodic operations, for example:

- Time-multiplexing seven-segment displays
- Periodic D/A conversion
- Periodic A/D conversion

Example 6.1 Write a few C functions that can create a time delay which is 50 μs, a multiple of 1 ms, a multiple of 10 ms, and a multiple of 100 ms, assuming that the timer clock source is 80 MHz.

Solution:

- For the 50-μs delay, set prescaler to 1, and the required timer count is 4000.
- For the time delay of 1 ms and 10 ms, set the prescaler to 79, then f_{CK_CNT} is 1 MHz. The timer count for creating a time delay of 1 ms and 10 ms are 1000 and 10,000, respectively.
- For the time delay of 100 ms, set the prescaler to 159, then f_{CK_CNT} is 500 kHz. The timer count for creating a 100-ms time delay is 50,000.

The following functions create the specified time delays:

```
// -----------------------------------------------------------------------------------------------------------
----

// This function creates a 50-μs  delay assuming that the clock

// input to the TIM7 is 80 MHz.
```

```
// -----------------------------------------------------------------------------------------------------------------
----
void delay50us(void)
{
    TIM7->PSC  = 0;              // set clock input prescaler to 1
    TIM7->ARR  = 4000;           // set up the timer count for 50 us delay
    TIM7->CNT  = 0;              // force TIM7 to count up from 0
    TIM7->EGR  = TIM_EGR_UG; // update PSC and ARR value
    TIM7->SR   = 0;              // clear the UIF flag
    TIM7->CR1  = TIM_CR1_ARPE + TIM_CR1_CEN; // enable TIM7 and ARR auto reload
    while(!(TIM7->SR & TIM_SR_UIF)); // wait until UIF flag is set
}

// -----------------------------------------------------------------------------------------------------------------
------------------------
// This function creates a delay that is a multiple of 1 ms assuming that the clock
// input to the TIM7 is 80 MHz.
// -----------------------------------------------------------------------------------------------------------------
------------------------
void delayby1ms(uint16_t k)
{
    TIM7->PSC  = 79;             // set clock input prescaler to 80
    TIM7->ARR  = 1000;           // set up the timer count for 1 ms delay
    TIM7->CNT  = 0;              // force TIM7 to count up from 0
    TIM7->EGR  = TIM_EGR_UG;     // update PSC and ARR value
    TIM7->SR   = 0;              // clear the UIF flag
    TIM7->CR1  = TIM_CR1_ARPE + TIM_CR1_CEN; // enable TIM7 and ARR auto reload
    while (k){ // stay here until multiple count is decremented to 0
        while (!(TIM7->SR & TIM_SR_UIF));
        TIM7->SR = 0;            // clear UIF flag to 0
```

```
        k--;
    }
}

// -------------------------------------------------------------------------------------------------------------
------------------------

// This function creates a delay that is a multiple of 1o ms assuming that the clock
// input to the TIM7 is 80 MHz.
// -------------------------------------------------------------------------------------------------------------
------------------------
void delayby10ms(uint16_t k)
{
    TIM7->PSC  = 79;               // set clock input prescaler to 80
    TIM7->ARR  = 10000;            // set up the timer count for 10 ms delay
    TIM7->CNT  = 0;                // force TIM7 to count up from 0
    TIM7->EGR  = TIM_EGR_UG;       // update PSC and ARR value
    TIM7->SR   = 0;                // clear the UIF flag
    TIM7->CR1  = TIM_CR1_ARPE + TIM_CR1_CEN; // enable TIM7 and ARR auto reload
    while(k){ // stay here until multiple count is decremented to 0
        while(!(TIM7->SR & TIM_SR_UIF));
        TIM7->SR = 0;              // clear UIF flag to 0
        k--;
    }
}

// -------------------------------------------------------------------------------------------------------------
-----------------------
// This function creates a delay that is a multiple of 100 ms assuming that the clock
// input to TIM7 is 80 MHz.
// -------------------------------------------------------------------------------------------------------------
```

```
-----------------------

void delayby100ms(uint16_t k)
{
    TIM7->PSC  = 159;              // set clock input prescaler to 160
    TIM7->ARR  = 50000;            // set up the timer count for the 100 ms delay
    TIM7->CNT  = 0;                // force TIM7 to count up from 0
    TIM7->EGR  = TIM_EGR_UG;       // update PSC and ARR value
    TIM7->SR   = 0;                // clear the UIF flag
    TIM7->CR1  = TIM_CR1_ARPE + TIM_CR1_CEN; // enable TIM7 and ARR auto reload
    while(k){ // stay here until multiple count is decremented to 0
        while(!(TIM7->SR & TIM_SR_UIF));
        TIM7->SR = 0;              // clear UIF flag to 0
        k--;
    }
}
```

Example 6.2 Write a sequence of C statements to configure TIM6 so that it can generate a TRGO output every 4 μs, assuming that the clock source to TIM6 is 80 MHz.

Solution: Let's set the timer clock prescaler to 8, then the TIM6 clock period is $1\text{ s} \div (80 \times 10^6 \div 8) = 100\text{ ns}$. 4 μs corresponds to 40 TIM6 clock cycles. The TIM6's update event (UEV) should be selected as the source of TRGO output. The following C statements will generate a TRGO pulse every 4 μs:

```
TIM6->PSC  = 7; // set prescaler to 8
TIM6->CR2  = TIM_CR2_MMS_1; // select update event as TRGO source
TIM6->ARR  = 39;
TIM6->CNT  = 0;
TIM6->EGR  = TIM_EGR_UG; // update PSC and ARR values
TIM6->SR   = 0;
TIM6->CR1  = TIM_CR1_ARPE + TIM_CR1_CEN; // enable TIM6 and auto-preload
```

6.5 General-Purpose Timers TIM2/TIM3/TIM4/TIM5

TIM2 and TIM5 are 32-bit timers, whereas TIM3 and TIM4 are 16-bit timers. All of them can count up, count down, or count up to the top and then count down to 0 with auto-reload capability. The default clock input to these 4 timers is the APB1 bus clock divided by a 16-bit prescaler.

Each timer has up to four independent channels for

- Input capture
- Output compare
- PWM generation (both edge- and center-aligned modes)
- One-pulse mode output

All of these four timers provide synchronization circuit to control the timer (via the TRGI input) with external signals and interconnect several timers together (via the TRGO signal).

6.5.1 TIME-BASE UNIT

Similar to TIM6 and TIM7, the time-base unit of the TIM2/TIM3/TIM4/TIM5 timer consists of three registers:

- Counter register (TIMx->CNT). Depending on the timer, TIMx->CNT may be 16-bit or 32-bit. Here, x can be 2, 3, 4, or 5. In the following+ discussion, x refers the TIM2~TIM5.
- Prescaler register (TIMx->PSC). This register is 16-bit. The clock input is divided by the value in the prescaler register. The resultant signal is used as the clock input of the counter register.
- Auto-reload register (TIMx->ARR). This register holds the **TOP value** of the counting process. The TIMx->CNT counts up to this value or counts down from this value.

Both the TIMx->PSC and TIMx->ARR have a shadow (buffer) register. The shadow register of the TIMx->PSC is used to prescale the timer input clock, whereas the shadow register of TIMx->ARR is used as the TOP value of the counting process. Shadow registers are updated when there is an UEV.

6.5.2 COUNTING MODES

The TIM2/TIM3/TIM4/TIM5 timer has three counting modes:

- Upcounting mode
- Downcounting mode
- Center-aligned mode

Upcounting Mode

In this mode, the counter counts from 0 to the top value held in the shadow register of the TIMx->ARR register, rolls over to 0, and then counts up again. The action of rolling over from the top value to 0 is called **timer overflow**. Unless disabled by the UDIS bit in the TIMx->CR1 register, the update event (UEV) is generated when the counter counts to the TOP value. The UEV causes the contents of the TIMx->PSC and TIMx->ARR register to be copied to their respective shadow registers.

An UEV can also be generated by setting the UG bit in the TIMx->EGR register. However, if the **update**

request source (**URS**) bit in the TIMx->CR1 register is set to 1, the setting of UG bit will not generate an UEV interrupt or DMA request.

When an UEV occurs, the UIF flag in the TIMx->SR register will be set to 1 under three conditions:

- At overflow or underflow and the UDIS bit in the TIMx->CR1 register is 0.
- TIMx->ARR is reinitialized by setting the UG bit in the TIMx->EGR register, and the URS and the UDIS bit in the TIMx->CR1 register are 0s.
- When TIMx->CNT is reinitialized by a trigger event and the URS and UDIS bit in the TIMx->CR1 register are 0s.

Downcounting Mode

The counter counts from the auto-reload value down to 0, restart from the auto-reload value and count down. An UEV can be generated at each counter underflow (the moment that counter counts down to 0) or by setting the UG bit in the TIMx->EGR register. The UEV event can be disabled by software by setting the UDIS bit in the TIMx->CR1 register. This is to avoid updating the shadow registers while writing new values in the preload registers. The counter restarts from the current auto-reload value, whereas the counter of the prescaler restarts from 0.

If the URS bit (update request selection) in the TIMx->CR1 register is set, setting the UG bit generates an UEV without setting the UIF flag (thus, no interrupt or DMA request is sent). This is to avoid generating both update and capture interrupts when clearing the counter on the capture event.

Center-Aligned Mode (Up/Down Counting)

In this mode, the counter counts from 0 to the **auto-reload value – 1**, generates a counter overflow event, then counts from the auto-reload value down to 1 and generates a counter underflow event. Then it restarts counting from 0.

Depending on the value of the **CMS field** in the **TIMx->CR1** register, there are three versions of center-aligned mode:

- CMS = 01. The output-compare interrupt flag (CC_nIF, n = 1, 2, 3, or 4) of channels configured in output is set when counter is counting down.
- CMS = 10. The output-compare interrupt flag of channels configured in output is set when counter is counting up.
- CMS = 11. The output-compare interrupt flag of channels configured in output is set when counter is counting up or down.

The UEV can be generated at each counter overflow and at each counter underflow or by setting the UG bit in the TIMx->EGR register. If the UEV is generated by setting the UG bit, the counter restarts counting from 0. The prescaler counter also restarts counting from 0.

Like in other two counting modes, the UEV can be disabled by setting the UDIS bit in the TIMx->CR1 register. The contents of TIMx->CR1, TIMx->EGR, and TIMx->SR register are shown in Figures 6.15, 6.16, and 6.17, respectively.

15	14	13	12	11	10	9	8
–	–	–	–	UIF-REMAP	–	CKD[1:0]	

Reset value = 0x0000
Offset = 0x00

7	6	5	4	3	2	1	0
ARPE	CMS[1:0]		DIR	OPM	URS	UDIS	CEN

UIFREMAP: UIF status bit remapping
0: No remapping. UIF bit is not copied to TIMx_CNT register bit 31.
1: Remapping enabled. UIF status is copied to TIMx_CNT register bit 31.

CKD[1:0]: Clock division
This field specifies the division ratio between the timer clock (CK_INT) frequency and the sampling clock used by the digital filters (ETR, Tix)
00: $t_{DTS} = t_{CK\_INT}$
01: $t_{DTS} = 2 \times t_{CK\_INT}$
10: $t_{DTS} = 4 \times t_{CK\_INT}$
11: reserved

ARPE: Auto reload preload enable
0: TIMx_ARR register is not buffered
1: TIMx_ARR register is buffered

CMS[1:0]: Center-aligned mode selection
00: Edge-aligned mode (CNT only counts up or down)
01: Center-aligned mode 1. The counter counts up and down alternately. Output compare interrupt flags of channels configured in output (CCxS=00 in TIMx_CCMR register) are set only when the counter is counting down.
10: Center-aligned mode 2. The counter counts up and down alternately. Output compare interrupt flags of channels configured in output are set only when the counter is counting up.
11: Center-aligned mode 3. The counter counts up and down alternately. Output compare interrupt flags of channels configured in output are set both when the counter is counting up and down.

Figure 6.15 TIMx control register 1 (TIMx_CR1)

15	14	13	12	11	10	9	8
–	–	–	–	UIF-REMAP	–	CKD[1:0]	

Reset value = 0x0000
Offset = 0x00

7	6	5	4	3	2	1	0
ARPE	CMS[1:0]		DIR	OPM	URS	UDIS	CEN

DIR: Direction (used only when the timer is in center-aligned or encoder mode).
0: counter is counting up
1: counter is counting down

OPM: One-pulse mode
0: Counter does not stop at update event
1: Counter stops counting at the next update event (clearing the bit CEN)

URS: Update request source
0: Any of the following events can generate an update event or DMA request if enabled:
(a) Counter overflow/underflow
(b) Setting the UG bit
(c) Update generation through the slave mode controller
1: Only counter overflow/underflow generates an update interrupt or DMA request.

UDIS: Update disable
0: UEV enabled. The update (UEV) event is generated by (a) counter overflow/underflow) (b) setting the UG bit (c) Update generation through the slave mode controller
1: UEV disabled. The update event is not generated, shadow registers keep their value (ARR, PSC, CCRx). However, the counter and the prescaler are reinitialized if the UG bit is set or if a hardware reset is received from the slave mode controller.

CEN: counter enable
0: counter disabled
1: Counter enabled
Trigger mode can set the CEN bit (i.e., start the timer) automatically by hardware.

Figure 6.15a TIMx control register 1 (TIMx_CR1)—(continued)

15	14	13	12	11	10	9	8	
–	–	–	–	–	–	–	–	Reset value = 0x0000
7	**6**	**5**	**4**	**3**	**2**	**1**	**0**	Offset = 0x14
–	TG	–	CC4G	CC3G	CC2G	CC1G	UG	

TG: Trigger generation

This bit is set by software to generate an event, it is automatically cleared by hardware.

0: No action

1: The TIF flag in the TIMx_SR register is set. Related interrupt or DMA transfer can occur if enabled.

CCxG: Capture/compare x generation (x = 1..4)

0: No action

1: A capture/compare event is generated from channel x:

if channel x is configured as **output**:

CCxIF flag is set, corresponding interrupt or DMA request is sent if enabled.

if channel x is configured as **input**:

The current value of the counter is captured in TIMx_CCR1 register. The CCxIF flag of corresponding interrupt or DMA request is sent if enabled. The CC1OF flag is set if the CC1IF flag was already high.

UG: Update generation

0: No action

1: Re-initialize the counter and generates an update of the registers. Note that the prescaler counter is cleared too (the prescaler ratio is not affected). The counter is cleared if the center-aligned mode is selected and DIR = 0 (upcounting), else it takes the TIMx_ARR value if DIR = 1 (downcounting).

Figure 6.16 TIMx event generation register (TIMx_EGR)

15	14	13	12	11	10	9	8	
–	–	–	CC4OF	CC3OF	CC2OF	CC1OF	–	Reset value = 0x0000
7	**6**	**5**	**4**	**3**	**2**	**1**	**0**	Offset = 0x10
–	TIF	–	CC4IF	CC3IF	CC2IF	CC1IF	UIF	

CCyOF: Capture/compare x overcapture flag (y = 1..4)

This bit is set by hardware only the corresponding channel is configured for input capture. It is cleared by software by writing it to '0'.

0: No overcapture has been detected

1: The counter value has been captured in TIMx_CCRy register while CCyIF flag was already set.

TIF: trigger interrupt flag

This flag is set by hardware on trigger event (active edge detected on TRIG input when the slave mode controller is enabled in all modes but gated mode). It is set when the counter starts or stops when gated mode is selected. It is cleared by software.

0: No trigger event occurred.

1: Trigger interrupt pending

CCyIF: Capture/compare y interrupt flag (y = 1..4)

If channel y is **configured for output**: This flag is set when the counter matches the compare value (in TIMx_CCRy register), with some exception in center-aligned mode (refer to the CMS bits in the TIMx_CR1 register) and in retriggerable one pulse mode. It is cleared using software.

0: No match;

1: The TIMx_CNT matches the TIMx_CCRy register.

If channel y is **configured for input**: This bit is set on a capture. It is cleared by software or by reading the TIMx_CCRy register.

0: No capture has occurred.

1: The contents of the TIMx_CNT has been captured in TIMx_CCRy register.

UIF: Update interrupt flag

0: No update occurred

1: Update interrupt pending. This bit is set when the registers are updated.

Figure 6.17 TIMx status register (TIMx_SR)

6.5.3 CLOCK SELECTION

The counter has four possible clock sources:

- Internal clock (CK_INT)
- External clock mode 1: External input pin (TIx)
- External clock mode 2: External trigger input (ETR)
- Internal trigger inputs (ITRx): Using one timer as prescaler for another timer. For example, the user can configure Timer 3 as the prescaler for Timer 2. This is illustrated in Figure 6.18.

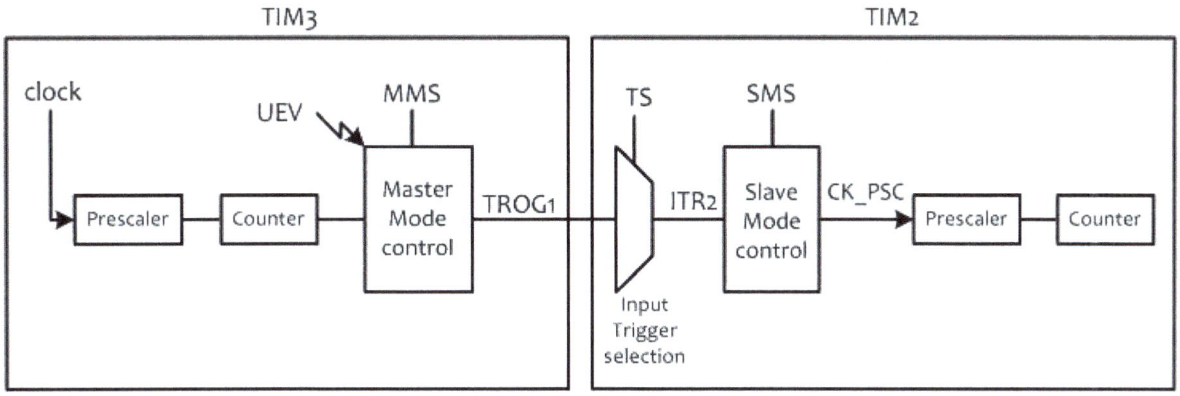

Figure 6.18 Using one timer as prescaler of another timer example

Internal Clock Source (CK_INT)

If the slave mode controller is disabled (the SMS field of the TIMx->SMCR register set to 000), then the CEN, DIR bits in the TIMx->CR1 and the UG bit of the TIMx->EGR register control the timer operation. As soon as the CEN bit is set to 1, the prescaler is clocked by the internal clock CK_INT. The CK_INT clock is the same as the APB1 bus clock.

External Clock Source Mode 1

The block diagram illustrating the input capture, prescaler, capture/compare register, and output control circuit is shown in Figure 6.19.

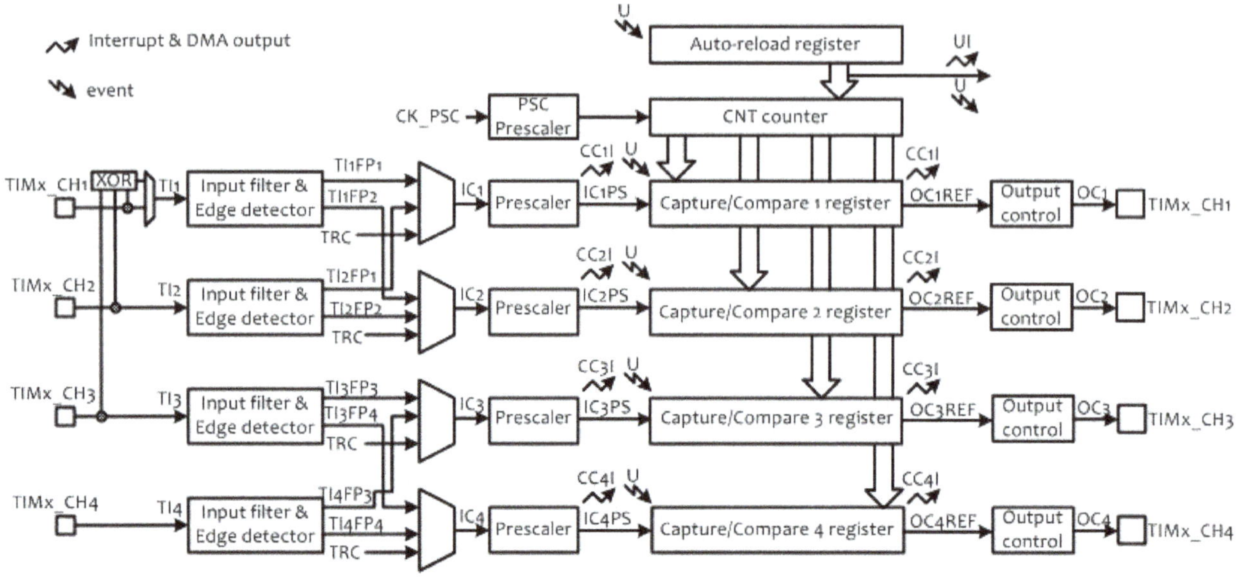

Figure 6.19 Block diagram of the 4 input capture/output compare channels of timer x

The **external clock source mode 1** is selected when the SMS[2:0] field in the TIMx->SMCR register is 111. The counter can count at each rising or falling edge on a selected input. The circuit diagram when TI2 (channel 2) input is selected as the clock input to TIMx is illustrated in Figure 6.20.

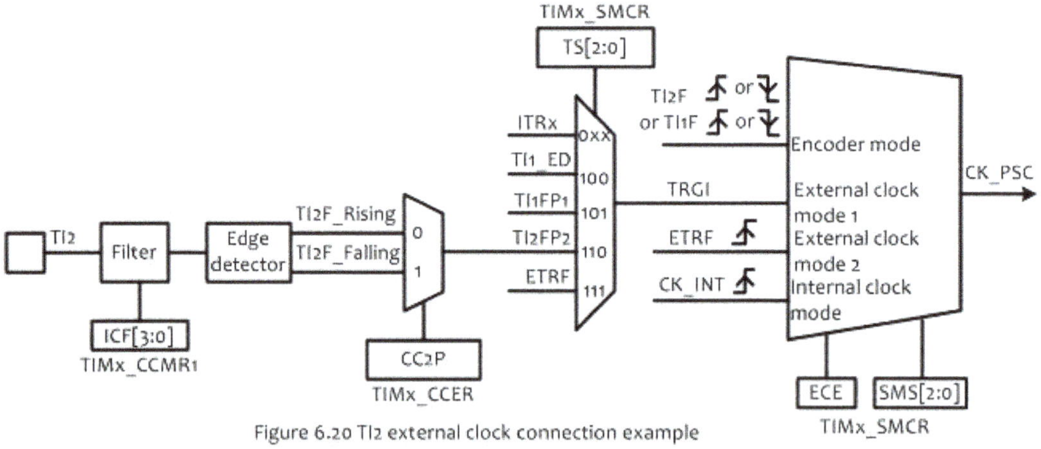

Figure 6.20 TI2 external clock connection example

The contents of the TIMx->SMCR and the TIMx->CCER register are shown in Figure 6.21 and 6.22, respectively.

31	30	29	28	27	26	25	24
--	--	--	--	--	--	--	--
23	**22**	**21**	**20**	**19**	**18**	**17**	**16**
--	--	--	--	--	--	--	SMS[3]
15	**14**	**13**	**12**	**11**	**10**	**9**	**8**
ETP	ECE	ETPS[1:0]		ETF[3]			
7	**6**	**5**	**4**	**3**	**2**	**1**	**0**
MSM	TS[2:0]			OCCS	SMS[2:0]		

Reset value = 0x0000
Offset = 0x08

ETP: External trigger polarity
- 0: ETR is non-inverted, active high or rising edge
- 1: ETR is inverted, active low or falling edge

ECE: external clock enable—this bit enables external clock mode 2
- 0: External clock mode 2 disabled
- 1: External clock mode 2 enabled. The counter is clocked by any active edge on the ETRF signal. (1) Setting the ECE bit has the same effect as selecting external clock mode 1 with TRGI connected to ETRF (SMS = 111 & TS = 111) (2) It is possible to simultaneously use external clock mode 2 with the following slave modes: reset mode, gated mode and trigger mode. TRGI must not be connected to ETRF in this case (TS bits must not be 111). (3) If external clock mode 1 and external clock mode 2 are enabled at the same time, the external clock input is ETRF.

ETPS[1:0]: External trigger prescaler

External trigger signal ETRF frequency must be at most ¼ of CK_INT frequency. A prescaler can be enabled to reduce ETRF frequency.

00: Prescaler OFF	01: ETRF frequency divided by 2
10: ETRF frequency divided by 4	11: ETRF frequency divided by 8

MSM: master/slave mode
- 0: No action
- 1: The effect of an event on the trigger input (TRGI) is delayed to allow a perfect synchronization between the current timer and its slaves (through TRGO).

Figure 6.21 TIMx slave mode control register (TIMx_SMCR)

31	30	29	28	27	26	25	24
–	–	–	–	–	–	–	–
23	**22**	**21**	**20**	**19**	**18**	**17**	**16**
–	–	–	–	–	–	–	SMS[3]
15	**14**	**13**	**12**	**11**	**10**	**9**	**8**
ETP	ECE	ETPS[1:0]		ETF[3]			
7	**6**	**5**	**4**	**3**	**2**	**1**	**0**
MSM	TS[2:0]			OCCS	SMS[2:0]		

Reset value = 0x0000
Offset = 0x08

ETF[3:0]: External trigger filter

This field defines the frequency used to sample ETRF signal and the length of the digital filter applied to ETRF. The digital filter is made of an event counter in which N consecutive events are needed to validate a transition on the output. **See Table 6.2.**

TS: trigger selection—this field selects the trigger input to be used to synchronize the counter. See **Table 6.3**. Internal trigger connection for different timers are shown in **Table 6.4**.

OCCS: OCREF clear selection

0: OCREF_CLR_INT is connected to the OCREF_CLR input

1: OCREF_CLR_INT is connected to ETRF

SMS: Slave mode selection

0000: slave mode disabled—the counter will be clocked by the internal clock.

0001: Encoder mode 1—counter counts up/down on TI1FP1 edge depending on TI2FP2 clock.

0010: Encoder mode 2—counter counts up/down on TI2FP2 edge depending on TI1FP1 clock.

0011: Encoder mode 3—counter counts up/down on both the TI1FP1 and TI2FP2 edge depending on the level of the other input.

0100: Reset mode—rising edge of the selected trigger input (TRGI) reinitializes the counter and generates an update of the registers.

0101: Gated mode—The counter clock is enabled when the trigger input is high. The counter stops (but is not reset) as soon as the trigger goes low. Both start and stop of the counter are controlled.

0110: Trigger mode—The counter starts at a rising edge of the trigger TRGI (but is not reset). Only the start of the counter is controlled.

0111: External clock mode 1—Rising edges of the selected trigger (TRGI) clock the counter.

1000: Combined reset + trigger mode—Rising edges of the selected trigger (TRGI) input reinitializes the counter, generates an update of the registers and starts the counter.

Figure 6.21a TIMx slave mode control register (TIMx_SMCR)—(continued)

Table 6.2 External trigger filter combinations

ETF[3:0]	Description	ETF[3:0]	Description
0000	No filter, sampling is done at f_{DTS}	1000	$f_{SAMPLING} = f_{DTS}/8$, N = 6
0001	$f_{SAMPLING} = f_{CK\_INT}$, N = 2	1001	$f_{SAMPLING} = f_{DTS}/8$, N = 8
0010	$f_{SAMPLING} = f_{CK\_INT}$, N = 4	1010	$f_{SAMPLING} = f_{DTS}/16$, N = 5
0011	$f_{SAMPLING} = f_{CK\_INT}$, N = 8	1011	$f_{SAMPLING} = f_{DTS}/16$, N = 6
0100	$f_{SAMPLING} = f_{DTS}/2$, N = 6	1100	$f_{SAMPLING} = f_{DTS}/16$, N = 8
0101	$f_{SAMPLING} = f_{DTS}/2$, N = 8	1101	$f_{SAMPLING} = f_{DTS}/32$, N = 5
0110	$f_{SAMPLING} = f_{DTS}/4$, N = 6	1110	$f_{SAMPLING} = f_{DTS}/32$, N = 6
0111	$f_{SAMPLING} = f_{DTS}/4$, N = 8	1111	$f_{SAMPLING} = f_{DTS}/32$, N = 8

Table 6.3 Trigger selection

TS[2:0]	Description
000	Internal trigger 0 (ITR0). Reserved
001	Internal trigger 1 (ITR1)
010	Internal trigger 2 (ITR2)
011	Internal trigger 3 (ITR3). Reserved
100	TI1 Edge detector (TI1F_ED)
101	Filtered Timer Input 1 (TI1FP1)
110	Filtered Timer Input 2 (TI2FP2)
111	External Trigger input (ETRF)

Table 6.4 TIMx internal trigger connection

Slave TIM	ITR0 (TS = 000)	ITR1 (TS = 001)	ITR2 (TS = 010)	ITR3 (TS = 011)
TIM2	TIM1	TIM8/OTG_FS SOF	TIM3	TIM4
TIM3	TIM1	TIM2	TIM5	TIM4
TIM4	TIM1	TIM2	TIM3	TIM8
TIM5	TIM2	TIM3	TIM4	TIM8

15	14	13	12	11	10	9	8	
CC4NP	–	CC4P	CC4E	CC3NP	–	CC3P	CC3E	Reset value = 0x0000
7	6	5	4	3	2	1	0	Offset = 0x20
CC2NP	–	CC2P	CC2E	CC1NP	–	CC1P	CC1E	

CCkNP: Capture/Compare k output polarity (k = 1..4)

CCk channel configured as output: CCkNP must be kept 0.

CCk channel configured as input: This bit is used in conjunction with CCkP to define TI_kFP1/ $TI_{k+1}FP1$ polarity. Refer to CCkP description.

CCkP: Capture/compare k output polarity (k = 1..4)

CCk configured as output:

0: OCk active high 1: OCk active low

CCk configured as input: CC_kNP/CC_kP bits select TI_kFP_k and $TI_{k+1}FP_k$ polarity for trigger or capture operations.

00: noninverted/rising edge. Circuit is sensitive to TI_kFP_k rising edge (capture, trigger in reset, external clock or trigger mode). TI_kFP_k is not inverted (trigger in gated mode, encoder mode)

01: Inverted/falling edge. Circuit is sensitive to TI_kFP_k falling edge (capture, trigger in reset, external clock trigger mode), TI_kFP_k is inverted (trigger in gated, encoder mode)

10: not used

11: noninverted/both edges. Circuit is sensitive to both edges of TI_kFP_k.

CCkE: Capture/compare k output enable

CCk channel configured as output:

0: Off – OCk is not active

1: On – OCk is output on the corresponding output pin

CCK channel configured as input: This bit determines if a capture of the counter value can actually be done into the input capture/compare register k ($TIMx\_CCR_k$) or not.

0: capture disabled 1: capture enabled

Figure 6.22 TIMx capture/compare enable register (TIMx_CCER)

Example 6.3 Configure the upcounter (take TIM2 as an example) in response to a rising edge on the TI2 input and write a sequence of C statements to implement it.

Solution:

The procedure is as follows:

Step 1

Configure channel 2 of TIM2 to detect rising edges on the TI2 input by writing the CC2S field in the TIM2->CCMR1 register to 01.

Step 2

Configure the input filter duration by writing the IC2F field in the TIMx->CCMR1 register to 0000 (here, we don't need a filter).

Step 3

Select rising edge by setting CC2P and CC2NP bits in the TIMx->CCER register to 0 and 0.

Step 4

Configure TIM2 to **external clock mode 1** by setting the SMS[2:0] field in the TIMx->SMCR register t0 111.

Step 5

Select TI2 as the input source by setting the TS field in the TIMx->SMCR register to 110.

Step 6

Enable TIM2 by setting the CEN bit in the TIMx_CR1 register to 1.

The following C statements achieve the desired configuration:

```
    TIM2->CCMR1    &=  ~(TIM_CCMR1_CC2S + TIM_CCMR1_IC2F);
    TIM2->CCMR1    |=   TIM_CCMR1_CC2S_0; // CC2S set to 01, IC2F set to 0000
    TIM2->CCER     &=  ~(TIM_CCER_CC2P + TIM_CCER_CC2NP);
    TIM2->SMCR     &=  ~(TIM_SMCR_SMS + TIM_SMCR_TS);
// SMS set to 111, TS set to 110
    TIM2->SMCR     |=   TIM_SMCR_SMS + TIM_SMCR_TS_1 + TIM_SMCR_TS_2;
    TIM2->CR1      |=   TIM_CR1_CEN; // enable TIM2 timer
```

External Clock Source Mode 2

This mode is selected by setting **ECE** bit in the TIMx->SMCR register to 1. The counter can count at each rising or falling edge on the external trigger input **ETR**. The block diagram of this mode is illustrated in Figure 6.23.

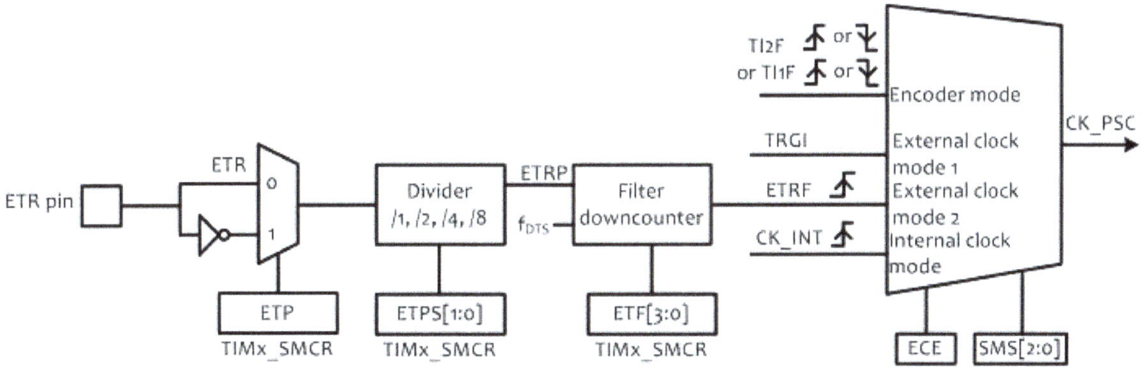

Figure 6.23 External trigger input block

Example 6.4 Describe how to configure the TIM2 to upcounting mode to count in every two rising edges on ETR and write a sequence of C statements to implement it.

Solution:

Step 1

Set the ETF[3:0] field in the TIMx->SMCR register to 0000 because no filter is needed.

Step 2

Set the prescaler to 2 by setting the ETPS[1:0] field in the TIMx->SMCR register to 01.

Step 3

Select rising edge detection on the ETR pin by clearing the ETP bit in the TIMx->SMCR register to 0.

Step 4

Enable external clock mode 2 by setting the ECE bit in the TIMx_SMCR register to 1.

Step 5

Enable the counter by setting the CEN bit in the TIMx_CR1 register.

The following C statements configure TIM2 to count every two ETR rising edges:

```
TIM2->SMCR     &= ~(TIM_SMCR_ETF + TIM_SMCR_ETPS + TIM_SMCR_ETP); // clear 3 fields
TIM2->SMCR     |= TIM_SMCR_ETPS_0 + TIM_SMCR_ECE; // set the ETPS field to 01, ECE = 1
TIM2->CR1      |= TIM_CR1_CEN; // enable TIM2
```

6.5.4 SIGNAL PINS RELATED TO TIM2/TIM3/TIM4/TIM5

Five signal pins are associated with each of these timers. Each timer has TIMx_CH1~TIMx_CH4 for input capture or output compare function and TIMx_ETR pin for external input. The pin assignment of these signals is present in Table 6.5. TIM5 does not have an ETR input.

Table 6.5 Pin assignment for TIM2.TIM3/TIM4/TIM5

Signal	Pin	Signal	Pin
TIM2_CH1	PA0 (AF1), PA5 (AF1), PA15 (AF1)	TIM4_CH1	PB6 (AF2), PD12 (AF2)
TIM2_CH2	PA1(AF1), PB3 (AF1)	TIM4_CH2	PB7 (AF2), PD13 (AF2)
TIM2_CH3	PA2 (AF1), PB10 (AF1)	TIM4_CH3	PB8 (AF2), PD14 (AF2)
TIM2_CH4	PA3 (AF1), PB11 (AF1)	TIM4_CH4	PB9 (AF2), PD15 (AF2)
TIM2_ETR	PA5 (AF2), PA15 (AF2)	TIM4_ETR	PE0 (AF2)
TIM3_CH1	PA6 (AF2), PB4 (AF2), PC6 (AF2), PE3 (AF2)	TIM5_CH1	PA0 (AF2)
TIM3_CH2	PA7 (AF2), PB5 (AF2), PC7 (AF2), PE4 (AF2)	TIM5_CH2	PA1 (AF2)
TIM3_CH3	PB0 (AF2), PC8 (AF2), PC8 (AF2), PE5 (AF2)	TIM5_CH3	PA2 (AF2)
TIM3_CH4	PB1 (AF2), PC9 (AF2), PC9 (AF2), PE6 (AF2)	TIM5_CH4	PA3 (AF2)
TIM3_ETR	PD2 (AF2), PE2 (AF2)	TIM5_ETR	

Note. **AF** stands for **alternate function**

6.5.5 CAPTURE/COMPARE CHANNELS

The capture/compare channels are very complicated. Each capture/compare channel is built around a capture/compare register (including a shadow register), an input stage for capture (with digital filter, multiplexing, and prescaler), and an output stage (with comparator and output control). The block diagram of the input stage of a capture/compare channel is shown in Figure 6.24.

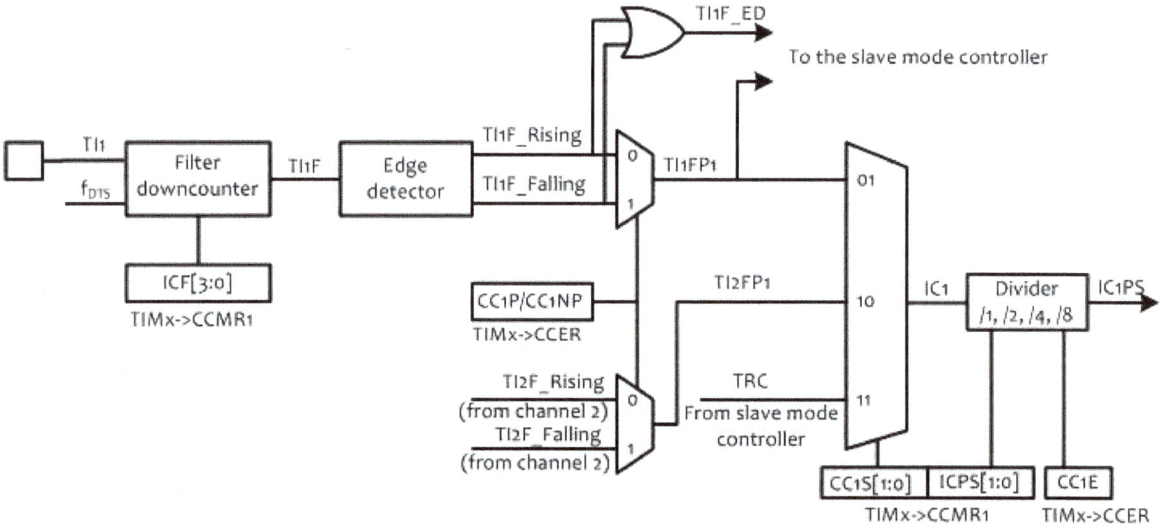

Figure 6.24 Input stage of the Capture/compare channel (channel 1 example)

The main circuit of the capture/compare channel is shown in Figure 6.25 (use channel 1 as an example). The capture/compare block is made of one preload register and one shadow register. Write and read always access the preload register.

In capture mode, captures are done in the shadow register, which is then copied into the preload register.

In compare mode, the contents of the preload register are copied into the shadow register, which is compared to the counter.

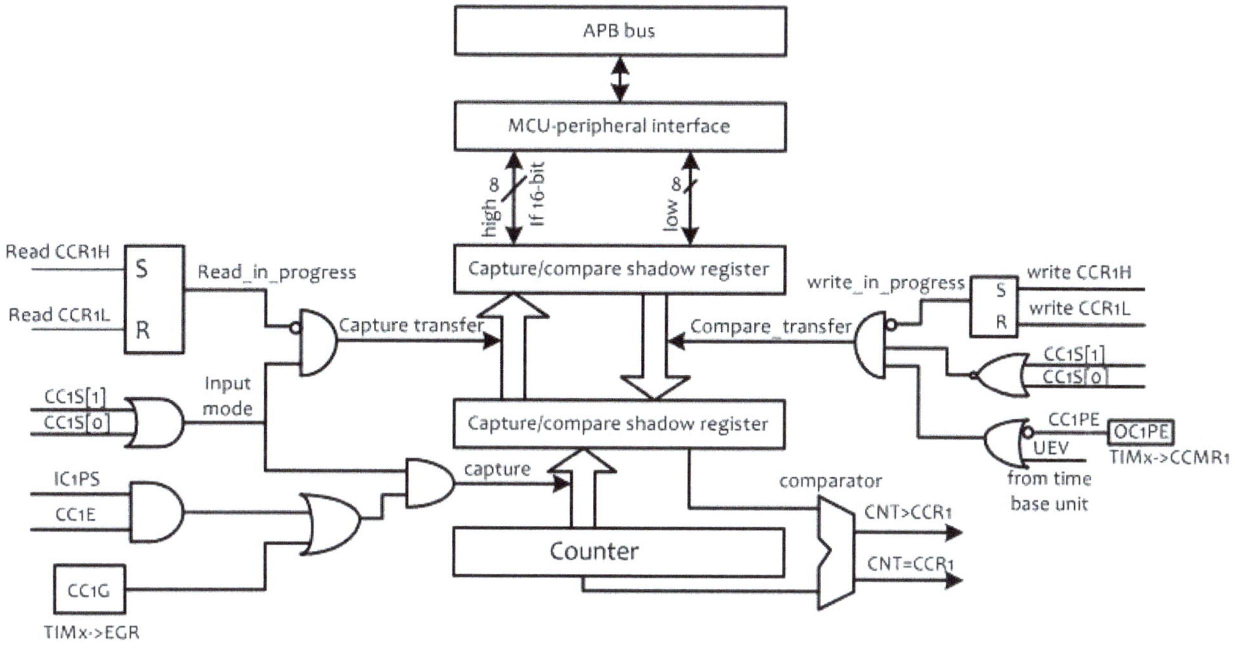

Figure 6.25 Capture/compare channel main circuit (channel 1 example)

The output stage generates an intermediate waveform OCxREF (shown in Figure 6.19) that is then used for reference. The block diagram of the output stage of capture/compare channel is shown in Figure 6.26.

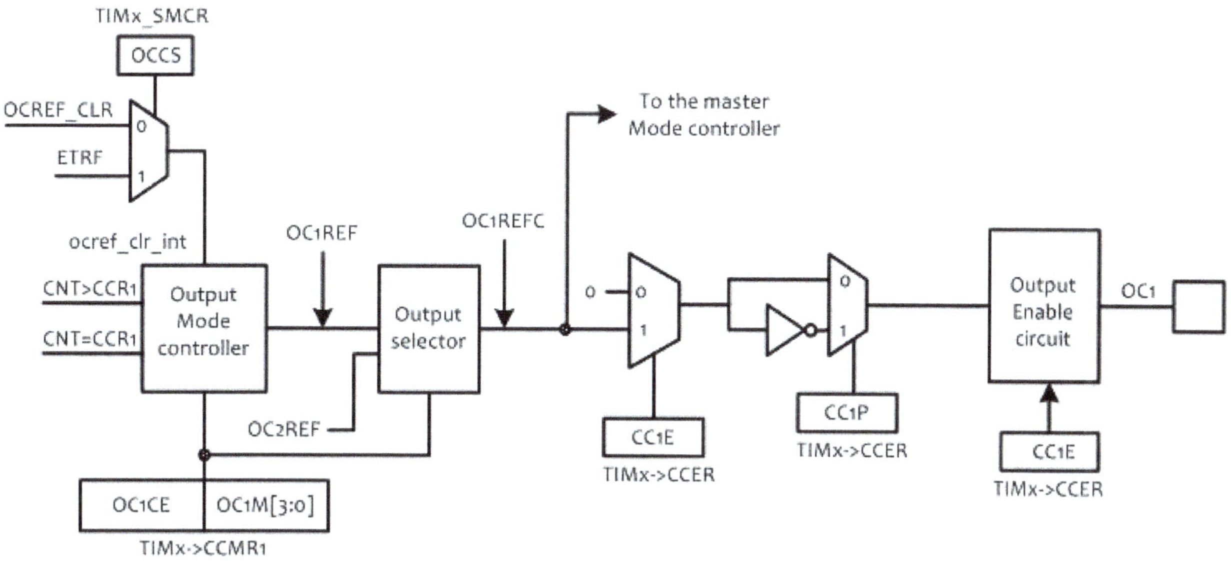

Figure 6.26 Output stage of the Capture/compare channel (channel 1 example)

6.5.6 INPUT CAPTURE MODE

In the input capture mode, the contents of the timer are copied into the capture/compare register (TIMx->C-CRy) when the selected transition is detected on the ICy signal. When a capture occurs, the associated CCy-IF flag in the TIMx->SR register is set and an interrupt or DMA request can be generated if they are enabled.

If a capture occurs while the CCyIF flag is already set, then the over-capture flag CCyOF in the TIMx->SR register will be set to 1. The CCyIF flag can be cleared by writing 0 to it or by reading the captured data stored in the TIMx->CCRy register.

31	30	29	28	27	26	25	24
							OC2M[3]

23	22	21	20	19	18	17	16
							OC1M[3]

Reset value = 0x0000
Address offset = 0x18

15	14	13	12	11	10	9	8
OC2CE	OC2M[2:0]			OC2PE	OC2FE	CC2S[1:0]	
IC2F[3:0]				IC2PSC[1:0]			

7	6	5	4	3	2	1	0
OC1CE	OC1M[2:0]			OC1PE	OC1FE	CC1S[1:0]	
IC1F[3:0]				IC1PSC[1:0]			

CC1S[1:0]: Capture/compare 1 selection
00: CC1 channel is configured as output.
01: CC1 channel is configured as input, IC1 is mapped on TI1.
10: CC1 channel is configured as input, IC1 is mapped on TI2.
11: CC1 channel is configured as input, IC1 is mapped on TRC. This mode is working only if an internal trigger input is selected through TS bit (TIMx_SMCR register)CC2S[1:0]: capture/compare 2 selection
00: CC2 channel is configured as output.
01: CC2 channel is configured as input, IC2 is mapped on TI2.
10: CC2 channel is configured as input, IC2 is mapped on TI1.
11: CC2 channel is configured as input, IC2 is mapped on TRC. This mode is working only if an internal trigger input is selected through the TS bit in the TIMx_SMCR register.

Output Compare Mode

OCyM[3]: output compare x mode – bit 3 (y = 1, 2)
OCyCE (y = 1 or 2): Output compare y clear enable
0: OCyREF is not affected by the ETRF input.
1: OCyREF is cleared as soon as the ETRF input is high.

Figure 6.27 TIMx capture/compare mode register 1 (TIMx_CCMR1)

31	30	29	28	27	26	25	24
							OC2M[3]

23	22	21	20	19	18	17	16
							OC2M[3]

15	14	13	12	11	10	9	8
OC2CE	OC2M[2:0]			OC2PE	OC2FE	CC2S[1:0]	
IC2F[3:0]				IC2PSC[1:0]			

7	6	5	4	3	2	1	0
OC1CE	OC1M[2:0]			OC1PE	OC1FE	CC1S[1:0]	
IC1F[3:0]				IC1PSC[1:0]			

Reset value = 0x0000
Address offset = 0x18

Output compare mode

OCyM[3:0]: output compare y mode (y = 1, 2)

These bits define the behavior of the OCyREF signal from which OCy and OCyN are derived. OCyREF is active high. OCy and OCyN active level depends on CCyP and CCyNP bits. CCyP and CCyNP are contained in the TIMx_CCER register.

Possible modes see **Table 6.5**.

OCyPE: output compare y preload enable (y = 1, 2)

0: preload register on TIMx_CCRy disabled. TIMx_CCRy can be written at anytime, the new value is taken in account immediately.

1: preload register on TIMx_CCRy enabled. Read/write operations to TIMx_CCRy access its preload register. TIMx_CCRy preload value is loaded in the active register at update event.

OCyFE: Output compare y fast enable (y = 1, 2)

This bit is used to accelerate the effect of an event on the trigger in input on the CC output.

0: CCy behaves normally depending on counter and CCRy values even when the trigger is ON. The minimum delay to activate CCy output when an edge occurs on the trigger input is 5 clock cycles.

1: An active edge on the trigger input acts like a compare match on CCy output. Then, OC is set to the compare level independently from the result of the comparison. Delay to sample the trigger input and to activate CCy output is reduced to 3 clock cycles.

Figure 6.27a TIMx capture/compare mode register 1 (TIMx_CCMR1)—(continued)

Table 6.6 Output compare y mode (OCyM: y = 1, 2)

OCyM[3:0]	Description (effect on comparison result between TIMx_CCRy and TIMx_CNT)
0000	Frozen—the comparison of TIMx_CCRy and TIMx_CNT has no effect on the output OCyREF.
0001	Set OCyREF to high when the value in TIMx_CCRy equals that of TIMx_CNT.
0010	Set OCyREF to low when the value in TIMx_CCRy equals that of TIMx_CNT.
0011	Toggle OCyREF signal when the value in TIMx_CCRy equals that of TIMx_CNT.
0100	Force OCyREF to low.
0101	Force OCyREF to high.
0110	**PWM mode 1.** When upcounting, OCyREF is high if TIMx_CNT < TIMx_CCRy, else OCyREF is low. When downcounting, OCyREF is low if TIMx_CNT > TIMx_CCRy, else OCyREF is high.
0111	**PWM mode 2.** When upcounting, OCyREF is low if TIMx_CNT < TIMx_CCRy, else OCyREF is high. When downcounting, OCyREF is high if TIMx_CNT > TIMx_CCRy, else OCyREF is low.
1000	**Retriggerable OPM mode 1.** In up-counting mode, the channel is active until a trigger event is detected (on TRGI signal). Then a comparison is performed as in OWM mode 1 and the channel becomes inactive again at the next update. In down-counting mode, the channel is inactive until a trigger is detected(on TRIGI signal). Then a comparison is performed as in PWM mode 1 and the channels become inactive again at the next update.
1001	**Retriggerable OPM mode 2.** In up-counting mode, the channel is inactive until a trigger event is detected (on TRGI signal). Then a comparison is performed as in PWM mode 2 and the channel becomes inactive again at the next update. In down-counting mode, the channel is active until a trigger event is detected (on TRGI signal). Then a comparison is performed as in PWM mode 1 and the channels becomes active again at the next update.
1010 & 1011	Not used
1100	**Combined PWM mode 1.** OCyREF has the same behavior as in PWM mode 1. OCyREFC is the logical OR of OC1REF and OC2REF.
1101	**Combined PWM mode 2.** OCyREF has the same behavior as in PWM mode 2. OCyREFC is the logical AND of OC1REF and OC2REF.
1110	**Asymmetric PWM mode 1.** OCyREF has the same behavior as in PWM mode 1. OC1REFC outputs OC1REF when the counter is counting up, OC2REF when it is counting down. OC2REF outputs OC2REF when the counter is counting up, OC1REF when it is counting down.
1111	**Asymmetric PWM mode 2.** OCyREF has the same behavior as in PWM mode 2. OC1REFC outputs OC1REF when the counter is counting up, OC2REF when it is counting down. OC2REFC outputs OC2REF when the counter is counting up, OC1REF when it is counting down.

31	30	29	28	27	26	25	24
							OC2M[3]

Reset value = 0x0000
Address offset = 0x18

23	22	21	20	19	18	17	16
							OC1M[3]

15	14	13	12	11	10	9	8
OC2CE	OC2M[2:0]			OC2PE	OC2FE	CC2S[1:0]	
IC2F[3:0]				IC2PSC[1:0]			

7	6	5	4	3	2	1	0
OC1CE	OC1M[2:0]			OC1PE	OC1FE	CC1S[1:0]	
IC1F[3:0]				IC1PSC[1:0]			

Input capture mode

ICyF[3:0]: input capture filter (y = 1, 2 channel)

This field defines the frequency to sample TI1 and the length of the digital filter applied to TI1.

0000: No filter, sampling is done at f_{DTS} 0001: $f_{SAMPLING} = f_{CK\_INT}$, N = 2
0010: $f_{SAMPLING} = f_{CK\_INT}$, N = 4 0011: $f_{SAMPLING} = f_{CK\_INT}$, N = 8
0100: $f_{SAMPLING} = f_{DTS}/2$, N = 6 0101: $f_{SAMPLING} = f_{DTS}/2$, N = 8
0110: $f_{SAMPLING} = f_{DTS}/4$, N = 6 0111: $f_{SAMPLING} = f_{DTS}/4$, N = 8
1000: $f_{SAMPLING} = f_{DTS}/8$, N = 6 1001: $f_{SAMPLING} = f_{DTS}/8$, N = 8
1010: $f_{SAMPLING} = f_{DTS}/16$, N = 5 1011: $f_{SAMPLING} = f_{DTS}/16$, N = 6
1100: $f_{SAMPLING} = f_{DTS}/16$, N = 8 1101: $f_{SAMPLING} = f_{DTS}/32$, N = 5
1110: $f_{SAMPLING} = f_{DTS}/32$, N = 6 1111: $f_{SAMPLING} = f_{DTS}/32$, N = 8

ICyPSC: Input capture y prescaler (y = 1, 2 channel)

The prescaler is reset as soon as CCyE = 0 (TIMx_CCER register).
00: No prescaler, capture on every edgve 01: capture is done once every 2 events
10: capture is done once every 4 events. 11: capture is done once every 8 events

Figure 6.27b TIMx capture/compare mode register 1 (TIMx_CCMR1)—(continued)

31	30	29	28	27	26	25	24
							OC4M[3]

23	22	21	20	19	18	17	16
							OC3M[3]

Reset value = 0x0000
Address offset = 0x1C

15	14	13	12	11	10	9	8
OC4CE	OC4M[2:0]			OC4PE	OC4FE	CC4S[1:0]	
IC4F[3:0]				IC4PSC[1:0]			

7	6	5	4	3	2	1	0
OC3CE	OC3M[2:0]			OC3PE	OC3FE	CC3S[1:0]	
IC3F[3:0]				IC3PSC[1:0]			

CC4S[1:0]: capture/compare 4 selection
- 00: CC4 channel is configured as output.
- 01: CC4 channel is configured as input, IC4 is mapped on TI4.
- 10: CC4 channel is configured as input, IC4 is mapped on TI3.
- 11: CC4 channel is configured as input, IC4 is mapped on TRC. This mode is working only if an internal trigger input is selected through the TS bit in the TIMx_SMCR register.

CC3S[1:0]: Capture/compare 3 selection
- 00: CC3 channel is configured as output.
- 01: CC3 channel is configured as input, IC3 is mapped on TI3.
- 10: CC3 channel is configured as input, IC3 is mapped on TI4.
- 11: CC3 channel is configured as input, IC3 is mapped on TRC. This mode is working only if an internal trigger input is selected through TS bit (TIMx_SMCR register)

Output Compare Mode

OCyM[3]: output compare x mode – bit 3 (y = 3, 4)

OCyCE: Output compare y clear enable (y = 3, 4)
- 0: OCyREF is not affected by the ETRF input.
- 1: OCyREF is cleared as soon as the ETRF input is high.

Figure 6.28 TIMx capture/compare mode register 2 (TIMx_CCMR2)

<table>
<tr><td>31</td><td>30</td><td>29</td><td>28</td><td>27</td><td>26</td><td>25</td><td>24</td></tr>
<tr><td></td><td></td><td></td><td></td><td></td><td></td><td></td><td>OC4M[3]</td></tr>
<tr><td>23</td><td>22</td><td>21</td><td>20</td><td>19</td><td>18</td><td>17</td><td>16</td></tr>
<tr><td></td><td></td><td></td><td></td><td></td><td></td><td></td><td>OC3M[3]</td></tr>
<tr><td>15</td><td>14</td><td>13</td><td>12</td><td>11</td><td>10</td><td>9</td><td>8</td></tr>
<tr><td>OC4CE</td><td colspan="3">OC4M[2:0]</td><td>OC4PE</td><td>OC4FE</td><td colspan="2" rowspan="2">CC4S[1:0]</td></tr>
<tr><td colspan="4">IC4F[3:0]</td><td colspan="2">IC4PSC[1:0]</td></tr>
<tr><td>7</td><td>6</td><td>5</td><td>4</td><td>3</td><td>2</td><td>1</td><td>0</td></tr>
<tr><td>OC3CE</td><td colspan="3">OC3M[2:0]</td><td>OC3PE</td><td>OC3FE</td><td colspan="2" rowspan="2">CC3S[1:0]</td></tr>
<tr><td colspan="4">IC3F[3:0]</td><td colspan="2">IC3PSC[1:0]</td></tr>
</table>

Reset value = 0x0000
Address offset = 0x1C

Output compare mode

OCyM[3:0]: output compare y mode (y = 3, 4)

These bits define the behavior of the OCyREF signal from which OCy and OCyN are derived. OCyREF is active high. OCy and OCyN active level depends on CCyP and CCyNP bits. CCyP and CCyNP are contained in the TIMx_CCER register.

Possible modes see Table 6.6.

OCyPE: output compare y preload enable (y = 3, 4)

0: preload register on TIMx_CCRy disabled. TIMx_CCRy can be written at anytime, the new value is taken in account immediately.

1: preload register on TIMx_CCRy enabled. Read/write operations to TIMx_CCRy access its preload register. TIMx_CCRy preload value is loaded in the active register at update event.

OCyFE: Output compare y fast enable (y = 3, 4)

This bit is used to accelerate the effect of an event on the trigger in input on the CC output.

0: CCy behaves normally depending on counter and CCRy values even when the trigger is ON. The minimum delay to activate CCy output when an edge occurs on the trigger input is 5 clock cycles.

1: An active edge on the trigger input acts like a compare match on CCy output. Then, OC is set to the compare level independently from the result of the comparison. Delay to sample the trigger input and to activate CCy output is reduced to 3 clock cycles.

Figure 6.28a TIMx capture/compare mode register 2 (TIMx_CCMR2)

Table 6.7 Output compare y mode (OCyM: y = 3, 4)

OCyM[3:0]	Description (effect on comparison result between TIMx_CCRy and TIMx_CNT)
0000	Frozen—the comparison of TIMx_CCRy and TIMx_CNT has no effect on the output OCyREF.
0001	Set OCyREF to high when the value in TIMx_CCRy equals that of TIMx_CNT.
0010	Set OCyREF to low when the value in TIMx_CCRy equals that of TIMx_CNT.
0011	Toggle OCyREF signal when the value in TIMx_CCRy equals that of TIMx_CNT.
0100	Force OCyREF to low.
0101	Force OCyREF to high.
0110	**PWM mode 1.** When upcounting, OCyREF is high if TIMx_CNT < TIMx_CCRy, else OCyREF is low. When downcounting, OCyREF is low if TIMx_CNT > TIMx_CCRy, else OCyREF is high.
0111	**PWM mode 2.** When upcounting, OCyREF is low if TIMx_CNT < TIMx_CCRy, else OCyREF is high. When downcounting, OCyREF is high if TIMx_CNT > TIMx_CCRy, else OCyREF is low.
1000	**Retriggerable OPM mode 1.** In up-counting mode, the channel is active until a trigger event is detected (on TRGI signal). Then a comparison is performed as in OWM mode 1 and the channel becomes inactive again at the next update. In down-counting mode, the channel is inactive until a trigger is detected(on TRIGI signal). Then a comparison is performed as in PWM mode 1 and the channels become inactive again at the next update.
1001	**Retriggerable OPM mode 2.** In up-counting mode, the channel is inactive until a trigger event is detected (on TRGI signal). Then a comparison is performed as in PWM mode 2 and the channel becomes inactive again at the next update. In down-counting mode, the channel is active until a trigger event is detected (on TRGI signal). Then a comparison is performed as in PWM mode 1 and the channels becomes active again at the next update.
1010 & 1011	Not used
1100	**Combined PWM mode 1.** OCyREF has the same behavior as in PWM mode 1. OCyREFC is the logical OR of OC3REF and OC4REF.
1101	**Combined PWM mode 2.** OCyREF has the same behavior as in PWM mode 2. OCyREFC is the logical AND of OC3REF and OC4REF.
1110	**Asymmetric PWM mode 1.** OCyREF has the same behavior as in PWM mode 1. OC3REFC outputs OC3REF when the counter is counting up, OC4REF when it is counting down. OC4REF outputs OC4REF when the counter is counting up, OC3REF when it is counting down.
1111	**Asymmetric PWM mode 2.** OCyREF has the same behavior as in PWM mode 2. OC3REFC outputs OC3REF when the counter is counting up, OC4REF when it is counting down. OC4REFC outputs OC4REF when the counter is counting up, OC3REF when it is counting down.

31	30	29	28	27	26	25	24
							OC4M[3]

23	22	21	20	19	18	17	16
							OC3M[3]

Reset value = 0x0000
Address offset = 0x1C

15	14	13	12	11	10	9	8
OC4CE	OC4M[2:0]			OC4PE	OC4FE	CC4S[1:0]	
IC4F[3:0]				IC4PSC[1:0]			

7	6	5	4	3	2	1	0
OC3CE	OC3M[2:0]			OC3PE	OC3FE	CC3S[1:0]	
IC3F[3:0]				IC3PSC[1:0]			

Input capture mode

ICyF[3:0]: input capture filter (y = 3, 4 channel)

This field defines the frequency to sample TIy and the length of the digital filter applied to TIy.

- 0000: No filter, sampling is done at f_{DTS}
- 0001: $f_{SAMPLING} = f_{CK\_INT}$, N = 2
- 0010: $f_{SAMPLING} = f_{CK\_INT}$, N = 4
- 0011: $f_{SAMPLING} = f_{CK\_INT}$, N = 8
- 0100: $f_{SAMPLING} = f_{DTS}/2$, N = 6
- 0101: $f_{SAMPLING} = f_{DTS}/2$, N = 8
- 0110: $f_{SAMPLING} = f_{DTS}/4$, N = 6
- 0111: $f_{SAMPLING} = f_{DTS}/4$, N = 8
- 1000: $f_{SAMPLING} = f_{DTS}/8$, N = 6
- 1001: $f_{SAMPLING} = f_{DTS}/8$, N = 8
- 1010: $f_{SAMPLING} = f_{DTS}/16$, N = 5
- 1011: $f_{SAMPLING} = f_{DTS}/16$, N = 6
- 1100: $f_{SAMPLING} = f_{DTS}/16$, N = 8
- 1101: $f_{SAMPLING} = f_{DTS}/32$, N = 5
- 1110: $f_{SAMPLING} = f_{DTS}/32$, N = 6
- 1111: $f_{SAMPLING} = f_{DTS}/32$, N = 8

ICyPSC: Input capture y prescaler (y = 3, 4 channel)

The prescaler is reset as soon as CCyE = 0 (TIMx_CCER register).

- 00: No prescaler, capture on every edgve
- 01: capture is done once every 2 events
- 10: capture is done once every 4 events.
- 11: capture is done once every 8 events

Figure 6.28b TIMx capture/compare mode register 2 (TIMx_CCMR2)—(continued)

Example 6.5 Describe how to configure TIM2 channel 1 to capture the timer value

TIM2->CNT into the TIM2->CCR1 register on the rising edge of the TI1 signal and write a sequence of C statements to implement it. There is no need to filter the input signal.

Solution:

The procedure is as follows:

Step 1

Select the TI1 input to capture (map TI1 signal to TIM2_CH1 pin) by setting the CC1S field of the TIM2->C-CMR1 register to 01.

Step 2

Disable filter by setting the IC1F field of the TIM2->CCMR1 register to 0000.

Step 3

Select the rising edge to capture by setting the CC1P and CC1NP bits in the TIM1->CCER register to 00.

Step 4

Program the input prescaler. In this example, we wish the capture to be performed at each valid transition, so the prescaler is disabled. Set the IC1PSC[1:0] field in the TIM2->CCMR1 to 00.

Step 5

Enable capture on channel 1 by setting the CC1E bit in the TIM2->CCER register.

Step 6

If needed, we can enable the capture interrupt on channel 1 or enable DMA transfer by setting the CC1DE bit in the TIM2->DIER register.

The following C statements implement Step 1 to Step 5:

```
TIM2->CCMR1  &=  ~(TIM_CCMR1_CC1S + TIM_CCMR1_IC1F + TIM_CCMR1_IC1PSC);
TIM2->CCMR1  |=  TIM_CCMR1_CC1S_0; // CC1S set to 01, other 2 field set to 00 & 0000
TIM2->CCER   &=  ~(TIM_CCER_CC1P + TIM_CCER_CC1NP); // CC1P & CC1NP set to 00
TIM2->CCER   |=  TIM_CCER_CC1E; // enable channel 1 capture on TIM2
TIM2->CR1    |= TIM_CR1_CEN; // enable TIM2
```

Input capture can be used to measure the pulse width of a signal (need not be periodic) and the period of a periodic signal. However, the PWM input mode makes this even easier.

6.5.7 PWM INPUT MODE

This mode is a special case of input capture mode. This mode is similar to the input capture mode with the following differences:

1. Two ICx signals are mapped on the same TIx input pin (refer to Figure 6.19, TI1FP1 and TI1FP2).
2. These two ICx signals are active on opposite edges (need to be set up).
3. One of the two TIxFP signals is selected as trigger input, and the slave mode controller is configured in reset mode. In reset mode, the trigger input forces the counter to 0.

The PWM input mode can be used only with the TIMx_CH1/TIMx_CH2 signals because only TI1FP1 and TI2FP2 are connected to the slave mode controller.

To measure the pulse width and duty cycle of a signal applied to TI1 signal, take the following steps after setting up the prescaler of the timer clock input:

Step 1

Select TI1 as the input for TIMx_CCR1 by setting the CC1S field in the TIMx_CCMR1 register to 01.

Step 2

Select the rising edge of the TI1FP1 signal for channel 1 capture and counter clear by setting the CC1P and CC1NP bit in the TIMx_CCER register to 00.

Step 3

Select TI1 as the input for TIMx_CCR2 by setting the CC2S field in the TIMx_CCMR1 register to 10.

Step 4

Select the falling edge of the TI1FP2 for channel 2 capture by setting the CC2P bit to 1 and CC2NP bit to 0 via the TIMx_CCER register.

Step 5

Select TI1FP1 as the trigger input by setting the TS field in the TIMx_SMCR register to 101.

Step 6

Configure the slave mode controller to reset mode by setting the SMS field in the TIMx_SMCR register to 100.

Step 7

Enable capture by setting the CC1E and CC2E bit in the TIMx_CCER register to 11.

Example 6.6 Measure the pulse width and duty cycle of a periodic signal connected to the TIM2_CH1 (PA0) pin, assuming that f_{CLK_INT} = 80 MHz.

Solution:

```
#include <stm32L475xx.h>

void sysClkInit(void);

int main(void)

{

    uint32_t period, duty;

    sysClkInit();

    GPIOA->MODER   &= ~(GPIO_MODER_MODE0);

    GPIOA->MODER   |= GPIO_MODER_MODE0_1; // configure PA0 for alternate function

    GPIOA->AFR[0]  &= ~(GPIO_AFRL_AFSEL0); // map PA0 to AF1 (TIM2_CH1)

    GPIOA->AFR[0]  |= GPIO_AFRL_AFSEL0_0; //   "

    // CC1S set to 01, CC2S field set to 10 → select TI1 as input of channel 1 & 2

    TIM2->CCMR1    = TIM_CCMR1_CC1S_0 + TIM_CCMR1_CC2S_1;

    TIM2->SMCR     &= ~(TIM_SMCR_TS + TIM_SMCR_SMS); // clear TS and SMS fields

    // select TI1FP1 (101) as trigger input & configure slave mode controller to reset mode

    TIM2->SMCR     |= TIM_SMCR_TS_0 + TIM_SMCR_TS_2 + TIM_SMCR_SMS_2;
```

```
    TIM2->PSC        = 3; // clock prescaler set to 4
    TIM2->ARR        = 100,000,000; // TOP value for counting
    TIM2->EGR        |= TIM_EGR_UG; // load PSC & ARR into their shadow registers
    TIM2->CNT        = 0; // force TIM2 to count from 0
    // Enable auto preload, select edge-aligned mode, select up-counting,
    // enable auto-reload, enable TIM2 to count
    TIM2->CR1        = TIM_CR1_ARPE + TIM_CR1_CEN;
    TIM2->SR         = 0; // clear all TIM2 flags
    TIM2->CCER       = 0;
    // capture TI1FP1 rising edge for channel 1, capture falling edge for channel 2,
    // enable capture on channel 1 & 2
    TIM2->CCER       = TIM_CCER_CC2P + TIM_CCER_CC1E + TIM_CCER_CC2E;
    while(!(TIM2->SR & TIM_SR_CC1IF)); // wait for the first rising edge to arrive
    TIM2->SR &= ~TIM_SR_CC1IF; // clear CC1IF flag
    while(!(TIM2->SR & TIM_SR_CC1IF));// wait for the second rising edge
    period      = TIM2->CCR1; // period in # of clock cycles
    duty        = (TIM2->CCR2 * 100) / period; // calculate the duty (0 to 100 percent)
    return 0;
}
```

6.5.8 FORCED OUTPUT MODE

The user can force the output compare signal to low or high (OCyREF and then OCy). The first step is to configure the timer channel to output by programing the CCxS field in the TIMx->CCMRy (x = 2..5, y = 1..2) register to 00. In the second step, the user needs to program the OCxM field in the TIMx->CCMRy register to **0100** or **0101** depending on whether the user wants to force the OCyREF signal to low or high.

The comparison between the TIMx->CCRy shadow register and the counter is still performed and allows the flag to be set. Interrupt and DMA request can be sent accordingly.

The following C statements force the TIM2_CH1 (**OC1**) pin to high:

```
    TIM2->CCMR1   &= ~(TIM_CCMR1_CC1S + TIM_CCMR1_OC1M);
    TIM2->CCMR1   |=  TIM_CCMR1_OC1M_2 + TIM_CCMR1_OC1M_0; // force OC1 pin high
```

6.5.9 OUTPUT COMPARE MODE

This mode is mainly provided to control an output waveform or indicating when a period of time has elapsed.

The contents of the capture/compare register and the counter are compared in every clock cycle. When there is a match, the OCy signal (see Figure 6.26) may be affected in the following manner depending upon the setting of the OCyM field in the TIMx->CCMRy register and the CCyP bit in the TIMx->CCER register:

- No change (OCyM field = 0000)
- Set active (OCyM field = 0001)
- Set inactive (OCyM field = 0010)
- Toggle (OCyM field = 0011)

On a compare match, the CCyIF flag in the TIMx_SR register is set to 1. An interrupt will be generated if the CCyIE bit in the TIMx->DIER register is set to 1. The contents of the

TIMx->DIER register are shown in Figure 6.29. A DMA request will be generated if the corresponding enable bit (CCyDE bit in the TIMx->DIER register and the CCDS bit in the TIMx->CR2 register) is set. The contents of the TIMx->CR2 register are shown in Figure 6.30.

In output compare mode, the update event (UEV) has no effect on OCyREF and OCy output. Output compare mode can also be used to output a single pulse if the single-pulse mode is selected.

15	14	13	12	11	10	9	8
--	TDE	--	CC4DE	CC3DE	CC2DE	CC1DE	UDE

7	6	5	4	3	2	1	0
	TIE		CC4IE	CC3IE	CC2IE	CC1IE	UIE

Reset value = 0x0000
Address offset = 0x0C

TDE: Trigger DMA request enable
0: Trigger DMA request disabled 1: Trigger DMA request enabled
CCyDE: Capture/Compare y DMA request enable (y = 1, 2, 3, 4)
0: CCy DMA request disabled 1: CCy DMA request enabled
UDE: Update DMA request enable
0: Update DMA request disabled 1: update DMA request enabled
TIE: Trigger interrupt enable
0: Trigger interrupt disabled 1: Trigger interrupt enabled
CCyIE: Capture/Compare y interrupt enable (y = 1, 2, 3, 4)
0: CCy interrupt disabled 1: CCy interrupt enabled
UIE: Update interrupt enable
0: Update interrupt disabled 1: Update interrupt enabled

Figure 6.29 TIMx DMA/Interrupt enable register (TIMx_DIER)

15	14	13	12	11	10	9	8
--	--	--	--	--	--	--	--

7	6	5	4	3	2	1	0
TI1S	MMS[2:0]			CCDS		--	--

Reset value = 0x0000
Address offset = 0x04

--

TI1S: TI1 selection
0: The TIMx_CH1 pin is connected to TI1
1: The TIMx_CH1, CH2, and CH3 are XORed before being connected to the TI1 input (see Figure 6.19)

CCDS: Capture/compare DMA selection
0: CCx DMA request sent when CCx event occurs
1: CCx DMA request sent when update event occurs

MMS[2:0]: Master mode selection
These bits select the information to be sent to slave timers for synchronization in master mode.
000: **Reset**. The UG bit from TIMx_EGR register is used as trigger output (TRGO). If the reset is generated by the trigger input then the signal on TRGO is delayed compared to the actual reset.
001: **Enable**. The counter enable signal, CNT_EN, is used as trigger output. This option allows several timers to be started at the same time or to control a window in which a slave timer is enabled. When configured in gated mode, CNT_EN signal is a logic OR of the CEN bit and the trigger input.
010: **Update**. The update event is selected as trigger output. In this case, a master timer can be used a prescaler for a slave timer.
011: **Compare pulse**. The trigger output send a positive pulse when the CC1IF flag is to be set, as soon as a capture or a compare match occurred.
100: **Compare**. OC1REF signal is used as trigger output (TRGO).
101: **Compare**. OC2REF signal is used as a trigger output (TRGO).
110: **Compare**. OC3REF signal is used as a trigger output (TRGO).
111: **Compare**. OC4REF signal is used as a trigger output (TRGO).

Figure 6.30 TIMx control register 2 (TIMx_CR2)

The output compare mode can be used to create time delay and generate waveforms.

Time Delay Generation

Example 6.7 Write a set of functions that use the 32-bit TIM5 to create time delays that are 50 μs, a multiple of 1 ms, a multiple of 10 ms, a multiple of 100 ms, respectively. Assume that the frequency of the APB1 bus clock is 80 MHz.

Solution:

For the delay of 50 μs, 1 ms, and 10 ms, we will set the prescale factor t0 8. For the delay of 100 ms, we will set the prescale factor to 80.

The following functions create the specified delays:

```
void OCdelay50us(void)

{
```

```
    TIM5->PSC    = 7;    // set clock prescaler to 8
    TIM5->ARR    = 500;  // delay count for 50µs
    TIM5->CCR1   = 500;
    TIM5->CNT    = 0;
    TIM5->SR     = 0;    // clear all flags
    TIM5->EGR    |= TIM_EGR_UG; // load ARR, PSC, CCR1 to their shadow registers
    TIM5->SMCR   = 0;    // disable slave mode
    TIM5->CCMR1 = TIM_CCMR1_OC1PE; // enable CCR1 preload
    TIM5->CR1    = TIM_CR1_ARPE +TIM_CR1_CEN; // enable auto reload preload,
    while(!(TIM5->SR & TIM_SR_CC1IF)); // wait for compare match
}
void OCdelayby1ms(uint16_t k)
{
    TIM5->PSC    = 7;    // set clock prescaler to 8
    TIM5->ARR    = 10000;          // delay count for 1 ms
    TIM5->CCR1   = 10000;
    TIM5->CNT    = 0;
    TIM5->SR     = 0;    // clear all flags
    TIM5->EGR    |= TIM_EGR_UG; // load ARR, PSC, CCR1 to their shadow registers
    TIM5->SMCR   = 0;    // disable slave mode
    TIM5->CCMR1 = TIM_CCMR1_OC1PE; // enable CCR1 preload
    TIM5->CR1    = TIM_CR1_ARPE +TIM_CR1_CEN; // enable auto reload preload,
    while(k){
        while(!(TIM5->SR & TIM_SR_CC1IF));
        TIM5->SR = 0; // clear CC1IF
        k--;
    }
}
```

```
void OCdelayby10ms(uint16_t k)
{
    TIM5->PSC    = 7;     // set clock prescaler to 8
    TIM5->ARR    = 100000;          // delay count for 10 ms
    TIM5->CCR1   = 100000;
    TIM5->CNT    = 0;
    TIM5->SR     = 0;     // clear all flags
    TIM5->EGR    |= TIM_EGR_UG; // load ARR, PSC, CCR1 to their shadow registers
    TIM5->SMCR   = 0;     // disable slave mode
    TIM5->CCMR1 = TIM_CCMR1_OC1PE; // enable CCR1 preload
    TIM5->CR1    = TIM_CR1_ARPE +TIM_CR1_CEN; // enable auto reload preload,
    while(k){
        while(!(TIM5->SR & TIM_SR_CC1IF));
        TIM5->SR = 0;     // clear CC1IF
        k--;
    }
}
void OCdelayby100ms(uint16_t k)
{
    TIM5->PSC    = 79;      // set clock prescaler to 80
    TIM5->ARR    = 100000;          // delay count for 100 ms
    TIM5->CCR1   = 100000;
    TIM5->CNT    = 0;
    TIM5->SR     = 0;       // clear all flags
    TIM5->EGR    |= TIM_EGR_UG; // load ARR, PSC, CCR1 to their shadow registers
    TIM5->SMCR   = 0;       // disable slave mode
    TIM5->CCMR1 = TIM_CCMR1_OC1PE; // enable CCR1 preload
    TIM5->CR1    = TIM_CR1_ARPE +TIM_CR1_CEN; // enable auto reload preload,
    while(k){
```

```
        while(!(TIM5->SR & TIM_SR_CC1IF));
        TIM5->SR = 0;       // clear CC1IF
        k--;
    }
}
```

Waveform Generation

A periodic square wave with 50% duty cycle can be easily created using the output compare function. Although periodic square wave with other duty cycle can also be created using the output compare function, it would be much easier using the PWM mode.

Example 6.8 Write a program to generate a 1-kHz periodic square wave with 50% duty cycle using TIM2_CH1 pin.

Solution:

By setting the TIM2 clock input prescaler to 8, TIM2 is counting with 10-MHz clock. In one cycle of the square wave, the waveform toggles twice. The same value is to be loaded into the TIM2->ARR and TIM2->CCR1 register so that TIM2 counts to the TOP value and toggles. This value is $10 \times 10^6 \div (10^3 \times 2) = 5000$.

The following program generates the specified waveform:

```
#include <stm32L475xx.h>
void sysClkInit(void);
int main (void)
{
    sysClkInit();  // initialize system clock to 80-MHz
// assign PA15 pin to TIM2_CH1 signal
    GPIOA->MODER   &= ~GPIO_MODER_MODE15; // clear the MODE15 field
    GPIOA->MODER   |= GPIO_MODER_MODE15_1; // assign PA15 pin to alternate function
    GPIOA->AFR[1]  &= ~GPIO_AFRH_AFSEL15;
    GPIOA->AFR[1]  |= GPIO_AFRH_AFSEL15_0; // assign to AF1-->TIM2_CH1
    TIM2->PSC      = 7; // divide timer clock input by 8
// set output frequency to 1 kHz
    TIM2->ARR      = 5000; // TOP value for TIM2 counting
    TIM2->CCR1               = 5000; // channel compare value
```

```
    TIM2->EGR       |= TIM_EGR_UG;
    // OC1 output toggle on compare match, OC1 preload enable
    TIM2->CCMR1     = TIM_CCMR1_OC1M_0 + TIM_CCMR1_OC1M_1 + TIM_CCMR1_OC1PE;
    TIM2->CCER      = TIM_CCER_CC1E; // enable TIM2 CC1 channel output
// select edge-aligned mode, enable timer, auto-reload
    TIM2->CR1       = TIM_CR1_ARPE + TIM_CR1_CEN;
    while(1);
}
```

Making Sound

By driving the digital waveform to a speaker (shown in Figure 6.31) with a frequency in the audible range (20 Hz to 20 kHz), a sound can be made.

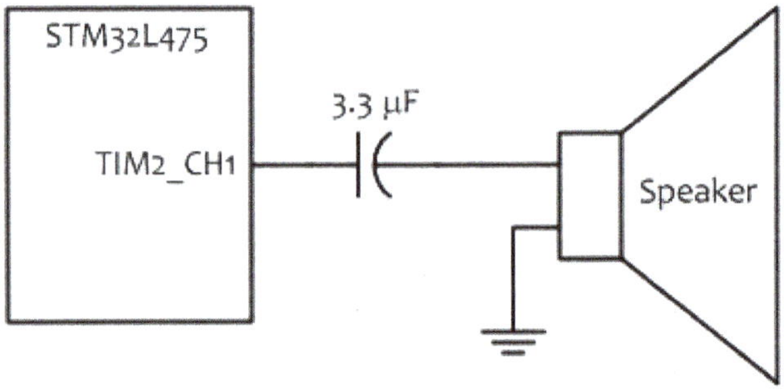

Figure 6.31 Circuit connection for a speaker

Example 6.9 Write a program to generate a 3-tone siren that alternates between 250 Hz, 500 Hz, and 1 kHz using the circuit shown in Figure 6.31. Each tone lasts for 0.5 second.

Solution: By setting the timer clock prescaler to 8, the values to be loaded into TIM2_ARR and TIM2_CCR1 for 250-Hz, 500-Hz, and 1-kHz tones are 20000, 10000, and 5000, respectively. The following C program will generate the specified 3-tone siren:

```
#include <stm32L475xx.h>
void delayby100ms(uint16_t k);
void sysClkInit(void);
int main (void)
{
    sysClkInit(); // initialize system clock to 80-MHz
```

```
    // assign PA15 pin to TIM2_CH1 signal
    GPIOA->MODER   &= ~GPIO_MODER_MODE15; // clear the MODE15 field
    GPIOA->MODER   |= GPIO_MODER_MODE15_1; // assign PA15 pin to alternate function
    GPIOA->AFR[1]  &= ~GPIO_AFRH_AFSEL15;
    GPIOA->AFR[1]  |= GPIO_AFRH_AFSEL15_0; // assign to AF1-->TIM2_CH1
    TIM2->PSC      = 7; // set Timer clock prescaler to 8
    // OC1 output toggle on compare match
    TIM2->CCMR1    = TIM_CCMR1_OC1M_0 + TIM_CCMR1_OC1M_1 + TIM_CCMR1_OC1PE;
    TIM2->CCER     = TIM_CCER_CC1E; // enable TIM2 CC1 channel output
    TIM2->CNT      = 0;
    // select edge-aligned mode, enable auto-reload, enable timer to count
    TIM2->CR1      = TIM_CR1_ARPE + TIM_CR1_CEN;
    while (1){
        TIM2->ARR  = 20000;        // set frequency to 250-Hz
        TIM2->CCR1                 = 20000;
        TIM2->EGR  |= TIM_EGR_UG; // load the new values into buffer of ARR and CCR1
        delayby100ms(5);           // play 250-Hz tone for 0.5 s
        TIM2->ARR  = 10000;        // set frequency to 500-Hz
        TIM2->CCR1                 = 10000;
        TIM2->EGR  |= TIM_EGR_UG; // load the new values into buffer of ARR and CCR1
        delayby100ms(5);           // play 500-Hz tone for 0.5 s
        TIM2->ARR  = 5000;         // set frequency to 1-kHz
        TIM2->CCR1                 = 5000;
        TIM2->EGR  |= TIM_EGR_UG; // load the new values into buffer of ARR and CCR1
        delayby100ms(5);           // play 1-kHz tone for 0.5 s
    }
}
```

Playing a Song

The program that generates a 3-tone siren can be modified to play a song. A music score consists of a sequence of notes. A note in the music score has two components: **pitch (frequency)** and **tempo (duration)**. The duration of a quarter note is 400 ms. The duration of other notes can be derived proportionately. The complete list of the music notes and their frequencies is given in Appendix B.

As we learned in the siren example, the frequency of a note is determined by the timer reload value. In the next example, we will represent the duration of a note as a multiple of 10 ms. The **delayby10ms(k)** function will be called to control the duration of each note.

A matrix is created to hold the music score. The number of rows equals the number of notes in the music score, and each row contains two components of each note: (1) the reload value and (2) the duration (a multiple of 10 ms). For every note, the program uses the output compare toggle-output mode of the timer to generate the digital waveform with the specified frequency and duration. One problem with this method is that contiguous identical notes become a single long note with the duration that equals the sum of those identical notes. This problem can be solved by inserting a short inaudible note between two adjacent identical notes. The rest note in the score is played by generating an inaudible note with the specified duration.

Example 6.10 Write a program and use the circuit shown in Figure 6.31 to play the song with the score shown in Figure 6.32.

Who is this

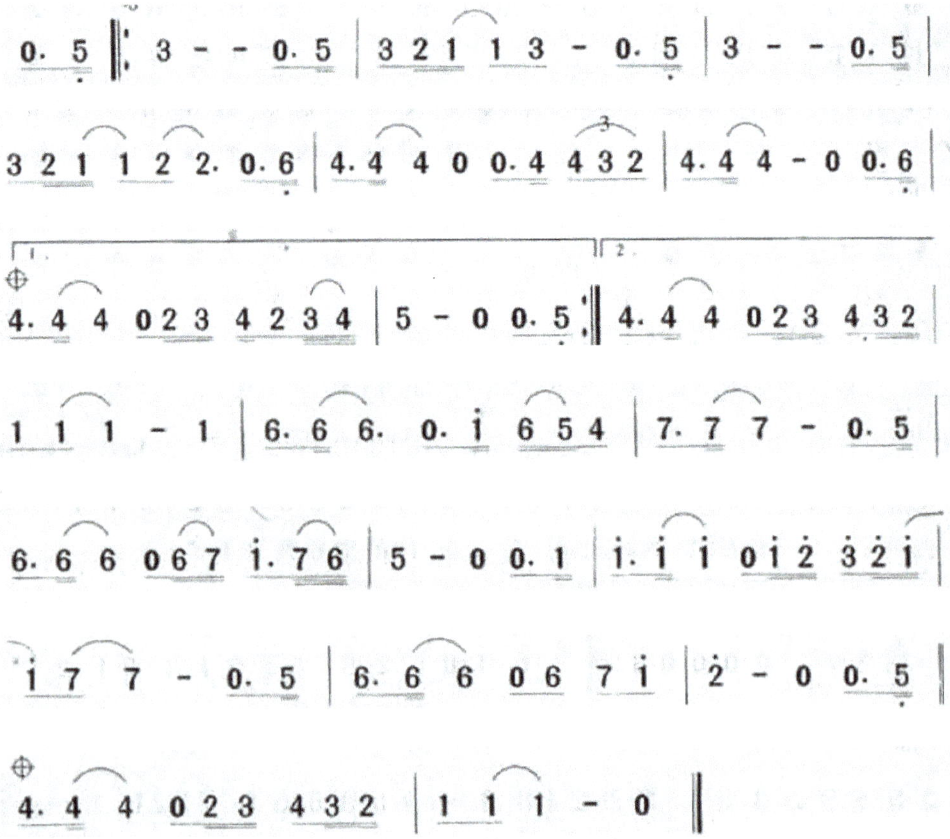

Figure 6.32 An old pop song score

Solution:

```
#include <stm32L475xx.h>
void sysClkInit(void);
void delayby10ms(uint16_t k);
// reload value for each note by setting the prescaler to 20
#define  G3   10204// = 4000000 ÷ (2 × 196)
#define  A3   9091       // = 4000000 ÷ (2 × 220)
#define  B3   8099       // = 4000000 ÷ (2 × 246.94)
#define  C4   7644       // 261.63 Hz
#define  C4S  7216       // 277.18 Hz
#define  D4F  7216       // 277.18 Hz
#define  D4   6811       // 293.66 Hz
#define  D4S  6428       // 311.13 Hz
#define  E4F  6428       // 311.13 Hz
#define  E4   6067       // 329.63 Hz
#define  F4   5727       // 349.23 Hz
#define  F4S  5410       // 369.66 Hz
#define  G4F  5410       // 369.66 Hz
#define  G4   5102       // 392 Hz
#define  G4S  4816       // 415.3 Hz
#define  A4F  4816       // 415.3 Hz
#define  A4   4545       // 440 Hz
#define  A4S  4290       // 466.16 Hz
#define  B4F  4290       // 466.16 Hz
#define  B4   4050       // 493.88 Hz
#define  C5   3822       // 523.25 Hz
#define  C5S  3608       // 554.37 Hz
#define  D5F  3608       // 554.37 Hz
#define  D5   3405       // 587.33 Hz
```

```
#define   D5S   3214          // 622.25 Hz
#define   E5F   3214          // 622.25 Hz
#define   E5    3033          // 659.26 Hz
#define   F5    2863          // 698.46 Hz
#define   F5S   2703          // 739.99 Hz
#define   G5F   2703          // 739.99 Hz
#define   G5    2551          // 783.99 Hz
#define   G5S   2408          // 830.61 Hz
#define   A5F   2408          // 830.61 Hz
#define   A5    2273          // 880 Hz
#define   A5S   2145          // 932.33 Hz
#define   B5F   2145          // 932.33 Hz
#define   B5    2025          // 987.77 Hz
#define   ZZ    50            // 40,000 Hz
uint16_t score[152][2] = {
          {G3,10},  {E4,120}, {ZZ,30},  {G4,10},  {E4,20},  {D4,10},
          {C4,30},  {E4,20},  {ZZ,70},  {G3,10},  {E4,120}, {ZZ,30},
          {G4,10},  {E4,20},  {D4,10},  {C4,30},  {D4,60},  {ZZ,30},
          {A3,10},  {F4,30},  {ZZ,2},   {F4,50},  {ZZ,70},  {F4,10},
          {ZZ,2},   {F4,13},  {E4,13},  {D4,13},  {F4,30},  {ZZ,2},
          {F4,50},  {ZZ,70},  {A3,10},  {F4,30},  {ZZ,2},   {F4,50},
          {ZZ,20},  {D4,10},  {E4,10},  {F4,10},  {D4,20},  {E4,5},
          {F4,5},   {G4,80},  {ZZ,70},  {G3,10},  {E4,120}, {ZZ,30},
          {G4,10},  {E4,20},  {D4,10},  {C4,30},  {E4,20},  {ZZ,70},
          {G3,10},  {E4,20},  {ZZ,30},  {G4,10},  {E4,20},  {D4,10},
          {C4,30},  {D4,60},  {ZZ,30},  {A3,10},  {F4,30},  {ZZ,2},
          {F4,50},  {ZZ,70},  {F4,10},  {ZZ,2},   {F4,13},  {E4,13},
          {D4,13},  {F4,30},  {ZZ,2},   {F4,50},  {ZZ,70},  {A3,10},
```

```
            {F4,30},  {ZZ,2},   {F4,50},  {ZZ,20},  {D4,10},  {E4,10},
            {F4,20},  {E4,10},  {D4,10},  {C4,20},  {ZZ,2},   {C4,60},
            {ZZ,40},  {C4,40},  {A4,30},  {ZZ,2},   {A4,50},  {ZZ,30},
            {C5,10},  {A4,10},  {G4,10},  {F4,20},  {B4,30},  {ZZ,2},
            {B4,50},  {ZZ,70},  {G4,10},  {A4,30},  {ZZ,2},   {A4,50},
            {ZZ,20},  {A4,10},  {B4,10},  {C5,30},  {B4,5},   {A4,5},
            {G4,80},  {ZZ,70},  {C4,10},  {C5,30},  {ZZ,2},   {C5,50},
            {ZZ,20},  {C5,10},  {D5,10},  {E5,20},  {D5,10},  {C5,30},
            {B4,60},  {ZZ,70},  {G4,10},  {A4,30},  {ZZ,2},   {A4,50},
            {ZZ,20},  {A4,20},  {B4,20},  {C5,20},  {D5,80},  {ZZ,70},
            {G3,10},  {F4,30},  {ZZ,2},   {F4,50},  {ZZ,20},  {D4,10},
            {E4,10},  {F4,20},  {E4,10},  {D4,10},  {C4,20},  {ZZ,2},
            {C4,50},  {0,40}};
int main (void)
{
    uint16_t j;
    sysClkInit();
    // assign PA15 pin to TIM2_CH1 signal
    GPIOA->MODER    &= ~GPIO_MODER_MODE15; // clear the MODE15 field
    GPIOA->MODER    |= GPIO_MODER_MODE15_1; // assign PA15 pin to alternate function
    GPIOA->AFR[1]   &= ~GPIO_AFRH_AFSEL15;
    GPIOA->AFR[1]   |= GPIO_AFRH_AFSEL15_0; // assign to AF1-->TIM2_CH1
    TIM2->PSC       = 19;        // set Timer clock prescaler to 20
    // OC1 output toggle on compare match
    TIM2->CCMR1     = TIM_CCMR1_OC1M_0 + TIM_CCMR1_OC1M_1 + TIM_CCMR1_OC1PE;
    TIM2->CCER      = TIM_CCER_CC1E; // enable TIM2 CC1 channel output
    TIM2->CNT       = 0;
    // select edge-aligned mode, enable auto-reload, enable timer to count
```

```
    TIM2->CR1          = TIM_CR1_ARPE + TIM_CR1_CEN;
    j = 0;
    while(score[j][0]){
        TIM2->ARR  = score[j][0];
        TIM2->CCR1= score[j][0];
        TIM2->EGR  |= TIM_EGR_UG; // load new values into buffer of ARR and CCR1
        delayby10ms(score[j][1]);
        j++;
    }
}
```

6.5.10 PWM MODE

Pulse-width modulation (PWM) mode allows you to generate a signal with a frequency determined by the value of the TIMx->ARR register and a duty cycle determined by the value of the TIMx->CCRy register.

The PWM mode can be selected independently for each channel by setting the OCxM field in the TIMx->C-CMRy register to either 110 (PWM mode 1) or 111 (PMW mode 2). The corresponding preload register must be enabled by setting the OCxPE bit in the

TIMx->CCMRy register. The auto-reload preload register (in upcounting and center-aligned modes) must also be enabled by setting the ARPE bit in the TIMx->CR1 register.

Because the preload registers are transferred to their shadow registers only when an update event (UEV) occurs, before starting the counter, the user must initialize all the registers by setting the UG bit in the TIMx->EGR register.

The OCx polarity is software-programmable using the CCxP bit in the TIMx->CCER register. It can be programmed as active high or active low. The OCx output is enabled by setting the CCxE bit in the TIMx->C-CER register.

The timer can generate PWM in edge-aligned mode or center-aligned mode depending on the CMS bits in the TIMx->CR1 register.

PWM Edge-Aligned Mode

The edge-aligned mode can be achieved by clearing the CMS[1:0] field in the TIMx->CR1 register to 00 and configuring the timer to either the upcounting mode (DIR bit = 0) or the downcounting mode (DIR bit = 1).

For PWM mode 1, during the upcounting interval, the reference PWM signal OCyREF (see Figure 6.19) is high as long as TIMx->CNT < TIMx->CCRy, else OCyREF signal is low.

During the downcounting interval, the reference signal OCyREF is low as long as TIMx->CNT > TIMx->C-CRx, else it is high. If the compare value in TIMx->CCRy is greater than the auto-reload value in TIMx->ARR, then OCyREF is held high 100% of the time.

For PWM mode 2, during the upcounting interval, the reference signal OCyREF is low as long as TIMx->CNT < TIMx->CCRx. During the downcounting interval, the reference signal OCyREF is high as long as TIMx->CNT > TIMx->CCRx.

Example 6.11 Write a C program to generate a 2-kHz PWM waveform with 40% duty cycle from the TIM2_CH1 pin (assigned to PA05 pin), assuming that the clock source for TIM2 is 80 MHz.

Solution:

By setting the timer clock prescaler to 8, the timer TOP value to set output frequency to 2 kHz is computed to be 5000. The value to be loaded into the TIM2->CCR1 register to set duty cycle to 40% is 2000.

The following program generates the specified PWM waveform:

```
#include <stm32L475xx.h>
void sysClkInit(void);
int main (void)
{
    sysClkInit();
    GPIOA->MODER   &= ~(GPIO_MODER_MODE5); // clear bit 10~11
    GPIOA->MODER   |=  GPIO_MODER_MODE5_1; // select alternate function
    GPIOA->AFR[0]  &= ~GPIO_AFRL_AFSEL5; // clear AFSEL5 field
    GPIOA->AFR[0]  |=  GPIO_AFRL_AFSEL5_0; // select AF1 (TIM2_CH1) function
    TIM2->PSC      =  7; // set timer clock prescaler to 8,
    TIM2->ARR      =  5000;        // set output frequency to 2 kHz
    TIM2->CCR1     =  2000; // set duty cycle to 40%
    TIM2->EGR      |=  TIM_EGR_UG; // transfer PSC, ARR, & CCR1 to their buffer
    // PWM mode 1, enable OC1 output, enable CCR1 preload, CC1S field selects output
    TIM2->CCMR1    =  TIM_CCMR1_OC1M_2 + TIM_CCMR1_OC1M_1 + TIM_CCMR1_OC1PE;
    TIM2->CCER     =  TIM_CCER_CC1E; // enable OC1 output, OC1 active high
    // edge-aligned mode, enable ARR preload, enable TIM2
    TIM2->CR1      =  TIM_CR1_ARPE + TIM_CR1_CEN;
    while(1);
}
```

PWM Center-Aligned Mode

Center-aligned mode is active when the CMS field in the TIMx->CR1 register is not 00. Depending on the value of the CMS field, the compare flag is set (CCnIF, n = 1...4) when the counter counts up (10), counts down (01), or both up and down (11). The DIR bit in the

TIMx->CR1 register is updated by hardware and must not be changed by software.

Example 6.12 Write a program and use the TIM5_CH1 pin to generate a 200-Hz periodic waveform with 30% duty cycle using the PWM **center-aligned mode 2** with the CMS field in the TIM5->CR1 register set to 10, assuming that the clock source to TIM5 is 80 MHz.

Solution:

By setting the prescaler factor to 8 (load 7 into TIM5->PSC), the value to be loaded into the TIM5->ARR to set waveform frequency to 200 Hz is calculated to be 25000 (= $80x10^6 \div 8 \div (2 \times 200)$). The value to be loaded into TIM5->CCR1 to set the duty cycle to 30% is 7500 (= 25000 × 30%). The following program generates the specified waveform:

```
#include <stm32L475xx.h>
void sysClkInit(void);
int main (void)
{
    sysClkInit();
    GPIOA->MODER  &= ~(GPIO_MODER_MODE0); // clear bit 0~1
    GPIOA->MODER  |=  GPIO_MODER_MODE0_1;  // select alternate function
    GPIOA->AFR[0] &= ~GPIO_AFRL_AFSEL0;    // clear AFSEL5 field
    GPIOA->AFR[0] |=  GPIO_AFRL_AFSEL0_1;  // select AF2 (TIM5_CH1) function
    TIM5->PSC     =  7;           // set timer clock prescaler to 8,
    TIM5->ARR     =  25000;       // set output frequency to 200 Hz
    TIM5->CCR1    =  7500;        // set duty cycle to 30%
    TIM5->EGR     |= TIM_EGR_UG;  // transfer PSC, ARR, & CCR1 to their buffer
    // PWM mode 1, enable OC1 output, enable CCR1 preload
    TIM5->CCMR1   =  TIM_CCMR1_OC1M_2 + TIM_CCMR1_OC1M_1 + TIM_CCMR1_OC1PE;
    TIM5->CCER    =  TIM_CCER_CC1E; // enable OC1 output, OC1 active high
    // center-aligned mode 2, enable ARR preload, enable TIM2
    TIM5->CR1     =  TIM_CR1_ARPE + TIM_CR1_CMS_1 + TIM_CR1_CEN;
    while(1);
}
```

6.5.11 ASYMMETRIC PWM MODE

This mode allows two center-aligned PWM signals to be generated with a programmable phase shift. The frequency of the generated waveform is determined by the value of the TIMx->ARR register and the duty cycle, and the phase-shifts are determined by a pair of TIMx->CCRy registers. One register controls the PWM during upcounting and the other register during downcounting. The PWM is adjusted every half PWM cycle:

- OC1REFC (or OC2REFC) is controlled by TIMx->CCR1 and TIMx->CCR2.
- OC3REFC (or OC4REFC) is controlled by TIMx->CCR3 and TIMx->CCR4.

Depending on the value of the OCxM field in the TIMx->CCMRy register, there are two versions of the asymmetric PWM mode:

- Asymmetric PWM mode 1 (OCxM = 1110)
- Asymmetric PWM mode 2 (OCxM = 1111)

The behavior of OC1REF~OC1REF4 and OC1REFC~OC4REFC in these two modes is summarized in Tables 6.8 and 6.9, respectively.

Table 6.8 Asymmetric PWM mode 1 signal summary

Signal	Behavior
OC1REF	Same behavior as in PWM mode 1
OC1REFC	Outputs OC1REF when counting is counting up, OC2REF when it is counting down
OC2REF	Same behavior as in PWM mode 1
OC2REFC	Outputs OC2REF when counting is counting up, OC1REF when it is counting down
OC3REF	Same behavior as in PWM mode 1
OC3REFC	Outputs OC3REF when counting is counting up, OC4REF when it is counting down
OC4REF	Same behavior as in PWM mode 1
OC4REFC	Outputs OC4REF when counting is counting up, OC3REF when it is counting down

Table 6.9 Asymmetric PWM mode 2 signal summary

Signal	Behavior
OC1REF	Same behavior as in PWM mode 2
OC1REFC	Outputs OC1REF when counting is counting up, OC2REF when it is counting down
OC2REF	Same behavior as in PWM mode 2
OC2REFC	Outputs OC2REF when counting is counting up, OC1REF when it is counting down
OC3REF	Same behavior as in PWM mode 2
OC3REFC	Outputs OC3REF when counting is counting up, OC4REF when it is counting down
OC4REF	Same behavior as in PWM mode 2
OC4REFC	Outputs OC4REF when counting is counting up, OC3REF when it is counting down

Examples of asymmetric PWM mode 1 and mode 2 are illustrated in Figure 6.33 and 6.34, respectively.

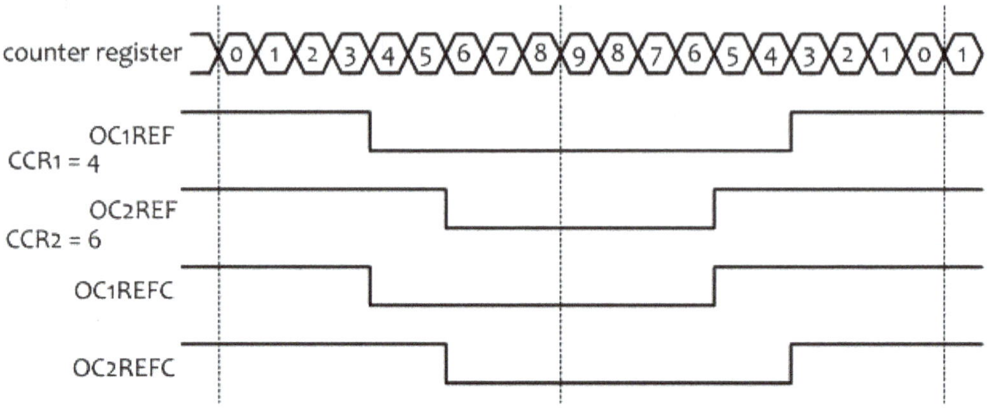

Figure 6.33 An example of asymmetric PWM mode 1

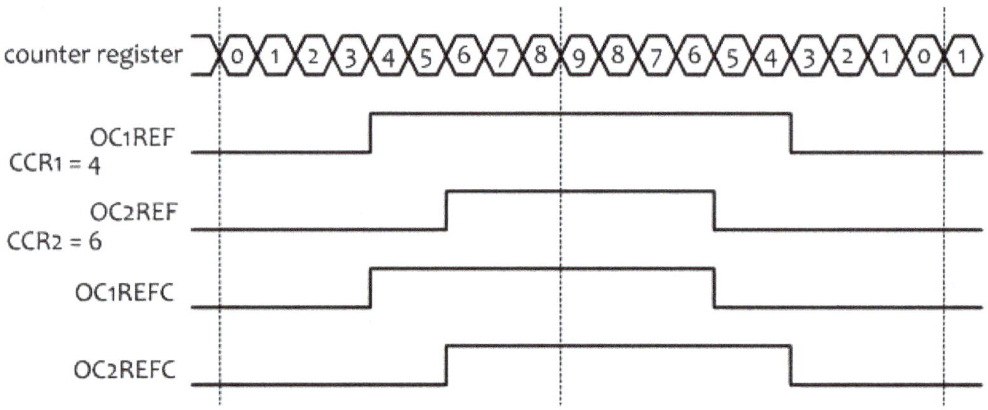

Figure 6.34 An example of asymmetric PWM mode 2

6.5.12 COMBINED PWM MODE

Combined PWM mode allows two edge- or center-aligned PWM signals to be generated with programmable delay and phase-shift between respective pulses. While the frequency of the generated waveform is determined by the value of the TIMx->ARR register, the duty cycle and delay are determined by the two TIMx->CCRy registers. The resultant signals, OCyREFC, are made of an OR or AND logical combination of two reference PWMs:

- OC1REFC (or OC2REFC) is controlled by TIMx->CCR1 and TIMx->CCR2.
- OC3REFC (or OC4REFC) is controlled by TIMx->CCR3 and TIMx->CCR4.

There are two versions of combined PWM mode:

- Combined PWM mode 1 (OCxM = 1100)
- Combined PWM mode 2 (OCxM = 1101)

The behavior of OC1REF~OC1REF4 and OC1REFC~OC4REFC in the combined PWM mode 1 and 2 is summarized in Table 6.10 and 6.11, respectively.

Table 6.10 Combined PWM mode 1 signal summary

Signal	Behavior
OC1REF	Same behavior as in PWM mode 1
OC1REFC	Logical OR of OC1REF and OC2REF
OC2REF	Same behavior as in PWM mode 1
OC2REFC	Logical OR of OC1REF and OC2REF
OC3REF	Same behavior as in PWM mode 1
OC3REFC	Logical OR of OC3REF and OC4REF
OC4REF	Same behavior as in PWM mode 1
OC4REFC	Logical OR of OC3REF and OC4REF

Table 6.11 Combined PWM mode 2 signal summary

Signal	Behavior
OC1REF	Same behavior as in PWM mode 2
OC1REFC	Logical AND of OC1REF and OC2REF
OC2REF	Same behavior as in PWM mode 2
OC2REFC	Logical AND of OC1REF and OC2REF
OC3REF	Same behavior as in PWM mode 2
OC3REFC	Logical AND of OC3REF and OC4REF
OC4REF	Same behavior as in PWM mode 2
OC4REFC	Logical AND of OC3REF and OC4REF

6.5.13 CLEARING THE OCYREF SIGNAL ON AN EXTERNAL EVENT

The user can clear the OCyREF signal of a given channel by setting the OCyCE bit in the

TIMx->CCMRy register to 1. The OCyREF signal remains low until the next update event (UEV) occurs. This function can only be used in output compare and PWM modes. It does not work in forced mode. Setting the OCyCE bit to 1 causes the OCyREF_CLR_INPUT signal to high and clears the OCyREF signal.

The OCREF_CLR_INPUT signal can be selected between the OCREF_CLR input and the ETRF (ETR after the filter) by configuring the OCCS bit in the TIMx->SMCR register.

To be used as the clear input of the OCxREF signal, the ETR signal must be configured as follows:

1. The external trigger prescaler should be kept off by setting the ETPS field in the TIMx->SMCR register to 00.
2. The external clock mode 2 must be disabled by clearing the ECE bit in the TIMx->SMCR register to 0.
3. The external trigger polarity (ETP) and the external trigger filter (ETF) can be configured according to the application's needs.

6.5.14 ONE-PULSE MODE

This mode allows the counter to be started in response to a stimulus (a trigger signal) and to generate a pulse with a programmable length after a programmable delay. The slave mode controller should be used to control the starting of the counter. The timer channel should be configured to output compare mode or PWM mode. The one-pulse mode is selected by setting the OPM bit in the TIMx->CR1 register. The one-pulse mode causes the timer to stop counting at the next update event (UEV).

A pulse can be correctly generated only if the compare value is different from the counter initial value (i.e., TIMx->CNT < TIMx->CCRy < TIMx->ARR).

Suppose we want to generate a single pulse on OC1 with a duration of t_{PULSE} at t_{DELAY} after it is triggered by a rising edge on the TI2 input, the following steps should be taken:

Step 1

Configure the timer clock properly and load a compare value into the TIM2->CCR1 register so that it creates a delay, which is equal to t_{DELAY}.

Step 2

Load an appropriate value into the TIM2->ARR register so that (TIM2->ARR – TIM2->CCR1) corresponds to the pulse width t_{PULSE}.

Step 3

Map the TI2FP2 signal to TI2 by setting the CC2S field in the TIM2->CCMR1 register to 01.

Step 4

Configure TI2FP2 as a trigger for the slave mode controller (TRGI) by setting the TS field in the TIM2->SMCR register to 110.

Step 5

Use TI2FP2 to start the counter by setting the SMS field in the TIM2->SMCR register to 110 (select trigger mode).

Step 6

Configure CCR1 to PWM mode 2 by setting the OC1M field in the TIMx->CCMR1 register to 0111. We can optionally enable the preload registers by setting OC1PE in the TIMx->CCMR1 and the ARPE bit in the TIMx->CR1 register to 1.

Step 7

Clear the CC2P and CC2NP bits in the TIMx->CCER register to 0 to detect the rising edge on TI2. Clear the DIR and CMS field in the TIMx->CR1 to 0. Set the OPM bit in the TIMx->CR1 to 1.

Example 6.13 Write a C program to generate a pulse with 10-ms delay and 10-ms pulse width after a rising edge on the TI1 edge is detected using TIM2, assuming that the internal clock source to TIM2 is 80 MHz.

Solution:

By setting the TIM2 clock input prescaler to 80 (PSC set to 79), the value to be loaded into TIM2->CCR1 is calculated to be 10,000. The value to be loaded into TIM2->ARR is computed to be 20,000.

The following program generates the specified one pulse:

```
#include <stm32L475xx.h>

void sysClkInit(void);

int main (void)

{
```

```
    sysClkInit();
    // configure PA1 and PA0 pin to be used as TIM2_CH1 and TIM2_CH2 pin
    GPIOA->MODER  &= ~(GPIO_MODER_MODE1 + GPIO_MODER_MODE0);
    GPIOA->MODER  |=  GPIO_MODER_MODE1_1 + GPIO_MODER_MODE0_1;
    GPIOA->AFR[0] &= ~(GPIO_AFRL_AFSEL1 + GPIO_AFRL_AFSEL0);
    GPIOA->AFR[0] |=  GPIO_AFRL_AFSEL1_0 + GPIO_AFRL_AFSEL0_0;
    TIM2->PSC     =   79; // set clock input prescaler to 80
    TIM2->CCR1    =   10000; // set delay to 10 ms
    TIM2->ARR     =   20000; // set pulse width to 10 ms
    TIM2->EGR     |=  TIM_EGR_UG; // load PSC, ARR, and CCR1 into their buffer
    TIM2->CCMR1   =   0;
    // IC2 mapped to TI2, OC1 set to PWM mode 2, set CC1 to output, enable OC1 preload
    TIM2->CCMR1   =   TIM_CCMR1_CC2S_0 + TIM_CCMR1_OC1M_2 +
                      TIM_CCMR1_OC1M_1 + TIM_CCMR1_OC1M_0 + TIM_CCMR1_OC1PE;
    TIM2->SMCR    =   0;
    // select TI2FP2 (TS[2:0] = 110) as a trigger, select trigger mode (SMS[3:0] = 0110)
    TIM2->SMCR    =   TIM_SMCR_TS_2 + TIM_SMCR_TS_1 + TIM_SMCR_SMS_2 +
                      TIM_SMCR_SMS_1;
    // detect the rising edge on TIM2_CH2 pin
    TIM2->CCER    &= ~(TIM_CCER_CC2P + TIM_CCER_CC2NP);
    // count up, internal clock mode, one pulse mode, enable auto reload preload
    TIM2->CR1     =   TIM_CR1_ARPE + TIM_CR1_OPM;
    while(1);
}
```

6.5.15 RETRIGGERABLE ONE-PULSE MODE (OPM)

In this mode, the counter is started as soon as a stimulus is detected and generates a pulse with a programmable length. There is no delay between the generation of the pulse and the detection of the stimulus. The pulse will be extended if a new trigger occurs before the previous one is completed. This situation is illustrated in Figure 6.35.

The timer must be in slave mode with the SMS field in the TIMx->SMCR register set to 1000 (combined reset + trigger mode) and the OCxM field in the TIMx->CCMRy register (y = 1 or 2) set to 1000 or 1001.

If the timer is configured in upcounting mode, the corresponding TIMx->CCRy register must be set to 0 and the TIMx->ARR register set to the pulse width. If the timer is configured in downcounting mode, the TIMx->CCRy register must be set to a value that is above or equal to TIMx->ARR.

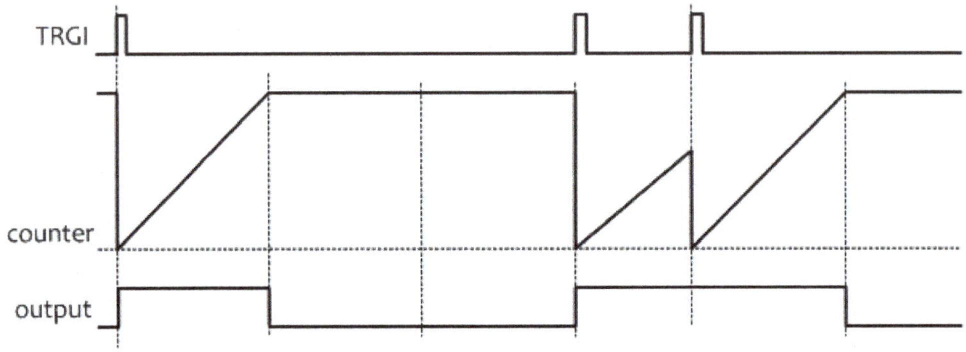

Figure 6.35 An example of retriggerable one pulse mode

6.5.16 ENCODER INTERFACE MODE

There are three encoder modes selected by the SMS field in the TIMx->SMCR register (x = 2…5):

- **Encoder mode 1**: The counter counts up/down on the TI1FP1 rising/falling edge depending on whether the TI2FP2 is low or high.
- **Encoder mode 2**: The counter counts up/down on the TI2FP2 rising/falling edge depending on whether the TI1FP1 level is low or high.
- **Encoder mode 3**: The counter counts up/down on both TI1FP1 and TI2FP2 edges depending on the level of the other input.

As shown in Figure 6.19, the TI2, TI3, and TI4 signals are connected to the TIMx_CH2, TIMx_CH3, and TIMx_CH4 pin, respectively. The TI1 signal can be driven by either the TIMx_CH1 signal or the XOR function of the TIMx_CH1, TIMx_CH2, and TIMx_CH3 signals. This choice is selected by clearing/setting the TI1S bit in the TIMx->CR2 register.

TI1FP1 and TI2FP2 signals are derived from the filtered and polarity-selected version of TI1 and TI2, respectively. The sequence of transitions of the two inputs is evaluated, and count pulses as well as the direction signal are generated. Depending on the sequence the counter counts up or down, the DIR bit in the TIMx->CR1 register is modified accordingly. The DIR bit is calculated at each transition on any input (TI1 or TI2), whether the counter is counting on TI1 only, TI2 only, or both TI1 and TI2.

Encoder interface mode acts simply as an external clock with direction selection. The counter just counts between 0 and the auto-reload value in the TIMx->ARR register. The user must configure TIMx->ARR before starting. The combination of the counting direction versus encoder signals are given in Table 6.12.

In this mode, the counter is modified automatically following the speed and the direction of the quadrature encoder, and its content, therefore, always represents the encoder's position. The count direction corresponds to the rotation direction of the connected sensor.

Table 6.12 Counting direction versus encoder signals

Active edge	Level on opposite signal (TI1FP1 for TI2, TI2FP2 for TI1)	TI1FP1		TI2FP2	
		Rising	Falling	Rising	Falling
Counting on TI1 only	high	Down	up	No count	No count
	low	up	Down	No count	No count
Counting on TI2 only	high	No count	No count	up	Down
	low	No count	No count	Down	up
Counting on TI1 and TI2	high	Down	up	up	Down
	low	up	Down	Down	up

An external incremental encoder can be connected directly to the MCU without external interface logic. However, comparators are normally used to convert the encoder's differential outputs to digital signals. This greatly increases noise immunity. The third encoder output, which indicates the mechanical zero position, may be connected to an external interrupt input and trigger a counter reset.

Example 6.14 Assume that TIM2 is configured to count up/down on TI1 and TI2 in encoder mode 3 and you are given the TI1 and TI2 waveforms as shown in Figure 6.36. Also assume that

- TI1FPI is mapped to TI1 (i.e., the CC1S field in the TIM2->CCMR1 register is set to 01)
- TI2FP2 is mapped to TI2 (i.e., the CC2S field in the TIM2->CCMR1 register is set to 01)
- TI1FP1 = TI1 (i.e., the CC1P and the CC1NP bit in the TIM2->CCER register are set t0 0)
- TI2FP2 = TI2 (i.e., the CC2P and the CC2NP bit in the TIM2->CCER register are set to 0)
- Both inputs are active on both rising and falling edges (i.e., the SMS field in the TIM2->SMCR register is set to 011—encoder mode 3).
- TIM2 is enabled (i.e., the CEN bit in the TIM2->CR1 register is set to 1)

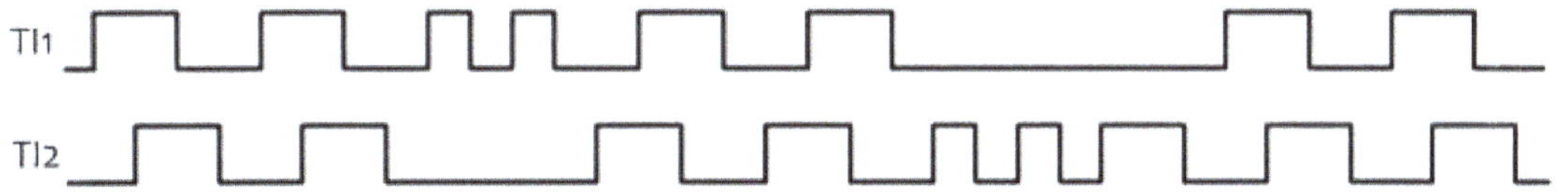

Figure 6.36 A sample TI1 and TI2 input waveform

What is the counter counting pattern? Draw the waveform to illustrate.

Solution:

The resultant counter counting pattern can be derived by referring to Table 6.12 and is shown in Figure 6.37.

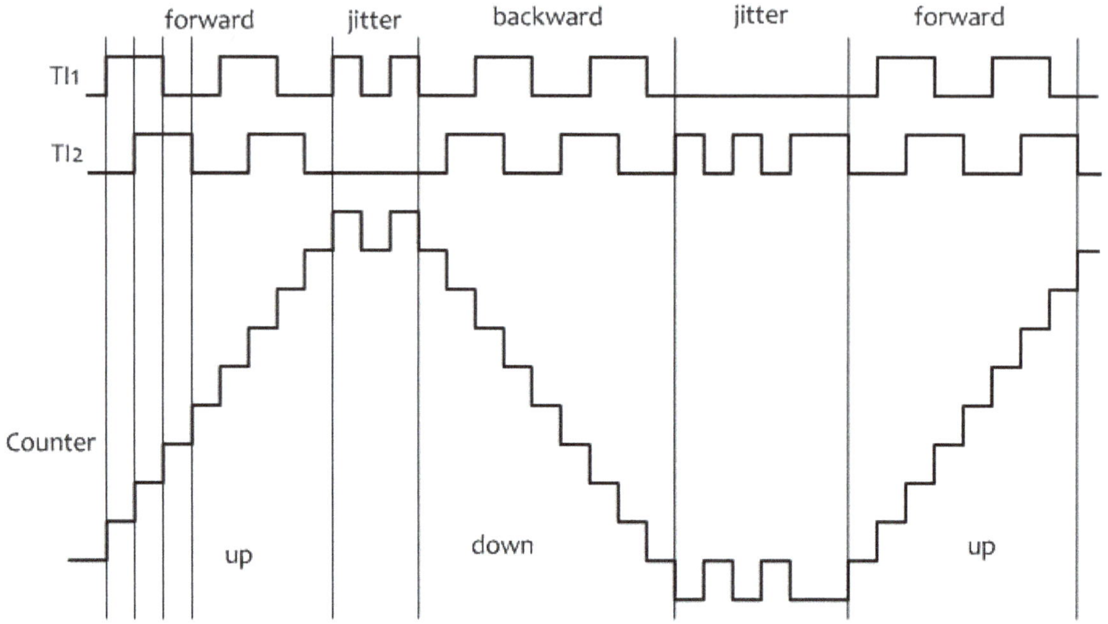

Figure 6.35 The resultant counting sequence for the given TI1 and TI2 input waveform in Figure 6.34

6.5.17 UIF BIT REMAPPING

The **UIFREMAP** bit in the TIMx->CR1 register forces a continuous copy of the update interrupt flag (UIF) to bit 31 (call it **UIFCPY**) of the timer counter register (TIMx->CNT[31]). This allows the processor to atomically read both the counter value and a potential roll-over condition signaled by the UIFCPY flag. It eases the calculation of angular speed by avoiding race conditions caused, for instance, by a processing shared between a background task (counter reading) and an interrupt (update interrupt).

There is no latency between the UIF and UIFCPY flag assertions. In a 32-bit timer implementation, when the UIFREMAP bit is set, bit 31 of the counter is overwritten by the UIFCPY flag on the read access.

6.5.18 TIMERS AND EXTERNAL TRIGGER SYNCHRONIZATION

The user can synchronize TIMx timers using an external trigger signal in several modes: reset mode, gated mode, and trigger mode.

Slave Mode: Reset Mode

The counter and prescaler are reinitialized in response to an event on a trigger input. Moreover, if the URS bit in the TIMx->CR1 register is 0, an update event (UEV) is generated. All the preloaded registers including TIMx->ARR and TIMx->CCRy are updated.

For example, the user can reset the TIM2 (to 0) by applying a rising edge on the TIM2_CH1 pin by taking the following actions:

Step 1

Configure the channel 1 to detect rising edges on the TI1 (TIM2_CH1 pin). If filter is not needed, set the IC1F field in the TIM2->CCMR1 register to 0000. Set the CC1S field in the TIM2->CCMR1 register to 01 to map IC1 to the TI1 pin. Clear the CC1P and CC1NP bit in the TIM2->CCER register to 0 so that only the rising edge will be detected.

Step 2

Configure the timer to **reset mode** by setting the **SMS field** in the **TIM2->SMCR** register to 100. Select TI1 as the input source by setting the TS field in the TIM2->SMCR register to 101.

Step 3

Start the counter by setting the CEN bit in the TIM2->CR1 register to 1.

After setting the CEN bit, TIM2 starts to count. When a rising edge on the TI1 pin is detected, the TIM2 counter is cleared and restarts from 0. In the meantime, the trigger flag is set (TIF flag in the TIM2->SR register) and an interrupt or a DMA request can be generated if they are enabled (by setting the TIE and TDE bits in the TIM2->DIER register). An example of the operation of the reset mode with TIMx->ARR set to 80 is illustrated in Figure 6.38.

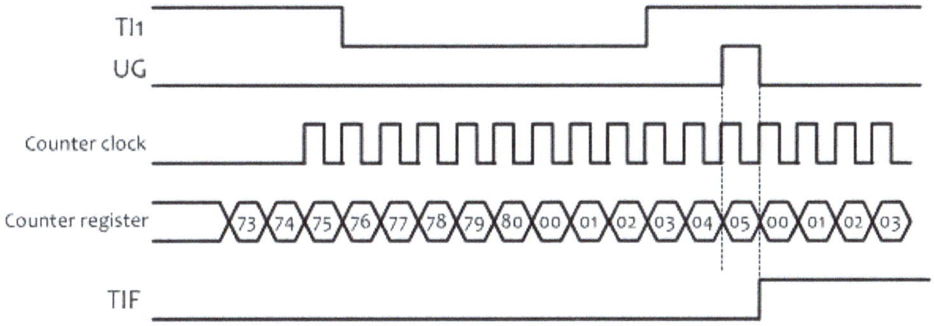

Figure 6.38 Reset mode counter waveforms and values

Slave Mode: Gated Mode

The counter can be enabled depending on the level of a selected input. The user can choose to enable the counter to count when the selected signal is either low or high. This mode can be used to measure the pulse width of an unknown signal. An example that illustrates the counter is enabled to count when the selected signal is high is shown in Figure 6.39. The procedure to set up the operation shown in Figure 6.39 is as follows:

Step 1

Configure the channel 1 to detect high levels on TI1. Set the CC1S field in the TIMx->CCMR1 register to 01 to select TI1 as the input capture source. Set the CC1P and CC1NP bit in the TIMx->CCER register to 0 to detect the rising edge.

Step 2

Configure the timer to operate in **gated mode** and select TI1 as the gating signal by setting the SMS and TS fields of the TIMx->SMCR register to 0101 and 101, respectively.

Step 3

Enable TIMx by setting the CEN bit in the TIMx->CR1 register to 1.

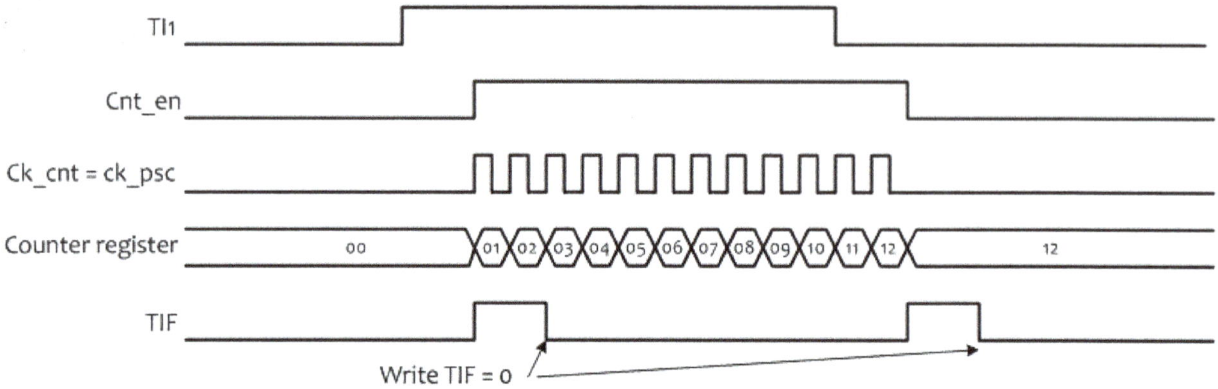

Figure 6.39 Gated mode counter waveforms and values

Slave Mode: Trigger Mode

A counter can be started to count by an event on a selected input. For example, the user can let TIM2 to count up in response to a rising edge on the TI2 input by taking the following steps:

Step 1

Configure the channel 2 to detect the rising edge on the TI2 input. If the input does not need any filter, set the IC2F field in the TIM2->CCMR1 register to 0000. Set the CC2S field in the TIM2->CCMR1 register to 01 to select the TI2 input. Set the CC2P and CC2NP bit in the

TIM2->CCMR2 register to 0 and 0.

Step 2

Configure TIM2 to operate in **trigger mode** and select TI2 as the trigger source by setting the SMS and TS field in the TIM2->SMCR register to 0110 and 110, respectively.

When a rising edge occurs on TI2, the counter starts counting on the internal clock and the TIF flag is set. An example of this mode is illustrated in Figure 6.40.

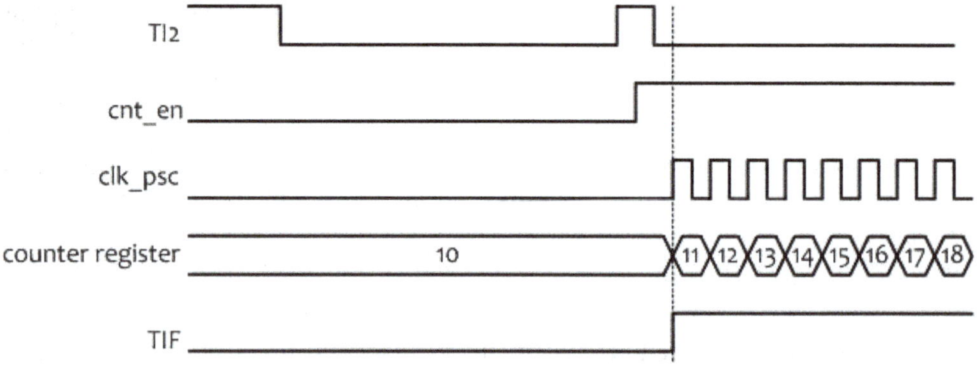

Figure 6.40 Trigger mode counter waveforms and values

Slave Mode: External Clock Mode 2 + Trigger Mode

The external clock mode 2 can be used in addition to another slave mode (except external clock mode 1 and encoder mode). In this case, the ETR signal is used as an external clock input, and another input can be selected as trigger input when operating in reset mode, gated mode, or trigger mode. It is recommended not to select ETR as TRGI through the TS bits of the TIMx->SMCR register.

One example is selecting the ETR input as the clock to TIM2 and use TI1 to start the TIM2 counter. The following procedure sets up this operation:

Step 1

Configure the ETR input by programming the TIM2->SMCR register as follows:

- Select no filter by setting the ETF field to 0000.
- Disable ETR prescaler by setting the ETPS field to 00.
- Detect the rising edge of the ETR signal by clearing the ETP bit to 0.
- Enable external clock mode 2 by setting the ECE bit.

Step 2

Configure channel 1 to detect the rising edge of the TI1 input by

- Disabling the TI1 filter by setting the IC1F field of the TIM2->CCMR1 register to 0000.
- Configuring the CC1 as input and mapping it to TI1 by setting the CC1S field in the TIM2->CCMR1 register to 01.
- Setting the CC1P and CC1NP bit in the TIM2->CCER register to 0.

Step 3

Configure the TIM2 to trigger mode by setting the SMS field in the TIM2->SMCR register to 110. Select TI1 as the trigger source by setting the TS field in the TIM2->SMCR register to 101.

A rising edge on the TI1 signal enables the counter and sets the TIF flag. The counter then counts on the ETR rising edges. This procedure is illustrated in Figure 6.41.

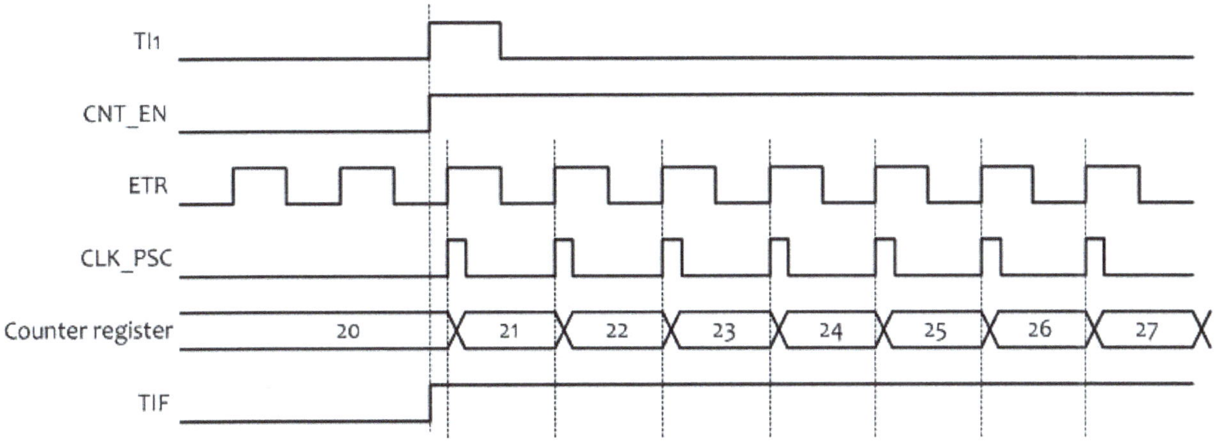

Figure 6.41 An example of External clock mode 2 + trigger mode

6.5.19 TIMER SYNCHRONIZATION

The TIMx timers are linked together internally for timer synchronization or chaining. When one timer is configured in master mode, it can reset, start, stop, or clock the counter of another timer configured in slave mode.

Using one Timer as the Prescaler for Another Timer

For example, the following procedure sets up TIM3 to be the prescaler of TIM2:

Step 1

Configure TIM3 to master mode so that it outputs a periodic trigger signal on each update event (UEV) by setting the MMS field in the TIM3->CR2 register to 010. Once this is done, a rising edge is output on the TRGO signal each time an UEV is generated.

Step 2

Connect the TRGO output of TIM3 to TIM2 by configuring TIM2 to slave mode using ITR2 as internal trigger. This is achieved by setting the **TS** field in the TIM2->SMCR register to **010**.

Step 3

Place the slave mode controller in **external clock mode 1** by setting the SMS field in the TIM2->SMCR register to **111**. This causes TIM2 to be clocked by the rising edge of the periodic TIM3 trigger signal.

Step 4

Enable both timers by setting the CEN bit of the TIM2->CR1 and TIM3->CR1 register.

The user can also select the OCx of a timer as the trigger output and use it to clock the counter of another timer.

Use One Timer to Enable Another Timer

The idea of this application is quite like the trigger mode described previously. The controlling timer must generate the TRGO signal, whereas the slave timer must be configured to the gated mode. The user should program the MMS field of the TIMx->CR2 to select a signal to be output to the TRGO.

For example, the following procedure uses the OC1REF from TIM3 to enable TIM2 to count:

Step 1

Set the MMS field of the TIM3->CR2 register to 100 to select OC1REF to be sent to the TRGO output.

Step 2

Configure the TIM3 OC1REF waveform properly. In this regard, the user is required to program TIM3->ARR, TIM3->CR1, TIM3->CCR1, TIM3->CCMR1, and so on.

Step 3

Set the TS field in the TIM2->SMCR register to 010 (select ITR2) to connect to the TRGO from TIM3.

Step 4

Configure TIM2 to gated mode by setting the SMS field in the TIM2->SMCR register to 101.

Step 5

Enable TIM2 and TIM3 by setting the CEN bit in the TIM2->CR1 and TIM3->CR1 register.

Use One Timer to Start Another Timer

The timer to be started must be configured to trigger mode, whereas the master timer can select one of the eight possible events to be sent to TRGO and start the slave timer. For example, the user can use the UEV of TIM3 to start TIM2 using the following procedure:

Step 1

Configure TIM3 to select its UEV as trigger output (TRGO) by setting the MMS field in the TIM3->CR2 register to 010.

Step 2

Configure the TIM3 period by loading an appropriate value into the TIM3->ARR register.

Step 3

Configure TIM2 to receive its trigger input from the ITR2 signal by setting the TS field of the TIM2->SMCR register to 010.

Step 4

Configure TIM2 to trigger mode by setting the SMS field in the TIM2->SMCR register to 110.

Step 5

Start TIM3 by setting the CEN bit in the TIM3->CR1 register to 1.

Starting Two Timers Synchronously in Response to an External Trigger

The user can use a trigger input to enable a timer and then use the generated enable signal to enable another timer. For example, we can use the TI1 input to enable TIM3 and then use the enable signal of TIM3 to enable TIM2. The procedure is as follows:

Step 1

Configure TIM3 master mode to send its Enable as trigger output by setting the MMS field in the TIM3->CR2 register to 001.

Step 2

Configure TIM3 slave mode to get its trigger input from TI1 by setting the TS field in the TIM3->SMCR register to 100.

Step 3

Configure TIM3 to trigger mode by setting the SMS field in the TIM3->SMCR register to 110.

Step 4

Configure TIM3 to master/slave mode by setting the **MSM** bit in the TIM3->SMCR register to 1.

Step 5

Configure TIM2 to get the input trigger from TIM3 by setting the TS field in the TIM2->SMCR register to 010 (see Tables 6.3 and 6.4).

Step 6

Configure TIM2 in trigger mode by setting the SMS field in the TIM2->SMCR register to 110.

When a rising edge occurs on TI1 (TIM3), both counters start counting synchronously on the internal clock and both TIF flags are set. An example is illustrated in Figure 6.42. In the figure, it can be seen that both counters are initialized to 0.

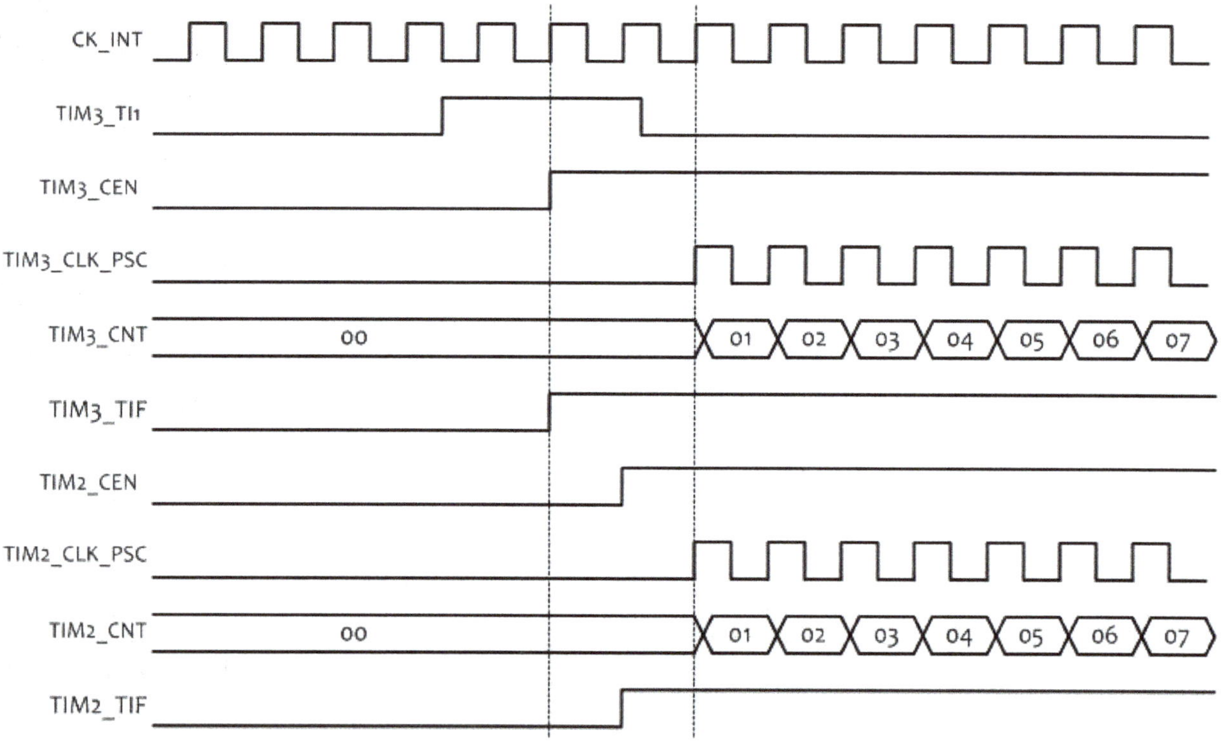

Figure 6.42 An example of using TI1 input of TIM3 to trigger TIM3 and TIM2

6.6 Driving the DC Motor

A DC motor is an analog motor and is available in just about any size and is therefore common to many applications, especially those that require a large torque. Because the speed and torque of DC motors can be controlled precisely over a wide range, they are used extensively in control systems as positioning devices. The DC motor has a permanent magnetic field, and its armature is a coil. When a voltage is applied to the armature, the motor begins to spin. The applied voltage level determines the speed of rotation.

Among the several variations of DC motors, the brushless DC motor is by far the most popular one. Brushless DC motors are commonly used where precise speed control is necessary, for example, computer disk drives, spindles within CD, DVD drives, and mechanisms within office products (such as fans, laser printers, and photocopiers). Modern brushless DC motors range in power from a fraction of a watt to many kilowatts. Larger brushless motors up to about 100-kW ratings are used in electric vehicles. They also find significant use in high-performance electric model aircraft. To provide control to the speed, Hall-effect sensors are often used to provide speed information to the microcontroller that controls the DC motor.

The STM32L475 can interface with the DC motor through a driver as shown in Figure 6.43. This configuration takes up only three I/O pins. The pin that controls the direction can be ordinary I/O pin, but the pin that controls the speed must be a PWM pin. The pin that receives the feedback must be an input capture pin.

Although some DC motors operate at 5 V or less, the STM32L475 cannot supply the required current to drive a motor directly. The minimum current requirement of any practical motor is much higher than any microcontroller can supply. Depending on the size and rating of the motor, a suitable driver chip must be selected to take control signals from the STM32L475 and deliver the necessary voltage and current to the motor.

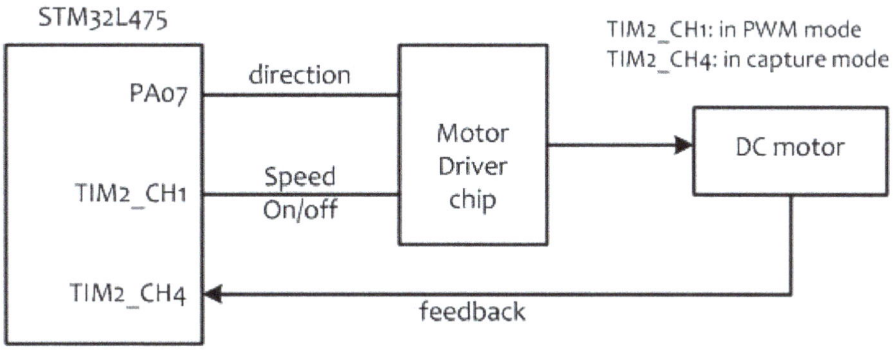

Figure 6.43 Simplified circuit for DC motor control

6.6.1 DC MOTOR DRIVER ICS

Standard motor driver chips are available in many current and voltage ratings. One example is the L293D from ST Microelectronics. The L293D has four channels and can output up to 1 A of current per channel with a supply voltage from 4.5 to 36 V. Each chip has a separate logic supply and uses a logical input (0 or 1) to enable or disable each channel. Input pins are clamped with diodes to protect against the static and back electromotive force (EMF) generated during the reversing of a motor. The pin assignment of the L293D is shown in Figure 6.44. There are two supply voltages: V_{CC1} and V_{CC2}. V_{CC1} is the logic supply voltage, which is normally connected to 5.0 V. The V_{CC2} signal is the output supply voltage and can be as high as 36 V. Drivers are enabled in pairs with drivers 1 and 2 enabled by the 1,2EN signal and drivers 3 and 4 enabled by the 3,4EN signal.

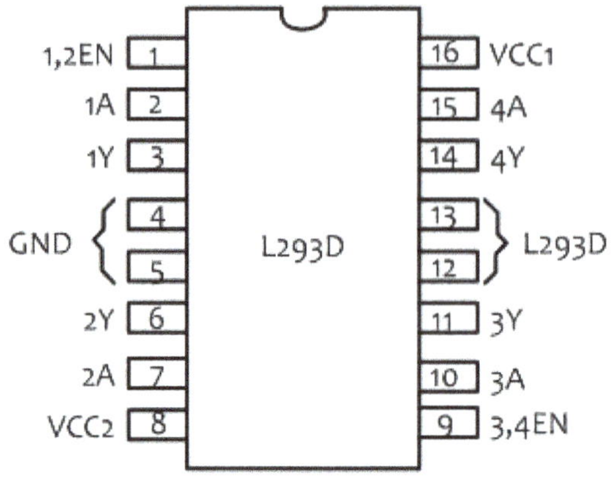

Figure 6.44 Motor driver L293D pin assignment

6.6.2 DRIVING A DC MOTOR USING THE L293D

A circuit that includes the STM32L475 and the L293D to drive the DC motor is shown in Figure 6.45. In the normal operation, the TIM2_CH1 pin outputs the PWM waveform, whereas the TIM2_CH2 pin outputs a 0 V. To rotate the DC motor in reverse direction, the TIM2_CH1 pin should be programmed to output a 0 V, whereas the TIM2_CH2 outputs a PWM output. To brake the motor (when the TIM_CH1 pin is outputting the PWM), the TIM2_CH1 pin should be programmed to output a 0 V, and the TIM2_CH2 to output to a 5 V for a duration that can stop the motor totally.

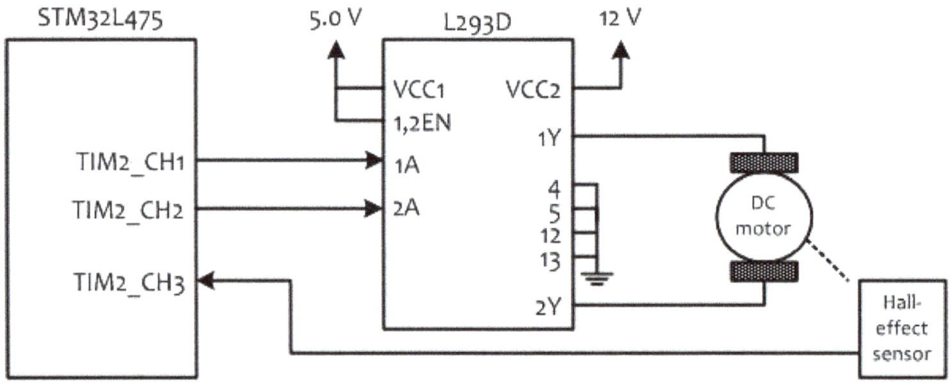

Figure 6.45 A DC motor control circuit that uses Hall-effect transistor

One way to provide feedback to the MCU is to add a Hall-effect sensor, as shown in Figure 6.45. By attaching two small magnets on the two edges (180° apart) of the DC motor and configuring the TIM2 channel 3 in capture mode, the STM32L475 will be able to measure the motor rotation speed. Whenever a magnet passes by the Hall-effect sensor, it induces a pulse. This pulse can be captured by the channel 3. The difference of these two consecutive captured edges gives the time for the motor to rotate half a cycle. The programs like those in Examples 6.10 and 6.11 can be used to generate PWM waveforms to drive the motor in the circuit shown in Figure 6.45.

Example 6.15 For the circuit shown in Figure 6.45, write a C function to measure the motor speed (in RPM), assuming that the TIM2 clock input has been set to 2 MHz. Assume that TIM2->ARR is loaded with 0x10000000.

Solution:

One minute is equal to 60,000,000 μs. Two pulses are captured in half a rotation. The captured value represents the duration of the time required for the DC motor to rotate half a cycle in the unit of number of clock cycles. The period of the TIM2 clock input is 0.5 μs (= 1 ÷ 2 MHz). Let **diff** be the difference of two captured edges, then the DC motor rotation speed is equal to 60,000,000 ÷ diff.

```
uint32_t motorRPM(void)
{
    uint32_t edge1, edge2, diff, rpm;
    TIM2->CCMR2   = TIM_CCMR2_CC3S_0; // TIM2_CH3 pin for capture
// enable TIM2_CH3 capture on falling edge
    TIM2->CCER    = TIM_CCER_CC3E + TIM_CCER_CC3P;
    TIM2->CR1     = TIM_CR1_ARPE + TIM_CR1_CEN; // enable TIM2
    TIM2->SR      = 0; // clear all flags
    while(!(TIM2->SR & TIM_SR_CC3IF)); // wait for first falling edge
    edge1         = TIM2->CCR3;
    TIM2->SR      = 0; // clear CC3IF flag
    while(!(TIM2->SR & TIM_SR_CC3IF)); // wait for 2nd falling edge
    edge2         = TIM1->CCR3;
// TIM2 overflows, assume TIM2->ARR is loaded with 0x10000000
    if (TIM2->SR & TIM_SR_UIF)
        diff      = edge2 + (0x10000000 - edge1); // TIM2 overflow occurred
    else //
        diff      = edge2 - edge1; // TIM2 did not overflow → edge2 > edge1
    rpm  = 60000000 / diff;
    return rpm;
}
```

6.7 Summary

Timer functions make many applications possible. With a timer, delay creation becomes much easier. Without a timer, signal parameter measurement and waveform generation become extremely difficult or even impossible. For many microcontrollers, capture, compare, and PWM are the three basic timer functions that they provide. Either the timer counter or the compare function can be used to create time delays. Capture function can be used to measure signal parameters such as pulse width, period, and duty cycle. Either compare function or PWM function can be used to generate waveforms.

The STM32L475 has five groups of timers:

- Basic timers: TIM6 and TIM7
- General-purpose timers: TIM2/TIM3/TIM4/TIM5
- General-purpose timers: TIM15/TIM16/TIM17
- Advanced control timers: TIM1/TIM8
- Low-power timer: LPTIM

Each of these timers has an **auto-reload register** (**TIMx_ARR**) that sets the **TOP** value, which a counter can count up to or count down from. For those timers that have the capture/compare channels, a capture/compare register (TIMx_CCRy) is included in each channel. When in capture mode, the TIMx_CCRy register holds the captured counter value. When in compare mode, it holds the value to be compared to the counter. Both the TIMx_ARR and TIMx_CCRy register have a shadow register (or buffer register). When they are enabled, the shadow register is updated in an **update event (UEV)**.

The master mode and/or slave mode of each of the general-purpose and advanced control timers can be enabled (both modes can be enabled at the same time). When the master mode is enabled, a timer can generate a trigger output (TRGO) to control other timers. When the slave mode is enabled, a timer can be controlled by other timer. Timers can achieve synchronization via these two modes.

Basic timers are very simple. Creating time delays is the main application of basic timers. General-purpose timers and advanced control timers support input capture, output compare, and PWM functions. General-purpose and advanced control timers can count up, count down, and count up and then count down. Some of these timers support encoder mode that can measure the motor position. A few timers also support dead-time insertion in their PWM mode. This function can be used in the bridge-type circuit that drives the DC motor [1].

PWM outputs are mainly used in applications that require average DC voltage level to be controlled. Examples include DC motor, fan speed, lamp brightness, and so on. The frequency of the PWM is not critical to these applications. The only exception might be the servo motor. A servo motor requires the driving signal to be set to certain frequency.

DC motors are used wherever precise speed control is required. The speed of the DC motor is controlled by changing the voltage applied to the DC motor. The PWM mode of the STM32L475 timers is suitable for this application. Almost every application that uses a DC motor requires it to reverse its direction of rotation or vary its speed. Reversing the direction is achieved by changing the polarity of the voltage applied to the motor. Sometimes there is a need to brake a DC motor. When a DC motor is turning, it picks up momentum. Turning off the voltage to the motor won't stop the motor immediately. To stop the DC motor abruptly, you need to reverse the voltage applied to the DC motor.

6.8 Exercises

E6.1 Write a function that uses TIM5 to generate a time delay of 17 ms, assuming that the internal clock source (i.e., APB1 bus clock) is 16MHz, 48 MHz, and 80 MHz.

E6.2 Write a sequence of C statements to configure TIM2 to generate a 50-Hz square waveform with 10% duty cycle from the TIM2_CH1 pin (assigned to PA5 pin), assuming that the internal clock source (i.e., APB1 bus clock) is 80 MHz. Use both the PWM edge-aligned mode and center-aligned mode.

E6.3 Continue with **E6.2**; what are the values to be loaded into TIM2->CCR1 to generate duty cycles of 5%, 5.5%, 6%, 6.5%, 7%, 7.5%, 8%, 8.5%, 9%, and 9.5%, respectively (use edge-aligned mode).

E6.4 Write a C program to configure TIM3 to generate an 800-Hz square waveform with 60% duty cycle from the TIM3_CH2 pin, assuming that the internal clock source (i.e., APB1 bus clock) is 80 MHz. Use both edge-aligned and center-aligned modes.

E6.5 Write a program to generate a 2-kHz digital waveform with a 60% duty cycle from the TIM2_CH4 pin, assuming that the internal clock source (i.e., APB1 bus clock) is 80 MHz. Use both edge-aligned and center-aligned modes.

E6.6 Write a program that uses the circuit shown in Figure 6.31 to play the song "Home, Sweet Home," assuming that the internal clock source (i.e., APB1 bus clock) is 80 MHz.

E6.7 Assume that TIM2 is configured to count up/down on TI1 and TI2 in encoder mode 3 and you are given the TI1 and TI2 waveform as shown in Figure E6.7. Also assume that

- CC1S= 01 (TIMx->CCMR1 register, TI1FP1 mapped on TI1)
- CC2S= 01 (TIMx->CCMR1 register, TI2FP2 mapped on TI2)
- CC1P and CC1NP = '1' (TIMx->CCER register, TI1FP1 inverted, TI1FP1=/TI1)
- CC2P and CC2NP = '0' (TIMx->CCER register, TI2FP2 noninverted, TI2FP2=TI2)
- SMS= 011 (TIMx->SMCR register, both inputs are active on both rising and falling edges)
- CEN= 1 (TIMx->CR1 register, Counter is enabled)

What is the counter counting pattern? Draw the waveform to illustrate.

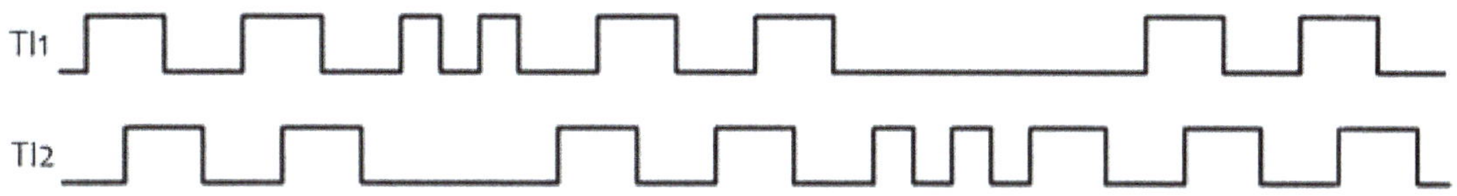

Figure E6.6 A sample TI1 and TI2 input waveform

E6.8 Assume that TIM2 is configured to count up/down on TI1 and TI2 in encoder mode 3 and you are given the TI1 and TI2 waveform as shown in Figure E6.8. Also assume that

- TI1FPI is mapped to TI1 (i.e., the CC1S field in the TIM2_CCMR1 register is set to 01)
- TI2FP2 is mapped to TI2 (i.e., the CC2S field in the TIM2_CCMR1 register is set to 01)
- TI1FP1 = TI1 (i.e., the CC1P and the CC1NP bit in the TIM2_CCER register are set t0 0)

- TI2FP2 = TI2 (i.2., the CC2P and the CC2NP bit in the TIM2_CCER register are set to 0)
- Both inputs are active on both rising and falling edges (i.e., the SMS field in the TIM2_SMCR register is set to 011—encoder mode 3).
- TIM2 is enabled (i.e., the CEN bit in the TIM2_CR1 register is set to 1)

What is the counter counting pattern? Draw the waveform to illustrate.

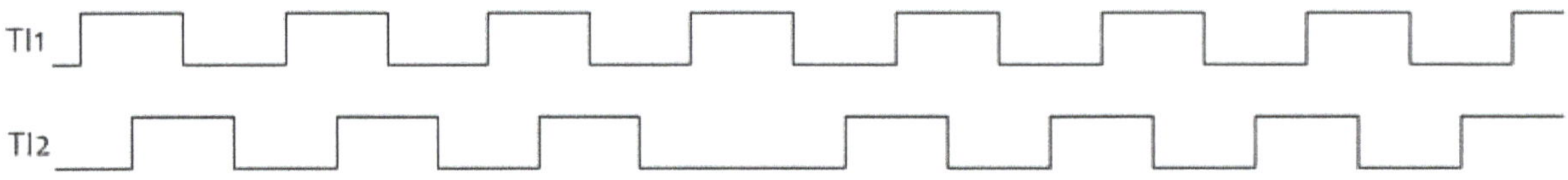

Figure E6.8 A sample TI1 and TI2 input waveform

E6.9 Assume that the TIM4_CH1 pin is connected to a speaker. Write a program to generate a 3-tone siren that alternates among the frequencies of 220, 440, and 880 Hz with each tone lasting for 0.5 second using PWM mode 1. Assume that the TIM4 internal clock source is 80 MHz.

E6.10 Write a program and use the TIM5_CH1 to generate a 400-Hz periodic waveform with 40% duty cycle using the PWM mode 2 along with **center-aligned mode 2** with the CMS field in the TIM5->CR1 register set to 10, assuming that the clock source to TIM5 is 80 MHz.

E6.11 To measure the frequency of a signal, the signal should be selected as the clock input for the timer selected to do the measurement. Write a program that uses TIM5 to measure the frequency of a signal.

E6.12 Write a sequence of C statements to generate the periodic waveform from the TIM2_CH1 pin with one cycle shown in Figure E6.12, assuming that the APB1 clock input is 80 MHz. Enable the asymmetric PWM mode 1 to generate the waveform.

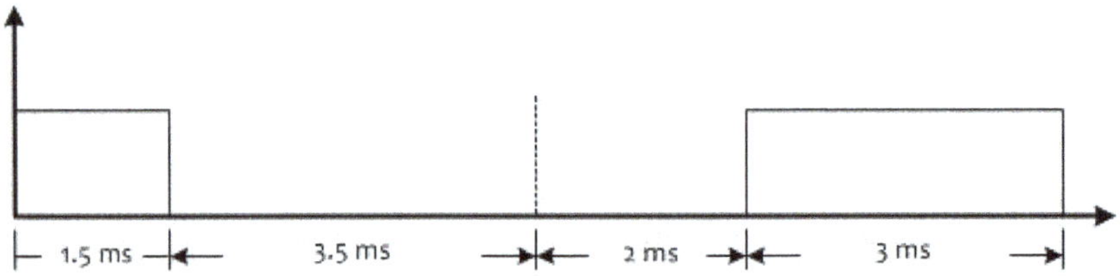

Figure E6.12 One cycle of the waveform to be generated using the asymmetric PWM mode 1

E6.13 Write a sequence of C statements to generate periodic waveform with one cycle shown in Figure E6.13 using the asymmetric PWM mode 2 from the TIM2_CH1 pin, assuming that the APB1 clock input is 80 MHz.

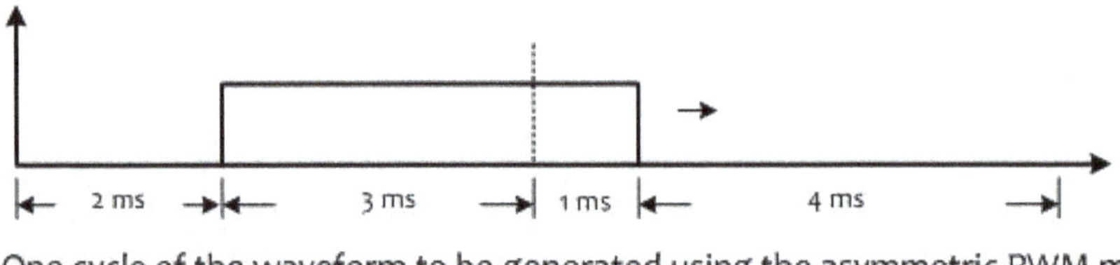

Figure E6.13 One cycle of the waveform to be generated using the asymmetric PWM mode 2

E6.14 Write a C program to generate a pulse with 1-ms delay and 1.5-ms pulse width from the TIM2_CH1 pin after a rising edge on the TIM2_CH2 pin is detected using TIM2, assuming the internal clock source to TIM2 is 80 MHz.

E6.15 Write a sequence of C statements to configure TIM2 so that it can generate a TRGO output every 1 ms, assuming that the clock source to TIM2 is 80 MHz.

6.9 Lab Assignments

L6.1 Three-Tone Siren Generation. Connect the TIM2_CH1 pin to a speaker. Write a program to generate a 3-tone siren with frequency alternating from 220 to 440 to 880 Hz, and this is repeated. Each tone lasts for half a second. Assume that the frequency of the TIM2 internal clock source is 80 MHz.

L6.2 DC Motor Driving Experiment. Connect the circuit as shown in Figure L6.2.

Write a program to configure the TIM2_CH1 to PWM mode 1. Start the TIM2_CH1 pin output from 30% duty cycle, then 40% duty cycle, then 50%, until the duty cycle reaches 90% with each duty cycle lasting for 10 seconds. Write down your observation about the DC motor rotation. A fan with a DC motor such as the one shown in Figure L6.2a can be used in this lab.

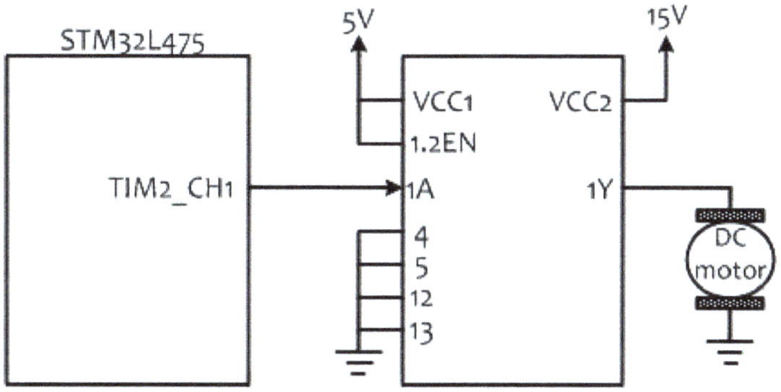

Figure L6.2 Circuit for driving a DC motor

Figure L6.2a A cooling fan with DC motor for lab 6.2

L6.3 Write a program and use the circuit shown in Figure 6.31 to play the song with the score shown in Figure L6.3.

Serenade of Green Island

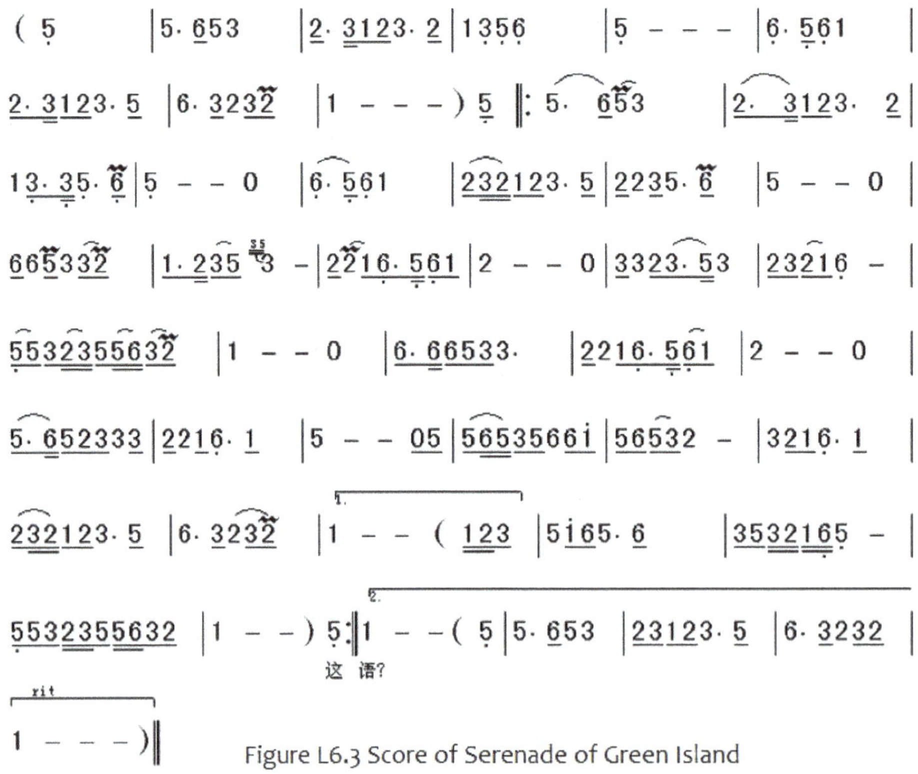

Figure L6.3 Score of Serenade of Green Island

7

Serial Peripheral Interface (SPI)

7.1 Objectives

After completing this chapter, you will be able to:

- Describe the SPI protocol.
- Configure the STM32L475 SPI operation parameters.
- Transmit and receive data using the SPI protocol.
- Interface with peripheral chips using the SPI interface.
- Use the SPI protocol to interface with the shift register such as the 74HC595.
- Use the SPI protocol to interface with the EEPROM chip such as the 25LC256.
- Use the SPI protocol to interface with the digital-to-analog converter (DAC) chip such as the MCP4922.

7.2 Introduction to SPI

The SPI is a synchronous communication protocol introduced by Motorola in mid-1980s to facilitate data communications between the microcontroller and peripheral chips. Because of its low software overhead, simple hardware connection, and good performance, all microcontrollers have provided the SPI as a standard interfacing peripheral. However, the SPI protocol is not a standard. Many semiconductor vendors implement this protocol slightly differently from the original SPI protocol from Motorola.

7.2.1 SPI DEVICE TYPES

In the SPI protocol, devices are divided into **masters** and **slaves**. A master can initiate data transfer and generate clock signal to synchronize data transfers whereas a slave can only respond to the data transfer requests. A microcontroller can serve both the role of a master and a slave whereas peripheral chips can only serve as slaves.

7.2.2 SPI SIGNALS

The SPI has four signals:

- **SCLK**. Serial clock. This signal is an output from the master device, which synchronizes data transfer under the SPI protocol.
- **MOSI**. Master out slave in. This signal is an output from the master device and input to the slave device.
- **MISO**. Master in slave out. This signal is an input to the master device and output from the slave device.
- **SS**. Slave select. This signal is an output from the master device to enable a slave device to respond to data transfer request. The SS signal is often asserted low for peripheral chips.

A circuit connection between a master and a slave is illustrated in Figure 7.1. In the figure, the same signals are tied together.

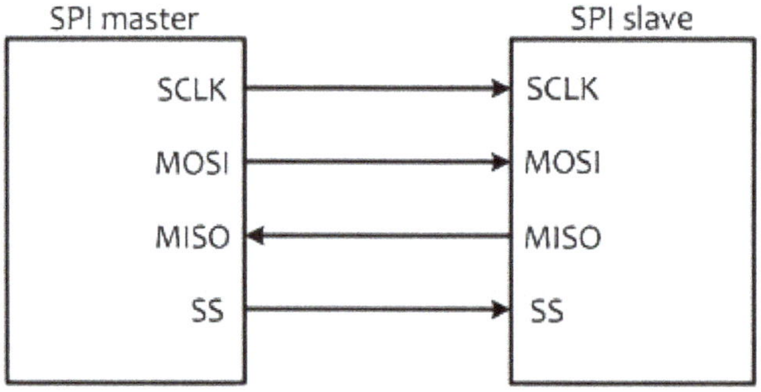

Figure 7.1 Single SPI master and single SPI slave connection

7.2.3 SPI DATA TRANSMISSION

The SPI master configures the clock, using a frequency supported by the slave device, typically up to 10 MHz. The master selects a slave device by asserting the SS signal to the target slave.

The SPI master starts a data transfer by **writing into the data register.** The master sends out a bit to the MOSI pin and the slave reads in every clock cycle, while at the same time, the slave sends back a bit on the MISO pin and the master reads it. Transmissions normally involve two shift registers of some given length (8 bits or 16 bits), one in the master device and one in the slave device; they are connected in a ring topology as shown in Figure 7.2. Data are usually shifted out most significant bit first. The master will trigger as many SCLK pulses as needed by the data transfer (8 or 16).

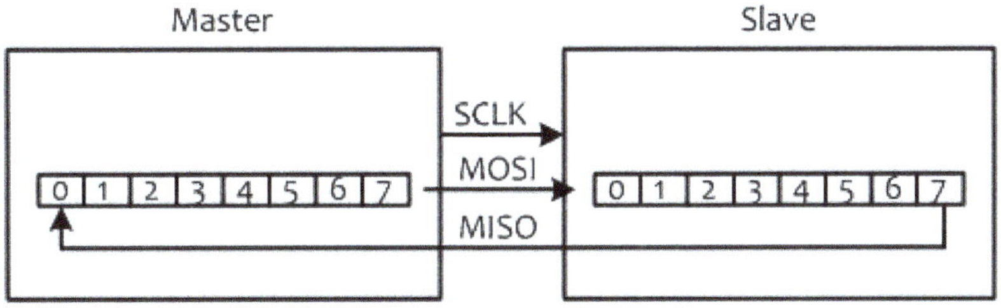

Figure 7.2 SPI data transfer operation

7.2.4 CLOCK POLARITY AND PHASE

The SPI master is required to specify the SCLK clock polarity when it is idle and the clock phase used in data transfers. The clock polarity and phase are named as CPOL and CPHA, respectively. The SCLK signal is idle low if CPOL is 0. Otherwise, it is idle high. The parameter CPHA specifies the clock edge that data (on MOSI and MISO pins) are sampled (or shifted). When CPHA is 0, data are sampled on the first edge in a SCLK cycle. Otherwise, data are sampled on the second edge. The combinations of CPOL and CPHA are shown in Figure 7.3.

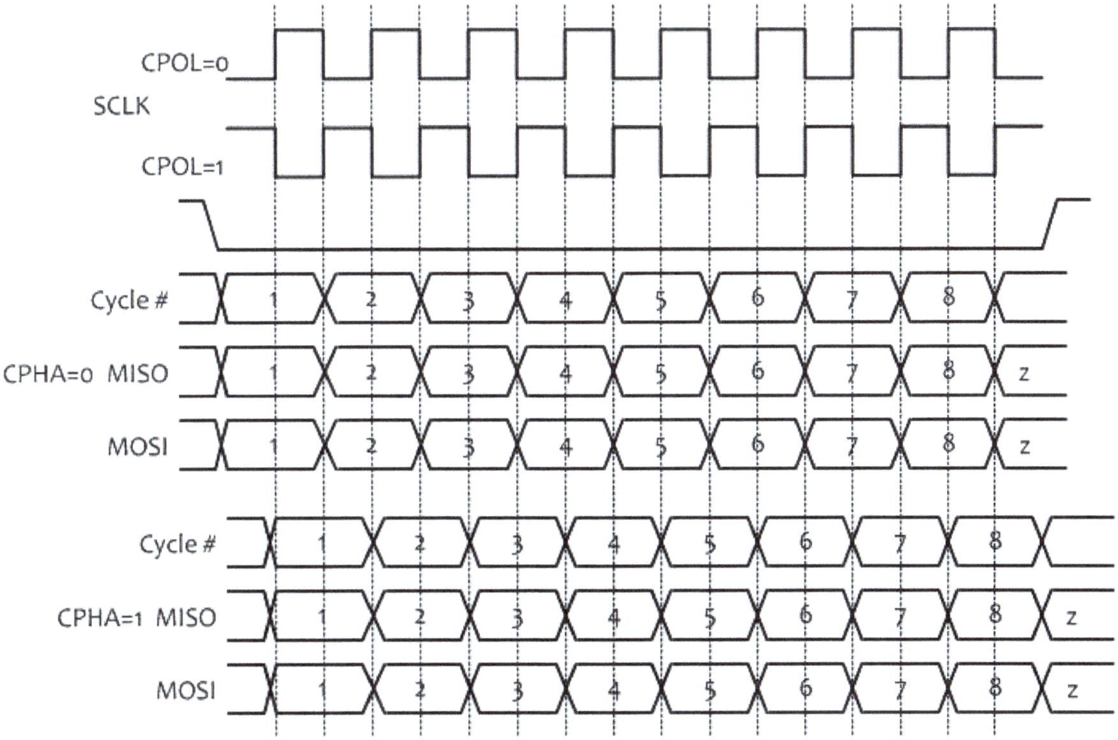

Figure 7.3 SPI clock polarity and phase combinations

7.2.5 DATA FRAME FORMAT

Data are transmitted and received frame by frame. Initially, a frame is 8 bits. However, the SPI is not a published standard. Different companies may implement the SPI protocol slightly differently. Nowadays, an SPI frame may be as short as 4 bits and as long as 16 bits.

A frame may be transmitted least significant bit (LSB) first or most significant bit (MSB) first. The frame size is configurable for many companies.

7.2.6 SPI BUS CONNECTION METHODS

When an embedded system has only one SPI slave device, the user can use the connection method shown in Figure 7.1. When there are multiple SPI slaves in a system, they can be connected to the microcontroller using the serial or parallel method.

When there are multiple identical SPI slaves in a system that the master needs to transfer or receive data to/from simultaneously, the serial connection method illustrated in Figure 7.4 is the most appropriate configuration.

In the **serial connection method**, the SCLK and SS signals from the master and slaves are tied together. The MOSI signal from the master and the first slave are tied together. The MISO signal from the first slave is connected to the MOSI signal of the second slave, and so on. The MISO signal of the last slave in the chain is connected to the same signal of the master. The serial connection method is also called **daisy-chained method.**

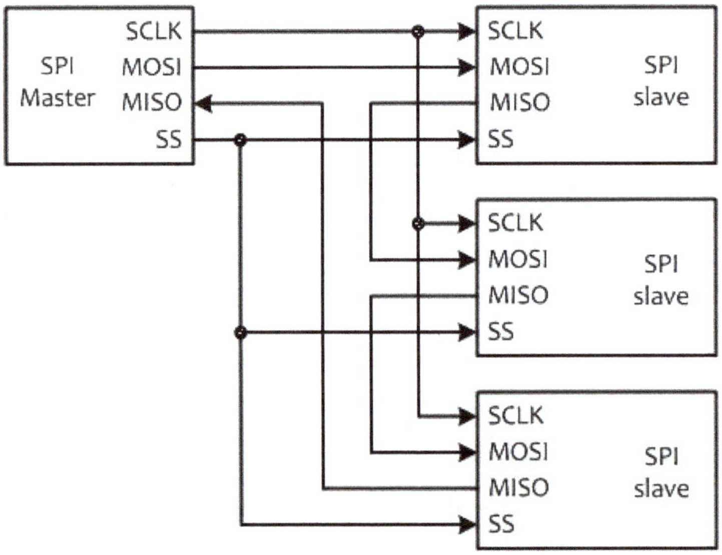

Figure 7.4 SPI serial connection method

When there are several different types of SPI slaves in a system, they are often accessed individually at different times. The **parallel connection method** illustrated in Figure 7.5 should be used. In this connection method, all identical signals (except for the SS signal) are tied together. The master uses as many I/O pins as the number of slaves for the SS signal. This method enables the master to perform data transfer with each individual SPI slave without going through any other SPI slave.

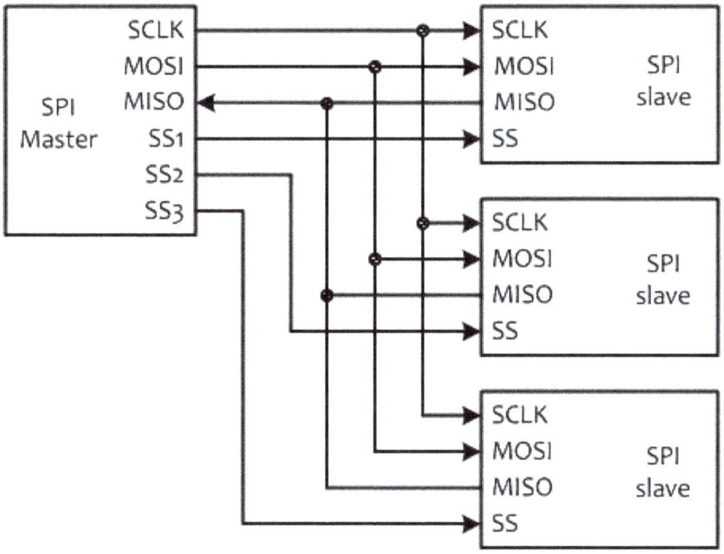

Figure 7.5 SPI parallel connection method

7.2.7 DUAL SPI [2]

Because the full-duplex nature of SPI is rarely used, an extension uses both data pins in a half-duplex configuration to send two data bits per clock cycle. Typically a command byte is sent requesting a response in dual mode, after which the MOSI line becomes SIO0 (serial I/O 0) and carries even bits, whereas the MISO line becomes SIO1 and carries odd bits. Data are still transmitted MSB first, but SIO1 carries bits 7, 5, 3, and 1 of each byte, whereas SIO0 carries bits 6, 4, 2, and 0.

This is particularly popular among SPI ROMs, which have to send a large amount of data, and comes in two variants:

- Dual read commands accept the send command and address from the master in single mode, and return the data in the dual mode.
- Dual I/O commands send the command in the single mode, then send the address and return the data in the dual mode.

7.2.8 QUAD SPI [2]

Whereas dual SPI reuses the existing serial I/O lines, quad SPI adds two more I/O lines (SIO2 and SIO3) and sends 4 data bits per clock cycle. Again, it is requested by a special command, which enables quad mode after the command itself is sent in the single mode. There are two variants:

- **SQI type 1**: The command is sent on the single-line mode but addresses and data are sent on four lines.
- **SQI type 2**: Commands and addresses are sent on a single line but data are sent/received on four lines.

All Cortex-M4 and Cortex-M7 devices from ST implement the QUADSPI interface. This interface method is implemented mainly for supporting data transfer with the flash memory with the SPI interface.

7.3 Features of the STM32L475 SPI Modules

The STM32L475 has three identical SPI modules. Each of these modules supports three data transfer modes: (a) full-duplex synchronous mode on three lines, (b) half-duplex synchronous mode on two lines (with bidirectional data line), and (c) simplex synchronous mode on two lines (with unidirectional data line).

Data frames can be from 4 to 16 bits. A data frame can be transferred most significant bit first, and in multimaster environment. The slave-select signal (SS) is named as NSS in the STM32L475 SPI. The NSS signal can be managed by software or hardware for both the SPI master or SPI slave (MCU only). This enables the dynamic change of master/slave operations and makes the multimaster operation possible.

The maximum frequency for the SPI is $f_{PCLK/2}$ in both the master and slave mode for the STM32L475. PCLK is the peripheral bus clock.

The STM32L475 SPI supports both the Motorola and TI versions of the SPI. Two 32-bit embedded Rx and Rx FIFO with DMA capability are included to facilitate data packing and unpacking during the data transfer phase.

7.4 The STM32L475 SPI Signal Assignment

Four signal pins are allocated to each SPI module. The signal pin usage is summarized in Table 7.1.

Table 7.1 STM32L475 SPI signal pins usage

Module	Signal function	Alternate function	pin
SPI1	MOSI	AF5	PA7, PB5, PE15
	MISO	AF5	PA6, PB4, PE14
	SCK	AF5	PA5, PB3, PE13
	NSS	AF5	PA4, PA15, PE12
SPI2	MOSI	AF5	PB15, PC3, PD4
	MISO	AF5	PB14, PC2, PD3
	SCK	AF5	PB10, PB13, PD1
	NSS	AF5	PB9, PB12, PD0
SPI3	MOSI	AF6	PB5, PC12
	MISO	AF6	PB4, PC11
	SCK	AF6	PB3, PC10
	NSS	AF6	PA4, PA15

7.5 The STM32L475 SPI Communications

The STM32L475 SPI supports the following communication environments:

- One master and one slave
- One master and multiple slaves
- Multiple masters and multiple slaves

7.5.1 COMMUNICATIONS BETWEEN ONE MASTER AND ONE SLAVE

The communication between one master and one slave can be proceeded in (a) full-duplex mode, (b) half-duplex mode, or (3) simplex mode.

Full-Duplex Communication

This mode should be used when the master and slave have data to be exchanged in both directions. The circuit connection is shown in Figure 7.6.

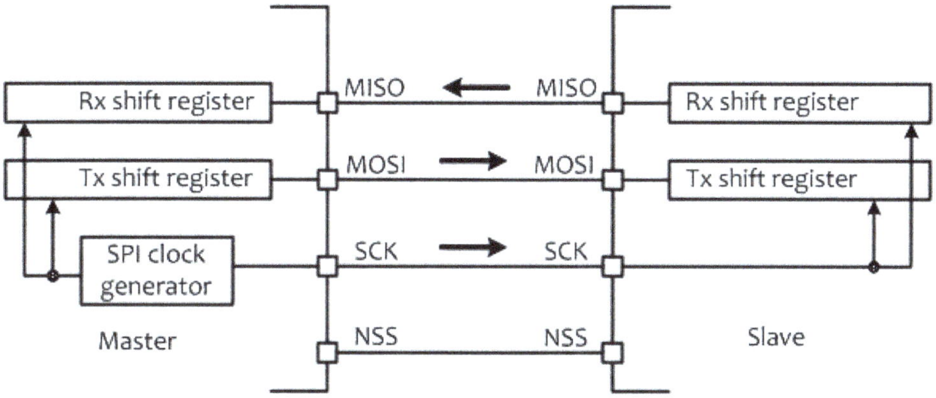

Figure 7.6 Full-duplex single master/single slave application

Half-Duplex Communication

The SPI can communicate in the half-duplex mode by setting the BIDIMODE bit in the SPIx->CR1 register. In this configuration, one single cross-connection line is used to link shift registers of the master and the slave together. During this communication, the data are synchronously shifted between the shift registers on the SCK clock edge in the transfer direction selected reciprocally by both the master and slave with the BIDIOE bit in the SPIx->CR1 registers. This configuration is shown in Figure 7.7. In this configuration, the master's MISO pin and the slave's MOSI pin are free for other application uses. The contents of the SPIx->CR1 register are shown in Figure 7.8.

A critical condition can happen when the data transfer direction is changed not synchronously between two nodes working at bidirectional mode and new transmitter accesses the common data line while former transmitter still keeps an opposite value on the line. Both nodes then fight while providing opposite output levels on the common line temporarily until the next node changes its direction settings correspondingly. Adding a serial resistor between the MOSI and MISO pins can limit the current flow and provide protection to the circuit.

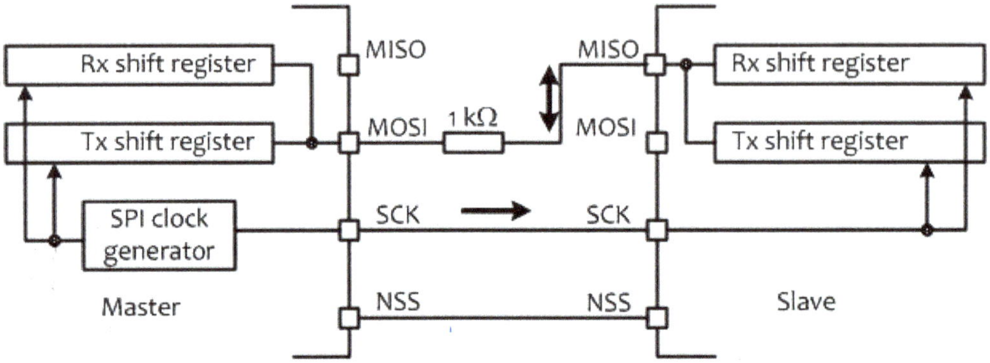

Figure 7.7 Half-duplex single master/single slave application

15	14	13	12	11	10	9	8
BIDI MODE	BIDIOE	CRCEN	CRC NEXT	CRCL	RXONLY	SSM	SSI

Reset value = 0x0000
Offset = 0x00

7	6	5	4	3	2	1	0
LSB FIRST	SPE	BR[2:0]			MSTR	CPOL	CPHA

BIDIMODE: Bidirectional data mode enable
 0: 2-line unidirectional data mode selected
 1: 1-line bidirectional data mode selected (keep RXONLY bit cleared)
BIDIOE: Output enable in bidirectional mode
 In master mode, the MOSI pin is used and in slave mode, the MISO pin is used.
 0: Output disabled (receive-only mode)
 1: Output enabled (transmit-only mode)
CRCEN: Hardware CRC calculation enable (written only when SPE = 0)
 0: CRC calculation disabled
 1: CRC calculation enabled
CRCNEXT: Transmit CRC next
 0: next transmit value is from Tx buffer
 1: next transmit value is from Tx CRC register
CRCL: CRC length
 0: 8-bit CRC length
 1: 16-bit CRC length
RXONLY: receive only mode enable
 This bit enables simplex communication, using a single unidirectional line to receive data exclusively. Keep BIDIMODE bit clear when receive only mode is active.
 0: full duplex (transmit and receive)
 1: output disabled (receive-only mode)
SSM: Software slave management
 0: software slave management disabled
 1: Software slave management enabled—NSS pin input is replaced with the value from SSI bit

Figure 7.8 SPI control register 1 (SPIx->CR1, x = 1, 2, 3)

15	14	13	12	11	10	9	8
BIDI MODE	BIDIOE	CRCEN	CRC NEXT	CRCL	RXONLY	SSM	SSI

7	6	5	4	3	2	1	0
LSB FIRST	SPE	BR[2:0]			MSTR	CPOL	CPHA

Reset value = 0x0000
Offset = 0x00

SSI: Internal slave select
This bit has effect only when the SSM bit is set. The value of this bit is forced to the NSS pin and the I/O value of the NSS pin is ignored.
LSBFIRST: Frame format
0: Data is transmitted/received with the MSB first
1: Data transmitted/received with the LSB first
SPE: SPI enable
0: peripheral disabled 1: Peripheral enabled
BR[2:0]: Baud rate control
000: $f_{PCLK}/2$ 001: $f_{PCLK}/4$ 010: $f_{PCLK}/8$ 011: $f_{PCLK}/16$
100: $f_{PCLK}/32$ 101: $f_{PCLK}/64$ 110: $f_{PCLK}/128$ 111: $f_{PCLK}/256$
MSTR: Master selection
0: slave configuration 1: master configuration
CPOL: Clock polarity
0: SCLK is idle low 1: SCLK is idle high
CPHA: Clock phase
0: The first clock transition in one cycle is the first data capture edge
1: The second clock transition in one cycle if the first data capture edge

Figure 7.8a SPI control register 1 (SPIx->CR1, x = 1, 2, 3)—(continued)

Simplex Communications

The SPI can communicate in simplex mode by setting the SPI **transmit-only** or **receive-only** using the RXONLY bit in the SPIx->CR1 register. This configuration is illustrated in Figure 7.9. In this configuration, only one line is used for the transfer between the shift registers of the master and slave.

- **Transmit-only mode (RXONLY = 0).** The configuration settings are the same as for full-duplex mode. The application has to ignore the information captured on the unused input pin.
- **Receive-only mode (RXONLY = 1).** In the slave configuration, the MISO output is disabled. The slave continues to receive data from the MOSI pin while its slave select signal is asserted. In the master configuration, the MOSI output is disabled and the pin can be used as a GPIO. The clock signal is generated continuously as long as the SPI is enabled. The only way to stop the clock is to clear the RXONLY bit or the SPE bit and wait until the incoming pattern from the MISO pin is finished and fills the data buffer structure, depending on its configuration.

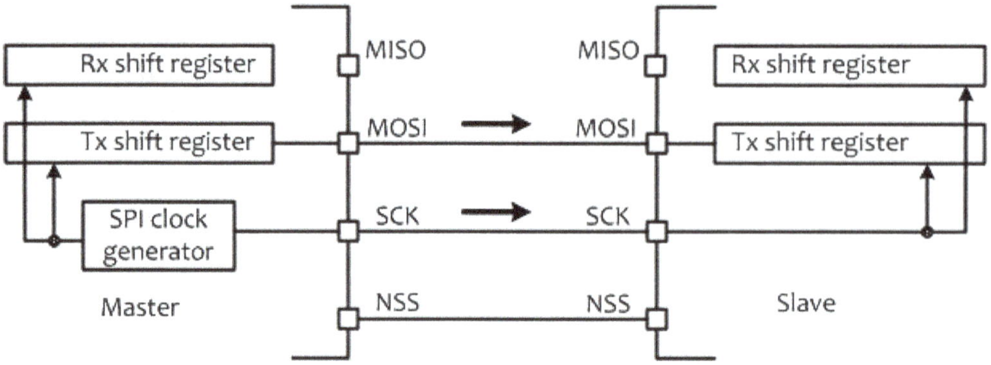

Figure 7.9 Simplex single master/single slave application (master in transmit-only/ slave in receive-only mode)

7.5.2 STANDARD SINGLE-MASTER, MULTISLAVE COMMUNICATION

This is the environment in which the microcontroller interfaces with several peripheral chips using the SPI interface. In this configuration, the STM32L475 is required to use GPIO pins to manage the slave select (or chip enable) input for the peripheral chips. Depending on the type of SPI peripheral chips, either the connection method in Figure 7.4 or 7.5 should be used.

7.5.3 MULTIMASTER COMMUNICATION

Although the SPI bus is not designed for a multimaster application, the user can still use the built-in feature which detects a potential conflict between two nodes trying to master the same bus at the same time. The NSS pin should be configured as an input for this purpose.

When nodes are not active, they stay at slave mode by default. Once one node wants to overtake control on the bus, it switches itself into master mode and applies active level on the slave select input of the other node via dedicated GPIO pin. After the session is completed, the active slave select signal is released and the node mastering the bus temporarily returns to passive slave mode waiting for the next session to start.

If two nodes raised their mastering request at the same time, a bus conflict event occurs (**a mode fault**). The user can then apply some simple arbitration process (for example, back off a random amount of time and retry) to resolve the conflict.

7.5.4 SLAVE SELECT (NSS) PIN MANAGEMENT

In slave mode, the NSS signal works as a standard **chip select** input and lets the slave communicate with the master. In master mode, NSS can be used as an output or input. As an input, it can prevent multimaster bus conflict, and as an output it can drive a slave select signal of a single slave.

The choice of hardware or software slave select is done by programming the SSM bit in the SPIx->CR1 register:

- **Software NSS Management** (SSM = 1). In this configuration, the slave select information is driven internally by the SSI bit in the SPIx->CR1 register. The external NSS pin is free for other application uses.
- **Hardware NSS Management** (SSM = 0). There are two possible configurations in this scheme differentiated by the setting of the SSOE bit in the SPIx->CR1 register:
  (a) NSS output enable (SSM = 0, SSOE = 1). This configuration is used when the MCU is programmed to be a master. The NSS pin is managed by the hardware. The NSS signal is driven low as soon as the SPI is enabled in master mode and is kept low until the SPI is disabled. A pulse can be generated between continuous communications if NSS pulse mode is activated (NSSP = 1). The NSSP bit is in the SPIx->CR2 register. The SPI cannot work in multimaster configuration with this NSS setting. The contents of the SPIx->CR2 register are shown in Figure 7.10.
  (b) NSS output disable (SSM = 0, SSOE = 0). If the MCU is acting as the master on the bus, this configuration supports the multimaster capability. If the NSS pin is pulled low in this mode, the SPI enters master mode fault state and the device is automatically reconfigured to the slave mode. In the slave mode, the NSS pin works as a standard **chip select** input and the slave is selected while the NSS signal is low.

15	14	13	12	11	10	9	8
--	LDMA_TX	LDMA_RX	FRXTH	DS[3:0]			

7	6	5	4	3	2	1	0
TXEIE	RXNEIE	ERRIE	FRF	NSSP	SSOE	TXDMAEN	RXDMAEN

Reset value = 0x0700
Offset = 0x04

LDMA_TX: Last DMA transfer for transmission
This bit is used in data packing mode, to define if the total number of data to transmit by DMA is odd or even.
0: Number of data to transfer is even. 1: Number of data to transfer is odd.
LDMA_RX: Last DMA transfer for reception
Used in data packing mode, to define if the total number of data to receive by DMA is odd or even.
0: Number of data to receive is even. 1: Number of data to receive is odd
FRXTH: FIFO reception threshold
0: RXNE event is generated if the FIFO level is greater than or equal to ½ (16-bit)
1: RXNE event is generated if the FIFO level is greater than or equal to ¼ (8-bit)
DS[3:0]: Data size

0000~0010: not used	0011: 4-bit	0100: 5-bit
0101: 6-bit	0110: 7-bit	0111: 8-bit
1000: 9-bit	1001: 10-bit	1010: 11-bit
1011: 12-bit	1100: 13-bit	1101: 14-bit
1110: 15-bit	1111: 16-bit	

TXEIE: Tx buffer empty interrupt enable
0: TXE interrupt disabled 1: TXE interrupt enabled

Figure 7.10 SPI control register 2 (SPIx->CR2, x = 1, 2, 3)

15	14	13	12	11	10	9	8	
--	LDMA_TX	LDMA_RX	FRXTH	DS[3:0]				Reset value = 0x0700 Offset = 0x04
7	**6**	**5**	**4**	**3**	**2**	**1**	**0**	
TXEIE	RXNEIE	ERRIE	FRF	NSSP	SSOE	TXDMAEN	RXDMAEN	

RXNEIE: RX buffer not empty interrupt enable
  0: RXNE interrupt disabled   1: RXNE interrupt enabled
ERRIE: Error interrupt enable
  0: Error interrupt is disabled   1: error interrupt enabled
FRF: Frame format (must be written when SPI is disabled)
  0: SPI Motorola mode   1: SPI TI mode
NSSP: NSS pulse management (used in master mode only)
  This bit allows the SPI to generate an NSS pulse between two consecutive data when doing continuous transfers. In single transfer, it forces NSS to go high after the transfer. This bit has no meaning if CPHA = 1 or FRF = 1.
  0: No NSS pulse   1: NSS pulse generated
SSOE: SS output enable
  0: SS output is disabled in master mode and the SPI can work in multimaster mode
  1: SS output is enabled in master mode and when SPI is enabled. The SPI cannot work in multi-master mode.
TXDMAEN: Tx buffer DMA enable
  When this bit is set, a DMA request is generated whenever the TXE flag is set
  0: Tx buffer DMA is disabled   1: Tx buffer DMA is enabled
RXDMAEN: Rx buffer DMA enable
  When this bit is set, a DMA request is generated whenever the RXNE flag is set.
  0:Rx buffer DMA is disabled   1: Rx buffer DMA is enabled

Figure 7.10a SPI control register 2 (SPIx->CR2, x = 1, 2, 3)—(continued)

7.5.5 HOW TO START DATA TRANSMISSION AND RECEPTION

- In **full-duplex mode** (BIDIMODE bit = 0 and RXONLY bit = 0):
  (a) The sequence begins when data are written into the SPIx->DR register.
  (b) The data are then loaded from the Tx buffer into the 8-bit shift register and then shifted out from the MOSI pin.
  (c) At the same time, the received data on the MISO pin is shifted in serially into the 8-bit shift register and then parallelly loaded into the SPIx->DR register (Rx buffer).

- In **unidirectional receive-only mode** (BIDIMODE bit = 0 and RXONLY bit = 1):
  (a) The sequence begins as soon as the SPE bit is set to 1.
  (b) Only the receiver is activated and the receiver data on the MISO pin are shifted in serially to the 8-bit shift register and then parallelly loaded into the SPIx->DR register (Rx buffer).

- In **bidirectional mode, when transmitting** (BIDIMODE bit = 1 and BIDIOE bit = 1):
  (a) The sequence begins when data are written into the SPIx->DR register (Tx buffer).
  (b) The data are then parallelly loaded from the Tx buffer into the 8-bit shift register and then shifted out serially from the MOSI pin.
  (c) No data are received.

- In **bidirectional mode, when receiving** (BIDIMODE bit = 1 and BIDIOE bit = 0):
  (a) The sequence begins as soon as the SPE bit is set to 1 and BIDIOE bit is set to 0.
  (b) The received data from the MOSI pin are shifted in serially to the 8-bit shift register and then parallelly loaded into the SPIx->DR register (Rx buffer).
  (c) The transmitter is not activated and no data are shifted out from the MOSI pin.

7.5.6 COMMUNICATION FORMATS

During the SPI communication, receive and transmit operations are performed simultaneously. The serial clock synchronizes the shifting and sampling of the information on the data lines. The communication format depends on the clock phase, the clock polarity, and the data frame format. To be able to communicate together, the master and slave devices must follow the same communication format.

Clock Polarity and Phase Control

The edge-triggered D flip-flop (shown in Figure 7.11) is the building block of a register. The value applied on the D input is transferred to the Q output on the rising (Figure 7.11a) or falling edge (Figure 7.11b). In the literature, the sentence "**data is sampled or shifted on the rising or falling clock edge**" refers to the fact that either the rising-edge-triggered or falling-edge-triggered D flip-flops is used.

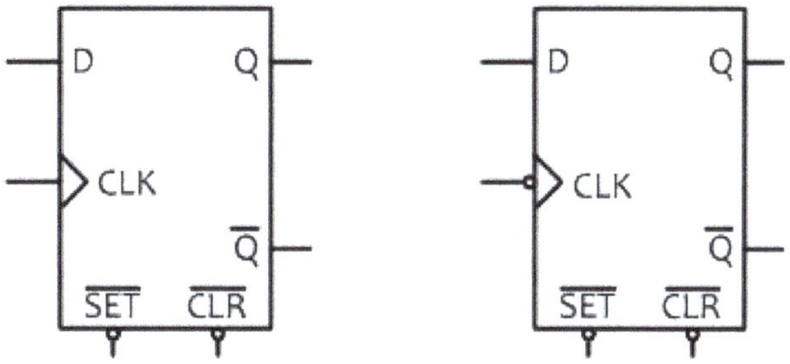

(a) rising-edge triggered (b) falling-edge triggered

Figure 7.11 Edge-triggered D flip-flop

The CLK input can be idle high or idle low. The word **idle** refers to the fact that the CLK input is not changed for a period of time.

For a rising-edge-triggered D flip-flop,

- If CLK is idle low, the D input is shifted (sampled) to the Q output on the immediate rising edge of CLK. That is, the first clock edge in a clock cycle samples the input data.
- If CLK is idle high, it must be pulled low and then pulled high in order to shift the D input to the Q output. That is, the second clock edge in a clock cycle samples the input data.

For a falling-edge-triggered D flip-flop,

- If CLK is idle low, it must be pulled high and then pulled low in order to shift the D input to the Q output. That is, the second clock edge in a clock cycle samples the input data.
- If CLK is idle high, the D input is shifted to the Q output on the immediate falling edge of CLK. That is, the first clock edge in a clock cycle samples the input data.

The STM32L475 SPI modules support both clock polarities. This option is selected by programming the **CPOL** bit in the SPIx->CR1 register. The SCK signal is idle low when the CPOL bit is 0. Otherwise, it is idle high.

The **CPHA** bit in the SPIx->CR1 register allows the user to choose the first (when CPHA = 0) or the second (when CPHA = 1) SCK edge to shift data. The SPI data clock for the STM32L475 is shown in Figure 7.3.

Data Frame Format

The SPI shift register of the STM32L475 can be set up to shift out data MSB-first or LSB-first, depending on the value of the **LSBFIRST** bit in the SPIx->CR1 register. The MSB-first format is selected if the LSBFIRST is 0. Otherwise, the LSB-first format is selected.

The processor writes into the 16-bit data register (SPIx->DR) in order to transmit a frame. To access the received data frame, the processor also reads from the SPIx->DR register. A data frame can be from 4 to 16 bits. The size of a data frame is selected by programming the DS field in the SPIx->CR1 register. The size setting applies to both transmission and reception.

7.5.7 DATA TRANSMISSION AND RECEPTION PROCEDURES

Receive FIFO (RXFIFO) and Transmit FIFO (TXFIFO)

Each SPI has a 32-bit RXFIFO and a 32-bit TXFIFO. These FIFOs enable the SPI to work in a continuous flow and prevent overruns when the data frame size is short. These FIFOs are used in all modes except for receive-only mode (slave or master) with CRC calculation enabled.

The handling of FIFOs depends on the data exchange mode (duplex, simplex), data frame format (number of bits in a frame), access size performed on the FIFO data registers (8 bit or 16 bit), and whether or not data packing is used when accessing the FIFOs.

A read access to the SPIx->DR register returns the oldest value stored in RXFIFO that has not been read yet. A write access to the SPIx->DR register stores the written data in the TXFIFO at the end of a send queue. The read access must always align with the RXFIFO threshold configured by the FRXTH bit in the SPIx->CR2 register. The FTLVL[1:0] and FRLVL[1:0] fields in the SPIx->SR register indicate the current occupancy level of both FIFOs. The contents of the SPIx->SR register are shown in Figure 7.12.

15	14	13	12	11	10	9	8
--	--	--	FTLVL[1:0]		FRLVL[1:0]		FRE
7	**6**	**5**	**4**	**3**	**2**	**1**	**0**
BSY	OVR	MODF	CRCERR	--	--	TXE	RXNE

Reset value = 0x0002
Offset = 0x08

FTLVL[1:0]: FIFO transmission level
  00: FIFO empty 01: ¼ FIFO 10: ½ FIFO 11: FIFO full
FRLVL[1:0]: FIFO reception level
  00: FIFO empty 01: ¼ FIFO 10: ½ FIFO 11: FIFO full
  These bits are not used in SPI receive-only mode while CRC is enabled
FRE: Frame format error (used for SPI in TI slave mode)
  0: No frame format error 1: A frame error occurred
BSY: Busy flag
  0: SPI is not busy 1: SPI is busy in communication or Tx buffer is not empty
OVR: Overrun flag
  0: No overrun occurred 1: Overrun occurred
MODF: mode fault
  0: No mode fault occurred 1: Mode fault occurred
CRCERR: CRC error flag
  0: CRC value received matches the SPIx_RXCRCR value
  1: CRC value received does not match the SPIx_RXCRCR value
TXE: transmit buffer empty
  0: Tx buffer not empty 1: Tx buffer empty
RXNE: receive buffer not empty
  0: Rx buffer empty 1: Rx buffer not empty

Figure 7.12 SPI status register (SPIx_SR, x = 1, 2, 3)

The RXNE bit in the SPIx->SR register should be used to manage the read access to the SPIx->DR register. The RXNE bit is set to 1 when data are stored in the RXFIFO and the threshold (defined by the FRXTH bit in the SPIx->CR2 register) is reached. When the RXNE bit is cleared, RXFIFO is considered to be empty. Similarly, the TXE bit in the SPIx->SR register is used to manage the write access of a data frame to be transmitted. The TXE bit is set when the TXFIFO level is less than or equal to half of its capacity. Otherwise, the TXE bit is cleared and the TXFIFO is considered as full. In this way, the RXFIFO can store up to four data frames, whereas the TXFIFO can only store up to three data frames when the data frame is not greater than 8 bits. This difference prevents the possible corruption of three 8-bit data frames already stored in the TXFIFO when software tries to write more data in 16-bit mode into TXFIFO. The setting of TXE and RXNE flags may generate interrupts if they are enabled.

If a data frame is received when the RXFIFO is full, an overrun event occurs and the OVR flag in the SPIx->SR register is set to 1. When there is an ongoing transaction, the BSY bit in the SPIx->SR register will be set to 1. When the SCK clock runs continuously, the BSY flag stays set between data frames at master but becomes low for a minimum duration of one SPI clock at the slave between two data frame transfers.

Sequence Handling

A few data frames can be passed in a single sequence to complete a message. When transmission is enabled, a sequence begins and continues while any data is present in the TXFIFO of the master. The clock signal is provided continuously by the master until the TXFIFO becomes empty; then it stops waiting for additional data.

In receive-only modes, half-duplex or simplex, the master starts the sequence immediately when both SPIs are enabled and the receive-only mode is activated. The clock signal is provided by the master and it does not stop until either the SPI or the receive-only mode is disabled by the master. The master receives data frames continuously up to this point.

Although the master can provide all the transactions in continuous mode, it has to consider the slave capability to handle data flow at any time. When necessary, the master should slow down and provide either a slower clock or separate frames or data sessions with sufficient delays. The SPI does not have an underflow error signal for the master or slave and data from the slave is always transacted and processed by the master even if the slave could not prepare it correctly in time. When data frames are shorter and the bus rate is high, it is preferable for the slave to use DMA.

Each sequence must be encased by the NSS pulse in parallel with the multislave system to select just one of the slaves for communication. In a single-slave system it is not necessary to control the slave using the NSS signal, but it is often better to provide the pulse here too, to synchronize the slave with the beginning of each data sequence.

When the BSY bit is set, it signifies an ongoing data frame transaction. When the dedicated frame transaction is finished, the RXNE flag is set. The received data frame is stored in the RXFIFO.

Procedure for Disabling SPI

Because of the existence of the TXFIFO and RXFIFO, the user should follow a safe procedure to disable the SPI so that no ongoing transactions are corrupted:

In receive-only mode

- Interrupt the receive flow by disabling the SPI (by clearing the SPE bit) in the specific time window while the last data frame is ongoing.
- Wait until BSY bit of the SPIx->SR register becomes 0 (the last data frame is processed).
- Read data until the FRLVL[1:0] field of the SPIx->SR register changes to 00.

In non-receive-only mode

- Wait until FTLVL[1:0] = 00 (no more data transmit).
- Wait until BSY bit of the SPIx->SR register becomes 0.
- Disable the SPI.
- Read data until FRLVL[1:0] field of the SPIx->SR register changes to 00.

If packing mode is used and an odd number of data frames with a format less than or equal to 8 bits has to be received, FRXTH must be set when FRLVL[1:0] = 01, in order to generate the RXNE event to read the last odd data frame and to keep good FIFO pointer alignment.

Data Packing

When the data frame size fits into one byte (shorter than or equal to 8 bits), data packing is used automatically when any 16-bit read or write access is performed on the SPIx->DR register. The double data frame pattern is handled in parallel in this case. At first, the SPI operates using the pattern stored in the least significant byte (LSB) of the accessed word and then with the other half stored in the most significant byte (MSB). Two data frames are sent after the single 16-bit access to the SPIx->DR register of the transmitter. The sequence can generate just one RXNE event in the receiver if the RXFIFO threshold is set to 16 bits (FRXTH bit = 0). The receiver then has to access both data frames by a single 16-bit read of the SPIx->DR register as a response to this single RXNE event. An example of data packing in FIFO for transmission and reception is illustrated in Figure 7.13.

The RXFIFO threshold setting and following read access must be always kept aligned at the receiver side, as data can be lost if it is not in line. A specific problem appears if an odd number of such "fit into one byte" data frames must be handled. On the transmitter side, writing the last data frame of any odd sequence with an 8-bit access to SPIx->DR register is enough. The receiver has to change the RXFIFO threshold level for the last data frame received in the odd sequence of frames in order to generate the RXNE event.

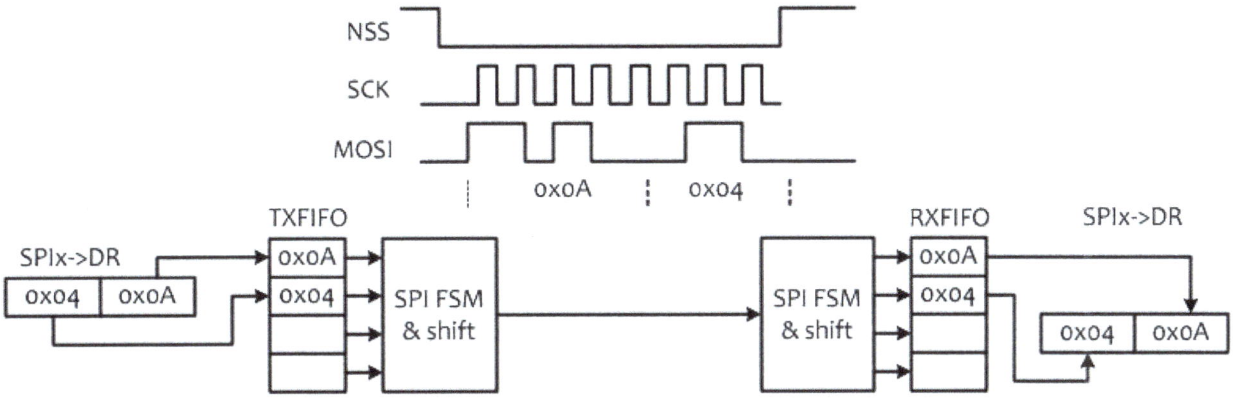

Figure 7.13 Packing data in FIFO for transmission and reception

Communication Using DMA

The STM32L475 SPI supports DMA data transfer. The DMA capability is enabled by setting the TXDMAEN and/or RXDMAEN bit in the SPIx->CR2 register. Separate DMA requests are issued to the Tx and Rx buffers:

- In transmission, a DMA request is issued each time TXE flag is set to 1. The DMA then writes to the SPIx->DR register.
- In reception, a DMA request is issued each time RXNE flag is set to 1. The DMA then reads the SPIx->DR register.

When the SPI is used only to transmit data, it is possible to enable only the SPI Tx DMA channel. In this case, the OVR flag is set because the data received is not read. When the SPI is used only to receive data, it is possible to enable only the SPI Rx DMA channel.

In transmission mode, when the DMA has written all the data to be transmitted (TCIF flag in the DMA->ISR register is set), the BSY flag can be monitored to ensure that the SPI communication is complete. This is required to avoid corrupting the last transmission before disabling the SPI or entering the STOP mode. The software must first wait until the FTLVL[1:0] field in the SPIx->SR register becomes 00 and then until the BSY flag becomes 0.

Packing with DMA

If the SPI transfers are managed by DMA, packing mode is enabled/disabled automatically depending on the PSIZE value configured for SPI TX and SPI RX DMA channel. If the DMA channel PSIZE value is equal to 16 bits and SPI data size is less than or equal to 8 bits, then packing mode is enabled. The DMA then automatically manages the write operations to the SPIx->DR register.

If data packing mode is used and the number of data frames to be transferred is not a multiple of 2, the LDMA_TX/LDMA_RX bits (in SPIx->CR2) must be set. The SPI then considers only one data frame for the transmission or reception to serve the last DMA transfer.

7.5.8 SPI STATUS FLAGS

The user application monitors the SPI bus using three status flags contained in the SPIx->SR register.

Tx Buffer Empty Flag (TXE)

The TXE flag is set whenever the TXFIFO has enough space to store data to be sent. This flag is set and stays at 1 as long as the TXFIFO level is lower than or equal to ½ of the FIFO depth.

An interrupt can be generated if the TXEIE bit in the SPIx->CR2 register is set. The TXE flag is cleared automatically when the TXFIFO level becomes greater than ½ of the FIFO depth. The TXE flag is 1 after a reset.

Rx Buffer Not Empty (RXNE)

The RXNE flag is set depending on the FRXTH bit value in the SPIx->CR2 register:

- If the **FRXTH bit is 1**, the RXNE bit will be set as long as the RXFIFO level is greater than or equal to ¼ the FIFO depth.
- If the **FRXTH bit is 0**, RXNE bit will be set as long as the RXFIFO level is greater than or equal to ½ the FIFO depth.

The RXNE flag is 0 after a reset. An interrupt will be generated if the RXNEIE bit in the SPIx->CR2 register is set to 1.

Busy Flag (BSY)

This flag is 0 after a reset. When the BSY flag is set, it indicates that an SPI data transfer is in progress. The BSY flag can be used in certain modes to detect the end of a transfer so that the software can disable the SPI or its peripheral clock before entering a low-power mode which does not provide a clock for the peripheral. This avoids corrupting the last transfer.

The BSY flag is cleared under any one of the following conditions:

- When the SPI is correctly disabled.
- When a fault is detected in master mode (MODF bit set to 1).
- In master mode, when it finishes a data transmission and no new data are ready to be sent.
- In slave mode, when the BSY flag is set to 0 for at least one SPI clock cycle between two data transfers.

7.5.9 SPI ERROR FLAGS

A SPI interrupt is generated if one of the following error flags is set and interrupt is enabled by setting the ERRIE bit in the SPIx->CR2 register.

Overrun Flag (OVR)

An overrun condition occurs when data are received by a master or slave and the RXFIFO has not enough space to store this received data. This can happen if the software or the DMA did not have enough time to read the previously received data or when space for data storage is limited, for example, the RXFIFO is not available when CRC is enabled in receive-only mode. In this case, the reception buffer is limited to a single data frame buffer.

When an overrun condition occurs, the newly received value does not overwrite the previous one in the RXFIFO. The newly received value is discarded and all data transmitted subsequently is lost. The OVR bit is cleared by reading the SPIx->DR register and followed by reading the SPIx->SR register.

Mode Fault (MODF)

Mode fault occurs when the master device has its internal NSS signal (NSS pin in NSS hardware mode, or SSI bit in NSS software mode) pulled low. Mode fault affects the SPI interface in the following ways:

- The MODF bit is set and an SPI interrupt is generated if the ERRIE bit in the SPIx->CR2 register is set.
- The SPE bit in the SPIx->CR1 register is cleared. This blocks all output from the device and disables the SPI interface.
- The MSTR bit in the SPIx->CR1 register is cleared, thus forcing the device into slave mode.

The MODF bit can be cleared by taking the following two steps:

Step 1. Read or write the SPIx->SR register when the MODF bit is set.

Step 2. Write to the SPIx->CR1 register.

CRC Error (CRCERR)

This flag is used to verify the validity of the value received when the CRCEN bit in the SPIx->CR1 register is set. The CRCERR flag in the SPIx->SR register is set if the value received in the shift register does not match the receiver SPIx->RXCRCR value. This flag is cleared by writing a 0 to it.

TI Mode Frame Format Error (FRE)

The STM32L475 SPI supports both the Motorola and TI frame formats. These frame formats differ only slightly. The difference will be discussed shortly. A TI mode frame format error is detected when an NSS pulse occurs during an ongoing communication when the SPI is operating in slave mode and configured to conform to the TI mode protocol. When this error occurs, the FRE flag in the SPIx->SR register is set. The SPI is not disabled when an error occurs, the NSS pulse is ignored, and the SPI waits for the next NSS pulse before starting a new transfer. The data may be corrupted since the error detection may result in the loss of two data bytes.

Reading the SPIx->SR register clears the FRE flag. An interrupt is generated if the ERRIE bit in the SPIx->CR2 register is set. In this case, the SPI should be disabled because data consistency is no longer guaranteed and communications should be reinitialized by the master when the slave SPI is enabled again.

7.5.10 NSS PULSE MODE

When the MCU interfaces with a peripheral chip using the SPI interface, it operates in the master mode. The MCU may use the NSS signal to enable SPI transfer to the peripheral chip. The peripheral chip with the SPI interface often needs its chip-enable (driven by the NSS signal) to be deasserted after receiving a frame from the MCU to trigger its internal operation. The NSS pulse mode can serve this purpose.

The NSS pulse mode takes effect only when the SPI interface is configured as Motorola SPI master with capture (or sample) on the first SCK edge. When activated, the NSS pulse is generated between two consecutive data frame transfers. The NSS pulse lasts for one SCK clock period at least. This mode is only useful for applications with a single master–slave pair. An example of NSS pulse mode is illustrated in Figure 7.14.

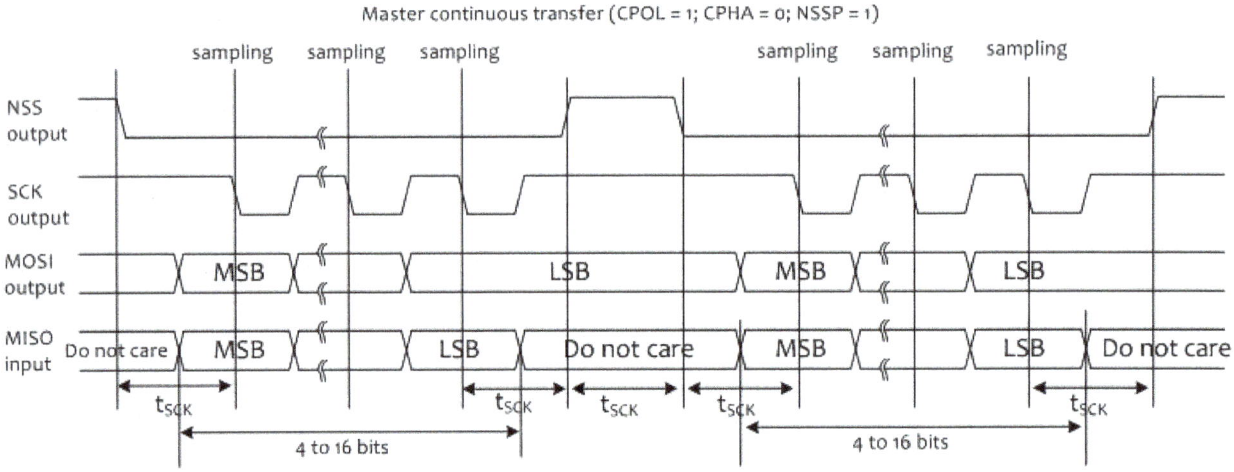

Figure 7.14 NSSP pulse generation in Motorola SPI master mode

7.5.11 TI MODE

The implementation of TI's SPI interface [5] differs from that of ST32L475 (Motorola SPI) mainly on the clock scheme:

- Falling edge without delay. The SPI transmits data on the falling edge of the SCK signal and receives data on the rising edge of the SCK signal.
- Falling edge with delay. The SPI transmits data one half-cycle ahead of the falling edge (i.e., on the rising edge) of the SCK signal and receives data on the falling edge of the SCK signal.
- Rising edge without delay. The SPI transmits data on the rising edge of the SCK signal and receives data on the falling edge of the SCK signal.
- Rising edge with delay. The SPI transmits data one-half cycle ahead of the rising edge (i.e., on the falling edge) of the SCK signal and receives data on the rising edge of the SCK signal.

Apparently, the SPI interface of TI transmits and receives data bits on different clock edges. The SPI of TI can transmit from 1 to 16 bits in one data frame.

The **FRF bit** in the SPIx->CR2 register can be used to configure the SPI to TI mode. The clock polarity and phase are forced to conform to the TI protocol requirements whatever the values set in the SPIx->CR1 register. The NSS signal management is also specific to the TI protocol.

In slave mode, the SPI baud rate prescaler is used to control the moment when the MISO pin state changes to HiZ (high impedance) when the current transaction finishes. Any baud rate can be used, making it possible to determine with optimal flexibility. However, the baud rate is generally set to the external master clock baud rate. The delay for the MISO signal to become HiZ ($t_{release}$) depends on internal resynchronization and on the baud rate value set using the BR[2:0] field in the SPIx->CR1 register. It is given by the formula:

$$t_{baud\_rate}/2 + 4 \times t_{pclk} < t_{release} < t_{baud\_rate} + 6 \times t_{pclk}$$

where pclk is the peripheral bus clock, t_{baud_rate} is period of SPI SCLK clock, and t_{pclk} is period of bus clock.

If the slave detects a misplaced NSS pulse during a data frame transaction, the TIFRE flag in the SPIx->SR register will be set to 1.

If the data size is equal to 4 or 5 bits, the master in full-duplex mode or transmit-only mode uses a protocol with one dummy data bit added after LSB. TI NSS pulse is generated above this dummy bit clock cycle instead of the LSB in each period. This feature is not available in Motorola mode.

7.5.12 CYCLIC REDUNDANCY CHECK (CRC)

The CRC, a **polynomial code**, is a widely used error-detection code. CRC codes treat bit strings as representation of polynomials with coefficients of 0 and 1 only. A k-bit frame is regarded as the coefficient list for a polynomial with k terms, ranging from x^{k-1} to x^0. Such a polynomial is said to be of degree **k – 1**. The high-order (leftmost) bit is the coefficient of x^{k-1}, the next bit is the coefficient of x^{k-2}, and so on. For example, 110001 has 6 bits and thus represents a six-term polynomial with coefficients 1, 1, 0, 0, 0, and 1: $1x^5 + 1x^4 + 0x^3 + 0x^2 + 0x^1 + 1x^0$.

Polynomial arithmetic is done modulo 2, according to the rules of algebraic field theory. It does not have carries for addition or borrows for subtraction. Both addition and subtraction are identical to XOR. For example, see Figure 7.15.

```
  10011011      01010101      11000011      01010101
+ 11001010    + 11001010    + 10101010    + 11111010
----------    ----------    ----------    ----------
  01010001      10011111      01101001      10101111
```

Figure 7.15 Examples of Modulo 2 long division

Long division is carried out in exactly the same way as it is in binary except that the subtraction is again done modulo 2. A divisor is said "to go into" a dividend if the dividend has as many bits as the divisor.

When the polynomial code method is employed, the sender and receiver must agree upon a **generator polynomial**, G(x), in advance. Both the high- and low-order bits of the generator must be 1. To compute the CRC for some frame with m bits corresponding to the polynomial M(x), the frame must be longer than the generator polynomial. The idea is to append a CRC to the end of the frame in such a way that the polynomial represented by the checksum frame is divisible by G(x). When the receiver gets the checksummed frame, it tries dividing it by G(x); if there is a remainder, there has been a transmission error.

The algorithm for computing the CRC is as follows:

Step 1

Let r be the degree of G(x). Append r zero bits to the low-order end of the frame, so it now contains **m + r** bits and corresponds to the polynomial $x^rM(x)$.

Step 2

Divide the bit string corresponding to G(x) into the bit string corresponding to $x^rM(x)$, using modulo 2 division.

Step 3

Subtract the remainder (which is always r or fewer bits) from the bit string corresponding to $x^rM(x)$ using modulo 2 subtraction. The result is the checksummed frame to be transmitted. Call it polynomial **T(x)**. The remainder is the CRC code.

Figure 7.16 illustrates the calculation of CRC for a frame 1101011111 using the generator $G(x) = x^4 + x + 1$.

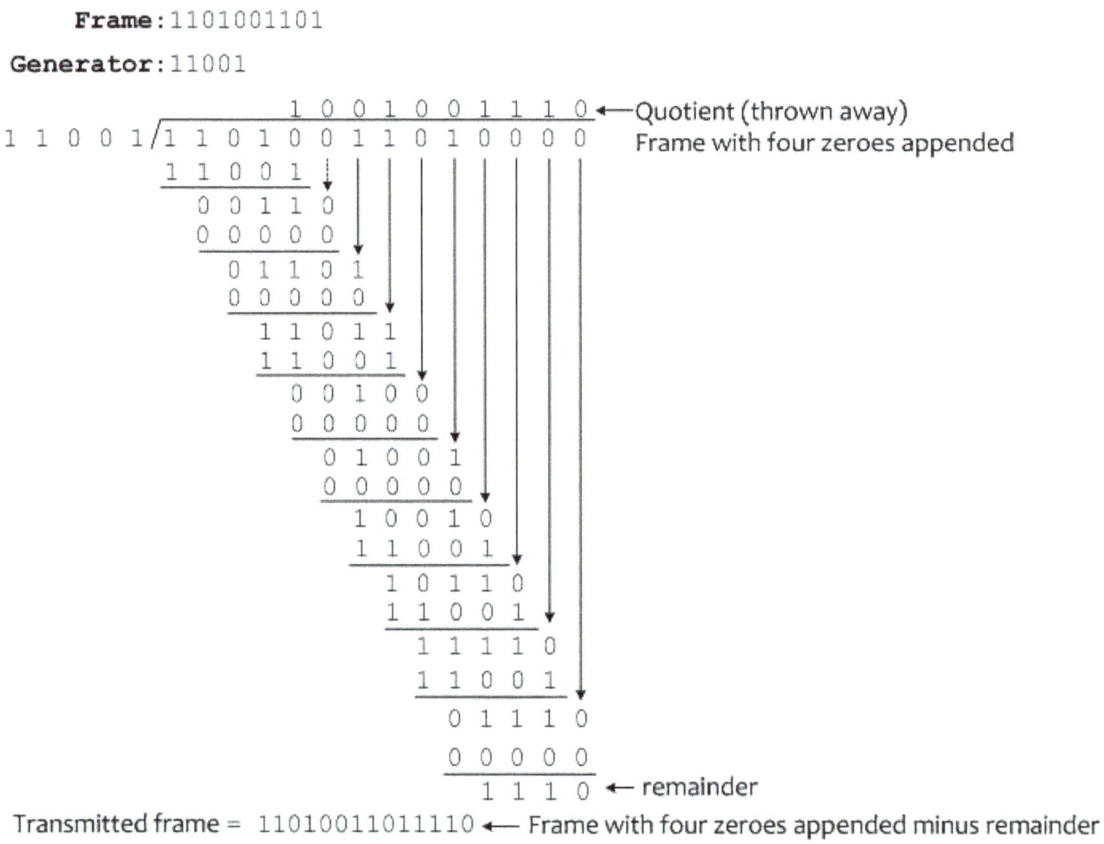

Figure 7.16 Example of CRC calculation

It should be clear that T(x) is divisible (modulo 2) by G(x). In any division problem, if you diminish the dividend by the remainder, what is left over is divisible by the divisor.

When receiving the frame, the receiver recalculates the CRC using the same generator polynomial. If the calculated CRC is identical to the received CRC, the frame is correctly received. Otherwise, the data frame has been corrupted and the receiver can request the sender to resend the frame.

The selection of the generator polynomial is the most important part of implementing the CRC algorithm. The polynomial must be chosen to maximize the error-detection capability while minimizing overall collision probability.

The most important attribute of the polynomial is its length (highest degree (exponent) + 1) because of its direct influence on the length of the computed check value.

The most commonly used polynomial lengths are:

- 9 bits (CRC-8)
- 17 bits (CRC-16)
- 33 bits (CRC-32)
- 65 bits (CRC-64)

A CRC is called an n-bit CRC when its check value is n-bit. For a given n, multiple CRCs are possible, each with a different generator polynomial. Such a polynomial has the highest degree n, and hence **n + 1** terms (the polynomial has a length of **n + 1**). The remainder has a length of **n**.

The design of the CRC polynomial depends on the maximum total length of the block to be protected (data + CRC bits), the desired error protection features, and the type of resources for implementing the CRC, as well as the desired performance. However, the discussion of these issues are beyond the scope of this text.

A summary of commonly used polynomial generators for CRC-8, CRC-16, and CRC-32 is given in Table 7.2.

Table 7.2 Summary of commonly used polynomial generators for CRC-8, CRC-16, and CRC-32

Name	Uses	Polynomial representation			
		Normal	Reversed	Reciprocal	Reversed reciprocal
CRC-8	DVB-S2	0xD5	0xAB	0x57	0xEA
		$x^8 + x^7 + x^6 + x^4 + x^2 + 1$			
CRC-8-AUTOSAR	Automotive integratrion, OpenSafety	0x2F	0xF4	0xE9	0x97
		$x^8 + x^5 + x^3 + x^2 + x + 1$			
CRC-8-Bluetooth	Wireless connectivity	0xA7	0xE5	0xCB	0xD3
		$x^8 + x^7 + x^5 + x^2 + x + 1$			
CRC-8-CCITT	ITU-T I.432.1; ATM HEC, ISDN HEC and cell delineation	0x07	0xE0	0xC1	0x83
		$x^8 + x^2 + x + 1$			
CRC-Dallas/Maxim	1-wire bus	0x31	0x8C	0x19	0x98
		$x^8 + x^5 + x^4 + 1$			
CRC-8-DARC	Data radio channel	0x39	0x9C	0x39	0x9C
		$x^8 + x^5 + x^4 + x^3 + 1$			
CRC-8-GSM-B	Mobile networks	0x49	0x92	0x25	0xA4
		$x^8 + x^6 + x^3 + 1$			
CRC-8-SAE J1850	AES3; OBD	0x1D	0xB8	0x71	0x8E
		$x^8 + x^4 + x^3 + x^2 + 1$			
CRC-8-WCDMA	Mobile network	0x9B	0xD9	0xB3	0xCD
		$x^8 + x^7 + x^4 + x^3 + x + 1$			
CRC-16-Chakravarty	Optimal for payload ≤ 64 bits	0x2F15	0xA8F4	0x51E9	0x978A
		$x^{16} + x^{13} + x^{11} + x^{10} + x^9 + x^8 + x^4 + x^2 + 1$			
CRC-16-ARINC	ACARS applications	0xA02B	0xD405	0xA80B	0xD015
		$x^{16} + x^{15} + x^{13} + x^5 + x^3 + x + 1$			
CRC-16-CCITT	X.25, V.41, HDLC FCS, XMODEM, Bluetooth, PACTOR, SD, DigRF, many others; known as CRC-CCITT	0x1021	0x8408	0x811	0x8810
		$x^{16} + x^{12} + x^5 + 1$			
CRC-16-CDMA2000	Mobile network	0xC867	0xE613	0xCC27	0xE433
		$x^{16} + x^{15} + x^{14} + x^{11} + x^6 + x^5 + x^2 + x + 1$			
CRC-16-DECT	Cordless telephones	0x0589	0x91A0	0x2341	0x82C4
		$x^{16} + x^{10} + x^8 + x^7 + x^3 + 1$			
CRC-16-T10-DIF	SCSI DIF	0x8BB7	0xEDD1	0xDBA3	0xC5DB
		$x^{16} + x^{15} + x^{11} + x^9 + x^8 + x^7 + x^5 + x^4 + x^2 + x + 1$			

Table 7.2a Summary of commonly used polynomial generators for CRC-8, CRC-16, and CRC-32—(continued)

Name	Uses	Polynomial representation			
		Normal	Reversed	Reciprocal	Reversed reciprocal
CRC-16-DNP	DNP, IEC 870, M-Bus	0x3D65	0xA6BC	0x4D79	0x9EB2
		$x^{16} + x^{13} + x^{12} + x^{11} + x^{10} + x^8 + x^6 + x^5 + x^2 + 1$			
CRC-16-IBM	Bisync, Modbus, USB, ANSI X3.28, SIA DC-07, many others	0x8005	0xA001	0x4003	0xC002
		$x^{16} + x^{15} + x^2 + 1$			
CRC-16-OpenSafety-A	Safety fieldbus	0x5935	0xAC9A	0x5935	0xAC9A
		$x^{16} + x^{14} + x^{12} + x^{11} + x^8 + x^5 + x^4 + x^2 + 1$			
CRC-16-OpenSafety-B	Safety fieldbus	0x755B	0xDAAE	0xB55D	0xBAAD
		$x^{16} + x^{14} + x^{13} + x^{12} + x^{10} + x^8 + x^6 + x^4 + x^3 + x^1 + 1$			
CRC-16-Profibus	Fieldbus networks	0x1DCF	0xF3B8	0xE771	0x8EE7
		$x^{16} + x^{12} + x^{11} + x^{10} + x^8 + x^7 + x^6 + x^3 + x^2 + x + 1$			
CRC-32	ISO 3309, ANSI X3.66, FIPS PUB 71, FED-STD-1003, ITU-T V.42, IEEE802-3, SATA, MPEG-2, PKZIP, Gzip, Bzip2, POSIX cksum, PNG, ZMODEM	0x04C11DB7	0xEDB88320	0xDB710641	0x82608EDB
		$x^{32} + x^{26} + x^{23} + x^{22} + x^{16} + x^{12} + x^{11} + x^{10} + x^8 + x^7 + x^5 + x^4 + x^2 + x + 1$			
CRC-32C (Castagnoli)	iSCSI, SCTP, G.hn payload, SSE4.2, Btrfs, ext4, Ceph	0x1EDC6F41	0x82F63B78	0x05EC76F1	0x8F6E37A0
		$x^{32} + x^{28} + x^{27} + x^{26} + x^{25} + x^{23} + x^{22} + x^{20} + x^{19} + x^{18} + x^{14} + x^{13} + x^{11} + x^{10} + x^9 + x^8 + x^6 + 1$			
CRC-32K (Koopman {1,3,28})	Excellent at Ethernet frame length, poor performance with long files	0x741B8CD7	0xEB31D82E	0xD663B05D	0xBA0DC66B
		$x^{32} + x^{30} + x^{29} + x^{28} + x^{26} + x^{20} + x^{19} + x^{17} + x^{16} + x^{15} + x^{11} + x^{10} + x^7 + x^6 + x^4 + x^2 + x + 1$			
CRC-32K_2 (Koopman {1,1,30})	Excellent at Ethernet frame length, poor performance with long files	0x32583499	0x992C1A4C	0x32583499	0x992C1A4C
		$x^{32} + x^{29} + x^{28} + x^{25} + x^{22} + x^{20} + x^{19} + x^{13} + x^{12} + x^{10} + x^7 + x^4 + x^3 + 1$			
CRC-32Q	Aviation; AIXM	0x814141AB	0xD5828281	0xAB050503	0xC0A0A0D5
		$x^{32} + x^{31} + x^{24} + x^{22} + x^{16} + x^{14} + x^8 + x^7 + x^5 + x^3 + x + 1$			

In Table 7.2, the generator polynomials are represented by four different hexadecimal numbers. Let's use CRC-8 to illustrate how those four numbers (normal, reverse, reciprocal, reversed reciprocal) are derived:

The coefficients of the polynomial $x^8 + x^7 + x^6 + x^4 + x^2 + 1$ are 111010101.

Normal representation

1. Drop the MSB: 111010101 → 11010101
2. Group four consecutive bits into one hexadecimal digit from left to right: 11010101 → 1101 0101 → **0xD5**

Reversed representation

1. Drop the MSB: 111010101 → 11010101
2. Reverse the coefficients from right to left: 11010101 → 10101011
3. Group four consecutive bits from left to right into one hexadecimal digit: 10101011 → 1010 1011 → **0xAB**

Reciprocal representation

1. Drop the LSB: 111010101 → 11101010
2. Reverse the coefficients: 11101010 → 01010111
3. Group four consecutive bits from left to right and write them in hexadecimal digits: 01010111 → 0101 0111 → **0x57**

Reversed reciprocal representation

1. Drop the LSB: 111010101 → 11101010
2. Group four consecutive bits from left to right and write them in hexadecimal digits: 11101010 → 1110 1010 → **0xEA**

7.5.13 CRC CALCULATION IN STM32L475 SPI

Two separate CRC calculators are implemented in order to check the reliability of transmitted and received data. The STM32 SPI offers CRC8 or CRC16 calculation for 8- or 16-bit data frame. That is, either 8-bit or 16-bit data frame can choose either CRC8 or CRC16 for error checking. For all other data frame lengths, no CRC is available.

To use CRC for error checking, the user is required to write the CRC generator polynomial into the 16-bit SPIx->CRCPR register. The polynomial value should be odd only. The reset value of this register is 0x0007. This value is used for both transmission and reception.

CRC calculation is enabled by setting the CRCEN bit in the SPIx->CR1 register before the SPI is enabled. The CRC value is calculated using an odd programmable polynomial on each bit. The calculation is processed on the sampling clock edge defined by the CPHA and CPOL bits in the SPIx->CR1 register. The calculated CRC value is checked automatically at the end of the data block as well as for transfer managed by the CPU or by the DMA.

When a mismatch is detected between the CRC calculated internally on the received data and the CRC sent by the transmitter, a CRCERR flag is set to indicate a data corruption error.

CRC Transfer Managed by CPU

Communication starts and continues normally until the last data frame has to be sent or received in the SPIx->DR register. Then the CRCNEXT bit in the SPIx->CR1 register has to be set to indicate that the CRC frame transaction will follow after the transaction of the currently processed data frame. The CRCNEXT bit must be set before the end of the last data frame transaction. CRC calculation is frozen during CRC transaction. The CRC corresponding to the blocks of frames to be transmitted is calculated and stored in the SPIx->TXCRCR register. The contents of the SPIx->TXCRCR register will be transmitted after the last data frame if the CRCNEXT bit has been set.

When receiving data frames, the SPI will compute the CRC (if CRC is enabled) corresponding to the data frames received so far. The computed CRC is stored in the SPIx->RXCRCR register. The received CRC is stored in the RXFIFO like a data byte or word. That is why in CRC mode only the reception buffer has to be considered as a single 16-bit buffer used to receive only one data frame at a time.

A CRC-format transaction usually takes one more frame to communicate at the end of data sequence. However, when setting an 8-bit data frame checked by a 16-bit CRC, two more frames are necessary to send the complete CRC.

When the last CRC data are received, an automatic check is performed comparing the received value and the value in the SPIx->RXCRCR register. Software has to check the CRCERR flag in the SPIx->SR register to determine if the data transfer was corrupted or not. The CRCERR flag is cleared by writing a 0 to it.

After the CRC reception, the CRC value is stored in the RXFIFO and must be read in the SPIx->DR register in order to clear the RXNE flag.

CRC Transfer Managed by DMA

When SPI communication is enabled with CRC communication and DMA mode, the transmission and reception of the CRC at the end of communication is automatic (with the exception of reading CRC data in receive-only mode). The CRCNEXT bit does not have to be handled by the software. The counter for the SPI transmission DMA channel has to be set to the number of data frames to transmit excluding the CRC frame. On the receiver side, the received CRC value is handled automatically by DMA at the end of the transaction but user must take care to flush out received CRC information from RXFIFO as it is always loaded into it. In full-duplex mode, the counter of the reception DMA channel can be set to the number of data frames to receive including the CRC, which means, for example, in the specific case of an 8-bit data frame checked by 16-bit CRC:

DMA_RX = Number of data frames + 2

In receive-only mode, the DMA reception channel counter should contain only the amount of data transferred, excluding the CRC calculation. Then based on the complete transfer from DMA, all the CRC values must be read back by software from FIFO as it works as a single buffer in this mode.

At the end of data and CRC transfers, the CRCERR flag in the SPIx->SR register is set if corruption occurred during data transfer. If packing mode is used, the LDMA_RX bit must be used to indicate whether the number of data frames is odd.

Resetting the SPIx->TXCRCR and SPIx->RXCRCR Values

The SPIx->TXCRCR and SPIx->RXCRCR values are cleared automatically when new data are sampled after a CRC phase. This allows the use of DMA circular mode (not available in receive-only mode) in order to transfer data without any interruption (several data blocks covered by intermediate CRC checking phases).

CRC checking is applicable only when both the master and the slave devices support this capability. Most peripheral chips with the SPI interface do not support the CRC generation and checking.

7.6 Writing Basic SPI Functions

Example 7.1 Write a function to initialize SPI1 with the following setting:

- Use PA7, PA6, and PA5 for MOSI, MISO, and SCK signal
- Select master mode

- Set baud rate to 2.5 MHz assuming that f_{PCLK} = 80 MHz
- Select unidirectional mode with CRC disabled
- Select full-duplex mode
- Shift MSB first in each SPI transfer
- Configure SCK to idle low and shift data on the rising edge (first edge)
- Disable DMA transfer
- 8- or 16-bit frame length (specified by incoming argument ds (0 = 8 bit; 1 = 16 bit)
- Select Motorola SPI mode
- No NSS pulse

Solution:

```
void spi_init(uint32_t ds)
{
    GPIOA->MODER   &= ~(GPIO_MODER_MODE5 + GPIO_MODER_MODE6 +
                       GPIO_MODER_MODE7); // clear bit 10 to 15
    // configure PA5, PA6, PA7 for alternate function
    GPIOA->MODER   |=  GPIO_MODER_MODE5_1 + GPIO_MODER_MODE6_1 +
                       GPIO_MODER_MODE7_1;
    // configure PA5, PA6, and PA7 for alternate function 5
    GPIOA->AFR[0]  &= ~(GPIO_AFRL_AFSEL7 + GPIO_AFRL_AFSEL6 +
                       GPIO_AFRL_AFSEL5);
    GPIOA->AFR[0]  |=  (GPIO_AFRL_AFSEL7_0 + GPIO_AFRL_AFSEL7_2 +
                       GPIO_AFRL_AFSEL6_0 + GPIO_AFRL_AFSEL6_2 +
                       GPIO_AFRL_AFSEL5_0 + GPIO_AFRL_AFSEL5_2);
    if (ds == 1)
        SPI1->CR2   =  SPI_CR2_DS_0 + SPI_CR2_DS_1 + SPI_CR2_DS_2 + SPI_CR2_DS_3;
    else
        SPI1->CR2   =  SPI_CR2_DS_0 + SPI_CR2_DS_1 + SPI_CR2_DS_2 +
                       SPI_CR2_FRXTH;
    SPI1->CR1       =  SPI_CR1_BR_2 + SPI_CR1_MSTR + SPI_CR1_SPE;
}
```

Example 7.2 Assuming that SPI1 has been configured to full-duplex mode, write a function to send a 16-bit value to the SPI1 (SPI1 is configured to use 16-bit data frames) and also a function to send an 8-bit value to the SPI1 (SPI1 is configured to use 8-bit data frames).

Solution: This function should make sure there is enough space in the TXFIFO before writing the 16-bit data in the SPI1->DR register:

```
void putHWSPI1 (uint16_t dw)
{
    while (!(SPI1->SR & SPI_SR_TXE)); // wait until there is enough space in TXFIFO
    SPI1->DR = dw;
}

void putchSPI1 (uint8_t bt)
{
    while (!(SPI1->SR & SPI_SR_TXE)); // wait until there is enough space in TXFIFO
    SPI1->DR = bt;
}
```

Example 7.3 Assuming that SPI1 is configured to full-duplex mode, write a function to read a byte from SPI1 and a function to read a 16-bit value from SPI1.

Solution: To read a byte or a halfword in full-duplex mode, the master must trigger clock pulses from the SCK pin. This can be done by writing into the SPI1->DR register.

```
// assume that SPI1 data frame size has been configured to 8 bits
uint8_t getByteSPI1 (void)
{
    while(!(SPI1->SR & SPI_SR_TXE));
    SPI1->DR = 0x00; // trigger 8 clock pulses from the SCK pin
    while(!(SPI1->SR & SPI_SR_RXNE)); // wait until a byte has been shifted in
    return ((uint8_t)SPI1->DR);
}
// assume that SPI1 data frame size has been configured to 16 bits
uint16_t getHWSPI1(void)
{
```

```
        while(!(SPI1->SR & SPI_SR_TXE));
        SPI1->DR = 0x0000; // trigger 16 clock pulses from the SCK pin
        while(!(SPI1->SR & SPI_SR_RXNE)); // wait until 16 bits have been shifted in
        return SPI1->DR;
    }
```

7.7 Simulating SPI Data Transfer Functions

An MCU can exchange data with a peripheral having the SPI interface by emulating the SPI protocol. To send data to the peripheral, the MCU is required to use one pin to carry the data bit stream and another pin to carry the clock signal. Another I/O pin may be needed to be used as the slave select signal. To receive data, the MCU is required to use an additional pin to carry incoming data bit stream. The same I/O pins used for SCK signal and slave select can be shared.

Example 7.4 Write a C function to configure Port C pins PC5, PC4, and PC3 to be used as MOSI (output), SCK (output), and MISO (input) pins. Also configure PC0~PC2 for output so that they can be used as slave select signals.

Solution:

```
    void setupPINs (void)
    {
        GPIOC->MODER &= ~0x0FFF; // clear the lower 12 bits
        // configure PC5, PC4, PC2~PC0 for output and PC3 for input
        GPIOC->MODER |= GPIO_MODER_MODE0_0 + GPIO_MODER_MODE1_0 +
                        GPIO_MODER_MODE2_0 + GPIO_MODER_MODE4_0 +
                        GPIO_MODER_MODE5_0;
    }
```

Example 7.5 Write a C function that can send out a byte serially by simulating the SPI protocol using two pins (PC05—data; PC04—clock). Also write a function that can send out a 16-bit value by simulating the SPI protocol using the same two pins.

Solution:

```
void put8bSPISim (uint8_t kx)
{
    uint32_t k;
```

```
    for(k = 0; k < 8; k++) {
        if((kx & 0x80)){
            GPIOC->BSRR = GPIO_BSRR_BS5;    // shift out a 1
            GPIOC->BSRR = GPIO_BSRR_BR4;    // generate a rising edge on PC4 pin
            GPIOC->BSRR = GPIO_BSRR_BS4;    // "
        }
        else {
            GPIOC->BSRR = GPIO_BSRR_BR5;    // shift out a 0
            GPIOC->BSRR = GPIO_BSRR_BR4;    // generate a rising edge on PC4 pin
            GPIOC->BSRR = GPIO_BSRR_BS4;    // "
        }
        kx = kx << 1; // make the next lower bit the most significant bit
    }
}
void put16bSPISim (uint8_t kx)
{
    uint32_t k;
    for (k = 0; k < 16; k++) {
        if((kx & 0x8000)){
            GPIOC->BSRR = GPIO_BSRR_BS5;    // set pin 5 high to shift out a 1
            GPIOC->BSRR = GPIO_BSRR_BR4;    // generate a rising edge on PC4 pin
            GPIOC->BSRR = GPIO_BSRR_BS4;    // "
        }
        else {
            GPIOC->BSRR = GPIO_BSRR_BR5;    // set pin 5 low to shift out a 0
            GPIOC->BSRR = GPIO_BSRR_BR4;    // generate a rising edge on PC4 pin
            GPIOC->BSRR = GPIO_BSRR_BS4;    // "
        }
```

```
            kx = kx << 1; // make the next lower bit the most significant bit
        }
}
```

Example 7.6 Write a C function that can shift in a byte of data by simulating the SPI protocol and a function that can shift in 16 bits using two pins (PC03—data; PC04—clock).

Solution:

```
uint8_t get8bSPISim (void)
{
    uint16_t k, cx;
    cx = 0;
    for(k = 0; k < 8; k++){
        GPIOC->BSRR    = GPIO_BSRR_BR4;    // generate a rising edge to shift
        GPIOC->BSRR    = GPIO_BSRR_BS4;    // in one bit
        if(GPIOC->IDR & GPIO_IDR_ID3)
            cx = (cx << 1) | 0x01; // shift in a 1
        else
            cx = (cx << 1); // shift in a 0
    }
    return (uint8_t)cx;
}

uint16_t get16bSPISim (void)
{
    uint16_t k, cx;
    cx = 0;
    for(k = 0; k < 16; k++){
        GPIOC->BSRR    = GPIO_BSRR_BR4;    // generate a rising edge to shift
        GPIOC->BSRR    = GPIO_BSRR_BS4;    // in one bit
        if(GPIOC->IDR & GPIO_IDR_ID3)
```

```
            cx = (cx << 1) | 0x01; // shift in a 1
        else
            cx = (cx << 1); // shift in a 0
    }
    return cx;
}
```

7.8 Using the 25LC256—An EEPROM with SPI Interface

The 25LC256 is an EEPROM with 256 Kbits capacity and has a 32,768 × 8-bit organization. That is, the chip has 32,768 locations and each location can store 8 bits of data. This chip has the SPI interface, which can shift data in/out at a rate up to 10 MHz.

By sending one address, the MCU can write up to 64 locations (a page) or read the whole chip. The chip can operate with a power supply ranging from 2.5 up to 5.5 V.

The chip has block-write protection capability. Either none, ¼, ½, or the whole chip can be configured to be write protected.

7.8.1 SIGNAL PINS

The pin assignment of the 25LC256 is shown in Figure 7.17.

- : chip select input
- SO: serial data output
- : write protection
- SI: serial data input
- SCK: serial clock input
- : the low voltage on this pin stops communication to this device.

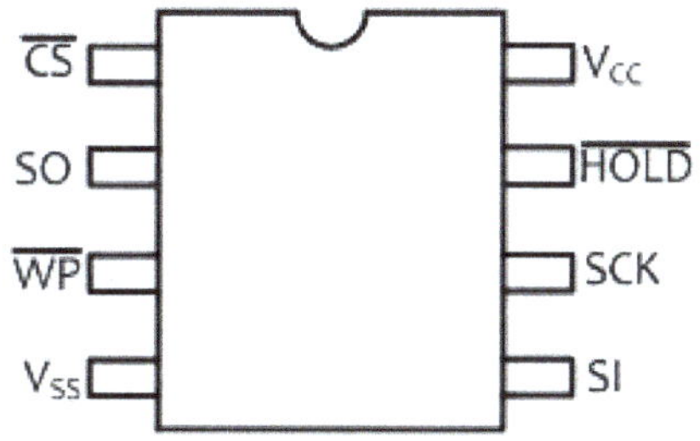

Figure 7.17 25LC256 pin assignment

7.8.2 PRINCIPLES OF OPERATIONS

To transfer data to/from the 25LC256, the pin must be pulled low and the /HOLD pin must be pulled high. Data are shifted into the chip on the rising edge of the SCK clock and SCK is idle low.

The 25LC256 has an instruction register and a status register to support its operation. Before performing any operation, the MCU is required to send an instruction (a command) to the chip. Instructions supported by the 25LC256 are listed in Table 7.3. When sending an instruction, the pin must be pulled low. After the instruction has been sent in, the pin must be pulled high for the chip to execute it.

Table 7.3 25LC256 instruction set

Instruction	Instruction code	Description
READ	0000 0011	Read data from memory array beginning at selected address
WRITE	0000 0010	Write data to memory array beginning at selected address
WRDI	0000 0100	Reset the write enable latch (disable write operation)
WREN	0000 0110	Set the write enable latch (enable write operation)
RDSR	0000 0101	Read status register
WRSR	0000 0001	Write status register

7.8.3 READ OPERATION

To read a random address, the following operations are performed:

1. Pull the signal low.
2. Send in the READ command.
3. Send in the 16-bit address (accompanied by 16 clock pulses on the SCK pin) from the SI pin.
4. Send in eight more clock pulses on the SCK pin to shift data out from the SO pin. The data stored in the memory at the next address can be read sequentially by continuing to provide clock pulses. The internal address pointer is automatically incremented to the next higher address after each byte of data is shifted out. When the highest address (0x7FFF) is reached, the address counter rolls over to 0x0000 allowing the read cycle to be continued indefinitely.
5. Pull the signal high to terminate the random read operation.

7.8.4 WRITE OPERATION

Before writing data, the MCU is required to enable write operation to the 25LC256 by sending the WREN command. This command sets the **write-enable latch** inside the status register.

After the write-enable latch has been set, the MCU must pull the signal low again and send in the **WRITE** instruction followed by the 16-bit address, and then the data to be written. Up to 64 bytes of data can be send to the device before an internal write cycle is necessary. The only restriction is that all of the bytes must reside in the same page.

By pulling the signal high after the LSB of the last data byte has been clocked in, the internal write operation will be started. An internal write operation takes about 5 ms to complete. While the internal operation is in progress, the STATUS register can be read back to check the status of the WPEN, WIP, WEL, BP1, and BP0 bits. A read attempt of a memory location will not be possible during a write cycle. When the write cycle is completed, the **write-enable latch** (**WEL**) is reset. The contents of the status register of the 25LC256 are shown in Figure 7.18.

7	6	5	4	3	2	1	0
WPEN	x	x	x	BP1	BP0	WEL	WIP
w/r				w/r	w/r	r	r

WPEN: write protection enable (nonvolatile)
  0: disable write protection   1: enable write protection if /WP pin is low.
BP1~BP0: block protection bits
  00: none of the memory block is write protected
  01: the memory block from 0x6000 to 0x7FFF is write protected.
  10: the memory block from 0x4000 to 0x7FFF is write protected.
  11: the whole memory array is write protected.
WEL: write enable latch
  0: write to the memory array and status register is prohibited.
  1: write to the memory array and status register is allowed.
WIP: write in progress
  0: no write operation is in progress.   1: a write operation is in progress.

Figure 7.18 Status register of the 25LC256

The MCU can read the status register by issuing the RDSR instruction and write to the status register by sending the WRSR instruction. The **WEL** and **WIP** bits are **volatile** whereas other bits are **nonvolatile**.

7.8.5 DATA PROTECTION

The 25LC256 is designed to prevent inadvertent write to the memory array. After power up, the write-enable latch is reset to prevent any write to the memory array. A write-enable instruction must be issued to set the WEL bit. After a byte write, page write, or a status register write, the WEL bit is reset. The signal must be pulled high after a write operation to start an internal write cycle.

Access to the memory array during an internal write cycle is ignored, and programming is continued. When the WPEN bit is set and the signal is low, the write operation to the nonvolatile bits (WPEN, BP1, BP0) of the status register and the protected memory block is disabled. The 25LC256 write protection function matrix is given in Table 7.4.

Table 7.4 25LC256 write protect function matrix

WEL	WPEN	WP pin	Protected Blocks	Unprotected Blocks	Status register
0	x	x	Protected	Protected	Protected
1	0	x	Protected	Writable	Writable
1	1	0 (low)	Protected	Writable	Protected
1	1	1 (high)	Protected	Writable	Writable

7.8.6 INTERFACING THE 25LC256 TO THE STM32L475

A possible circuit connection between the STM32L475 and the 25LC256 is shown in Figure 7.19.

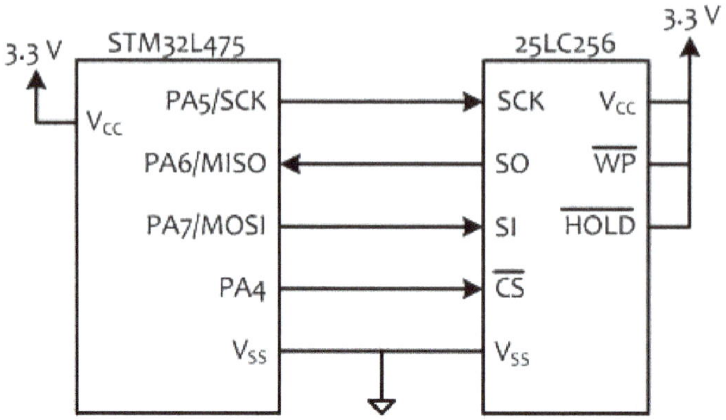

Figure 7.19 Circuit connection between the 25LC256 and the STM32L475

Example 7.7 Write a C function that writes a byte into the specified location in the EEPROM and a C function that reads the value of the specified location in EEPROM. Assume that the C function in Example 7.1 has been called to set the data frame size to 8 bits.

Solution: The C function in Example 7.1 initializes SPI1 to shift data at 2.5 MHz.

```
#define  WREN    0x06    // Set write-enable latch
#define  WRITE   0x02
#define  READ    0x03
#define  RDSR0x05 // read EEPROM status register
#define  WRSR    0x01    // write EEPROM status register
#define  WRDI    0x04    // reset the write-enable latch
void WrByteEE (uint16_t addr, uint8_t val)
{
    uint8_t temp, temp1, adH, adL;
// Step 1. Set the write-enable latch to 1
    GPIOA->BSRR = GPIO_BSRR_BR4; // enable SPI transfer to EEPROM
    putchSPI1(WREN);
    GPIOA->BSRR = GPIO_BSRR_BS4; // execute WREN command
    temp1 = SPI1->DR; // clean out the data in RXFIFO
// Step 2. Send the write EE command
    GPIOA->BSRR = GPIO_BSRR_BR4; // enable SPI transfer to EEPROM
    putchSPI1(WRITE);
```

```
    temp1 = SPI1->DR; // clean out the data in RXFIFO
// Step 3. Send out address of the location to be written
    adH = (uint8_t)(addr >> 8);
    adL = (uint8_t)(addr & 0x00FF);
    putchSPI1(adH);
    temp1 = SPI1->DR; // clean out the data in RXFIFO
    putchSPI1(adL);
    temp1 = SPI1->DR; // clean out the data in RXFIFO
// Step 4. Send the value to be written
    putchSPI1(val);
    temp1 = SPI1->DR; // clean out the data in RXFIFO
    GPIOA->BSRR = GPIO_BSRR_BS4; // start writing value into memory array
// Step 5. Wait until internal write cycle is completed before returning
    do {
        GPIOA->BSRR = GPIO_BSRR_BR4; // enable SPI transfer to EEPROM
        putchSPI1(RDSR);
        temp1 = SPI1->DR; // clean out the data in RXFIFO
        temp = getchSPI1();
        GPIOA->BSRR = GPIO_BSRR_BS4;
    } while(temp & 0x01); // continue if WIP bit is still true
}
uint8_t RdByteEE (uint16_t addr)
{
    uint8_t     tmp, tmp1, adH, adL;
// Step 1. Send READ command
    GPIOA->BSRR = GPIO_BSRR_BR4; // enable SPI transfer
    putchSPI1(READ);
    tmp1 = SPI1->DR; // clear the RXFIFO
// Step 2. Send address of EEPROM location to read
```

```
    adH = (uint8_t)(addr >> 8); // extract upper half of address
    adL = (uint8_t)(addr & 0x00FF);      // extract lower half of address
    putchSPI1(adH);
    temp1 = SPI1->DR; // clear the RXFIFO
    putchSPI1(adL);
    temp1 = SPI1->DR; // clear the RXFIFO
// Step 3. Read the value and return
    tmp = getchSPI1();
    GPIOA->BSRR = GPIO_BSRR_BS4; // terminate SPI transfer
    return tmp;
}
```

7.9 Using the MCP4922—a DAC with SPI Interface

The MCP4922 from Microchip is a 12-bit voltage output digital-to-analog converter (DAC) with a flexible SPI interface. The MCP4922 has an output settling time (or DAC conversion time) of 4.7 μs. A D/A conversion is started by writing a 16-bit value into the chip. The 16-bit value consists of 4 control bits and 12 data bits. Designed for a wide range of supply voltages, the MCP4922 can operate with a power supply from 2.7 to 5.5 V. The MCP4922 is available in several types of packages, including PDIP, SOIC, MSOP, and TSSOP.

7.9.1 SIGNAL PINS

The pin assignment and functional block of the MCP4922 are shown in Figure 7.20.

The functions of the MCP4922 signals are as follows:

- AV_{SS}: Analog ground
- V_{DD}: Power supply
- V_{REFA}, V_{REFB}: Reference voltage for channels A and B
- : Chip select
- SDI: Serial data input
- : Latch DAC input. When this signal is low, the contents of the input latch registers are transferred to the DAC registers. This signal can be tied low if data transfer on the rising edge of the signal is desired.
- : Shut down input. When this signal is low, the MCP4922 is in the low-power standby mode.
- V_{OUTA}, V_{OUTB}: DAC outputs. The DAC output amplifiers drive these pins with a range of AV_{SS} to V_{DD}.

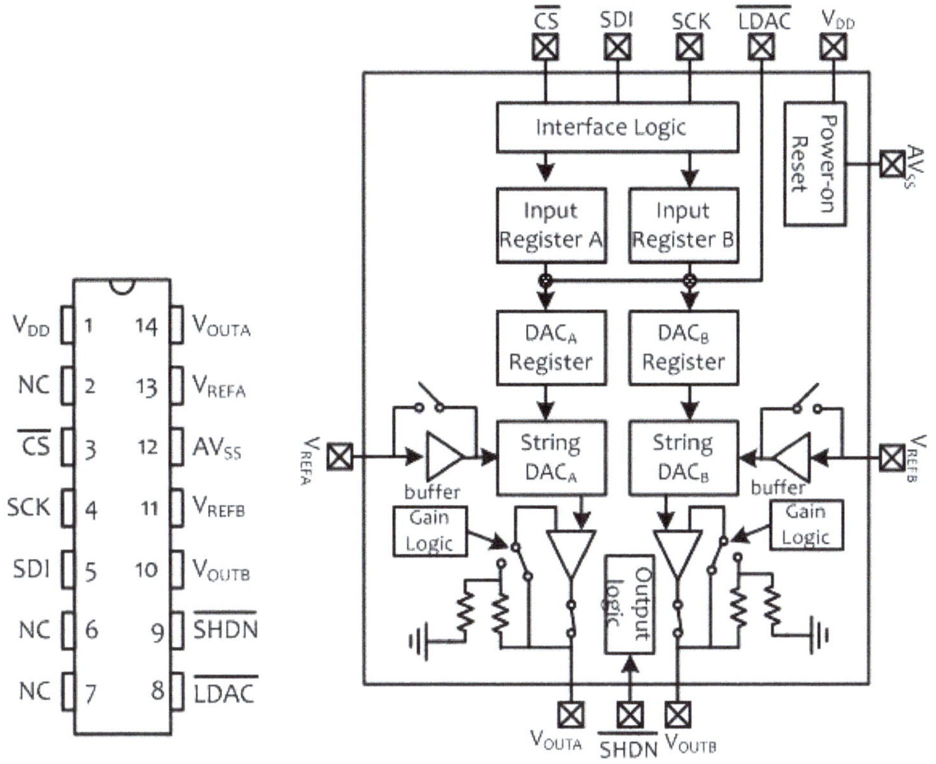

(a) Pin assignment (b)Functional block diagram

Figure 7.20 The MCP4922 DAC pins and block diagram

7.9.2 DATA FORMAT

The microcontroller sends in a 16-bit frame that consists of 4 bits of command and 12 bits of data to the MCP4922 to start a D/A conversion. The contents of the 16-bit data frame are shown in Figure 7.21. The control bit allows the user to shut down the MCP4922 to save power when it is not needed.

15	14	13	12	11	10	9	8	7	6	5	4	3	2	1	0
$\overline{A}$/B	BUF	$\overline{GA}$	$\overline{SHDN}$	D11	D10	D9	D8	D7	D6	D5	D4	D3	D2	D1	D0

$\overline{A}$/B: DAC_A or DAC_B select
- 0 = write to DAC_A
- 1 = write to DAC_B

BUF: V_{REF} input buffer control
- 0 = buffered
- 1 = unbuffered

$\overline{GA}$: output gain select bit
- 0 = gain is 2 ($V_{OUT} = 2 * V_{REF} * D / 4096$)
- 1 = gain is 1 ($V_{OUT} = V_{REF} * D / 4096$)

$\overline{SHDN}$: output power down control bit
- 0 = output buffer is disabled. Output is in high impedance
- 1 = output buffer is enabled

D11~D0: DAC data bits

Figure 7.21 Input data format for the MCP4922 DAC

The value to be sent to the MCP4922 to generate VOUT output from either V_{OUTA} or V_{OUTB} pin is

$$\text{Code} = 4096 \times V_{OUT} / (GA \times V_{REF})$$

where,

- GA is gain (1 or 2)
- V_{REF} is the reference voltage

Suppose that a 2-V output is to be generated from the V_{OUTA} pin and that V_{REF} is set to 3.3 V); the value to be sent to the MCP4922 is computed as follows:

- Select Channel A → set bit 15 to 0
- Select unbuffered mode (set bit 14 to 0)
- Set gain to 1 (set bit 13 to 1)
- Enable output buffer (set bit 12 to 1)
- 2 V corresponds to the digital value (lowest 12 bits) of 4096 × 2 ÷ 3.3 = 2482 = 0x9B2
- The value to be sent to the MCP4922 is 0011 1001 1011 0010 = **0x39B2**. (If the voltage is to be generated from the V_{OUTB} pin, then send **0xB9B2** to the MCP4922.)

7.9.3 INTERFACING THE MCP4922 WITH THE STM32L475

A typical connection between the MCP4922 and the STM32L475 is shown in Figure 7.22.

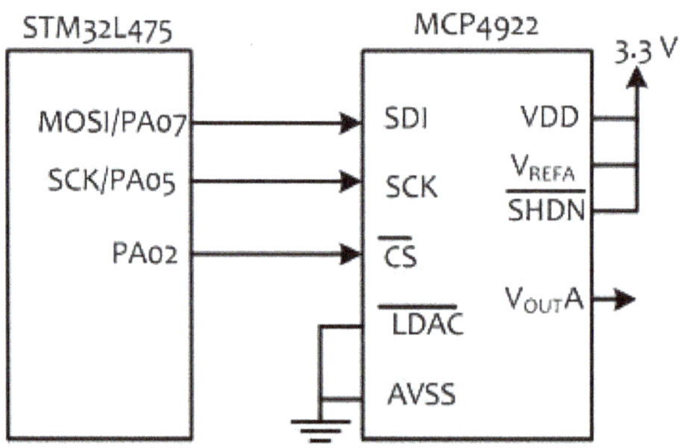

Figure 7.22 Circuit connection between the STM32L475 and MCP4922

For the circuit connection shown in Figure 7.22, the highest 4 bits of the 16-bit value to be sent to the MCP4922 are

- Bit 15: 0 → select channel A
- Bit 14: 0 → select unbuffered mode
- Bit 13: 1 → set gain to 1
- Bit 12: 1: → select normal mode (not shutdown)

If the user wants both the V_{OUTA} and V_{OUTB} pin to produce output, then bit 15 should be alternated between 0 and 1 and V_{REFB} should also be tied to V_{DD}. The lower 12 bits to be sent are proportional to the voltage to be generated.

Example 7.8 Write a C program to generate a sawtooth waveform specified in Figure 7.23 from the V_{OUTA} pin. Divide one cycle of a waveform into 60 segments (61 points).

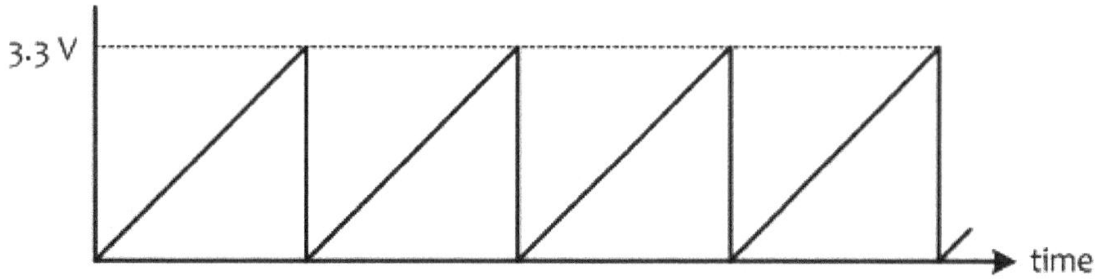

Figure 7.23 Waveform to be geneated

Solution: The MCP4922 requires a D/A conversion time of 4.7 μs; the MCU is required to provide at least this amount of time between sending two consecutive values to the MCP4922. By setting the SCK frequency to 2.5 MHz (= 80MHz / 32), each 16-bit value takes 6.4 μs to shift into the MCP4922.

The maximum value that can be represented by 12 bits is 4095. The quotient of 4095 divided by 60 is 68.25. The values to be sent to the MCP4922 are 0x3000, 0x3044, 0x3088, . . ., 0x3FFF. The C program that can generate the specified waveform is as follows:

```
#include <stm32L475xx.h>

#include "spiUtil.h"

void sysClkInit(void);

void putHWSPI1(uint16_t dw);

uint16_t sawtooth[ ]=

    { 0x3000, 0x3044, 0x3088, 0x30CD, 0x3111, 0x3155, 0x319A, 0x31DE,

      0x3222, 0x3266, 0x32AB, 0x32EF, 0x3333, 0x3377, 0x33BC, 0x3400,

      0x3444, 0x3489, 0x34CD, 0x3511, 0x3555, 0x359A, 0x35DE, 0x3622,

      0x3666, 0x36AB, 0x36EF, 0x3733, 0x3777, 0x37BC, 0x3800, 0x3844,

      0x3889, 0x38CD, 0x3911, 0x3955, 0x399A, 0x39DE, 0x3A22, 0x3A66,

      0x3AAB, 0x3AEF, 0x3B33, 0x3B77, 0x3BBC, 0x3C00, 0x3C44, 0x3C89,

      0x3CCD, 0x3D11, 0x3D55, 0x3D9A, 0x3DDE, 0x3E22, 0x3E66, 0x3EAB,

      0x3EEF, 0x3F33, 0x3F77, 0x3FBC, 0x3FFF};
```

```
int main (void)
{
    uint16_t j;
    sysClkInit();
    openSPI1(1);
    GPIOA->MODER &= ~GPIO_MODER_MODE2; // configure PA02 pin for output
    GPIOA->MODER |= GPIO_MODER_MODE2_0; // "
    while(1) {
        for(j = 0; j < 61; j++){
            GPIOA->BSRR = GPIO_BSRR_BR2; // enable SPI transfer to MCP4922
            putHWSPI1(sawtooth[j]);
            GPIOA->BSRR = GPIO_BSRR_BS2; // start D/A conversion
        }
    }
}
```

Example 7.9 Write a C program to generate voltage waveforms from both the V_{OUTA} and V_{OUTB} pins as shown in Figure 7.24 using the circuit connection shown in Figure 7.22.

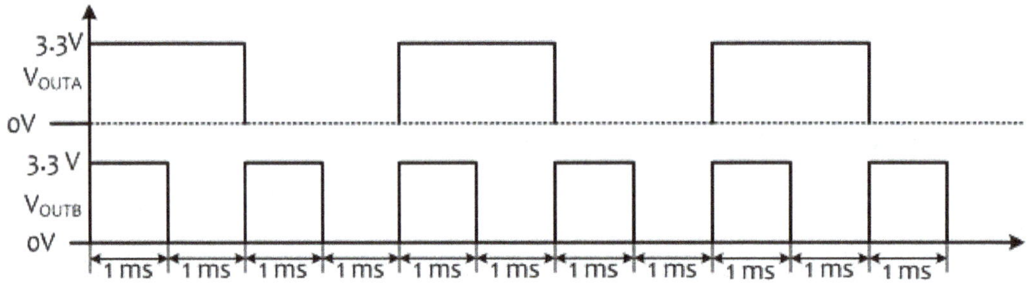

Figure 7.24 Waveform to be generated

Solution: The 12-bit value to generate a 3.3 V output is 0xFFF whereas the value to generate a 0 V output is 0x000. The following program will produce the specified waveform:

```
#include <stm32L475xx.h>
void sysClkInit(void);
```

```
#include "delays.h"
#include "spiUtil.h"
int main (void)
{
    sysClkInit();
    openSPI1(1);
    GPIOA->MODER      &= ~GPIO_MODER_MODE2; // configure PA02 pin for output
    GPIOA->MODER      |= GPIO_MODER_MODE2_0; //    "
        while(1){
            GPIOA->BSRR   = GPIO_BSRR_BR2; // enable SPI transfer to MCP4922
            putHWSPI1(0x3FFF); // generate 3.3 V from VOUTA
            GPIOA->BSRR   = GPIO_BSRR_BS2; // start DAC to generate 3.3 V from VOUTA
            GPIOA->BSRR   = GPIO_BSRR_BR2; // enable SPI transfer to MCP4922
            putHWSPI1(0xBFFF); // generate 3.3 V from VOUTB
            GPIOA->BSRR   = GPIO_BSRR_BS2; // start DAC
            delayby1ms(1);          // wait for 1 ms
            GPIOA->BSRR   = GPIO_BSRR_BR2; // enable SPI transfer
            putHWSPI1(0xB000); // generate 0 V from VOUTB
            GPIOA->BSRR   = GPIO_BSRR_BS2; // start DAC
            delayby1ms(1);          // wait for 1 ms
            GPIOA->BSRR   = GPIO_BSRR_BR2; // enable SPI transfer
            putHWSPI1(0x3000); // generate 0 V from VOUTA
            GPIOA->BSRR   = GPIO_BSRR_BS2; // start DAC
            GPIOA->BSRR   = GPIO_BSRR_BR2; // enable SPI transfer
            putHWSPI1(0xBFFF); // generate 3.3 V from VOUTB pin
            GPIOA->BSRR   = GPIO_BSRR_BS2; // start DAC
            delayby1ms(1);
            GPIOA->BSRR   = GPIO_BSRR_BR2; // enable SPI transfer
            putHWSPI1(0xB000); // generate 0 V from VOUTB
```

```
            GPIOA->BSRR    = GPIO_BSRR_BS2; // start DAC
            delayby1ms(1);           // wait for 1 ms
        }
}
```

7.10 Interfacing with the Shift Register 74HC595

One of the applications of a shift register is to convert data from parallel to serial and vice versa. As shown in Figure 7.25, the 74HC595 is a CMOS 8-stage serial shift register with a storage register and 3-state outputs. The shift register accepts serial data and provides a serial output. The shift register also provides parallel data to the 8-bit latch. The shift register and the latch have different clock sources. This device also has an asynchronous reset input. The maximum shift clock frequency is 30 MHz at room temperature (25°C) and the power supply is in the range from 2 to 6 V. The maximum DC current output of each pin is 35 mA and the maximum current that this chip can supply is 75 mA.

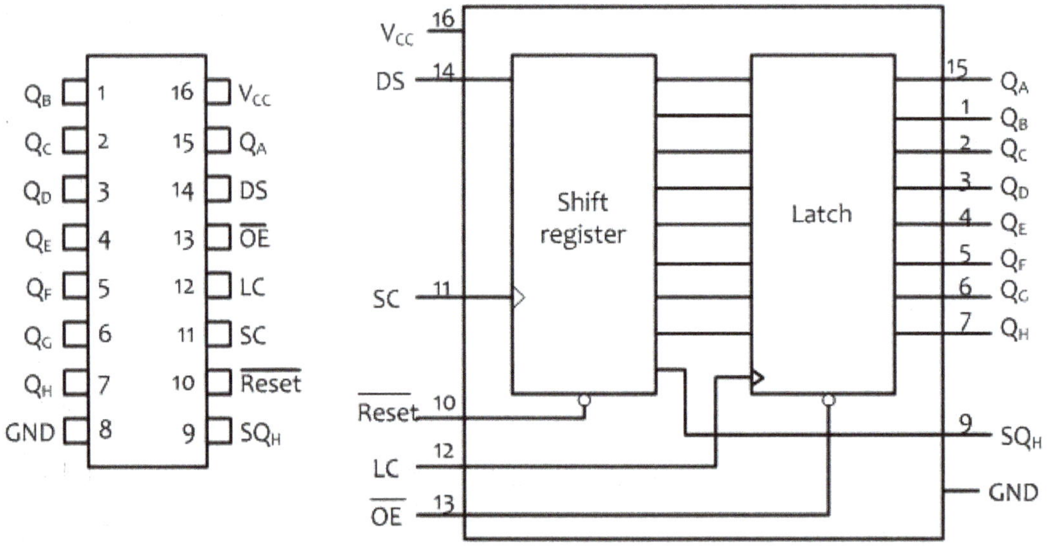

Figure 7.25 The 74HC595 block diagram and pin assignment

The functions of the pins in Figure 7.25 are as follows:

- DS: Serial data input. The data on this pin are shifted into the 8-bit shift register.
- SC: Shift clock. The rising edge of this signal causes the data at the serial input pin to be shifted into the shift register.
- : Reset input. A low on this pin clears the shift register portion of this device only. The 8-bit latch is not affected.
- LC: Latch clock. The rising edge of this signal loads the contents of the shift register into the output latch.

- : Output enable. A low on this pin allows the data from the latch to be presented at the output pins Q_A~Q_H.
- Q_A~Q_H: Noninverted, tri-state latch outputs.
- SQ_H: Serial data output. This is the output of the eighth stage of the 8-bit shift register. This output does not have tri-state capability.

The 74HC595 is designed to shift in 8-bit data serially and then transfer it to the latch to be used as parallel data. This chip can be used to add parallel output ports to a microcontroller. Both connection methods shown in Figures 7.4 and 7.5 can be used in appropriate applications.

Example 7.10 Describe how to use two 74HC59s to interface with the STM32L475 to drive eight common-cathode seven-segment displays, assuming that the STM32L475 is running at 80 MHz.

Solution: One way to use two 74HC595s to drive eight seven-segment displays is shown in Figure 7.26. These two 74HC595s are cascaded together with the first one driving the segment patterns and the second one driving the common cathode of all the seven-segment displays.

The SCK signal is used as the shift clock (SC) whereas the PA03 pin drives the latch clock (LC). One of the outputs QH~QA of the 74HC595 #2 must be pulled low in order to turn on the connected seven-segment display. The user can apply the time-multiplexing technique to this circuit to display multiple digits simultaneously.

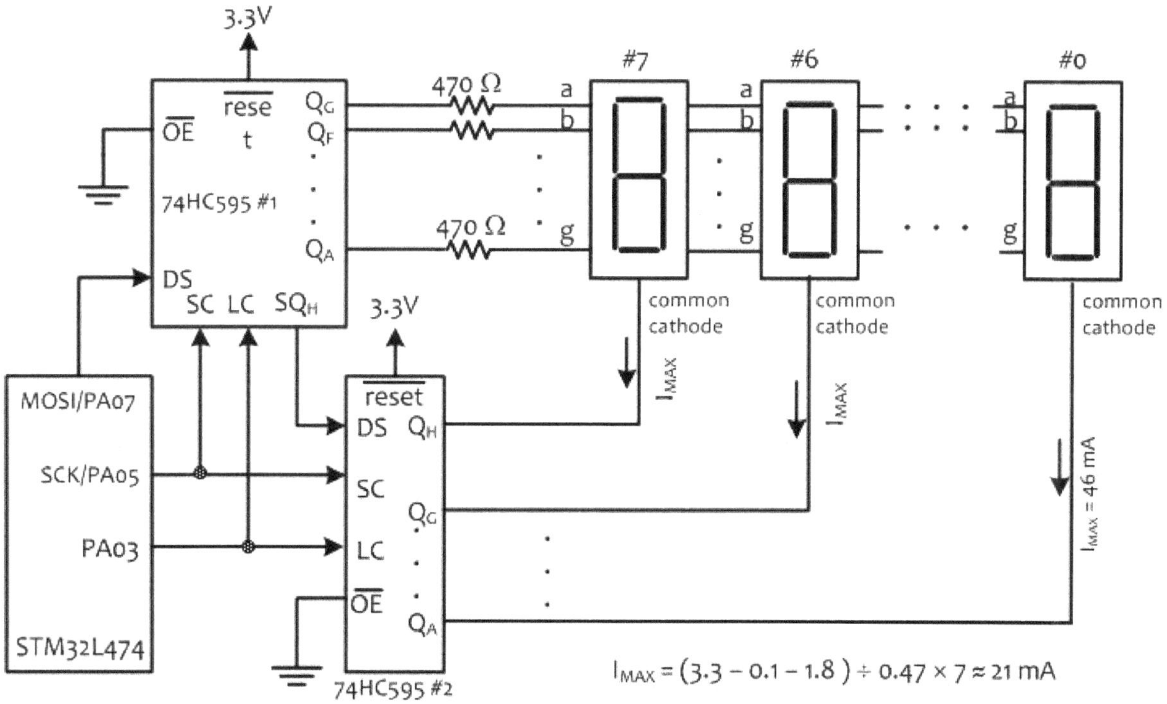

Figure 7.26 Two 74HC595s together drive eight seven-segment displays

Example 7.11 Write a C program to display 12345678 on display #7 to #0 in Figure 7.26.

Solution: The value to turn on display #7~#0 are $0111\ 1111_2$(or 0x7F), $1011\ 1111_2$(0r 0xBF), $1101\ 1111_2$ (or 0xDF), $1110\ 1111_2$ (or 0xEF), $1111\ 0111_2$ (or oxF7), $1111\ 1011_2$ (or 0xFB), $1111\ 1101_2$ (or 0xFD), and 1111

1110_2 (or 0xFE), respectively. The segment pattern of 1 is 0x30. To display 1 on display #7, we are required to send the value 0x7F30 to the SPI1. The values to be sent for other digits on corresponding displays can be figured out similarly.

The following C program will display 12345678 on display #7 to #0 using the time-multiplexing technique:

```
#include <stm32L475xx.h>
#include "delays.h"
#include "spiUtil.h"
void sysClkInit(void);
uint16_t dispTab[8] = {0x7F30, 0xBF6D, 0xDF79, 0xEF33, 0xF75B, 0xFB5F, 0xFD70, 0xFE7F};
int main (void)
{
    uint16_t j;
    sysClkInit();
    openSPI1(1);
    GPIOA->MODER  &= ~GPIO_MODER_MODE3; // configure PA03 pin for output
    GPIOA->MODER  |=  GPIO_MODER_MODE3_0; //       "
    while(1){
        for(j = 0; j < 8; j++) {
            putHWSPI1(dispTab[j]); // send out display select and segment patterns
            GPIOA->BSRR   = GPIO_BSRR_BR3; // copy data to output latch
            GPIOA->BSRR   = GPIO_BSRR_BS3;
            delayby1ms(1); // wait for 1 ms
        }
    }
}
```

7.11 Summary

When high-speed data transfer is not needed, using serial data transfer allows us to make the most of the limited number of I/O pins available on the MCU device. Serial data transfer can be performed asynchronously or synchronously. The SPI is a synchronous protocol introduced by Motorola for data exchange between the microcontroller and peripheral chips.

In the SPI protocol, a device (must be a microcontroller) is responsible for initiating the data transfer and generating the clock pulses for synchronizing data transfer. This device is referred to as the **SPI master**. All other devices in the same system are referred to as **SPI slaves**. The SPI module (of a master or a slave) uses three signals to carry out data transfer:

- SCK: a clock signal for synchronizing data transfer
- MOSI: serial data output from the master (an input to the slave)
- MISO: serial data input to the master (an output from the slave)

An SPI slave device normally needs a slave-select (SS, sometimes also called chip-select (CS)) signal to enable its operation.

To transfer data to one or multiple SPI devices, the MCU writes data into the SPI data register and appropriate number of clock pulses are generated to shift out data from the MOSI pin. If the MISO pin of the MCU is also connected (to the same pin of the slave), then the same number of bits are also shifted into the SPI data register.

The STM32L475 implements three identical SPI modules (SPI1, SPI2, and SPI3). The SPI module includes the TXFIFO and RXFIFO and DMA capability to support data packing and unpacking. However, these also add complexity to the use of the SPI function. The STM32L475 SPI implementation also includes the CRC checking to improve the reliability of applications that deal with extensive data storage and communication operations. The user is required to specify a CRC generator polynomial for the CRC circuit to generate the CRC code to be transmitted during the transmission phase. The same polynomial will also be used to generate a CRC code from the received data stream to be compared with the received CRC during the reception phase. To utilize CRC checking, both the master and the slave must be an MCU. A non-MCU slave cannot perform CRC checking.

For some peripheral chips, the MCU is required to send several data frames to the peripheral before reading back the data frame. In the full-duplex mode, the MCU and the peripheral exchange data frames in each data frame transfer. The application should clean up the dummy data frames stored in the RXFIFO to ensure that the intended data frame is read back.

The shift register 74HC595, the EEPROM chip 25LC256, and the DAC chip MCP4922 are used to illustrate the SPI interfacing techniques and applications.

7.12 Exercises

E7.1 Modify the C function in Example 7.1 to configure SPI2 so that SPI2 operates with the following parameters:

- Use PB15, PB14, and PB10 pins for MOSI, MISO, and SCK signals.
- Select master mode and disable all interrupts.
- SCK idle high and shift data on the falling edge.
- Shift data LSB first.
- Data frame is either 8 bit or 16 bit (using the incoming parameter **ds** to specify, when ds = 0, data size is 8 bit; otherwise, data is 16 bit)
- Set data baud rate to 1.25 MHz assuming that the peripheral bus clock is 80 MHz.
- Enable TX DMA and RX DMA.
- Disable CRC checking.

E7.2 Modify the C function in Example 7.1 to configure SPI3 so that SPI3 operates with the following parameters:

- Use PC12, PC11, and PC10 pins for MOSI, MISO, and SCK signals.
- Select master mode and enable all SPI interrupts.
- Configure SCK to be idle low and shift data on the rising edge.
- Shift data MSB first.
- Set baud rate to 5 MHz assuming that the peripheral bus clock is 80 MHz.
- Enable TXDMA and RXDMA.
- Enable CRC and set CRC polynomial to be $x^8 + x^7 + x^6 + x^4 + x^2 + 1$.

E7.3 The 74HC165 is another SPI-compatible shift register. This chip has both serial and parallel inputs and is often used to expand the number of input ports for the microcontroller. The block diagram of the 74HC165 is shown in Figure E7.3. The operation of this chip is illustrated in Table E7.3. The 74HC165 can be cascaded. To cascade multiple 74HC165s, connect the Q7 output of a 74HC165 to the DS input of its adjacent 74HC165. All 74HC165s should share the same shift clock CP. Suppose we want to use two 74HC165s to interface with two DIP switches so that four hex digits can be read by the STM32L475. Describe the circuit connection and write a sequence of C statements to read data from two DIP switches.

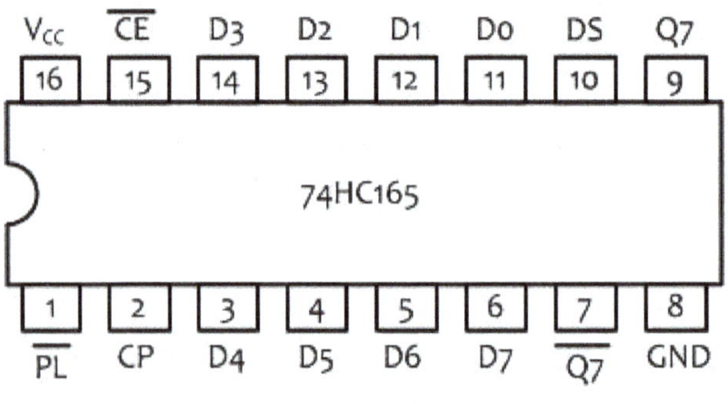

Figure E7.3 The 74HC165 pin assignment

Table E7.3 Function table of the 74HC165

Operating mode	inputs					Qn flip-flops		Outputs	
	$\overline{PL}$	$\overline{CE}$	CP	Ds	D0-D7	Q0	Q1-Q6	Q7	$\overline{Q7}$
parallel load	L	X	X	X	L	L	L-L	L	H
	L	X	X	X	H	H	H-H	H	L
Serial shift	H	LL	↑	l	X	L	q0-q5	q6	$\overline{q6}$
	H		↑	h	X	H	q0-q5	q6	$\overline{q6}$
hold	H	H	X	X	X	q0	q1-q6	q7	$\overline{q7}$

E7.4 For the circuit shown in Figure 7.26, write a C program to display the following patterns forever with each pattern lasting for 800 ms assuming that the STM32L475 is running at 80 MHz:

12345678
23456789
34567890
45678901
56789012
67890123
78901234
89012345
90123456
01234567

E7.5 Modify the C function **WrByteEE** in Example 7.7 so that it can write a block of data into the 25LC256 starting from the specified address. The prototype of the new function is "void **WrPageEE** (uint16_t addr, uint8_t *ptr, uint8_t byteCnt)." The argument **addr** is the address of the first location in EEPROM to be written into. The argument **ptr** points to the block of data to be written. The argument **byteCnt** specifies the number of bytes to be written.

E7.6 Modify the C function **RdByteEE** in Example 7.7 so that it can read back a block of data from the 25LC256 starting from the specified address. The prototype of the new function is "void **RdBlockEE** (uint16_t addr, uint8_t *ptr, uint16_t byteCnt)." The argument **addr** is the address of the first location in EEPROM to be read from. The argument **ptr** points to the buffer to hold the read back data and the argument **byteCnt** specifies the number of bytes to be read.

E7.7 Write a program that uses the circuit shown in Figure 7.22 to generate a waveform shown in Figure E7.7 from the V_{OUTB} pin. Only two cycles of the periodic waveform are shown.

E7.8 The AD7814 is an SPI-compatible 10-bit plus sign digital temperature sensor made by Analog Devices. The datasheet of this chip can be downloaded from the website at www.analog.com. Show the circuit connection between the AD7814 and the STM32L475. Write a C program that reads temperature once every second and convert the temperature reading into a string so that it can be displayed on the LCD.

E7.9 Real-time clock (RTC) is used in many applications due to its capability of keeping track of time-of-day. The DS1390 is an RTC chip with the 4-wire SPI interface made by Maxim Semiconductor. The datasheet of

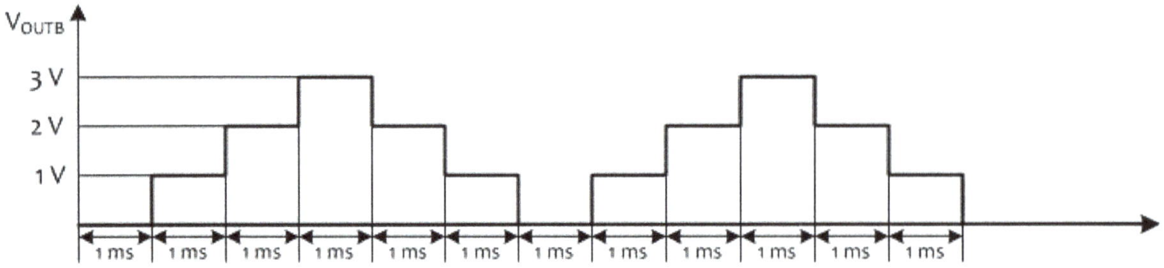

Figure E7.7 Waveform to be generated from V_{OUTB} pin

the DS1390 can be downloaded from the website www.maxim-ic.com. Describe how to connect this chip to the STM32L475.

E7.10 Write a C function to transfer the current time-of-day to the DS1390 circuit described in E7.9. This function has an incoming argument *ptr that points to the string that represents the current time-of-day. The string is represented as an ASCII string yy:MM:dd:DD:hh:mm:ss:fs. The ":" character is used to separate different time fields. The word **fs** stands for fraction seconds (tenths and hundredths seconds).

E7.11 Write a C function to read out the current time-of-day from the DS1390 and format it into an ASCII string so that it can be displayed on the LCD. Display the time-of-day in the 24-hour format: hh:mm:ss:D-D:dd:yy.

E7.12 Write a program that uses the circuit shown in Figure 7.22 to generate a sine wave and triangular wave from the V_{OUTA} and V_{OUTB} pins, respectively. Divide one cycle of the waveform into 60 points.

7.13 Lab Assignments

L7.1 Use the MCP4922 to interface with the STM32L475 to generate a sine wave from the V_{OUTA} pin and a triangular wave from the V_{OUTB} pin. Divide one cycle of the sine wave and the triangular wave into 60 uniformly spaced points. Display the waveforms using an oscilloscope.

L7.2 Use two 74HC595s and the STM32L475 to drive six seven-segment displays and display the following patterns forever with each row lasting for 600 ms:

654321
765432
876543
987654
098765
109876
210987
321098
432109
543210

8 Universal Synchronous Asynchronous Receiver Transmitter (USART)

8.1 Objectives

After you finish this chapter, you will be able to

- Describe the four aspects of the RS-232 standard.
- Describe the NULL modem.
- Describe and explain virtual COM port.
- Understand the functions supported by the USART, UART, and LPUART modules.
- Configure the baud rate for the USART modules.
- Configure the USART operation parameters.
- Reference the registers of any USART module.
- Invoke USART utility functions to perform data transmission and reception.
- Use infrared light to transmit and receive data.
- Use USART and infrared light emitter and receiver to perform data communications.

8.2 Introduction

Almost all the microcontrollers provide universal synchronous asynchronous receiver transmitter (USART) module to support data communications with other microcontrollers or PCs. The synchronous mode may not be supported by all microcontrollers. For those microcontrollers that do not support the synchronous mode, the USART name is reduced to UART.

The earliest UART only supports the RS-232 interface, which allows the microcontroller to communicate with another microcontroller or a PC. More recent microcontrollers utilize the USART module to support more and more functions. For example, quite a few microcontrollers have used the USART module to support the LIN, ModBus, Smart card, infrared communication, and so on.

Since the USART supports the RS-232 interface from the beginning, a brief discussion on RS-232 will be included in this Chapter.

8.3 The RS-232 Standard

The RS-232 standard was established in 1960 by the Electronic Industry Association (EIA) to facilitate the data communication between two computers. This standard requires a computer to be connected to a modem when performing data communications. It has been revised several times since then. The acronym **RS** stands for recommended standard. Up to the fifth revision, EIA is the control organization of this standard. The current version is TIA-232F, which was issued in 1997. The control organization has been transferred to the Telecommunication Industry Association (TIA).

An RS-232 serial port was once a standard feature of a personal computer, used for connections to modems, printers, mice, data storage, uninterruptable power supplies, and other peripheral devices. RS-232, when compared to later interfaces such as RS-422, RS-485, and Ethernet, has lower transmission speed, short maximum cable length, large voltage swing, large standard connectors, no multipoint capability, and limited multidrop capability. In modern personal computers, USB has displaced RS-232 from most of its peripheral interface roles. Most computers no longer come equipped with RS-232 ports and must use either an external USB-to-DB9 converter or an internal expansion card with one or more serial ports to connect to RS-232 peripherals. Nevertheless, thanks to their simplicity and past ubiquity, RS-232 interfaces are still used—particularly in industrial machines, networking equipment, and scientific instruments where a short-range, point-to-point, low-speed wired data connection is adequate.

We refer to the standard RS-232 and TIA-232 throughout this text. In data communication terms, both computers and terminals are called **data terminal equipment** (DTE), whereas modems, bridges, and routers are referred to as **data communication equipment** (DCE).

There are four aspects to the TIA-232 standards:

1. Electrical specifications. The voltage level, rise time, and fall time of each signal, achievable data rate, and the distance of communication are specified.
2. Functional specifications. The function of each signal is specified.
3. Mechanical specifications. The number of pins, the shape, and dimensions of the connectors are specified.
4. Procedural specifications. The sequence of events for transmitting data based on the functional specifications of the interface is specified.

8.3.1 TIA-232 ELECTRICAL SPECIFICATIONS

The following electrical specifications of the TIA-232 are of interest to us:

1. Data Rates. The TIA-232 standard supports data rates of up to 20,000 bits per second (the usual upper limit is 19,200 baud). The TIA-232 standard did not set any fixed baud rate. The commonly used baud rate values are 2,400, 4,800, 9,600, and 19,200.
2. Signal State Voltage Assignments. Voltages of –3 V to –25 V with respect to signal ground are considered logic 1 (referred to as the ***mark*** condition), whereas voltages of +3 V to +25 V are considered logic 0 (referred to as the ***space*** condition). The range of voltages between –3 V and +3 V is considered **transition region** for which a signal state is not assigned.
3. Signal Transfer Distance. The standard requires the TIA-232 implementation to transfer data correctly up to 15 m. Greater distance can be achieved with good design.

8.3.2 FUNCTIONAL SPECIFICATIONS

The TIA-232 standard specifies 22 signals. These signals are divided into six categories:

1. *Signal Ground and Shield.*
2. *Primary Communications Channel.* This is used for data interchange and includes flow control signals.
3. *Secondary Communications Channel.* When implemented, this is used for control of the remote modem, requests for retransmission when errors occur, and governance over the setup of the primary channel.
4. *Modem Status and Control Signals.* These signals indicate modem status and provide intermediate checkpoints as the telephone voice channel is established.
5. *Transmitter and Receiver Timing Signals.* If a synchronous protocol is used, these signals provide timing information for the transmitter and receiver, which may operate at different baud rates.
6. *Channel Test Signals.* Before data are exchanged, the channel may be tested for its integrity and the baud rate automatically is adjusted to the maximum rate that the channel could support.

Signal Ground

Pins 7 and 1 and the shell are included in this category. Cables provide separate paths for each, but internal wiring often connects pin 1 and the cable shell/shield to the signal ground on pin 7. All signals are referenced to a common ground, as defined by the voltage on pin 7. This conductor may or may not be connected to the protective ground inside the DCE device.

Primary Communication Channel

Pin 2 carries the *transmit data* (TxD) signal, which is active when data are transmitted from the DTE device to the DCE device. When no data are transmitted, the signal is held in the mark condition (logic 1, negative voltage).

Pin 3 carries the *received data* (RxD), which is active when the DTE device receives data from the DCE device. When no data are received, the signal is held in the mark condition.

Pin 4 carries the *request to send* (RTS) signal, which is asserted (logic 0, positive voltage) to prepare the DCE device for accepting transmitted data from the DTE device. Such preparation might include enabling the receive circuits or setting up the channel direction in half-duplex applications. When the DCE is ready, it acknowledges by asserting the CTS signal.

Pin 5 carries the *clear to send* (CTS) signal, which will be asserted (logic 0) by the DCE device to inform the DTE device that transmission may begin. RTS and CTS commonly are used as handshaking signals to moderate the flow of data into the DCE device.

Secondary Communication Channel

Pin 14 is the *secondary transmitted data* (STxD). Pin 16 is the *secondary received data* (SRxD). Pin 19 carries the *secondary request to send* (SRTS) signal. Pin 13 carries the *secondary clear to send* (SCTS) signal. These signals are equivalent to the corresponding signals in the primary communications channel. The baud rate, however, typically is much lower in the secondary channel, for increased reliability.

Modem Status and Control Signals

This group includes the following signals:

Pin 6—DCE Ready (DSR). When originating from a modem, this signal is asserted (logic 0) when all the following three conditions are satisfied:

1. The modem is connected to an active telephone line that is off hook.
2. The modem is in data mode, not voice or dialing mode.
3. The modem has completed dialing or call setup functions and is generating an answer.

If the line goes off-hook, a fault condition is detected, or a voice connection is established, and the DCE ready signal is de-asserted (logic 1).

Pin 20—DTE Ready (DTR). This signal is asserted (logic 0) by the DTE device when it wishes to open a communication channel. If the DCE device is a modem, the assertion of DTR prepares the modem to be connected to the telephone circuit and once connected, maintains the connection. When DTR is de-asserted, the modem is switched to *on-hook* to terminate the connection (same as placing the phone back on the telephone socket).

Pin 8—Received Line Signal Detector (CD). Also called *carrier detect*, this signal is relevant when the DCE device is a modem. It is asserted (logic 0) by the modem when the telephone line is off-hook, a connection has been established, and an answer tone is being received from the remote modem. The signal is de-asserted when no answer tone is being received or when the answer tone is of inadequate quality to meet the local modem's requirements.

Pin 12—Secondary Received Line Signal Detector (SCD). This signal is equivalent to the CD (pin 8) signal but refers to the secondary channel.

Pin 22—Ring Indicator (RI). This signal is relevant when the DCE device is a modem and is asserted (logic 0) when a ringing signal is being received from the telephone line. The assertion time of this signal will equal approximately the duration of the ring signal, and it will be de-asserted between rings or when no ringing is present.

Pin 23—Data Signal Rate Selector. This signal may originate in either the DTE or DCE devices (but not both) and is used to select one of two prearranged baud rates. The assertion condition (logic "0") selects the higher baud rate.

Transmitter and Receiver Timing Signals

This group consists of the following signals:

Pin 15—Transmitter Signal Element Timing (TC). Also called a *transmitter clock*, this signal is relevant only when the DCE device is a modem and is operating with a synchronous protocol. The modem generates this clock signal to control exactly the rate at which data are send on TxD (pin 2) from the DTE device to the DCE device. The logic 1 to logic 0 (negative to positive) transition on this line causes a corresponding transition to the next data element on the TxD line. The modem generates this signal continuously, except when it is performing internal diagnostic functions.

Pin 17—Receiver Signal Element Timing (RC). Also called a *receiver clock*, this signal is similar to TC, except that it provides timing information for the DTE receiver.

Pin 24—Transmitter Signal Element Timing (ETC). Also called an *external transmitter clock* with timing signals provided by the DTE device for use by a modem, this signal is used only when TC and RC (pins 15 and 17) are not in use. The logic 1 to logic 0 transition indicates the time center of the data element. Timing signals will be provided whenever the DTE is turned on, regardless of other signal conditions.

Channel Test Signals

This group consists of the following signals:

Pin 18—Local Loopback (LL). This signal is generated by the DTE device and is used to place the modem into a test state. When LL is asserted (logic 0, positive voltage), the modem redirects its modulated output signal, which normally is fed into the telephone line, and back into its receiving circuitry. This enables data generated by the DTE to be echoed back through the local modem to check the condition of the modem circuitry. The modem asserts its test mode signal on pin 25 to acknowledge that it has been placed in LL condition.

Pin 21—Remote Loopback (RL). This signal is generated by the DTE device and is used to place the remote modem into a test state. When RL is asserted (logic 0), the remote modem redirects its received data back to its transmitted data input, thereby demodulating the received data and returning it to its source. When the DTE initiates such a test, transmitted data are passed through the local modem, the telephone line, the remote modem, and back, to exercise the channel and confirm its integrity. The remote modem signals the local modem to assert test mode on pin 25 when the remote loopback test is underway.

Pin 25—Test Mode (TM). This signal is relevant only when the DCE device is a modem. When asserted (logic 0), it indicates that the modem is in an LL or RL condition. Other internal self-test conditions also may cause the TM signal to be asserted, depending on the modem and the network to which it is attached.

8.3.3 TIA-232 MECHANICAL SPECIFICATIONS

The TIA-232 uses a 25-pin D-type connector (DB25). However, only a small subset of the 25 signals is used, a 9-pin connector (DB9) is used in most PCs. The signal assignment of DB9 is shown in Figure 8.1. The DB9 is not part of the TIA-232 standard. Today, USB bus has become the most popular serial bus used in personal computers (PC). Most PCs no longer provide the DB9 connector. To use the UART port to communicate with the PC, the user will need to purchase a DB9-to-USB converter or an add-on serial card that plugs into the PCI bus on the PC.

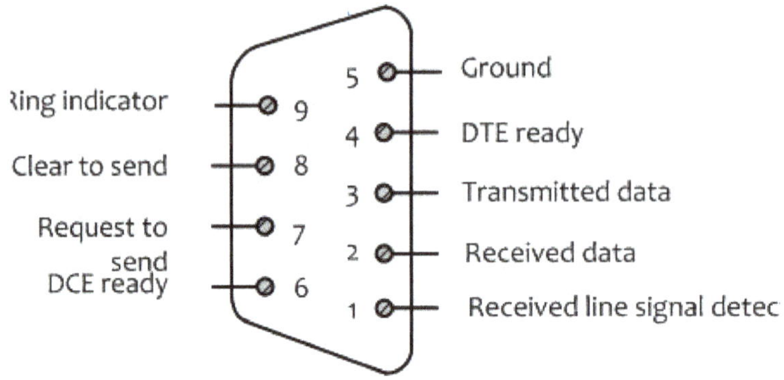

Figure 8.1 TIA-232E DB9 connector and signal assignment

8.3.4 TIA-232 PROCEDURAL SPECIFICATIONS

The sequence of events that occurs during data transmission using the TIA-232 standard can be understood best by studying examples. Two examples are used to explain the procedure.

In the first example, two DTEs are connected with a point-to-point link using a modem. The modem requires only the following circuits to operate:

- Signal ground (GND)
- Transmitted data (TxD)
- Received data (RxD)
- Request to send (RTS)
- Clear to send (CTS)
- Data set ready (DSR)
- Carrier detect (CD)

Before the DTE can transmit data, the DSR circuit must be asserted to indicate that the modem is ready to operate. This signal should be asserted before the DTE attempts to make a request to send data. The DSR pin can be connected to the power supply of the DCE to indicate that it is switched on and ready to operate.

When a DTE has data to send, it asserts the RTS signal. The modem responds, when ready, with the CTS signal asserted, indicating that data may be transmitted. If the arrangement is half-duplex, the assertion of the RTS signal also inhibits the receive mode. The DTE sends data to the local modem bit serially. The local modem modulates the data into the carrier signal and transmits the resultant signal over the dedicated communication lines. Before sending out modulated data, the local modem sends out a carrier signal to the remote modem so that it is ready to receive the data. The remote modem detects the carrier and asserts the CD signal. The assertion of the CD signal tells the remote DTE that the local modem is transmitting. The remote modem receives the modulated signal, demodulates it to recover the data, and sends it to the remote DTE over the RxD pin.

A point-to-point asynchronous circuit connection is shown in Figure 8.2. After the local DTE finishes data transmission, it drops the RTS signal, and the local modem then drops the CTS signal. The local modem also drops the carrier. The remote modem detects the loss of carrier; it then drops the CD signal, which then terminates the whole data transmission process.

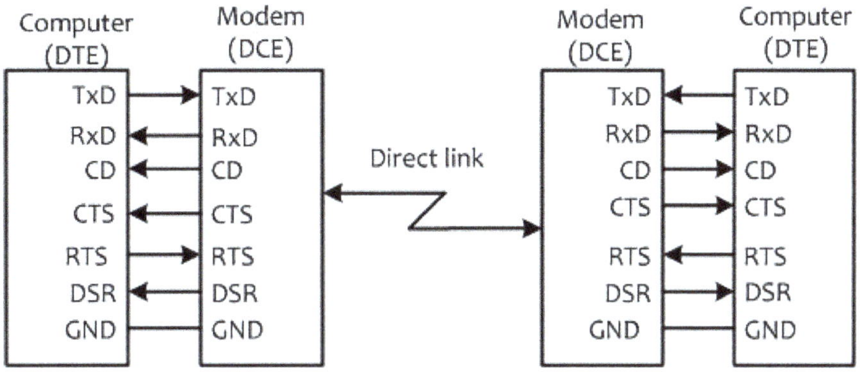

Figure 8.2 Point-to-point asynchronous connection

The next example involves two computers exchanging data through a public telephone line. One of the computers (initiator) must dial the phone (automatically or manually) to establish the connection, just like people talking over the phone. Two additional signals are required for this application:

- Data terminal ready (DTR)
- Ring indicator (RI)

The data transmission in this setting is divided into three phases:

Phase 1

Connection Establishment. The following events occur in this phase:

1. The transmitting computer asserts the DTR signal to indicate to the local modem that it is ready to make a call.
2. The local modem opens the phone line and dials the destination number. The number can be stored in the modem or transmitted to the modem by the computer via the TxD pin.
3. The remote modem detects a ring on the phone line and asserts the RI signal to inform the remote computer that a call has arrived.
4. The remote computer asserts the DTR signal to accept the call.
5. The remote modem answers the call by sending a carrier signal to the local modem via the phone line. It also asserts the DSR signal to inform the remote computer that it is ready for data transmission.
6. The local modem asserts both the DSR and CD signals to indicate that the connection is established and it is ready for data communication.

7. For full-duplex data communication, the local modem also sends a carrier signal to the remote modem. The remote modem then asserts the CD signal.

Phase 2

Data Transmission. The following events occur during this phase.

1. The local computer asserts the RTS signal when it is ready to send data.
2. The local modem responds by asserting the CTS signal.
3. The local computer sends data bit serially to the local modem over the TxD pin. The local modem then modulates its carrier signal to transmit data to the remote modem.
4. The remote modem receives the modulated signal from the local modem, demodulates it to recover the data, and forwards it to the remote computer over the RxD pin.

Phase 3

Disconnection. Disconnection requires only two steps.

1. When the local computer has finished the data transmission, it drops the RTS signal.
2. The local modem then de-asserts the CTS signal and drops the carrier (equivalent to hanging up the phone).

The circuit connection for this example is shown in Figure 8.3. A timing signal is not required in an asynchronous transmission.

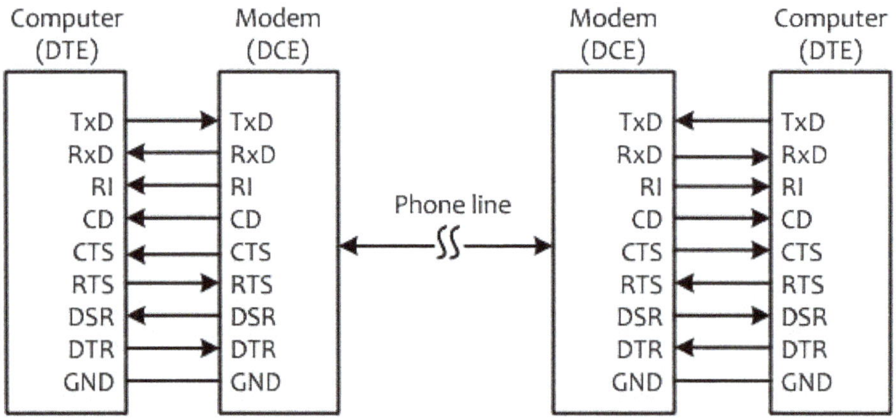

Figure 8.3 Asynchronous connection over public phone line

8.3.5 DATA FORMAT

Using the TIA-232 protocol, data are transferred character by character. Each character is preceded by a start bit (low), followed by eight or nine data bits, and terminated by a stop bit (high). The data format of an 8-bit character is shown in Figure 8.4.

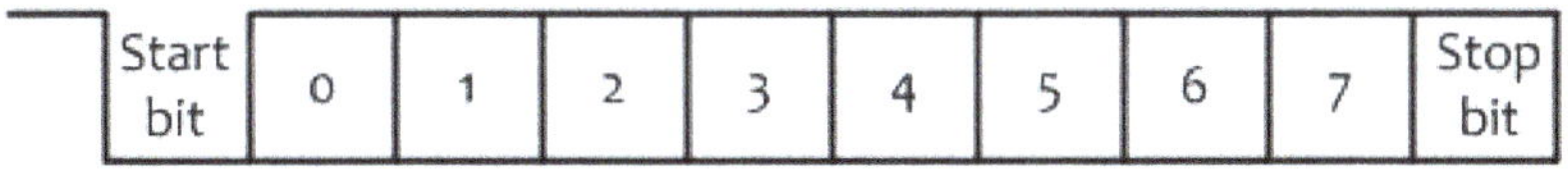

Figure 8.4 The format of a character

As shown in Figure 8.4, the least significant bit is transmitted first, and the most significant bit is transmitted last. The stop bit is high. The start bit and the stop bit identify the start and the end of a character.

Since there is no clock information in the asynchronous format, the receiver uses a clock signal with a frequency that is a multiple (can be 8 or 16) of the data rate to sample the incoming data to detect the arrival of the start bit and determine the logical value of each data bit. A clock with a frequency that is 16 times the data rate can tolerate a frequency difference in the clocks slightly more than 3% at the transmitter and receiver.

Detecting the arrival of a start bit is similar among all microcontrollers:

When the RxD pin is idle (high) for at least three sampling times and then is followed by a low voltage, the UART will look at the third, fifth, and seventh samples after the first low sample (these are called verification samples). If the majority of these three samples are low, then the eighth, ninth, and tenth samples will be checked. If the majority function of these three samples is also low, then a valid start bit is detected. This process is illustrated in Figure 8.5. Otherwise, the UART will restart the process. After detecting a valid start bit, the UART starts to shift in data bits.

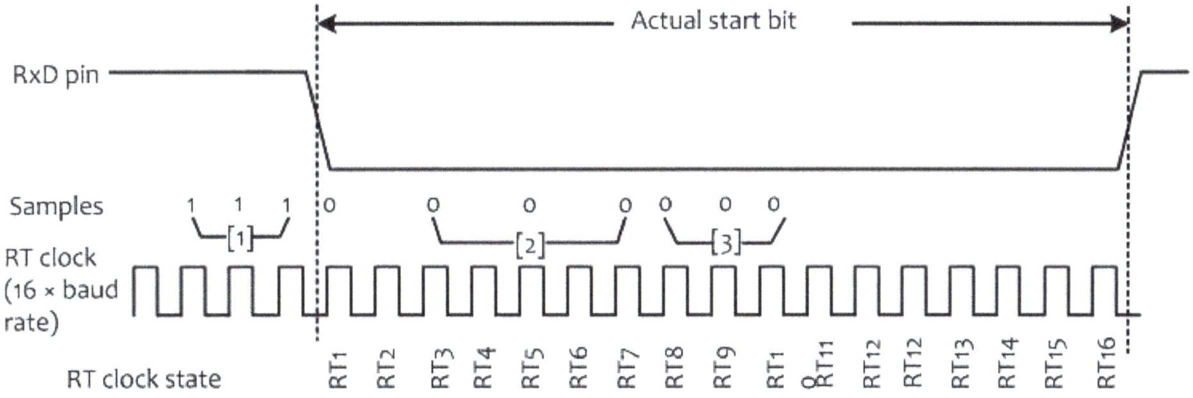

1. A 0 following three 1s.
2. Majority of samples 3, 5, and 7 are 0s.
3. Majority of samples 8, 9, and 10 are 0s

Figure 8.5 Detection of start bit (ideal case)

The method for determining the data bit value is also similar for most microcontrollers:

The UART uses a clock with a frequency which is 16 times (most often) that of the data rate to sample the RxD signal. If the majority of the seventh, eighth, and ninth samples are 1s, then the data bit is determined to be 1. Otherwise, the data bit is determined to be 0.

The stop bit is high. Using this format, it is possible to transfer data character by character without any gap.

The term *baud rate* is defined to be the number of bit changes per second. Since the RS-232 standard uses a *non-return-to-zero* (NRZ) encoding method, baud rate is identical to bit rate. In an NRZ code, a logic 1 bit is sent as a high voltage and a logic 0 bit is sent as a low voltage. When a logic 1 follows another logic 1 during a data transfer, the voltage does not drop to zero before it goes high.

8.3.6 UART DETECTABLE ERRORS

A UART can detect the following two types of communication errors:

- **Framing Error**: The situation that a character is not terminated by a stop bit is referred to as a framing error.
- **Receiver Overrun Error**: This error occurs when a new character arrives before the previously received character read by the CPU.

8.3.7 NULL MODEM CONNECTION

When two DTE devices are located side by side and use the TIA-232 interface to exchange data, there really is no reason to use two modems to connect them. However, the TIA-232 standard does not allow the direct connection of two DTEs. To make this scheme work, a *null modem* is needed. The null modem interconnects leads in such a way as to fool both DTEs into thinking that they are connected to modems. The null modem connection is shown in Table 8.1.

In Table 8.1, the signals of DTE1 and DTE2 that are to be wired together are listed in the same row. The transmitter-timing and receiver-timing signals are not needed in asynchronous data transmission. Ring indicator is not needed either, because the transmission is not through a public phone line.

Table 8.1 Null modem connection

Signal Name	DTE 1		DTE 2		Signal Name
	DB25 pin	DB9 pin	DB9 pin	DB25 pin	
FG (frame ground)	1	-	-	1	FG
TD (transmit data)	2	3	2	3	RD
RD (receive data)	3	2	3	2	TD
RTS (request to send)	4	7	8	5	CTS
CTS (clear to send)	5	8	7	4	RTS
SG (signal ground)	7	5	5	7	SG
DSR (data set ready)	6	6	4	20	DTR
CD (carrier detect)	8	1	4	20	DTR
DTR (data terminal ready)	20	4	1	8	CD
DTR (data terminal ready)	20	4	6	6	DSR

8.3.8 CONNECTING UART TO THE RS-232 INTERFACE

The RS-232 interface can be used for two MCUs or between one MCU and a PC to exchange data. This method has been widely used in university laboratories for communicating a microcontroller demo board with a PC. Because the UART modules of any microcontroller use a positive voltage (2.0~5.5 V) and 0 V to represent logic 1 and 0, respectively, they cannot be connected directly to the RS-232 interface. A voltage translation circuit, which is called the RS-232 transceiver, is needed to translate the voltage levels of the UART signals (RxD and TxD) to and from those of the corresponding RS-232 signals.

The RS-232 transceivers are available from vendors including MAXIM, SIPEX, National Semiconductor, Philips, STMicroelectronics, Intersil, etc.). These companies produce TIA-232 transceiver chips that can operate with a single voltage supply over a range from 3.0 to 5.5 V.

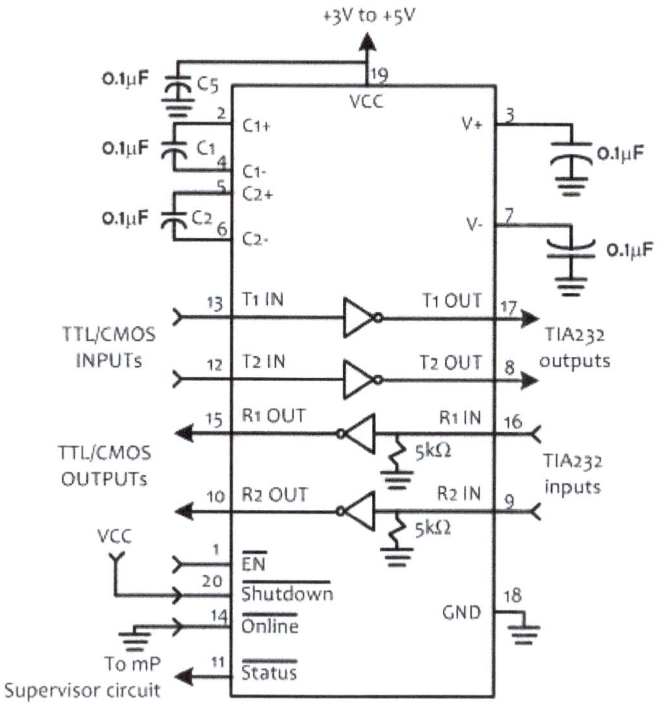

Figure 8.6 SP3223E Typical operating circuit

The SP3223E series from Sipex is discussed in this section. The pin assignment and the use of each pin are illustrated in Figure 8.6. Adding a TIA-232 transceiver chip will allow an MCU to use the UART module to communicate with the TIA-232 interface circuit. The circuit shown in Figure 8.7 is used in many MCU demo boards. A null-modem connection is followed to allow the use of a straight-through cable to communicate with a PC.

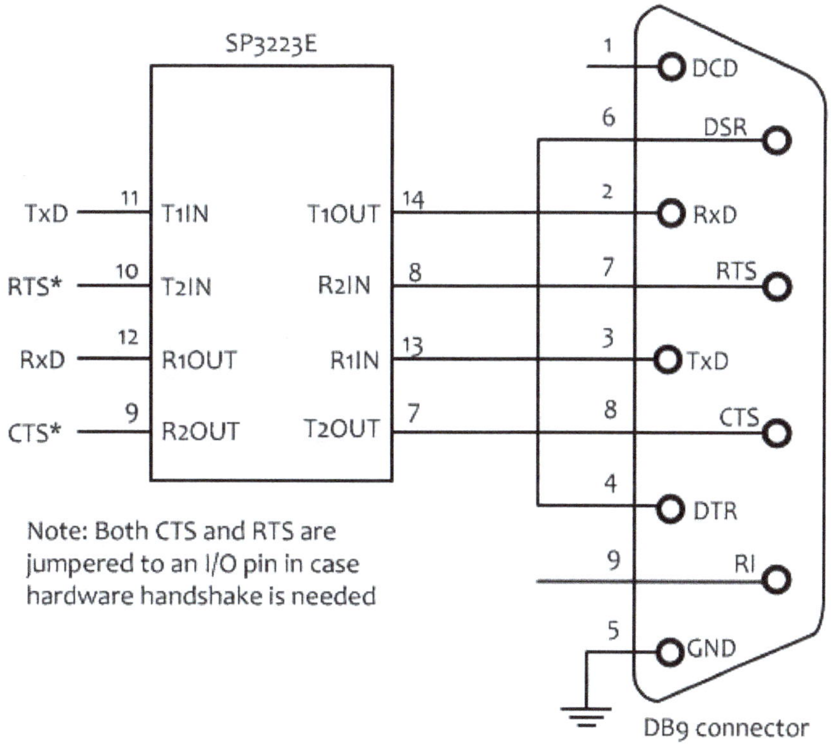

Figure 8.7 Diagram of UART and TIA232 DB9 connector wiring in a demo board

COM PORT

Before 2005, most PCs still included one or two COM ports with which the user can use the RS-232 interface to connect to peripheral devices. During this period, the microcontroller demo boards would include a 9-pin RS-232 connector to allow the application program on the demo board to utilize the PC monitor and keyboard to perform input and output during the software debugging phase. A serial cable connects the COM port on the demo board and that on the PC.

After 2005, fewer and fewer PCs provided COM ports. PC vendors preferred using USB ports to replace COM ports because USB ports are much faster and not as bulky as the COM ports. But computer engineers still need them. Several companies provided a simple solution to this issue. This solution consists of a conversion module and the appropriate wires and connectors. The conversion module consists of the circuit that interfaces with the UART signals and the circuit that implements the USB protocol and is usually implemented on an IC chip. The module uses wires or connector to connect to the serial port of the demo board and the USB connector to connect to a PC. An example of a USB-to-serial converter is shown in Figures 8.8a and 8.8b. To use this solution, the microcontroller demo board must have an RS-232 9-pin connector. A driver program must be installed on the PC. After the driver is installed, a new USB-to-Serial COM Port device will appear on the Ports of the PC (an example is shown in Figure 8.9).

The FT232R is an example of USB to serial UART interface IC from FTDI Inc. This chip has been used to implement the virtual COM port by many users.

Figure 8.8a USB-to-Serial cable (conversion module invisible)

Figure 8.8b USB-to-Serial cable with conversion module visible

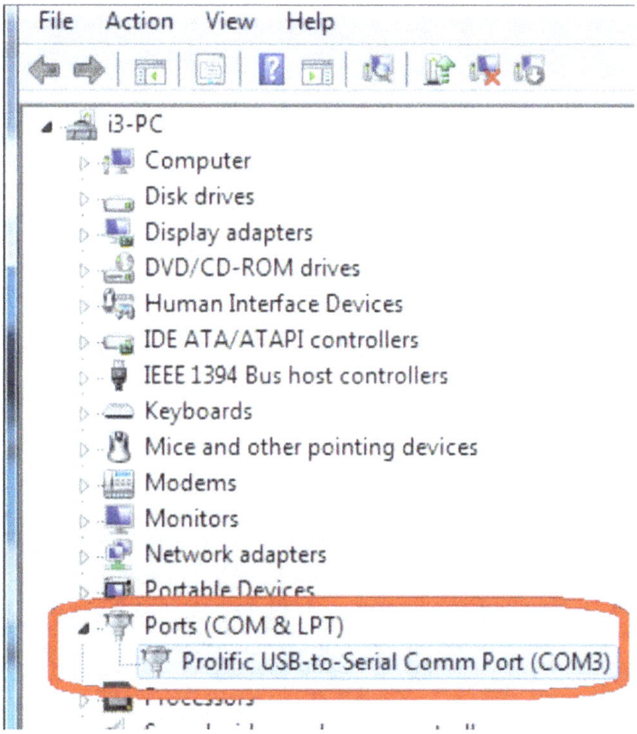

Figure 8.9 Adding a serial port to the PC

To allow the microcontroller demo board to display information using the PC monitor, the user is required to run a terminal emulation program on the PC, for example, Tera Term, PuTTY, SecureCRT, AlphaCom, TtyEmulator, etc. To start a terminal emulation program such as Tera Term, click on its icon. The startup screen is similar to that in Figure 8.10. Select **Serial** (instead of **TCP/IP**) by clicking on the circle to the left of the word **Serial** and click **OK**. The screen is changed (shown in Figure 8.11) to allow for setting the communication parameters such as baud rate, parity, number of stop bits, flow control, and so on. To set the communication parameters, select the menu **Setup→serial port...** as shown in Figure 8.12. An example of parameter setting is shown in Figure 8.13. You need to connect the demo board to the PC when performing this configuration, otherwise, the **Serial** option won't be available.

Once the user starts the terminal emulator software on the PC and sets the baud rate, parity, number of stops, flow control, etc. on the terminal emulator, the application running on the demo board can start to transmit data to and from the UART port. The parameters on the UART module of the demo board must be set to be identical to those of the terminal emulator running on the PC.

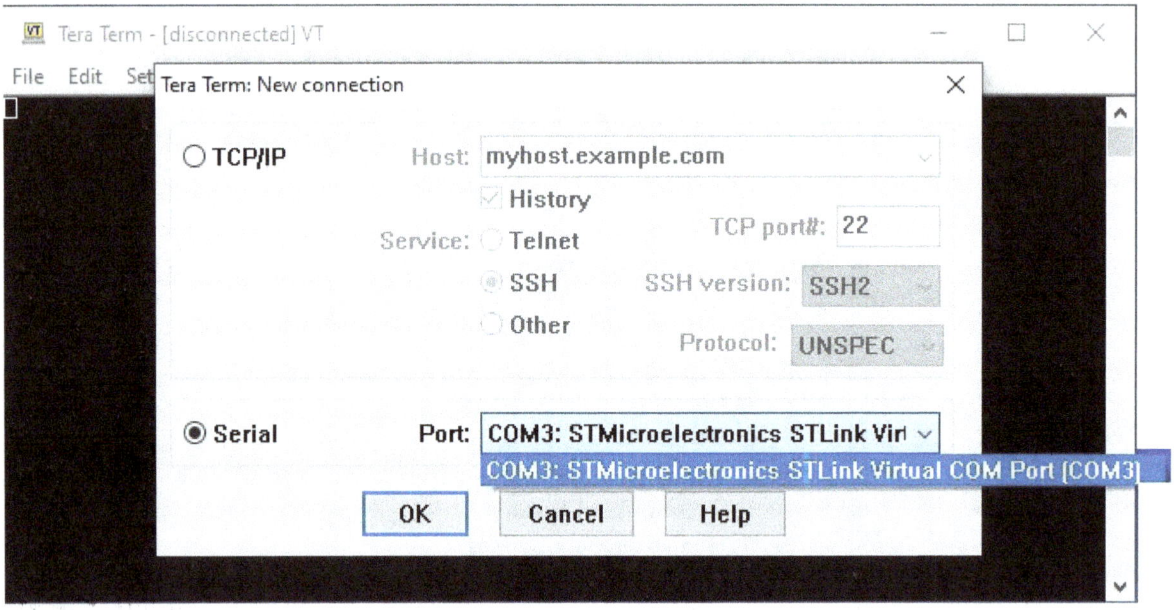

Figure 8.10 Start screen of Tera Term (a terminal emulator)

Figure 8.11 Tera Term terminal emulation screen

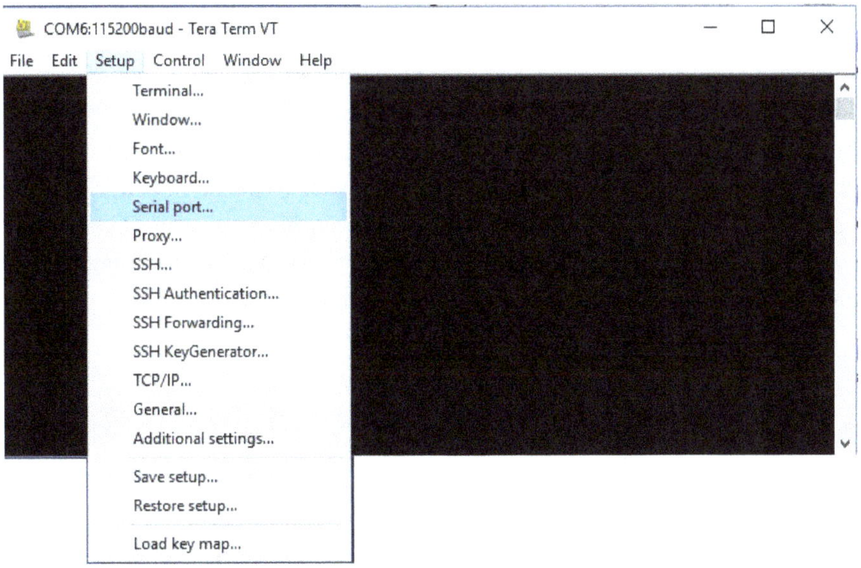

Figure 8.12 Menu for setting up communication parameters

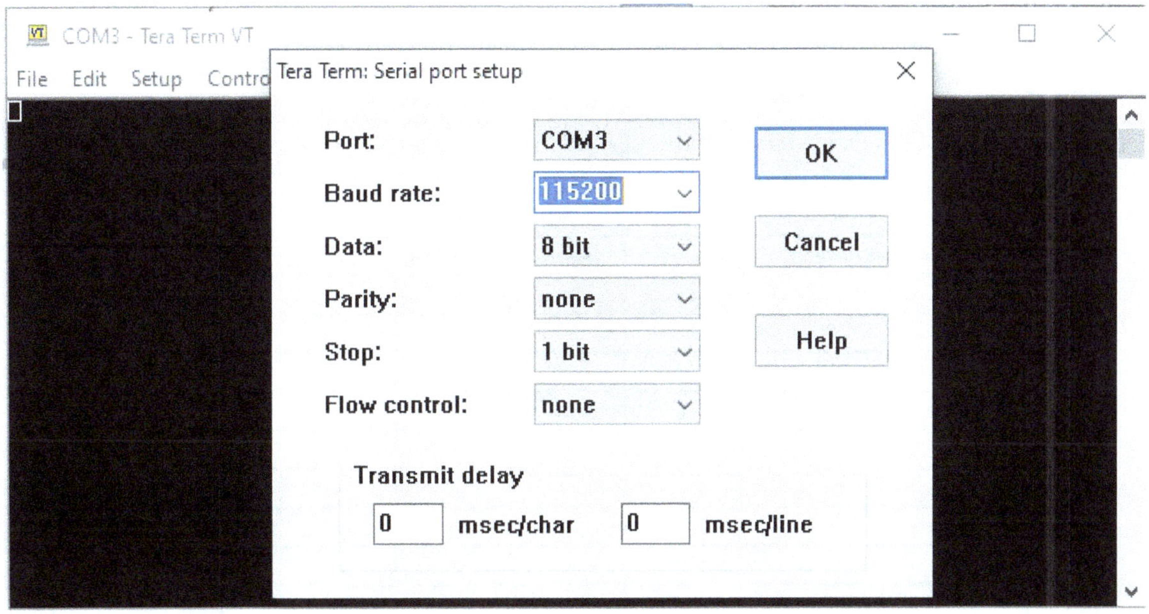

Example 8.13 An example of Tera Term parameter setting

The use of USB-to-serial converter does not reduce the number of connectors required for the demo board. There are at least three connectors being used on the demo board when the user is carrying out program debugging activities:

1. The first connector is used to connect the debug adaptor to the PC and the demo board.
2. The second connector is used by the MCU on the demo board to carry out data communications between the USART and the PC (utilizing the PC monitor and keyboard).
3. The third connector is used for supplying power to the demo board.

Reducing the number of connectors on the demo board is of great interest to the MCU vendors who also provide MCU demo boards to their users. The USB cable itself carries a 5-V power with maximum current limited at 0.5 A. This voltage can be used to power the demo board. In the last few years, more and more MCU vendors integrate the debug adapter on the demo board. When doing this, they also include the USB-to-serial converter circuit on the demo board. Nowadays, many MCU demo boards use a single USB connector to connect to the PC. This USB cable enables the user to perform program downloading, debugging, UART (terminal) I/O with the PC, and obtain power supply from the PC. To realize this, the MCU demo board is required to have a circuit that converts the USB signals to the corresponding UART signals, debug signals, and the power supply signal required by the demo board.

8.4 Introduction to the STM32L475 USART Modules

The STM32L475 implements three USARTs, two UARTs, and one low-power UART (LPUART). These modules support asynchronous and synchronous communications. In asynchronous mode, the USART or UART module also supports multiprocessor communication, local interconnect network (LIN), Infrared communications, smartcard application, and ModBus communications. The supported synchronous communication is like the SPI discussed in Chapter 7 and hence won't be discussed in this chapter. The LIN protocol, ModBus communication, and the smartcard applications are beyond the scope of this Chapter and won't be discussed in this chapter either.

The features of these USARTs, UARTs, and the LPUART are summarized in Table 8.2.

Table 8.2 STM32L4x5 USART/UART/LPUART features

USART modes/features	USART1	USART2	USART3	UART4	UART5	LPUART1
Hardware flow control for modem	X	X	X	X	X	X
Continuous communication using DMA	X	X	X	X	X	X
Multiprocessor communication	X	X	X	X	X	X
Synchronous mode	X	X	X	-	-	-
Smartcard mode	X	X	X	-	-	-
Single-wire half-duplex communication	X	X	X	X	X	X
IrDA SIR ENDEC block	X	X	X	X	X	-
LIN mode	X	X	X	X	X	-
Dual clock domain and wakeup from stop mode	X	X	X	X	X	X
Receiver timeout interrupt	X	X	X	X	X	-
Modbus communication	X	X	X	X	X	-
Auto baud rate detection	X (4 modes)					-
Driver Enable	X	X	X	X	X	X
LPUART/USART data length	7^(1), 8 and 9 bits					

Note. 1. In 7-bit data length mode, Smartcard mode, LIN master mode and auto baud rate (0x7F and 0x55 frames) detection are not supported.

The block diagram of a USART is shown in Figure 8.14. In Figure 8.14, the USART has five signals that need to be assigned to I/O pins:

- **TX**: *transmit data*. This pin carries the data bit to be transmitted.
- **RX**: *receive data*. This pin carries the input data bit.
- **RTS/DE**: *request to send / driver enable*. When used as the RTS signal, it indicates that USART is ready to send data. When used as the driver enable signal, it activates the transmission mode of the external transceiver (in RS485 control mode).
- **CTS**: *clear to send*. When asserted (low), CTS enables the USART to transmit data.
- **CK**: *clock output*. This pin outputs the transmit data clock for synchronous transmission corresponding to SPI master mode. In parallel, data can be received synchronously on RX pin. This can be used to control peripherals that have shift registers. Like in SPI, the clock phase and polarity are software programmable. In smartcard mode, the CK output can provide the clock to the smartcard.

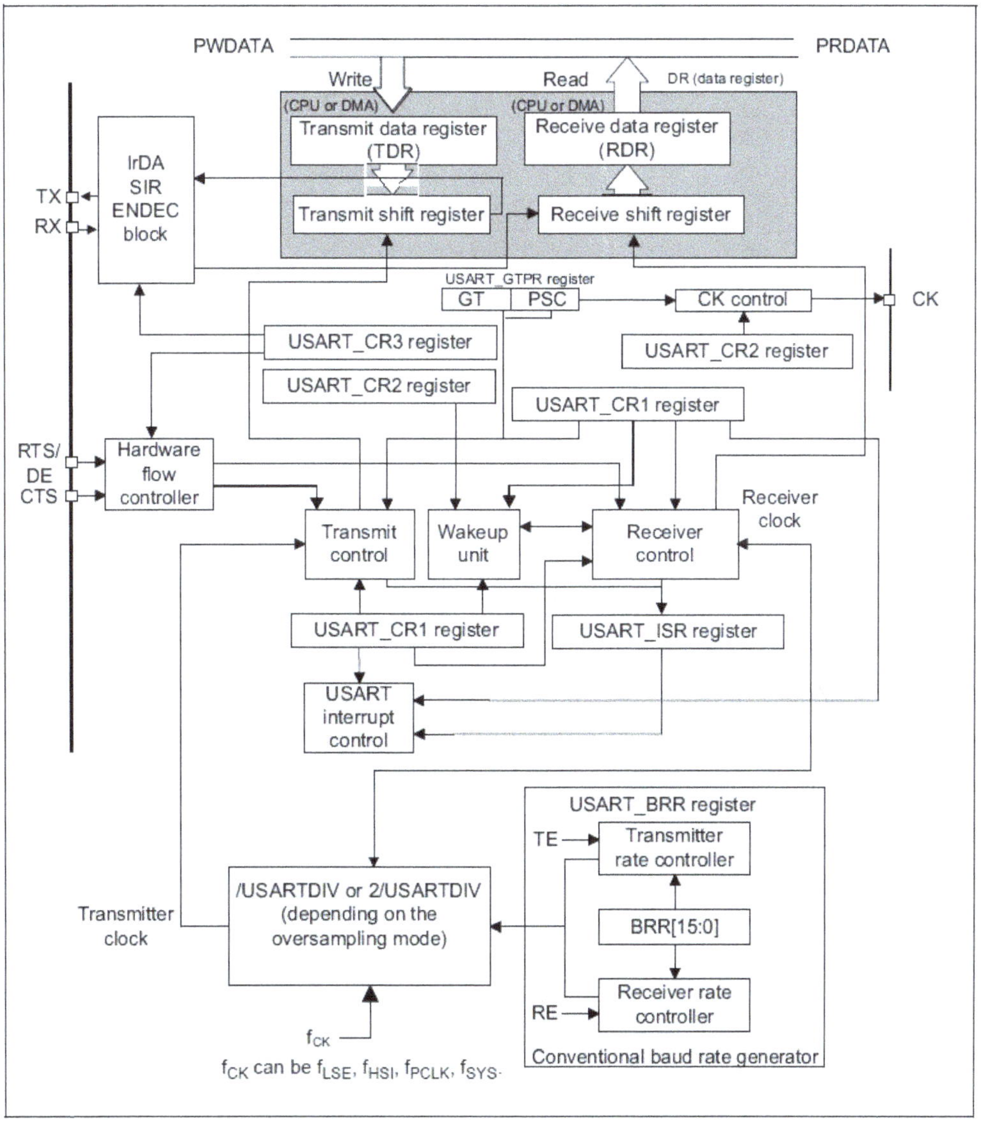

Figure 8.14 The USART block diagram

8.5 USART Operation

8.5.1 USART REGISTERS

Although USARTs, UARTs, and the LPUART modules do not support the same functions, they do have the same number of registers to support their operations. The Keil μVision IDE provides the following struct data type in the **stm32L475xx.h** header file to be used by the user:

```
typedef struct
{
    __IO      uint32_t     CR1;     // USART control register 1
    __IO      uint32_t     CR2;     // USART control register 2
    __IO      uint32_t     CR3;     // USART control register 3
    __IO      uint32_t     BRR;     // USART baud rate register
    __IO      uint16_t     GTPR;    // USART guard time and prescaler register
    uint16_t  RESERVED2;            // reserved 0x12—address offset
    __IO      uint32_t     RTOR;    // USART receive time out register
    __IO      uint16_t     RQR;     // USART request register
    uint16_t  RESERVED3;            // reserved, 0x1A
    __IO      uint32_t     ISR;     // USART interrupt and status register
    __IO      uint32_t     ICR;     // USART interrupt flag clear register
    __IO      uint16_t     RDR;     // USART receive data register
    uint16_t  RESERVED4;            // reserved 0x26
    __IO      uint16_t     TDR;     // USART transmit data register
    uint16_t  RESERVED5;            // reserved 0x2A
} USART_typeDef;
```

A pointer is declared to each of the USARTs, UART, and LPUART module (in **stm32L475xx.h**) so that the registers contained in these modules can be accessed. These pointers are

- USART1
- USART2
- USART3
- UART4
- UART5
- LPUART1

Although the names of the pointers to these modules are not uniform, we will use USARTx to refer to them to simplify the discussion. For example, we will use **USARTx->CR1** to refer to the control register 1 (CR1) of any one of these modules.

8.5.2 USART CHARACTER FRAME

The STM32L475 USART supports character length of 7, 8, or 9 bits. The 7-bit character cannot be used in Smartcard, LIN master mode, and autobaud rate detection.

An **Idle character** is represented by an entire frame of "1"s (including all the stop bits). A **Break character** is represented by "0"s of the whole frame period. At the end of the break frame, the transmitter inserts 2 stop bits. Examples of character frames (with 1 stop bit), Idle frame, and Break frame are shown in Figure 8.15. If parity is used, then the parity bit occupies the position of the most significant bit.

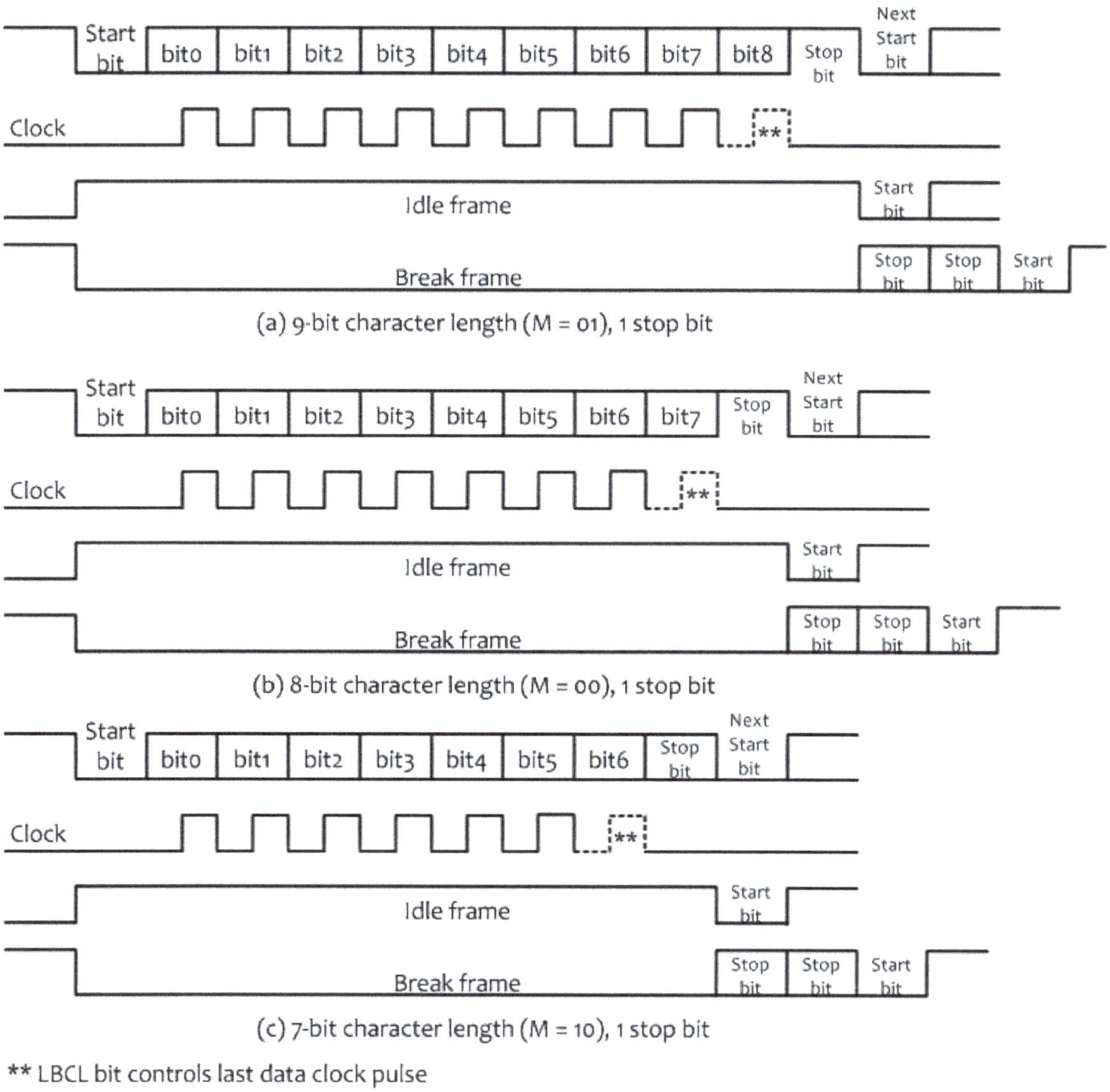

Figure 8.15 Character length programming

A character may be 7, 8, or 9 bits, which is selected by the M[1:0] field in the USARTx->CR1 register. By default, the start bit is low, and the stop bit is high. These values can be inverted. The number of stop bits is programmed via the STOP[1:0] field in the USARTx->CR2 register. The contents of registers USARTx->CR1 and USARTx->CR2 are shown in Figures 8.16 and 8.17, respectively.

In synchronous mode, the user has the option to select whether the clock pulse associated with the last data bit transmitted (MSB) is to be output on the CK pin (shown in Figure 8.15). This option is selected by the LBCL bit of the USARTx->CR2 register.

31	30	29	28	27	26	25	24
--	--	--	M1	EOBIE	RTOIE	DEAT[4:3]	

23	22	21	20	19	18	17	16
DEAT[2:0]			DEDT[4:0]				

15	14	13	12	11	10	9	8
OVER8	CMIE	MME	M0	WAKE	PCE	PS	PEIE

7	6	5	4	3	2	1	0
TXEIE	TCIE	RXNEIE	IDLEIE	TE	RE	UESM	UE

Reset value = 0x0000 0000
Offset = 0x00

M1M0: Word length
- 00: 1 start bit, 8 data bits, n stop bits — 01: 1 start bit, 9 data bits, n stop bits
- 10: 1 start bit, 7 data bits, n stop bits — 11: reserved

EOBIE: End of block interrupt enable (used by Smartcard mode)
- 0: Interrupt is inhibited — 1: interrupt enabled
- An USART interrupt is generated when the EOBF flag in the USARTx_ISR register is set.

RTOIE: Receiver timeout interrupt enable
- 0: Receiver timeout interrupt disabled — 1: Receiver timeout interrupt enabled

DEAT: Driver enable assertion time
- This field defines the time between the activation of the DE (driver enable) signal and the beginning of the start bit. It is expressed in sample time units (1/8 or 1/16 bit duration, depending on the oversampling rate. This field can only be written when USART is disabled.

DEDT: Driver enable de-assertion time
- This field defines the time between the end of the last stop bit, in a transmitted message, and the de-activation of the DE (driver enable) signal. It is expressed in sample time units (1/8 or 1/16 bit duration, depending on the oversampling rate). If the USARTx_TDR register is written during the DEDT time, the new data is transmitted only when the DEDT and DEAT times have been elapsed.

OVER8: Oversampling mode
- 0: Oversampling by 16 — 1: Oversampling by 8

CMIE: Character match interrupt enable
- 0: Interrupt is inhibited — 1: character match interrupt enabled

MME: Mute mode enable
- 0: Receiver in active mode permanently
- 1: Receiver can switch between mute and active mode.

WAKE: Receiver wake up method
- 0: Idle line — 1: Address mark

Figure 8.16 USART control register 1 (USARTx_CR1)

31	30	29	28	27	26	25	24
--	--	--	M1	EOBIE	RTOIE	DEAT[4:3]	
23	**22**	**21**	**20**	**19**	**18**	**17**	**16**
DEAT[2:0]			DEDT[4:0]				
15	**14**	**13**	**12**	**11**	**10**	**9**	**8**
OVER8	CMIE	MME	M0	WAKE	PCE	PS	PEIE
7	**6**	**5**	**4**	**3**	**2**	**1**	**0**
TXEIE	TCIE	RXNEIE	IDLEIE	TE	RE	UESM	UE

Reset value = 0x0000 0000
Offset = 0x00

PCE: Parity control enable
When parity is enabled, the parity bit is inserted at the most significant bit position.
0: Parity control disabled 1: Parity control enabled.

PS: Parity selection
0: Even parity 1: Odd parity

PEIE: PE interrupt enable
0: Parity error interrupt inhibited 1: Parity error interrupt enabled

TXEIE: Transmit data register empty interrupt enable
0: Interrupt disabled 1: interrupt enabled

TCIE: Transmit completion interrupt enable
0: Interrupt disabled 1: TC interrupt enabled

RXNEIE: RXNE interrupt enable
0: Interrupt disabled 1: RXNE interrupt enabled

IDLEIE: IDLE interrupt enable
0: Interrupt is disabled 1: IDLE interrupt enabled

TE: Transmitter enable
0: Transmitter is enabled 1: Transmitter is enabled

RE: Receiver enable
0: Receiver is disabled 1: Receiver is enabled and begins searching start bit

UESM: USART enable in Stop mode
0: USART not able to wake up the MCU from the Stop mode
1: USART able to wake up the MCU from the Stop mode as long as the USART clock source is either HSI16 or LSE.

UE: USART enable
0: USART disabled, low power mode 1: USART enabled

Figure 8.16a USART control register 1 (USARTx_CR1)—(continued)

31	30	29	28	27	26	25	24
ADD[7:4]				ADD[3:0]			
23	22	21	20	19	18	17	16
RTOEN	ABRMOD[1:0]		ABREN	MSBFIRST	DATAINV	TXINV	RXINV
15	14	13	12	11	10	9	8
SWAP	LINEN	STOP[1:0]		CLKEN	CPOL	CPHA	LBCL
7	6	5	4	3	2	1	0
--	LBDIE	LBDL	ADDM7	--	--	--	--

Reset value = 0x0000 0000
Offset = 0x04

ADD[7:0]: Address of the USART node
This field gives the address of the USART node or a character code to be recognized. This is used in multiprocessor communication during Mute mode or stop mode, for wakeup with address mark detection. The MSB of the character sent by the transmitter should be equal to 1. It may also be used for character detection during normal reception, mute mode inactive. In this case, the whole received character (8-bit) is compared to the ADD[7:0] and the CMF flag is set on match.

RTOEN: Receiver time out enable
0: Receiver timeout feature disabled   1: Receiver timeout feature enabled
When this feature is enabled, the RTOF flag in the USARTx_ISR register is set if the RX line is idle for the duration programmed in the RTOR register.

ABRMOD[1:0]: Auto baud rate mode
00: Measurement of the start bit is used to detect the baud rate
01: Falling edge to falling edge measurement.
10: 0x7F frame detection   11: 0x55 frame detection

ABREN: Auto baud rate enable
0: Auto baud rate detection is disabled
1: Auto baud rate detection is enabled

MSBFIRST: most significant bit first
0: Data is received/transmitted least significant bit first
1: Data is received/transmitted most significant bit first

DATAINV: Binary data inversion
0: Logical data from data register is transmitted/received in positive logic (1 = high)
1: Logical data from data register is transmitted/received in negative logic (0 = high)

TXINV: TX pin active level inversion
0: TX pin signal works using the standard logic levels (VDD = 1/idle, Gnd = 0/mark)
1: TX pin signal values are inverted. (VDD = 0/mark, Gnd = 1/idle)

Figure 8.17 USART control register 2 (USARTx_CR2)

31	30	29	28	27	26	25	24
ADD[7:4]				ADD[3:0]			

23	22	21	20	19	18	17	16
RTOEN	ABRMOD[1:0]		ABREN	MSBFIRST	DATAINV	TXINV	RXINV

15	14	13	12	11	10	9	8
SWAP	LINEN	STOP[1:0]		CLKEN	CPOL	CPHA	LBCL

7	6	5	4	3	2	1	0
--	LBDIE	LBDL	ADDM7	--	--	--	--

Reset value = 0x0000 0000
Offset = 0x04

RXINV: RX pin active level inversion (must be written when UE = 0)
0: RX pin signal works using the standard logic levels (VDD = 1/idle, Gnd= 0/mark)
1: RX pin signal values are inverted. (VDD=0/mark, Gnd=1/idle).
SWAP: Swap TX/RX pin (must be written when UE = 0)
0: TX/RX pins are used as defined in standard pinout.
1: The TX and RX pins functions are swapped.
LINEN: LIN mode enable (must be written when UE = 0)
0: LIN disabled 1: LIN mode enabled
STOP[1:0]: STOP bits (must be written when UE = 0)
00: 1 stop bits 01: 0.5 stop bits 10: 2 stop bits 11: 1.5 stop bits
CLKEN: Clock enable
0: CK pin disabled 1: CK pin enabled
CPOL: Clock polarity
0: CK pin idle low 1: CK pin idle high
CPHA: Clock phase
0: Data is shifted on the first clock edge
1: Data is shifted on the second clock edge
LBCL: Last bit clock pulse
0: The clock pulse of the last data bit is not output to the CK pin
1: The clock pulse of the last data bit is output to the CK pin
LBDIE: LIN break detection interrupt enable
0: Interrupt is inhibited
1: Interrupt is generated whenever the LBDF flag is set to 1
LBDL: LIN break detection length
0: 10-bit break detection 1: 11-bit break detection
ADDM7: 7-bit address detection/4-bit address detection
0: 4-bit address detection 1: 7-bit address detection (in 8-bit data mode)

Figure 8.17a USART control register 2 (USARTx_CR2)—(continued)

8.5.3 USART TRANSMITTER

In Figure 8.14, the processor writes the data to be transmitted into the **TDR register** via the PWDATA bus. The data in the TDR register are then transferred to the **transmit shift register**. The circuit around the transmit shift register adds a start bit, and an appropriate number of stop bits (0.5 to 2) to the data character and shifts it out via the TX pin. The frequency of the transmit clock is the baud rate.

The number of stop bits can be 0.5, 1, 1.5, and 2. Among them, the 0.5 and 1.5 stop bits are used only in Smartcard mode.

To transmit data, both the USART module and the transmitter must be enabled. The transmitter is enabled by setting the TE bit in the USARTx->CR1 register to 1 whereas the USARTx module is enabled by setting the UE bit in the same register to 1.

The user can request to send a break character by setting the SBKRQ bit in the USARTx->RQR register. To free the CPU from the chore of copying data to be transmitted, the user can enable transmit DMA transfer by setting the DMAT bit in the USARTx->CR3 register to 1. A transmit DMA request is triggered by the TXE event (i.e., when the TXE flag is set to 1). The contents of the USARTx->CR3 and USARTx->RQR registers are shown in Figures 8.18 and 8.19, respectively.

31	30	29	28	27	26	25	24
--	--	--	--	--	--	--	--
23	**22**	**21**	**20**	**19**	**18**	**17**	**16**
--	WUFIE	WUS		SCARCNT[2:0]			
15	**14**	**13**	**12**	**11**	**10**	**9**	**8**
DEP	DEM	DDRE	OVRDIS	ONEBIT	CTSIE	CTSE	RTSE
7	**6**	**5**	**4**	**3**	**2**	**1**	**0**
DMAT	DMAR	SCEN	NACK	HDSEL	IRLP	IREN	EIE

Reset value = 0x0000 0000
Offset = 0x08

WUFIE: Wakeup from stop mode interrupt enable
- 0: Interrupt is disabled
- 1: An USART interrupt is generated when the WUF flag in the USARTx_ISR register is set to 1

WUS[1:0]: Wakeup from stop mode interrupt flag selection
- 00: WUF active on address match (as defined by ADDR[7:0] and ADDM7)
- 01: Reserved
- 10: WUF active on start bit detection 11: WUF active on RXNE
- If USART does not support wakeup from stop feature, this field will be forced to 0.

SCACNT[2:0] Smartcard auto-retry count
- This bit-field specifies the number of retries in transmit and receive, in Smartcard mode. In transmission mode, it specifies the number of automatic retransmission retries, before generating a transmission error (FE bit set). In reception mode, it specifies the number of erroneous reception trials, before generating a reception error (RXNE & PE bits set)

DEP: Driver enable polarity selection
- 0: DE signal is active high 1: DE signal is active low

DEM: Driver enable mode
- 0: DE function is disabled 1: DE function is enabled

DDRE: DMA disable on reception error
- 0: DMA is not disabled in case of reception error. The corresponding error flag is set but RXNE flag is kept 0 preventing receiver from overrun.
- 1: DMA is disabled following a reception error. The corresponding error flag is set, as well as RXNE. The DMA request is masked until the error flag is cleared. The software must first disable the DMA request (DMAR=0) or clear RXNE before clearing the error flag.

Figure 8.18 USART control register 3 (USARTx->CR3)

31	30	29	28	27	26	25	24	
--	--	--	--	--	--	--	--	Reset value = 0x0000 0000
23	**22**	**21**	**20**	**19**	**18**	**17**	**16**	Offset = 0x08
--	WUFIE	WUS		SCARCNT[2:0]				
15	**14**	**13**	**12**	**11**	**10**	**9**	**8**	
DEP	DEM	DDRE	OVRDIS	ONEBIT	CTSIE	CTSE	RTSE	
7	**6**	**5**	**4**	**3**	**2**	**1**	**0**	
DMAT	DMAR	SCEN	NACK	HDSEL	IRLP	IREN	EIE	

OVRDIS: Overrun disable

0: Overrun error flag, ORE, is set when received data is not read before receiving new data.

1: Overrun functionality is disabled. If new data is received while the RXNE flag is set, the ORE flag is not set and the new received data overwrites the previous content of the USARTx_RDR register.

ONEBIT: One sample bit method enable

0: Three sample bits are taken to detect the arrival of the start bit & determine the logic value of a data bit.

1: One sample bit method is used

CTSIE: CTS interrupt enable

0: Interrupt is inhibited

1: An interrupt is generated whenever the CTSIF flag in the USARTx_ISR register is set to 1.

CTSE: CTS enable

0: CTS hardware flow control is disabled

1: CTS mode enabled, data is transmitted only when CTS input is asserted (tied to 0). If the CTS input is de-asserted, while data is being transmitted, then the transmission is completed before stopping. If data is written into the data register while CTS is de-asserted, the transmission is postponed until CTS is asserted.

RTSE: RTS enable

0: RTS hardware flow control disabled.

1: RTS interrupt enabled, data is only requested when there is space in receive buffer. The transmission of data is expected to cease after the current character has been transmitted. The RTS output is asserted (low) when a data can be received.

DMAT: DMA enable transmitter.

0: DMA is disabled for transmission. 1: DMA is enabled for transmission.

Figure 8.18a USART control register 3 (USARTx->CR3)—(continued)

31	30	29	28	27	26	25	24
--	--	--	--	--	--	--	--
23	**22**	**21**	**20**	**19**	**18**	**17**	**16**
--	WUFIE	WUS		SCARCNT[2:0]			
15	**14**	**13**	**12**	**11**	**10**	**9**	**8**
DEP	DEM	DDRE	OVRDIS	ONEBIT	CTSIE	CTSE	RTSE
7	**6**	**5**	**4**	**3**	**2**	**1**	**0**
DMAT	DMAR	SCEN	NACK	HDSEL	IRLP	IREN	EIE

Reset value = 0x0000 0000
Offset = 0x08

DMAR: DMA enable receiver
0: DMA is disabled for reception. 1: DMA is enabled for reception.
SCEN: Smartcard mode enable (not available in UART4 & UART5)
0: Smartcard mode disabled 1: Smartcard mode enabled.
NACK: Smartcard NACK enable (not available in UART4 & UART5)
0: NACK transmission in case of parity error is disabled
1: NACK transmission in case of parity error is enabled
HDSEL: Half-duplex selection
0: Half duplex mode is not selected 1: Half duplex mode is selected.
IRLP: IrDA low-power
0: Normal IrDA mode 1: Low-power IrDA mode
IREN: IrDA mode enable
0: IrDA disabled 1: IrDA enabled
EIE: Error interrupt enable (any of FE, ORE, NF bit set to 1)
0: Error interrupt disabled
1: An interrupt is generated whenever DMAR = 1 in USARTx->CR3 and FE=1 or ORE=1 or NF=1 in the USARTx->ISR register.

Figure 8.18b USART control register 3 (USARTx->CR3)—(continued)

31	30	29	28	27	26	25	24
--	--	--	--	--	--	--	--
23	**22**	**21**	**20**	**19**	**18**	**17**	**16**
--	--	--	--	--	--	--	--
15	**14**	**13**	**12**	**11**	**10**	**9**	**8**
--	--	--	--	--	--	--	--
7	**6**	**5**	**4**	**3**	**2**	**1**	**0**
--	--	--	TXFRQ	RXFRQ	MMRQ	SBKRQ	ABRRQ

Reset value = 0x0000 0000
Offset = 0x18

TXFRQ: Transmit data flush request
Writing this bit sets the TXE flag. This allows to discard the transmit data. This bit must be used only in Smartcard mode, when data has not been sent due to errors (NACK) and the FE flag is active in the USARTx->ISR register.
RXFRQ: Receive data flush request
Writing 1 to this bit clears the RXNE flag. This allows to discard the received data without reading it, and avoid an overrun condition.
MMRQ: Mute mode request
Writing 1 to this bit puts the USART in mute mode and sets the RWU flag.
SBKRQ: Send break request
Writing 1 to this bit sets the SBKF flag and request to send a BREAK on the line, as soon as transmit machine is available.
ABRRQ: Auto baud rate request
Writing 1 to this bit resets the ABRF flag in the USARTx->ISR register and request an automatic baud rate measurement on the next received data frame.

Figure 8.19 USART request register (USARTx->RQR)

Before writing data into the USARTx->TDR register, the user is required to make sure that the transmit data register empty bit (TXE) in the USARTx->ISR register is 1. The TXE flag may generate an interrupt request if it is enabled. The flags in the USARTx->ISR register can be cleared by writing 1 to the corresponding bit in the USARTx->ICR register. The contents of the USARTx->ISR and USARTx->ICR registers are shown in Figures 8.20 and 8.21, respectively.

31	30	29	28	27	26	25	24
–	–	–	–	–	–	–	–
23	**22**	**21**	**20**	**19**	**18**	**17**	**16**
–	REACK	TEACK	WUF	RWU	SBKF	CMF	BUSY
15	**14**	**13**	**12**	**11**	**10**	**9**	**8**
ABRF	ABRE	–	EOBF	RTOF	CTS	CTSIF	LBDF
7	**6**	**5**	**4**	**3**	**2**	**1**	**0**
TXE	TC	RXNE	IDLE	ORE	NF	FE	PE

Reset value = 0x0200 00C0
Offset = 0x1C

All of these flags can be cleared by writing a 1 to the corresponding bit in the USARTx_ICR register.

REACK: Receive enable acknowledge flag
  0: receiver has not been enabled 1: receiver has been enabled
  This bit can be used to verify that USART is ready for reception before entering stop mode.

TEACK: Transmit enable acknowledge flag
  0: Transmitted has not been enabled 1: Transmitter has been enabled

WUF: Wakeup from Stop mode flag
  0: No wakeup event has been detected.
  1: A wakeup event has been detected since last time this flag was cleared.

RWU: Receiver wakeup from mute mode
  0: Receiver is in active mode 1: Receiver is in mute mode

SBKF: Send break flag
  This bit indicates that a send break character was requested.
  0: No break character is transmitted. 1: Break character will be transmitted.

CMF: character match flag
  0: No character match has occurred. 1: A character match has occurred.

BUSY: Busy flag
  0: USART is idle 1: Reception is on going.

ABRF: Auto baud rate flag
  This bit is set when the automatic baud rate has been set (RXNE will also be set) or when the auto baud rate operation was completed without success (ABRE, RXNE, and FE are set).

ABRE: Auto baud rate error
  This bit is set if the baud rate measurement failed (baud rate out of range or character comparison failed). This bit is cleared by software.

EOBF: End of block
  0: End of block not reached 1: End of block (number of characters) reached

RTOF: Receiver timeout (used in Smartcard mode)
  0: Timeout value not reached 1: timeout value reached without any data reception

Figure 8.20 Interrupt and status register (USARTx_ISR)

31	30	29	28	27	26	25	24
--	--	--	--	--	--	--	--
23	22	21	20	19	18	17	16
--	REACK	TEACK	WUF	RWU	SBKF	CMF	BUSY
15	14	13	12	11	10	9	8
ABRF	ABRE	--	EOBF	RTOF	CTS	CTSIF	LBDF
7	6	5	4	3	2	1	0
TXE	TC	RXNE	IDLE	ORE	NF	FE	PE

Reset value = 0x0200 00C0
Offset = 0x1C

All of the flags can be cleared by writing a 1 to the corresponding bit in the USARTx_ICR register.

CTS: CTS flag
0: CTS line set 1: CTS line reset

CTSIF: CTS interrupt flag—if the CTSE bit is set, this bit is set when the CTS input toggles.
0: No change occurred on the CTS line 1: A change occurred on the CTS line

LBDF: LIN break detection flag
0: LIN break not detected 1: LIN break detected

TXE: transmit data register empty
0: transmit data register not empty 1: transmit data register is empty

TC: transmission complete
0: transmission is not complete (at least, the transmit shift register is not empty)
1: both the transmit data register and the transmit shift register are empty.

RXNE: Receive data register is not empty
0: Receive data register is empty (No data has been received)
1: Received data is ready to be read.

IDLE: Idle line detected
0: No idle line is detected 1: Idle line is detected

ORE: Overrun error
0: No overrun error 1: Overrun error is detected.

NF: Start bit noise detection flag
0: No noise is detected 1: Noise is detected

FE: framing error
0: No framing error is detected 1: Framing error or break character is detected

PE: Parity error
0: No parity error 1: Parity error has occurred.

Figure 8.20a Interrupt and status register (USARTx->ISR)—(continued)

31	30	29	28	27	26	25	24
--	--	--	--	--	--	--	--
23	**22**	**21**	**20**	**19**	**18**	**17**	**16**
--	--	--	WUCF	--	--	CMCF	--
15	**14**	**13**	**12**	**11**	**10**	**9**	**8**
--	--	--	EOBCF	RTOCF	--	CTSCF	LBDCF
7	**6**	**5**	**4**	**3**	**2**	**1**	**0**
--	TCCF	--	IDLECF	ORECF	NCF	FECF	PECF

Reset value = 0x0000 0000
Offset = 0x20

WUCF: Wakeup from stop mode clear flag
Writing 1 to this bit clears the WUF flag in the USARTx->ISR register.
CMCF: Character match clear flag
Writing 1 to this bit clears the CMF flag in the USARTx->ISR register.
EOBCF: End of block clear flag
Writing 1 to this bit clears the EOB flag in the USARTx->ISR register.
RTOCF: Receiver time-out clear flag
Writing 1 to this bit clears the RTOF flag in the USARTx->ISR register.
CTSCF: CTS clear flag
Writing 1 to this bit clears the CTSIF flag in the USARTx->ISR register.
LBDCF: LIN break detection clear flag
Writing 1 to this bit clears the LBDF flag in the USARTx->ISR register.
TCCF: Transmission complete clear flag
Writing 1 to this bit clears the TC flag in the USARTx->ISR register.
IDLECF: Idle line detected clear flag
Writing 1 to this bit clears the IDLE flag in the USARTx->ISR register.
ORECF: Overrun error clear flag
Writing 1 to this bit clears the ORE flag in the USARTx->ISR register.
NCF: Noise detected clear flag
Writing 1 to this bit clears the NF flag in the USARTx->ISR register.
FECF: Framing error clear flag
Writing 1 to this bit clears the FE flag in the USARTx->ISR register.
PECF: Parity error clear flag
Writing 1 to this bit clears the PE flag in the USARTx->ISR register.

Figure 8.21 Interrupt flag clear register (USARTx->ICR)

8.5.4 USART RECEIVER

Before receiving data, both the USART and the receiver must be enabled. The receiver is enabled by setting the RE bit in the USARTx->CR1 register.

Once enabled, the receiver uses either 16 or 8 times the baud rate to sample the incoming data from the RX pin. Once the start bit is detected, the receiver shifts in the programmed number of data bits and verifies the stop and/or the parity bit. Parity checking is optional. Disregarding the error condition, the data character in the receive shift register will be transferred to the receive data register (USARTx->RDR) and the **receive data register not empty bit** (**RXNE**) in the USARTx->ISR register will be set to 1.

Errors can occur during the reception process. Reception errors are recorded in the USARTx->ISR register. The possible errors are

1. **Framing error**—represented by the FE flag. This error is detected by the missing stop bit.

2. **Parity error**—represented by the PE flag. This error is detected by the incorrectly received parity bit.
3. **Noise error**—represented by the NF flag. In Figure 8.5, this error occurs when the three samples are not identical.
4. **Receiver overrun**—represented by the ORE flag. This error occurs when a character is received while the RXNE bit is 1. Data won't be transferred from the shift register to the RDR register until the RXNE bit is 0. When an overrun occurs, the RDR contents will not be lost but the shift register will be overwritten. After this point, any data received during overrun is lost.

Reception error flags can be cleared by setting the corresponding clear request bit in the USARTx->ICR register to 1.

In Figure 8.5, three samples are taken and the majority function of these three samples is used to determine the arrival of the start bit and the logic value of any data bit. However, the STM32L475 also allows the user to use one sample to detect the arrival of a start bit and determine the logic value of a data bit. To use this option, set the ONEBIT bit in the USARTx->CR3 register to 1.

DMA transfer is also supported in USART reception. The reception DMA is enabled by setting the DMAR bit in the USARTx->CR3 register to 1. A reception DMA request is triggered by the RXNE event (i.e., when this bit is set to 1).

8.5.5 USART BAUD RATE GENERATION

Although the transmitter and receiver do not use a common clock signal to synchronize data transfer in asynchronous mode, they do need a clock signal to shift out and shift in data. The transmitter and the receiver need to use the same clock frequency during the transmission and reception process. Because the USART module uses the NRZ (nonreturn to zero) method to encode data, the data baud rate is the same as the clock frequency.

The MCU writes a value into the 16-bit register USARTx->BRR to set the baud rate (or frequency) of the USART module. Let **USARTDIV** be the value to divide the USART incoming clock frequency f_{CK}. The baud rate to be generated can be derived in the following manner:

For standard USART mode (including SPI mode), there are two cases:

Case 1: Oversampling by 16 (reception)

$$\text{Tx/Rx Baud} = f_{CK} \div \text{USARTDIV}$$

Case 2: Oversampling by 8 (reception)

$$\text{Tx/Rx Baud} = (2 \times f_{CK}) \div \text{USARTDIV}$$

For Smartcard, LIN, and IrDA modes (oversampling by 16)

$$\text{Tx/Rx Baud} = f_{CK} \div \text{USARTDIV}$$

When oversampling by 16 is used, the value to be written into the USARTx->BRR register is USARTDIV.

When oversampling by 8 is used,

- The lowest three bits of the value to be written into the USARTx->BRR register is the same as the lowest 4 bits of USARTDIV, that is, USARTDIV[3:0] shifted to the right one place.
- The bit 3 of the USARTx->BRR register must be forced to 0.
- The upper 12 bits of the USARTx->BRR register (BRR[15:4]) are the same as USARTDIV[15:4].

Example 8.1 If we want to set the USART1 baud rate to 115,200 for transmission and reception using oversampling by 16 method and oversampling by 8 method, what value should be written into the USARTx->BRR register, respectively, if f_{CK} = 80 MHz?

Solution:

1. Oversampling by 16
   USARTDIV = 80,000,000 / 115,200 = 694.44 ≈ 694 = 0x2B6
   BRR = USARTDIV = 0x2B6
2. Oversampling by 8
   USARTDIV = 2 * 80,000,000 / 115,200 = 1,388.888 ≈ 1,389 = 0x56D
   BRR[3:0] = 0xD >> 1 = 0x6
   BRR = 0x566

Error Calculation Programming Baud Rates

Because the USART clock frequency (f_{CK}) may not be divisible by the desired baud rate, the resultant baud rate obtained from the previous method may not be equal to the desired baud rate. A few examples of the desired baud rates and the actual resultant baud rates for f_{CK} = 80 MHz are given in Table 8.3.

Table 8.3 Error calculation for programming baud rates at f_{CK} = 80 MHz

Baud rate		Oversampling by 16 (OVER8 = 0)			Oversampling by 8 (OVER8 = 1)		
S. No	Desired	Actual	BRR	% Error = (calculated - Desired)B. rate / Desired B. Rate)	Actual	BRR	% Error
1	2.4 Kbps	2.4 Kbps	0x8235	0	2.4 Kbps	0x10465	0
2	9.6 Kbps	9.6 Kbps	0x208D	0	9.6 Kbps	0x4115	0
3	19.2 Kbps	19.198 Kbps	0x1047	0.01	19.201 Kbps	0x2086	0
4	38.4 Kbps	38.406 Kbps	0x823	0.0160	38.397 Kbps	0x1043	0
5	57.6 Kbps	57.595 Kbps	0x56D	0.0087	57.595 Kbps	0xAD5	0
6	115.2 Kbps	115.274 Kbps	0x2B6	0.0064	115.190 Kbps	0x566	0.009
7	230.4 Kbps	230.548 Kbps	0x15B	0.0064	230.548 Kbps	0x2B3	0.06
8	460.8 Kbps	459770 Kbps	0xAE	0.22	461.095 Kbps	0x155	0.064
9	921.6 Kbps	919540 Kbps	0x57	0.224	919.540 Kbps	0xA7	0.22
10	2 Mbps	2 Mbps	0x28	0	2 Mbps	0x50	0

Tolerance of USART Receiver to Clock Deviation

In asynchronous mode, both the transmitter and receiver are required to use the same baud rate to perform data communications. Due to several reasons, the actual clock frequencies of the transmitter's clock and the receiver's clock may deviate from the expected frequency. As long as the deviation of the actual clock frequency from the desired frequency is within the tolerance of the receiver, data communication can be correctly carried out.

The causes which contribute to the total deviation include:

- DTRA: Deviation due to the transmitter error (which also includes the deviation of the transmitter's local oscillator)
- DQUANT: Error due to the baud rate quantization of the receiver
- DREC: Deviation of the receiver's local oscillator
- DTCL: Deviation due to the transmission line
- DWU: Error due to sampling point deviation when the wakeup from Stop mode is used.

The tolerance of the USART receiver to clock deviation as a function of the character length and BRR[3:0] value is given in Tables 8.4 and 8.5.

Table 8.4 Tolerance of the USART receiver when BRR[3:0] = 0000

M bits (character length setting)	OVER8 bit = 0		OVER8 bit = 1	
	ONEBIT = 0	ONEBIT = 1	ONEBIT = 0	ONEBIT = 1
00	3.75%	4.375%	2.50%	3.75%
01	3.41%	3.97%	2.27%	3.41%
10	4.16%	4.86%	2.77%	4.16%

Table 8.5 Tolerance of the USART receiver when BRR[3:0] is different from 0000

M bits (character length setting)	OVER8 bit = 0		OVER8 bit = 1	
	ONEBIT = 0	ONEBIT = 1	ONEBIT = 0	ONEBIT = 1
00	3.33 %	3.88 %	2 %	3 %
01	3.03 %	3.53 %	1.82 %	2.73 %
10	3.7 %	4.31 %	2.22 %	3.33 %

USART Auto Baud Rate Detection

The USART is able to detect and automatically set the USARTx->BRR register value based on the reception of one character. Automatic baud rate detection is useful under two circumstances:

1. The communication speed is unknown in advance.
2. The system is using a relatively low accuracy clock source and this mechanism allows the correct baud rate to be obtained without measuring the clock deviation.

The clock source frequency must be compatible with the expected communication speed. When oversampling by 16 is chosen, the measured baud rate must be between $f_{CK}/65,536$ and $f_{CK}/16$. When oversampling by 8 is chosen, the measured baud rate must be between $f_{CK}/65,536$ and $f_{CK}/8$.

Before starting auto baud rate detection, the auto baud rate detection mode must be chosen. The auto baud rate detection mode is selected by programming the ABRMOD[1:0] field in the USARTx->CR2 register.

There are four auto baud rate detection modes:

- **Mode 0**. Any character starting with a bit 1. In this case, the USART measures the duration of the start bit (falling edge to rising edge).

- **Mode 1**. Any character starting with a **10xx** bit pattern. In this case, the USART measures the duration of the start bit and that of the first data bit. The measurement is done falling edge to falling edge, ensuring better accuracy in the case of slow signal slopes.
- **Mode 2**. A 0x7F character frame (it may be a 0x7F character in LSB-first mode or a 0xFE in MSB-first mode). In this case, the baud rate is updated first at the end of the start bit and then at the end of bit 6 (based on the measurement done from falling edge to falling edge: BR6).
- **Mode 3**. A 0x55 character frame. In this case, the baud rate is updated at the end of start bit (BRs), then at the end of bit 0 (based on the measurement done from falling edge to falling edge: BR0), and finally at the end of bit 6 (BR6). Bit 0 is sampled at BRs, bit 1 to bit 6 are sampled at BR0, and further bits of the character are sampled at BR6.

where, BRs refers to the measured baud rate of start bit and BR_k refers to the measured baud rate of bit k.

Before activating auto baud rate detection, the user is required to load a nonzero value into the USART->BRR register. The auto baud rate detection is started by setting the ABREN bit in the USART->CR2 register. The USART will then wait for the first character on the RX line. The auto baud rate operation is indicated by the setting of the **ABRF** flag in the USART->ISR register. If the line is noisy, the correct baud rate detection cannot be guaranteed. In this case, the BRR value may be corrupted and the **ABRE** error flag will be set. This also happens if the communication speed is not compatible with the automatic baud rate detection range (bit duration not between 16 and 65,536 clock periods (oversampling by 16) and not between 8 and 65,536 clock periods (oversampling by 8)). The RXNE interrupt signals the end of the operation.

8.5.6 USART PIN ASSIGNMENT

Depending on the operation mode, the USART module may need to use up to five signal pins. The USART signal pin assignment is shown in Table 8.6.

Table 8.6 USART signal pins usage

Module	Signal function	Alternate function	pin	Module	Signal function	Alternate function	pin
USART1	TX	AF7	PA9, PB6	UART4	TX	AF8	PA0, PC10
	RX	AF7	PA10, PB7		RX	AF8	PA1, PC11
	CK	AF7	PA8, PB5		RTS_DE	AF8	PA15, PB3
	RTS_DE	AF7	PA12, PB3		CTS	AF8	PB7
	CTS	AF7	PA11, PB4	UART5	TX	AF8	PC12
USART2	TX	AF7	PA2, PD5		RX	AF8	PD2
	RX	AF7	PA3, PD6		RTS_DE	AF8	PB4
	CK	AF7	PA4, PD7		CTS	AF8	PB5
	RTS_DE	AF7	PA1, PD4	LPUART1	TX	AF8	PB11, PC1
	CTS	AF7	PA0, PD3		RX	AF8	PB10, PC0
USART3	TX	AF7	PB10, PC4, PC10, PD8		RTS_DE	AF8	PB12
	RX	AF7	PB11, PC5, PC11, PD9		CTS	AF8	PB13
	CK	AF7	PB0, PB12, PC12, PD10				
	RTS_DE	AF7	PB1, PB14, PD2				
	CTS	AF7	PA6, PB4, PB13, PD11				

8.5.7 WRITING BASIC USART FUNCTIONS

Before using the USART to carry out input/output operations, the user is required to configure the operation parameters of the USART module and then either invoke the library functions or write his/her own functions for data transfer.

Example 8.2 Write a C function to configure USART1 to operate at 115,200 baud, use character frame with 8 data bits, one stop bit, and no parity. Use 16 times oversampling and the majority of three samples to detect start bit and determine data bit values. Assign the TX and RX signals to the PB6 and PB7 pins. Enable both the transmitter and receiver and then also enable the USART1.

Solution: The function is as follows:

```
void initUSART1 (void)
{
// configure PB6 and PB7 for alternate function
    GPIOB->MODER &= ~(GPIO_MODER_MODE6 + GPIO_MODER_MODE7);
    GPIOB->MODER |= GPIO_MODER_MODE6_1 + GPIO_MODER_MODE7_1;
// Assign PB6 and PB7 pins to alternate function 7
    GPIOB->AFR[0]  &= ~(GPIO_AFRL_AFSEL6 + GPIO_AFRL_AFSEL7); // clear bits 24~31
    GPIOB->AFR[0]  |= (GPIO_AFRL_AFSEL6_2 + GPIO_AFRL_AFSEL6_1 +
          GPIO_AFRL_AFSEL6_0 + GPIO_AFRL_AFSEL7_2 + GPIO_AFRL_AFSEL7_1 +
          GPIO_AFRL_AFSEL7_0);
// select 8 data bits, 16 times oversampling
    USART1->CR1    &= ~(USART_CR1_M1 + USART_CR1_M0 + USART_CR1_OVER8);
    USART1->BRR    = 0x2B6; // set baud rate to 115,200 baud
    USART1->CR2    &= ~(USART_CR2_STOP); // select one stop bit
// use three samples to detect start bit, determine data bit values
    USART1->CR3    &= ~(USART_CR3_ONEBIT);
// enable USART1, enable transmitter, receiver
    USART1->CR1    |= USART_CR1_UE + USART_CR1_TE + USART_CR1_RE;
}
```

Example 8.3 Write a C function that outputs a character to the USART1 module using the polling method.

Solution: The MCU is required to wait until the USART1->TDR register is empty before it writes data into the USART1->TDR register.

```
void putchUSART1(char cx)
{
    while(!(USART1->ISR & USART_ISR_TXE));
    USART1->TDR = (uint16_t)cx;
}
```

Example 8.4 Write a C function that outputs a NEWLINE character. A newline character is a combination of a line feed character (LF) and a carriage return (CR) character.

Solution: This function simply outputs the LF character and then outputs the CR character by calling the putchUSART1 function.

```
void newlineUSART1 (void)
{
    putchUSART1(0x0D);      // output CR
    putchUSART1(0x0A);      // output LF
}
```

Example 8.5 Write a C function that outputs a string terminated by a NULL character to the USART1 module using the polling method. The pointer to the string to be output is passed to this function.

Solution: Using the polling method, this function simply calls the putchUSART1 function repeatedly until the end of the string is reached.

```
void putsUSART1(char *ptr)
{
    while(*ptr){
        putchUSART1(*ptr++);
    }
}
```

Example 8.6 Write a C function that reads a character from USART1 using the polling method.

Solution: This function waits until a character has been shifted into the USART1->RDR register (indicated by the setting of the RXNE flag in the USART1->ISR register) and then returns it to the caller.

```
char getchUSART1 (void)
{
    while (!(USART1->ISR & USART_ISR_RXNE));
    return ((char)USART1->RDR);
}
```

Example 8.7 Write a C function that reads a string from the USART1 module using the polling method. A pointer to a buffer to hold the received string is passed to this function.

Solution: This function calls the getchUSART1 function repeatedly until the **enter** character is received.

```
#define ENTER  0x0D      // ASCII code of the ENTER character
#define BS     0x08      // ASCII code of the BACKSPACE character
#define SPACE  0x20      // ASCII code of the SPACE character
void getsUSART1 (char *ptr)
{
    char cx;
    while ((cx = getchUSART1()) != ENTER) { // received an ENTER character?
        *ptr  = cx;
        putchUSART1(cx);      // echo the received character
        if (cx == BS) { // received a backspace character?
            putchUSART1(SPACE); // clear the character to be backspaced
            putchUSART1(BS);
            ptr--;
        }
        else ptr++;
    }
    *ptr = 0;                 // terminate the string with a NULL character
}
```

Number Conversion

A number is represented in binary format and must be converted to a BCD string before it can be output to the USART module. A string read in from the USART module (often entered from the keyboard) must be converted to a binary representation before it can be processed by the microcontroller.

Example 8.8 Write a C function that converts a binary number into an ASCII string terminated by a NULL character.

Solution: The procedure to convert a binary number to a decimal ASCII is as follows:

Step 1. Divide the given number by 10.

Step 2. Add 0x30 to the remainder.

Step 3. Append the resultant value to a buffer.

Step 4. Replace the number by the quotient.

Repeat this procedure until the quotient is 0. Reverse the resultant string and add a NULL character to the end of the string.

The C function that implements this algorithm is as follows:

```
void int2ASCII (int ix, char *ptr)
{
    char sign, *p;
    uint16_t    len, j;
    sign        = '+';
    len         = 0;
    p           = ptr;
    if (ix < 0) { // find the magnitude for a negative number
        sign  = '-';
        ix    = -ix;
    }
    do { // convert every decimal digit into ASCII code
        *ptr  = (ix % 10) + '0';
        ptr++;
        len++;
        ix    /= 10;
```

```
    } while (ix != 0);
    if (sign == '-') {
        *ptr   = '-';
        ptr++;
        len++;
    }
    for (j = 0; j < len/2; j++) { // reverse the string by swapping
        p[len]= p[j];        // p[len] is a temporary storage
        p[j]          = p[len - j - 1];
        p[len - j - 1] = p[len];
    }
    p[len] = 0;  // terminate the string with a NULL character
}
```

Example 8.9 Write a C function that converts a decimal string into its binary equivalent. The pointer to the string is passed to this function.

Solution: Let **val** represent the binary value of the decimal string and **sign** indicate the sign of the decimal string. Assume that **ptr** points to the decimal string to be converted.

The algorithm to convert the decimal string to its binary equivalent is as follows:

Step 1

```
    val ← 0;
```

Step 2

```
if (*ptr == '-') {
    sign ← '-';
    ptr++;}
```

Step 3

```
do {
    val ← val × 10 + *ptr - 0x30;
    ptr++;
```

```
} while (*ptr != 0);
```

Step 4

```
if (sign == '-')
    val = -val;
```

The function that implements this algorithm is as follows:

```
int ASCII2Int (char *ptr)
{
    int         val    = 0;
    uint8_t     sign = '+';
    if (*ptr == '-') {
        sign   = '-';
        ptr++;      // move to the first decimal digit
    }
    while (*ptr != 0) {
        val = val * 10 + *ptr - '0';
        ptr++;
    }
    if (sign == '-')
        val    = - val;
    return val;
}
```

Example 8.10 Write a C function that outputs an integer to the USART1 module.

Solution: The C function that performs the specified operation is as follows:

```
void USART1_puti (int ix) // output an integer to USART1
{
    char  sarr[12];
    int2ASCII (ix, sarr); // convert the integer to an ASCII string
    putsUSART1 (sarr);
}
```

Example 8.11 Write a C function that inputs an integer from the USART1 module.

Solution: This function will perform the specified operation in two steps:

Step 1

Read in an ASCII string that represents the integer.

Step 2

Convert the ASCII string into its equivalent binary value and return it to the caller.

The function is as follows:

```
int USART1_geti (void)
{
    char sarr[12];
    getsUSART1 (sarr);
    return (ASCII2Int (sarr));
}
```

To facilitate the reuse of the functions created in Examples 8.2 to 8.11, we will use a file called **USART1_util.c** to store these functions and use a file called **USART1_util.h** to store the prototype declarations of these functions.

These functions can be tested using the virtual COM port described in Section 8.3.9.

Example 8.12 Write a program to compute the **greatest common divisor** (**gcd**) of two nonnegative integers entered from the keyboard and display the gcd on the terminal window generated by **tera term.** This program is to be run on the **B-L475E-IOT01A** demo board.

Solution: The **gcd** of two nonnegative integers can be found by using the Euclidean algorithm. This algorithm is as follows:

Step 1

Get the numbers **m** and **n**.

Step 2

If (n == 0), return the value of m as the answer and stop; otherwise, proceed to Step 3.

Step 3

Divide m by n and assign the value of the remainder to r.

Step 4

Assign the value of n to m and the value of r to n. Go to Step 2.

The program is as follows:

```
#include <stm32L475xx.h>
#include "USART1_util.h"
void sysClkInit(void);
int gcd(int ax, int bx);
void main (void)
{
    char *msg1 = "Want to continue?";
    char *msg2 = "Enter the first number: ";
    char *msg3 = "Enter the second number: ";
    char *msg4 = "The gcd is ";
    char cx;
    int    n1, n2, k;
    sysClkInit();
    initUSART1();
    while(1) {
        newlineUSART1();
        putsUSART1(msg1);       // ask user whether to continue
        cx = getchUSART1();
        if(cx == 'n')
            break;              // not to continue
        newlineUSART1();
        putsUSART1(msg2);       // Remind the user to enter the first number
        n1    = USART1_geti();  // read the first number (entered from keyboard)
        newlineUSART1();
        putsUSART1(msg3);       // Remind the user to enter the second number
        n2    = USART1_geti();  // read the second number (entered from keyboard)
        k     = gcd(n1, n2);    // compute the GCD
        newlineUSART1();
```

```
            putsUSART1(msg4);       // output the computed GCD
            USART1_puti(k);         //  "
        }
}
int gcd(int ax, int bx)
{
        int     i, temp;
        if(ax > bx){
                temp    = ax;
                ax      = bx;
                bx      = temp;
        }
        while(ax != 0){
                i       = bx / ax;
                temp  = bx % ax;
                if (temp == 0)
                        return ax;
                bx      = ax;
                ax      = temp;
        }
}
```

A few examples of the program execution are shown in Figure 8.22.

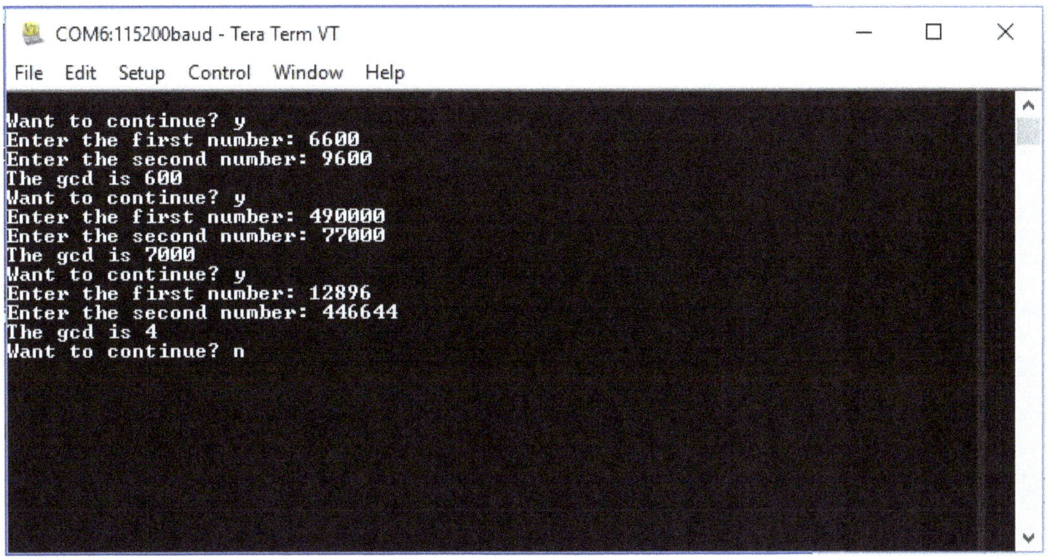

Figure 8.22 A few examples of gcd computation

8.5.8 USART INTERRUPTS

A USART module has many possible interrupt sources. Each interrupt source is represented by a flag in the USARTx->ISR register. If a USART interrupt flag is set and the corresponding enable bit in one of the three control registers (USARTx->CR1, USARTx->CR2, or USARTx->CR3) is also set, then an interrupt will be requested to the MCU. An USART interrupt flag can be cleared by writing a 1 to the corresponding bit in the USARTx->ICR register.

A USART module has 12 interrupt sources but only one interrupt vector is assigned to each USART module. The USART interrupt service routine needs to poll the interrupt flags in order to identify the cause of the interrupt before it can take appropriate action. The USART interrupt sources are listed in Table 8.7.

Example 8.13 Write an interrupt-driven version of the putsUSART1(char *ptr) function.

Solution: Using this approach, we need a function to be called to start the string output process. This function saves a copy of the string pointer to a global pointer and then enables the TXE and USART1 interrupt. This function assumes that interrupts have been enabled globally.

We also need to write an interrupt service routine for USART1, which checks whether the USART1 interrupt is caused by the TXE event. If the interrupt is indeed caused by the TXE event, then the service routine checks whether the string has been totally output. If yes, then the service routine disables the TXE and USART1 interrupt. Otherwise, the service routine writes the next character to the USART1->TDR register and also increments str_ptr, and returns.

```
char *str_ptr;

void putsUSART1_int(char *ptr)
```

```
{
    str_ptr          = ptr;                    // copy the pointer of the string to be output
    USART1->CR1     |= USART_CR1_TXEIE;        // enable TXE interrupt
    NVIC_SetPriority(USART1_IRQn, 0);          // put USART1 interrupt to highest priority
    NVIC_EnableIRQ(USART1_IRQn);               // enable USART1 interrupt
}
void USART1_IRQHandler(void)
{
    if(USART1->ISR & USART_ISR_TXE){
        if(*str_ptr == 0){ // reach the end of string then disable TXE interrupt
            USART1->CR1 &= ~USART_CR1_TXEIE; // disable TXE interrupt
            NVIC_DisableIRQ(USART1_IRQn);
        } else {
            USART1->TDR = *str_ptr++; // output the next character
        }
    }
}
```

Table 8.7 USART interrupt requests

Interrupt event	interrupt flag	interrupt enable bit
Transmit data register empty	TXE	TXEIE
CTS interrupt	CTSIF	CTSIE
Transmission complete	TC	TCIE
Receive data register not empty (data ready to be read)	RXNE	RXNEIE
Overrun error detected	ORE	
Idle line detected	IDLE	IDLEIE
Parity error	PE	PEIE
LIN break	LBDF	LBDIE
Noise flag, overrun error and framing error in multibuffer communication	NF, ORE, or FE	EIE
Character match	CMF	CMIE
Receiver timeout	RTOF	RTOIE
End of block	EOBF	EOBIE
Wakeup from stop mode	WUF[(1)]	WUFIE

1. The WUF interrupt is active only in Stop mode.

8.5.9 DMA SUPPORT IN USART

The STM32L475 USART has DMA support for data transmission and reception. The functionalities and configuration of DMA are described in Appendix C. To use DMA to carry out USART data transmission or reception, the following two steps must be followed:

Step 1

Set up the DMA transfer parameters including the source and destination addresses for the transfer, the transfer count, the size of each transfer, etc.

Step 2

Enable USART DMA transmission and/or USART DMA reception.

Example 8.14 Write a DMA version of the putsUSART1(char *ptr) function.

Solution: The USART1 transmitter DMA transmission is controlled by DMA2 module channel 6. We need to follow the two steps described previously. A function to count the total number of characters to be transmitted is also required.

```
uint32_t char_cnt(char *ptr)
{
    uint32_t cnt;
    cnt = 0;
    while(*ptr){
        cnt++;
        ptr++;
    }
    return cnt;
}
void putsUSART1_DMA(char *ptr)
{
    DMA2_CSELR->CSELR &= ~DMA_CSELR_C6S; // clear bit 0 to 20
// assign USART1 Transmitter to channel 6
    DMA2_CSELR->CSELR |= 0x02 << DMA_CSELR_C6S_Pos;
// assign USART1->TDR to destination
    DMA2_Channel6->CPAR = (uint32_t)(USART1 + 0x28);
```

```
    DMA2_Channel6->CMAR = (uint32_t)ptr; // assign string to be output to source
    DMA2_Channel6->CNDTR = char_cnt(ptr);// count number of characters to be output
    DMA2_Channel6->CCR = 0;
    DMA2_Channel6->CCR = DMA_CCR_PL_1 + DMA_CCR_MINC + DMA_CCR_DIR +
                DMA_CCR_EN; // DMA high priority, 8-bit transfer, memory address increment
    USART1->ICR = USART_ICR_TCCF; // clear the TCF flag in the USART1->ISR register
    USART1->CR3 |= USART_CR3_DMAT; // enable USART DMA transmission
}
```

8.6 Infrared Communication with USART

8.6.1 INTRODUCTION TO INFRARED LIGHT

Infrared (IR) light is electromagnetic radiation with a wavelength longer than that of the visible light, but shorter than that of microwaves. The frequency of IR light ranges from 300 GHz to 400 THz and the wavelength of IR light varies from about 750 nm (the **near infrared**) to 1 millimeter (the **far infrared**).

IR transmission systems are widely used in short-range communications. A common application of IR is in remote control systems for televisions, VCRs, DVD players, and set-top boxes. IR transmitters are usually relatively directional, cheap, lightweight, reliable, and easy to manufacture. The main disadvantage is that the IR light cannot penetrate solid objects. However, this disadvantage may be a plus because the IR system in one room will not interfere with similar systems in nearby rooms, and the possibility of eavesdropping is far lower than with radio-based systems.

8.6.2 BASICS OF IR COMMUNICATION

IR sources are all around us. The sun, light bulb, or anything with heat has components in the IR spectrum. When we use the TV remote control, an IR LED transmits information to the TV. So, how does the IR receiver in our TV pick out signals from our remote control among all the ambient IR light? The answer is that the IR signal is modulated. Modulating a signal is like assigning a pattern to our data, so that the receiver knows what to listen.

A common modulation scheme for IR communication is called **38-kHz modulation**. There are very few natural sources that have the regularity of a 38-kHz signal, so an IR transmitter sending data at that frequency would stand out among the ambient IR. The 38-kHz modulated data is the most common, but other frequencies can be used. Suppose we have a data waveform as shown in Figure 8.23. After modulated with IR light, the resultant waveform becomes that shown in Figure 8.24. After transmission, the data waveform must be restored to that in Figure 8.23 at the receiver.

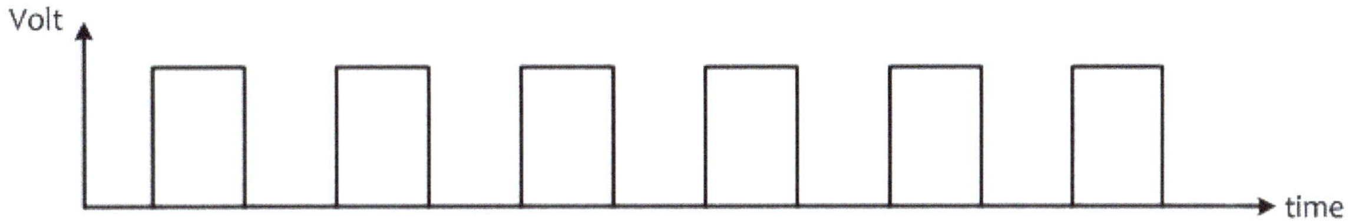

Figure 8.23 Original data waveform

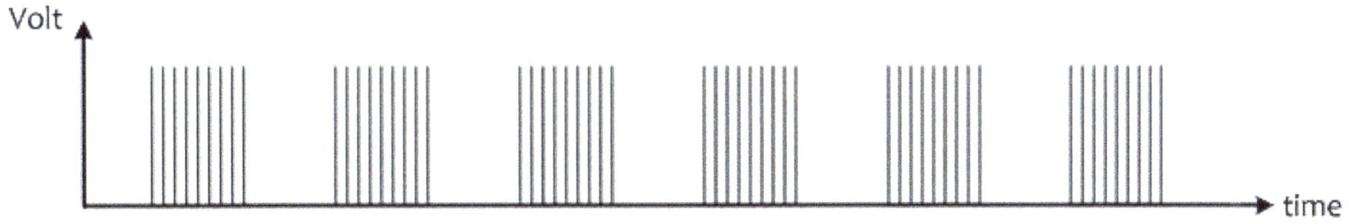

Figure 8.24 Data waveform after modulated with IR

TRANSMISSION AND RECEPTION CIRCUIT

A 555 timer chip can be used to generate a 38-kHz waveform to modulate the IR light. The 555 timer should be set up to operate in the astable mode. An example circuit for generating a 38-kHz waveform and modulating the IR light is shown in Figure 8.25. In the circuit, once the push button is pressed, the 38-kHz output will be applied to the IR LED and causes it to emit the modulated IR light. When the push button is released, the IR LED stops emitting the IR light. The IR emitter TSAL4400 in Figure 8.25 emits an IR light with 940 nm wavelength whenever the voltage at the Q pin is high.

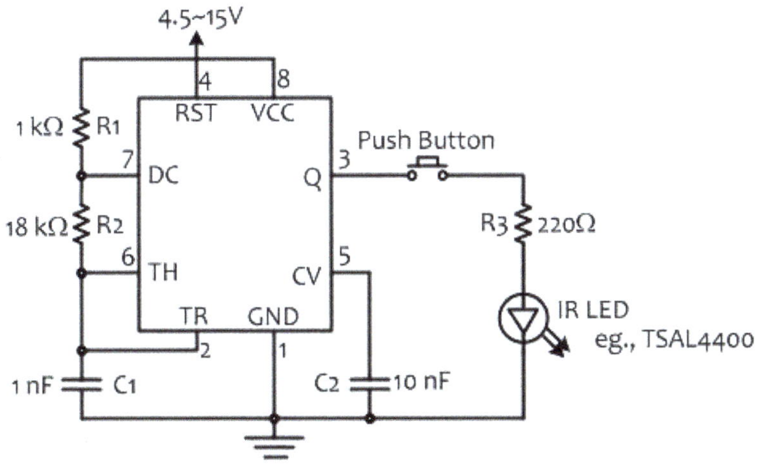

Figure 8.25 A 555 circuit for generating 38-kHz waveform and modulate the IR light

To receive the 38-kHz modulated IR light, an IR receiver such as TSOP14238, TSOP1738, or TSOP38238 is required. Each of these receivers has three pins: Vs (power supply), GND, and OUT. After TSOP1738 (or other IR receiver chip) is powered up, the OUT pin voltage is high when there is no IR light coming in. An example circuit that uses TSOP1738 for receiving IR light is shown in Figure 8.26. As soon as the TSOP1738 detects IR light, the voltage on the OUT pin drops to low, causes the PNP transistor to turn on, and lights the LED. The LED indicates whether the TSOP1738 detects the IR light because the IR light is invisible.

The user can construct both the circuits in Figures 8.25 and 8.26. Whenever the user presses the button at the IR transmitter circuit, the LED in Figure 8.26 will glow.

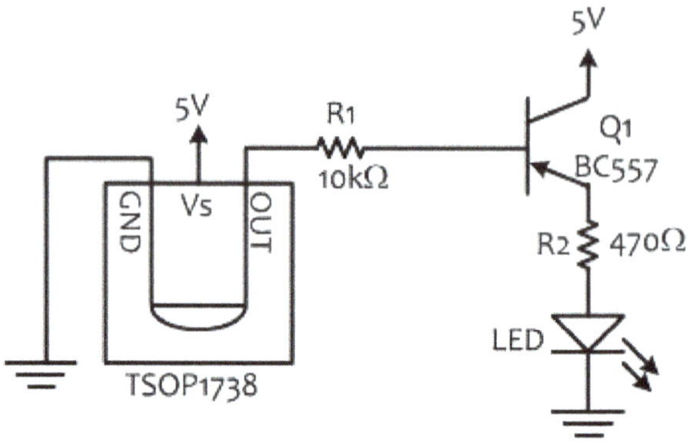

Figure 8.26 An example of IR receiver circuit

8.6.4 THE IRDA

IrDA is the abbreviation for the **Infrared Data Association**, a nonprofit organization for setting standards in IR serial computer connections. IrDA was established in 1993 to set and support hardware and software standards which create infrared communication links. The Association's charter is to create an interoperable, low-cost, low-power, half-duplex, serial data interconnection standard that supports a walk-up, point-to-point user model that is adaptable to a wide range of applications and devices.

In June 1994, IrDA published the IrDA standards, which include the **Serial Infrared** (**SIR**) **Link** specification, the **Link Access Protocol** (**IrLAP**) specification, and the **Link Management Protocol** (**IrLMP**) specification. IrDA released extensions to SIR standard including 4 Mbit/s in October 1995. The IrDA Standard Specification has been expanded to include high-speed extensions of 1.152 and 4.0 Mbit/s data rates.

8.6.5 THE IRDA STANDARD

The current IrDA physical layer standard is version 1.4 and includes all changes and add-ons up to VFIR (very fast infrared) with 16 Mbits.

IrDA Transmission

The transmission in an IrDA-compatible mode (sometimes called **SIR mode** for **serial IR**) uses the RS-232 port of all IBM PC compatibles in the old days. In the SIR mode, the bit pulse is shortened to 3/16 of its original bit length for power-saving requirements, an infrared-emitting diode is driven to transmit an optical signal to the receiver.

This type of transmission covers the data range up to 115.2 kbits/s which is the maximum data rate supported by standard UARTs. The minimum demand for transmission speed for IrDA is only 9,600 bit/s. All transmissions must be started at this frequency to enable compatibility. Higher speeds are a matter of negotiation of the ports after establishing the links.

Higher speeds require special interfaces, which operate at 1.152 Mbits/s and use a similar pulse-shortening process as in the RS232-related mode, but with a pulse reduction to 1/4 of the original pulse length. The fastest data rate supported by IrDA is 4.0 Mbits/s (often called **FIR** mode), operating with 125-ns pulses in a 4-PPM (PPM = Pulse-Position Modulation) mode. In this chapter, we will only focus on the SIR link with speed up to 115.2 kbits/s.

The typical interface for SIR mode is shown in Figure 8.27. Optical output power and receiver sensitivity are set to a level where a point-and-shoot activity (±15°) is sufficient for point-to-point communication but prevents the pollution of the ambient by straying needless power. Transmission over a distance of at least 1 m is ensured. The data to be transmitted by the UART port go out from the Tx pin, are reshaped by the **Pulse shaping block**, and are then forwarded to the transmitter. The IR transmitter (also called IR emitter) then sends out the corresponding modulated IR light. The IR receiver detects the IR light and forwards it to the ENDEC, which reshapes the signal and feeds it to the UART port.

For frequencies (or baud rate) up to 115.2 kbits/s, the minimum output intensity is defined with 40 mW/sr. For higher speeds, a higher output intensity of 100 mW/sr minimum is used. The sensitivity thresholds are 40 and 100 mW/m^2 for SIR and FIR, respectively. The wavelength chosen for the standard is between 850 and 900 nm.

An example of IR ENDEC is the TOIM4232 from Vishay Semiconductor. An example of IR transceiver is the TFDU4100 from Vishay Semiconductor. The TFDU4100 includes an IR emitter and an IR receiver in one package.

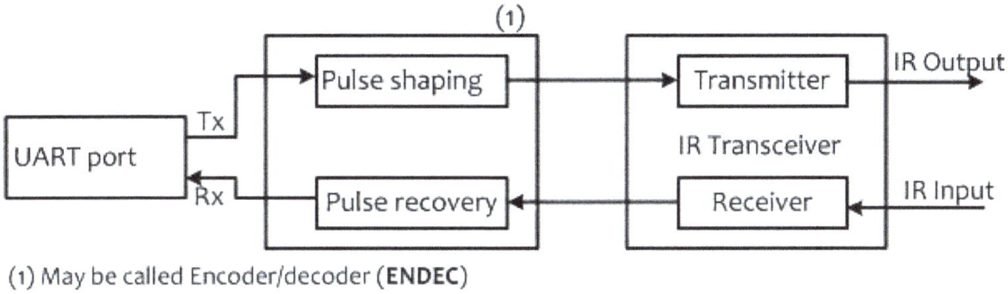

Figure 8.27 Block diagram of one-end of the overall SIR link

IrDA Standard—Physical Layer

In SIR mode, the data are represented by optical pulses between 1.6 μs and 3/16 of the bit length of the RS-232 data pulse in SIR mode. Pulse-length reduction is also applied in the higher frequency modes. The optical radiant intensity and detector sensitivity are adjusted to guarantee a point-to-point transmission in a cone of ±15° over a distance of at least 1 m. The radiant intensity and sensitivity of the front end can be increased to ensure a transmission over 3 m.

Since data are transmitted frame by frame via the UART (or USART) port, it is beneficial to compare a data frame from the UART port and that of the SIR mode. Data are encoded using **return to zero, inverted** (**RZI**) scheme in IR frame. A comparison of UART frame and an IR frame is shown in Figure 8.28.

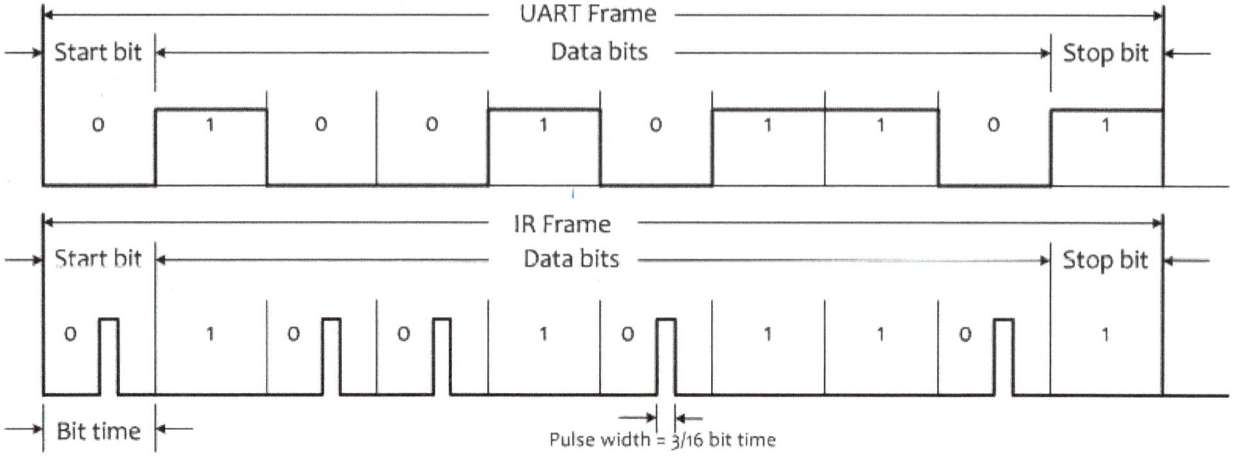

Figure 8.28 A comparison of a UART frame and an IR frame

A UART frame (in Figure 8.28) is shifted out from the Tx pin in Figure 8.27 and is converted into an IR frame and drives the IR transmitter (IR emitter) to send out the frame in the form of IR light. A reverse process is performed for the reception of an IR frame.

In Figure 8.28, the nominal IR pulse width is 3/16 of the bit time. However, in regular data transmission, the actual IR pulse width may not be exactly equal to 3/16 of the bit time. A range of minimal and maximal pulse durations is acceptable. The acceptable minimal and maximal IR frame pulse durations at different baud rates are specified in Table 8.8.

Table 8.8 Signaling rate and pulse duration specification

Signaling rate	Modulation	Tolerance rate % of rate	Pulse Duration Minimum	Pulse Duration Nominal	Pulse Duration Maximal
2.4 kbits/s	RZI*	±0.87	1.41 μs	78.13 μs	88.55 μs
9.6 kbits/s	RZI*	±0.87	1.41 μs	19.53 μs	22.13 μs
19.2 kbits/s	RZI*	±0.87	1.41 μs	9.77 μs	11.07 μs
38.4 kbits/s	RZI*	±0.87	1.41 μs	4.88 μs	5.96 μs
57.6 kbits/s	RZI*	±0.87	1.41 μs	3.26 μs	4.34 μs
115.2 kbits/s	RZI*	±0.87	1.41 μs	1.63 μs	2.23 μs
0.576 Mbits/s	RZI*	±0.1	295.2 ns	434.0 ns	520.8 ns
1.152 Mbits/s	RZI*	±0.1	147.6 ns	217.0 ns	260.4 ns
4.0 Mbits/s Single pulse Double pulse	 4 PPM 4 PPM	 ±0.01 ±0.01	 115.0 ns 240.0 ns	 125.0 ns 250.0 ns	 135.0 ns 260.0 ns
16 Mbits/s	HHH (1.13)	±0.01	38.3 ns	41.7 ns	45.0 ns

RZI*: return to zero inverted

8.6.6 USART IRDA SIR ENDEC BLOCK

All the USART and UART modules of the STM32L475 implement an SIR-compatible IR ENDEC module to allow the STM32L475 to interface with an IR transceiver directly to perform IR wireless communication.

The IrDA mode is selected by setting the IREN bit in the USARTx->CR3 register to 1. In IrDA mode, the following bits must be cleared:

- LINEN, STOP, and CLKEN bits in the USARTx->CR2 register.
- SCEN and HDSEL bits in the USARTx->CR3 register.

The SIR ENDEC module uses the RZI (Return to Zero Inverted) encoding scheme to encode the NRZ (Non-Return to Zero) transmit bit stream output from USART. USART supports only bit rates up to 115.2 kbps for SIR ENDEC. In normal mode the transmitted pulse width is specified as 3/16 of a bit time.

The SIR receive decoder demodulates the return-to-zero bit stream from the infrared detector and outputs the received NRZ serial bit stream to the USART.

IrDA is a half-duplex communication protocol. If the transmitter is busy (when the USART is sending data to the IrDA encoder), any data on the IrDA receive line is ignored by the IrDA decoder and if the receiver is busy (when the USART is receiving decoded data from the IrDA decoder), data on the Tx pin from the USART to IrDA are not encoded. The transmit encoder output has the opposite polarity to the decoder input. In Table 8.8, the IrDA specification requires the acceptance of pulses greater than 1.41 μs. In IrDA mode, the STOP bit field in the USARTx->CR2 register must be configured to 1 stop bit.

8.6.7 THE IR TRANSCEIVER TFDU4101

The block diagram of the TFDU IR transceiver is shown in Figure 8.29.

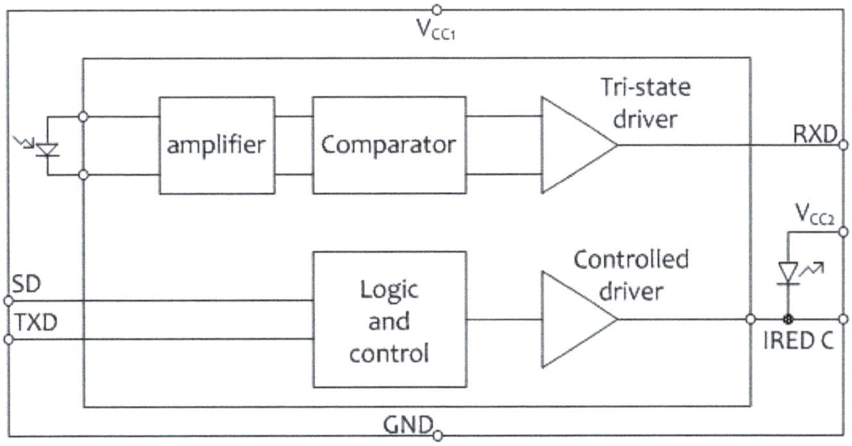

Figure 8.29 The block diagram of TFDU4101

The functions of signals in Figure 8.29 are as follows:

- **Pin 1: V_{CC2} (IR LED anode)**. The anode of IR LED is connected to this pin. This pin should be connected to the power supply via a resistor to set the IR LED current.

- **Pin 2: IRED Cathode.** This pin is connected to the internal driver. There is no need to make external connection to this pin.
- **Pin 3: TXD.** This pin is a Schmitt-trigger input and is used to transmit serial data when the SD pin is low. An on-chip protection circuit disables the LED driver if the TXD pin is asserted for longer than 50 μs.
- **Pin 4: RXD.** This pin is received data output. This pin is push-pull CMOS driver output capable of driving standard CMOS or TTL loads.
- **Pin 5: SD.** This pin is the shut-down input and should be grounded for normal operation.
- **Pin 6: V_{CC1}.** Supply voltage. Supply voltage can be from 2.4 to 5.5 V.
- **Pin 7: NC.** No connection.
- **Pin 8: GND.** Ground pin.

A possible circuit connection between the STM32L475 and the TFDU4101 is illustrated in Figure 8.30. This circuit allows the STM32L475 to perform data communication using IR light.

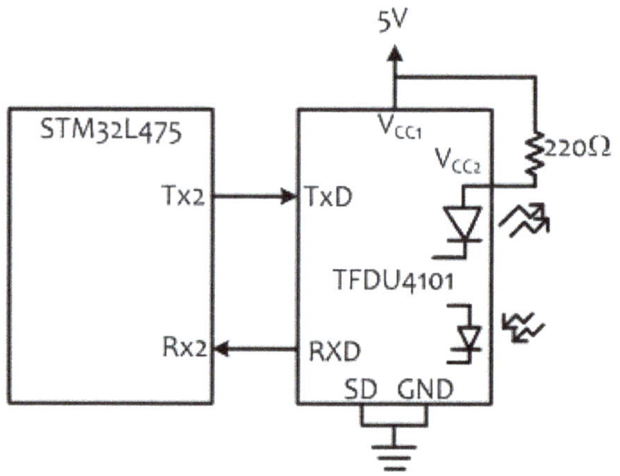

Figure 8.30 Circuit connection between USART2 and TFDU4101

Example 8.15 Write a C function to configure USART2 to operate at 38,000 baud, use character frame with 8 data bits, one stop bit, and no parity. Use 16 times oversampling and the majority of three samples to detect start bit and determine data bit values. Assign the TX and RX signals to the PA2 and PA3 pins. Enable both the transmitter and receiver and then also enable the USART2. Enable IrDA support.

Solution:

```
void usart2Init_IR(void)
{
// configure PA2 and PA3 for Tx2, Rx2 (alternate function 7)
    GPIOA->MODER    &= ~(GPIO_MODER_MODE2 + GPIO_MODER_MODE3);
    GPIOA->MODER    |=  GPIO_MODER_MODE2_1 + GPIO_MODER_MODE3_1;
    GPIOA->AFR[0]   &= ~(GPIO_AFRL_AFSEL2 + GPIO_AFRL_AFSEL3);
    GPIOA->AFR[0]   |=  (GPIO_AFRL_AFSEL2_2 + GPIO_AFRL_AFSEL2_1 +
```

```
                        GPIO_AFRL_AFSEL2_0 + GPIO_AFRL_AFSEL3_2 +
                        GPIO_AFRL_AFSEL3_1 + GPIO_AFRL_AFSEL3_0);
// select 8 data bits, 16 times oversampling
    USART2->CR1     =   0;
    USART2->BRR     =   2105; // set baud rate to 38 Kbps
    USART2->CR2     =   0;       // select one STOP bit
    USART2->CR3     =   USART_CR3_IREN; // enable IrDA mode
// enable USART2, enable transmitter, receiver
    USART2->CR1     |=  USART_CR1_UE + USART_CR1_TE + USART_CR1_RE;
}
```

8.7 Summary

The USART (or UART) module is provided by every microcontroller from all vendors. The earliest UART was designed to use the RS-232 standard to facilitate the communication between computers via telephone lines. However, the later USARTs were designed to support more and more functionalities, for example, LIN, Modbus communication, Smartcard, Infrared, and so on. At the minimum, all the USART implementation supports the asynchronous data transmission mode. The traditional C library I/O functions such as printf and scanf can be implemented using the USART module asynchronous mode. The printf function has been proved to be very useful for program execution and debugging.

When operating in asynchronous mode, the application has the option to select oversampling by 16 or oversampling by 8 to detect the arrival of the start bit and determine the logic value of data bits. Data are transmitted character by character. Each character is framed by a start and 0.5 to 2 stop bits before being sent out. If parity is enabled, then the parity bit occupies the most significant bit of the data character.

Data transmission is started by writing data into the USARTx->TDR register. Data should be written into the USARTx->TDR register only when the TXE bit in the USARTx->ISR register is set. Data reception is enabled by setting the RE bit and the UE bit in the USARTx->CR1 register. When the RXNE bit in the USARTx->ISR register is set, the application can read the character held in the USARTx->RDR register.

Data transmission and reception can be performed by using polling method (checking the TXE and RXNE flag), interrupt-driven method, or DMA method.

Two STM32L475s can communicate via the USART ports in either asynchronous mode or the IrDA mode. To transmit data via the USART port, the MCU writes data into the USARTx->TDR register after making sure that the TXE bit in the USARTx->ISR register is empty is 1. To receive data via the USART module, the MCU makes sure that the RXNE flag in the USARTx->ISR register is 1 and reads the USARTx->RDR register. Data transmission and reception can be done using the polling, DMA, or interrupt-driven approach.

8.8 Exercises

E8.1 If we want to set the USART baud rate to 38,400 and 66,800 for transmission and reception using oversampling by 16 and oversampling by 8, what value should be written into the USARTx->BRR register, respectively, if $\mathbf{f_{CK} = 48\ MHz}$?

E8.2 Write an interrupt-driven version of getsUSART1 function for USART1 module.

E8.3 Write a DMA-driven version of the getsUSART1 function for USART1 module.

E8.4 Write a C function that outputs a 16-bit unsigned integer as four hexadecimal digits to the USART1 module.

E8.5 Write a C function that outputs a 32-bit unsigned integer as eight hexadecimal digits to the USART1 module.

E8.6 Write a C function that reads in four hexadecimal digits (each digit is represented as an ASCII code) from the USART1 module and returns its binary value to the caller. The first digit read in is the most significant digit whereas the last digit read in is the least significant digit.

E8.7 Write a C function that reads in eight hexadecimal digits (each digit is represented as an ASCII code) from the USART1 module and returns its equivalent 32-bit binary value. The first digit read in is the most significant digit whereas the last digit read in is the least significant digit.

E8.8 Write a program that invokes appropriate USART1 functions to test whether a number entered by the user from the PC keyboard is a prime number. The program performs the following operations:

1. Output the message "Want to continue? y/n: ".
2. Read in the answer entered from the keyboard. If the answer is **n**, exit.
3. Output the message "Enter a natural number: "
4. You enter a number from the keyboard and the program reads it in.
5. Output the message "The entered number ", followed by the **entered number**, "is (is not) prime.", depending on whether it is prime.
6. Go to Step 1.

8.9 Lab Assignments

L8.1 Write a program that invokes appropriate USART1 functions to perform the following operations:

1. Output the message "Want to continue? Type y/n: ".
2. Read in the answer. If the answer is **y**, continue. Otherwise, exit.

3. Output the message "What is your name?"
4. Read in the answer and store it in a buffer.
5. Output the message "My name is ", followed by the **name entered** in Step 4.
6. Output the message "What is your major?"
7. Read in the answer and save it in a buffer.
8. Output the message "My major is ", followed by the **major entered** in Step 7.
9. Go to Step 1

L8.2 Time-of-day update and display. Start the **Tera Term** program to operate at the baud rate of 115,200. Write a program to initialize the USART1 with baud rate set to 115,200 and perform the following operations:

Step 1

Initialize system clock and the USART1.

Step 2

Call the putsUSART1() function to output a message to remind the user to enter the current time of day in the format of **hh:mm:ss** (the colon characters are included).

Step 3

Call the getsUSART1() function to read in the time (entered from the PC keyboard) and save the time in a buffer.

Step 4

Output the message **Current time is hh:mm:ss**, where, hh, mm, and ss are the time components that your program read in from the keyboard.

Step 5

Stay in an infinite loop and perform the following operations:

- Call a delay function to wait for one second.
- Update the current time of day.
- Redisplay the current time of day.

When updating the current time of day, backspace the screen by eight places and redisplay the new time.

L8.3 Construct the circuit shown in Figures 8.25 and 8.26. Press the push button in Figure 8.25 and watch the change in the circuit in Figure 8.26. Use a TV remote control and press a few keys and watch the response in the circuit shown in Figure 8.26.

9

Digital-to-Analog Converter

9.1 Objectives

After completing this chapter, you should be able to

- Understand the general features of a DAC.
- Understand the applications of a DAC.
- Set up DAC parameters to perform D/A conversion.
- Generate waveforms using the DAC.
- Superimpose a triangle or linear feedback shift register noise on top of a regularly generated waveform.

9.2 Introduction

A digital-to-analog converter (DAC) is a circuit that can convert a digital value into a voltage. The number of bits that encodes a value to be converted into a voltage is called the **resolution** of the DAC. The resolution of a DAC is often smaller than the length of the data register that holds the value to be converted. Therefore, the value to be converted can be stored left-aligned or right-aligned in the data register. A **reference** voltage is required for the D/A conversion. The reference voltage can be obtained internally or externally (from an I/O pin). A DAC may have one or multiple outputs.

DAC is often used in data communication systems that transmit and receive analog data such as voice or image. Voice or image is first converted to voltage using a sensor. The voltage output from the sensor is then converted to a digital value, which will be placed in a data frame, and sent to the destination. At the destination, the overhead of the data frame will be removed, and data will be converted back to the original analog physical quantity using a DAC and other appropriate circuits.

Because a DAC is capable of converting a digital value to a voltage, it can also be used to generate stimuli waveforms to test the functionalities and characteristics of certain circuits.

9.3 The Features of the STM32L475 DAC

The STM32L475 has two DACs with 12-bit resolution. Each DAC has the following features:

- Each DAC has one output.
- 12-bit data to be converted can be written into the DAC either right- or left-aligned. Eight-bit data can only be written into the DAC right-aligned.
- Data to be converted can be sent to the DAC using DMA transfer.
- D/A conversion can be started automatically, started by software, or triggered by external events.
- The DAC offers sample and hold mode for low-power operation in the STOP mode.
- DAC has a buffer circuit before the output pin. This buffer circuit can be bypassed.
- The DAC output can be connected to internal peripheral such as the analog comparator (AC) or the analog-to-digital converter (ADC).

In the literature, the DAC1 is also called **DAC channel 1** whereas the DAC2 is also called **DAC channel 2**.

9.4 The Operation of the STM32L475 DAC

9.4.1 DAC SIGNAL PINS

The DAC has the following signal pins:

- V_{REF+}: This is the positive analog reference input to the DAC. This reference voltage cannot be higher than V_{DDA}.
- V_{DDA}: Analog supply voltage.
- V_{SSA}: Analog supply ground.
- DAC_OUTx (x = 1 or 2): DAC channel x voltage output. DAC_OUT1 is assigned to PA4 pin whereas DAC_OUT2 is assigned to PA5 pin. If these two signals are enabled, the PA4 and PA5 pins will be used as DAC_OUT1 and DAC_OUT2 automatically.

9.4.2 DAC REGISTER NAMING IN C

A struct data type is defined for the DAC registers in the **STM32L475xx.h** header file:

```
typedef struct
{
    __IO    uint32_t    CR;            // DAC control register
```

```
    __IO  uint32_t  SWTRIGR;    // DAC software trigger register
    __IO  uint32_t  DHR12R1;    // Channel 1 12-bit right-aligned data holding register
    __IO  uint32_t  DHR12L1;    // Channel 1 12-bit left-aligned data holding register
    __IO  uint32_t  DHR8R1;     // Channel 1 8-bit right-aligned data holding register
    __IO  uint32_t  DHR12R2;    // Channel 2 12-bit right-aligned data holding register
    __IO  uint32_t  DHR12L2;    // Channel 2 12-bit left-aligned data holding register
    __IO  uint32_t  DHR8R2;     // Channel 2 8-bit right-aligned data holding register
    __IO  uint32_t  DHR12RD;    // Dual DAC 12-bit right-aligned data holding register
    __IO  uint32_t  DHR12LD;    // Dual DAC 12-bit left-aligned data holding register
    __IO  uint32_t  DHR8RD;     // Dual DAC 8-bit right-aligned data holding register
    __IO  uint32_t  DOR1;       // DAC channel 1 data output register
    __IO  uint32_t  DOR2;       // DAC channel 2 data output register
    __IO  uint32_t  SR;         // DAC status register
    __IO  uint32_t  CCR;        // DAC calibration control register
    __IO  uint32_t  MCR;        // DAC mode control register
    __IO  uint32_t  SHSR1;      // DAC sample and hold sample-time register 1
    __IO  uint32_t  SHSR2;      // DAC sample and hold sample-time register 2
    __IO  uint32_t  SHHR;       // DAC sample and hold hold-time register
    __IO  uint32_t  SHRR;       // DAC sample and hold refresh-time register
} DAC_TypeDef;
```

With the following macro definitions, the user can use either the pointer **DAC** or **DAC1** to access DAC registers:

```
#define  PERIPH_BASE       ((uint32_t)0x40000000U)     // peripheral base address
#define  APB1PERIPH_BASE   PERIPH_BASE
#define  DAC_BASE          (APB1PERIPH_BASE + 0x7400U)
#define  DAC1_BASE         (APB1PERIPH_BASE + 0x7400U)
#define  DAC               ((DAC_TypeDef *) DAC1_BASE)
#define  DAC1              ((DAC_TypeDef *) DAC1_BASE)
```

9.4.3 DATA FLOW INSIDE THE DAC

To allow user the flexibility of choosing the data alignment method when sending data to DAC, the data flow for the DAC module is divided into three stages:

- Data holding register in the front end. There are nine registers for the user to choose the alignment mode and channel mode. These registers are listed in Table 9.1.
- Data holding registers in the middle stage. There are two registers in this stage: DHR1 and DHR2. DHR1 is the data holding register for DAC1 whereas DHR2 is the data holding register for DAC2. These two registers are not user addressable.
- Data output registers in the third stage. There are two data output registers, one for each DAC channel. DAC->DOR1 is DAC channel 1 data output register whereas DAC->DOR2 is DAC channel 2 data output register. DAC->DOR1 and DAC->DOR2 are read-only.

Table 9.1 DAC data holding registers

Register symbol	Description
DAC->DHR8R1	DAC channel 1 8-bit right-aligned data holding register
DAC->DHR12R1	DAC channel 1 12-bit right-aligned data holding register
DAC->DHR12L1	DAC channel 1 12-bit left-aligned data holding register
DAC->DHR8R2	DAC channel 2 8-bit right-aligned data holding register
DAC->DHR12R2	DAC channel 2 12-bit right-aligned data holding register
DAC->DHR12L2	DAC channel 2 12-bit left-aligned data holding register
DAC->DHR8RD	Dual DAC 8-bit right-aligned data holding register
DAC->DHR12RD	Dual DAC 12-bit right-aligned data holding register
DAC->DHR12LD	Dual DAC 12-bit left-aligned data holding register

Only the data holding registers in the front end are accessible to the user. A value written into one of the holding registers in the front end will be transferred to either DHR1 (channel 1) or DHR2 (channel 2) automatically depending on which DAC is chosen. The transfer of value from the middle stage to the third stage can be automatic or nonautomatic depending on the DAC starting mode that the user chooses. It can be (1) automatic, (2) software triggered, or (3) external event triggered. Once a value is transferred to one of the output register in the third stage, digital-to-analog conversion is started.

9.4.4 DAC DATA FORMAT

When only a single channel x (x = 1 or 2) is selected for operation, there are three possibilities:

- 8-bit right alignment: Data to be converted is to be loaded into the DAC->DHR8Rx[7:0] bits, which will be stored in the DHRx[11:4] bits in the middle stage.
- 12-bit left alignment: Data to be converted is to be loaded into the DAC->DHR12Lx[15:4] bits, which will be stored in the DHRx[11:0] bits in the middle stage.
- 12-bit right alignment: Data to be converted is to be loaded into the DAC->DHR12Rx[11:0] bits, which will be stored in the DHRx[11:0] bits in the middle stage.

Data holding registers in the front end in single-channel mode are illustrated in Figure 9.1.

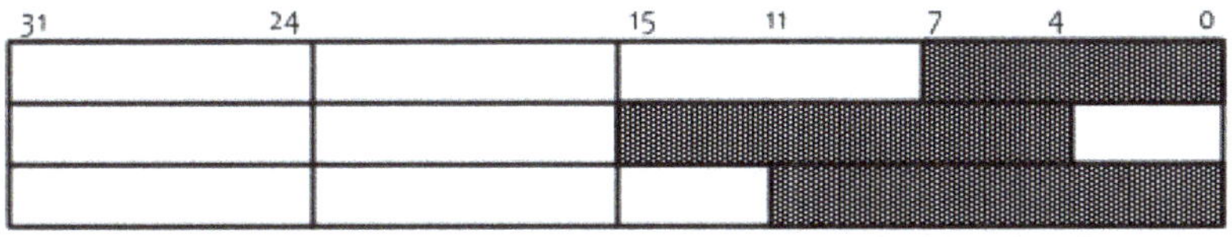

Figure 9.1 DAC front end data holding registers in single channel mode

When both channels (**dual-channel mode**) are used at the same time, there are also three possibilities:

- 8-bit right alignment: Data for channel 1 are to be loaded into the DAC->DHR8RD[7:0] bits and data for channel 2 are to be loaded into the DAC->DHR8RD[15:8] bits. The value of DAC->DHR8RD[7:0] will be transferred to the DHR1[11:4] bits whereas the value of DAC->DHR8RD[15:8] will be transferred to the DHR2[11:4] bits.
- 12-bit left alignment: Data for channel 1 are to be loaded into the DAC->DHR12LD[15:4] bits and data for channel 2 are to be loaded into the DAC->DHR12LD[31:20] bits. The value of DAC->DHR12LD[15:4] will be transferred to DHR1[11:0] whereas the value of DAC->DHR12LD[31:20] will be transferred to DHR2[11:0].
- 12-bit right alignment: Data for channel 1 are to be loaded into DAC->DHR12RD[11:0] and data for channel 2 are to be loaded into DAC->DHR12RD[27:16]. The value of DAC->DHR12RD[11:0] will be transferred to DHR1[11:0] whereas the value of DAC->DHR12RD[27:16] will be transferred to DHR2[11:0].

Data holding registers in the front end in dual-channel mode are shown in Figure 9.2.

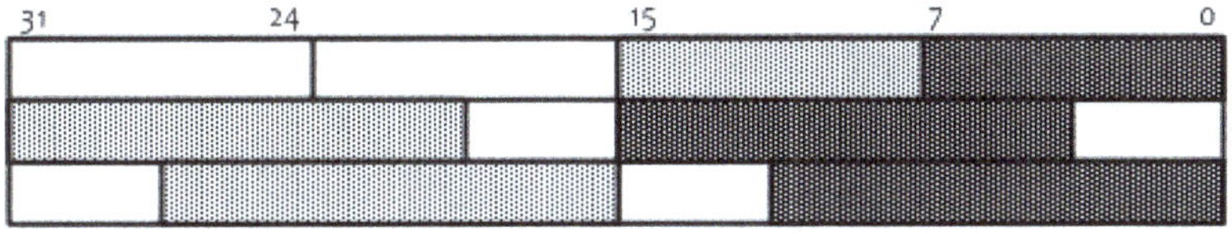

Figure 9.2 DAC front end data holding registers in dual-channel mode

9.4.5 D/A CONVERSION

The value stored in the data holding register (DHRx, x = 1 or 2) in the middle stage may or may not be transferred to the data output register (DAC->DORx) automatically depending on whether the trigger mode is enabled. The trigger mode is enabled by setting the TENx bit (x = 1 or 2) in the DAC->CR register.

If trigger mode is disabled, the value in the DHRx register will be transferred to the DAC->DORx register after one APB1 clock cycle. If trigger mode is enabled, then the value in the DHRx register will be transferred to the DAC->DORx register only when a trigger event has occurred. Once the DAC->DORx register is loaded with the contents of the DHRx register, the analog output voltage becomes available after a time $t_{SETTLING}$. This process is illustrated using nontrigger mode in Figure 9.3. In worst case, it takes 3 μs for DAC_OUT to reach final value ±0.5LSB.

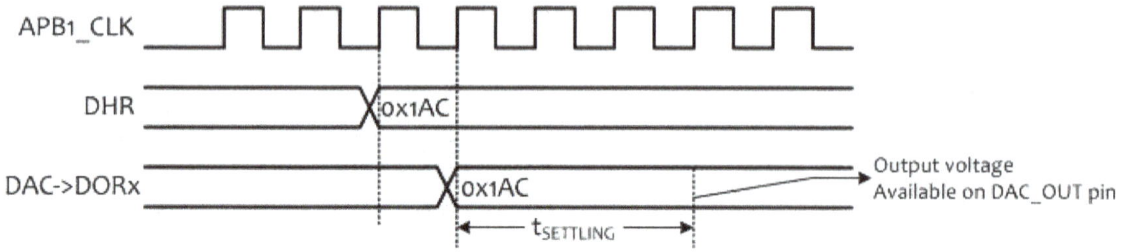

Figure 9.3 Timing diagram for conversion with trigger disabled (TEN=0)

The analog output voltage on each DAC channel pin is determined by the following equation:

$$DAC_{output} = V_{REF} \times DOR \div 4095 \text{ (255 for 8-bit resolution)}$$

or

$$DOR = DAC_{output} \div V_{REF} \times 4095 \text{ (256 for 8-bit resolution)}$$

Example 9.1 Answer the following questions assuming that V_{REF} = 3.3 V:

(1) What value should be written into the DAC->DHR8R1 register if we want to generate a 2 V output from the DAC_OUT1 pin?
(2) What value should be written into the DAC->DHR12R1 register if we want to generate a 1.2 V output from the DAC_OUT1 pin?
(3) What value should be written into the DAC->DHR12L2 register if we want to generate a 2.2 V output from the DAC_OUT2 pin?
(4) What value should be written into the DAC->DHR8RD register if we want to generate 1.5 and 2.4 V outputs from the DAC_OUT1 and DAC_OUT2 pins, respectively?
(5) What value should be written into the DAC->DHR12RD register if we want to generate 1.9 and 2.9 V outputs from the DAC_OUT1 and DAC_OUT2 pins, respectively?
(6) What value should be written into the DAC->DHR12LD register if we want to generate 1.8 and 2.7 V outputs from the DAC_OUT1 and DAC_OUT2 pins, respectively?

Solution:

(1) The 8-bit value to be written into DAC->DHR8R1 register is 2 ÷ 3.3 × 255 = 154.54 ≈ 155. This value is to be written into the lowest 8 bits → DAC->DHR8R1 = 155.
(2) Right-alignment format is used. The value to be written is 1.2 ÷ 3.3 × 4095 = 1489.09 ≈ 1489. This value is to be written into the lowest 12 bits → DAC->DHR12R1 = 1489.
(3) Left-alignment format is used. The value to be written is 2.2 ÷ 3.3 × 4095 = 2730. This value is to be written into bits 15~04 → DAC->DHR12L2 = (2730 << 4) = 43680 (or 0xAAA0).
(4) The value to be written into DAC->DHR8RD[7:0] is 1.5 ÷ 3.3 × 255 = 115.9 ≈ 116 = 0x74. The value to be written into DAC->DHR8RD[15:8] is 2.4 ÷ 3.3 × 255 = 185.45 ≈ 185 = 0xB9. The statement to make the assignment is DAC->DHR8RD = 0xB974.
(5) The value to be written into DAC->DHR12RD[11:0] is 1.9 ÷ 3.3 × 4095 = 2357.72 ≈ 2358 = 0x0936. The value to be written into DAC->DHR12RD[27:16] is 2.9 ÷ 3.3 × 4095 = 3599 = 0x0E0F. The statement to make the assignment is DAC->DHR12RD = 0x0E0F0936.
(6) The value to be written into DAC->DHR12LD[15:4] is 1.8 ÷ 3.3 × 4095 = 2233.63 ≈ 2234 = 0x8BA. The value to be written into DAC->DHR12LD[31:20] is 2.7 ÷ 3.3 × 4095 = 3350.45 ≈ 3350 (0xD16).

The statement to make the assignment is DAC->DHR12LD = (0x0D16 << 20 + 0x08BA << 4) = 0xD1608BA0.

9.4.6 DAC TRIGGER SELECTION

If the TENx (x = 1 or 2) bit (in DAC->CR register) is set, conversion can be started by an external event or software. The TSELx[2:0] field in the DAC->CR register selects the trigger source. Each time a DAC interface detects a rising edge on the selected trigger source, the last data stored in the DAC->DHRx register are transferred to the DAC->DORx register three APB1 clock cycles after the trigger event. Once data are transferred to the DAC->DORx register, the D/A conversion starts. The contents of the DAC->CR register are shown in Figure 9.4.

31	30	29	28	27	26	25	24
--	CEN2	DMAUDRIE2	DMAEN2	MAMP2[3:0]			
	r/w	r/w	r/w	r/w	r/w	r/w	r/w

23	22	21	20	19	18	17	16
WAVE2[1:0]		TSEL[2:0]			TEN2	--	EN2
r/w	r/w	r/w	r/w	r/w	r/w		r/w

15	14	13	12	11	10	9	8
--	CEN1	DMAUDRIE1	DMAEN1	MAMP1[3:0]			
	r/w	r/w	r/w	r/w	r/w	r/w	r/w

7	6	5	4	3	2	1	0
WAVE1[1:0]		TSEL1[2:0]			TEN1	--	EN1
r/w	r/w	r/w	r/w	r/w	r/w		r/w

Reset value = 0x0000 0000
Addr offset = 0x00

CENx(x = 1 or 2): DAC channel x calibration enable
This bit can be written only if ENx = 0.
0: DAC channel x is in normal operating mode   1: DAC channel x is in calibration mode
DMAUDRIEx(x = 1 or 2): DAC channel x DMA underrun interrupt enable
0: DAC channel x DMA underrun interrupt disabled
1: DAC channel x DMA underrun interrupt enabled
DMAENx(x = 1 or 2): DAC channel x DMA enable
0: DAC channel x DMA mode disabled   1: DAC channel x DMA mode enabled
MAMPx[3:0]: DAC channel x (x = 1 or 2) mask/amplitude selector
These bits are written to select mask in wave generation mode or amplitude in triangle generation mode. See Table9.2.

Figure 9.4 DAC Control register (DAC->CR)

31	30	29	28	27	26	25	24
–	CEN2	DMAUDRIE2	DMAEN2	MAMP2[3:0]			
	r/w	r/w	r/w	r/w	r/w	r/w	r/w
23	22	21	20	19	18	17	16
WAVE2[1:0]		TSEL[2:0]			TEN2	–	EN2
r/w	r/w	r/w	r/w	r/w	r/w		r/w
15	14	13	12	11	10	9	8
–	CEN1	DMAUDRIE1	DMAEN1	MAMP[3:0]			
	r/w	r/w	r/w	r/w	r/w	r/w	r/w
7	6	5	4	3	2	1	0
WAVE1[1:0]		TSEL1[2:0]			TEN1	–	EN1
r/w	r/w	r/w	r/w	r/w	r/w		r/w

Reset value = 0x0000 0000
Addr offset = 0x00

WAVEx[1:0]: DAC channel x (x = 1 or 2) noise/triangle wave generation enable
00: wave generation disabled   01: Noise wave generation enabled
1x: Triangle wave generation enabled.
TSELx[2:0]: DAC channel x (x = 1 or 2) trigger selection
000: Timer 6 TRGO event   001: Timer 8 TRGO event   010: Timer 7 TRGO event
011: Timer 5 TRGO event   100: Timer 2 TRGO event   101: Timer 4 TRGO event
110: External line 9   111: Software trigger
Software trigger is generated by setting the SWTRIGx bit in the DAC->SWTRGR register to 1. The contents of the DAC->SWTRGR register are shown in Figure 9.5.
TENx: DAC channel x (x = 1 or 2) trigger enable
0: DAC channel x trigger disabled—DHRx register is transferred to DAC->DORx in one APBx cycle.
1: DAC channel x trigger enable and the contents of DHRx register are transferred to DAC->DORx register three APB1 clock cycles after the trigger event
ENx: DAC channel x (x = 1 or 2) enable
0: DAC channel x disabled   1: DAC channel x enabled

Figure 9.4a DAC Control register (DAC->CR)—(continued)

Table 9.2 DAC Channel x (1 or 2) mask/amplitude selector

MAMPx[3:0]	Description
0000	Unmask bits of LFSR/triangle amplitude equal to 1
0001	Unmask bits[1:0] of LFSR/triangle amplitude equal to 3
0010	Unmask bits[2:0] of LFSR/triangle amplitude equal to 7
0011	Unmask bits[3:0] of LFSR/triangle amplitude equal to 15
0100	Unmask bits[4:0] of LFSR/triangle amplitude equal to 31
0101	Unmask bits[5:0] of LFSR/triangle amplitude equal to 63
0110	Unmask bits[6:0] of LFSR/triangle amplitude equal to 127
0111	Unmask bits[7:0] of LFSR/triangle amplitude equal to 255
1000	Unmask bits[8:0] of LFSR/triangle amplitude equal to 511
1001	Unmask bits[9:0] of LFSR/triangle amplitude equal to 1023
1010	Unmask bits[10:0] of LFSR/triangle amplitude equal to 2047
≥1011	Unmask bits[11:0] of LFSR/triangle amplitude equal to 4095

31	30	29	28	27	26	25	24
--	--	--	--	--	--	--	--
	r/w	r/w	r/w	r/w	r/w	r/w	r/w
23	**22**	**21**	**20**	**19**	**18**	**17**	**16**
--	--	--	--	--	--	--	--
r/w	r/w	r/w	r/w	r/w	r/w		r/w
15	**14**	**13**	**12**	**11**	**10**	**9**	**8**
--	--	--	--	--	--	--	--
	r/w	r/w	r/w	r/w	r/w	r/w	r/w
7	**6**	**5**	**4**	**3**	**2**	**1**	**0**
--	--	--	--	--	--	SWTRIG2	SWTRIG1
r/w	r/w	r/w	r/w	r/w	r/w		r/w

Reset value = 0x0000 0000
Addr offset = 0x04

SWTRIGx: DAC channel x software trigger (x = 1 or 2)
0: No trigger
1: Trigger a DAC
This bit is cleared by hardware once the DHRx register value has been loaded into the DAC->DORx register (one APB1 clock cycle later).

Figure 9.5 DAC software trigger register (DAC->SWTRGR)

9.4.7 DMA REQUEST

Data to be converted can be transferred to the DAC using the DMA. Each DAC channel is serviced by one DMA channel.

A DAC DMA request is generated when an external trigger (but not a software trigger) occurs while the DMAENx bit in the DAC->CR register is set. The value of the DHRx register is then transferred to the DAC->DORx register.

In dual mode, if both DMAENx bits are set, two DMA requests are generated. If only one DMA request is needed, we should set only the corresponding DMAENx bit. In this way, the application can manage both DAC channels in dual mode by using one DMA request and a unique DMA channel.

DMA Underrun

DMA requests are not queued. If a second external trigger arrives before the acknowledgement for the first external trigger is received (first request), then no new request is issued and the DMA channel x underrun flag DMAUDRx in the DAC->SR register is set, reporting the error condition. The DAC channel x continues to convert old data. The contents of the DAC->SR register are shown in Figure 9.6.

The software should clear the DMAUDRx flag by writing 1 to the flag, clear the DMAEN bit of the used DMA channel and reinitialize both the DMA and DAC channel x to restart the transfer correctly. The software should modify the DAC trigger conversion frequency or lighten the DMA workload to avoid a new DMA underrun. Finally, the DAC conversion could be resumed by enabling both DMA data transfer and conversion trigger. An interrupt may be generated if the corresponding DMAUDRIEx bit in the DAC->CR register is set.

31	30	29	28	27	26	25	24
BWST2	CAL_FLAG2	DMAUDR2	–	–	–	–	–

Reset value = 0x0000 0000
Addr offset = 0x34

23	22	21	20	19	18	17	16
–			–		–	–	–

15	14	13	12	11	10	9	8
BWST1	CAL_FLAG1	DMAUDR1	–	–	–	–	–

7	6	5	4	3	2	1	0
–	–	–	–	–	–	–	–
						r/w	r/w

BWSTx: DAC channel x busy writing sample time flag (x = 0 or 2)
This bit is set just after sample & hold mode enable and is set each time the software writes the DAC->SHSRx register, it is cleared when the write operation of DAC->SHSRx is complete.
0: There is no write operation of DAC->SHSRx ongoing: DAC->SHSRx can be written.
1: There is a write operation of DAC->SHSRx ongoing: DAC->SHSRx cannot be written
CAL_FLAGx: DAC channel x calibration offset status (x = 1 or 2)
0: calibration trimming value is greater than the offset correction value
1: calibration trimming value is lower than the offset correction value
DMAUDRx: DAC channel x DMA underrun flag (x = 1 or 2)
0: No DMA underrun error condition occurred for DAC channel x
1: DMA underrun error condition occurred for DAC channel x (i.e., the currently selected trigger is driving DAC channel x conversion at a frequency higher than the DMA service capability rate).

Figure 9.6 DAC status register (DAC->SR)

9.4.8 NOISE GENERATION

When using the DAC to generate signals to test a circuit, it is desirable to make the signal more complicated. The STM32L475 DAC has the capability to generate a noise to be superimposed on top of the generated output. The amplitude is also variable. This capability is implemented using a **linear feedback shift register (LFSR)**.

The DAC noise generation function is enabled by setting the WAVEx[1:0] field in the DAC->CR register to **01**. The preloaded value in the LFSR is 0xAAA. This register is updated three APB1 clock cycles after each trigger event, following a specific calculation algorithm.

The LFSR value can be masked out by the MAMPx[3:0] field in the DAC->CR register before being added to the DHRx register. The resultant sum is then transferred to the DAC->DORx register to be converted to a voltage. The value in the MAMPx[3:0] field determines the number of the lowest bits in the LFSR register that can be added to the DHRx register. For example, if MAMPx[3:0] = 0011, then the rightmost (lowest) 4 bits of the LFSR is added to the DHRx register.

If the LFSR content is 0x0000, a 1 is injected into it. This is the **antilock** mechanism. The noise generation function can be disabled by clearing the WAVEx field to **00**. The LFSR register calculation algorithm is illustrated in Figure 9.7.

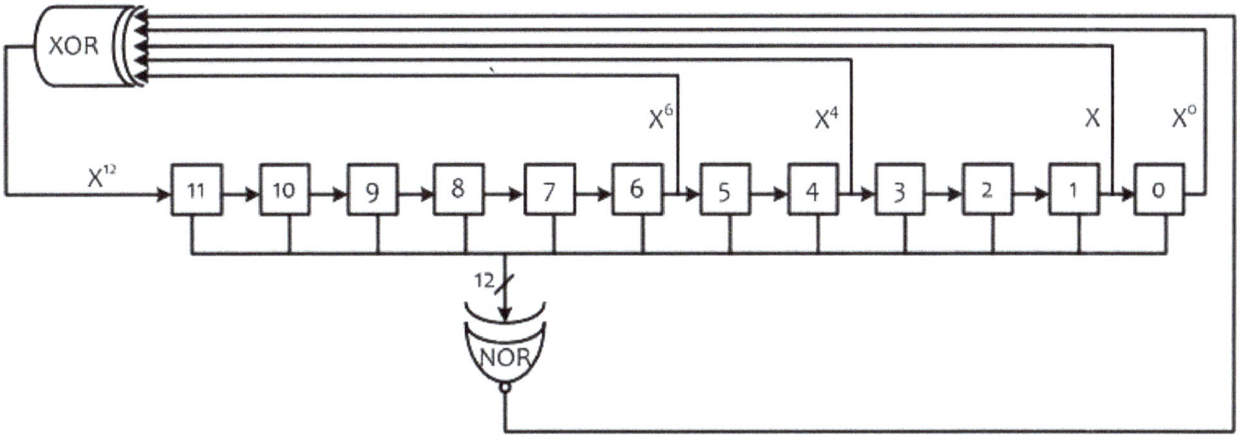

Figure 9.7 DAC LFSR register calculation algorithm

9.4.9 TRIANGLE WAVE GENERATION

It is possible to add a triangular waveform with a small amplitude on top of a DC or slowly changing signal. This feature is selected by setting the WAVEx[1:0] field in the DAC->CR register to **10**. The amplitude of the triangle is set by programming the MAMPx[3:0] field in the DAC->CR register. An internal triangle counter is incremented three APB1 clock cycles after each trigger event. The value of this counter is then added to the DHRx register without overflow and the sum is transferred to the DAC->DORx register. The triangle counter is incremented as long as it is less than the maximum amplitude defined by the MAMPx[3:0] field. Once the programmed amplitude is reached, the counter is decremented down to 0, then incremented again, and so on.

The DAC triangle wave generation is illustrated in Figures 9.8 and 9.9.

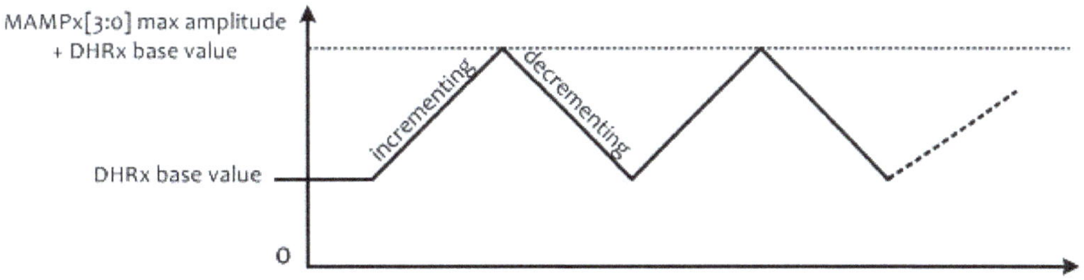

Figure 9.8 DAC triangle wave generation

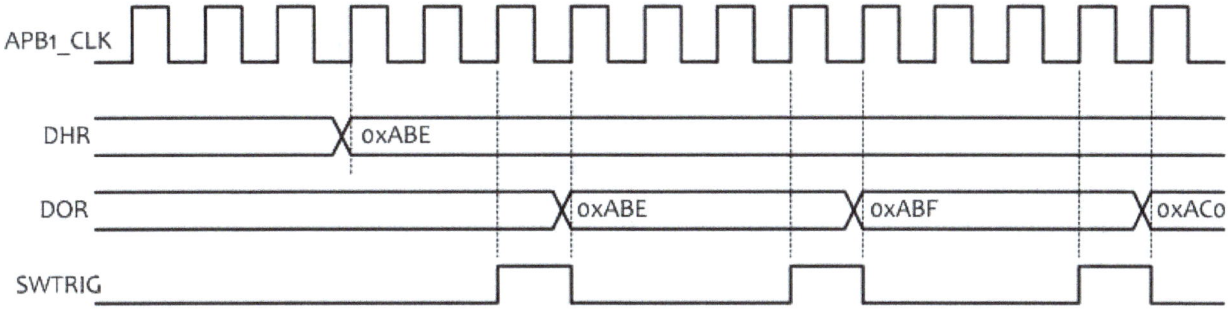

Figure 9.9 DAC conversion (SW trigger enabled) with triangle wave generation

9.4.10 DAC CHANNEL MODES

Each DAC channel has two operation modes: **normal mode** and **hold mode**. There is a buffer between the DAC output and the DAC_OUTx pin. The user can choose to bypass this buffer if it is not needed. The output buffer boosts the DAC drive capability.

Before enabling the output buffer, the voltage offset needs to be calibrated. This calibration is performed at the factory (loaded after reset) and can be adjusted by software during application operation.

The MODEx[2:0] field in the DAC->MCR register sets the DAC channel mode. The contents of the DAC->MCR register are shown in Figure 9.10. Four combinations of the MODEx[2:0] field configure the DAC to the normal mode and the remaining four combinations put DAC in the sample and hold mode.

Normal Mode

Two combinations of the MODEx[2:0] enable the output buffer whereas the other two combinations disable the output buffer:

- Output buffer enabled
  (1) 000: DAC is connected to the external pin
  (2) 001: DAC is connected to external pin and on-chip peripherals
- Output buffer disabled
  (1) 010: DAC is connected to the external pin
  (2) 011: DAC is connected to on-chip peripherals

31	30	29	28	27	26	25	24
–	–	–	–	–	–	–	–
23	**22**	**21**	**20**	**19**	**18**	**17**	**16**
–			–		MODE2[2:0]		
					r/w	r/w	r/w
15	**14**	**13**	**12**	**11**	**10**	**9**	**8**
–	–	–	–	–	–	–	–
7	**6**	**5**	**4**	**3**	**2**	**1**	**0**
–	–	–	–	–	MODE1[2:0]		
					r/w	r/w	r/w

Reset value = 0x0000 0000
Addr offset = 0x3C

MODEx[2:0]: DAC channel x mode (x = 1 or 2)
Can be written only when DAC is disabled and not in calibration mode
DAC channel x in normal mode
000: DAC channel x is connected to external pin with buffer enabled
001: DAC channel x is connected to external pin and to on-chip peripheral with buffer enabled
010: DAC channel x is connected to external pin with buffer disabled
011: DAC channel x is connected to on-chip peripherals with buffer disabled
DAC channel x in sample & hold mode
100: DAC channel x is connected to external pin with buffer enabled
101: DAC channel x is connected to external pin and to on-chip peripherals with buffer enabled
110: DAC channel x is connected to external pin and to on-chip peripherals with buffer disabled
111: DAC channel x is connected to on-chip peripherals with buffer disabled

Figure 9.10 DAC mode control register (DAC->MCR)

Sample and Hold Mode

In this mode, the DAC core circuit converts data on the trigger event and then holds the converted voltage on a capacitor. When not converting, the DAC core circuit and buffer are turned off and the DAC output is tri-stated, reducing the overall power consumption.

A new **stabilization period** (T_{STAB_BON} or T_{STAB_BOFF} depending on the buffer state) is needed before each new conversion. In this mode, the DAC core and all corresponding logic and registers are driven by the **low-speed clock** (**LSI**) in addition to the APB bus clock, allowing to use the DAC channels in deep low-power modes such as the STOP mode.

The operation of the sample and hold mode can be divided into three phrases:

- **Sample phase.** The sample/hold element, which is a capacitor, is charged to the desired voltage. The charging time depends on the capacitance value. The sampling time is configured via the TSAMx[9:0] field in the DAC->SHSRx register.
- **Hold phase.** In this phase, the DAC output channel is tri-stated, and the DAC core circuit and the buffer are turned off, to reduce the power consumption. The hold time is set via the THOLDx[9:0] field in the DAC->SHHR register.
- **Refresh phase.** The refresh time is configured via the TREFx[7:0] field in the DAC->SHRR register.

The contents of the DAC->SHSR1, DAC->SHSR2, DAC->SHHR, and DAC->SHRR registers are shown in Figures 9.11, 9.12, 9.13, and 9.14, respectively.

31	30	29	28	27	26	25	24
–	–	–	–	–	–	–	–

Reset value = 0x0000 0000
Addr offset = 0x40

23	22	21	20	19	18	17	16
–	–	–	–	–	–	–	–

15	14	13	12	11	10	9	8
–	–	–	–	–	–	TSAMPLE1[9:8]	

7	6	5	4	3	2	1	0
TSAMPLE1[7:0]							
						r/w	r/w

TSAMPLE1[9:0]: DAC channel 1 sample time (only valid in sample and hold mode)
This field can be written when the DAC channel 1 is disabled or also during normal operation. In the later case, the write can be done only when BWSTx of DAC->SR register is low. If BWSTx = 1, the write operation is ignored.

Figure 9.11 DAC sample and hold sample time register 1 (DAC->SHSR1)

31	30	29	28	27	26	25	24
–	–	–	–	–	–	–	–
23	22	21	20	19	18	17	16
–	–	–	–	–	–	–	–
15	14	13	12	11	10	9	8
–	–	–	–	–	–	TSAMPLE2[9:8]	
7	6	5	4	3	2	1	0
TSAMPLE2[7:0]							
						r/w	r/w

Reset value = 0x0000 0000
Addr offset = 0x44

TSAMPLE2[9:0]: DAC channel 2 sample time (only valid in sample and hold mode)
This field can be written when the DAC channel 2 is disabled or also during normal operation. In the later case, the write can be done only when BWSTx of DAC->SR register is low. If BWSTx = 1, the write operation is ignored.

Figure 9.12 DAC sample and hold sample time register 2 (DAC->SHSR2)

31	30	29	28	27	26	25	24
–	–	–	–	–	–	THOLD2[9:8]	
23	22	21	20	19	18	17	16
THOLD2[7:0]							
15	14	13	12	11	10	9	8
–	–	–	–	–	–	THOLD1[9:8]	
7	6	5	4	3	2	1	0
THOLD1[7:0]							
						r/w	r/w

Reset value = 0x0001 0001
Addr offset = 0x48

THOLDx[9:0]: DAC channel x hold time (x = 1 or 2, only valid in sample and hold mode)
Hold time = (THOLD[9:0]) x T_{LSI}

Figure 9.13 DAC Sample and Hold hold time register (DAC->SHHR)

31	30	29	28	27	26	25	24
–	–	–	–	–	–	–	–
23	22	21	20	19	18	17	16
TREFRESH2[7:0]							
15	14	13	12	11	10	9	8
–	–	–	–	–	–	–	–
7	6	5	4	3	2	1	0
TREFRESH1[7:0]							
						r/w	r/w

Reset value = 0x0001 0001
Addr offset = 0x4C

TREFRESHx[7:0]: DAC channel x refresh time (x = 1 or 2, only valid in sample and hold mode)
Hold time = (TREFRESH[7:0]) x T_{LSI}

Figure 9.14 DAC Sample and Hold refresh time register (DAC->SHRR)

The timings for three phases are represented in units of LSI clocks. As an example, consider configuring a sample time of 350 μs, hold time of 2 ms, and refresh time of 120 μs assuming that f_{LSI} = 32 kHz.

The period of LSI clock is 1 / 32 kHz = 30.5 μs.

1. Sample time = 350 μs ÷ 30.5 μs ≈ 11 → SAMx[9:0] = 11.
2. Hold time = 2 ms ÷ 30.5 μs ≈ 62 → THOLDx[9:0] = 62.
3. Refresh time = 120 μs ÷ 30.5 μs ≈ 4 → SHRRx[7:0] = 4.

The actual sample time and refresh time must be calculated from the information given in the datasheet. The formulas for computing these parameters when the buffer is enabled and disabled are given in Table 9.3.

Table 9.3 Sample and refresh timings

Buffer State	$t_{sampling(1)(3)}$	$t_{refresh(2)(3)}$
Enabled	$T_{stab\text{-}BON} + (10 * R_{BON} * C_{load})$	$T_{stab\text{-}BON} + (R_{BON} * C_{load}) * \ln(2 * N_{lsb})$
Disabled	$T_{stab\text{-}BOFF} + (10 * R_{BOFF} * C_{load})$	$T_{stab\text{-}BOFF} + (R_{BOFF} * C_{load}) * \ln(2 * N_{lsb})$

Note: 1. In the above formula the settling to the desired code value with ½ LSB or accuracy requires 10 constant time for 12 bits resolution. For 8 bits resolution, the settling time is 7 constant time.
2. The tolerated voltage drop during the hold phase "**Vd**" is represented by the number of LSBs after the capacitor discharging with the output leakage current. The settling back to the desired value with ½ LSB error accuracy requires $\ln(2 * N_{lsb})$ constant time in DAC.
3. The parameters $T_{stab\text{-}BON}$, $T_{stab\text{-}BOFF}$, R_{BON}, R_{BOFF} are specified in datasheet.

Example 9.2 Assume that C_{load} = 100 nF, V_{DDA} = 3.0 V, $T_{STB\text{-}BON}$ = 7 μs, R_{BON} = 2 kΩ. Find $t_{sampling}$, $t_{refresh}$, and t_{hold} when the buffer is enabled.

Solution:

$t_{sampling} = T_{STAB\text{-}BON} + (10 \times R_{BON} \times C_{load}) = 7\ \mu s + (10 \times 2 \times 10^3 \times 100 \times 10^{-9}) = 2.007\ ms$

$t_{refresh} = T_{STAB\text{-}BON} + (R_{BON} \times C_{load}) \times \ln(2 \times N_{LSB}) = 7\ \mu s + (2 \times 10^3 \times 100 \times 10^{-9}) \times \ln(2 \times 10)$

$= 606.1\ \mu s\ (N_{LSB} = 10)$

In the **hold phase**,

- One LSB corresponding to 3 V ÷ 4095 = 0.00073 V.
- During the hold phase, the voltage degradation (D_V) shouldn't be larger than 10 × LSB (=0.0073 V).
- The voltage degradation of the C_{load} is given by the following equation:
  $D_V = i_{leak} \times t_{hold} \div C_{load} = 0.0073\ V$
  In the worst case, i_{leak} is at most 150 nA.
  Therefore,

$t_{hold} = 0.0073 \times 100 \times 10^{-9} \div (150 \times 10^{-9}) = 4.867\ ms.$

The DAC output waveform in the sample and hold mode is best illustrated using a timing diagram. An example timing diagram is shown in Figure 9.15.

- In the first sampling phase in Figure 9.15, the DAC performs a conversion and charges the holding capacitor from 0 V to the voltage V_1. The magnitude of V_1 is determined by the value written into the front-end hold register.

- In the hold phase, the DAC is turned off and its output goes to tri-state and the capacitor holds the voltage using the charge across its two plates. The charge across the capacitor will leak over time and the voltage across the capacitor degrades as shown.
- During the refresh phase, the voltage across the holding capacitor is restored to its most recent peak value.
- In the second hold phase, the voltage across the holding capacitor degrades again due to the leakage current.
- In the second sampling phase, a new value is written into the front-end hold register, which causes the DAC to perform another D/A conversion. This time a smaller value is written into the front-end hold register, and hence, a smaller voltage is generated from the DAC output.

All sample and hold phases are interruptible and any change in the DHRx register will trigger immediately a new sample phase. Another way of representing the relationship of DAC mode, buffer enabling, and output connections is given in Table 9.4.

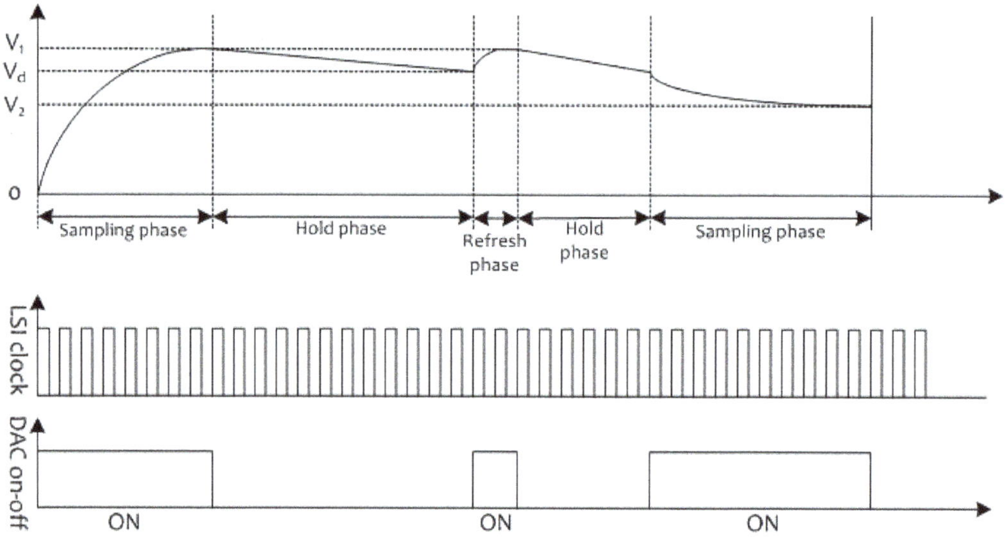

Figure 9.15 An example pf DAC sample and hold mode phase diagram

Table 9.4 Channel output modes summary

MODEx[2:0]	Mode	Buffer	Output connections
000	Normal mode	Enabled	Connected to external pin
001			Connected to external pin and to on-chip peripherals (e.g. AC)
010		Disabled	Connected to external pin
011			Connected to on-chip peripherals (e.g., comparators)
100	Sample & hold mode	Enabled	Connected to external pin
101			Connected to external pin and to on-chip peripherals (e.g. AC)
110		Disabled	Connected to external pin and to on-chip peripherals (e.g. AC)
111			Connected to on-chip peripherals (e.g., comparators)

AC stands for analog comparator

9.4.11 DAC CHANNEL BUFFER CALIBRATION

The output of an N-bit DAC can be expressed as follows:

$$V_{OUT} = ((D \div 2^N) \times G \times V_{REF}) + V_{OS}$$

where,

V_{OUT} is the analog voltage output.

D is the digital value to be converted.

G is the gain of the DAC. Ideally, G = 1.

V_{REF} is the DAC reference voltage.

V_{OS} is the offset voltage. Ideally, $V_{OS} = 0$ V.

The offset voltage V_{OS} may differ from device to device and introduce an absolute offset error on the analog output. Calibration is needed by a trimming technique to compensate for the V_{OS}. Calibration is valid only when the DAC channel is operating with buffer enabled.

The buffer output will be disconnected from pin internal/external connections and put in the tristate mode (HiZ). The buffer will act as a comparator, to sense the middle-code value 0x800 and compare it to $V_{REF+}/2$ signal through an internal bridge, and then toggle its output signal to 0 or 1 depending on the comparison result (CAL_FLAGx bit).

The DAC buffer offset is factory trimmed. The default value of the OTRIMx[4:0] field in the DAC->CCR register is the factory trimming value and it is loaded once DAC digital interface is reset. If the operating conditions differ from nominal factory trimming conditions and in particular when V_{DD}/V_{DDA} voltage, temperature, V_{REF+} values change, the user can perform additional trimming using software.

The procedure for calibrating the DAC output buffer is as follows:

Step 1

Disable the DAC by clearing the ENx bit in the DAC->CR register.

Step 2

Select a DAC mode in which the output buffer is enabled. The MODEx[2:0] field should be 000, or 001, or 100, or 101.

Step 3

Load 0x800 into DAC->DHR12Rx[11:0].

Step 4

Start DAC calibration by setting the CENx bit of the DAC->CR register to 1.

Step 5

Apply the following calibration algorithm:

- Write a code into the OTRIMx[4:0] field in the DAC->CCR register starting from 00000.
- Wait for the $t_{OFFTRIMmax}$ delay.
- Check if CAL_FLAGx bit in the DAC->SR register is set to 1.
- If the CAL_FLAGx bit in the DAC->SR register is 1, the trimming code OTRIMx[4:0] is found and will be used during normal operation to compensate for the output value; else, increment OTRIMx[4:0] and repeat these four steps.

Step 5 can be changed to use successive approximation method to speed up the calibration process. A $t_{OFFTRIMmax}$ delay is needed to ensure that the correct value of CAL_FLAGx bit is read. The $t_{OFFTRIMmax}$ delay can be found in the device's datasheet. The contents of the

DAC->CCR register are shown in Figure 9.16.

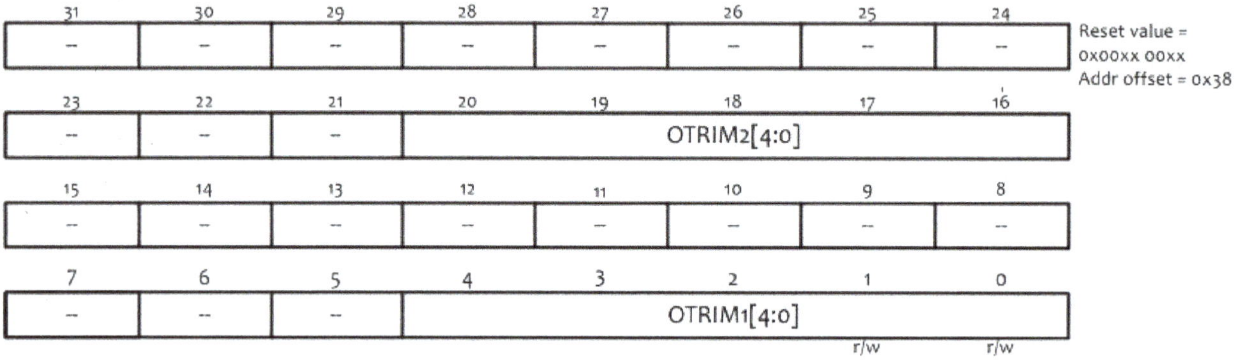

OTRIMx[4:0]: DAC channel x offset trimming value (x = 1 or 2)

Figure 9.16 DAC calibration control register (DAC->CCR)

Example 9.3 Write a sequence of C statements to configure the DAC channel 1 to generate a waveform as shown in Figure 9.17 assuming that the function **delayby1ms (k)** is available for your use, where k is the multiple of 1 ms. V_{REF} is 3.3 V. Use 12-bit resolution.

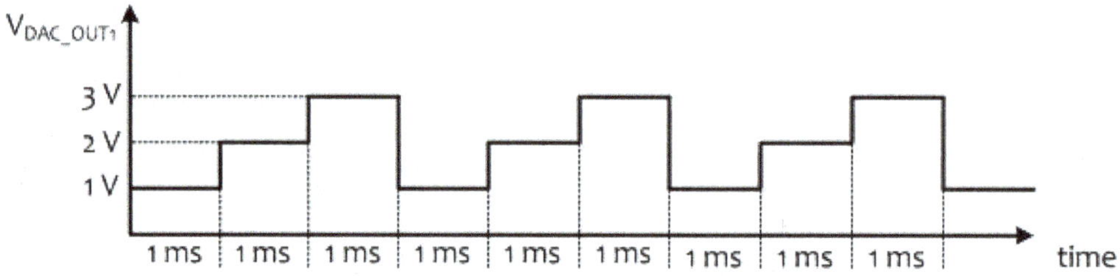

Figure 9.17 Waveform to be generated

Solution:

The value to generate 1, 2, and 3 V are computed as follows:

$$D(1\ V) = 4095 \times 1 \div 3.3 \approx 1241$$

$$D(2\ V) = 4095 \times 2 \div 3.3 \approx 2482$$

$$D(3\ V) = 4095 \times 3 \div 3.3 \approx 3723$$

The C statements to generate the specified waveform are as follows:

```
DAC->CR = DAC_CR_EN1; // enable DAC channel 1
DAC->MCR = 0; // set DAC channels 1 and 2 to normal mode with buffer enabled
while(1) {
    DAC->DHR12R1 = 1241;
    delayby1ms(1);
    DAC->DHR12R1 = 2482;
    delayby1ms(1);
    DAC->DHR12R1 = 3723;
    delayby1ms(1);
}
```

Example 9.4 Write a sequence of C statements to generate the waveform shown in Figure 9.18 using both channels of the DAC assuming that the function delayby1ms (k) is available for your use, where k is the multiple of 1 ms. V_{REF} is 3.3 V. Use 12-bit resolution.

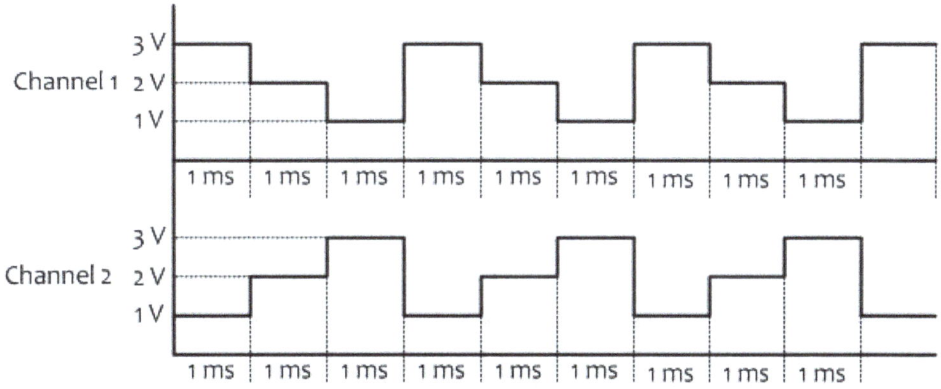

Figure 9.18 Waveform to be generated

Solution:

The values to generate 1, 2, and 3 V output from DAC with V_{REF} equals 3.3 V are 1241 (0x4D9), 2482 (0x9B2), and 3723 (0xE8B), respectively.

The value to be written into DAC_DHR12RD to generate 3 and 1 V from DAC_OUT1 and DAC_OUT2 is 0x04D90E8B.

The value to be written into DAC_DHR12RD to generate 2 and 2 V from DAC_OUT1 and DAC_OUT2 is 0x09B209B2.

The value to be written into DAC_DHR12RD to generate 1 and 3 V from DAC_OUT1 and DAC_OUT2 is 0x0E8B04D9.

The C statements to generate the specified waveform is as follows:

```
DAC->CR = DAC_CR_EN1 + DAC_CR_EN2; // enable both channels
DAC->MCR = 0; // set both DAC channels to normal mode with buffer enabled
while(1){
    DAC->DHR12RD = 0x04D90E8B;
    delayby1ms(1);
    DAC->DHR12RD = 0x09B209B2;
    delayby1ms(1);
    DAC->DHR12RD = 0x0E8B04D9;
    delayby1ms(1);
}
```

Example 9.5 Write a C program to generate a periodic sinusoidal waveform with magnitude between 0 and V_{REF} Volts using 12-bit resolution and store the value right-aligned. To approximate the sine wave, divide one cycle of sine wave into 60 points.

Solution: By dividing one cycle into 60 points, two adjacent points are separated by 6°. We need to calculate the sine function from 0° up to 354°. We don't need to calculate the sine function of 360° because it is the same as that at o°. After sending the value of one point, we need to call a delay function to wait for at least 3 μs to allow the D/A conversion to complete.

Because the range of the sine function is from −1 to 1 but the DAC cannot generate negative voltage outputs, we need to add 1 to the sine function value (shift up the sine wave) in order to find out the value to be sent to the DAC. For example, sine(6°) = 0.1045, then the 12-bit value to be sent to the DAC for sine(6°) = $(1+0.1045) \times 4095 \div 2 = 2261.52 \approx 2262$ = 0x8D6. The values for other degrees can be computed similarly.

The C program that generates a periodic sine wave is as follows:

```
#include <stm32L475xx.h>
void sysClkInit(void);
uint32_t sine[60] = {
    0x0800, 0x08D6, 0x09A9, 0x0A78, 0x0B40, 0x0BFF,
    0x0CB3, 0x0D5A, 0x0DF1, 0x0E78, 0x0EED, 0x0F4E,
    0x0F9B, 0x0FD2, 0x0FF4, 0x0FFF, 0x0FF4, 0x0FD2,
```

```
        0x0F9B, 0x0F4E, 0x0EED, 0x0E78, 0x0DF1, 0x0D5A,
        0x0CB3, 0x0BEF, 0x0B40, 0x0A78, 0x09A9, 0x08D6,
        0x0800, 0x0728, 0x0656, 0x0587, 0x04BF, 0x0400,
        0x034C, 0x02A5, 0x020E, 0x0187, 0x0112, 0x00B1,
        0x0064, 0x002D, 0x000B, 0x0000, 0x000B, 0x002D,
        0x0064, 0x00B1, 0x0112, 0x0187, 0x020E, 0x02A5,
        0x034C, 0x0400, 0x04BF, 0x0587, 0x0656, 0x0729};
void wait3us(void);
int main (void)
{
        uint32_t j;
        sysClkInit();
        DAC->CR = DAC_CR_EN1; // enable DAC channel 1
        DAC->MCR = 0; // set DAC channels 1 and 2 to normal mode with buffer enabled
        while(1){
            for(j = 0; j < 60; j++){
                DAC->DHR12R1 = sine[j];
                wait3us();
            }
        }
}
void wait3us(void)
{
    .... // statements to generate roughly 3 us delay
}
```

Example 9.6 Write a C program to generate the waveform shown in Figure 9.19 assuming that VREF = 3.3 V. Assume that TIM7 operates with an 80 MHz clock source.

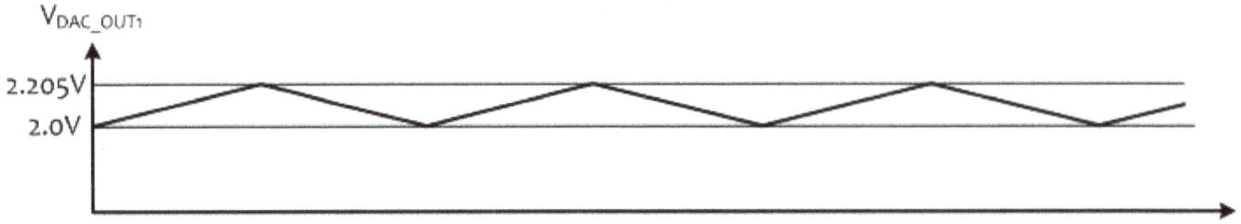

Figure E9.19 Waveform to be generated

Solution: This waveform can be generated by:

1. Load (= 2 × 4095 ÷ 3.3) ≈ 2482 = 0x9B2 into the DAC->DHR12R1 register.
2. Enable trigger and select TIM7 (set TSEL[2:0] to 010) as the trigger source.
3. Set WAVE1[1:0] to 10 to enable triangle waveform generation.
4. Set MAMP1[3:0] to 0111 so that triangle magnitude can go up to 0.205 V (= 3.3 × 255 ÷ 4095).
5. Stay in an infinite loop and generate a software trigger once every 4 μs.

The C program that generates the specified waveform is as follows:

```
#include <stm32L475xx.h>
void sysClkInit(void);
void initTIM7 (void);
int main (void)
{
    sysClkInit();
    DAC->DHR12R1 = 0x9B2; // value to produce 2 V
    DAC->MCR = 0; // normal mode, enable output buffer
    DAC->CR = DAC_CR_MAMP1_2 + DAC_CR_MAMP1_1 + DAC_CR_MAMP1_0 +
          DAC_CR_WAVE1_1 + DAC_CR_TSEL1_1 + DAC_CR_TEN1 + DAC_CR_EN1;
    initTIM7();
    while(1){ // perform other operations
          ....
    }
}
void initTIM7 (void)
{
    TIM7->PSC     = 0; // set prescaler to 1
    TIM7->ARR     = 319; // it takes 4 μs to count to this value
```

```
    TIM7->CR1    = TIM_CR1_ARPE; // enable ARR buffer
    TIM7->CR2    = TIM_CR2_MMS_1; // select update event as TRGO
    TIM7->EGR    |= TIM_EGR_UG;
    TIM7->CR1    |= TIM_CR1_CEN; // enable TIM7 to count
}
```

Example 9.7 Use TIM6 to generate TRGO as the trigger source for DAC1. Set up TIM6 properly so that the trigger is generated every 4 μs. Assume that the frequency of the clock source to TIM6 is 80 MHz.

Solution: Use 8 as the prescaler to the clock source of TIM6. By setting TIM6->ARR to 39, the TRGO from TIM6 will be generated every 4 μs. The following C statements should be used to replace the while loop in Example 9.6:

```
    TIM6->PSC    = 7;                  // set prescaler to 8
    TIM6->ARR    = 39;
    TIM6->EGR    |= TIM_EGR_UG;        // update prescaler and ARR
    TIM6->CR2    = TIM_CR2_MMS_1;      // select Update event as the source of TRGO
    TIM6->CR1    |= TIM_CR1_ARPE + TIM_CR1_CEN; // enable TIM6
    DAC->CR      &= ~DAC_CR_TSEL1 ; // select Timer 6 TRGO event as trigger source
    DAC->CR      |= DAC_CR_TEN1;       // enable DAC channel 1 trigger
```

Example 9.8 Modify Example 9.5 to use DMA function to transfer data to be converted to the DAC so that the processor can continue to perform other operation. Assume that the STM32L475 system clock is 80 MHz.

Solution:

```
#include <stm32L475xx.h>
void sysClkInit(void);
void dmaSetup(void);
uint32_t sine[60] = {
        0x0800, 0x08D6, 0x09A9, 0x0A78, 0x0B40, 0x0BFF,
        0x0CB3, 0x0D5A, 0x0DF1, 0x0E78, 0x0EED, 0x0F4E,
        0x0F9B, 0x0FD2, 0x0FF4, 0x0FFF, 0x0FF4, 0x0FD2,
        0x0F9B, 0x0F4E, 0x0EED, 0x0E78, 0x0DF1, 0x0D5A,
```

```
        0x0CB3, 0x0BEF, 0x0B40, 0x0A78, 0x09A9, 0x08D6,
        0x0800, 0x0728, 0x0656, 0x0587, 0x04BF, 0x0400,
        0x034C, 0x02A5, 0x020E, 0x0187, 0x0112, 0x00B1,
        0x0064, 0x002D, 0x000B, 0x0000, 0x000B, 0x002D,
        0x0064, 0x00B1, 0x0112, 0x0187, 0x020E, 0x02A5,
        0x034C, 0x0400, 0x04BF, 0x0587, 0x0656, 0x0729};
int main (void)
{
    sysClkInit();
    dmaSetup();
// enable DMA to DAC1, enable and select TIM6 TRGO trigger to DAC,
// enable  DAC channel 1
    DAC->CR      = DAC_CR_DMAEN1 + DAC_CR_TEN1 + DAC_CR_EN1;
    DAC->MCR     = 0; // set DAC channels 1 and 2 to normal mode with buffer enabled
// set up TIM6 to generate a trigger from TRGO every 4 us (trigger DMA transfer to DAC)
    TIM6->PSC    = 7; // set TIM6 clock input frequency to 10 MHz
    TIM6->ARR    = 39; // TIM6 generates update event every 4 us
    TIM6->EGR    |= TIM_EGR_UG; // update prescaler and ARR
    TIM6->CR2    = TIM_CR2_MMS_1; // select update event as the source of TRGO
    TIM6->CR1    |= TIM_CR1_ARPE + TIM_CR1_CEN; // enable TIM6 and its auto reload
    while(1);
}
void dmaSetup(void)
{
    DMA1_CSELR->CSELR        &=  ~DMA_CSELR_C3S; // assign DAC1 to DMA1 Channel 3
    DMA1_CSELR->CSELR        |=  (0x06 << DMA_CSELR_C3S_Pos);        //      "
    DMA1_Channel3->CMAR      =   (uint32_t)sine;
    DMA1_Channel3->CPAR      =   (uint32_t)&DAC1->DHR12R1;
```

```
    DMA1_Channel3->CNDTR =     60;
    DMA1_Channel3->CCR     &=  ~(DMA_CCR_PL + DMA_CCR_MSIZE + DMA_CCR_PSIZE);
// set Channel 3 to highest priority, set memory and peripheral size to 32 bits,
// data transfer from memory to peripheral, circular mode, enable Channel 3
    DMA1_Channel3->CCR     |=  DMA_CCR_PL_1 + DMA_CCR_MSIZE_1 +
                               DMA_CCR_PSIZE_1 + DMA_CCR_MINC + DMA_CCR_DIR +
                               DMA_CCR_CIRC + DMA_CCR_EN;
}
```

9.5 Dual-Channel DAC Conversion

Dual-channel registers DHR8RD, DHR12RD, and DHR12LD are implemented for efficient use of data bus bandwidth in applications that require two DAC channels at the same time. Eleven conversion modes are possible when using these two DAC channels and dual registers. However, all the conversion modes can be obtained using separate DHRyyyx registers (yyy can be 8R, 12R, or 12L and x can be 1 or 2) if needed.

9.5.1 INDEPENDENT TRIGGER WITHOUT WAVE GENERATION

The procedure for this conversion mode is as follows:

Step 1

Set both the TEN1 and TEN2 bits in the DAC->CR register to 1 to enable trigger to both DAC channels.

Step 2

Configure different trigger sources by setting the TSEL1[2:0] and TSEL2[2:0] bit fields in the DAC->CR register to different values.

Step 3

Load values to be converted into the desired front-end dual-channel hold register (DAC->DHR8RD, DAC->DHR12D, or DAC->DHR12LD).

Step 4

When a DAC channel 1 trigger arrives, the DHR1 register is transferred to the DAC->DOR1 register three APB1 bus clock cycles later.

Step 5

When a DAC channel 2 trigger arrives, the DHR2 register is transferred to the DAC->DOR2 register three APB1 bus clock cycles later.

9.5.2 INDEPENDENT TRIGGER WITH SINGLE LFSR GENERATION

The procedure for this conversion mode is as follows:

Step 1

Set both the TEN1 and TEN2 bits in the DAC->CR register to 1 to enable trigger to both DAC channels.

Step 2

Configure different trigger sources by setting the TSEL1[2:0] and TSEL2[2:0] bit fields in the DAC->CR register to different values.

Step 3

Program two DAC channel WAVEx[1:0] bit fields to 01 and the same LFSR mask value in the MAMPx[3:0] bit fields of the DAC->CR register.

Step 4

Load the dual DAC channel data into the desired front-end dual-channel DHR register (DHR8RD, DRH12RD, or DHR12LD).

Step 5

When a DAC channel 1 trigger arrives, the LFSR1 counter with the mask is added to the DHR1 register and the sum is transferred to the DAC->DOR1 register and the LFSR1 counter is updated.

Step 6

When a DAC channel 2 trigger arrives, the LFSR2 counter with the mask is added to the DHR2 register and the sum is transferred to the DAC->DOR2 register and the LFSR2 counter is updated.

9.5.3 INDEPENDENT TRIGGER AND DIFFERENT LFSR GENERATION

The procedure for this conversion mode is as follows:

Step 1

Set both the TEN1 and TEN2 bit in the DAC->CR register to 1 to enable trigger to both DAC channels.

Step 2

Set the TSEL1[2:0] and TSEL2[2:0] bit fields in the DAC->CR register to different values so that two DAC channels have different trigger sources.

Step 3

Configure both DAC channel WAVEx[1:0] bit fields to 01 and set different LFSR mask values in the MAMP1[3:0] and MAMP2[3:0] bit fields in the DAC->CR register.

Step 4

Load the dual DAC channel data into the desired front-end DHR register (DHR8RD, DRH12RD, or DHR12LD).

Step 5

When a DAC channel 1 trigger arrives, the LFSR1 counter with the mask is added to the DHR1 register and the sum is transferred to the DAC->DOR1 register and the LFSR1 counter is updated.

Step 6

When a DAC channel 2 trigger arrives, the LFSR2 counter with the mask is added to the DHR2 register and the sum is transferred to the DAC->DOR2 register and the LFSR2 counter is updated.

9.5.4 INDEPENDENT TRIGGER AND SINGLE TRIANGLE GENERATION

The procedure for this conversion mode is as follows:

Step 1

Set both the TEN1 and TEN2 bits in the DAC->CR register to 1 to enable trigger to both DAC channels.

Step 2

Set the TSEL1[2:0] and TSEL2[2:0] bit fields in the DAC->CR register to different values so that two DAC channels have different trigger sources.

Step 3

Configure both DAC channel WAVEx[1:0] bit fields to **1x** and the same value in the MAMP1[3:0] and MAMP2[3:0] bit fields.

Step 4

Load the dual DAC channel data into the desired front-end DHR register (DHR8RD, DRH12RD, or DHR12LD).

Step 5

When a DAC channel 1 trigger arrives, the DAC channel 1 triangle counter is added to the DHR1 register and the sum is transferred to the DAC->DOR1 register. The DAC channel 1 triangle counter is then updated.

Step 6

When a DAC channel 2 trigger arrives, the DAC channel 2 triangle counter is added to the DHR2 register and the sum is transferred to the DAC->DOR2 register. The DAC channel 2 triangle counter is then updated.

9.5.5 INDEPENDENT TRIGGER WITH DIFFERENT TRIANGLE GENERATION

The procedure for this conversion mode is as follows:

Step 1

Set both the TEN1 and TEN2 bits in the DAC->CR register to 1 to enable trigger to both DAC channels.

Step 2

Set the TSEL1[2:0] and TSEL2[2:0] bit fields in the DAC->CR register to different values so that two DAC channels have different trigger sources.

Step 3

Set the WAVE1[1:0] and WAVE2[1:0] bit field in the DAC->CR register to 1x and set the MAMP1[3:0] and MAMP2[3:0] bit fields to different values.

Step 4

Load the dual DAC channel data into the desired front-end DHR register (DHR8RD, DRH12RD, or DHR12LD).

Step 5

When a DAC channel 1 trigger arrives, the DAC channel 1 triangle counter is added to the DHR1 register and the sum is transferred to the DAC->DOR1 register. The DAC channel 1 triangle counter is then updated.

Step 6

When a DAC channel 2 trigger arrives, the DAC channel 2 triangle counter is added to the DHR2 register and the sum is transferred to the DAC->DOR2 register. The DAC channel 2 triangle counter is then updated.

9.5.6 SIMULTANEOUS SOFTWARE START

The procedure for this conversion mode is as follows:

Step 1

Load the dual DAC channel data into the desired front-end DHR register (DHR8RD, DRH12RD, or DHR12LD).

Step 2

Set both the SWTRIG1 and SWTRIG2 bits in the DAC->SWTRGR register to 1.

In this configuration, one APB1 clock cycle later, the DHR1 and DHR2 registers are transferred to DAC->DOR1 and DAC->DOR2, respectively, and the conversion is started.

9.5.7 SIMULTANEOUS TRIGGER WITHOUT WAVE GENERATION

The procedure for this conversion mode is as follows:

Step 1

Set both the TEN1 and TEN2 bit in the DAC->CR register to 1 to enable trigger to both DAC channels.

Step 2

Set the TSEL1[2:0] and TSEL2[2:0] bit fields in the DAC->CR register to the same value so that both DAC channels have the same trigger source.

Step 3

Load the dual DAC channel data to the desired front-end DHR register (DHR8RD, DRH12RD, or DHR12LD).

Step 4

When a trigger arrives, the contents of the DHR1 and DHR2 registers are transferred to

DAC->DOR1 and DAC->DOR2, respectively, after three APB1 bus clock cycles.

9.5.8 SIMULTANEOUS TRIGGER WITH SINGLE LFSR GENERATION

The procedure for this conversion mode is as follows:

Step 1

Enable trigger to both DAC channels by setting both the TEN1 and TEN2 bits in the DAC->CR register to 1.

Step 2

Set the TSEL1[2:0] and TSEL2[2:0] bit fields in the DAC->CR register to the same value so that both DAC channels have the same trigger source.

Step 3

Set both the WAVE1[1:0] and WAVE2[2:0] fields in the DAC->CR register to 01 and load the same LFSR mask value to the MAMP1[3:0] and MAMP2[3:0] bit fields in the DAC->CR register.

Step 4

Load the dual DAC channel data to the desired front-end HDR register (DHR8RD, DRH12RD, or DHR12LD).

Step 5

When a trigger arrives, the LFSR1 counter, with the same mask, is added to the DHR1 register and the sum is transferred to the DAC->DOR1 register. The LFSR1 counter is then updated.

Step 6

At the same time, the LFSR2 counter, with the same mask, is added to the DHR2 register and the sum is transferred to the DAC->DOR2 register. The LFSR2 counter is then updated.

9.5.9 SIMULTANEOUS TRIGGER WITH DIFFERENT LFSR GENERATION

The procedure for this conversion mode is as follows:

Step 1

Enable trigger to both DAC channels by setting the TEN1 and TEN2 bits in the DAC->CR register to 1.

Step 2

Set the TSEL1[2:0] and TSEL2[2:0] bit fields in the DAC->CR register to the same value so that both DAC channels have the same trigger source.

Step 3

Configure the two DAC channel WAVEx[1:0] bits as 01 and set different LFSR mask values using the MAMP1[3:0] and MAMP2[3:0] bit fields in the DAC->CR register.

Step 4

Load the dual DAC channel data into the desired DHR register (DAC->DHR8RD,

DAC->DHR12RD, DAC->DHR12LD).

Step 5

When a trigger arrives, the LFSR1 counter, with the mask configured by MAMP1[3:0], is added to the DHR1 register and the sum is transferred to the DAC->DOR1 register. The LFSR1 counter is then updated.

Step 6

At the same time, the LFSR2 counter, with the mask configured by MAMP2[3:0], is added to the DHR2 register and the sum is transferred to the DAC->DOR2 register. The LFSR2 counter is then updated.

Example 9.9 Write a C program to generate waveforms from DAC_OUT1 and DAC_OUT2 pins with the following characteristics assuming that $V_{REF} = 3.3$ V:

1. DAC_OUT1: superimpose an LFSR noise with magnitude equals 0.205 V (MAMP1[3:0] = 0111) on top of a 1-V DC voltage.
2. DAC_OUT2: superimpose an LFSR noise with magnitude equals 0.412 V (MAPM2[3:0] = 1000) on top of a 2-V DC voltage

Two waveforms are triggered by the update event of TIM7 every 4 μs.

Solution:

1. The WAVE1[1:0] and WAVE2[1:0] fields must be set to 01.
2. The TSEL1[2:0] and TSEL1[2:0] fields must be set to 010

The following C program will generate the specified waveform:

```
#include <stm32L475xx.h>

void sysClkInit(void);

void wait4us(void);

int main (void)

{

    sysClkInit();

    DAC->MCR = 0;

    // DAC level for DAC_OUT1 and DAC_OUT2 are set to 1 and 2 V

    DAC->DHR12RD = 0x09B204D9;

    DAC->CR =

        DAC_CR_WAVE1_0 + DAC_CR_MAMP1_0 + DAC_CR_MAMP1_1 + DAC_CR_MAMP1_2 +

        DAC_CR_WAVE2_0 + DAC_CR_MAMP2_3 +

        DAC_CR_TSEL1_1 + DAC_CR_TSEL2_1 +

        DAC_CR_TEN1 + DAC_CR_TEN2 + DAC_CR_EN1 + DAC_CR_EN2;

    initTIM7();

    while(1){

        ... // perform other operations

    }

}

void initTIM7 (void)

{

    TIM7->PSC    = 0;               // set prescaler to 1

    TIM7->ARR    = 319;             // it takes 4 µs to count to this value

    TIM7->CR1    = TIM_CR1_ARPE;    // enable ARR buffer

    TIM7->CR2    = TIM_CR2_MMS_1;   // select update event as TRGO

    TIM7->EGR    |= TIM_EGR_UG;     // update buffers
```

```
    TIM7->CR1     |= TIM_CR1_CEN;        // enable TIM7 to count
}
```

9.5.10 SIMULTANEOUS TRIGGER WITH SINGLE TRIANGLE GENERATION

The procedure for this conversion mode is as follows:

Step 1

Enable trigger to both DAC channels by setting the TEN1 and TEN2 bits in the DAC->CR register to 1.

Step 2

Set the TSEL1[2:0] and TSEL2[2:0] bit fields in the DAC->CR register to the same value so that both DAC channels have the same trigger source.

Step 3

Set the WAVE1[1:0] and WAVE2[1:0] bit fields in the DAC->CR register to **1x** and store the same maximum amplitude value to the MAMP1[3:0] and MAMP2[3:0] fields in the DAC->CR register.

Step 4

Load the dual DAC channel data into the desired front-end DHR register (DAC->DHR8RD,

DAC->DHR12RD, DAC->DHR12LD).

Step 5

When a trigger arrives, the DAC channel 1 triangle counter is added to the DHR1 register and the sum is transferred to DAC->DOR1. The DAC channel 1 triangle counter is then updated.

Step 6

At the same time, the DAC channel 2 triangle counter is added to the DHR2 register and the sum is transferred to DAC->DOR2. The DAC channel 2 triangle counter is then updated.

9.5.11 SIMULTANEOUS TRIGGER WITH DIFFERENT TRIANGLE GENERATION

The procedure for this conversion mode is as follows:

Step 1

Enable trigger to both DAC channels by setting the TEN1 and TEN2 bits in the DAC->CR register to 1.

Step 2

Set the TSEL1[2:0] and TSEL2[2:0] bit fields in the DAC->CR register to the same value so that both DAC channels have the same trigger source.

Step 3

Set the WAVE1[1:0] and WAVE2[1:0] fields in the DAC->CR register to **1x** and write different values to the MAMP1[3:0] and MAMP2[3:0] fields in the DAC->CR register.

Step 4

Load the dual DAC channel data into the desired front-end DHR register (DAC->DHR8RD,

DAC->DHR12RD, DAC->DHR12LD).

Step 5

When a trigger arrives, the DAC channel 1 triangle counter is added to the DHR1 register and the sum is transferred to the DAC->DOR1 register. The DAC channel 1 triangle counter is then updated.

Step 6

At the same time, the DAC channel 2 triangle counter is added to the DHR2 register and the sum is transferred to the DAC->DOR2 register. The DAC channel 2 triangle counter is then updated.

9.6 Summary

DAC is a circuit that can convert a digital value to a voltage. The digital value to be converted is limited to a number encoded using **n** bits. The value **n** is the **resolution** of the DAC. A DAC also requires a reference voltage to perform the conversion.

The STM32L475 has two digital-to-analog converters. In the STM32L475 literature, these two DACs are also called two DAC channels. Each DAC channel has one output. Each DAC channel also has an output buffer, which can boost the output drive current. The D/A conversion takes 3 μs in the worst case for its output to reach the final value ±0.5LSB. After sending a value to be converted, the application is required to wait for 3 μs before sending the next value to be converted. To provide this time delay, the user has three options:

1. Option 1: Use a dummy loop to create a delay slightly longer than 3 μs.
2. Option 2: Call a timer function to create a delay slightly longer than 3 μs.
3. Option 3: Configure a timer to generate a trigger output ($TRGO_n$) every 3 μs to trigger a DMA channel to transfer data to the DAC.

The user can choose one of these options to send the next value to be converted to the DAC.

There are three methods to start the D/A conversion: (1) automatic—simply write the value into one of the front-end hold register and let it be converted, (2) software trigger-by setting the SWTRIG1 or SWTRIG2 bit in the DAC->SWTRIGR register, (3) external event trigger.

The STM32L475 DAC allows the user to superimpose a noise or a small triangle signal on top of a base signal. The resultant waveform can be used as a stimulus to test a circuit.

The user can use the DAC one channel at a time or both channels at the same time. The user can also include noise or triangle generation when both channels are used. There are eleven possible operation modes for dual channel operations.

9.7 Exercises

E9.1 Write a C program to generate the waveform shown in Figure E9.1 using DAC channel 2 assuming that V_{REF} = 3.3 V. Divide one cycle into 60 points.

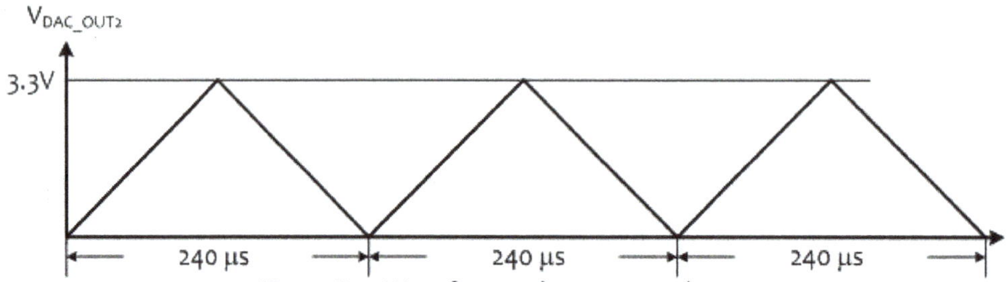

Figure E9.1 Waveform to be generated

E9.2 Write a C program to generate the waveform shown in Figure E9.2 from DAC_OUT1 pin assuming that V_{REF} = 3.3 V. Divide one cycle into 60 points and use DMA to transfer the data (in an array) to be converted to DAC.

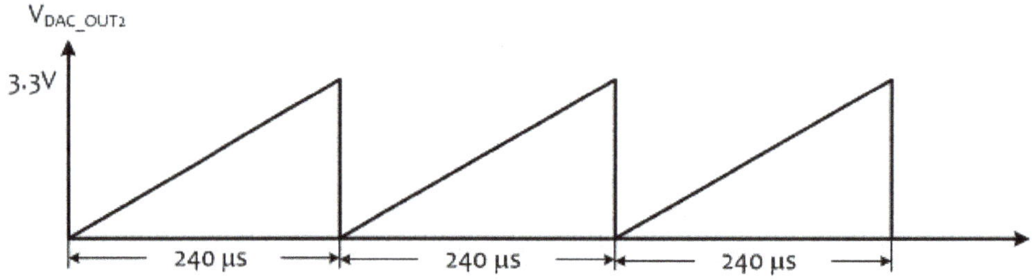

Figure E9.02 Waveform to be generated

E9.3 Write a C program to generate a saw-tooth waveform (shown in Figure E9.2) from the DAC_OUT1 pin and a sine waveform (Example 9.5) from DAC_OUT2 pin assuming that V_{REF} = 3.3 V. Divide each cycle into 60 points.

E9.4 Supposing the initial value in LFSR is $0000\ 0000\ 0001_2$, refer to Figure 9.7, write down the values of the LFSR register after the first 12 events.

E9.5 Write a C program to generate waveforms from DAC_OUT1 and DAC_OUT2 pins with the following characteristics assuming that V_{REF} = 3.3 V:

1. DAC_OUT1: superimpose a triangle wave with magnitude equals 0.1023 V (MAMP1[3:0] = 0110) on top of a 1.8-V DC voltage.
2. DAC_OUT2: superimpose a triangle wave with magnitude equals 0.824 V (MAPM2[3:0] = 1001) on top of a 2.5-V DC voltage.

Two waveforms are triggered by the same software trigger every 4 µs.

E9.6 Write a C program to generate waveforms from DAC_OUT1 and DAC_OUT2 pins with the following characteristics assuming that V_{REF} = 3.3 V:

1. DAC_OUT1: superimpose an LFSR noise with magnitude equals 0.205 V (MAMP1[3:0] = 0111) on top of a 1-V DC voltage.
2. DAC_OUT2: superimpose a triangle noise with magnitude equals 0.412 V (MAPM2[3:0] = 1000) on top of a 2-V DC voltage.

Two waveforms are triggered by the TIM2 TRGO trigger event every 4 μs. Assume that the clock source to TIM2 is 80 MHz.

9.8 Lab Assignments

L9.1 Write a program to generate a sine wave (output from PA4 pin). Divide a cycle of the sine wave into 60 points. Use DMA transfer to send the data to be converted to the DAC1. Use external trigger (TIM6) to trigger the DMA transfer every 4 μs. The DMA must be configured to circular mode. Display the waveforms using the oscilloscope.

L9.2 Write a C program to generate a sine wave from the DAC_OUT1 pin and a triangular wave from DAC_OUT2 pin, respectively, and connect V_{REF} to 3.3 V. Display both waveforms using the oscilloscope. Use DMA function to transfer the data to be converted.

L9.3 Write a C program to generate waveforms from DAC_OUT1 and DAC_OUT2 pins with the following characteristics assuming that V_{REF} = 3.3 V:

1. DAC_OUT1: superimpose a triangle wave with magnitude equals 0.205 V (MAMP1[3:0] = 255) on top of a 1.8-V DC voltage.
2. DAC_OUT2: superimpose a triangle wave with magnitude equals 0.412 V (MAPM2[3:0] = 511) on top of a 2.5-V DC voltage.

Two waveforms are triggered by the TIM6 update event (TIM6->CNT == TIM6->ARR) every 5 μs. Display both waveforms using the oscilloscope.

10

Analog-to-Digital Converter

10.1 Objectives

After completing this chapter, you should be able to:

- Explain the A/D conversion process.
- Interpret the A/D conversion result.
- Perform signal conditioning for sensor output.
- Configure GPIO pins to carry analog signals to be converted.
- Place analog channels into regular group or injected group.
- Start A/D conversion using external event or software trigger.
- Configure ADC to operate at different modes.

10.2 Introduction

Many embedded applications need to deal with nonelectric quantities, such as weight, humidity, pressure, weight, mass flow, airflow, temperature, light intensity, and speed. These quantities are analog in nature because they have a continuous set of values over a given range, in contrast to the discrete values of digital signals. To enable the microcontroller to process these quantities, they need to be represented in digital forms; thus, an analog-to-digital converter is required.

10.2.1 A DATA ACQUISITION SYSTEM

An analog-to-digital converter (ADC) only can deal with electric voltage. A nonelectric quantity must be converted to a voltage before A/D conversion can be performed. The conversion of a nonelectric quantity to a voltage requires the use of a **transducer**. In general, a transducer is a device that converts the quantity from one form to another. For example, a temperature sensor is a transducer that can convert the temperature into a voltage. A **load cell** is the transducer that can convert a weight into a voltage.

A transducer may not generate an output voltage in the range suitable for A/D conversion. This may happen when the range of a nonelectric quantity of interest is converted to a very narrow range of voltage output. Since the range of voltage is very narrow, the nonelectric quantity will be converted into a very small range of digital values. Thus, significant error might be introduced when translating the A/D result back to the original nonelectric quantity.

If the transducer output is from 0 V to a small voltage (e.g., 50 mV), we can use a voltage amplifier (also referred to as a **voltage scaler**) to amplify it to an appropriate magnitude that can take advantage of the full dynamic range (0 to $2^n - 1$, n is the number of bits that represents the A/D conversion result) of the A/D converter. If the transducer output range is from a voltage to another slightly larger voltage (e.g., from 2.0 V to 2.05 V), then we need a circuit that can shift and scale this voltage to an appropriate range (e.g., **0V** ~ $\mathbf{V_{REF}}$) so that it can be converted by the ADC and then properly processed by the computer. The circuit that performs the task of shifting and scaling is called **signal-conditioning circuit**. The overall A/D process is illustrated in Figure 10.1.

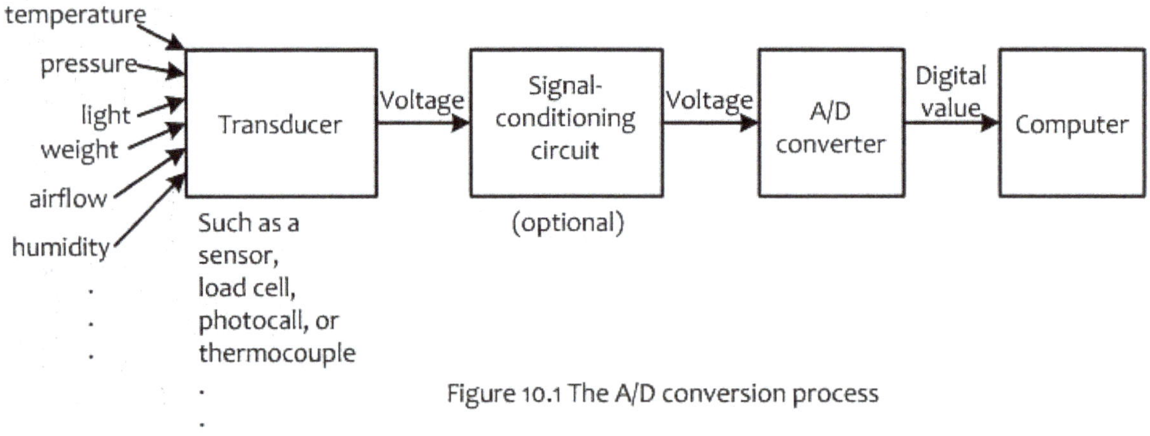

Figure 10.1 The A/D conversion process

10.2.2 ANALOG VOLTAGE AND DIGITAL CODE CHARACTERISTIC

An ideal ADC should demonstrate the linear input/output relationship shown in Figure 10.2. However, the output characteristic shown in Figure 10.2 is unrealistic because it requires the ADC to use an infinite number of bits to represent the conversion result. The output characteristic of an ideal ADC using n bits to represent the conversion result is shown in Figure 10.3. An n-bit ADC has 2^n possible output code values. The area between the dotted line and the staircase is called the **quantization error**. The value of $V_{DD}/2^n$ is the **resolution** of this ADC. Using n bits to represent the conversion result, the average conversion error is $V_{DD}/2^{n+1}$ if the converter is perfectly linear. This value corresponds to half of the least significant bit of the conversion result. For a real ADC, the output characteristic may have **nonlinearity** (the staircase may have unequal steps in some values) and **nonmonotonicity** (higher voltage may have smaller code).

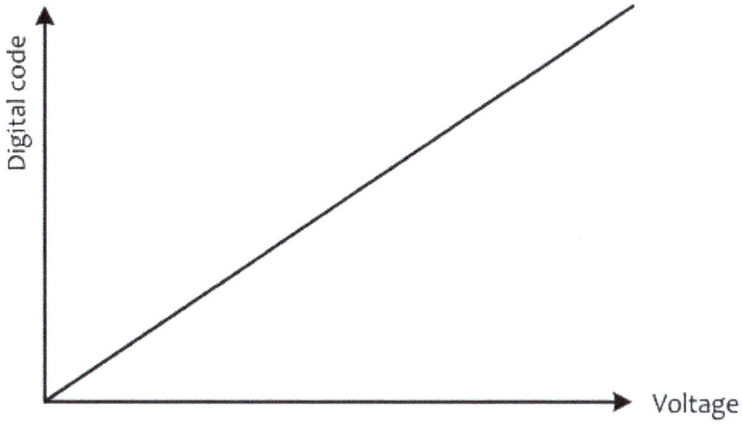

Figure 10.2 An ideal A/D converter output characteristic

Obviously, the more bits are used to represent the A/D conversion result, the smaller the conversion error will be. Most microcontrollers use 8 bits, 10 bits, or 12 bits to represent the conversion result. Some microcontrollers (mainly 8051 variants from Silicon Laboratory, TI, and Analog Devices) use 16 bits or even 24 bits to represent conversion results. Whenever the on-chip A/D converter cannot provide the required accuracy, an external A/D converter should be considered.

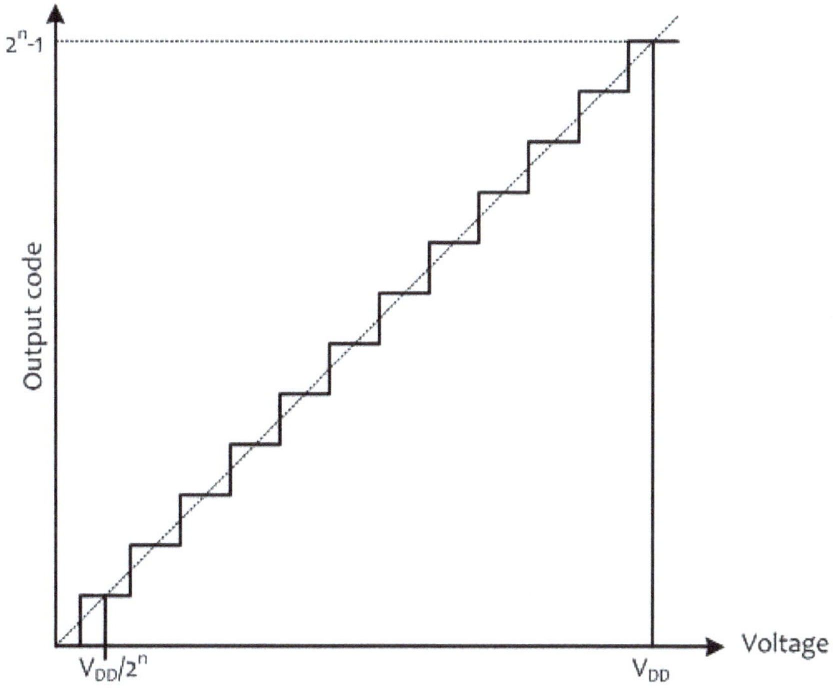

Figure 10.3 Output characteristic of an ideal n-bit A/D converter

10.2.3 A/D CONVERSION ALGORITHM

Many A/D conversion algorithms have been developed in the past. These algorithms can be divided into four categories:

1. Parallel (flash) ADC
2. Slope and double-slope ADC
3. Sigma-delta ADC
4. Successive-approximation ADC

Parallel (Flash) ADC

In this type of ADC, 2^n comparators are used. One of the inputs to each comparator is the input voltage to be converted; the other input corresponds to the voltage that represents one of the 2^n combinations of n-bit values. The comparator output will be high whenever the analog input (to be converted) is higher than the voltage that represents one of the 2^n combinations of the n-bit value. **The largest n-bit value that causes the comparator output to become true is selected as the A/D conversion value through a priority encoder**. It is obvious that this type of ADC will be very fast. However, they require a lot of hardware resources to implement and therefore are not suitable for implementing high-resolution ADCs. This type of ADC is often used in applications that require high speed but low resolution, such as a video signal. Over the years, many variations to this approach have been proposed to produce high-speed ADCs. The most commonly used technique is to pipeline a flash ADC, which will reduce the amount of hardware required while still achieving high conversion speed.

Slope and Double-Slope A/D Converters

This type of ADC is used in Microchip Technology PIC14000 microcontrollers in which the charging and discharging of a capacitor is used to perform A/D conversion. It requires relatively simple hardware and is popular in low-speed applications, such as digital multimeters. In addition, a high resolution (10-bit to 16-bit) can be achieved.

Sigma-Delta ADCs

This type of ADC uses the oversampling technique to perform A/D conversion. It has good noise immunity and can achieve high resolution. Sigma-delta ADCs are becoming more and more popular in implementing high-resolution ADCs. The only disadvantage is the slow conversion speed. However, this weakness is improving because of advancements in the CMOS technology.

Successive-Approximation ADCs

The successive-approximation method approximates the analog signal to n-bit code in **n** steps. It may be used for applications with large DC noise, such as an electrocardiograph. The block diagram of this method is shown in Figure 10.4.

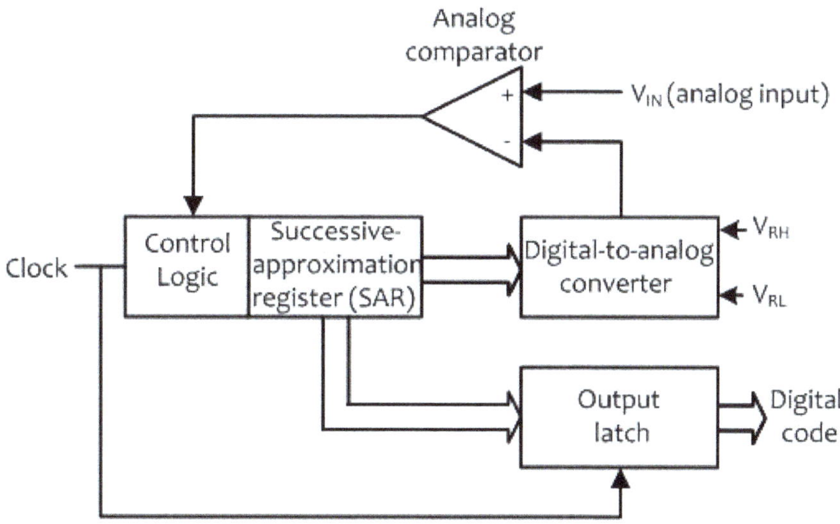

Figure 10.4 Block diagram of a successive approximation A/D converter

It first initializes the successive-approximation register (SAR) to 0 and then performs a series of guessing, starting with the most significant bit and proceeding toward the least significant bit. The algorithm of the successive-approximation method is illustrated in Figure 10.5. For every bit of the SAR, the algorithm performs the following operations:

- Guesses the bit to be a 1.
- Converts the value of the SAR register to an analog voltage.
- Compares the D/A output with the analog input and clears the bit to 0 if the D/A output is larger (which indicates that the guess is wrong).

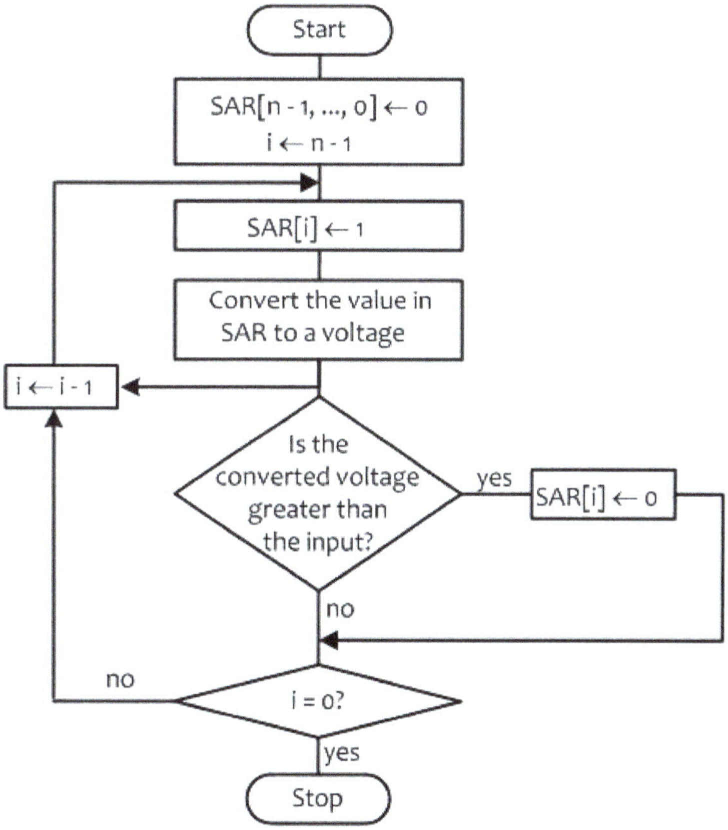

Figure 10.5 Successive-approximation A/D conversion method

Because of its balanced speed and precision, this method has become one of the most popular A/D conversion methods. Most microcontrollers use this method to implement the ADC. The STM32L475 MCUs also use this technique to implement ADCs.

10.2.4 INTERPRETING THE A/D CONVERSION RESULT

An ADC needs a **low reference voltage** (V_{RL}) and a **high reference voltage** (V_{RH}) to perform the conversion. The V_{RL} voltage is often set to ground, whereas the V_{RH} voltage is often set to V_{DD}. Some microcontrollers simply tie V_{RL} to the ground voltage and leave only the V_{RH} voltage programmable. Most ADCs are **ratiometric** for the following reasons:

- A 0-V (or V_{RL}) analog input is converted to the digital code of n 0s.
- A V_{DD} (or V_{RH}) analog input is converted to the digital code of $2^n - 1$.
- A k-V input (or V_{RL} + k) will be converted to the digital code of $k \times (2^n - 1) \div V_{DD}$.

Here, n is the number of bits used to represent the A/D conversion result.

The A/D conversion result would be most accurate if the value of the analog signal covers the whole voltage range from V_{RL} to V_{RH}. The A/D conversion result k corresponds to an analog voltage V_K given by the following equation:

$$V_K = V_{RL} + (\text{range} \times k) \div (2^n - 1) \qquad (10.1)$$

where range = $V_{RH} - V_{RL}$.

Example 10.1 Suppose that there is a 12-bit ADC with V_{RL} = 1 V and V_{RH} = 4 V. Find the corresponding voltage values for the A/D conversion results of 50, 160, 750, 1000, 1500, and 2800.

Solution: Range = $V_{RH} - V_{RL}$ = 4 V − 1 V = 3 V.

The voltages corresponding to the A/D conversion results of 50, 160, 750, 1000, and 2800 are:

$V(50) = 1\text{ V} + (3 \times 50) \div (2^{12} - 1) = 1 + 0.037 = 1.037\text{ V}$

$V(160) = 1\text{ V} + (3 \times 160) \div (2^{12} - 1) = 1 + 0.117 = 1.117\text{ V}$

$V(750) = 1\text{ V} + (3 \times 750) \div (2^{12} - 1) = 1 + 0.549 = 1.549\text{ V}$

$V(1000) = 1\text{ V} + (3 \times 1000) \div (2^{12} - 1) = 1 + 0.733 = 1.733\text{ V}$

$V(1500) = 1\text{ V} + (3 \times 1500) \div (2^{12} - 1) = 1 + 1.099 = 2.099\text{ V}$

$V(2800) = 1\text{ V} + (3 \times 2800) \div (2^{12} - 1) = 1 + 2.051 = 3.051\text{ V}$

In the discussion of the next two subsections, we assume that V_{RL} and V_{RH} have been set to 0 V and V_{DD}, respectively.

10.2.5 SCALING CIRCUIT

Some of the transducer output voltages are in the range of 0 ~ V_Z, where $V_Z < V_{DD}$. Because V_Z sometimes can be much smaller than V_{DD}, the A/D converter cannot take advantage of the available full dynamic range (0 to $2^n - 1$, where n is the number of bits used to represent the conversion result), and therefore conversion results can be very inaccurate. The voltage scaling (amplifying) circuit can be used to improve the accuracy because it allows the ADC to utilize its full dynamic range. The diagram of a voltage scaling circuit is shown in Figure 10.6. Because the input impedance of an OP AMP is extremely large, the current that flows through the resistor R_2 will be the same as the current that flows through R_1. In addition, the voltage at the inverting input terminal (same as the voltage drop across R_1) would be the same as that at the noninverting terminal (V_{IN}). Therefore, the voltage gain of this circuit is given by the following equation:

$$A_V = V_{OUT} \div V_{IN} = (R_1 + R_2) \div R_1 = 1 + R_2/R_1 \quad (10.2)$$

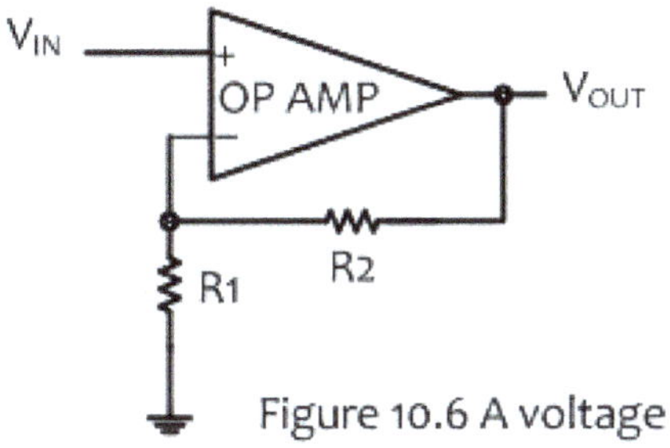

Figure 10.6 A voltage scaler

Example 10.2 Suppose that the transducer output voltage ranges from 0 V to 200 mV. Choose the appropriate values for R_1 and R_2 to scale this range to 0 ~ 5 V.

Solution: 5 V ÷ 200 mV = 25 $\therefore R_2/R_1 = 24$

By setting R_2 and R_1 to 24 kΩ and 1 kΩ, respectively, we obtain an R_2/R_1 ratio of 24 and achieve the desired scaling goal.

10.2.6 VOLTAGE TRANSLATION CIRCUIT

Some transducers have output voltage in the range of V_1 ~ V_2 (V_1 can be negative and V_2 can be higher or lower than V_{DD}) instead of 0 V ~ V_{DD}. The accuracy of A/D conversion can be improved by using a circuit that shifts and scales the transducer output so that it falls in the full range of 0 V ~ V_{DD}.

An OP AMP circuit that can shift and scale the transducer output is shown in Figure 10.7c. This circuit consists of a summing circuit (Figure 10.7a) and an inverting circuit (Figure 10.7b). The voltage V_{IN} comes from the transducer output and V_1 is an adjusting voltage. By choosing appropriate values for V_1 and resistors R_0, R_1, R_2, and R_f, the desired voltage shifting and scaling can be achieved. Equation 10.5 shows that the resistance R_0 is an independent variable and can be set to a convenient value.

Example 10.3 Choose appropriate resistor values and the adjusting voltage V_1 so that the circuit shown in Figure 10.7c can shift the voltage from the range of −1.2 V to 3.0 V to the range of 0 V to 5 V.

Solution:

Applying Equation 10.5:

$$0 = -1.2 \times (R_f/R_1) - (R_f/R_2) \times V_1 \quad (1)$$

$$5 = 3.0 \times (R_f/R_1) - (R_f/R_2) \times V_1 \quad (2)$$

(2) – (1) → $R_f = 25R1/21$

2.4 × (1) + (2) → Set V_1 to –5V, then $R_2 = 3.5R_f$

By choosing R_0 = 10 kΩ, R1 = 2.8 kΩ, R_2 = 11.7 kΩ, R_f = 3.33 kΩ, and V_1 = –5V, we can translate and scale the voltage from the specified range to the desired range. This example tells us that the selection of resistors and the voltage V1 is a trial-and-error process at best.

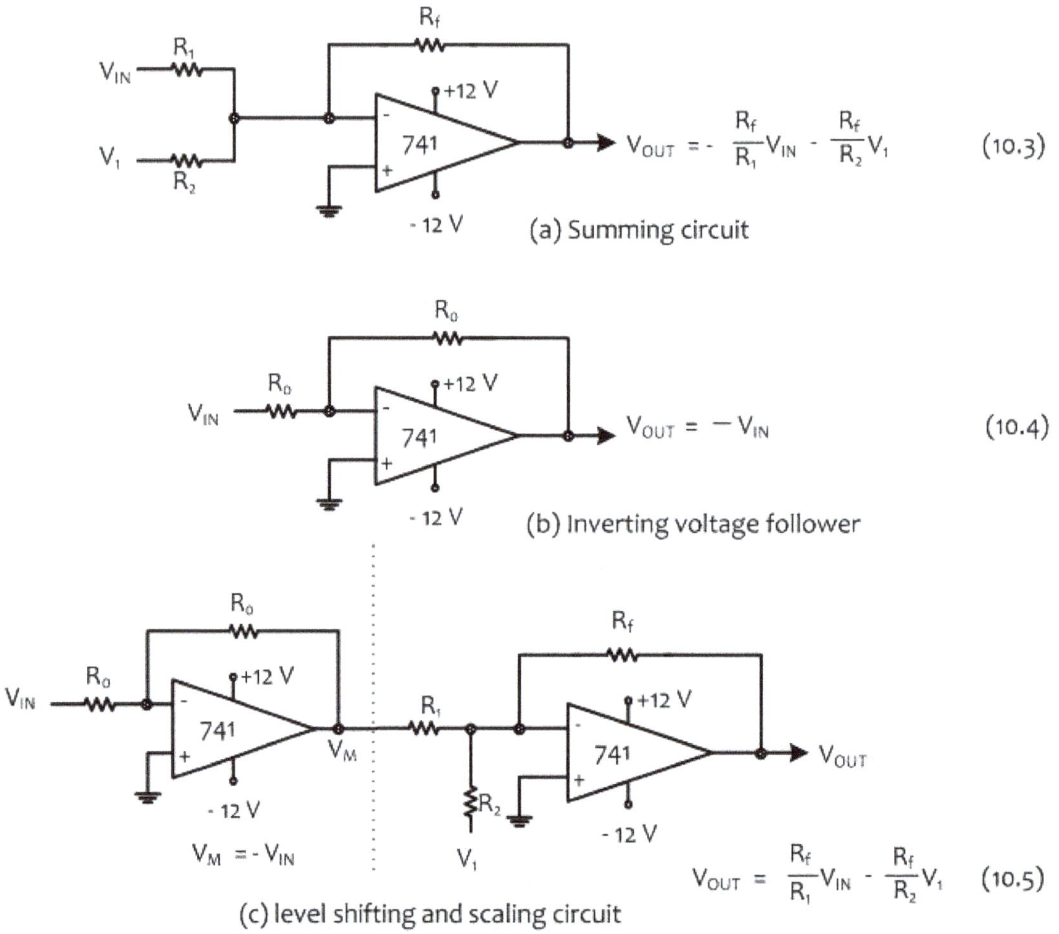

Figure 10.7 Level shifting and scaling circuit

10.3 Features of the STM32L475 ADC

The STM32L475 has three ADCs (ADC1~ADC3) that use successive approximation method to perform the conversion. A voltage input that can be converted by the ADC is referred to as a **channel**. Each ADC may have internal and external input channels. The number of internal and external channels available in each ADC is given in Table 10.1. ADC1 and ADC2 can operate in dual mode.

Table 10.1. Number of input channels of each ADC

ADC	Fast channels[1]	slow channels[1]	Internal channels
ADC1	5	11	3 (V_{REFINT})[2], V_{TS}[3], V_{BAT}[4]/3)
ADC2	5	11	2 (DAC1, DAC2)
ADC3	4	8	4 (V_{TS}[3], V_{BAT}[4]/3, DAC1, DAC2)

Note.

1. These channels are connected to I/O pads.
2. Internal reference voltage
3. Internal temperature sensor
4. V_{BAT} monitoring channel ($V_{BAT}/3$)—V_{BAT} is the backup battery input pin.

The A/D conversion can be performed in 12, 10, 8, or 6-bit resolution. A few channels have shorter conversion time and hence are called **fast channels**. Other channels are referred to as **slow channels**. At 12-bit resolution, the fast channel has a conversion time of 0.188 μs. At the same resolution, the slow channel takes 0.238 μs to convert. The ADC conversion time can be reduced by reducing the resolution. For example, choosing the 10-bit resolution, the conversion time of the fast channel is reduced to 0.16 μs. The conversion time is independent of the AHB bus clock frequency.

The ADC input can be configured to **single-ended** mode or **differential** mode. In differential mode, one input (channel) is designated as the positive input, whereas the other input is designated as the negative input. The ADC converts the difference of these two voltages into a digital value. The single-ended input mode can be considered as the differential mode with negative input grounded.

In a real application, an ADC may need to perform A/D conversion on several analog inputs regularly. These inputs are referred to as **regular channels**. However, the ADC may also need to perform conversions on other analog inputs occasionally. When the ADC perform conversions on this type of inputs, it cannot perform conversion on the regular channels. These channels are referred to as **injected channels**. Each ADC may accept up to **four** injected channels.

The A/D conversion on the regular channel or the injected channel can be **started** by software or hardware trigger signals. The polarity (rising or falling edge or both edges) of the hardware trigger signal is programmable.

The A/D converter supports several conversion modes. Each ADC can convert a single channel or a sequence of channels. In the single mode, one trigger signal starts the conversion of all the selected channels once per trigger. However, the continuous mode will convert the selected channels continuously per trigger.

The DMA transfer can be used to save A/D conversion results in SRAM. ADC1 and ADC2 share the same interrupt vector, whereas ADC3 has its own interrupt vector. An interrupt can be generated at ADC ready; end of sampling; end of each conversion; end of a sequence of conversions; analog watchdog 1, 2, or 3; or overrun events.

The STM32L475 ADC supports the watchdog function which can be configured to detect any channel input falling out of the selected range. ADC1 and ADC2 can be configured to operate in the **dual mode**. The range of the analog input is $V_{REF-} \leq V_{IN} \leq V_{REF+}$. The ADC power supply must be between 1.62V and 3.6V.

10.4 External Signal Pins for the STM32L475 ADC

The following signal pins are provided to support the ADC operation:

V_{DDA}: Analog power supply input. This voltage must be in the range from 1.62 V to 3.6 V.

V_{SSA}: Analog supply ground. V_{SSA} is the same as V_{SS}.

V_{REF+}: High reference voltage for the ADC. It must be no lower than 1.62 V and no higher than analog power supply V_{DDA}.

V_{REF-}: Low reference voltage for the ADC. This voltage must be tied to analog supply ground V_{SSA}.

V_{INP}[18:0]: Positive input channels. These signals are either connected to external channels ADC_IN$_i$ or internal channels.

V_{INN}[18:0]: Negative input channels. These channels are either connected to V_{REF-} or external channels ADC_IN$_{i-1}$.

The GPIO pins that can be used for ADC input channels are listed in Table 10.2. Two steps must be performed to configure these pins for ADC channels:

Step 1 Configure these pins to analog mode by programming the GPIOx->MODER register.

Step 2 Connect these pins to ADC channels by programming the GPIOx->ASCR register.

Table 10.2 ADC Input channel pin assignment

GPIO Pin	ADC Channel	GPIO Pin	ADC Channel
PA0	ADC12[(1)]_IN5	PC0	ADC123[(2)]_IN1
PA1	ADC12[(1)]_IN6	PC1	ADC123[(2)]_IN2
PA2	ADC12[(1)]_IN7	PC2	ADC123[(2)]_IN3
PA3	ADC12[(1)]_IN8	PC3	ADC123[(2)]_IN4
PA4	ADC12[(1)]_IN9	PC4	ADC12[(1)]_IN13
PA5	ADC12[(1)]_IN10	PC5	ADC12[(1)]_IN14
PA6	ADC12[(1)]_IN11	PB0	ADC12[(1)]_IN15
PA7	ADC12[(1)]_IN12	PB1	ADC12[(1)]_IN16

Note

1. ADC module 1 and 2. PA0 pin serves as the channel 5 input for ADC1 and ADC2 module
2. ADC module 1, 2, and 3. PC0 serves as the channel 1 input for ADC1, ADC2, and ADC3

For ADC1, V_{REFINT}, V_{TS} and $V_{BAT/3}$ are the inputs of channel 0, 17, and 18.

For ADC2, the DAC1 and DAC2 internal outputs are the channel 17 and channel 18 inputs. The channel 16 (PB1 pin) is the negative input when the channel 15 is configured to differential mode. However, when channel 16 is configured to differential mode, its negative input is V_{SSA}. ADC2 has no channel 0 input.

For ADC3, DAC1, DAC2, V_{TS}, and $V_{BAT/3}$ are the inputs of channel 14, 15, 17, and 18, respectively. ADC3 does not have channel 0 and channel 16 input.

10.5 ADC Registers

Each ADC has its own set of registers. There are three registers that are used to configure the parameters for all three ADCs. The header file STM32L475xx.h defines a struct data type with the tag **ADC_TypeDef** to allow users to access each registers contained in a specific ADC module. The contents of the tag ADC_TypeDef are as follows:

```
typedef struct
{
    __IO uint32_t   ISR;            // ADC interrupt and status register
    __IO uint32_t   IER;            // ADC interrupt enable register
    __IO uint32_t   CR;             // ADC control register
    __IO uint32_t   CFGR;           // ADC configure register 1
    __IO uint32_t   CFGR2;          // ADC configure register 2
    __IO uint32_t   SMPR1;          // ADC sampling time register 1
    __IO uint32_t   SMPR2;          // ADC sampling time register 2
         uint32_t   RESERVED1;      // reserved
    __IO uint32_t   TR1;            // ADC analog watchdog 1 threshold register
    __IO uint32_t   TR2;            // ADC analog watchdog 2 threshold register
    __IO uint32_t   TR3;            // ADC analog watchdog 3 threshold register
         uint32_t   RESERVED2;      // reserved
    __IO uint32_t   SQR1;           // ADC group regular sequencer register 1
    __IO uint32_t   SQR2;           // ADC group regular sequencer register 2
    __IO uint32_t   SQR3;           // ADC group regular sequencer register 3
    __IO uint32_t   SQR4;           // ADC group regular sequencer register 4
    __IO uint32_t   DR;             // ADC group regular data register
    __IO uint32_t   RESERVED3;      // reserved
    __IO uint32_t   RESERVED4;      // reserved
    __IO uint32_t   JSQR;           // ADC injected sequencer register
    __IO uint32_t   RESERVED5[4];   // reserved
    __IO uint32_t   OFR1;           // ADC offset register 1
    __IO uint32_t   OFR2;           // ADC offset register 2
```

```
    __IO uint32_t   OFR3;           // ADC offset register 3
    __IO uint32_t   OFR4;           // ADC offset register 4
    __IO uint32_t   RESERVED6[4];   // reserved
    __IO uint32_t   JDR1;           // ADC group injected rank 1 data register
    __IO uint32_t   JDR2;           // ADC group injected rank 2 data register
    __IO uint32_t   JDR3;           // ADC group injected rank 3 data register
    __IO uint32_t   JDR4;           // ADC group injected rank 4 data register
    __IO uint32_t   RESERVED7[4];   // reserved
    __IO uint32_t   AWD2CR;         // ADC analog watchdog 2 configuration register
    __IO uint32_t   AWD3CR;         // ADC analog watchdog 3 configuration register
    __IO uint32_t   RESERVED8;      // reserved
    __IO uint32_t   RESERVED9;      // reserved
    __IO uint32_t   DIFSEL;         // ADC differential mode configuration register
    __IO uint32_t   CALFACT;        // ADC calibration register
} ADC_TypeDef;
```

Another struct data type with the tag **ADC_Common_TypeDef** is defined to allow the access of the three common registers:

```
typedef   struct
{
    __IO uint32_t   CSR;            // ADC common status register
         uint32_t   RESERVED;       // reserved
    __IO uint32_t   CCR;            // ADC common configuration register
    __IO uint32_t   CDR;            // ADC common group regular data register
} ADC_Common_TypeDef;
```

Three pointers **ADC1**, **ADC2**, and **ADC3** are defined to allow users to access registers contained in the struct with the tag of ADC_TypeDef. The pointer **ADC123_COMMON** is defined to allow the user to access registers common to all three ADCs.

10.6 ADC Clock Source

The input clock source is the same for all three ADCs. There are two ways for ADCs to choose the clock source:

1. Select from one of three clock sources: **system clock**, **PLLSAI1**, or **PLLSAI2**. To choose this clock scheme, reset the CKMODE[1:0] field in the ADC123_COMMON->CCR register to 00. After selecting this clock source, the working ADC clock can be further divided by a factor of 1, 2, 4, 8, 16, 32, 64, 128, or 256 by programming the PRESC[3:0] field of the ADC123_COMMON->CCR register. The advantage of choosing this clock source is that the user can use the highest frequency 80 MHz to control the ADC operation.
2. Select AHB bus clock divided by 1, 2, or 4 according to the CKMODE[1:0] bit field of the ADC123_COMMON->CCR register.

The contents of the ADC123_COMMON->CCR register are shown in Figure 10.8. The ADC clock scheme is illustrated in Figure 10.9.

31	30	29	28	27	26	25	24
–	–	–	–	–	–	–	CH18SEL
23	**22**	**21**	**20**	**19**	**18**	**17**	**16**
CH17SEL	VREFEN	PRESC[3:0]				CKMODE[1:0]	
15	**14**	**13**	**12**	**11**	**10**	**9**	**8**
MDMA[1:0]		DMACFG	–	DELAY[3:0]			
7	**6**	**5**	**4**	**3**	**2**	**1**	**0**
–	–	–	DUAL[4:0]				

Reset value = 0x0000 0000
Offset Addr= 0x08

CH18SEL: CH18 selection (can be written only when ADC is disabled)
  0: V_{BAT} channel disabled. 1: V_{BAT} channel enabled.
CH17SEL: CH17 selection (can be written only when ADC is disabled)
  0: Temperature sensor channel disabled 1: Temperature sensor channel enabled
VREFEN: V_{REFINT} enable (can be written only when ADC is disabled)
  0: V_{REFINT} channel disabled. 1: V_{REFINT} channel enabled.
PRESC[3:0]: ADC prescaler (common to all ADCs)
  See Table 10.1.
CKMODE[1:0]: ADC clock mode
  00: CK_ADCx (x = 1,2,3). ADC clock is selected from SYSCLK, PLLSAI1, or PLLSAI2.
  01: HCLK/1 is selected as ADC clock. This configuration must be enabled only if the AHB clock prescaler is set to 1 (HPRE[3:0] = 0xxx in RCC->CFGR register).
  10: HCLK/2 (synchronous clock mode) 11: HCLK/4 (synchronous clock mode)
MDMA[1:0]: Direct memory access mode for dual ADC mode
  00: MDMA disabled 01: reserved
  10: MDMA mode enabled for 12 and 10-bit resolution
  11: MDMA mode enabled for 8 and 6-bit resolution
DMACFG: DMA configuration (for dual ADC mode, effective only if DMAEN=1)
  0: DMA one shot mode selected. 1: DMA circular mode selected.
DELAY[3:0]: Delay between two sampling phases
  These bits are used in dual interleaved modes. See Table 10.2.
DUAL[4:0]: Dual ADC operation mode selection
  See Table 10.3.

Figure 10.8 ADC common control register (ADC123->CCR)

Table 10.3 ADC prescaler

PRESC[3:0]	ADC clock frequency
0000	Input ADC clock not divided
0001	Input ADC clock divided by 2
0010	Input ADC clock divided by 4
0011	Input ADC clock divided by 6
0100	Input ADC clock divided by 8
0101	Input ADC clock divided by 10
0110	Input ADC clock divided by 12
0111	Input ADC clock divided by 16
1000	Input ADC clock divided by 32
1001	Input ADC clock divided by 64
1010	Input ADC clock divided by 128
1011	Input ADC clock divided by 256
other	reserved

Table 10.4 Delay bits versus ADC resolution

DELAY[3:0]	12-bit resolution	10-bit resolution	8-bit resolution	6-bit resolution
0000	$1 \times T_{ADC\_CLK}$	$1 \times T_{ADC\_CLK}$	$1 \times T_{ADC\_CLK}$	$1 \times T_{ADC\_CLK}$
0001	$2 \times T_{ADC\_CLK}$	$2 \times T_{ADC\_CLK}$	$2 \times T_{ADC\_CLK}$	$2 \times T_{ADC\_CLK}$
0010	$3 \times T_{ADC\_CLK}$	$3 \times T_{ADC\_CLK}$	$3 \times T_{ADC\_CLK}$	$3 \times T_{ADC\_CLK}$
0011	$4 \times T_{ADC\_CLK}$	$4 \times T_{ADC\_CLK}$	$4 \times T_{ADC\_CLK}$	$4 \times T_{ADC\_CLK}$
0100	$5 \times T_{ADC\_CLK}$	$5 \times T_{ADC\_CLK}$	$5 \times T_{ADC\_CLK}$	$5 \times T_{ADC\_CLK}$
0101	$6 \times T_{ADC\_CLK}$	$6 \times T_{ADC\_CLK}$	$6 \times T_{ADC\_CLK}$	$6 \times T_{ADC\_CLK}$
0110	$7 \times T_{ADC\_CLK}$	$7 \times T_{ADC\_CLK}$	$7 \times T_{ADC\_CLK}$	$6 \times T_{ADC\_CLK}$
0111	$8 \times T_{ADC\_CLK}$	$8 \times T_{ADC\_CLK}$	$8 \times T_{ADC\_CLK}$	$6 \times T_{ADC\_CLK}$
1000	$9 \times T_{ADC\_CLK}$	$9 \times T_{ADC\_CLK}$	$8 \times T_{ADC\_CLK}$	$6 \times T_{ADC\_CLK}$
1001	$10 \times T_{ADC\_CLK}$	$10 \times T_{ADC\_CLK}$	$8 \times T_{ADC\_CLK}$	$6 \times T_{ADC\_CLK}$
1010	$11 \times T_{ADC\_CLK}$	$10 \times T_{ADC\_CLK}$	$8 \times T_{ADC\_CLK}$	$6 \times T_{ADC\_CLK}$
1011	$12 \times T_{ADC\_CLK}$	$10 \times T_{ADC\_CLK}$	$8 \times T_{ADC\_CLK}$	$6 \times T_{ADC\_CLK}$
other	$12 \times T_{ADC\_CLK}$	$10 \times T_{ADC\_CLK}$	$8 \times T_{ADC\_CLK}$	$6 \times T_{ADC\_CLK}$

Table 10.5 Dual ADC operation mode selection

DUAL[4:0]	Operation mode description
00000	Independent mode
00001 to 01001	Dual mode, master and slave ADCs working together
00001	Combined regular simultaneous + injected simultaneous mode
00010	Combined regular simultaneous + alternate trigger mode
00011	Combined interleaved mode + injected simultaneous mode
00100	Reserved
00101	Injected simultaneous mode only
00110	Regular simultaneous mode only
00111	Interleaved mode only
01001	Alternate trigger mode only
other	Reserved

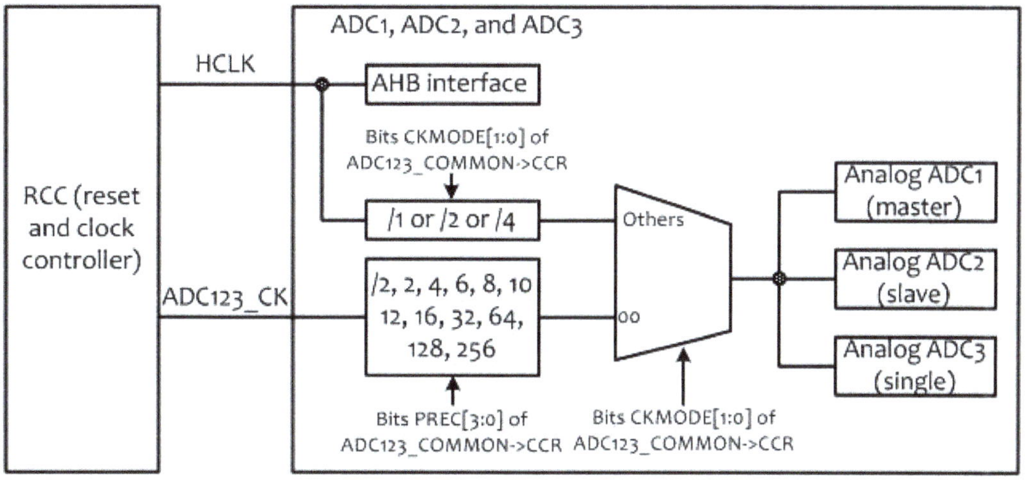

Figure 10.9 ADC clock scheme

10.7 ADC Operation

The operation and parameters of ADCs are described in detail in the following sections:

10.7.1 START THE ADC MODULE

After a reset, the ADC module is in the **deep-power-down mode** in which its power supply is internally switched off and the DEEPPWD bit in the ADCx->CR register is set to 1.

To start the ADC, the first thing to do is to exit the deep-power-down mode by clearing the DEEPPWD bit. The next step is to enable the ADC internal voltage regulator by setting the ADVREGEN bit in the ADCx->CR register to 1. It will take $T_{ADCVREG\_STUP}$ (about 20 ms) for the ADC voltage regulator to stabilize and function. After this delay the user can perform a calibration to the ADC if he/she feels that there is such a need. Otherwise, the application can enable the ADC and start to perform the conversion. The ADC is enabled by setting the ADEN bit in the ADCx->CR register to 1. Once the ADRDY bit in the ADCx->ISR register is set, the ADC is ready for use.

After finishing the ADC conversion, the application can disable the ADC by clearing the ADEN bit. If there is a need to save more power, the application can enter the deep-power-down mode by setting the DEEPPWD bit to 1.

The contents of the ADCx->CR register are shown in Figure 10.10.

31	30	29	28	27	26	25	24
ADCAL	ADCALDIF	DEEPPWD	ADVREGEN	--	--	--	--
23	**22**	**21**	**20**	**19**	**18**	**17**	**16**
--	--	--	--	--	--	--	--
15	**14**	**13**	**12**	**11**	**10**	**9**	**8**
--	--	--	--	--	--	--	--
7	**6**	**5**	**4**	**3**	**2**	**1**	**0**
--	--	JADSTP	ADSTP	JADSTART	ADSTART	ADDIS	ADEN

Reset value = 0x2000 0000
Offset Addr= 0x08

ADCAL: ADC calibration

Setting this bit starts the ADC calibration. Calibration is performed on differential mode if the ADCALDIF bit is 1. Otherwise, calibration applies to single-ended mode. After calibration is complete, this bit is cleared to 0.

0: Calibration is complete. 1: A calibration is on-going

ADCALDIF: Differential mode calibration

0: Setting the ADCAL bit will launch a calibration in single-ended input mode.

1: Setting the ADCAL bit will launch a calibration in differential input mode.

DEEPPWD: Deep-power-down enable

0: ADC not in deep-power-down. 1: ADC in deep-power-down.

ADVREGEN: ADC voltage regulator enable

0: ADC voltage regulator disabled. 1: ADC voltage regulator enabled.

JADSTP: ADC stop of injected conversion command

Setting this bit causes the ADC to stop and discard an ongoing injected conversion. This bit is cleared when the injected conversion is effectively discarded.

0: No ADC stop injected conversion command ongoing.

1: Write 1 to this bit discards an ongoing regular ADC conversion. Read 1 means that an JADSTP command is ongoing.

ADSTP: ADC stop of regular conversion command

Setting this bit causes ADC to stop and discard an ongoing regular conversion. This bit is cleared when the regular conversion is effectively discarded.

0: No ADC stop regular conversion command ongoing.

1: Write 1 to this bit discards an ongoing regular conversion. Read 1 means that an ADSTP command is in progress.

Figure 10.10 ADC control register (ADCx->CR)

31	30	29	28	27	26	25	24
ADCAL	ADCALDIF	DEEPPWD	ADVREGEN	--	--	--	--
23	22	21	20	19	18	17	16
--	--	--	--	--	--	--	--
15	14	13	12	11	10	9	8
--	--	--	--	--	--	--	--
7	6	5	4	3	2	1	0
--	--	JADSTP	ADSTP	JADSTART	ADSTART	ADDIS	ADEN

Reset value = 0x2000 0000
Offset Addr= 0x08

JADSTART: ADC start of injected conversion
If software trigger is selected, setting this bit starts the ADC conversion of injected channels. If hardware trigger mode is selected, the ADC conversion will be started when this bit has been set and the selected trigger source occurs.
0: No ADC injected conversion is ongoing.
1: Write 1 to start injected conversion (may or may not start immediately). Read 1 means that the ADC is operating and eventually converting an injected channel.
ADSTART: ADC start of regular conversion
If software trigger is selected, setting this bit starts the ADC conversion of the regular channels. If hardware trigger mode is selected, the ADC conversion will be started when this bit has been set and the selected trigger source occurs.
0: No ADC regular conversion is ongoing.
1: Write 1 to start regular conversions (may or may not start immediately). Read 1 means that ADC is operating and may eventually converting a regular channel.
ADDIS: ADC disable command
Setting this bit disables the ADC and put it in power-down state. This bit is cleared once the ADC is disabled (ADEN is also cleared).
0: no ADDIS command is ongoing.
1: Write 1 to disable the ADC. Read 1 means that an ADDIS command is in progress.
ADEN: ADC enable control
The ADC will be effectively ready to operate once the flag ADRDY flag has been set.
0: ADC is disabled 1: Write 1 to enable ADC

Figure 10.10a ADC control register (ADCx->CR)—(continued)

Example 10.4 Write a sequence of C statements to start and enable the ADC1 assuming that the function **delay50us()** is available for your use.

Solution:

The following C statements will perform the specified operations:

```
ADC1->CR    &= ~ADC_CR_DEEPPWD;    // clear the DEEPPWD flag
ADC1->CR    |= ADC_CR_ADVREGEN;    // enable ADC voltage regulator
delay50us ();
ADC1->CR    |= ADC_CR_ADEN;        // enable ADC1
while(!(ADC1->ISR & ADC_ISR_ADRDY));  // wait until ADC1 is ready
```

10.7.2 CHANNEL MODE CONFIGURATION

Channels can be configured to be either single-ended or differential inputs by programming the DIFSEL[15:1] field in the ADCx->DIFSEL register. This configuration must be done when the ADC is disabled. The DIFSEL[18:16] bits are fixed to single-ended channels (internal channels only) and are always read as 0.

In **single-ended input mode**, the analog voltage to be converted for channel i is the difference between the external voltage ADC_INi (positive input) and V_{REF-} (negative input).

In **differential input mode**, the analog voltage to be converted for channel i is the difference between the external voltage ADC_IN_i (positive input) and ADC_IN_{i+1} (negative input). When ADC is configured to operate in the differential mode, both inputs should be biased at $(V_{REF+})/2$.

Some channels are shared among ADC1, ADC2, and ADC3. This can make the channel on the other ADC unusable. The only exception is the interleaved mode for the ADC master and slave. The contents of the ADCx->DIFSEL register are shown in Figure 10.11.

31	30	29	28	27	26	25	24	
--	--	--	--	--	--	--	--	Reset value = 0x0000 0000
23	22	21	20	19	18	17	16	Offset Addr= 0xB0
--	--	--	--	--	DIFSEL[18:16]			
15	14	13	12	11	10	9	8	
DIFSEL[15:8]								
7	6	5	4	3	2	1	0	
DIFSEL[7:0]								

DIFSEL[18:16]: Differential mode channels 18 to 16.
  These bits are read only. These channels are forced to the single-ended input mode.
DIFSEL[15:1]: Differential mode for channels 15 to 1
  These bits are set and cleared by software. They allow the user to configure a channel to the single-ended or differential mode.
  DIFSEL[i] = 0: ADC analog input channel i is configured in the single-ended mode.
  DIFSEL[i] = 1: ADC analog input channel i is configured in the differential mode.
  These bits can only be configured when the ADC is disabled.
DIFSEL[0]: Differential mode for channel 0
  This bit is read only. This channel is forced to the single-ended input mode.

Figure 10.11 ADC Differential mode selection register (ADCx->DIFSEL)

To use a port pin as an analog channel, the user is required to (1) configure the pin for analog mode (by programming the GPIOx->MODER register), and (2) connect the pin to the ADC input. The pin i of any GPIOx (x = A–E & H) can be configured for channel i.

Example 10.5 Write a sequence of C statements to configure the pins PA1, PA2, and PA3 of the GPIOA as channels 6, 7, and 8 in single-ended mode of the ADC1 module.

Solution: The following C statements will perform the specified configuration:

```
GPIOA->MODER  |=  GPIO_MODER_MODE1 + GPIO_MODER_MODE2 +
```

```
                    GPIO_MODER_MODE3;
                    // configure PA1, PA2, & PA3 to analog mode
GPIOA->ASCR     |=  (GPIO_ASCR_ASC1 + GPIO_ASCR_ASC2 + GPIO_ASCR_ASC3);
                    // connect PA1, PA2, and PA3 to ADC input
ADC1 ->DIFSEL   &= ~(ADC_DIFSEL_DIFSEL_6 + ADC_DIFSEL_DIFSEL_7 +
                    ADC_DIFSEL_DIFSEL_8); // set channels 6, 7, and 8 to single-ended
                                          // mode
```

Example 10.6 Write a sequence of C statements to configure PC0, and PC2 to differential mode channels of ADC2.

Solution:

```
// configure PC0, PC1, PC2, & PC3 to analog mode
GPIOC->MODER  |=  GPIO_MODER_MODE0 + GPIO_MODER_MODE1 +
                  GPIO_MODER_MODE2 + GPIO_MODER_MODE3;
// connect PC0, PC1, PC2, and PC3 to ADC input
GPIOC->ASCR   |=  GPIO_ASCR_ASC0 + GPIO_ASCR_ASC1 + GPIO_ASCR_ASC2 +
                  GPIO_ASCR_ASC3;
// configure PC0, & PC2 to the differential mode inputs of ADC2 (ADC2_IN1 & IN3)
ADC2->DIFSEL  |=  ADC_DIFSEL_DIFSEL_1 + ADC_DIFSEL_DIFSEL_3;
```

When ADC2_IN1 and ADC2_IN3 are configured to differential mode, then ADC2_IN2 and ADC2_IN4 channels are selected automatically.

10.7.3 ADC CALIBRATION

There are offset errors in the ADC module due to the processor bandgap variation from chip to chip. To eliminate this offset error, the semiconductor manufacturer provides a calibration procedure for the ADC. A 7-bit calibration factor is used in this procedure. A default calibration factor is calculated during the chip manufacturing process and stored in the on-chip nonvolatile memory. This calibration factor is loaded into every ADC module in the power on process. During the ADC conversion process, the ADC applies the calibration factor stored in the ADC module to make the conversion more accurate. The ADC also includes a manual calibration procedure which allows the user to recalculate the calibration factor if the user suspects that the default calibration factor is not good enough.

There are two kinds of calibration: single-ended input calibration and differential input calibration. The resultant single-ended input calibration factor will be used to remove the offset error for the single-ended conversion whereas the produced differential input calibration factor will be used to remove the offset error when differential input conversion is performed.

The manual calibration is initiated by setting the ADCAL bit in the ADCx->CR register to 1. If the ADCALDIF bit in the ADCx->CR register is 0, a single-ended input calibration is performed. Otherwise, a differential input calibration is performed. The ADCAL bit will be cleared when the calibration process completes. The associated calibration factor is stored internally in the ADC and also in the bits CALFACT_S[6:0] or CALFACT_D[6:0] of the ADCx->CALFACT register depending on whether the calibration is single-ended or differential input. The contents of the ADCx->CALFACT register are shown in Figure 10.12.

When an A/D conversion is launched, the calibration factor stored in the ADCx->CALFACT register is injected into the ADC module only if the internal analog calibration factor differs from the one stored in CALFACT_S for single-ended input channel or bits CALFACT_D for differential input channel.

Example 10.7 Modify the sequence of C statements in Example 10.4 to perform single-ended calibration.

Solution:

```
ADC1->CR  &= ~ADC_CR_DEEPPWD;          // clear the DEEPPWD flag
ADC1->CR  |= ADC_CR_ADVREGEN;          // enable ADC voltage regulator
delay50us (); // wait for voltage regulator to become stable
ADC1->CR  &= ~ADC_CR_ADEN;             // disable ADC1
while(ADC1->CR & ADC_CR_ADEN);         // wait until ADEN bit is cleared
ADC1->CR  &= ~ADC_CR_ADCALDIF;         // select single-ended calibration mode
ADC1->CR  |= ADC_CR_ADCAL;             // start ADC calibration
while(ADC1->CR & ADC_CR_ADCAL);        // wait until calibration is done
ADC1->CR  |= ADC_CR_ADEN;              // enable ADC1
while(!(ADC1->ISR & ADC_ISR_ADRDY));   // wait for ADC1 to become ready
```

The calibration factor can be written if the ADC is enabled but not converting (ADEN = 1 and ADSTART = 0 and JADSTART = 0). Then, at the next start of conversion, the calibration factor will automatically be injected into the ADC. This loading is transparent and does not add any cycle latency to the start of the conversion. It is recommended to recalibrate when V_{REF+} voltage changes more than 10%.

31	30	29	28	27	26	25	24
--	--	--	--	--	--	--	--
23	**22**	**21**	**20**	**19**	**18**	**17**	**16**
--	CALFACT_D[6:0]						
15	**14**	**13**	**12**	**11**	**10**	**9**	**8**
--	--	--	--	--	--	--	--
7	**6**	**5**	**4**	**3**	**2**	**1**	**0**
	CALFACT_S[6:0]						

Reset value = 0x0000 0000
Offset Addr= 0xB4

CALFACT_D[6:0]: Calibration factors in differential mode
Once the differential input calibration is complete, this field is replaced with the calibration factor. Software can also write a new calibration factor to this field. If the new calibration factor is different from the current one stored in the ADC, it will then be applied once a new differential calibration is launched.

CALFACT_S[6:0]: Calibration factors in single-ended mode
Once a single-ended calibration is complete, this field is replaced with the calibration factor. Software can also write a new calibration factor to this field. If the new calibration factor is different from the current one stored in the ADC, it will then be applied once a new single-ended calibration is launched.

Figure 10.12 ADC Calibration factors register (ADCx->CALFACT)

The software can write a new value into the ADCx->CALFACT register as long as the ADC is enabled but not converting.

10.7.4 ADC ON-OFF CONTROL

Once the ADC gets out of the deep-power-down mode and the voltage regulator is functioning, the ADC module can be enabled by setting the ADEN bit in the ADCx->CR register to 1. The ADC needs t_{STAB} of time to stabilize before it can perform conversion accurately. When the ADC is stabilized, the **ADRDY** bit in the ADCx->ISR register will be set.

The ADC can be disabled by setting the ADDIS bit in the ADCx->CR register. Before setting the ADDIS bit, the software is required to make sure that no conversion is ongoing. The procedure to stop the ADC is as follows:

Step 1

Check both the ADSTART and the JADSTART bit in the ADCx->CR register are 0 to ensure that no conversion is ongoing. If there is any ongoing regular or injected conversion, discard it by setting the ADSTP or JADSTP bit in the ADCx->CR register. The user is required to wait until the ADSTP or JADSTP bit clears to 0 to make sure that the ongoing conversion has been discarded.

Step 2

Set the ADDIS bit to 1.

Step 3

If required by the application, wait until the ADEN bit becomes 0. This ensures that the ADC is effectively disabled.

10.7.5 CONSTRAINTS WHEN WRITING THE ADC CONTROL BITS

The software is allowed to write the clock control bits to configure and enable the ADC clock, the control bits DIFSEL in the ADCx->DIFSEL register and the control bits ADCAL and ADEN in the ADCx->CR register, only if the ADC is disabled.

The control bits ADSTART, JADSTART, and ADDIS of the ADCx->CR register can be written only if the ADC is enabled. To disable the ADC, the user must ensure that there is no pending conversion request.

For all other control bits of the ADCx->CFGR, ADCx->SMPRy, ADCx->TRy, ADCx->SQRy, ADCx->J-DRy, ADCx->OFRy, and ADCx->IER registers (x = 1 to 3; y = 1 up to 4):

- Control bits related to configuration of regular conversions can be written only if the ADC is enabled (ADEN bit = 1) and there is no regular conversion ongoing (ADSTART bit = 0)
- Control bits related to configuration of injected conversions can be written only if the ADC is enabled and there is no ongoing injected conversion (JADSTART bit = 0).

The software is allowed to write the control bits ADSTP and JADSTP of the ADCx->CR register only if the ADC is enabled and eventually converting and if there is no pending request to disable the ADC (i.e., ADSTART or JADSTART = 1 and ADDIS = 0).

10.7.6 CHANNEL SELECTION

Each ADC has up to 19 multiplexed channels. Five channels (ADC_IN1–5) are fast inputs and up to ten channels (ADC_IN6–15) are slow inputs. They are all assigned to GPIO pads. All ADCs are also connected to five internal analog inputs:

- Internal reference V_{REFINT}: connected to ADC1_IN0.
- Internal temperature sensor (V_{TS}): connected to ADC1_IN17 and ADC3_IN17.
- VBAT monitoring channel ($V_{BAT}/3$): connected to ADC1_IN18 and ADC3_IN18.
- DAC1 internal channel: connected to ADC2_IN17 and ADC3_IN14.
- DAC2 internal channel: connected to ADC2_IN18 and ADC3_IN15.

To convert one of the internal analog channels, the corresponding analog sources must be enabled by programming the VREFEN, CH17_SEL, or CH18_SEL bits in the ADC123_COMMON->CCR register. To convert an input channel coming from the GPIO pad, it is necessary to configure the corresponding GPIOx->ASCR register in addition to the I/O configuration in the analog mode.

When a set of analog inputs is to be converted with the same frequency, they can be put into a group and be converted by the same ADC. This group of inputs is called **regular group**. If there is another set of inputs (no more than four) to be converted at the same frequency but much less frequently than the previous group, this set of inputs can be put into another group. If this group of inputs are to be converted also by the same ADC, then they must be inserted into the sequence of the regular group every now and then. This group is then called the **injected group**.

A group consists of a sequence of conversions that can be done on any channel and in any order. For example, a regular group may consist of a conversion sequence in this order: ADC_IN5, ADC_IN10, ADC_IN2, ADC_IN3, ADC_IN15, ADC_IN15, ADC_IN7.

A regular group is composed of up to 16 conversions. The regular channels and their order in the conversion sequence are selected using the ADCx->SQRy (y = 1–4) registers. The total number of conversions in the regular group is written in the **L[3:0]** field in the ADCx->SQR1 register.

An injected group is composed of up to four conversions. The injected channels and their order in the conversion sequence are selected using the ADCx->JSQR register. The total number of conversions in the injected group is written in the L[1:0] bits in the ADCx->JSQR register.

Any ADCx->SQRy register must not be modified when regular conversions can occur (may need to be triggered). To modify any ADCx->SQRy register, the ADC regular conversions must be stopped first by setting the ADSTP bit in the ADCx->CR register.

The ADCx->JSQR register can be modified on the fly while the injected conversions are occurring. The contents of the ADCx->SQR1, ADCx->SQR2, ADCx->SQR3, ADCx->SQR4, and ADCx->JSQR are shown in Figures 10.13–10.17, respectively.

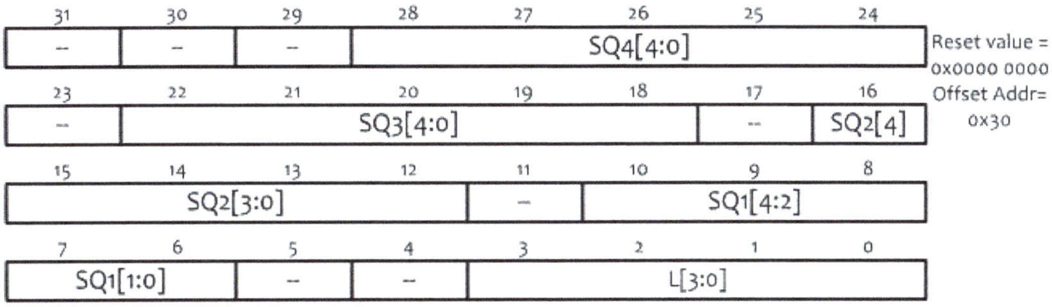

SQn[4:0]: nth conversion in regular sequence (n = 1..4)

These bits are written by software with the channel number (0..18) assigned as the nth in the regular conversion sequence.

Software is allowed to write these bits only when ADSTART=0.

L[3:0]: Regular channel sequence length

These bits define the total number of conversions in the regular channel conversion sequence.

0000: 1 conversion

0001: 2 conversions

....

1111: 16 conversions.

Figure 10.13 ADC Regular sequence register 1 (ADCx->SQR1)

31	30	29	28	27	26	25	24
--	--	--	SQ14[4:0]				
23	**22**	**21**	**20**	**19**	**18**	**17**	**16**
--	SQ13[4:0]					--	SQ12[4]
15	**14**	**13**	**12**	**11**	**10**	**9**	**8**
SQ12[3:0]				--	SQ11[4:2]		
7	**6**	**5**	**4**	**3**	**2**	**1**	**0**
SQ11[1:0]		--	SQ10[4:0]				

Reset value = 0x0000 0000
Offset Addr= 0x38

SQn[4:0]: nth conversion in regular sequence (n = 9..5)
These bits are written by software with the channel number (0..18) assigned as the nth in the regular conversion sequence.
Software is allowed to write these bits only when ADSTART=0.

Figure 10.14 ADC Regular sequence register 3 (ADCx->SQR3)

31	30	29	28	27	26	25	24
--	--	--	SQ14[4:0]				
23	**22**	**21**	**20**	**19**	**18**	**17**	**16**
--	SQ13[4:0]					--	SQ12[4]
15	**14**	**13**	**12**	**11**	**10**	**9**	**8**
SQ12[3:0]				--	SQ11[4:2]		
7	**6**	**5**	**4**	**3**	**2**	**1**	**0**
SQ11[1:0]		--	SQ10[4:0]				

Reset value = 0x0000 0000
Offset Addr= 0x38

SQn[4:0]: nth conversion in regular sequence (n = 14..10)
These bits are written by software with the channel number (0..18) assigned as the nth in the regular conversion sequence.
Software is allowed to write these bits only when ADSTART=0.

Figure 10.15 ADC Regular sequence register 3 (ADCx->SQR3)

31	30	29	28	27	26	25	24
--	--	--	--	--	--	--	--
23	**22**	**21**	**20**	**19**	**18**	**17**	**16**
--	--	--	--	--	--	--	--
15	**14**	**13**	**12**	**11**	**10**	**9**	**8**
--	--	--	--	--	SQ16[4:2]		
7	**6**	**5**	**4**	**3**	**2**	**1**	**0**
SQ16[1:0]		--	SQ15[4:0]				

Reset value = 0x0000 0000
Offset Addr= 0x3C

SQn[4:0]: nth conversion in regular sequence (n = 15..16)
These bits are written by software with the channel number (0..18) assigned as the nth in the regular conversion sequence.
Software is allowed to write these bits only when ADSTART=0.

Figure 10.16 ADC Regular sequence register 4 (ADCx->SQR4)

31	30	29	28	27	26	25	24
–	JSQ4[4:0]					–	JSQ3[4]
23	**22**	**21**	**20**	**19**	**18**	**17**	**16**
JSQ13[3:0]				--	JSQ2[4:2]		
15	**14**	**13**	**12**	**11**	**10**	**9**	**8**
JSQ2[1:0]		--	JSQ1[4:0]				
7	**6**	**5**	**4**	**3**	**2**	**1**	**0**
JEXTEN[1:0]		JEXTSEL[3:0]				JL[1:0]	

Reset value = 0x0000 0000
Offset Addr= 0x4C

JSQn[4:0]: nth conversion in the injected sequence (n = 1..4)
These bits are written by software with the channel number (0..18) assigned as the nth in the injected conversion sequence. Software is allowed to write these bits at any time, once the ADC is enabled (ADEN=1).

JEXTEN[1:0]: External trigger enable and polarity selection for injected channels
00: If JQDIS=0 (queue enabled), hardware and software trigger detection disabled.
If JQDIS=1 (queue disabled), hardware trigger detection disabled. Conversion can be launched by software.
01: hardware trigger detection on the rising edge
10: hardware trigger detection on the falling edge
11: hardware trigger detection on both the rising and falling edges

JEXTSEL[3:0]: External trigger selection for injected group
These bits select the external event used to trigger the start of conversion of an injected group (the meanings of events are given in Table 10.6):

0000: event 0	0001: event 1	0010: event 2	0011: event 3
0100: event 4	0101: event 5	0110: event 6	0111: event 7
1000: event 8	1001: event 9	1010: event 10	1011: event 11
1100: event 12	1101: event 13	1110: event 14	1111: event 15

JL[1:0]: Injected channel sequence length
These bits define the total number of conversions in the injected channel conversion sequence.
00: 1 conversion 01: 2 conversions 10: 3 conversions 11: 4 conversions

Figure 10.17 ADC injected sequence register (ADCx->JSQR)

Table 10.6 External triggers for injected channels of ADC1, ADC2, and ADC3

Name	Source	Type	JEXTSEL[3:0]
JEXT0	TIM1_TRGO event	Internal signal from on-chip timer	0000
JEXT1	TIM1_CC4 event	Internal signal from on-chip timer	0001
JEXT2	TIM2_TRGO event	Internal signal from on-chip timer	0010
JEXT3	TIM2_CC1 event	Internal signal from on-chip timer	0011
JEXT4	TIM3_CC4 event	Internal signal from on-chip timer	0100
JEXT5	TIM4_TRGO event	Internal signal from on-chip timer	0101
JEXT6	EXTI line 15	External pin	0110
JEXT7	TIM8_CC4 event	Internal signal from on-chip timer	0111
JEXT8	TIM1_TRGO2 event	Internal signal from on-chip timer	1000
JEXT9	TIM8_TRGO event	Internal signal from on-chip timer	1001
JEXT10	TIM8_TRGO2 event	Internal signal from on-chip timer	1010
JEXT11	TIM3_CC3 event	Internal signal from on-chip timer	1011
JEXT12	TIM3_TRGO event	Internal signal from on-chip timer	1100
JEXT13	TIM3_CC1 event	Internal signal from on-chip timer	1101
JEXT14	TIM6_TRGO event	Internal signal from on-chip timer	1110
JEXT15	TIM15_TRGO event	Internal signal from on-chip timer	1111

Example 10.8 Write a sequence of C statements to configure and place PC0, PC1, PB0, PA1, PA4, PC3 into the regular group and PC4 and PA6 in the injected group.

Solution:

The following C statements perform the specified configuration (without enabling the trigger):

```
GPIOA->MODER   |= GPIO_MODER_MODE1 + GPIO_MODER_MODE4 +
                  GPIO_MODER_MODE6;
GPIOA->ASCR    |= GPIO_ASCR_ASC1 +GPIO_ASCR_ASC4 + GPIO_ASCR_ASC6;
GPIOB->MODER   |= GPIO_MODER_MODE0;
GPIOB->ASCR    |= GPIO_ASCR_ASC0;
GPIOC->MODER   |= GPIO_MODER_MODE0 + GPIO_MODER_MODE1 +
                  GPIO_MODER_MODE3 + GPIO_MODER_MODE4;
GPIOC->ASCR    |= GPIO_ASCR_ASC0 + GPIO_ASCR_ASC1 + GPIO_ASCR_ASC3 +
                  GPIO_ASCR_ASC4;
ADC1->DIFSEL   &= ~(ADC_DIFSEL_DIFSEL_1 + ADC_DIFSEL_DIFSEL_2 +
                  ADC_DIFSEL_DIFSEL_4 + ADC_DIFSEL_DIFSEL_6 +
                  ADC_DIFSEL_DIFSEL_9 + ADC_DIFSEL_DIFSEL_11 +
                  ADC_DIFSEL_DIFSEL_13 + ADC_DIFSEL_DIFSEL_15);
// // regular group has six channels
ADC1->SQR1     =  ADC_SQR1_L_2 + ADC_SQR1_L_1 + // regular sequence contains 6
                  ADC_SQR1_SQ1_0 +                       // CH1
                  ADC_SQR1_SQ2_1 +                       // CH2
                  ADC_SQR1_SQ3_3 + ADC_SQR1_SQ3_2 +      // CH15
                  ADC_SQR1_SQ3_1 + ADC_SQR1_SQ3_0        // "
                  ADC_SQR1_SQ4_2 + ADC_SQR1_SQ4_1;       // CH6
ADC1->SQR2     =  ADC_SQR2_SQ5_3 + ADC_SQR2_SQ5_0 +      // CH9
                  ADC_SQR2_SQ6_2;                        // CH4
// injected group has two input channels (channel 13 and channel 11)
ADC1->JSQR     =  ADC_JSQR_JL_1 +
                  ADC_JSQR_JSQ1_3 + ADC_JSQR_JSQ1_2 + ADC_JSQR_JSQ1_0 +
                  ADC_JSQR_JSQ2_3 + ADC_JSQR_JSQ2_1 + ADC_JSQR_JSQ2_0;
```

10.7.7 CHANNEL SAMPLING TIME

There is a capacitor at every input channel of the ADC. This capacitor, which is called **sampling capacitor**, holds the voltage to be converted at a constant level. Before the conversion, the ADC must establish a direct connection between the voltage source to be converted and the sampling capacitor. Enough **sampling time** must be provided for the sampling capacitor to be charged to the level of the voltage source to be converted.

Each channel may have different sampling time, which is programmed via the SMP[2:0] bit in the ADCx->SMPR1 and ADCx->SMPR2 registers. The possible sampling time values are as follows:

- SMP[2:0] = 000: 2.5 ADC clock cycles
- SMP[2:0] = 001: 6.5 ADC clock cycles
- SMP[2:0] = 010: 12.5 ADC clock cycles
- SMP[2:0] = 011: 24.5 ADC clock cycles
- SMP[2:0] = 100: 47.5 ADC clock cycles
- SMP[2:0] = 101: 92.5 ADC clock cycles
- SMP[2:0] = 110: 247.5 ADC clock cycles
- SMP[2:0] = 111: 640.5 ADC clock cycles

The total conversion time is calculated as follows:

$$T_{CONV} = \text{Sampling time} + 12.5 \text{ ADC clock cycles}$$

Example 10.9 Assume that f_{ADC_CLK} = 80 MHz and the selected sampling time is 2.5 ADC clock cycles, what will be the conversion time for the 12-bit resolution?

Solution: Using the successive approximation method, it takes 12.5 ADC clock cycles to perform the conversion.

$T_{ADC\_CLK} = 1 / 80\text{MHz} = 12.5$ ns

$T_{CONV} = (2.5 + 12.5)$ ADC clock cycles = 15 ADC clock cycles = 187.5 ns (for fast channels)

At the end of the sampling time, the EOSMP bit in the ADCx->ISR register will be set to 1. The contents of the ADCx->ISR, ADCx->SMPR1, and ADCx->SMPR2 registers are shown in Figures 10.18–10.20, respectively.

31	30	29	28	27	26	25	24	
--	--	--	--	--	--	--	--	Reset value = 0x2000 0000
23	**22**	**21**	**20**	**19**	**18**	**17**	**16**	Offset Addr= 0x00
--	--	--	--	--	--	--	--	
15	**14**	**13**	**12**	**11**	**10**	**9**	**8**	
--	--	--	--	--	JQOVF	AWD3	AWD2	
7	**6**	**5**	**4**	**3**	**2**	**1**	**0**	
AWD1	JEOS	JEOC	OVR	EOS	EOC	EOSMP	ADRDY	

JQOVF: Injected context queue overflow

This bit is set when an overflow of the injected queue of context occurs.

0: No injected context queue overflow occurred.

1: Injected context queue overflow has occurred.

AWDn: Analog watchdog n flag (n = 1..3)

This bit is set when the converted voltage is outside the range defined by the fields LTn[7:0] and HTn[7:0] of the ADCx->TRn register.

0: No analog watchdog n event occurred 1: Analog watchdog n event occurred.

JEOS: Injected channel end of sequence flag

This bit is set at the end of the conversions of all injected channels in the group. It is cleared by writing 1 to it.

0: Injected conversion sequence not complete.

1: Injected conversion sequence complete.

JEOC: Injected channel end of conversion

This bit is set at the end of each injected conversion of a channel when a new data is available in the corresponding ADCx_JDRy register. It is cleared by writing 1 to it or by reading the corresponding ADCx_JDRy register.

0: Injected channel conversion not complete.

1: Injected channel conversion complete.

OVR: ADC overrun

This bit is set when a new conversion has completed while the EOC flag is already set. It is cleared by writing 1 to it.

0: No overrun occurred. 1: Overrun has occurred.

Figure 10.18 ADC Interrupt and status register (ADCx->ISR)

31	30	29	28	27	26	25	24	
--	--	--	--	--	--	--	--	Reset value = 0x2000 0000
23	22	21	20	19	18	17	16	Offset Addr= 0x00
--	--	--	--	--	--	--	--	
15	14	13	12	11	10	9	8	
--	--	--	--	--	JQOVF	AWD3	AWD2	
7	6	5	4	3	2	1	0	
AWD1	JEOS	JEOC	OVR	EOS	EOC	EOSMP	ADRDY	

EOS: End of regular sequence flag
This bit is set at the end of the conversions of a regular sequence of channels. It is cleared by writing 1 to it.
0: Regular conversion sequence not complete.
1: Regular conversion sequence complete

EOC: End of conversion flag
This bit is set at the end of each regular conversion of a channel when a new data is available in the ADCx->DR register. It is cleared by writing 1 to it or reading the ADCx->DR register.
0: Regular channel conversion not complete.
1. Regular channel conversion complete.

EOSMP: End of sampling flag
This bit is set during the conversion of any channel at the end of the sampling phase.
0: Not at the end of the sampling phase. 1: End of sampling phase reached.

ADRDY: ADC ready
This bit is set after the ADC has been enabled and when the ADC reaches a state where it is ready to accept conversion requests. It is cleared by writing 1 to it.
0: ADC not yet ready to start conversion. 1: ADC is ready to start conversion.

Figure 10.18a ADC Interrupt and status register (ADCx->ISR)—(continued)

31	30	29	28	27	26	25	24	
--	--	SMP9[2:0]			SMP8[2:0]			Reset value = 0x0000 0000
23	22	21	20	19	18	17	16	Offset Addr= 0x14
SMP7[2:0]			SMP6[2:0]			SMP5[2:1]		
15	14	13	12	11	10	9	8	
SMP5[0]	SMP4[2:0]			SMP3[2:0]			SMP2[2]	
7	6	5	4	3	2	1	0	
SMP2[1:0]		SMP1[2:0]			SMP0[2:0]			

SMPy[2:0]: Channel y sampling time selection (y = 9..0)
These bits select the sampling time for the associated channel.
000: 2.5 ADC clock cycles 001: 6.5 ADC clock cycles 010: 12.5 ADC clock cycles
011: 24.5 ADC clock cycles 100: 47.5 ADC clock cycles 101: 92.5 ADC clock cycles
110: 247.5 ADC clock cycles 111: 640.5 ADC clock cycles

Figure 10.19 ADC Sampling time register 1 (ADCx->SMPR1)

31	30	29	28	27	26	25	24
–	–	–	–	–	SMP18[2:0]		
23	**22**	**21**	**20**	**19**	**18**	**17**	**16**
SMP17[2:0]			SMP16[2:0]			SMP15[2:1]	
15	**14**	**13**	**12**	**11**	**10**	**9**	**8**
SMP15[0]	SMP14[2:0]			SMP13[2:0]			SMP12[2]
7	**6**	**5**	**4**	**3**	**2**	**1**	**0**
SMP12[1:0]		SMP11[2:0]			SMP10[2:0]		

Reset value = 0x0000 0000
Offset Addr= 0x18

SMPy[2:0]: Channel y sampling time selection (y = 18..10)

These bits select the sampling time for the associated channel.

000: 2.5 ADC clock cycles 001: 6.5 ADC clock cycles 010: 12.5 ADC clock cycles
011: 24.5 ADC clock cycles 100: 47.5 ADC clock cycles 101: 92.5 ADC clock cycles
110: 247.5 ADC clock cycles 111: 640.5 ADC clock cycles

Figure 10.20 ADC Sampling time register 2 (ADCx->SMPR2)

For each channel, the SMP[2:0] bits must be set to satisfy the minimum sampling time as specified in the ADC characteristics section of the datasheets. The I/O analog switches resistance increases when the V_{DDA} voltage is too low. This requires the sampling time to be adapted accordingly. This resistance can be minimized at low V_{DDA} by enabling an internal voltage booster with the BOOSTEN bit in the SYSCFG->CFGR1 register.

10.7.8 SINGLE CONVERSION MODE

In the single conversion mode, all the channels in a sequence (regular or injected) will be converted once with a trigger (software or hardware). To enter the single conversion mode, clear the CONT bit in the ADCx->CFGR register.

When the software trigger mode is selected, setting the ADSTART bit in the ADCx->CR register starts the conversion for each regular channel once, whereas setting the JADSTART bit in the ADCx->CR register starts the conversion for each injected channel once. The ADSTART and JADSTART bits are cleared at the end of a conversion sequence.

Inside the regular sequence, after each conversion is complete:

- The conversion result is stored in the 16-bit ADCx->DR register.
- The EOC flag in the ADCx->ISR register is set.
- An interrupt is generated if the EOCIE bit in the ADCx->IER register is set.

Inside the injected sequence, after each conversion is complete:

- The conversion result is stored in one of the four 16-bit ADCx->JDRy registers.
- The JEOC (end of injected conversion) flag in the ADCx->ISR register is set.
- An interrupt is generated if the JEOCIE bit in the ADCx->IER register is set.

After the regular sequence is complete:

- The EOS (end of regular sequence) flag in the ADCx->ISR register is set.
- An interrupt is generated if the EOSIE bit in the ADCx->IER register is set.

After the injected sequence is complete:

- The JEOS (end of injected sequence) flag in the ADCx->ISR register is set.
- An interrupt is generated if the JEOSIE bit in the ADCx->IER register is set.

Then the ADC stops until a new external regular or injected trigger occurs or until bit ADSTART or JADSTART is set again.

10.7.9 CONTINUOUS CONVERSION MODE

Continuous conversion mode is entered by setting the CONT bit to 1. This mode applies to regular channels only. When a software or hardware regular trigger event occurs, the ADC performs once all the regular conversions of the channels and then automatically restarts and continuously converts each channel of the sequence. Either the setting of the ADSTART bit in the ADCx->CR register or an external trigger event starts the conversion.

Inside the regular sequence, after each conversion is complete:

- The conversion result is stored in the 16-bit ADCx->DR register.
- The EOC flag in the ADCx->ISR register is set.
- An interrupt is generated if the EOCIE bit in the ADCx->IER register is set.

After the sequence of conversion is complete:

- The EOS flag in the ADCx->ISR register is set.
- An interrupt is generated if the EOSIE bit in the ADCx->IER register is set.

Then a new sequence restarts immediately and the ADC continuously repeats the conversion sequence. It is not possible to have both discontinuous mode and continuous mode enabled. Injected channels cannot be converted continuously. The only exception is when an injected channel is configured to be converted automatically after regular channels in continuous mode (by setting the JAUTO bit in the ADCx->CFGR register). The contents of the ADCx->CFGR register are shown in Figure 10.21.

31	30	29	28	27	26	25	24
JQDIS	AWD1CH[4:0]					JAUTO	JAWD1EN
23	**22**	**21**	**20**	**19**	**18**	**17**	**16**
AWD1EN	AWD1SGL	JQM	JDISCEN	DISCNUM[2:0]			DISCEN
15	**14**	**13**	**12**	**11**	**10**	**9**	**8**
–	AUTDLY	CONT	OVRMOD	EXTEN[1:0]		EXTSEL3	EXTSEL2
7	**6**	**5**	**4**	**3**	**2**	**1**	**0**
EXTSEL1	EXTSEL0	ALIGN	RES[1:0]		DFSDMCFG	DMACFG	DMAEN

Reset value = 0x8000 0000
Offset Addr= 0x0C

JQDIS: Injected queue disable
0: injected queue enabled 1: injected queue disabled
AWD1CH[4:0]: Analog watchdog 1 channel selection
These bits select the input channel to be guarded by the analog watchdog.
00000: ADC analog input channel 0 monitored by AWD1 (available in ADC1 only)
00001: ADC analog input channel 1 monitored by AWD1
....
10010: ADC analog input channel 18 monitored by AWD1
The channel selected by AWD1CH must be also selected into the SQRi or JSQRi registers.
JAUTO: Automatic injected group conversion
0: Automatic injected group conversion disabled
1: Automatic injected group conversion enabled
This bit can be written only when ADSTART = 0 and JADSTART = 0.
JAWD1EN: Analog watchdog 1 enable on injected channels
0: Analog watchdog 1 disabled on injected channel.
1: Analog watchdog 1 enabled on injected channels
This bit can be written only when JADSTART = 0.
AWD1EN: Analog watchdog 1 enable on regular channels
0: Analog watchdog 1 disabled on regular channels
1: Analog watchdog 1 enabled on regular channels
AWD1SGL: Enable the watchdog 1 on a single channel or on all channels
0: Analog watchdog 1 enabled on all channels
1: Analog watchdog 1 enabled on a single channel
The single channel to be watched is specified in AWD1CH[4:0].
JQM: JSQR queue mode
This bit defines how an empty queue is managed.
0: JSQR mode 0: The queue is never empty and maintains the last written configuration into JSQR.
1: JSQR mode 1: The queue can be empty and when this occurs, the software and hardware triggers of the injected sequence are both internally disabled just after the completion of the last valid injected sequence.

Figure 10.21 ADC configuration register (ADCx->CFGR)

31	30	29	28	27	26	25	24
JQDIS	AWD1CH[4:0]					JAUTO	JAWD1EN
23	**22**	**21**	**20**	**19**	**18**	**17**	**16**
AWD1EN	AWD1SGL	JQM	JDISCEN	DISCNUM[2:0]			DISCEN
15	**14**	**13**	**12**	**11**	**10**	**9**	**8**
--	AUTDLY	CONT	OVRMOD	EXTEN[1:0]		EXTSEL3	EXTSEL2
7	**6**	**5**	**4**	**3**	**2**	**1**	**0**
EXTSEL1	EXTSEL0	ALIGN	RES[1:0]		DFSDMCFG	DMACFG	DMAEN

Reset value = 0x8000 0000
Offset Addr= 0x0C

JDISCEN: Discontinuous mode on injected channels
0: Discontinuous mode on injected channels disabled
1: Discontinuous mode on injected channels enabled
It is not possible to use both auto-injected mode and discontinuous mode simultaneously: the bits DISCEN and JDISCEN must be kept cleared when JAUTO bit is set. When dual mode is enabled, the JDISCEN bit of the slave ADC is equal to the JDISCEN bit of master ADC.

DISCNUM[2:0]: Discontinuous mode channel count
These bits specify the number of regular channels to be converted in discontinuous mode, after receiving an external trigger.
000: 1 channel 001: 2 channels ... 111: 8 channels
These bits can be written only when ADSTART = 0. When dual mode is enabled, the bits DISCNUM[2:0] of the slave ADC is equal to the DISCNUM[2:0] bits of the master ADC.

DISCEN: Discontinuous mode for regular channels
0: Discontinuous mode for regular channels disabled
1: Discontinuous mode for regular channels enabled
It is not possible to use both auto-injected mode and discontinuous mode simultaneously. When JAUTO bit is set, both the DISCEN and JDISCEN bits must be cleared.

AUTDLY: Delayed conversion mode
0: Auto-delayed conversion mode off 1: Auto-delayed conversion mode on
When dual mode is enabled, the AUTDLY of the slave is equal to the AUTDLY bit of the master ADC.

CONT: Single/continuous mode for regular conversions
0: Single conversion mode 1: Continuous conversion mode
It is forbidden to set both DISCEN = 1 and CONT = 1.

OVRMOD: Overrun mode
0: ADCx->DR register is preserved with the old data when an overrun is detected.
1: ADCx->DR register is overwritten with the last conversion result when an overrun is detected.

EXTEN[1:0]: External trigger enable and polarity selection for regular channels
00: Hardware trigger detection disabled 01: Hardware trigger detection on the rising edge.
10: Hardware trigger detection on the falling edge
11: Hardware trigger detection on both the rising and falling edges

Figure 10.21a ADC configuration register (ADCx->CFGR)

31	30	29	28	27	26	25	24
JQDIS	AWD1CH[4:0]					JAUTO	JAWD1EN

23	22	21	20	19	18	17	16
AWD1EN	AWD1SGL	JQM	JDISCEN	DISCNUM[2:0]			DISCEN

15	14	13	12	11	10	9	8
--	AUTDLY	CONT	OVRMOD	EXTEN[1:0]		EXTSEL3	EXTSEL2

7	6	5	4	3	2	1	0
EXTSEL1	EXTSEL0	ALIGN	RES[1:0]		DFSDMCFG	DMACFG	DMAEN

Reset value = 0x8000 0000
Offset Addr= 0x0C

DISCEN: Discontinuous mode for regular channels
0: Discontinuous mode for regular channels disabled
1: Discontinuous mode for regular channels enabled
It is not possible to use both auto-injected mode and discontinuous mode simultaneously. When JAUTO bit is set, both the DISCEN and JDISCEN bits must be cleared.

AUTDLY: Delayed conversion mode
0: Auto-delayed conversion mode off 1: Auto-delayed conversion mode on
When dual mode is enabled, the AUTDLY of the slave is equal to the AUTDLY bit of the master ADC.

CONT: Single/continuous mode for regular conversions
0: Single conversion mode 1: Continuous conversion mode
It is forbidden to set both DISCEN = 1 and CONT = 1.

OVRMOD: Overrun mode
0: ADCx->DR register is preserved with the old data when an overrun is detected.
1: ADCx->DR register is overwritten with the last conversion result when an overrun is detected.

EXTEN[1:0]: External trigger enable and polarity selection for regular channels
00: Hardware trigger detection disabled 01: Hardware trigger detection on the rising edge.
10: Hardware trigger detection on the falling edge
11: Hardware trigger detection on both the rising and falling edges

Figure 10.21b ADC configuration register (ADCx->CFGR)

Table 10.7 External triggers for regular channels of ADC1, ADC2, and ADC3

Name	Source	Type	EXTSEL[3:0]
EXT0	TIM1_CC1 event	Internal signal from on-chip timer	0000
EXT1	TIM1_CC2 event	Internal signal from on-chip timer	0001
EXT2	TIM1_CC3 event	Internal signal from on-chip timer	0010
EXT3	TIM2_CC2 event	Internal signal from on-chip timer	0011
EXT4	TIM3_TRGO event	Internal signal from on-chip timer	0100
EXT5	TIM4_CC4 event	Internal signal from on-chip timer	0101
EXT6	EXTI line 11	External pin	0110
EXT7	TIM8_TRGO event	Internal signal from on-chip timer	0111
EXT8	TIM8_TRGO2 event	Internal signal from on-chip timer	1000
EXT9	TIM1_TRGO event	Internal signal from on-chip timer	1001
EXT10	TIM1_TRGO2 event	Internal signal from on-chip timer	1010
EXT11	TIM2_TRGO event	Internal signal from on-chip timer	1011
EXT12	TIM4_TRGO event	Internal signal from on-chip timer	1100
EXT13	TIM6_TRGO event	Internal signal from on-chip timer	1101
EXT14	TIM15_TRGO event	Internal signal from on-chip timer	1110
EXT15	TIM3_CC4 event	Internal signal from on-chip timer	1111

10.7.10 STARTING CONVERSIONS

Software starts the ADC regular conversion by setting the ADSTART bit in the ADCx->CR register to 1. When the ADSTART bit is set, the conversion starts either (1) immediately if the EXTEN field of the ADCx->CFGR register is 00 (software trigger) or (2) at the next active edge of the selected regular hardware trigger if the EXTEN field is not 00.

Software starts ADC injected conversions by setting the JADSTART bit in the ADCx->CR register to 1. When the JADSTART bit is set, the conversion starts either (1) immediately if the JEXTEN field is 00 (software trigger), or (2) at the next active edge of the selected injected hardware trigger if the JEXTEN field of the ADCx->JSQR register is not 00.

In **auto-injection mode** (JAUTO bit in the ADCx->CFGR register set to 1), use ADSTART bit to start the regular conversions followed by the auto-injected conversions (the JADSTART bit in the ADCx->CR register must be kept cleared).

The ADSTART and JADSTART bits also provide information on whether any ADC operation is currently ongoing. The ADC can be reconfigured when both the ADSTART and JADSTART bits are 0, indicating that the ADC is idle.

In the single mode with software trigger, the ADSTART bit will be cleared at the end of any regular conversion sequence (EOS assertion) or at any end of subgroup processing if DISCEN bit = 1. In all other cases, the ADSTART bit is cleared after execution of the ADSTP procedure asserted by software.

In the continuous mode, the ADSTART bit is not cleared by hardware with the assertion of the EOS flag in the ADCx->ISR register because the sequence is automatically relaunched.

When a hardware trigger is selected in the single mode, the ADSTART bit is not cleared by hardware with the assertion of the EOS flag to help the software which does not need to reset the ADSTART bit again for the next hardware trigger event. This ensures that no further hardware triggers are missed.

In the single mode with software trigger, the JADSTART bit is cleared at the end of any injected conversion sequence or at the end of any subgroup processing if JDISCEN = 1. In all other cases, the JADSTART bit is cleared after the execution of the JADSTP procedure asserted by the software.

10.7.11 STOPPING AN ONGOING CONVERSION

Occasionally the application needs to stop A/D conversions. The regular conversions can be stopped by setting the ADSTP bit, and the injected conversions can be stopped by setting the JADSTP bit. Both bits are in the ADCx->CR register.

Stopping conversions will reset the ongoing ADC operation. After that, the ADC can be reconfigured to prepare for a new operation.

It is possible to stop injected conversions while regular conversions are still operating and vice versa. This allows, for example, reconfiguration of the injected conversion sequence and triggers while regular conversions are still operating and vice versa.

When the ADSTP bit is set, any ongoing regular conversion is aborted with partial result discarded. The ADCx->DR register is not updated with the current conversion.

When the JADSTP bit is set, any ongoing injected conversion is aborted with partial result discarded. The ADCx->JDRy register is not updated with the current conversion. The scan sequence is also aborted and reset.

Once this procedure is complete, bits ADSTP/ADSTART (in case of regular conversion), or JADSTP/JADSTART (in case of injected conversion) are cleared by hardware and the software must poll ADSTART (or JADSTART) until the bit is reset before assuming that the ADC is completely stopped.

In auto-injection mode (JAUTO bit = 1), setting the ADSTP bit aborts both regular and injected conversions.

10.7.12 CONVERSION ON EXTERNAL TRIGGER AND TRIGGER POLARITY

A conversion or a sequence of conversions can be triggered either by software or by an external event (e.g., timer capture, input pins). If the EXTEN[1:0] field in the ADCx->CFGR register or the JEXTEN[1:0] field in the ADCx->JSQR register is not 00, external events are able to trigger a conversion with the selected polarity.

When the injected queue is enabled (bit JQDIS = 0 in ADCx->CFGR), injected software triggers are not possible.

The regular trigger selection is effective once the ADSTART bit has been set and the injected trigger selection is effective once the JADSTART bit has been set.

Any hardware triggers that occur while a conversion is ongoing are ignored. If the ADSTART bit is 0, any regular hardware triggers are ignored. If the JADSTART bit is 0, any injected hardware triggers are ignored.

The trigger polarity of regular conversions is specified by programming the EXTEN[1:0] field in the ADCx->CFGR register shown in Figure 10.21b. The trigger polarity of injected conversions is specified by programming the JEXTEN[1:0] field in the ADCx->JSQR register shown in Figure 10.17.

The polarity of the injected trigger can be changed on the fly when the queue is enabled. The EXTSEL[3:0] field in the ADCx->CFGR register selects the event that can trigger conversion for a regular group, whereas the JEXTSEL[3:0] field in the ADCx->JSQR register selects the event that can trigger conversion for a injected group. A regular group conversion can be interrupted by an injected trigger. In dual mode the trigger setting of the slave ADC follows that of the master ADC.

Example 10.10 Assume that the frequency of the clock source to the TIM2 and ADC1 is 48 MHz. Write a sequence of C statements to configure ADC1 regular group to be triggered by the TIM2 TRGO output (select the update event) every 1 ms.

Solution:

Let us set the TIM2 clock prescaler to 6 (PSC = 5), then the frequency of the clock input to TIM2 is 8 MHz. The clock period is 125 ns. The duration of 1 ms corresponds to 8000 TIM2 clock cycles.

The following C statements performs the specified configuration:

```
ADC1->CFGR    &= ~(ADC_CFGR_EXTEN + ADC_CFGR_EXTSEL);
```

```
// select TIM2_TRGO (event 11) rising edge as external trigger source
    ADC1->CFGR   |= ADC_CFGR_EXTEN_0 + ADC_CFGR_EXTSEL_3 +
                    ADC_CFGR_EXTSEL_1 + ADC_CFGR_EXTSEL_0;
    TIM2->PSC    =  5;
    TIM2->ARR    =  8000; // value to create 1 ms delay
    TIM2->EGR    |= TIM_EGR_UG; // update prescaler and ARR shadow
    TIM2->CR2    =  TIM_CR2_MMS_1; // select update event as the source of TRGO
    TIM2->CR1    |= TIM_CR1_ARPE + TIM_CR1_CEN; // enable TIM2 and its auto reload
```

10.7.13 INJECTED CHANNEL MANAGEMENT

Injected channels can be converted by trigger inputs and automatically after the regular sequence.

Triggered Injection Mode

To use triggered injection, the JAUTO bit in the ADCx->CFGR register must be cleared:

1. Start the conversion of a group of regular channels either by an external trigger or by setting the ADSTART bit in the ADCx->CR register.
2. If an external injected trigger occurs, or if the JADSTART bit in the ADCx->CR register is set during the conversion of a regular group of channels, the current conversion is reset and the ADC starts to convert the injected channel sequence (all the injected channels are converted once).
3. Then the conversion of the regular group of channels are resumed from the last interrupted regular channel.
4. If a regular event occurs during an injected conversion, the injected conversion is not interrupted, but the regular sequence is executed at the end of the injected sequence.

When using triggered injection, one must ensure that the interval between trigger events is longer than the injected sequence conversion time.

Auto-injection Mode

If the JAUTO bit in the ADCx->CFGR register is set, the channels in the injected group are automatically converted after the regular group of channels. This can be used to convert a sequence of up to 20 conversions programmed in the ADCx->SQR and ADCx->JSQR registers. In this mode, external trigger on injected channels must be disabled.

In this mode, the ADSTART bit in the ADCx->CR register must be set to start regular conversions, followed by injected conversions. The JADSTART bit in the ADCx->CR register must be cleared. Setting the ADSTP bit aborts both regular and injected conversions.

If the CONT bit in the ADCx->CFGR register is also set in addition to the JAUTO bit, regular channels followed by injected channels are continuously converted.

It is not possible to use both auto-injected and discontinuous modes simultaneously. When the DMA is used for exporting regular sequencer's data in the JAUTO mode, it is necessary to program it in circular mode. If the CIRC bit in the DMA$_x$_Channel$_n$->CCR register is reset (single-shot mode), the JAUTO sequence will be stopped upon DMA transfer complete event.

10.7.14 DISCONTINUOUS MODE

The user can use the discontinuous mode to **convert a subset of channels** in the selected sequence with one external trigger at a time in regular or injected channel mode.

Regular Group Mode

This mode is enabled by setting the DISCEN bit in the ADCx->CFGR register. It is used to convert a short sequence (subgroup) of **n** conversions ($n \le 8$) that is part of the sequence of conversions selected in the ADCx->SQR1...ADCx->SQR4 registers. The value **n** is specified using the DISCNUM[2:0] field in the ADCx->CFGR register.

When an external trigger occurs, it starts the next **n** conversions selected in the ADCx->SQR1...ADCx->SQR4 registers until all the conversions in the sequence are done. The total sequence length is specified by the L[3:0] field in the ADCx->CFGR register.

Example 10.11 Let the channels to be converted = {2, 3, 5, 6, 7, 9, 10, 11, 12}, n = 3, and DISCEN = 1. What will happen if four external triggers occur (assume that two triggers are separated each other long enough)?

Solution:

- When the first trigger occurs, channels 2, 3, and 5 are converted.
- When the second trigger occurs, channels 6, 7, and 9 are converted.
- When the third trigger occurs, channels 10, 11, and 12 are converted and an EOS event is generated after the conversion of channel 12.
- When the fourth trigger occurs, channels are 2, 3, and 5 are converted.

Example 10.12 Let the channels to be converted = {2, 3, 5, 6, 7, 9, 10, 11, 12}, n = 3 and DISCEN bit = 0. What will happen when a trigger occurs?

Solution:

- When a trigger occurs, the complete sequence is converted: channel 2, then 3, 5, 6, 7, 9, 10, 11, and 12. Each conversion generates an EOC event and the last conversion also generates an EOS event.
- All the next trigger events will relaunch the complete sequence.

When a regular group is converted in discontinuous mode, **no rollover occurs** (the last subgroup of the sequence can have less than **n** conversions).

Injected Group Mode

This mode is enabled by setting the JDISCEN bit in the ADCx->CFGR register. It converts the sequence selected in the ADCx->JSQR register, channel by channel, after an external injected trigger event. This is equivalent to discontinuous mode for regular channels where **n** is fixed at 1.

When an external trigger occurs, it starts the next conversion selected in the ADCx->JSQR registers until all the conversions in the sequence are done.

Example 10.13 Suppose injected channels to be converted = {2, 4, 6}, and the JDISCEN bit = 1, what will happen when four triggers one after another arrives?

Solution:

- When the first trigger occurs, channel 2 is converted (a JEOC event is generated).
- When the second trigger occurs, channel 4 is converted (a JEOC event is generated).
- When the third trigger occurs, channel 6 is converted (a JEOC event and a JEOS event are generated).
- When the fourth trigger occurs, channel 2 is converted (a JEOC event is generated).

When all injected channels have been converted, the next trigger starts the conversion of the first injected channel.

10.7.15 QUEUE OF CONTEXTS FOR INJECTED CONVERSIONS

The injected sequence option provides flexibility to the ADC to perform A/D conversions. However, it only allows up to four channels to be converted. Some applications may need to perform conversions on more than four channels every now and then. The queue of context feature makes this possible.

A context consists of:

1) Configuration of the injected triggers (the JEXTEN[1:0] and JEXTSEL[3:0] fields in the ADCx->JSQR register)
2) Definition of the injected sequence (the JSQ1[4:0]...JSQ4[4:0] and JL[1:0] fields in the ADCx->JSQR register)

A queue of context is implemented to anticipate up to 2 contexts for the next injected sequence of conversions. This feature enables the user to inject up to 8 channels to the regular sequence to be converted. The JQDIS bit in the ADCx->CFGR register must be cleared to enable this feature. Only hardware-triggered conversions are possible when the context queue is enabled.

The **user writes the context into the queue via the ADCx->JSQR register**. Up to two contexts can be written into the queue. That queue has two buffers. The operation of the queue of contexts is as follows:

1. The ADCx->JSQR register can be written at any moment even when injected conversions are ongoing.
2. Each data written into the ADCx->JSQR register is stored in the queue of contexts.
3. At the beginning, the queue is empty and the first write access into the JSQR register immediately changes the context and the ADC is ready to receive injected triggers.
4. Once an injected sequence is complete, the queue is consumed and the context changes according to the next JSQR parameters stored in the queue. This new context is applied for the next injected sequence of conversions.
5. A queue overflow occurs when writing into register JSQR while the queue is full. The overflow condition is indicated by the setting of JQOVF flag in the ADCx->ISR register. The context that caused overflow is ignored and the queue of context is unchanged. An interrupt can be generated if the

JQOVFIE bit in the ADCx->IER register is set. The contents of the ADCx->IER register are shown in Figure 10.22.

6. Depending on the setting of the JQM bit in the ADCx->CFGR register, there are two possible outcomes when the queue becomes empty:
   (1) If JQM = 0, the queue is empty immediately after enabling the ADC, after that it can never become empty during the normal operation. The queue always maintains the last active context and any further valid start of injected sequence will be served according to the last active context.
   (2) If JQM = 1, the queue can be empty after the end of an injected sequence or if the queue is flushed. When this occurs, there is no more context in the queue and hardware triggers are disabled. Therefore, any further hardware injected triggers are ignored until the software rewrites a new context into the ADCx->JSQR register.
7. Reading the ADCx->JSQR register returns the current context which is active at that moment. When the queue context is empty, the ADCx->JSQR register is read as 0x0000.
8. To flush the context queue by setting the JADSTP or disabling the ADC by setting the ADDIS bit in the ADCx->CR register, (1) if JQM = 0, the queue is maintained with the last active context, (2) If JQM = 1, the queue becomes empty and triggers are ignored.

When configured in discontinuous mode (JDISCEN = 1), only the last trigger of the injected sequence changes the context and consumes the queue. Assume that the queue contains two contexts and each context specifies three channels to be converted, then the outcomes of six triggers are as follows:

- First trigger: discontinuous, sequence 1: context 1 consumed, first conversion carried out.
- Second trigger: discontinuous, sequence 1: second conversion carried out.
- Third trigger: discontinuous, sequence 1: third conversion carried out.
- Fourth trigger: discontinuous, sequence 2, context 2 consumed, first conversion carried out.
- Fifth trigger: discontinuous, sequence 2, second conversion carried out.
- Sixth trigger: discontinuous, sequence 2, third conversion carried out.

31	30	29	28	27	26	25	24
--	--	--	--	--	--	--	--
23	**22**	**21**	**20**	**19**	**18**	**17**	**16**
--	--	--	--	--	--	--	--
15	**14**	**13**	**12**	**11**	**10**	**9**	**8**
--	--	--	--	--	JQOVFIE	AWD3IE	AWD2IE
7	**6**	**5**	**4**	**3**	**2**	**1**	**0**
AWD1IE	JEOSIE	JEOCIE	OVRIE	EOSIE	EOCIE	EOSMPIE	ADRDYIE

Reset value = 0x0000 0000
Offset Addr= 0x04

JQOVFIE: Injected context queue overflow interrupt enable
  0: Injected context queue overflow interrupt disabled
  1: Injected context queue overflow interrupt enabled
AWDnIE: Analog watchdog n interrupt enable (n = 1..3)
  0: Analog watchdog n interrupt disabled
  1: Analog watchdog n interrupt enabled
JEOSIE: End of injected sequence of conversions interrupt enable
  0: JEOS interrupt disabled   1: JEOS interrupt enabled
JEOCIE: End of injected conversion interrupt enable
  0: JEOC interrupt disabled   1: JEOC interrupt enabled
OVRIE: Overrun interrupt enable
  0: Overrun interrupt disabled   1: Overrun interrupt enabled
EOSIE: End of regular sequence of conversions interrupt enable
  0: EOS interrupt disabled   1: EOS interrupt enabled
EOCIE: End of regular conversion interrupt enable
  0: EOC interrupt disabled   1: EOC interrupt enabled
EOSMPIE: End of sampling flag interrupt enable for regular conversions
  0: EOSMP interrupt disabled   1: EOSMP interrupt enabled
ADRDYIE: ADC ready interrupt enable
  0: ADRDY interrupt disabled   1: ADRDY interrupt enabled

Figure 10.22 ADC Interrupt and status register (ADCx->IER)

10.7.16 PROGRAMMABLE RESOLUTION—FAST CONVERSION MODE

The resolution can be configured to be either 12, 10, 8, or 6 by programming the RES[1:0] field in the ADCx->CFGR register. By choosing lower resolution, the user can achieve faster conversion. The ADC conversion time consists of the channel sampling time and the time spent on the successive approximation process.

The relationships of ADC timing with respect to resolution are summarized in Table 10.8.

Table 10.8 ADC conversion time timing vs resolution

RES (bits)	TSAR (ADC clock cycles)	T_{SAR} (ns) at f_{ADC}=80MHz	T_{CONV} (ADC clock cycles) (with sampling time = 2.5 ADC clock cycles)	T_{CONV} (ns) at f_{ADC} = 80 MHz
12	12.5 ADC clock cycles	156.25 ns	15 ADC clock cycles	187.5 ns
10	10.5 ADC clock cycles	131.25 ns	13 ADC clock cycles	162.5 ns
8	8.5 ADC clock cycles	106.25 ns	11 ADC clock cycles	137.5 ns
6	6.5 ADC clock cycles	81.25 ns	9 ADC clock cycles	112.5 ns

10.7.17 DATA MANAGEMENT

Data Alignment

The ALIGN bit in the ADCx->CFGR register selects the alignment of the data stored after conversion. Data can be right- (ALIGN = 0) or left-aligned (ALIGN = 1).

When left-alignment is selected, data are aligned on a half-word basis except when the resolution is set to 6-bit. In that case, data are aligned on a byte basis.

Left-alignment is not supported in oversampling mode. When the ROVSE and/or JOVSE bit in the ADCx->CFGR2 is set, the ALIGN bit value is ignored and the ADC only provides right-aligned data. The contents of the ADCx->CFGR2 register are shown in Figure 10.23.

31	30	29	28	27	26	25	24
--	--	--	--	--	--	--	--
23	**22**	**21**	**20**	**19**	**18**	**17**	**16**
--	--	--	--	--	--	--	--
15	**14**	**13**	**12**	**11**	**10**	**9**	**8**
--	--	--	--	--	ROVSM	TROVS	OVSS[3]
7	**6**	**5**	**4**	**3**	**2**	**1**	**0**
OVSS[2:0]			OVSR[2:0]			JOVSE	ROVSE

Reset value = 0x0000 0000
Offset Addr= 0x10

ROVSM: Regular oversampling mode (can be written only when no conversion is ongoing)
- 0: Continued mode. When injected conversions are triggered, the oversampling is temporarily stopped and continued after the injection sequence. The oversampling buffer is maintained during injected sequence.
- 1: Resumed mode. When injected conversions are triggered, the current oversampling is aborted and resumed from start after the injected sequence.

TROVS: Triggered regular oversampling
- 0: All oversampled conversions for a channel are done consecutively following a trigger.
- 1: Each oversampled conversion for a channel needs a new trigger.

OVSS[3:0]: Oversampling shift

0000: No shift	0001: Shift 1 bit	0010: shift 2 bits	0011: shift 3 bits
0100: shift 4 bits	0101: shift 5 bits	0110: shift 6 bits	0111: shift 7 bits
1000: shift 8 bits	other codes: reserved		

OVSR[2:0]: Oversampling ratio

000: 2x	001: 4x	010: 8x	011: 16x
100: 32x	101: 64x	110: 128x	111: 256x

JOVSE: Injected oversampling enable
- 0: Injected oversampling disabled   1: Injected oversampling enabled

ROVSE: Regular oversampling enable
- 0: Regular oversampling disabled   1: Regular oversampling enabled

Figure 10.23 ADC configuration register 2 (ADCx->CFGR2)

Offset

An offset y (y = 1, 2, 3, 4) can be applied to a channel by setting the OFFSETy_EN bit in the ADCx->OFRy register (y = 1 to 4). The channel to which the offset will be applied is programmed into the OFFSETy_CH[4:0] field of the ADCx->OFRy register. The contents of the ADCx->OFRy register are shown in Figure 10.24. The offset computation needs to consider the resolution. The adjustment is illustrated in Table 10.9. In this case, the converted value is decreased by the user-specified offset written in the OFFSETy[11:0] field. The result may be a negative value so the read data is signed and the sign-extended (SEXT) bit represents the extended sign value.

31	30	29	28	27	26	25	24
OFFSETy_EN	OFFSETy_CH[4:0]					--	--
23	**22**	**21**	**20**	**19**	**18**	**17**	**16**
--	--	--	--	--	--	--	--
15	**14**	**13**	**12**	**11**	**10**	**9**	**8**
--	--	--	--	OFFSETy[11:8]			
7	**6**	**5**	**4**	**3**	**2**	**1**	**0**
OFFSETy[7:0]							

Reset value = 0x0000 0000
Offset Addr= 0x60 + 0x04 × (y − 1)

OFFSETy_EN: Offset y enable
This bit enable/disables the offset programmed into bits OFFSETy[11:0].
0: OFFSETy[11:0] disabled 1: OFFSETy[11:0] enabled

OFFSETy_CH[4:0]: channel selection for the data offset y
This field specifies the channel to which the offset programmed into bits OFFSETy[11:0] will apply.

OFFSETy[11:0]: Data offset y for the channel programmed into the OFFSETy_CH[4:0] field
The value of this field is to be subtracted from the raw converted data when converting a channel (can be regular or injected). The conversion result can be read from ADCx->DR or ADCx->JDRy register.

Figure 10.24 ADC Offset y register (ADCx->OFRy, y = 1 to 4)

Table 10.9 Offset computation versus data resolution

Resolution (RES[1:0])	Subtraction between raw converted data and offset		Result	Comments
	Raw converted data, left aligned	Offset		
00: 12-bit	DATA[11:0]	OFFSET[11:0]	Signed 12-bit data	--
01: 10-bit	DATA[11:2], 00	OFFSET[11:0]	Signed 12-bit data	The user must configure OFFSET[1:0] to 00
10: 8-bit	DATA[11:4], 0000	OFFSET[11:0]	Signed 12-bit data	The user must configure OFFSET[3:0] to 0000
10: 6-bit	DATA[11:6], 000000	OFFSET[11:0]	Signed 12-bit data	The user must configure OFFSET[5:0] to 000000

Offset correction is not supported in oversampling mode. When ROVSE and/or JOVSE bit is set, the value of the OFFSETy_EN bit in the ADCx->OFRy register is ignored.

When reading data from the ADCx->DR or from the ADCx->JDRy (y = 1–4) register corresponding to channel i, there are two possibilities:

1. If one of the offsets is enabled (bit OFFSETy_EN = 1) for the corresponding channel, the read data is signed.
2. If none of the four offsets is enabled for this channel, the read data is not signed.

The signed conversion result with offset enabled using right alignment is illustrated in Figure 10.25, whereas the signed conversion result with offset enabled using left alignment is illustrated in Figure 10.26.

12-bit data

bit15								bit7							bit 0
SEXT	SEXT	SEXT	SEXT	D11	D10	D9	D8	D7	D6	D5	D4	D3	D2	D1	D0

10-bit data

bit15								bit7							bit 0
SEXT	SEXT	SEXT	SEXT	SEXT	SEXT	D9	D8	D7	D6	D5	D4	D3	D2	D1	D0

8-bit data

bit15								bit7							bit 0
SEXT	SEXT	SEXT	SEXT	SEXT	SEXT	SEXT	SEXT	D7	D6	D5	D4	D3	D2	D1	D0

6-bit data

bit15								bit7							bit 0
SEXT	SEXT	SEXT	SEXT	SEXT	SEXT	SEXT	SEXT	SEXT	SEXT	D5	D4	D3	D2	D1	D0

Figure 10.25 Right aligned signed conversion data with offset enabled

12-bit data

bit15								bit7							bit 0
SEXT	D11	D10	D9	D8	D7	D6	D5	D4	D3	D2	D1	D0	0	0	0

10-bit data

bit15								bit7							bit 0
SEXT	D9	D8	D7	D6	D5	D4	D3	D2	D1	D0	0	0	0	0	0

8-bit data

bit15								bit7							bit 0
SEXT	D7	D6	D5	D4	D3	D2	D1	D0	0	0	0	0	0	0	0

6-bit data

bit15								bit7							bit 0
SEXT	SEXT	SEXT	SEXT	SEXT	SEXT	SEXT	SEXT	SEXT	D5	D4	D3	D2	D1	D0	0

Figure 10.26 Left aligned signed conversion data with offset enabled

Example 10.14 Write a sequence of C statements to set up the offset 152 (= $2^7 + 2^4 + 2^3$) into channel 9.

Solution:

The following statement sets up the specified offset for channel 9:

```
ADC->OFR1   =   ADC_OFR1_OFFSET1_EN +
                ADC_OFR1_OFFSET1_CH_3 + ADC_OFR1_OFFSET1_CH_0 +
                152;
```

ADC Overrun

The overrun flag (the OVR bit in the ADCx->ISR register) is set when the regular converted data was not read (by the CPU or DMA) before new converted data became available. An interrupt may be generated if the OVRIE bit in the ADCx->IER register is 1.

When an overrun condition occurs, the ADC is still operating and can continue to convert unless the software decides to stop and reset the sequence by setting the bit ADSTP in the ADCx->CR register to 1. The OVR flag can be cleared by writing 1 to it.

It is possible to configure whether data is preserved or overwritten when an overrun event occurs by programming the **OVRMOD** bit in the ADCx->CFGR register:

- OVRMOD = 0. The overrun event preserves the data register from being overwritten. The old data is maintained and the new conversion result is discarded and lost. If the OVR flag remains set, any further conversion will occur but the conversion result will be discarded.
- OVRMOD = 1. The data register is overwritten with the latest conversion result and the previous unread data is lost. If the OVR flag remains at 1, any further conversions will operate normally and the ADCx->DR register will always contain the latest conversion data.

Managing a Sequence of Conversion without Using the DMA

This situation is suitable when the conversions are very slow. In this case, the EOC flag in the ADCx->ISR register and its interrupt are used to handle conversion data. Each time a conversion is complete, the EOC flag is set and the ADCx->DR register can be read. The OVRMOD bit should be set to 0 to manage overrun.

Managing Conversions using DMA

Using DMA can avoid the loss of data already stored in the ADCx->DR register. When the DMA mode is enabled, a DMA request is generated after each conversion of a channel. This allows the transfer of the converted data from the ADCx->DR register to the destination location selected by the software.

Overrun can still occur when DMA is used. When overrun occurs because the DMA could not serve the DMA transfer request in time, the ADC stops generating DMA requests and the data corresponding to the new conversion is not transferred by the DMA. At this point, all the data transferred to the SRAM are valid.

Depending on the configuration of OVRMOD bit, the contents of the ADCx->DR register are either preserved or overwritten. The DMA transfer requests are blocked until the OVR flag is cleared.

The user can choose either the DMA one-shot mode or DMA circular mode. In one-shot mode, the DMA is programmed to transfer a fixed number of data. In circular mode, DMA will transfer continuously.

DMA One-Shot Mode

In this mode, the ADC generates a DMA transfer request each time a new conversion result is available and stops generating DMA requests once the preprogrammed transfer count has been decremented to 0.

When the DMA transfer is complete:

- The contents of the ADC data register are frozen.
- Any ongoing conversion is aborted with partial result discarded.
- No new DMA request is issued to the DMA control.
- DMA is stopped.

DMA Circular Mode

In this mode, the ADC generates a DMA transfer request each time a new conversion data is available in the data register. When the programmed transfer count is decremented to 0, it will be reloaded with the programmed value and the process continues. This mode is especially suitable for those applications that need to perform A/D conversions continuously.

Example 10.15 Write a sequence of C statements to set up DMA transfer (64 words in one-shot mode) for the ADC1. Assume that the word array **adcResult[64]** has been declared to hold the conversion result.

Solution:

```
DMA1_CSELR->CSELR        &= ~DMA_CSELR_C1S; // map ADC1 to DMA1 channel 1
DMA1_Channel1->CMAR      =  (uint32_t)adcResult;
DMA1_Channel1->CPAR      =  (uint32_t)ADC1 + 64;
DMA1_Channel1->CNDTR     =  64;
DMA1_Channel1->CCR       &= ~(DMA_CCR_PL + DMA_CCR_MSIZE + DMA_CCR_PSIZE);
DMA1_Channel1->CCR       |= DMA_CCR_PL_1 + DMA_CCR_MSIZE_1 +
                            DMA_CCR_PSIZE_1 + DMA_CCR_MINC + DMA_CCR_EN;
ADC1->CFGR               &= ~ADC_CFGR_DMACFG; // select DMA one-shot mode
ADC1->CFGR               |= ADC_CFGR_DMAEN; // enable ADC DMA transfer
```

10.7.18 AUTO-DELAYED CONVERSION MODE

This mode is enabled when the AUTDLY bit in the ADCx->CFGR register is set. When the application is clocked at very low frequency, there is a risk of getting the ADC overrun. The auto-delayed conversion mode can simplify the software as well as to optimize the performance of an application that runs at a very low frequency.

When the AUTDLY is set, a new conversion can start only if all the previous conversion results have been taken care of:

1. There is only one data register to hold the conversion result. Therefore, for regular conversions, a new conversion can be started only when the value in the ADCx->DR register has been read or after the EOC flag in the ADCx->ISR register has been cleared.
2. There are four data registers to hold the results of injected conversions and an injected sequence contains no more than four channels to be converted. Therefore, a new injected conversion can be started when the JEOS bit in the ADCx->ISR register has been cleared.

This is the way how the ADC automatically adapts the speed of the ADC to the speed of the system (CPU) which reads the data. A delay is inserted after each regular conversion and after each sequence of the injected conversions. During a conversion, a hardware trigger event (for the same group of conversions) occurring during this delay is ignored.

This is not true for software triggers where it remains possible during this delay to set the bits ADSTART or JADSTART to restart a conversion: it is up to the software to read the data before launching a new conversion.

No delay is inserted between conversions of different groups (a regular conversion followed by an injected conversion or conversely):

- If an injected trigger occurs during the automatic delay of a regular conversion, the injected conversion starts immediately.
- Once the injected sequence is complete, the ADC waits for the delay (if not ended) of the previous regular conversion before launching a new regular conversion.

For auto-injected mode (JAUTO = 1), a new regular conversion can start only when the automatic delay of the previous injected sequence of conversions has ended (i.e., the JEOS bit has been cleared). This is to ensure that the software can read all the data of a given sequence before starting a new sequence.

10.7.19 ANALOG WINDOW WATCHDOG (AWD)

The ADC provides three analog watchdogs to monitor whether some channels remain within a specified voltage range.

The register ADCx->TRn (n = 1–3) specifies the high and low threshold for analog watchdog n. If the converted value is higher than the high threshold or lower than the low threshold, the AWD_n flag in the ADCx->ISR register will be set. An interrupt will be generated if the AWD$_n$IE bit in the ADCx->IER register is set to 1. The contents of the ADCx->TR1, ADCx->TR2, and ADCx->TR3 registers are shown in Figures 10.27 and 10.28.

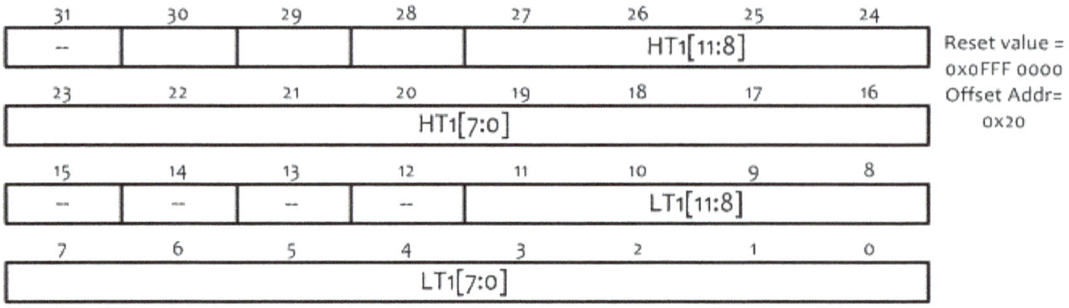

HT1[11:0]: Analog watchdog 1 high threshold
These bits can be written only when there is no ongoing conversion.
LT1[11:0]: Analog watchdog 1 low threshold
These bits can be written only when there is no ongoing conversion.

Figure 10.27 ADC Watchdog threshold register 1 (ADCx->TR1)

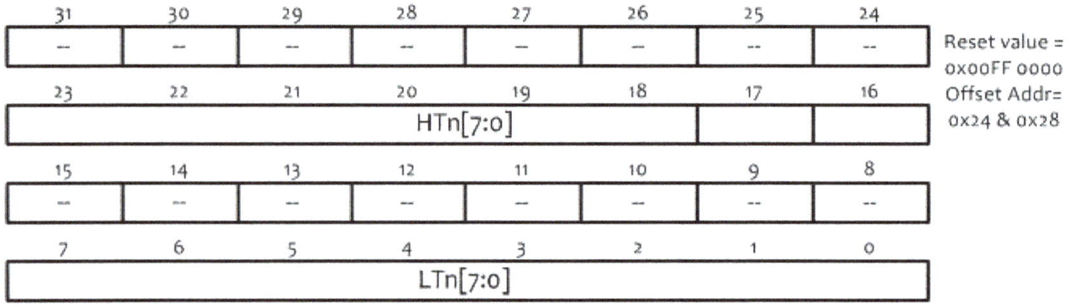

HTn[7:0]: Analog watchdog 1 high threshold (n = 2 or 3)
These bits can be written only when there is no ongoing conversion.
LTn[7:0]: Analog watchdog 1 low threshold (n = 2 or 3)
These bits can be written only when there is no ongoing conversion.

Figure 10.28 ADC Watchdog threshold register n (ADCx->TRn, n = 2 or 3)

Analog Watchdog 1

The analog watchdog 1 must be enabled before it can operate. The AWD1 is enabled by setting the AWD1EN bit in the ADCx->CFGR register. The analog channels to be monitored are configured by programming the AWD1SGL, AWD1EN, and JAWD1EN bits in the ADCx->CFGR register. The possible channel selection combinations are summarized in Table 10.10.

Table 10.10 Analog watchdog 1 channel selection

Channels monitored by the analog watchdog 1	AWD1SGL bit	AWD1EN bit	JAWD1EN bit
None	x	0	0
All injected channels	0	0	1
All regular channels	0	1	0
All regular and injected channels	0	1	1
Single[(1)] injected channel	1	0	1
Single[(1)] regular channel	1	1	0
Single[(1)] regular or injected channel	1	1	1

Note. 1. Selected by the AWD1CH[4:0] field in the ADCx->CFGR register

When converting data with a resolution less than 12 bits, the least significant bits of the threshold values must be kept cleared because the comparison is performed on the full 12-bit raw converted data. The setting of thresholds for all four resolutions are shown in Table 10.11.

Table 10.11 Analog watchdog 1 comparison

Resolution RES[1:0]	Analog watchdog comparison between		Comments
	Raw converted data left aligned (1)	Thresholds	
00: 12-bit	DATA[11:0]	LT1[11:0] and HT1[11:0]	--
01: 10-bit	DATA[11:2], 00	LT1[11:0] and HT1[11:0]	LT1[1:0] and HT1[1:0] must be et to 00
10: 8-bit	DATA[11:4], 0000	LT1[11:0] and HT1[11:0]	LT1[3:0] and HT1[3:0] must be set to 0000
11: 6-bit	DATA[11:6],000000	LT1[11:0] and HT1[11:0]	LT1[5:0] and HT1[5:0] must be set to 000000

Note. 1. The watchdog comparison is performed on the raw converted data before any alignment and before applying any offsets.

Example 10.16 Write a sequence of C statements to configure the ADC1 to monitor the channel 1 voltage whether the voltage is lower than 0.8 V or higher than 2.7 V. Assume that V_{REF} = 3.3 V and use 12-bit resolution.

Solution:

0.8 V will be converted to 0.8 ÷3.3 × 4095 = 993 = 0x3E1

2.7 V will be converted to 2.7 ÷3.3 × 4095 = 3350 = 0xD16

The sequence of C statements to monitor channel 1 not lower than 0.8 V or higher than 2.7 V is as follows:

```
    ADC1->TR1    = 0x0D1603E1; // set up low and high thresholds
    ADC1->CFGR  &= ~(ADC_CFGR_AWD1CH);
// watch ADC channel 1, and enable analog watchdog 1
    ADC1->CFGR  |= ADC_CFGR_AWD1CH_0 + ADC_CFGR_AWD1SGL + ADC_CFGR_AWD1EN;
```

Watchdogs 2 and 3

These two analog watchdogs can monitor multiple channels by programming the corresponding bits in the AWDyCH [18:0] (y = 2 or 3) field of the ADCx->AWDyCR register (y = 2 or 3). The corresponding watchdog is enabled if any bit of the AWDyCH [18:0] field is set. These two analog watchdogs use 8-bit resolution. They use the highest 8 bits of the threshold registers (HTy[7:0] and LTy[7:0]). Analog watchdog 2 and 3 comparisons for different resolutions are shown in Table 10.11.

Table 10.12 Analog watchdog 2 and 3 comparison

Resolution RES[1:0]	Analog watchdog comparison between		Comments
	Raw converted data left aligned (1)	Thresholds	
00: 12-bit	DATA[11:4]	LTx[7:0] and HTx[7:0]	DATA[3:0] are not relevant for comparison
01: 10-bit	DATA[11:4]	LTx[7:0] and HTx[7:0]	DATA[3:2] are not relevant for comparison
10: 8-bit	DATA[11:4]	LTx[7:0] and HTx[7:0]	--
11: 6-bit	DATA[11:6],00	LTx[7:0] and HTx[7:0]	User must configure LTx[1:0] & HTx[1:0] to 00

Note. 1. The watchdog comparison is performed on the raw converted data before any alignment and before applying any offsets.

ADCx_AWDy_OUT Signal Output Generation

Each analog watchdog is associated with an internal hardware signal ADCx_AWDy_OUT which is directly connected to the ETR input of some on-chip timers. When an analog watchdog is enabled, the associated ADCx_AWDy_OUT signal will be pulled high if a monitored analog conversion result is outside the programmed thresholds. Otherwise, it is pulled low.

The ADCx_AWDy_OUT signal is reset when the ADC is disabled (when setting ADDIS bit to 1). The AWDy flag has no influence on the generation of the ADCx_AWDy_OUT signal. This signal can toggle while the AWDy flag remains at 1 if the software did not clear the flag. This is demonstrated in Figure 10.29.

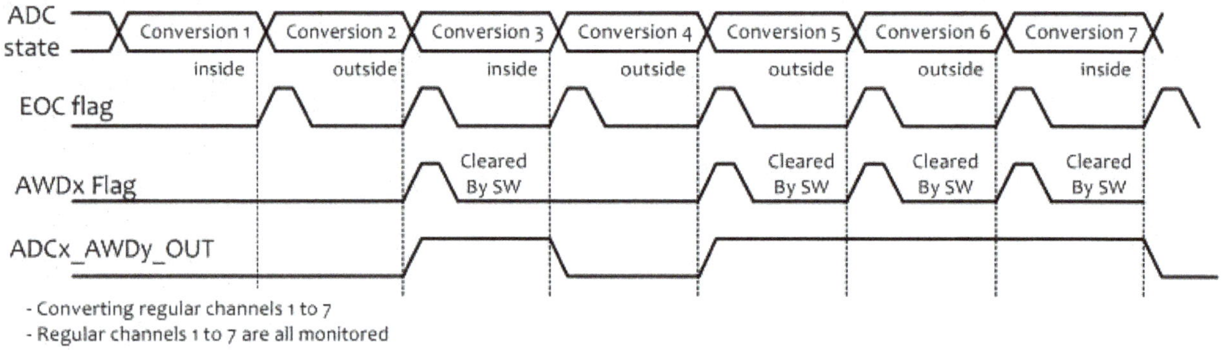

Figure 10.29 Example of ADCx_AWDy_OUT signal generation

10.7.20 OVERSAMPLER

This unit can handle multiple conversions and average them into a single value with increased data width, up to 16 bits.

The oversampler generates a result in the following format:

$$\text{Result} = \frac{1}{M} \times \sum_{n=0}^{n=N-1} \text{Conversion}(t_n)$$

where,

N is the oversampling ratio defined by the OVSR[2:0] field in the ADCx->CFGR2 register. N can be from 2 to 256.

M is the division coefficient defined using the OVSS[3:0] field in the ADCx->CFGR2 register. M specified the amount of right shift up to 8 bits.

The summation unit can yield a result up to 20 bits (256 × 12-bit), which is first shifted right. It is then truncated to the 16 bits, rounded to the nearest value, before being written into the ADCx->DR register.

A possible combination of M and N are given in Table 10.13.

Table 10.13 Maximum output results versus N and M (grey cells indicate truncation)

Over sampling ratio	Max Raw Data	No shift OVSS = 0000	1-bit shift OVSS = 0001	2-bit shift OVSS = 0010	3-bit shift OVSS = 0011	4-bit shift OVSS = 0100	5-bit shift OVSS = 0101	6-bit shift OVSS = 0110	7-bit shift OVSS = 0111	8-bit shift OVSS = 1000
2x	0x1FFE	0x1FFE	0x0FFF	0x0800	0x0400	0x0200	0x0100	0x0080	0x0040	0x0020
4x	0x3FFC	0x3FFC	0x1FFE	0x0FFF	0x0800	0x0400	0x0200	0x0100	0x0080	0x0040
8x	0x7FF8	0x7FF8	0x3FFC	0x1FFE	0x0FFF	0x0800	0x0400	0x0200	0x0100	0x0080
16x	0xFFF0	0xFFF0	0x7FF8	0x3FFC	0x1FFE	0x0FFF	0x0800	0x0400	0x0200	0x0100
32x	0x1FFE0	0xFFE0	0xFFF0	0x7FF8	0x3FFC	0x1FFE	0x0FFF	0x0800	0x0400	0x0200
64x	0x3FFC0	0xFFC0	0xFFE0	0xFFF0	0x7FF8	0x3FFC	0x1FFE	0x0FFF	0x0800	0x0400
128x	0x7FF80	0xFF80	0xFFC0	0xFFE0	0xFFF0	0x7FF8	0x3FFC	0x1FFE	0x0FFF	0x0800
256x	0xFFF00	0xFF00	0xFF80	0xFFC0	0xFFE0	0xFFF0	0x7FF8	0x3FFC	0x1FFE	0x0FFF

There are no changes for conversion timings in oversampled mode: the sample time is maintained equal during the whole oversampling sequence. A new data is generated at every N conversion, with an equivalent delay equal to $\mathbf{N \times T_{CONV} = N \times (t_{SMPL} + t_{SAR})}$. For the flags related to conversion:

- The end of sampling phase (EOSMP) flag is set after each sampling phase.
- The end of conversion (EOC) flag is set once at every N conversion, when the oversampled result is available.

- The end of sequence (EOS) flag is set once the sequence of the oversampled data is completed (i.e., after N x sequence length conversions).

Single ADC Operating Modes Support When Oversampling

In oversampling mode, most of the ADC operating modes are maintained:

- Single or continuous mode conversions
- ADC conversions start either by software or with triggers
- ADC stop during a conversion (abort)
- Data read via CPU or DMA with overrun detection
- Low-power modes (AUTDLY)
- Programmable resolution: in this case, the reduced conversion values are accumulated, truncated, rounded, and shifted in the same way as 12-bit conversions are.

The alignment mode is not available when working with oversampling data. The ALIGN bit in the ADCx->CFGR register is ignored and data are always provided right aligned.

Offset correction is not supported in oversampling mode. When ROVSE and/or JOVSE bit in the ADCx->CFGR2 register is set, the value of the OFFSETy_EN bit in the ADCx->OFRy register is ignored.

Behavior of an Analog Watchdog in Oversampling

When oversampling is in effect, the analog watchdog functionality is maintained with two differences:

1. The RES[1:0] field in the ADCx->CFGR register is ignored and comparison is always done on using the full 12-bit values HTy[11:0] and LTy[11:0].
2. The comparison is performed on the most significant 12-bit of the 16-bit oversampled results ADCx->DR[15:4].

Triggered Mode

The oversampling mode can achieve basic filtering function and serve as a notch filter to reject constant parasitic frequencies coming from power supply. For this purpose, the user can enable the discontinuous mode by setting the **TROVS** bit in the ADCx->CFGR2 register. An example of triggered oversampling conversion is shown in Figure 10.30.

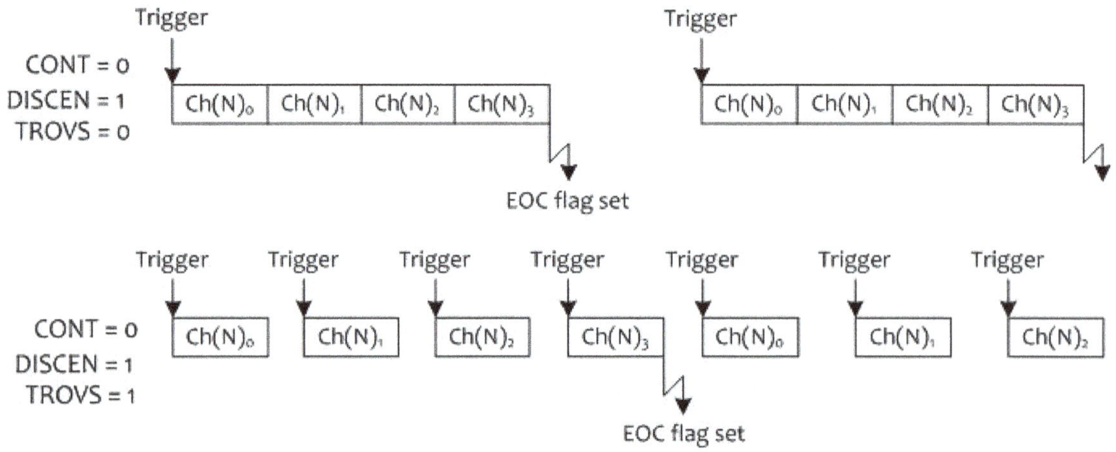

Figure 10.30 Triggered regular oversampling mode (TROVS bit = 1)

Oversampling Regular Channels Only

The regular oversampling mode bit ROVSM defines how the regular oversampling sequence is resumed if it is interrupted by injected conversion:

- **Continued mode**: The accumulation restarts from the last valid data (prior to the conversion abort request due to the injected trigger). This ensures that oversampling will be completed whatever the injection frequency.
- **Resumed mode**: The accumulation restarts from 0 (previous conversion results are ignored). This mode guarantees that all data used for oversampling were converted back to back within a single time slot. Care must be taken to have an injection trigger period longer than the oversampling period.

Oversampling Injected Channels Only

The injected oversampling mode bit JOVSE enables oversampling solely for conversions in the injected sequencer.

Oversampling Regular and Injected Channels

When both the ROVSE and JOVSE bits in the ADCx->CFGR2 register are set, the oversampling of both the regular and injected channels is enabled. In this case, the regular oversampling mode is forced to the **resumed mode** as illustrated in Figure 10.31. In Figure 10.31, M and N refer to the analog channels to be converted.

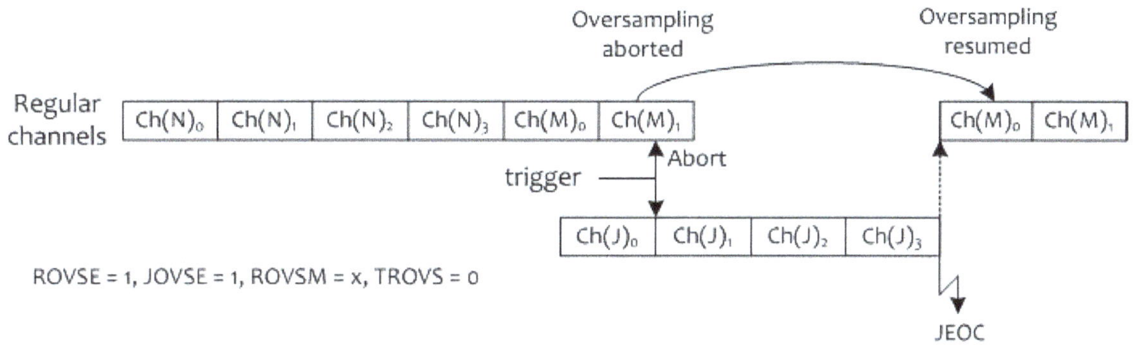

Figure 10.31 Regular and injected oversampling modes used simultaneously

Triggered Regular Oversampling with Injected Conversions

It is possible to have oversampling regular mode with injected conversions. In this case, the injected mode oversampling must be disabled and the ROVSM bit is ignored (resumed mode is forced). When a trigger event for the injected channels occurs, the ongoing regular conversion (oversampling mode) will be aborted and then resumed by a trigger event.

Auto-injected Mode

It is possible to oversample auto-injected sequences and have all conversion results stored in registers to save a DMA resource. This mode is available only with both regular and injected oversampling active, i.e., the JAUTO, ROVSE, and JOVSE bits must all be set to 1. It is also possible to have the triggered mode enabled, using the TROVS bit.

Dual ADC Modes Support When Oversampling

It is possible to have oversampling enabled when working in dual ADC configuration, for the injected simultaneous mode and regular simultaneous mode. In this case, the two ADCs must be programmed with the same settings (including oversampling).

All other dual ADC modes are not supported when either regular or injected oversampling is enabled (ROVSE = 1 or JOVSE = 1).

10.7.21 DUAL ADC MODES

When a device has two ADCs or more, dual modes can be used. ADC1 and ADC2 can be used together in dual mode. In dual ADC mode, the start of conversion is triggered alternately or simultaneously by the ADC master to the ADC slave, depending on the mode selected by the bits DUAL[4:0] in the **ADC common configuration register** (ADC123_COMMON->CCR). There are seven possible combinations for dual ADC mode:

- Injected simultaneous mode
- Regular simultaneous mode
- Interleaved mode
- Alternate trigger mode
- Injected simultaneous mode + regular simultaneous mode
- Regular simultaneous mode + alternate trigger mode
- Injected simultaneous mode + interleaved mode

In the dual mode, the bits CONT, AUTDLY, DISCEN, DISCNUM[2:0], JDISCEN, JQM, JAUTO of the ADCx->CFGR register are shared between the master and the slave ADCs. The bits in the slave ADC are always equal to the corresponding bits of the master ADC.

To start a conversion in the dual mode, the user must program the bits EXTEN, EXTSEL, JEXTEN, JEXTSEL of the master ADC only, to configure a software or hardware trigger and a regular or injected trigger.

In the regular or interleaved mode, once the user sets the ADSTART or the ADSTP bit of the master ADC, the same bit of the slave ADC is also automatically set. However, the ADSTART or the ADSTP bit of the slave ADC is not necessarily cleared at the same time as the master ADC bit.

In the injected simultaneous or alternate trigger modes: once the user sets the JADSTART or the JADSTP bit of the master ADC, the same bit of the slave ADC is also automatically set. However, the JADSTART or JADSTP bit of the slave ADC is not necessarily cleared at the same time as the master ADC.

In the dual mode, the conversion results of the master and slave ADCs can be read together from the **ADC common data register** (ADC123_common->CDR); The status bits can be read in parallel by reading the **dual-mode status register** (ADC123_COMMON->CSR). The contents of the ADC123_COMMON->CDR and ADC123_COMMON->CSR registers are shown in Figure 10.32 and 10.33, respectively.

31	30	29	28	27	26	25	24
RDATA_SLV[15:8]							
23	**22**	**21**	**20**	**19**	**18**	**17**	**16**
RDATA_SLV[7:0]							
15	**14**	**13**	**12**	**11**	**10**	**9**	**8**
RDATA_MST[15:8]							
7	**6**	**5**	**4**	**3**	**2**	**1**	**0**
RDATA_MST[7:0]							

Reset value = 0x0000 0000
Offset Addr= 0x0C

RDATA_SLV[15:0]: Regular data of the slave ADC
In dual mode, these bits contain the regular data of the slave ADC.
RDATA_MST[15:0]: Regular data of the master ADC
In dual mode, these bits contain the regular data of the master ADC

Figure 10.32 ADC Common regular data register for dual mode (ADC123_COMMON_CDR)

31	30	29	28	27	26	25	24
--	--	--	--	--	JQOVF_SLV	AWD3_SLV	AWD2_SLV
23	**22**	**21**	**20**	**19**	**18**	**17**	**16**
AWD1_SLV	JEOS_SLV	JEOC_SLV	OVR_SLV	EOS_SLV	EOC_SLV	EOSMP_SLV	ADRDY_SLV
15	**14**	**13**	**12**	**11**	**10**	**9**	**8**
--	--	--	--	--	JQOVF_MST	AWD3_MST	AWD2_MST
7	**6**	**5**	**4**	**3**	**2**	**1**	**0**
AWD1_MST	JEOS_MST	JEOC_MST	OVR_MST	EOS_MST	EOC_MST	EOSMP_MST	ADRDY_MST

Reset value = 0x0000 0000
Offset Addr= 0x00

JQOVF_SLV: Injected context queue overflow flag of the slave ADC
This bit is a copy of the JQOVF bit in the corresponding ADCx->ISR register.
AWD3_SLV: Analog watchdog 3 flag of the slave ADC
This bit is a copy of the AWD3 bit in the corresponding ADCx->ISR register.
AWD2_SLV: Analog watchdog 2 flag of the slave ADC
This bit is a copy of the AWD2 bit in the corresponding ADCx->ISR register.
AWD1_SLV: Analog watchdog 1 flag of the slave ADC
This bit is a copy of the AWD1 bit in the corresponding ADCx->ISR register.
JEOS_SLV: End of injected sequence flag of the slave ADC
This bit is a copy of the JEOS bit in the corresponding ADCx->ISR register.
JEOC_SLV: End of injected conversion flag of the slave ADC
This bit is a copy of the JEOC bit in the corresponding ADCx->ISR register.
OVR_SLV: Overrun flag of the slave ADC
This bit is a copy of the OVR bit in the corresponding ADCx->ISR register.
EOS_SLV: End of regular sequence flag of the slave ADC
This bit is a copy of the EOS bit in the corresponding ADCx->ISR register.
EOC_SLV: End of regular conversion of the slave ADC
This bit is a copy of the EOC bit in the corresponding ADCx->ISR register.
EOSMP_SLV: End of sampling phase flag of the slave ADC
This bit is a copy of the EOSMP bit in the corresponding ADCx->ISR register.
ADRDY_SLV: Slave ADC ready
This bit is a copy of the ADRDY bit in the corresponding ADCx->ISR register.

Figure 10.33 ADC common status register (ADC123_COMMON->CSR)

31	30	29	28	27	26	25	24
–	–	–	–	–	JQOVF_SLV	AWD3_SLV	AWD2_SLV
23	**22**	**21**	**20**	**19**	**18**	**17**	**16**
AWD1_SLV	JEOS_SLV	JEOC_SLV	OVR_SLV	EOS_SLV	EOC_SLV	EOSMP_SLV	ADRDY_SLV
15	**14**	**13**	**12**	**11**	**10**	**9**	**8**
–	–	–	–	–	JQOVF_MST	AWD3_MST	AWD2_MST
7	**6**	**5**	**4**	**3**	**2**	**1**	**0**
AWD1_MST	JEOS_MST	JEOC_MST	OVR_MST	EOS_MST	EOC_MST	EOSMP_MST	ADRDY_MST

Reset value = 0x0000 0000
Offset Addr= 0x00

JQOVF_MST: Injected context queue overflow flag of the master ADC
This bit is a copy of the JQOVF bit in the corresponding ADCx->ISR register.
AWD3_MST: Analog watchdog 3 flag of the master ADC
This bit is a copy of the AWD3 bit in the corresponding ADCx->ISR register.
AWD2_MST: Analog watchdog 2 flag of the master ADC
This bit is a copy of the AWD2 bit in the corresponding ADCx->ISR register.
AWD1_MST: Analog watchdog 1 flag of the master ADC
This bit is a copy of the AWD1 bit in the corresponding ADCx->ISR register.
JEOS_MST: End of injected sequence flag of the master ADC
This bit is a copy of the JEOS bit in the corresponding ADCx->ISR register.
JEOC_MST: End of injected conversion flag of the master ADC
This bit is a copy of the JEOC bit in the corresponding ADCx->ISR register.
OVR_MST: Overrun flag of the master ADC
This bit is a copy of the OVR bit in the corresponding ADCx->ISR register.
EOS_MST: End of regular sequence flag of the master ADC
This bit is a copy of the EOS bit in the corresponding ADCx->ISR register.
EOC_MST: End of regular conversion of the master ADC
This bit is a copy of the EOC bit in the corresponding ADCx->ISR register.
EOSMP_MST: End of sampling phase flag of the master ADC
This bit is a copy of the EOSMP bit in the corresponding ADCx->ISR register.
ADRDY_MST: Master ADC ready
This bit is a copy of the ADRDY bit in the corresponding ADCx->ISR register.

Figure 10.33a ADC common status register (ADC123_COMMON->CSR)—(continued)

Injected Simultaneous Mode

This mode is selected when the **DUAL[4:0] field** of the ADC123_COMMON->CCR register is set to **00101**. This mode converts an injected group of channels of the master and the slave ADCs. The external trigger source is selected by programming the JEXTSEL[3:0] field of the ADCx->JSQR register.

In this mode, the user must convert sequences with the same length or ensure that the interval between triggers is longer than the longer one of the two sequences. Otherwise, the ADC with the shorter sequence may restart while the ADC with the longer sequence is completing the previous conversions.

Regular conversions can be performed on one or both ADCs. In that case, they are independent of each other and are interrupted when an injected event occurs. They are resumed at the end of the injected conversion group.

At the end of the injected sequence of conversion event (JEOS) on the master ADC, the converted data is stored in the master ADCx->JDRy registers and the JEOS flag on the master is set. Similarly, at the end of the injected sequence of conversion event on the slave ADC, the converted data are stored in the slave ADCz->JDRy registers and the JEOS flag on the slave ADC is set. If the duration of the master injected sequence is equal to the duration of the slave injected one, it is possible to enable only one of the two JEOS interrupts and read both converted data (from master ADCx->JDRy and slave ADCz->JDRy registers).

If the **JDISCEN** bit in the ADCx->CFGR register is set, each simultaneous conversion of the injected sequence requires an injected trigger event to occur. This mode can be combined with the auto delay mode (AUDLY bit = 1):

1. Once simultaneous injected sequence of conversions has ended, a new injected trigger event is accepted only if both JEOS bits of the master and the slave ADC have been cleared. Any new injected trigger events occurring during the ongoing injected sequence and the associated delay phase are ignored.
2. Once a regular sequence of conversions of the master ADC has ended, a new regular trigger event of the master ADC is accepted only if the master data register has been read. Any new regular events occurring for the master ADC during the ongoing regular sequence and the associated delay phases are ignored. The same behavior for regular sequences occurs on the slave ADC.

Regular Simultaneous Mode with Independent Injected

This mode is selected when the **DUAL field** is set to **00110**. This mode is applied to a regular group of channels. The external trigger is selected using the EXTSEL[3:0] field in the ADCx->CFGR register to start the conversion. When the external trigger occurs, it is also provided to the slave ADC simultaneously. Both the regular group in the master ADC and the slave ADC are converted.

In this mode, independent injected conversions are supported. An injection request (either on the master or on the slave) will abort the current simultaneous conversions, which are restarted once the injected conversion is completed. The user should not convert the same channel on two different ADCs. In this mode, the user must convert sequences with the same length or ensure that the interval between two triggers is longer than the longer conversion time of the two sequences. Otherwise, the ADC with a shorter sequence may restart while the ADC with a longer sequence is completing the previous conversions.

The conversion results can be read using the EOC interrupt on the master and the slave ADC. If the duration of the master regular sequence is equal to that of the slave ADC, then enabling either the master or slave EOC interrupt can read both results from the ADC123_COMMON->CDR register.

It is also possible to read the regular conversion results using the DMA. There are two ways to read the conversion results using DMA:

1. Use two DMA channels—one for the master and one for the slave. One DMA channel reads the ADCx->DR register of the master and another DMA channel reads the ADCz->DR register of the slave ADC.
2. Use the MDMA mode. The user is required to program the MDMA[1:0] field of the ADC123_COMMON->CCR register according to the selection resolution. A single DMA channel is used. A single DMA request is generated each time both the master and slave EOC events have occurred, and the ADC common data register is transferred. Both EOC flags are cleared when the DMA reads the ADC123_COMMON->CDR register. In this mode, the user must program the same number of conversions in the master's sequence as in the slave's sequence.

If the discontinuous mode is enabled (by setting the DISCEN bit in the ADCx->CFGR register) for the regular channels and **n** is the number of channels specified in the DISCNUM field, then a regular trigger event is required at every **n** conversion.

Regular simultaneous mode can be combined with AUTDLY mode:

- Once a simultaneous conversion of the sequence has ended, the next conversion in the sequence is started only if the common data register (or the regular data register) has been read.
- Once a simultaneous regular sequence of conversions has ended, a new regular trigger event is accepted only if the common data register has been read. Any new regular trigger events occurring during the ongoing regular sequence and the associated delay phases are ignored.

To use regular simultaneous mode combined with AUTDLY mode, the user must ensure that:

1. The number of conversions in the master's sequence equals that of the slave.
2. For each simultaneous conversion of the sequence, the length of the conversion of the slave ADC is shorter than that of the conversion of the master ADC. Note that the length of the sequence depends on the number of channels to convert and the sampling time and the resolution of each channels.

Interleaved Mode with Independent Injected Channels

This mode is selected when the DUAL[4:0] field is set to 00111. In this mode, the master and the slave ADCs perform conversions on regular channels (usually one channel) alternately. The external trigger source applies to the regular channel of the master ADC.

When an external trigger occurs,

- The master ADC starts immediately.
- The slave ADC starts after a delay of several ADC clock cycles after the sampling phase of the master ADC has completed.

The minimum delay that separates 2 conversions in the interleaved mode is configured in the DELAY field of the ADC123_COMMON->CCR register. The delay starts to count after the end of the sampling phase of the master conversion. This way, an ADC cannot start a conversion if the complementary ADC is still sampling its input. An example of the interleaved mode is shown in Figure 10.34.

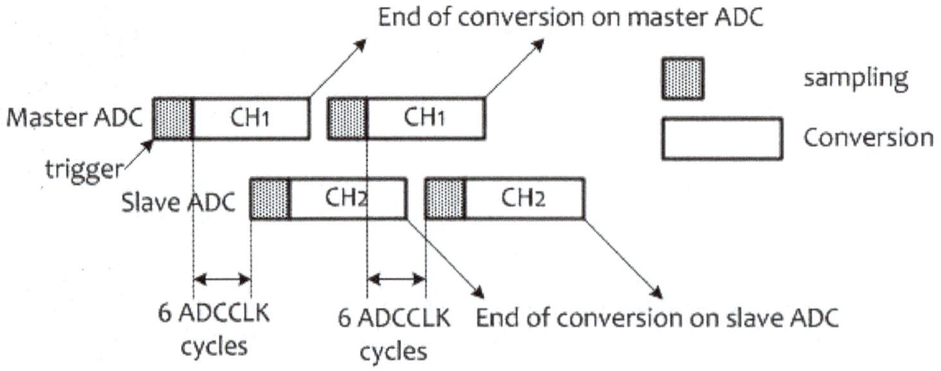

Figure 10.34 Example of interleave mode on one channel in continuous mode conversion

If the CONT bit (in the ADCx->CFGR register) is set on both the master and the slave ADCs, the selected regular channels of both ADCs are continuously converted. The setting of the EOC flags on both the master and slave ADCs can be used by software (via interrupt mechanism) to read the conversion results. If the duration of the conversions inside the sequence are compatible so that a master conversion is always followed by a slave conversion, then the user can enable only the slave EOC interrupt and read the conversion results from the ADC123_COMMON->CDR register.

It is also possible to have the regular data transferred by DMA. However, to do so, it is mandatory to use the MDMA mode:

- Depending on the resolution, configure the MDMA[1:0] field to 10 (12- or 10-bit) or 11 (8- or 6-bit).
- Select the DMA channel, which is assigned to the master ADC to read the common data register (ADC123_COMMON->CDR).
- A single DMA request is generated each time both master and slave EOC events have occurred.
- Both EOC flags are cleared when the DMA reads the ADC123_COMMON->CDR register.

If the DISCEN bit in the ADCx->CFGR register is set to 1, a trigger event is required to trigger **n** simultaneous conversions. Here, n is defined by the DISCNUM field in the ADCx->CFGR register of the master ADC. In this mode, injected conversions are supported. When injection occurs, both the master and the slave regular conversions are aborted and the sequence is restarted from the master. This situation is illustrated in Figure 10.35.

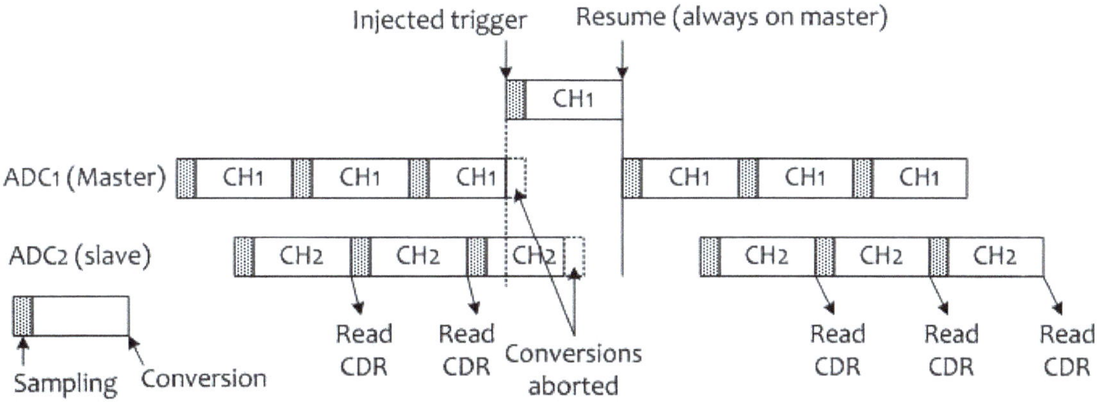

Figure 10.35 Example of interleave conversion with injection

Alternate Trigger Mode

This mode is selected when the DUAL[4:0] field is set to **01001**. This mode can be started only on an **injected group**. The source of the external trigger (JEXTSEL[3:0] in the ADCx->JSQR register) comes from the injected group multiplexer of the master ADC.

Depending on the setting of the JDISCEN bit in the ADCx->JSQR register, there are two options for the operation of this mode. If the **JDISCEN bit is 0**, the ADCs operate in the following manner:

- When the first trigger occurs, all injected master ADC channels in the group are converted.

- When the second trigger occurs, all injected slave ADC channels in the group are converted.
- And so on.

If the **JDISCEN bit is 1**, the ADCs operate in the following manner:

- When the first trigger occurs, the first injected channel of the master ADC is converted.
- When the second trigger occurs, the first injected channel of the slave ADC is converted.
- And so on.

Combined Regular/Injected Simultaneous Mode

This mode is selected when the DUAL[4:0] field is set to 00001. It is possible to interrupt the simultaneous conversion of a regular group to start the simultaneous conversion of an injected group. In this mode, the user must convert sequences with the same length or ensure that the interval between triggers is longer than the longer conversion time of the two sequences.

Combined Regular Simultaneous + Alternate Trigger Mode

This mode is selected when the DUAL[4:0] field is set to 00010. It is possible to interrupt the simultaneous conversion of a regular group to start the alternate trigger conversion of an injected group.

The injected alternate conversion is immediately started after the injected event. If a regular conversion is already running, the regular conversions of all ADCs (master/slave) are stopped and resumed at the end of the injected conversion.

In combined regular simultaneous + alternate trigger mode, one must convert sequences of the same length or ensure the interval between triggers to be longer than the long conversion time of the two sequences. Otherwise, the ADC with the shorter sequence may restart while the ADC with the longer sequence is completing the previous conversions.

If a trigger occurs during an injected conversion that has interrupted a regular conversion, the alternate trigger is served. An example is illustrated in Figure 10.36.

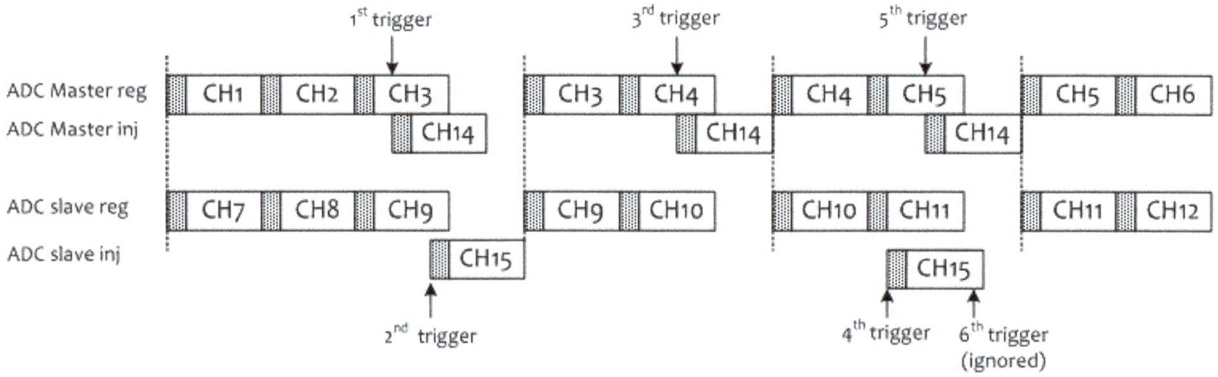

Figure 10.36 Example of trigger occurring during injected conversion

Combined Injected Simultaneous Plus Interleaved

This mode is selected by setting the DUAL[4:0] field to 00011. It is possible to interrupt an interleaved conversion with a simultaneous injected event. In this case, the interleaved conversion is interrupted immediately and the simultaneous injected conversion starts. At the end of the injected sequence the interleaved conversion is resumed. When the interleaved regular conversion resumes, the first regular conversion which is performed is always the master's one. In this mode, it is mandatory to use the common data register to read the regular conversion result with a single read access. An example is shown in Figure 10.37.

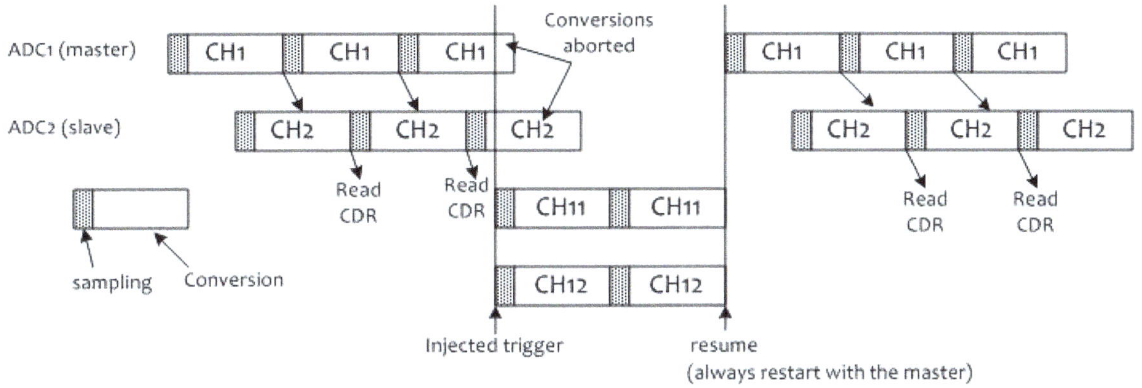

Figure 10.37 Two interleave channels (Ch1, Ch2) with injected sequence CH11, Ch12

DMA Requests in Dual ADC Mode

In all dual ADC modes, it is possible to use two DMA channels (one for the master, and one for the slave) to transfer the conversion results.

In simultaneous regular and interleaved modes, it is also possible to save one DMA channel and transfer both results using a single DMA channel. This must be done using the MDMA mode. The user must take care to configure properly the duration of the master and slave conversions so that a DMA request is generated and served for reading both data (master + slave) before a new conversion is available.

Overrun Detection

In dual mode, if an overrun is detected on one of the ADCs, the DMA requests are no longer issued to ensure that all the data transferred to the RAM are valid. It may happen that the EOC flag corresponding to one ADC remains set because the data register of this ADC contains valid data.

Stopping the Conversions in Dual ADC Modes

The user must set the ADSTP/JADSTP bit of the master ADC to stop the conversions of both ADCs in dual ADC mode. The ADSTP bit in the slave ADC has no effect in dual ADC mode. Once both ADCs are effectively stopped, the ADSTART and JADSTART bits of the master and slave ADCs are both cleared by hardware.

10.7.22 TEMPERATURE SENSOR

The temperature sensor can be used to measure the junction temperature of the microcontroller. The temperature sensor is internally connected to the ADC1_IN17 and ADC3_IN17 input channels. The sensor can be put in power down mode when it is not used.

The temperature sensor operates in the temperature range from −40°C to 125°C and is precise to ±2°C. Before using the temperature sensor, the CH17SEL bit in the ADC123_COMMON->CCR register must be set. Enough sampling time must be provided before the A/D conversion is started.

The junction temperature of the microcontroller can be derived from the following equation:

Temperature in °C = (110°C − 30°C) ÷ (TS_CAL2 − TS_CAL1) × (TS_DATA − TS_CAL1) + 30°C

where,

1. TS_CAL2 is the temperature sensor calibration value acquired at 110°C and is stored at 0x1FFF75CA~0x1FFF75CB.
2. TS_CAL1 is the temperature sensor calibration value acquired at 30°C and is stored at 0x1FFF75A8~0x1FFF75A9.
3. TS_DATA is the actual temperature sensor output converted by ADC.

Both the temperature sensor and the ADC have start time. To minimize the delay, the ADEN and CH17SEL bits should be set at the same time. The value of TS_CAL1 and TS_CAL2 can be read by using the expression of *((uint16_t *)0x1FFF75A8) and *((uint16_t *)0x1FFF75CA), respectively.

10.7.23 VBAT SUPPLY MONITORING

To measure the V_{BAT} supply voltage, the CH18SEL bit in the ADC123_COMMON->CCR register must be set to 1. The voltage at the V_{BAT} pin is internally divided by 3 before being connected to the ADC1_IN18 or ADC3_IN18 input channel. The user also needs to lookup the sampling time of $V_{BAT}/3$ before using it.

10.7.24 MONITORING THE INTERNAL VOLTAGE REFERENCE

The internal reference voltage (V_{REFINT}) can be monitored by connecting it to the ADC1 channel 0 (ADC1_IN0). The user is required to lookup the sampling time of V_{REFINT} before carrying out the measurement.

Calculating the Actual V_{DDA} using V_{REFINT}

The V_{DDA} power supply voltage applied to the microcontroller may be subject to variation or not precisely known. The embedded internal voltage reference V_{REFINT} and its calibration data acquired by the ADC during the manufacturing process at V_{DDA} = 3.3 V can be used to evaluate the actual V_{DDA} level.

The actual V_{DDA} level can be calculated using the following equation:

$$V_{DDA} = 3.0\text{ V} \times V_{REFINT\_CAL} \div V_{REFINT\_DATA}$$

where,

1. V_{REFINT_CAL} is the V_{REFINT} calibration value and is stored at 0x1FFF75AA~0x1FFF75AB.
2. V_{REFINT_DATA} is the actual V_{REFINT} output value converted by ADC.

The value of V_{REFINT_CAL} can be read by using the expression of *((uint16_t *)0x1FFF75AB).

10.7.25 ADC INTERRUPTS

ADC1 and ADC2 share an interrupt vector number (ADC1_2_IRQn), whereas the ADC3 has its own interrupt vector number ADC3_IRQn.

Each ADC has the following interrupt sources, and each interrupt source has its own flag:

- After ADC power-up and the ADC is ready (ADRDY flag)
- At the end of any conversion for regular groups (EOC flag)
- At the end of a sequence of conversions for regular group (EOS flag)
- At the end of any conversion for injected groups (JEOC flag)
- At the end of a sequence of conversions for injected groups (JEOS flag)
- When an analog watchdog detection occurs (AWD1, AWD2, and AWD3 flags)
- When the end of sampling phase occurs (EOSMP flag)
- When the data overrun occurs (OVR flag)
- When the injected sequence context queue overflows (JQOVF flag)

These flags are recorded in the ADCx->ISR register and their corresponding enable bits are recorded in the ADCx->IER register.

10.8 Measuring Voltage Using the ADC

We can use the ADC to measure a voltage. A circuit that connects the output of a potentiometer to the STM32L475 channel 2 is shown in Figure 10.38.

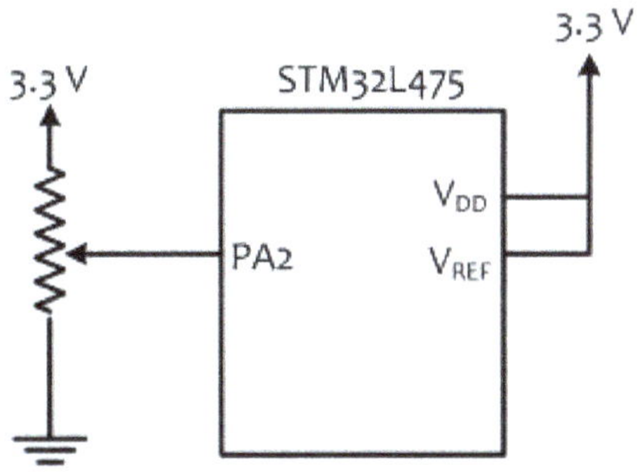

Figure 10.38 Potentiometer circuit connection

Example 10.17 Write a program to measure the voltage output of the potentiometer once every second. Output the voltage from USART1. Assume that the clock source is SYSCLK running at 80 MHz.

Solution:

The A/D conversion result of 3.3V using 12-bit resolution is 4095. To convert from A/D conversion result back to voltage, we need to divide the A/D conversion result by 1241 (= 4095 ÷ 3.3).

The C program that performs the specified operation is as follows:

```
#include <stm32L475xx.h>

void  sysClkInit(void);
```

```
void  initUSART1(void);
void  adc1Init(void);
void  init_val(void);
void  putchUSART1(uint8_t cx);
void  newlineUSART1(void);
void  putsUSART1(uint8_t *ptr);
void  delayby100ms(uint16_t k);
uint8_t title[] = "Voltage = ";
uint8_t value[6];
int main(void)
{
    uint16_t tmp1, tmp2;
    sysClkInit(); // initialize SYSCLK to 80 MHz
    initUSART1(); // set USART1 baud rate to 115200
    adc1Init();
    while(1){
        init_val();
        ADC1->CR |= ADC_CR_ADSTART; // start a new A/D conversion
        while(!(ADC1->ISR & ADC_ISR_EOC)); // wait for ADC to complete
        value[0] = (uint8_t)ADC1->DR/1241 + 0x30; // integer digit in ASCII
        tmp1 = ADC1->DR % 1241;
        value[2] = (tmp1 * 10)/1241 + 0x30; // fractional digit in ASCII
        tmp2 = (tmp1 * 10) % 1241;
        if(tmp2 > 620){ // perform rounding to get more accurate voltage
            value[2]++; // round up
            if (value[2] == 0x3A) {
                value[0]++; // round up to integer digit
                value[2] = 0x30; // fractional digit is 0 after rounding up
            }
        }
        newlineUSART1();
```

```
            putsUSART1(title);
            putsUSART1(value);
            delayby100ms(10); // wait for one second
    }
}
void adc1Init(void)
{
    uint32_t j;
    GPIOA->MODER |= GPIO_MODER_MODE2;          // configure PA2 for analog function
    GPIOA->ASCR  |= GPIO_ASCR_ASC2;            // connect PA2 pin to ADC channel 7
    ADC1->CR     &= ~ADC_CR_DEEPPWD;           // get out of deep power down mode
    ADC1->CR     |= ADC_CR_ADVREGEN;           // enable ADC voltage regulator
    for(j = 0; j < 300; j++);                  // wait for regulator to be stabilized
    ADC1->CR     |= ADC_CR_ADEN;               // enable ADC
    while(!(ADC1->ISR & ADC_ISR_ADRDY));       // wait for ADC1 to become ready
    ADC1->DIFSEL &= ~(ADC_DIFSEL_DIFSEL_7); // select single-ended mode
    ADC1->SQR1   = ADC_SQR1_L_0 +              // one channel in the regular group
                    ADC_SQR1_SQ1_2 + ADC_SQR1_SQ1_1 + ADC_SQR1_SQ1_0;
                                               // put PA2 in regular group
    ADC1->SMPR1  = 0x01 << 21;    // set channel 7 sample time to 6.5 ADC clock cycles
    ADC1->CFGR   = 0;             // select software trigger, right aligned, 12-bit resolution
}
void init_val(void)
{
    value[0]    = '0';
    value[1]    = '.';
    value[2]    = '0';
    value[3]    = ' ';
    value[4]    = 'V';
    value[5]    = 0;
}
```

10.9 Temperature Measurement Using the TC1047A

The TC1047A from Microchip Technology is a three-pin temperature sensor whose voltage output is proportional to the measured temperature. The TC1047A can accurately measure temperature from −40°C to 125°C with a power supply from 2.7 V to 5.5 V.

The voltage range of the TC1047A is 0.1 V to 1.75 V for temperature from −40°C to 125°C. The voltage versus temperature relationship is shown in Figure 10.39. The T1047A has a 10 mV/°C voltage slope output response.

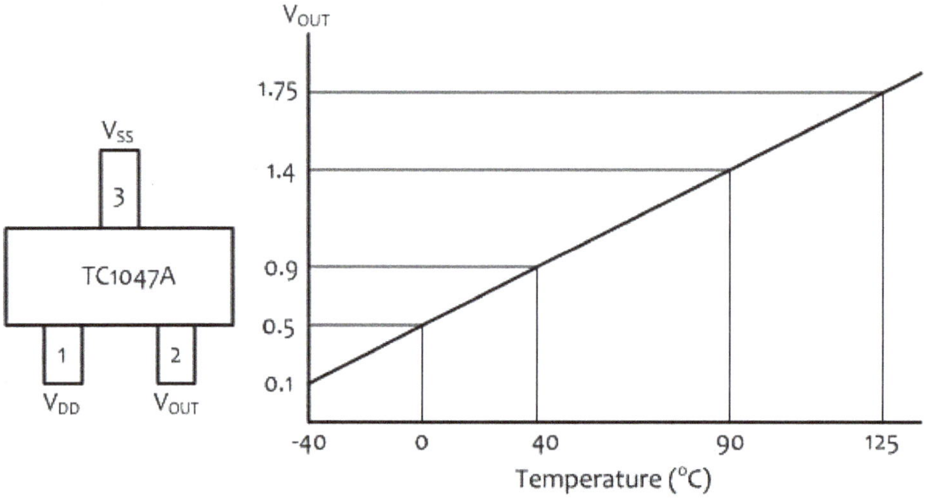

Figure 10.39 TC1047A VOUT vs. temperature characteristic

Example 10.18 Describe a circuit connection and write the required program to build a digital temperature thermometer using the STM32L475 and the TC1047A. Output the temperature in three integral and one fractional digits to the USART1 port once every second. Assume that the clock source is SYSCLK running at 80 MHz.

Solution: The circuit connection is shown in Figure 10.40. The external reference voltage can be provided by using a Zener diode or a resistor circuit. Two possible circuits are shown in Figure 10.41. A Zener diode with very tight breakdown voltage tolerance (0.07%) must be chosen in Figure 10.41(b). For the resistor ratio circuit shown in Figure 10.41(a), resistors with very tight tolerance (0.25% or smaller) should be used too.

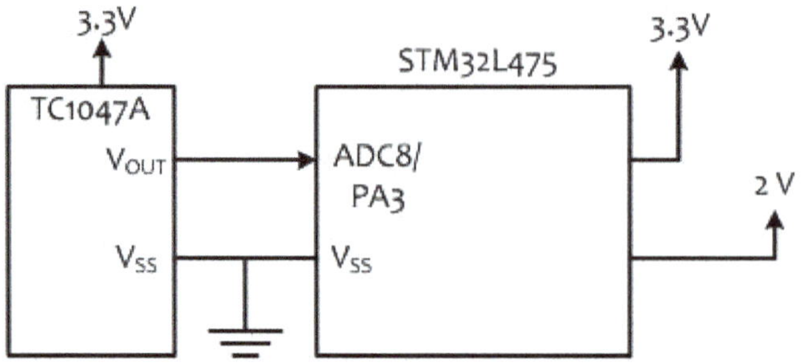

Figure 10.40 Circuit connection between STM32L475 and TC1047A

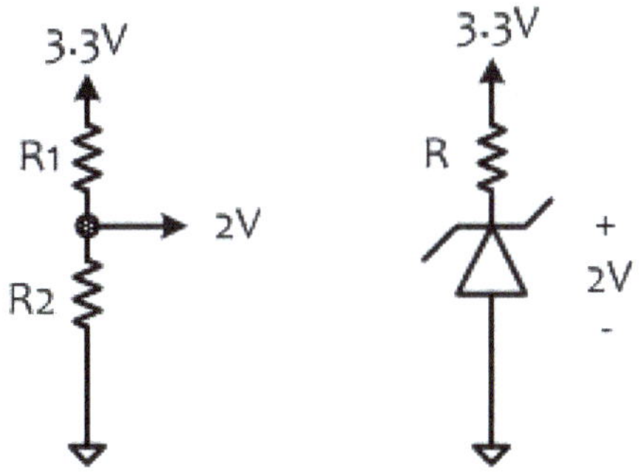

Figure 10.41 Circuit for reference voltage

The voltage 0.1 V will be converted to $0.1 \times 4095 \div 2 = 205$.

The voltage 1.75 V will be converted to $1.75 \times 4095 \div 2 = 3583$.

The range of A/D conversion result is 3583 – 205 = 3378. The temperature span is 125°C – (−40°C) = 165°C. The divide factor to translate the A/D conversion result back to temperature is 3378 ÷ 165 = 20.5. To avoid real number division, we will multiply the ADC conversion result by 10 and then divide the product by 205. We will enable the offset mode to channel 3 and set the offset to be 205 so that this value is subtracted from the conversion result in the ADC1->DR register.

After the A/D conversion, the following message will be output to the USART1:

Temperature = xxx.y °C

The following program performs the specified operation:

```
#include <stm32L475xx.h>
void     sysClkInit(void);
void     initUSART1(void);
void     adc1Init(void);
void     init_val(void);
void     putchUSART1(uint8_t cx);
void     newlineUSART1(void);
void     putsUSART1(uint8_t *ptr);
void     delayby100ms(uint16_t k);
uint8_t  title[14] = "Temperature = ";
uint8_t  value[8];
int main(void)
{
```

```
int tmp1, tmp2;
sysClkInit(); // initialize SYSCLK to 80 MHz
initUSART1(); // set USART1 baud rate to 115200
adc1Init();
while(1){
    init_val();
    ADC1->CR |= ADC_CR_ADSTART; // start a new A/D conversion
    while(!(ADC1->ISR & ADC_ISR_EOC)); // wait for ADC to complete
    tmp1 = (ADC1->DR * 10) / 205;
    tmp2 = (ADC1->DR * 10) % 205;
    value[4] = (tmp2 * 10)/205 + 0x30; // compute the fractional digit
    if ((tmp2 * 10)%205 > 102 ){
        value[4]++; // round up fractional digit
        if(value[4] == 0x3A){
            value[4] = 0x30;
            tmp1++;
        }
    }
    tmp1 = tmp1 - 40;
    if(tmp1 < 0){ // temperature is between -40°C and 0°C
        tmp1 = -tmp1;
        if(value[4] != 0x30){
            value[4] = 0x3A - value[4] + 0x30;
            tmp1--;
        }
        value[0] = 0x2D; // ASCII of minus sign
        value[2] = tmp1 % 10 + 0x30; // one's digit
        tmp1 /= 10;
        if (tmp1 != 0)
```

```
                value[1] = tmp1 + 0x30;
        }
        else { // temperature is above 0°C
            value[2] = tmp1 % 10 + 0x30; // one's digit
            tmp1 /= 10;
            if(tmp1 != 0){
                value[1] = tmp1 % 10 + 0x30; // ten's digit
                tmp1 /= 10;
            }
            if(tmp1 != 0)    // hundred's digit
                value[0] = 0x31;
        }
        newlineUSART1();
        putsUSART1(title);
        putsUSART1(value);
        delayby100ms(10); // wait for one second
    }
}
void adc1Init(void)
{
    uint32_t j;
    GPIOA->MODER   |=  GPIO_MODER_MODE3;    // configure PA3 for analog function
    GPIOA->ASCR    |=  GPIO_ASCR_ASC3;      // connect PA3 pin to ADC channel 8
    ADC1->CR       &= ~ADC_CR_DEEPPWD;      // get out of deep power down mode
    ADC1->CR       |=  ADC_CR_ADVREGEN;     // enable ADC voltage regulator
    for(j = 0; j < 300; j++);  // wait for regulator to be stabilized
    ADC1->CR       |=  ADC_CR_ADEN;  // enable ADC
    while(!(ADC1->ISR & ADC_ISR_ADRDY));    // wait for ADC1 to become ready
    ADC1->DIFSEL   &= ~ADC_DIFSEL_DIFSEL_8; // select single-ended mode
```

```
    ADC1->SQR1     =  ADC_SQR1_L_0 + // one channel in the regular group
                      ADC_SQR1_SQ1_3;        // put channel 8 (PA3) in regular group
    ADC1->SMPR1    =  0x01 << 24; // Set channel 8 sample time to 6.5 ADC clock cycles
    ADC1->CFGR     =  0;   // select software trigger, right aligned, 12-bit resolution
// enable OFFSET to Channel 8 and set offset to 205
    ADC1->OFR1     =  ADC_OFR1_OFFSET1_EN + ADC_OFR1_OFFSET1_CH_3 + 205;
}
void init_val(void)
{
    value[0]   = 0x20; // space character
    value[1]   = 0x20; // space character
    value[2]   = 0x30; // digit 0
    value[3]   = ':';
    value[4]   = 0x30; // digit 0
    value[5]   = 248;  // ASCII of degree character
    value[6]   = 'C';
    value[7]   = 0;    // NULL character
}
```

10.10 Summary

Data acquisition is an important application for the computer. Many of the physical quantities are non-electric. Before they can be processed by the computer, they must be converted into electric voltage. This work is performed by a sensor. Once the nonelectric quantity is converted into electric voltage, the analog to digital converter (ADC) on the computer can take over and convert it into a digital value, which is further processed by the computer.

An ADC requires two reference voltages to perform the conversion. The low reference voltage (V_{RL}) is often tied to the ground. The high reference voltage (V_{RH}) is assigned to one of the GPIO pins and must be supplied by the user. The sensor output voltages should be connected to certain GPIO pins, which have been configured for analog inputs to the ADC. The GPIO pins that have been configured into analog inputs are also called ADC channels.

The STM32L475 has three ADC modules. Each ADC module can handle up to 19 analog inputs. Most of the inputs are from GPIO pins. Some inputs are internal voltages. Analog inputs can be single-ended or differential. A/D conversion result can be represented as a 12-bit, 10-bit, 8-bit, or 6-bit value. A channel can be configured to operate in the offset mode. In this mode, the user can specify a value to be subtracted from the conversion result. This can slightly simplify the ADC result processing. The ADC also supports oversampling on the conversion. In this operation, multiple conversions are performed on the same analog input and the sum of these conversions is shifted by a specified number of places. This operation may be able to eliminate the noise on the analog inputs.

The analog inputs must be placed in two groups: regular and injected group. The analog inputs in the regular group will be converted regularly (or periodically), whereas the inputs in the injected group are not converted regularly.

To perform an A/D conversion, take the following steps:

Step 1

Get out the deep power down mode by clearing the DEEPPWD bit in the ADC->CR register.

Step 2

Enable the ADC voltage regulator and wait until it becomes stabilized.

Step 3

Perform an optional calibration (single-ended and/or differential mode).

Step 4

Enable the ADC module by setting ADEN bit in the ADCx->CR register and wait until the ADRDY bit in the ADC->ISR is set.

Step 5

Perform all other configurations, including: (a) configuring analog input pins, (b) placing analog inputs in regular and/or injected group, (c) selecting resolution, (d) enabling/disabling oversampling, (e) enabling offset mode, (f) selecting result alignment mode, (g) setting up analog watchdog mode, (h) selecting trigger mode (software or external trigger), (i) enabling/disabling interrupt, (j) DMA transfer, and (k) others.

Step 6

Start the A/D conversion.

Step 7

Process the A/D conversion result.

Whenever the application requires the conversion of a continuous analog signal into discrete time signal samples, the sampling rate is extremely important. The minimal sampling rate is determined by the **Nyquist theorem**. If f_{max} is the highest frequency of the signal component of the analog signal, then the user should sample the signal at a rate at least $2 \times f_{max}$ in order to faithfully represent the signal in the digital samples.

10.11 Exercises

E10.1 Design a circuit that can scale the voltage from the range of 0 mV ~ 100 mV to the range of 0 V ~ 3.3 V.

E10.2 Design a circuit that can shift and scale the voltage from the range of −80 mV ~ 160 mV to the range of 0 V ~ 3.3 V.

E10.3 Design a circuit that can shift and scale the voltage from the range of −50 mV ~ 75 mV to the range of 0 V ~ 3.3 V.

E10.4 Design a circuit that can shift and scale the voltage from the range of 1.5 V ~ 1.6 V to the range of 0 V ~ 3.3 V.

E10.5 Suppose there is a 10-bit ADC with V_{RL} and V_{RH} set to 0 V and 5 V, respectively. Find the corresponding voltage values for the A/D conversion results of 50, 175, 300, 600, 768, and 900, respectively.

E10.6 Suppose that there is a 12-bit A/D converter with V_{RL} and V_{RH} set to 1.5 V and 3.3 V respectively. Find the corresponding voltage values for the A/D conversion results of 80, 200, 480, 960, 1600, 2048, 3200, and 3900, respectively.

E10.7 Write a sequence of C statements to configure GPIO pins PB0, PA2, PC3, PB1, PA5, PA6, PC0, PC2, PC5 into analog channels. Place PB1, PA5, PA6, PC0, PC2, PC5 into regular group and place PB0, PA2, and PC3 into the injected group. Configure all channels to single-ended mode.

E10.8 Write a sequence of C statements to configure GPIO pins PA1, PA2, PC5, PB1, PC4, PA6, PA7, PA0, PA3 into analog channels. Place PA2, PC5, PB1, PC4, PA7 into regular group and place PA1, PA6, PA0, and PA3 into the injected group. Configure all channels to single-ended mode.

E10.9 Assume that the frequency of the clock source to the TIM6 and ADC1 are 80 MHz. Write a sequence of C statements to configure ADC1 regular group to be triggered by the TIM6 TRGO output (select the update event) every 1 ms.

E10.10 Write a sequence of C statements that use watchdog 1 to detect whether the channel 5 input is either lower than 0.5 V or higher than 2.9 V assuming that 12-bit resolution is used and V_{REF} = 3.3 V.

E10.11 Write a sequence of C statements that use all four ADC1->OFRy registers to enable offset mode for analog channels 1, 3, 5, and 9. Set their offset values to corresponding to 0.2 V, 0.4 V, 0.1 V, and 0.6 V assuming V_{REF} is 3.3 V.

E10.12 Write a sequence of C statements to enable the ADC1 EOC interrupt and also write the interrupt handling routine (void ADC1_2_IRQHandler (void);). The ADC1 interrupt handling routine adds ADC1->DR to the global variable sumADC. When the ADC1->DR has been added to sumADC 100 times, it computes sumADC/100, disables ADC1 interrupt, and then returns.

E10.13 Write a C program to measure the STM32L475 chip temperature once per second and output the temperature to USART1 in the following format:

MCU temperature = xxx.y °C

E10.14 Assume you are given the following two contexts to be written into the Queue of context:

Context 1:

JEXTEN[1:0] = 01

JEXTSEL[3:0] = 0010

JSQ1[4:0] = 00100

JSQ2[4:0] = 01010

JSQ3[4:0] = 00111

JSQ4[4:0] = 01000

JL[1:0] = 11

Context 2:

JEXTEN[1:0] = 10

JEXTSEL[3:0] = 0101

JSQ1[4:0] = 00001

JSQ2[4:0] = 01111

JSQ3[4:0] = 01011

JSQ4[4:0] = 00110

JL[1:0]

Write a sequence of C statements to place these two contexts into the injected queue of context.

E10.15 Write a sequence of C statements to set up the offset of 200 into channel 4 and set up the offset of 120 into channel 6.

E10.16 Write a sequence of C statements to configure the ADC1 to monitor all the regular channels whether their voltages are lower than 0.4 V or higher than 2.4 V. Assume that V_{REF} = 3.3 V and use 12-bit resolution.

E10.17 Write a sequence of C statement to monitor whether the current relative humidity is below 10% and higher than 75% using the analog watchdog 1 of ADC1. Assume that the humidity sensor outputs corresponding to 0% and 100% are 0 V and 2.8 V and V_{REF} = 3.3 V.

E10.18 Assume that the frequency of the clock source to the TIM2 and ADC1 are 80 MHz. Write a sequence of C statements to configure **ADC1 injected group** to be triggered by the TIM2 TRGO output (select the update event) every 10 ms. Place channels 2, 9, 11, and 15 into the injected group.

10.12 Lab Assignments

L10.1 Ambient Temperature Measurement. Use the TC1047A and the STM32L475 together to measure the temperature. Connect the TC1047A voltage output to PA1 pin and connect the V_{REF} to V_{DD} (3.3 V). Write a program to perform the appropriate initialization, measure the temperature once per 100 ms and display the temperature on the Terminal window (TERA Term).

L10.2 Potentiometer Voltage Measurement. Use a potentiometer and connect its top voltage to the same as the VREF (3.3 V) on the STM32L475 and connect its center tap output to the PA2 pin (set to analog channel 7). Write a program to perform the required initialization and perform the voltage measurement once every 200 ms. Display the voltage on the terminal window on the PC (output the voltage value to USART1).

L10.3 MCU Chip Temperature Measurement. Write a C program to measure the chip temperature using the on-chip temperature sensor and output the temperature to the USART1 in the following format:

MCU temperature is xxx.y °C

L10.4 ADC and DAC conversion Verification. Write a program to configure DAC1 and ADC2 to function properly. For DAC1, feed the data to be converted using 12-bit right-aligned format. The DAC1 output is the channel 17 input of ADC2. Set V_{REF} to 3.3 V (connect to V_{DD}).

Configure USART1 to operate at 115200 baud. Run the Tera Term on the PC and also set its baud rate to 115200. Send 200, 400, 600, ..., 4000 to be converted by the DAC. Perform conversion of each value by following the following procedure:

Step 1

Send one value to be converted by DAC1.

Step 2

Output the message "DAC1 convert xxxx to voltage."

Step 3

Wait for half of a second, start the ADC2 conversion.

Step 4

Wait for half of a second, read out the conversion result and output the message "ADC conversion result is xxxx."

Step 5

Go to step 1.

Set the ADC sampling time to at least 6.5 ADC clock cycles.

11 Inter-Integrated Circuit (I²C)

11.1 Objectives

After finishing this chapter, you will be able to

- Describe I²C protocols in general.
- Describe I²C signal components.
- Select appropriate pull-up resistors for the SCL and SDA lines.
- Perform SCL clock timing configuration for different I²C modes.
- Write functions to configure STM32L475 I²C parameters.
- Write I²C interrupt service routine.
- Use I²C to interface with the serial EEPROM AT24LC64B.
- Use I²C to interface with the humidity/temperature sensor HTS221.
- Use I²C to interface with the barometric pressure/temperature sensor LPS22HB.

11.2 Introduction to the I2C Interface

I²C (Inter-Integrated Circuit) is a two-wire bus protocol developed by Philips in 1982. It is mainly used for attaching lower-speed peripheral ICs to processors and microcontrollers in short-distance and intra-board communication. Like many other industrial protocols, I²C has gone through several revisions:

- In 1982, the 100-kHz I²C protocol was created as a simple internal bus system for building control electronics with various Philips chips. Only two bus lines are required: a **serial data line** (**SDA**) and a **serial clock line** (**SCL**).

- In 1992, the standardized version 1 of I²C was published. This version supported both 100-kHz (**standard mode**) and 400-kHz bus (**fast mode**) speeds and added 10-bit addressing in addition to the original 7-bit addressing.
- In 1998, version 2 of I²C was introduced. The 3.4-MHz bus speed (**high-speed mode**) and the power-saving requirements were added to the protocol.
- In 2000, version 2.1 was announced with a minor cleanup to the version 2.
- In 2007, version 3 was published. The 1-MHz bus speed (referred to as **fast-mode-plus** [Fm+]) and a device ID mechanism were added.
- In 2012, version 4 was published. The 5-MHz **ultra-fast mode** (UFm) was added. This mode uses the push–pull logic without pull-up resistors for the USDA (data) and USCL (clock) lines and adds an assigned manufactured ID table. It is only a unidirectional bus. Version 5 of I²C was also released in the same year by correcting some errors in the previous version.
- In 2014, version 6, the latest version, was released. Two graphs with errors in version 5 were corrected.

A typical I²C topology is shown in Figure 11.1. The I²C has the following features:

- Devices connected to the I²C bus can be a master or a slave.
- Multiple masters and multiple slaves can be connected to the same I²C bus.
- The number of ICs that can be connected to the same bus is limited only by the maximum bus capacitance.
- Addresses are used to select a slave to carry out data communication at a time.
- For a single master I²C system, the SCL line can be push-pull if there are no devices on the bus which would stretch the clock.
- The logic level of V_{IH} and V_{IL} are not fixed but set to 0.7 V_{DD} and 0.3 V_{DD}, respectively.

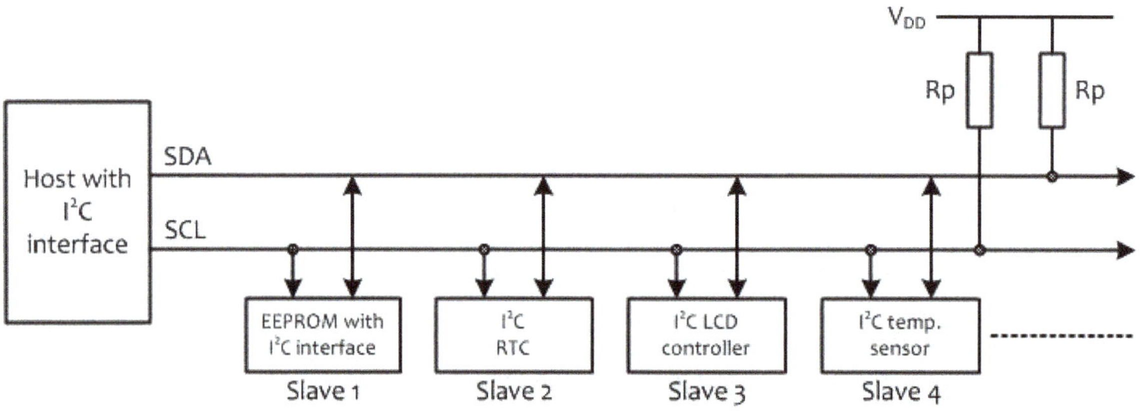

Figure 11.1 I²C bus interfacing block diagram

11.2.1 DATA TRANSMISSION IN I2C BUS

In an I²C system, data transmission is carried out byte by byte. A data transmission is started by the **start condition** generated by a master. A **slave address** follows the start condition, and it must be acknowledged by the targeted slave. The slave address can be 7 bits or 10 bits. A 10-bit address is transmitted in two bytes.

After the address, data are transmitted byte-by-byte either from the master to the slave or from the slave to the master. Every byte except the last byte must be acknowledged by the receiver. If the master is a receiver, it will not acknowledge the last-received byte. The slave will acknowledge every byte that it receives.

The master generates a **stop condition** to terminate a data transfer. The master does not need to give up the bus if it intends to change the data transmission direction with the same slave or carry out data communication with a different slave. The master generates a **restart condition** (also called **repeated start** condition) in order to switch from one slave to another or change data transfer direction with the same slave.

11.2.2 I2C SIGNAL COMPONENTS

An I²C transfer consists of a few basic signal components. Each of these signal components is described in the following:

START Condition

The first signal component to be generated during a transfer is the start condition. As illustrated in Figure 11.2, a start condition is represented by pulling the SDA signal low when the SCL signal is high. An I²C master uses this signal to indicate its intention to start a new data transfer.

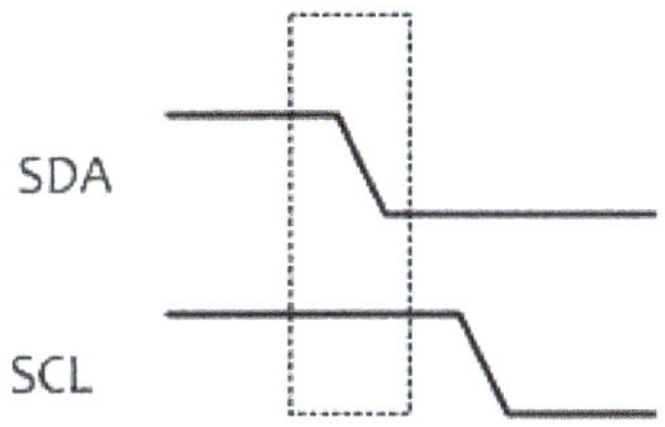

Figure 11.2 I²C Start condition

STOP Condition

A stop condition is represented by the SDA signal going high when the SCL signal is high. The stop condition indicates that the current data transfer on the I²C bus is to be terminated. A stop condition is shown in Figure 11.3.

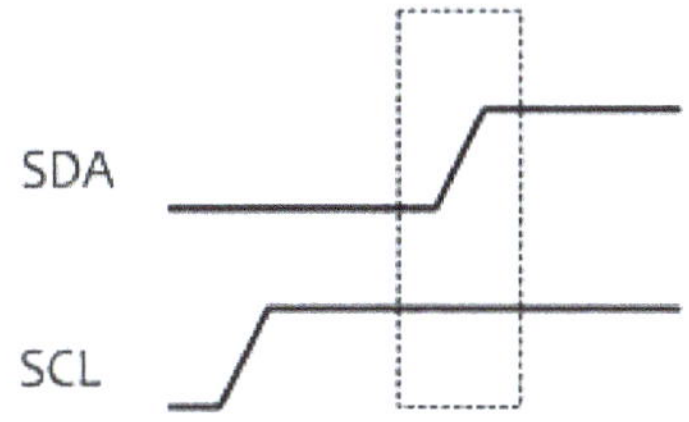

Figure 11.3 I²C Stop condition

Repeated START (RESTART) Condition

When a master device finishes the current data transfer and intends to change the data transfer direction with the current selected slave or exchange data with a different slave device without releasing the bus, it can generate a **Repeated START Condition**. A repeated start condition is also called a **RESTART** condition.

Illustrated in Figure 11.4, a RESTART condition is a start condition generated after a previous START condition without a stop condition inserted between them.

Figure 11.4 I²C **RESTART** condition

Data

Data are transferred byte by byte on the I^2C bus. Every data byte must be followed by an acknowledgement. Data are sent in a way that the most significant data byte is sent first and that byte is considered valid only when the SCL clock is high. When the SCL signal is low, data are allowed to change. The waveform of a data byte on the I^2C bus is shown in Figure 11.5.

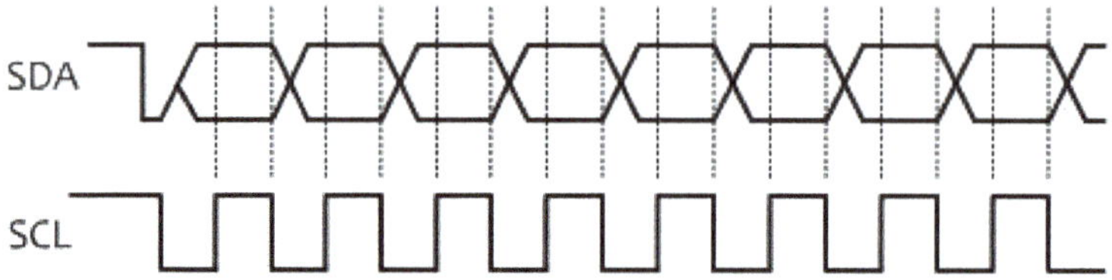

Note. Data bit is always stable when clock (SCL) is high

Figure 11.5 I^2C bus data elements

Address

A master initiates a data transfer by addressing a slave on the bus and indicating whether it wants to transmit or receive data. The I^2C addresses can be 7-bit or 10-bit. A 7-bit address is followed by the R/bit (0 = write; 1 = read) and sent together in a frame. A 7-bit wide address space theoretically allows 128 I^2C addresses. However, some addresses are reserved for special purposes. Thus, only 112 addresses are available for the 7-bit address scheme. The reserved 7-bit addresses are listed in Table 11.1.

Table 11.1 I^2C reserved addresses (x = don't care; 1 = high; 0 = low)

Slave address	$R/\overline{W}$ bit	Description
0000 000	0	General call address[1]
0000 000	1	START byte[2]
0000 001	x	CBUS address[3]
0000 010	x	Reserved for different bus format[4]
0000 011	x	Reserved for future purposes
0000 1xx	x	Hs-mode master code
1111 1xx	1	Device ID
1111 0xx	x	10-bit slave addressing

Note.

[1] The general call address is used for several functions including software reset.

[2] No device is allowed to acknowledge at the reception of the START byte.

[3] The CBUS address has been reserved to enable the inter-mixing of CBUS compatible and I^2C-bus compatible devices in the same system. I^2C compatible devices are not allowed to respond on reception of this address.

[4] The address reserved for a different bus format is included to enable I^2C and other protocols to be mixed. Only I^2C bus compatible devices that can work with such formats and protocols are allowed to respond to this address.

A 10-bit address is transferred as two bytes with the highest two address bits sent as bit 2 (A9) and bit 1 (A8) in the first byte and the lower 8 address bits sent in the second byte. The 7-bit address and 10-bit address are illustrated in Figure 11.6.

A6	A5	A4	A3	A2	A1	A0	R/$\overline{W}$

Figure11.6a I²C 7-bit addressing

1	1	1	1	0	A9	A8	R/$\overline{W}$

A7	A6	A5	A4	A3	A2	A1	A0

Figure 11.6b I²C 10-bit addressing

Acknowledge Condition (ACK)

Each data byte transferred on the I²C bus must be acknowledged positively or negatively. A **positive acknowledgment** (**ACK**) is bringing the SDA signal low while the SCL signal is high during the 9th clock pulse of a data byte transfer.

A **negative acknowledgment** (**NACK**) is leaving the SDA signal high while the SCL signal is high during the 9th clock pulse of a data byte transfer. The ACK and NACK signals are illustrated in Figure 11.7.

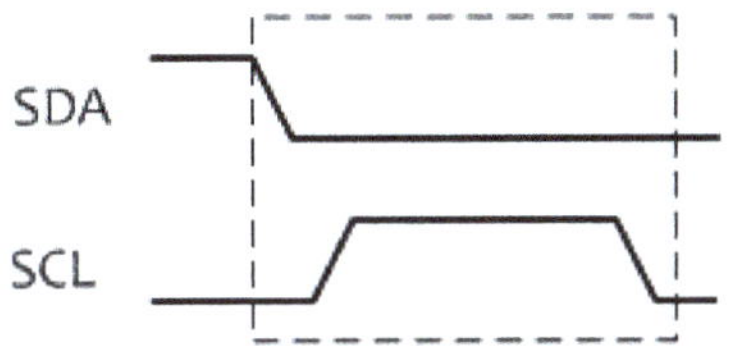

Figure 11.7a ACK condition

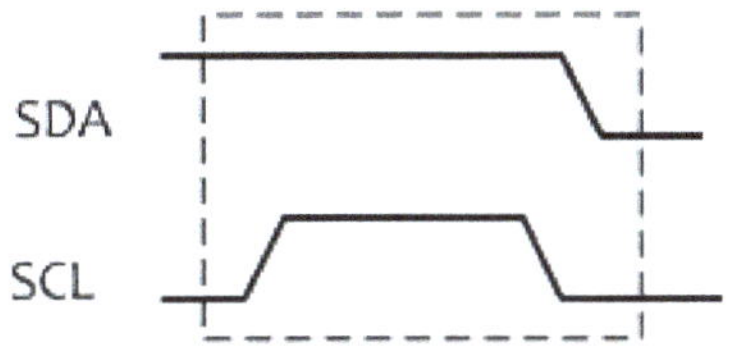

Figure 11.7b NACK condition

11.2.3 I2C DATA TRANSFER FORMAT

Data transfer in the I²C interface can be carried out as follows:

1. Master transmitter transmits data to a slave receiver.
2. Master reads data from a slave.
3. *Combined format.* Data transfer direction may change in this format, and the master may switch from one slave to another.

The possible data transfer formats are described in the following:

Master Transmitter and Slave Receiver—7-bit Addressing

The data transfer in this format starts with the transmission of the START condition, followed by the slave address and the R/ bit, which is set to 0. The selected slave acknowledges positively and then the master starts to transmit data byte after byte with each byte acknowledged by the slave. When the master finishes transmitting the last byte, it generates a STOP condition to terminate the transaction. This format is illustrated in Figure 11.8.

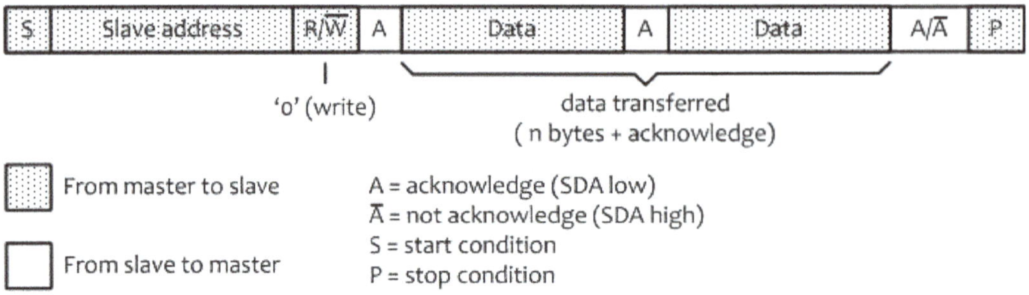

Figure 11.8 A master transmitter addressing a slave receiver with a 7-bit address. The transfer direction is not changed

Master Receiver and Slave Transmitter—7-bit Addressing

In this format, the master transmits the START condition, followed by the slave address byte with the R/bit set to 1. This byte is acknowledged positively by the slave. Slave starts to transmit data bytes with each byte (except the last byte) acknowledged positively by the master. After receiving the last data byte, the master generates a STOP condition to terminate the reception transaction. The process is illustrated in Figure 11.9.

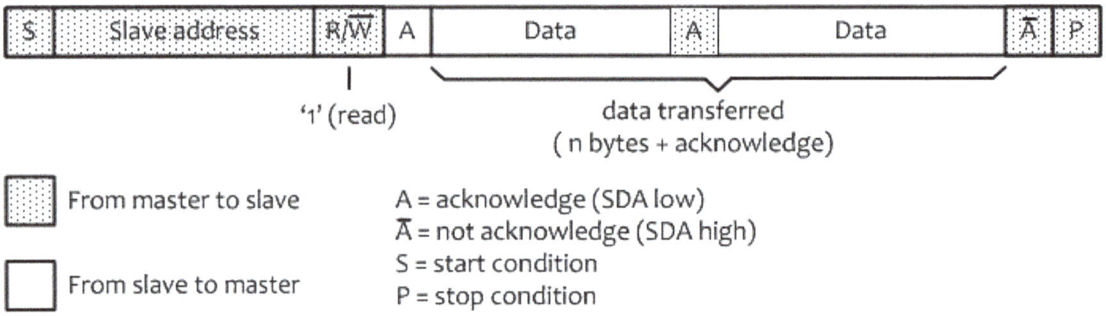

Figure 11.9 A master receives data bytes with a 7-bit address.

Combined Format—7-bit addressing

A RESTART condition is required in this format. There are quite a few combinations:

- A master sends data to a slave and then reads data from the same slave.
- A master receives data from a slave and then sends data to the same slave.
- A master sends data to a slave and then sends data to another slave.
- A master sends data to a slave and then reads data from another slave.
- A master reads data from a slave and then reads data from another slave.
- A master reads data from a slave and then sends data to another slave.

This format is illustrated in Figure 11.10.

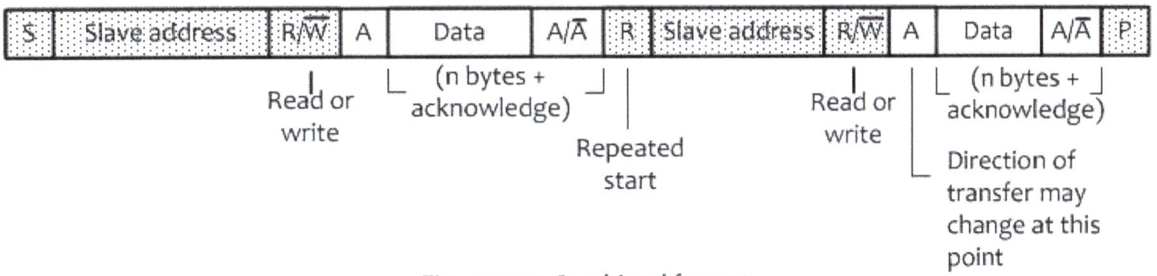

Figure 11.10 Combined format

Master Transmitter to Slave Receiver—10-bit Addressing

In this format, the address is transmitted in two bytes. This format is illustrated in Figure 11.11.

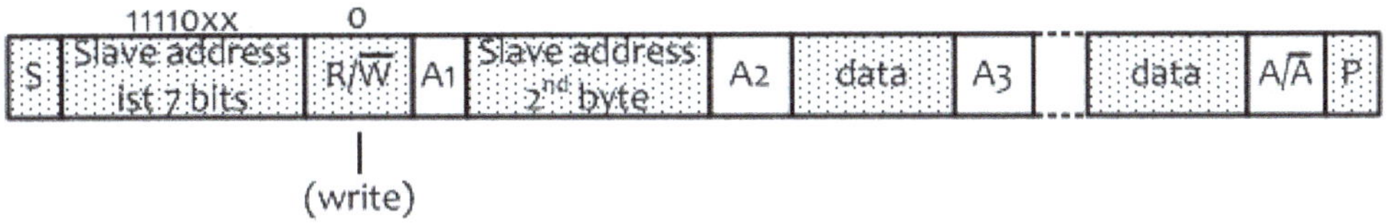

Figure 11.11 A master transmitter addresses a slave receiver with a 10-bit address

Master Receiver and Slave Transmitter—10-bit Addressing

In this format, a RESTART condition is required to be generated to turn around the data transmission direction as shown in Figure 11.12.

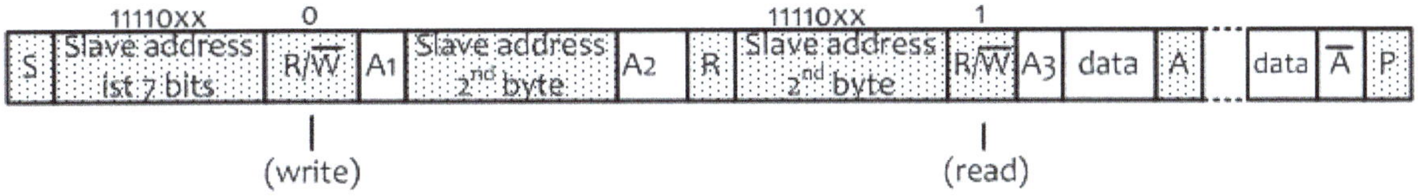

Figure 11.12 A master receiver addresses a slave transmitter with a 10-bit address

Combined Format Master Writes to Slave and Reads from the Same Slave—10-bit Addressing

A restart condition is required to turn around the data transmission direction as shown in Figure 11.13.

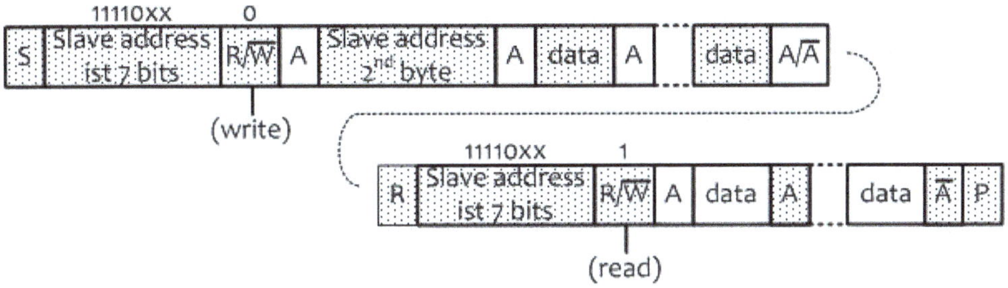

Figure 11.13 **Combined format.** A master addresses a slave with a 10-bit address, then transmits data to this slave and reads data from this slave.

Combined Format Master Writes to Two Different Slaves—10-bit Addressing

In this format, the master is required to generate a RESTART condition to switch from one slave to another. This formation is illustrated in Figure 11.14.

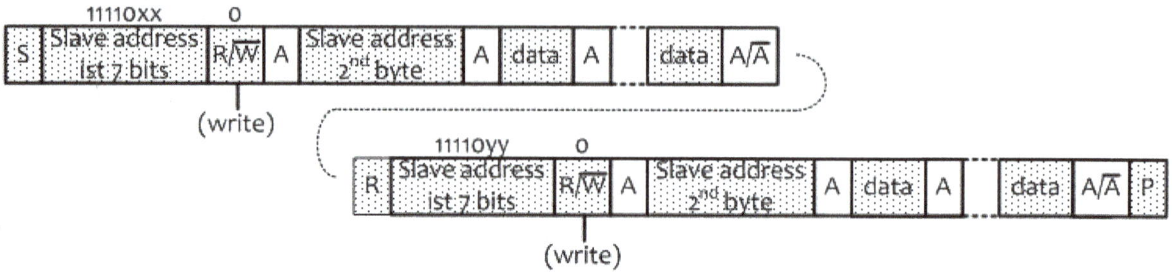

Figure 11.14 **Combined format.** A master transmits data to two slaves, both with 10-bit addresses.

Combined Format—One with 7-bit Addressing and the Other with 10-bit Addressing

Both 7-bit addressing and 10-bit addressing can be mixed in the same system. Figure 11.15 demonstrates an example of a master that sends data to two slaves: one with 7-bit address and the other with the 10-bit address.

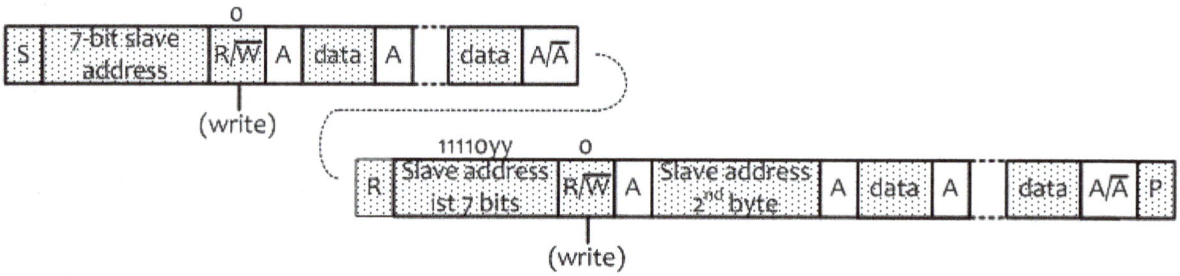

Figure 11.15 **Combined format.** A master transmits data to two slaves, one with 7-bit address, and one with 10-bit address.

11.2.4 ISSUES IN I2C DATA TRANSMISSION

The I²C protocol allows multiple masters to coexist in the same system, but only one master is allowed to control the bus at a time. When there are multiple masters in the same system, it is common that multiple masters attempt to start data transfer at about the same time. In this situation, these masters must first arbitrate for the use of the I²C bus. Before the arbitration process is completed, there is no common clock yet. These masters must work together to synchronize their clock signal.

I²C Bus Arbitration

In the event that two or more master devices attempt to begin a transfer at about the same time, an arbitration scheme is employed to force one or more masters to give up the bus. The master devices continue transmitting until one master attempts to send a high while the other transmits a low. The resultant bus voltage level is low. The master attempting to transfer a high signal will detect a low on the SDA line and give up the bus by switching off its data-output stage.

The winning master continues its transmission without interruption. This arbitration scheme is nondestructive: One device always wins, and no data are lost. An example of the arbitration process is shown in Figure 11.16.

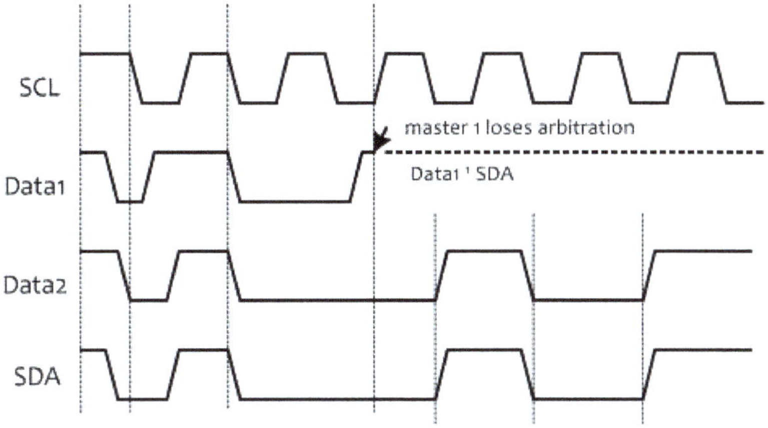

Figure 11.16 Arbitration procedure of two masters

I²C Bus Synchronization

When multiple I²C masters start data transfer on the bus and before the arbitration process is completed, all masters generate their own clocks on the SCL line to transfer messages. Data are valid during the high period of the clock. A defined clock is needed for the **bit-by-bit arbitration** procedure to take place.

The SCL signal is generated by counting down a programmable reload value using the instruction clock signal. Clock synchronization is performed by using the **wire-and** connection of the I²C interfaces to the SCL line. A **high-to-low** transition on the SCL line causes the devices concerned to start counting off their low period, and once a device clock has gone low, it will hold the SCL line in that state until the high state is reached (CLK1 in Figure 11.17). The **low-to-high** transition of this clock may not change the state of the SCL line if another clock (CLK2) is still within its low period.

The SCL line will be held low by the device with the longest low period. Devices with shorter low periods enter a **high-wait state** during this time. When all devices concerned have counted off their low periods, the clock line will be released and go high. All devices will then start counting off their high period. The high period will be dominated by the device with the shortest high period.

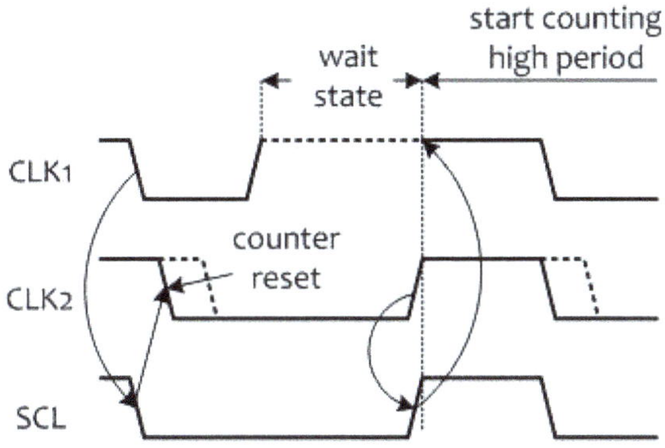

Figure 11.17 Clock synchronization during the arbitration procedure

Handshaking

Clock synchronization mechanism can be used as a handshake in data transfer. Slave devices may hold the SCL line low after the completion of a 1-byte transfer. In such a case, it halts the bus clock and forces the master clock into wait state until the slave releases the SCL line. The master device also can hold the SCL line low to indicate that it needs more time to handle a byte.

Clock Stretching

Clock stretching slows down a transaction by holding the SCL line low. The transaction cannot continue until the line is released high again. Clock stretching is optional; in fact, most slave devices do not include an SCL driver, so they are unable to stretch the clock.

On the byte level, a device can receive bytes of data at a fast rate but needs more time to store the received byte or prepare for another byte to be transmitted. Slaves can then hold the SCL line low after reception and acknowledgment of a byte to force the master into a wait state until the slave is ready for the next byte transfer in a type of handshake procedure.

On the bit level, a device such as a microcontroller with or without limited hardware for the I^2C bus can slow the bus clock by extending each clock low period. The speed of any master is adapted to the internal operating rate of this device.

In high-speed mode, this handshake feature can only be used on the byte level.

11.2.5 PULL-UP RESISTOR (RP) CALCULATION

The choice of the pull-up resistor value must meet the I^2C bus rise time requirement. The pull-up resistor cannot be too small or too large. A small (a strong pull-up) resistor prevents the I^2C pin on an IC from being able to drive low. A very large resistor may cause the I^2C bus signal rise time to exceed the maximum requirement.

The supply voltage limits the minimum value of resistor R_P due to the minimum **sink current** (I_{OL}) of 3 mA for standard mode and fast mode or 20 mA for fast-mode-plus. At the minimum sink current, V_{OL} is no higher than 0.4 V. $R_{P(min)}$ as a function of V_{DD} is shown in Figure 11.18. The traces in Figure 11.18 are calculated using the following equation:

$$R_{P(min)} = (V_{DD} - V_{OL(max)}) \div I_{OL} \text{ ------ } (11.1)$$

The bus rise time is a function of power supply voltage, the bus capacitance, and the pull-up resistor. The **bus rise time** is defined as the time it takes for the voltage on the bus line capacitance to rise from 0.3 V_{DD} to 0.7 V_{DD}. The voltage V_{IH} is defined as the lowest input voltage to be recognized as high and is defined to be 0.7 V_{DD}, whereas the voltage V_{IL} is the highest voltage to be considered as low and is defined to be 0.3 V_{DD}.

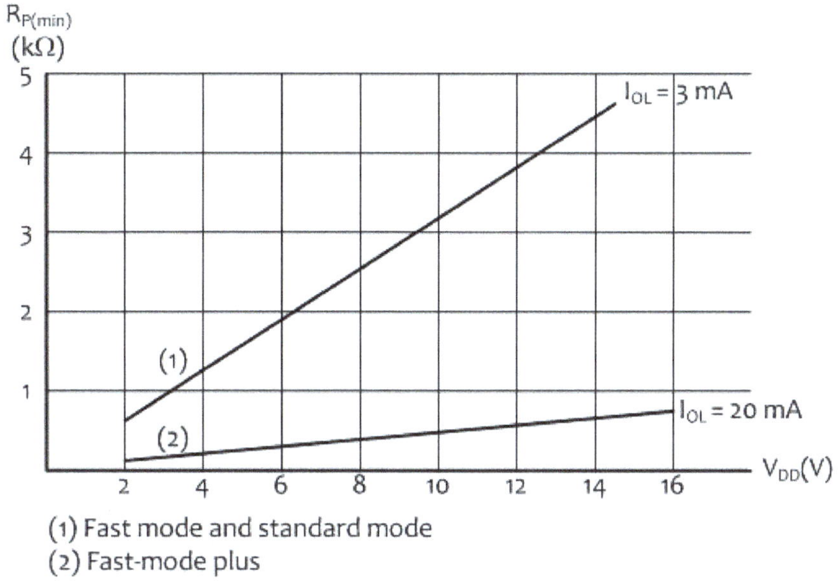

Figure 11.18 $R_{P(min)}$ as a function of V_{DD}

Since the pull-up resistor and the bus capacitance together form a RC circuit, the voltage across the bus line capacitance over time is $V(t) = V_{DD}(1 - e^{-t/RC})$, where t is the time since the charging has started.

Let $V(t_1) = 0.3 \times V_{DD} = V_{DD}(1 - e^{-t1/RC})$; then $t_1 = 0.3566749 \times RC$

$V(t_2) = 0.7 \times V_{DD} = V_{DD}(1 - e^{-t2/RC})$; then $t_2 = 1.2039729 \times RC$

Then the rise time is $t_r = t_2 - t_1 = 0.8473 \times RC$. The maximum allowable pull-up resistor can be calculated by plugging in the bus rise time as follows:

$R_{P(MAX)} = t_r \div (0.8473 \times C_B)$ --- (11.2)

The relationship between $R_{P(MAX)}$ and the bus capacitance (C_B) in standard mode, fast mode, and fast-mode -plus is shown in Figure 11.19.

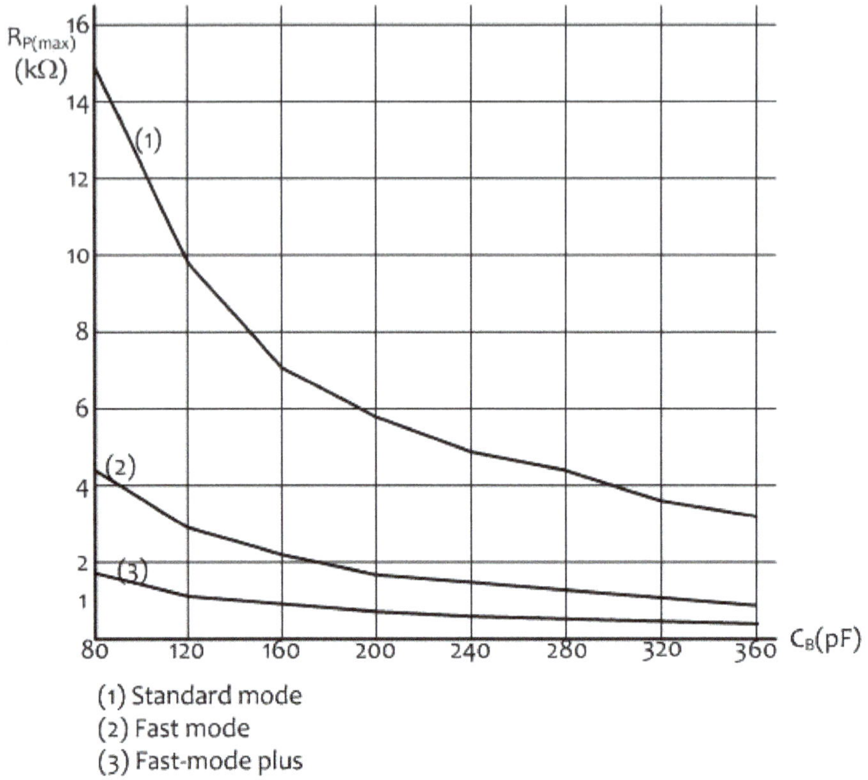

Figure 11.19 $R_{P(MAX)}$ as a function of bus capacitance

The bus line rise time (t_r), the maximum capacitive (C_b) load on the bus line, and output low voltage (V_{OL}) for the I²C standard mode, fast mode, and fast-mode-plus are given in Table 11.2.

Table 11.2 I²C parameters from I2C specifications

Parameter		Standard mode (max)	Fast mode (max)	Fast mode plus (max)	unit
t_r	Rise time of both SDA and SCL signals	1000	300	120	ns
C_b	Capacitive load for each bus line	400	400	550	pF
V_{OL}	Low-level output voltage (at 3mA current sink, V_{CC} > 2V)	0.4	0.4	0.4	V
	Low-level output voltage (at 2mA current sink, $V_{CC} \leq$ 2V)	–	0.2 x V_{CC}	0.2 x V_{CC}	V

Speed versus Power Trade-Off

Once the minimum and maximum values of the pull-up resistor have been calculated, the decision for the value of resistor can be made based on the trade-off between the speed and the power budget. A smaller resistor offers a higher speed because of a smaller RC delay. A larger resistor results in a lower power consumption.

Example 11.1 The I²C standard requires the signal **rise time** for SCL and SDA in the **fast mode** and **fast-mode-plus** to be no larger than 300 ns and 120 ns, respectively. Calculate the $R_{P(MIN)}$ and $R_{P(MAX)}$ for the fast mode and fast-mode-plus assuming that V_{DD} is 3.3V, C_B = 200 pF, V_{OL} = 0.4V, and $\mathbf{I_{OL}}$ for fast mode and fast-mode-plus are 3 mA and 20 mA, respectively.

Solution:

For the fast mode:

$R_{P(MAX)} = t_r / (0.8473 \times C_B) = 300 \text{ ns} / (0.8473 \times 200 \text{ pF}) = 1.77 \text{ kW}$

$R_{P(MIN)} = (3.3 \text{ V} - 0.4 \text{ V}) \div 3 \text{ mA} = 967\ \Omega$

For the fast-mode-plus:

$R_{P(MAX)} = t_r / (0.8473 \times C_B) = 120 \text{ ns} / (0.8473 \times 200 \text{ pF}) = 708\ \Omega$

$R_{P(MIN)} = (3.3 \text{ V} - 0.4 \text{ V}) \div 20 \text{ mA} = 145 \text{ W}$

We can select any available resistor value between $R_{P(MIN)}$ and $R_{P(MAX)}$. The value of the pull-up resistor can be selected based on the trade-off for the power consumption and speed.

11.3 The STM32L475 I2C Features

The STM32L475 I²C module is compatible to the I²C specification revision 3. It supports standard mode, fast mode, and fast-mode-plus (Fm+). It is also SMBus (system management bus) and PMBus (power management bus) compatible. Both the 7-bit and 10-bit addressing are supported.

The STM32L475 implements three I²C modules: I²C1, I²C2, and I²C3. The features of these three I²C modules are summarized in Table 11.3.

Table 11.3 STM32L4x5 I²C implementation

I²C features	I²C1	I²C2	I²C3
7-bit addressing mode	x	x	x
10-bit addressing mode	x	x	x
Standard-mode (up to 100 kbits/s)	x	x	x
Fast-mode (up to 400 kbits/s)	x	x	x
Fast-mode plus with 20 mA output drive (up to 1 Mbits/s)	x	x	x
Independent clock	x	x	x
SMBus	x	x	x
Wakeup from stop 0 mode	x	x	x
Wakeup from stop 1 mode	x	x	x
Wakeup from stop 2 mode	-	-	x

To support the operation of I²C bus, two signal pins are assigned to each I²C module. To support the operation of SMBus, an additional signal pin is assigned to each I²C module. The pin assignment to each I²C module is summarized in Table 11.4.

Table 11.4 I²C signal pins assignment

I²C Module	Signal function	Alternate function	I/O pin
I²C1	I²C1_SMBA	AF4	PB5
	I²C1_SCL	AF4	PB6, PB8
	I²C1_SDA	AF4	PB7, PB9
I²C2	I²C2_SMBA	AF4	PB12
	I²C2_SCL	AF4	PB10, PB13
	I²C2_SDA	AF4	PB11, PB14
I²C3	I²C3_SMBA	AF4	PB2
	I²C3_SCL	AF4	PC0
	I²C3_SDA	AF4	PC1

The block diagram of the I²C module is shown in Figure 11.20.

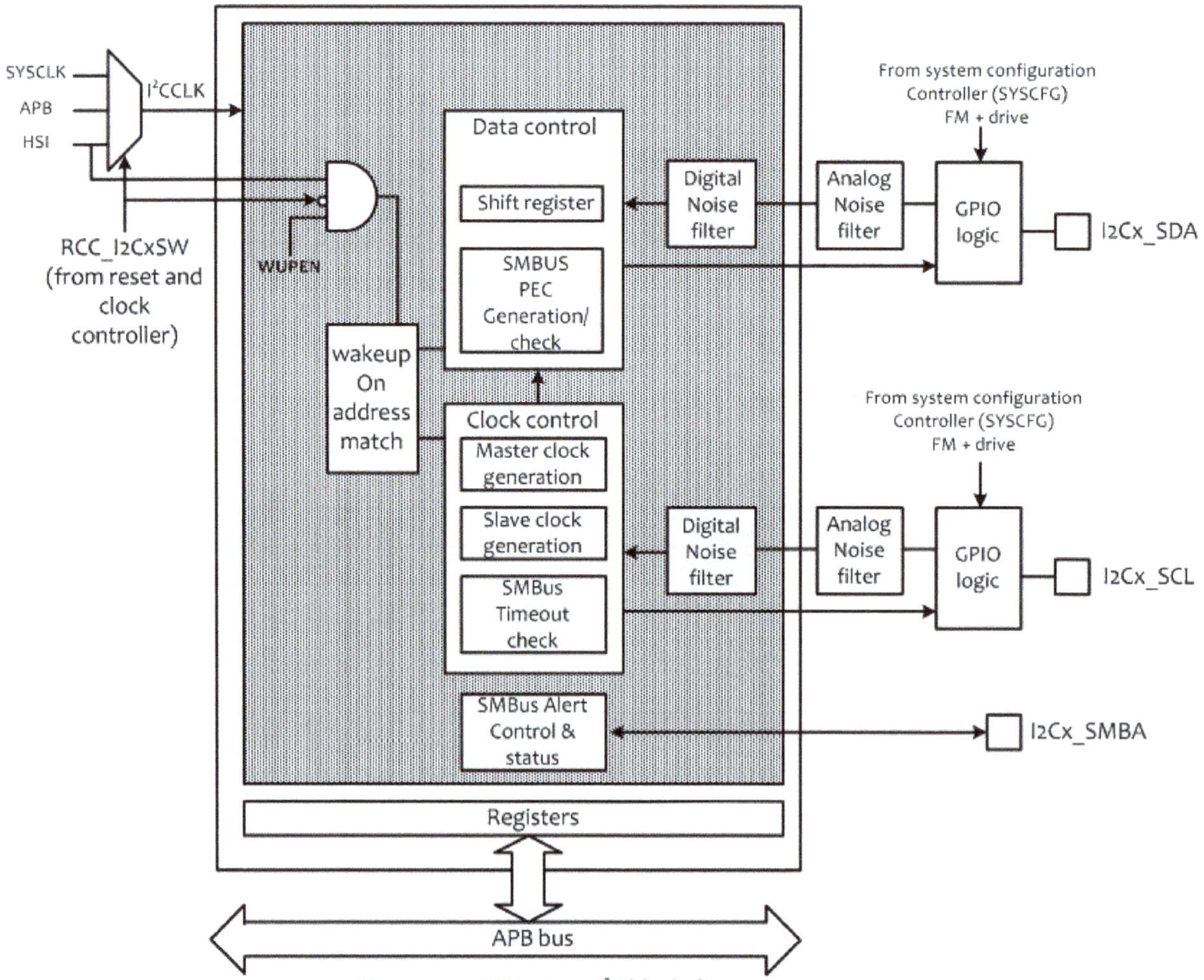

Figure 11.20 STM32L475 I²C block diagram

11.4 STM32L475 I2C Clock Generation

When the I²C module is configured to operate in master mode, it will generate the SCL clock to control the data transfer on the I²C bus. As shown in Figure 11.20, the I²C kernel is clocked by the I²CxCLK signal (x = 1, 2, or 3). I²CxCLK can be selected from APB1, HSI16, or SYSCLK. In the following discussion, we will simply use **I2CCLK** to refer to the I²C clock source.

The setting of the SCL clock must satisfy the following requirements:

$t_{LOW} > 4\times t_{I2CCLK} + t_{filters}$ ------ (11.3)

$t_{HIGH} > t_{I2CCLK}$ ------ (11.4)

where

t_{LOW} is the SCL low time

t_{HIGH} is the SCL high time

$t_{filters}$, when enabled, is the sum of delays brought by the analog filter and digital filter.

Maximum analog filter delay is 260 ns. Digital filter delay is DNF × t_{I2CCLK}.

11.4.1 BASIC I2C TIMING UNIT

To simplify the I²C timing configuration, the I2CCLK clock is prescaled by a factor and used as the basic timing unit. All other timing parameters are represented as a multiple of this unit. The prescaler is **PRESC + 1**, where PRESC is a field in the I2Cx->TIMINGR register.

11.4.2 NOISE FILTERS

If the I²C is used in a noisy environment, the user must configure the noise filters to filter out the noise on the SCL and SDA bus lines. By default, an analog filter is present on the SDA and SCL inputs. This analog filter is compliant with the I²C specification that requires the suppression of spikes with a pulse width up to 50 ns in fast mode and fast-mode-plus. The analog filter can be disabled by setting the ANFOFF bit in the I2Cx->CR1 register.

Digital noise filter can be enabled by programming the DNF[3:0] field in the I2Cx->CR1 register. When the digital filter is enabled, the level of the SCL and SDA lines is internally changed only if they remain stable for more than **DNF × I2CCLK** periods. This allows the user to suppress spikes with a programmable length of 1 to 15 I2CCLK periods.

11.4.3 I2C TIMINGS

The timing of data transmission is controlled by the SCL signal. At a specified speed mode (standard mode, fast mode, fast-mode-plus, etc.), the SCL signal has its own typical period. However, when data are being transferred, the SCL waveform changes to meet the timing requirements of different conditions. For example, data setup time and data hold time requirements on the SDA signal relative to the SCL clock. All timing parameters are represented as a multiple of the period of the I2CCLK clock multiplied by a prescaler defined in the I2Cx->TIMINGR register.

Minimal SCL Period

When there is only one master in the I²C bus and there is no data transaction, then the cycle time of the SCL clock is equal to the sum of the following four parameters as shown in Figure 11.21:

- t_{SYNC1}: This is the delay from the moment that the circuit forces the SCL clock to go low until the moment that the SCL clock is detected to be low.
- t_{SYNC2}: This is the delay from the moment that the circuit releases the SCL clock to go high until the moment that the SCL clock is detected to be high.
- t_{SCLH}: This is the interval that the SCL clock is high (high interval). This parameter is defined by the SCLH field in the I2Cx->TIMINGR register. The length of the SCL high interval is (SCLH + 1) × (PRESC + 1) × t_{I2CCLK}, where PRESC is also a field in the I2Cx->TIMINGR register.
- t_{SCLL}: This is the minimal interval that SCL clock is low (low interval). The actual SCL low interval can be longer if it is forced low by any I²C slave or master. This parameter is defined by the SCLL field in the I2Cx->TIMINGR register. The length of the SCL low interval is (SCLL + 1) × (PRESC + 1) × t_{I2CCLK}. The SCL may be stretched low by the master or the slave.

In this condition, the period of the master SCL clock is given as follows:

$$t_{SCL} = t_{SYNC1} + t_{SYNC2} + \{[(SCLH + 1) + (SCLL + 1)] \times (PRESC + 1) \times t_{I2CCLK}\} \quad \text{---- (11.5)}$$

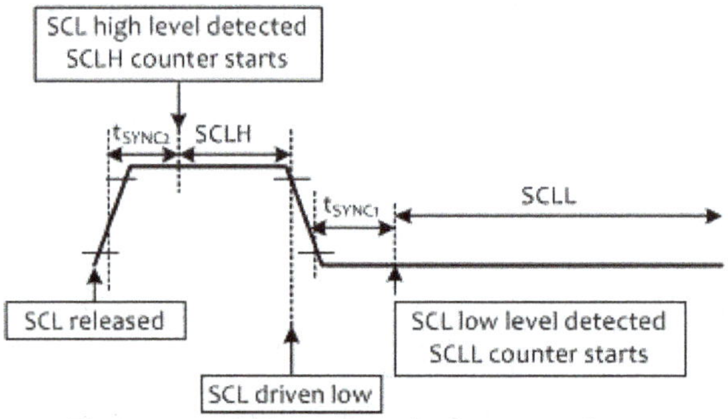

Figure 11.21 SCL master clock generation

The high interval (t_{HIGH}) and low interval (t_{LOW}) for the SCL clock for different I²C modes are given in Table 11.5.

The duration of $\mathbf{t_{SYNC1}}$ depends on these parameters:

- SCL falling edge
- When enabled, input delay induced by the analog filter
- When enabled, input delay induced by the digital filter: DNF × t_{I2CCLK}
- Delay due to SCL synchronization with I2CCLK clock (2 to 3 I2CCLK periods)

The duration of $\mathbf{t_{SYNC2}}$ depends on these parameters:

- SCL rising edge

- When enabled, input delay induced by the analog filter
- When enabled, input delay induced by the digital filter: DNF × t_{I2CCLK}
- Delay due to SCL synchronization with I2CCLK clock (2 to 3 I2CCLK periods)

Data Setup Time Requirement

When data are transmitted on the I²C bus, data setup time and data hold time must be satisfied in order for data to be transmitted correctly.

In I²C bus, data can only change when the SCL clock is low. As shown in Figure 10.22a, the delay from the moment that data become stable until the SCL clock starts to rise is called the **data setup time** ($t_{SU:STA}$). However, it takes time for data on the SDA bus to change until it becomes stable. We need to use a circuit to hold the SCL clock low from the moment that data on the SDA line start to change until data setup time is satisfied. This amount of time is called **SCL delay time** (t_{SCLDEL}). The t_{SCLDEL} delay is configured by programming the SCLDEL[3:0] field in the I2Cx->TIMINGR register. The parameter SCLDEL must be set to a value such that:

$$\{[t_{r(max)} + t_{SU:DAT(min)}] / [(PRESC + 1) \times t_{I2CCLK}]\} - 1 <= SCLDEL \quad \text{---- (11.6)}$$

where

$t_{r(max)}$ is the maximum data rise time on the SDA line. The delay time for SDA signal starts to change until it becomes stable and is normally determined by the rise time because data fall time is normally shorter. I²C bus data rise time and setup time for three operation modes are given in Table 11.5.

Table 11.5 I2C-SMBus specification clock timing

Symbol	Parameter	Standard-mode (Sm)		Fast-Mode (Fm)		Fast-Mode Plus (Fm+)		SMBus		unit
		Min.	Max	Min.	Max	Min.	Max	Min.	Max	
f_{SCL}	SCL clock frequency	–	100	–	400	–	1000	–	100	kHz
$t_{HD:STA}$	Hold time (repeated) START condition	4.0	–	0.6	–	0.26	–	4.0	–	µs
$t_{SU:STA}$	Set-up time for a repeated START condition	4.7	–	0.6	–	0.26	–	4.7	–	µs
$t_{SU:STO}$	Set-up time for STOP condition	4.0	–	0.6	–	0.26	–	4.0	–	µs
t_{BUF}	Bus free time between a STOP and START condition	4.7	–	1.3	–	0.5	–	4.7	–	µs
t_{LOW}	Low interval of the SCL clock	4.7	–	1.3	–	0.5	–	4.7	–	µs
t_{HIGH}	High interval of the SCL clock	4.0	–	0.6	–	0.26	–	4.0	50	µs
t_r	Rise time of both SDA and SCL signals	–	1000	–	300	–	120	–	1000	ns
t_f	Fall time of both SDA and SCL signals	–	300	–	300	–	120	–	300	ns
$t_{HD:DAT}$	Data hold time	0	–	0	–	0	–	0.3	–	µs
$t_{VD:DAT}$	Data valid time	–	3.45	–	0.9	–	0.45	–	–	µs
$t_{SU:DAT}$	Data setup time	250	–	100	–	50	–	250	–	ns

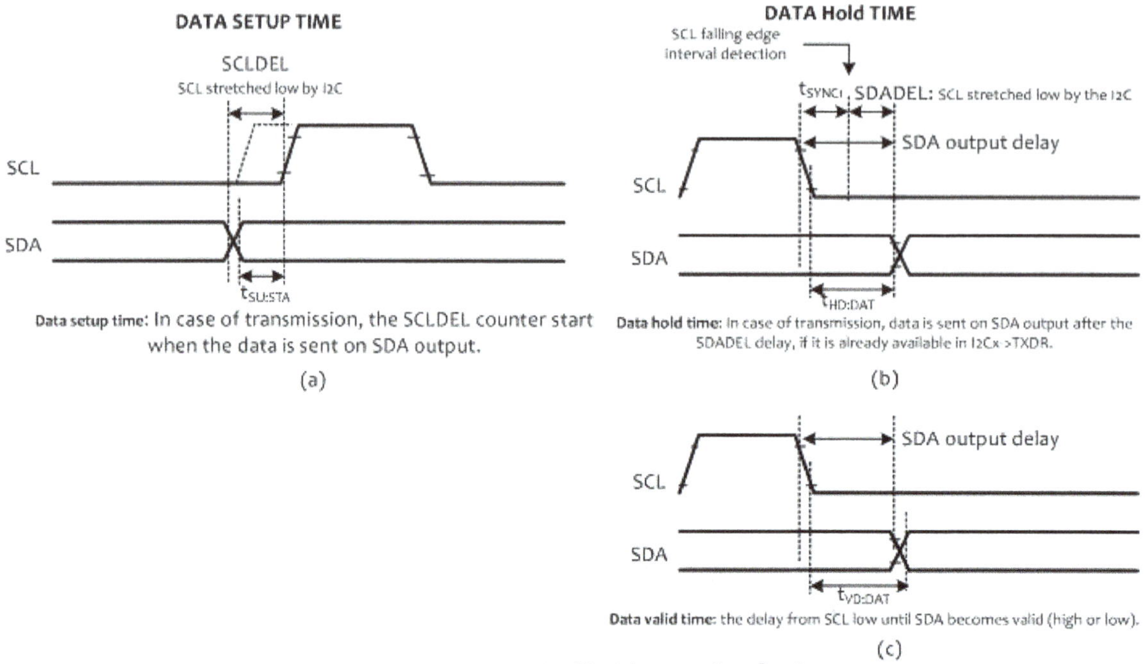

Figure 10.22 Data setup time and hold times for I²C data transmission

Data Hold Time Requirement

The data on the SDA line cannot change immediately after the SCL goes low. It needs to stay stable for at least $t_{HD:DAT}$ before it changes value to ensure correct data communication. In Figure 11.22b, the data hold time does not include the fall time of the SCL clock. After including the SCL fall time (t_f), it is called **data output delay** (t_{SDADEL}). This delay is provided by counting off the value in the SDADEL[3:0] field in the I2Cx->TIMINGR register. The contents of the I2Cx->TIMINGR register are shown in Figure 10.23.

The user must program the SDADEL parameter in a way that the following two requirements are satisfied:

$\{t_{f(max)} + t_{HD:DAT(min)} - t_{AF(min)} - [(DNF + 3) \times t_{I2CCLK}]\} / \{(PRESC + 1) \times t_{I2CCLK}\} \leq SDADEL$ --- (11.7)

$SDADEL \leq \{t_{HD:DAT(max)} - t_{AF(max)} - [(DNF + 4) \times t_{I2CCLK}]\} / \{(PRESC + 1) \times t_{I2CCLK}\}$ --- (11.8)

$t_{AF(min)}$ / $t_{AF(max)}$ are part of the equation only when the analog filter is enabled.

The maximum $t_{HD:DAT}$ is the maximum of $t_{VD:DAT}$ less of the SDA transition time (= max(t_r, t_f)). This maximum must only be met if the device does not stretch the LOW period (t_{LOW}) of the SCL signal. If the clock stretches the SCL, the data must be valid by the setup time before it releases the clock.

The SDA rising edge is usually the worst case, so in this case the previous equation becomes:

$SDADEL \leq \{t_{VD:DAT(max)} - t_{r(max)} - t_{AF(max)} - [(DNF + 4) \times t_{I2CCLK}]\} / \{(PRESC + 1) \times t_{I2CCLK}\}$ --- (11.9)

$t_{AF(max)}$ is part of the equation only if the analog filter is enabled.

31	30	29	28	27	26	25	24
PRESC[3:0]				--	--	--	--
23	**22**	**21**	**20**	**19**	**18**	**17**	**16**
SCLDEL[3:0]				SDADEL[3:0]			
15	**14**	**13**	**12**	**11**	**10**	**9**	**8**
SCLH[7:0]							
7	**6**	**5**	**4**	**3**	**2**	**1**	**0**
SCLL[7:0]							

Reset value = 0x0000 0000
Addr offset = 0x10

This register must be configured when the I²C is disabled (PE = 0).

PRESC[3:0]: Timing prescaler

This field is used to divide the I²CCLK clock to generate t_{PRESC} used for data setup and hold counters and for SCL high and low level counters.

$t_{PRESC} = (PRFESC + 1) \times t_{I2CCLK}$

SCLDEL[3:0]: Data setup time

This field is used to generate a delay t_{SCLDEL} between SDA edge and SCL rising edge. In master mode and in slave mode with NOSTRETCH = 0, the SCL line is stretched low during t_{SCLDEL}. $t_{SCLDEL} = (SCLDEL + 1) \times t_{PRESC}$. t_{SCLDEL} is used to generate $t_{SU:DAT}$ timing.

SDADEL[3:0]: Data hold time

This field is used to generate the delay t_{SDADEL} between SCL falling edge and SDA edge. In master mode and slave mode with NOSTRETCH=0, the SCL line is stretched low during t_{SDADEL}. $t_{SDADEL} = SDADEL \times t_{PRESC}$. SDADEL is used to generate $t_{HD:DAT}$ timing.

SCLH[7:0]: SCL high period (master mode)

This field is used to generate the SCL high period in master mode.

$t_{SCLH} = (SCLH + 1) \times t_{PRESC}$. SCLH is also used to generate $t_{SU:STO}$ and $t_{HD:STA}$ timing.

SCLL[7:0]: SCL low period (master mode)

This field is used to generate the SCL low period in master mode.

$t_{SCLL} = (SCLL + 1) \times t_{PRESC}$. SCLL is also used to generate t_{BUF} and $t_{SU:STA}$ timings.

Figure 11.23 I²C timing register (I²Cx->TIMINGR, x = 1, 2, or 3)

Example 11.2 Select a set of values to be programmed into the I2Cx->TIMINGR register so that the I²C module can operate at **fast mode** assuming that f_{I2CCLK} = 80 MHz.

Solution:

Set PRESC to 9. Enable analog filter and set DNF to 3. In Table 11.5, t_{rmax} = 300 ns, $t_{SU:DAT(min)}$ = 100 ns. t_{I2CCLK} = 12.5 ns for f_{I2CCLK} = 80 MHz

To select a value for SCLDEL, apply equation 11.6,

$SCLDEL \geq \{[t_{r(max)} + t_{SU:DAT(min)}] / [(PRESC + 1) \times t_{I2CCLK}]\} - 1$

SCLDEL ≥ (300 + 100)/(10 x 12.5) – 1 = 3.2 – 1 = 2.2 (**set SCLDEL to 3**)

To select a value for SDADEL, apply Equation 11.9:

$SDADEL \leq \{t_{VD:DAT(max)} - t_{r(max)} - 260 - [(DNF + 4) \times t_{I2CCLK}]\} / \{(PRESC + 1) \times t_{I2CCLK}\}$

In Table 11.5, $t_{VD:DAT(max)}$ = 900 ns, $t_{r(max)}$ = 300 ns. PRESC = 9, & t_{I2CCLK} = 12.5 ns.

Set DNF to 3, then the right-hand side of Equation 11.9 is

SDADEL ≤ [900 – 300 – 260 – (7 x 12.5)] / {(9 + 1) x 12.5} = 2.02 → **set SDADEL to 2**. This value also satisfies the requirement in Equation 11.7 (**SDADEL ≥ 1.4**).

To select a value for SCLL, $t_{SCLL(min)}$ = 1.3 ms ≤ (SCLL + 1) x 125 ns → **set SCLL to 10**

To select a value for SCLH, $t_{SCLH(min)}$ = 600 ns ≤ (SCLH + 1) x 125 ns → **set SCLH to 4**

The resultant SCL frequency is slightly less than 400 kHz.

Example 11.3 Select a set of values to be programmed into the I2Cx->TIMINGR register so that the I²C module can operate at **fast-mode-plus** assuming that f_{I2CCLK} = 80 MHz.

Solution:

One of the possible setting is as follows:

Set PRESC to 5, disable analog filter, set DNF to 2. t_{I2CCLK} = 12.5 ns. (PRESC + 1) ×t_{I2CCLK} = 75 ns.

To select a value for SCLDEL, apply Equation 11.6 and refer to Table 11.5,

$$SCLDEL \geq \{[t_{r(max)} + t_{SU:DAT(min)}] / [(PRESC + 1) \times t_{I2CCLK}]\} - 1$$

$$SCLDEL \geq \{[120ns + 50\ ns] / [(5 + 1) \times 12.5ns]\} - 1$$

SCLDEL ≥ 1.2 → set **SCLDEL to 2**

To select a value for SDADEL, apply Equations 11.7 and 11.8 and refer to Table 11.5,

$$SDADEL \geq \{t_{f(max)} + t_{HD:DAT(min)} - t_{AF(min)} - [(DNF + 3) \times t_{I2CCLK}]\} / \{(PRESC + 1) \times t_{I2CCLK}\}$$

$$SDADEL \geq 0.77$$

$$SDADEL \leq \{t_{VD:DAT(max)} - t_{r(max)} - t_{AF(max)} - [(DNF + 4) \times t_{I2CCLK}]\} / \{(PRESC + 1) \times t_{I2CCLK}\}$$

$$SDADEL \leq 3.4$$

Set **SDADEL to 2**

To select a value for SCLL, $t_{SCLL(min)}$ ≥ 500 ns → SCLL ≥ 5.6. Set **SCLL to 6**.

To select a value for SCLH, $t_{SCLH(min)}$ ≥ 260 ns → SCLH ≥ 2.5. Set **SCLH to 3**.

Example 11.4 Write a C statement to configure the I2C2->TIMINGR register using the timing parameters computed in Example 11.2.

Solution:

In Example 11.3, PRESC = 9, SCLDEL = 3, SDADEL = 2, SCLH = 4, and SCLL = 10

The C statement is as follows:

```
I2C2->TIMINGR = (9 << I2C_TIMINGR_PRESC_Pos) + (3 << I2C_TIMINGR_SCLDEL_Pos) +
                (2 << I2C_TIMINGR_SDADEL_Pos) + (4 << I2C_TIMINGR_SCLH_Pos) +
                (10 << I2C_TIMINGR_SCLL_Pos);
```

11.5 Data Transfer in I2C

Data transfer is managed through transmit and receive data registers and a shift register. Depending on whether the I²C module initiates or reacts to the transfer and the direction of data transfer, the I²C module may operate in four different modes:

- Master transmitter
- Master receiver
- Slave transmitter
- Slave receiver

By default, the I²C module operates in slave mode. The interface automatically switches from slave to master when it generates a START condition, and from master to slave if an arbitration loss or a STOP condition occurs.

11.5.1 DATA RECEPTION

Input data are shifted in from the SDA line. After the 8th SCL pulse, the shift register is copied into the I2Cx->RXDR register if it is empty. The I2Cx->RXDR register is empty if the RXNE bit in the I2Cx->ISR register is 0. If the RXNE bit is 1, the SCL line is stretched low until the CPU reads the I2Cx->RXDR register. This situation is illustrated in Figure 11.24.

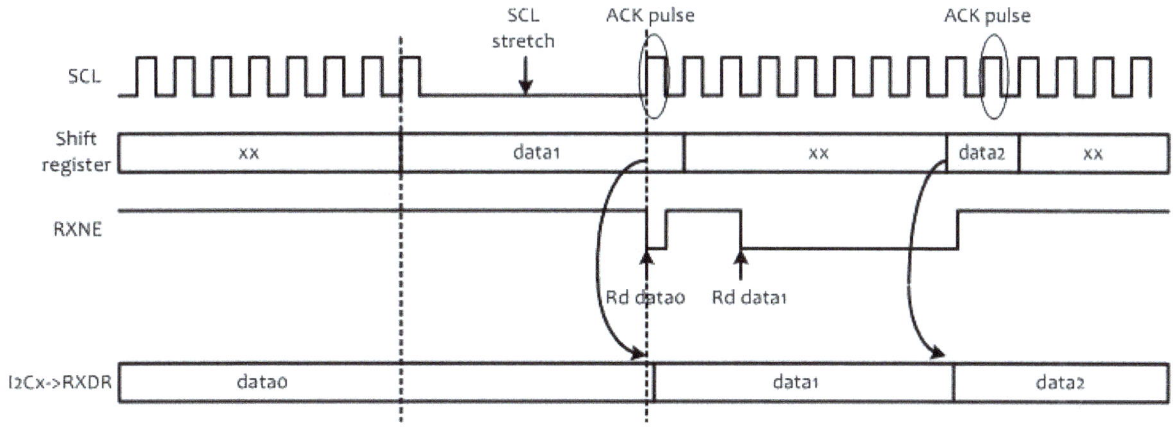

Figure 11.24 I2C data reception example

11.5.2 DATA TRANSMISSION

When the TXE bit in the I2Cx->ISR register is 1, the CPU can write a byte into the I2Cx->TXDR register. If the TXE bit is 1, the SCL line will be stretched low until the I2Cx->TXDR register is written into. Once the I2Cx->TXDR register is written into, its contents will be copied to the shift register if the shift register is not busy shifting. It takes 8 SCL pulses to shift out the data in the shift register, and the I^{2}C module expects to get back an ACK pulse in the 9th SCL pulse. This process is illustrated in Figure 11.25. The contents of the I2Cx->ISR register are shown in Figure 11.26.

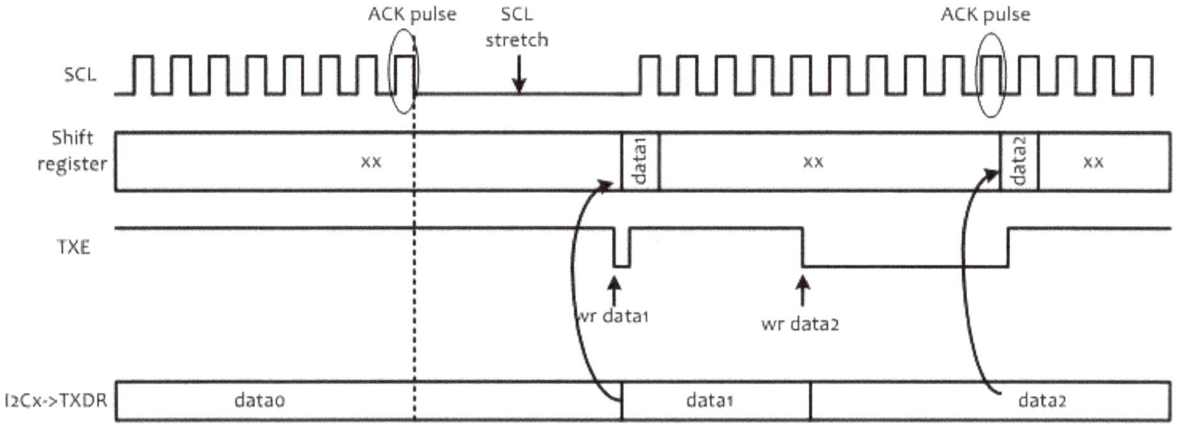

Figure 11.25 I^{2}C data transmission process

11.5.3 COMMUNICATION FLOW

In master mode, the I^{2}C module initiates a data transfer and generates the SCL signal. An I^{2}C transfer always begins with a START condition and ends with a STOP condition. Both conditions must be generated by the software. In slave mode, I^{2}C can recognize its own address (7-bit or 10-bit), and the general call address (all 0s). The general call and SMBus addresses can be enabled and disabled by software. The I^{2}C module is enabled by setting the PE bit in the I2Cx->CR1 register. The contents of the I2Cx->CR1 register are shown in Figure 11.27.

31	30	29	28	27	26	25	24
--	--	--	--	--	--	--	--
23	**22**	**21**	**20**	**19**	**18**	**17**	**16**
ADDCODE[6:0]							DIR
15	**14**	**13**	**12**	**11**	**10**	**9**	**8**
BUSY	--	ALERT	TIMEOUT	PECERR	OVR	ARLO	BERR
7	**6**	**5**	**4**	**3**	**2**	**1**	**0**
TCR	TC	STOPF	NACKF	ADDR	RXNE	TXIS	TXE

Reset value = 0x0000 0001
Addr offset = 0x18

ADDCODE[6:0]: Address match code (Slave mode)
These bits are updated with the received address when an address match event occurs (ADDR=1). In the case of a 10-bit address, ADDCODE provides the 10-bit header followed by the 2 msbs of the address

DIR: transfer direction (slave mode)
This flag is updated when an address match event occurs (ADDR=1)
0: Write transfer, slave enters receiver mode
1: Read transfer, slave enters transmitter mode

BUSY: Bus busy
This flag indicates that a communication is in progress on the bus. It is set when a START condition is detected. It is cleared when a STOP condition is detected, or when PE = 0.

ALERT: SMBus alert (SMBus mode only)
This flag is when SMBHEN=1, ALERTEN=1 and a SMBALERT event (falling edge) is detected on SMBA pin. It is cleared by setting the ALERTCF bit.

TIMEOUT: Timeout or t_{LOW} detection flag (SMBus mode only)
This flag is set when a timeout or extended clock timeout occurred. It is cleared by setting the TIMEOUTCF bit.

PECERR: PEC error in reception (SMBus mode only)
This flag is set when the received PEC does not match with the PEC register content. A NACK is automatically sent after the wrong PEC reception. It is cleared by writing a 1 to the PECCF bit.

Figure 11.26 I²C interrupt and status register (I²Cx->ISR)

31	30	29	28	27	26	25	24
--	--	--	--	--	--	--	--
23	**22**	**21**	**20**	**19**	**18**	**17**	**16**
ADDCODE[6:0]							DIR
15	**14**	**13**	**12**	**11**	**10**	**9**	**8**
BUSY	--	ALERT	TIMEOUT	PECERR	OVR	ARLO	BERR
7	**6**	**5**	**4**	**3**	**2**	**1**	**0**
TCR	TC	STOPF	NACKF	ADDR	RXNE	TXIS	TXE

Reset value = 0x0000 0001
Addr offset = 0x18

TCR: Transfer complete reload
Transfer complete (master mode)
This flag is set when RELOAD=1, and NBYTES data have been transferred.
It is cleared when NBYTES field is written to a non-zero value.

TC: Transfer complete
This flag is set when RELOAD=0, AUTOEND=0 and NBYTES data have been transferred.
It is cleared when START bit or STOP bit is set.

STOPF: Stop detection flag
This flag is set when a STOP condition is detected on the bus and the peripheral is involved in the transfer: (1) either as a master, provided that the STOP condition is generated by the peripheral (2)as a slave, provided that the peripheral has been addressed previously during this transfer

NACKF: Not acknowledge received flag
This flag is set when a NACK is received after a byte transmission. It is cleared by writing a 1 to the NACKCF bit.

ADDR: Address matched (slave mode)
This bit is set as soon as the received slave address matched with one of the enabled slave addresses. It is cleared by writing a 1 to the ADDRCF bit.

RXNE: Receive data register not empty (receivers)
This bit is set whenever the received data is copied into the I2Cx->RXDR register, and is ready to be read. It is cleared when I2Cx->RXDR is read.

TXIS: Transmit interrupt status (transmitters)
This bit is set when the I2Cx->TXDR register is empty and the data to be transmitted must be written in the I2Cx->TXDR register. It is cleared when the data is written into I2Cx->TXDR register.

TXE: Transmit data register is empty (transmitters)
This bit is set to 1 when the I2Cx->TXDR register is empty. This bit can be written to 1 by software in order to flush the transmit data register I2Cx->TXDR.

Figure 11.26a I^2C interrupt and status register (I^2Cx->ISR)—(continued)

31	30	29	28	27	26	25	24
--	--	--	--	--	--	--	--
23	**22**	**21**	**20**	**19**	**18**	**17**	**16**
PECEN	ALERTEN	SMBDEN	SMBHEN	GCEN	WUPEN	NOSTRETCH	SBC
15	**14**	**13**	**12**	**11**	**10**	**9**	**8**
RXDMAEN	TXDMAEN	--	ANFOFF	DNF			
7	**6**	**5**	**4**	**3**	**2**	**1**	**0**
ERRIE	TCIE	STOPIE	NACKIE	ADDRIE	RXIE	TXIE	PE

Reset value = 0x0000 0000
Addr offset = 0x00

PECEN: PEC enable (an SMBus feature only)
  0: PEC calculation disabled 1: PEC calculation enabled
ALERTEN: SMBus alert enable
  0: SMBus alert disabled
  1: Drives SMBus pin low and alert response address header enables: 0000 1100xx followed by ACK.
SMBDEN: SMBus device default address enable (only used for SMBus)
  0: Device default address disabled. Address 0b1100001x is NACKed.
  1: Device default address enabled. Address 0b1100001x is ACKed.
SMBHEN: SMBus host address enable
  0: Host address disabled. 0b0001000x is NACKed.
  1: Host address enabled. Address 0b0001000x is ACKed.
GCEN: General call enable
  0: General call disabled. Address 0b00000000 is NACKed
  1: General call enabled. Address 0b00000000 is ACKed
WUPEN: wakeup from stop mode enable
  0: Wakeup from stop mode disabled 1: Wakeup from stop mode enabled
NOSTRETCH: Clock stretching disable
  0: Clock stretching enabled 1: Clock stretching enabled
SBC: Slave byte control (used to enable hardware byte control in slave mode)
  0: Slave byte control disabled 1: slave byte control enabled
RXDMAEN: DMA reception requests enable
  0: DMA mode disabled for reception 1: DMA mode enabled for reception
TXDMAEN: DMA transmission requests enable
  0: DMA mode disabled for transmission 1: DMA mode enabled for transmission
ANFOFF: Analog noise filter OFF
  0: Analog noise filter enabled 1: Analog noise filter disabled

Figure 11.27 I^2C control register 1 (I^2Cx->CR1)

31	30	29	28	27	26	25	24
--	--	--	--	--	--	--	--
23	**22**	**21**	**20**	**19**	**18**	**17**	**16**
PECEN	ALERTEN	SMBDEN	SMBHEN	GCEN	WUPEN	NOSTRETCH	SBC
15	**14**	**13**	**12**	**11**	**10**	**9**	**8**
RXDMAEN	TXDMAEN	--	ANFOFF	DNF			
7	**6**	**5**	**4**	**3**	**2**	**1**	**0**
ERRIE	TCIE	STOPIE	NACKIE	ADDRIE	RXIE	TXIE	PE

Reset value = 0x0000 0000
Addr offset = 0x00

DNF: Digital noise filter—digital filter, when enabled, will filter spikes with a length of up to DNF[3:0] * t_{I2CCLK}. If analog is also enabled, digital filter is added to analog filter

0000: Digital filter disabled

0001: Digital filter enabled and filtering capability up to 1 t_{I2CCLK}

....

1111: Digital filter enabled and filtering capability up to 15 t_{I2CCLK}.

ERRIE: Error interrupts enable (ARLO, BERR, OVR, TIMEOUT, PECERR, ALERT)

0: Error detection interrupts disabled 1: Error detection interrupts enabled

TCIE: Transfer complete interrupt enable

0: Transfer complete interrupt disabled 1: Transfer complete interrupt enabled

STOPIE: STOP detection interrupt enable

0: Stop detection (STOPF) interrupt disabled

1: Stop detection (STOPF) interrupt enabled

NACKIE: Not acknowledge received interrupt enable

0: NACKF received interrupts disabled 1: NACK received interrupts enabled

ADDRIE: Address match interrupt enable (slave only)

0: Address match (ADDR) interrupts disabled

1: Address match (ADDR) interrupts enabled

RXIE: RX interrupt enable

0: Receive (RXNE) interrupt disabled 1: Receive (RXNE) interrupt enabled

TXIE: TX interrupt enable

0: Transmit (TXIS) interrupt disabled 1: Transmit (TXIS) interrupt enabled

PE: peripheral enable (I2C module enable)

0: Peripheral disable 1: Peripheral enable

When PE = 0, the I2C SCL and SDA lines are released

Figure 11.27a I^2C control register 1 (I^2Cx->CR1)—(continued 1)

11.5.4 MASTER COMMUNICATION INITIALIZATION

To initiate communication using the I²C, the user must program the following parameters for the addressed slave in the I2Cx->CR2 register:

- Address mode (ADD10): Select 7-bit or 10-bit slave address
- Slave address (SDAA[9:0]) to be sent
- Transfer direction (RD_WRN)
- HEAD10R bit: This is in case of 10-bit address read. The user must configure the HEAD10R bit to indicate whether to send the complete address sequence or only the 10-bit header in case of a direction change.
- The number of bytes to be transferred (NBYTES[7:0]). If the number of bytes to be transferred is equal to or greater than 255 bytes, NBYTES[7:0] must be initially filled with 0xFF.

After the previous parameters have been programmed, the user sets the START bit in the I2Cx->CR2 register to start the data transfer. All the above bit fields cannot be changed when the START bit is set. The contents of the I2Cx->CR2 register are shown in Figure 11.28.

31	30	29	28	27	26	25	24
--	--	--	--	--	PECBYTE	AUTOEND	RELOAD
23	22	21	20	19	18	17	16
NBYTES							
15	14	13	12	11	10	9	8
NACK	STOP	START	HEAD10R	ADD10	RD_WRN	SADD[9:8]	
7	6	5	4	3	2	1	0
SADD[7:0]							

Reset value = 0x0000 0000
Addr offset = 0x04

PECBYTE: packet error checking byte (this bit has no effect in slave mode when SBC=0)
0: No PEC transfer
1: PEC transmission/reception is requested
AUTOEND: Automatic end mode (has effect only in master mode)
0: software end mode. TC flag is set when NBYTES data are transferred, stretching SCL low.
1: Automatic end mode. A stop condition is automatically sent when NBYTES data are transferred.
RELOAD: NBYTES reload mode
0: The transfer is completed after the NBYTES data transfer (STOP or RESTART will follow).
1: The transfer is not completed after NBYTES data transfer (NBYTES will be reloaded). TCR flag is set when NBYTES data are transferred, stretching SCL low.
NBYTES: number of bytes
The number of bytes to be transferred/received is programmed here. This field is don't care in slave mode with SBC=0.
NACK: NACK generation (slave mode)
0: an ACK is sent after current received byte
1: an NACK is sent after the current received byte
When an overrun occurs in slave receiver NOSTRETCH mode, a NACK is automatically generated whatever the NACK value.

Figure 11.28 I²C control register 2 (I²Cx->CR2)

31	30	29	28	27	26	25	24
--	--	--	--	--	PECBYTE	AUTOEND	RELOAD
23	22	21	20	19	18	17	16
NBYTES							
15	14	13	12	11	10	9	8
NACK	STOP	START	HEAD10R	ADD10	RD_WRN	SADD[9:8]	
7	6	5	4	3	2	1	0
SADD[7:0]							

Reset value = 0x0000 0000
Addr offset = 0x04

STOP: Stop generation (used in master mode)
- 0: No stop generation 1: stop generation after current byte transfer

START: Start generation
- 0: No start generation 1: Restart/start generation
- If the I²C is already in master mode with AUTORELOAD = 0, setting this bit generates a RESTART condition when RELOAD=0, at the end of NBYTES transfer. Otherwise, setting this bit will generate a START condition once the bus is free.

HEAD10R: 10-bit address header only read direction (master receiver mode)
- 0: The master sends the complete 10-bit slave address sequence—Start + 2 bytes 10-bit address in write direction + Restart + 1st 7 bits of the 10-bit address, followed by Read direction
- 1: The master only sends the 1st 7 bits of the 10-bit address, followed by Read direction.

ADD10: 10-bit addressing mode (valid in master mode)
- 0: The master operates in 7-bit addressing mode
- 1: The master operates in 10-bit addressing mode

RD_WRN: Transfer direction
- 0: Master requests a write transfer
- 1: Master requests a read transfer

SADD[9:8]: Slave address bit 9:8 (valid in master mode)
- In 7-bit addressing mode (ADD10=0): these bits are don't care
- in 10-bit addressing mode (ADD10=1): These two bits are the bit 9:8 of the slave.

SADD[7:1]: Slave address bit 7:1 (valid in master mode)
- In 7-bit addressing mode: These bits should be written with the 7-bit slave address.
- In 10-bit address mode: These bits should be written with the slave address bits 7:1.

SADD0: Slave address bit 0
- In 7-bit addressing mode: don't care. In 10-bit addressing: the bit 0 of the slave address.

Figure 11.28a I²C control register 2 (I²Cx->CR2)—(continued 1)

Once the START bit in the I2Cx->CR2 register is set, the master I²C circuit automatically sends the START condition followed by the slave address as soon as it detects that the bus is free (BUSY bit = 0) and after a delay of t_{BUF}(Table 11.5).

In case of an arbitration loss, the master automatically switches back to slave mode and can acknowledge its address if it is addressed as a slave. The START bit is cleared once the slave address has been sent. The START bit is also reset if an arbitration loss occurs.

The same procedure applies to a RESTART condition. I²C data communication should be interrupt driven.

11.5.5 INITIALIZATION OF A MASTER RECEIVER ADDRESSING 10-BIT ADDRESS SLAVE

If 10-bit slave address is used, the user can choose to send the complete read sequence by clearing the HEAD10R bit in the I2Cx->CR2 register. In this case, the master sends START + slave address 10-bit header Write + slave address 2nd byte + RESTART + slave address 10-bit header Read. A 10-bit address read access with HEAD10R=0 is shown in Figure 11.29.

Figure 11.29 10-bit address read access with HEAD10R=0

If the master addresses a 10-bit address slave, transmits data to this slave, and then reads data from the same slave, a master transmission flow must be done first. Then a restart is set with the 10-bit slave address configured with HEAD10R=1. In this case, the master sends this sequence: RESTART + slave address 10-bit header Read. A 10-bit address read after write to the same slave is shown in Figure 11.30.

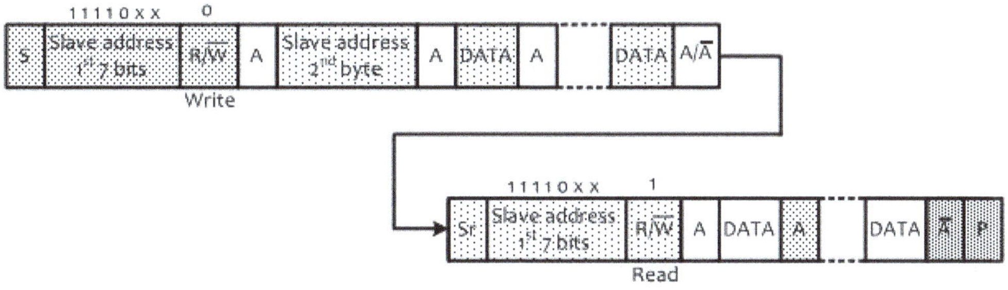

Figure 11.30 10-bit address read access with HEAD10R=1

11.5.6 HARDWARE TRANSFER MANAGEMENT

I²C has a byte counter to manage byte transfer and to close communication in various modes such as:

- NACK, STOP, and RESTART generation in master mode
- ACK control in slave receiver mode
- PEC generation/checking when SMBus feature is supported

The byte counter is always used in master mode. Byte counter is disabled in slave mode by default, but it can be enabled by setting the SBC (slave byte control) bit in the I2Cx->CR2 register.

The number of bytes to be transferred is written into the NBYTES[7:0] field in the I2Cx->CR2 register. If the number of bytes to be transferred is greater than 255, or if a receiver wants to control the ACK value of a received data byte, the reload mode must be selected by setting the RELOAD bit in the I2Cx->CR2 register. In the reload mode, the TCR flag will be set to 1 once the number of bytes programmed in the NBYTES field has been transferred, and an optional interrupt may be requested. The SCL clock is stretched as long as the TCR flag is set. The TCR flag is cleared when a non-zero value is written into the NBYTES field. When the NBYTES counter is reloaded with the last number of bytes, the RELOAD bit must be cleared.

In master mode with the RELOAD bit cleared, the byte counter can be used in two modes:

1. **Automatic end mode.** This mode is selected when the AUTOEND bit in the I2Cx->CR2 register is 1. In this mode, the master automatically sends a STOP condition once the number of bytes programmed in the NBYTES[7:0] field has been transferred. An example of an I²C master transmitter that transmits two bytes in automatic end mode is shown in Figure 11.31.
2. **Software end mode.** This mode is selected by setting the AUTOEND bit to 0. Software action is expected once the number of bytes programmed in the NBYTES[7:0] field has been transferred. The TC flag is set, and an interrupt is generated if the TCIE bit is set. The SCL signal is stretched as long as the TC flag is set. The TC flag is cleared if the START or STOP bit in the I2Cx->CR2 register is set. This mode must be used if the master wants to send a RESTART condition. An example of this mode is shown in Figure 11.32.

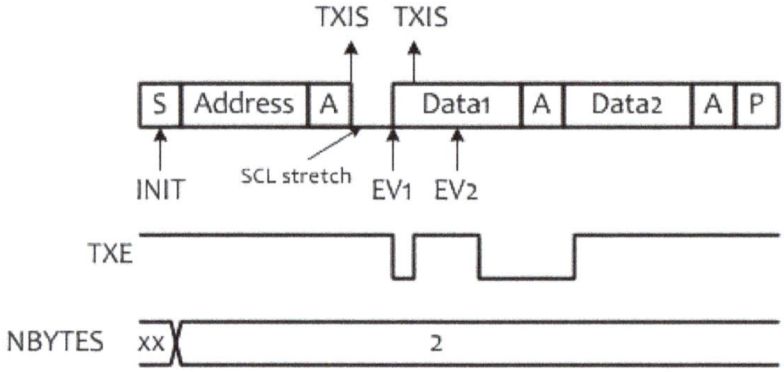

INIT: program slave address, set NBYTES = 2, set AUTOEND to 1, set START
EV1: TXIS ISR (interrupt service routine): write data1
EV2: TXIS ISR: write data2
P: STOP condition is generated automatically.

Figure 11.31 Example of master transmitter transmits 2 bytes in automatic end mode

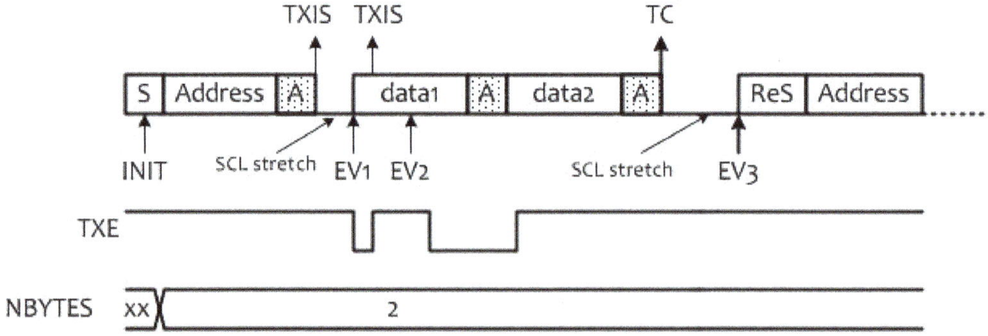

INIT: program slave address, set NBYTES = 2, set AUTOEND to 0, set START
EV1: TXIS ISR (interrupt service routine): write data1
EV2: TXIS ISR: write data2
EV3: TC ISR: program slave address, program NBYTES = N, set START

Figure 11.32 Example of master transmitter transmits 2 bytes in software end mode

11.5.7 MASTER TRANSMITTER

The TXIS flag is set after each byte transmission, after the 9th SCL pulse when an ACK is received. An interrupt may be generated if the TXIE bit in the I2Cx->CR1 register is also set. The flag is cleared if the CPU writes the next data byte into the I2Cx->TXDR register. The TXIS flag is not set when a NACK is received.

If the total number of bytes to be sent is greater than 255, reload mode must be selected by setting the RELOAD bit in the I2Cx->CR2 register. In this case, when NBYTES[7:0] bytes of data have been transferred, the TCR flag is set and the SCL line is stretched low until the NBYTES[7:0] field is written to a non-zero value.

When the RELOAD bit is 0 and NBYTES of data have been transferred:

- In automatic end mode, a STOP condition is automatically sent.
- In software end mode, the TC flag in the I2Cx->ISR register is set and the SCL line is stretched low in order to perform software actions:
    - A RESTART condition can be requested by setting the START bit in the I2Cx->CR2 register with the proper slave address configuration and the number of bytes to be transferred.
    - A STOP condition can be requested by setting the STOP bit in the I2Cx->CR2 register. Setting the STOP bit clears the TC flag, and the STOP condition is sent on the I²C bus.

If a NACK is received and the TXIS flag is not set, a STOP condition is automatically sent. The NACKF flag in the I2Cx->ISR register is set, and an interrupt may be generated if the NACKIE bit is set.

The transmission processes for I²C master with NBYTES ≤ 255 and NBYTES > 255 are illustrated in Figure 11.33 and 11.34, respectively.

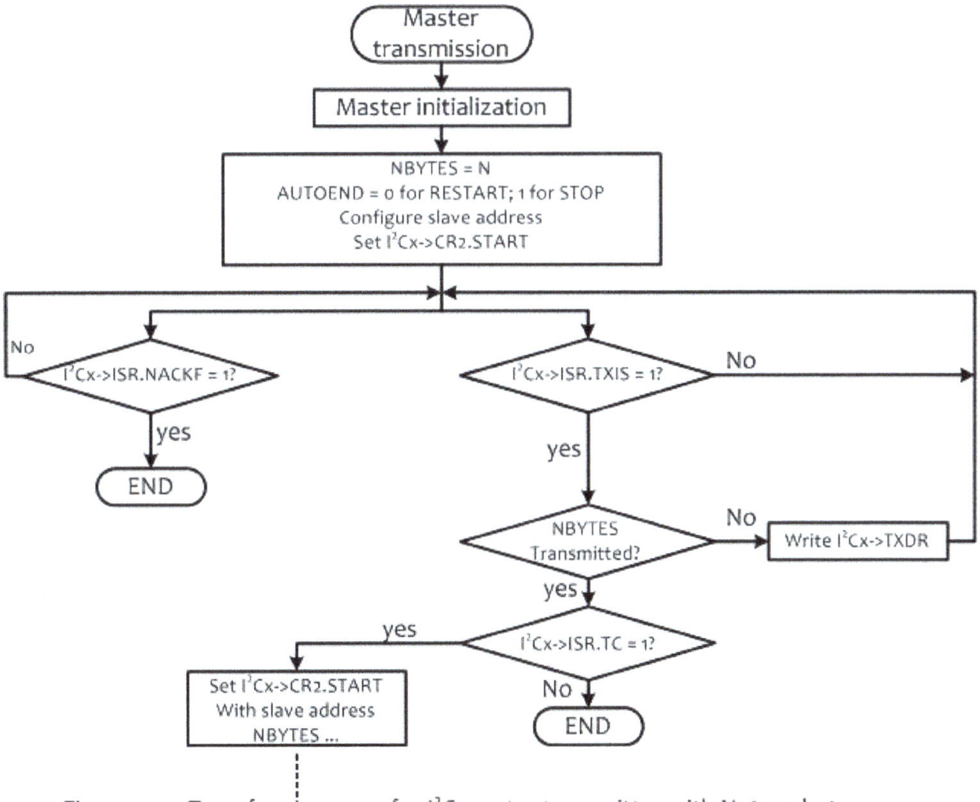

Figure 11.33 Transfer sequence for I²C master transmitter with N ≤ 255 bytes

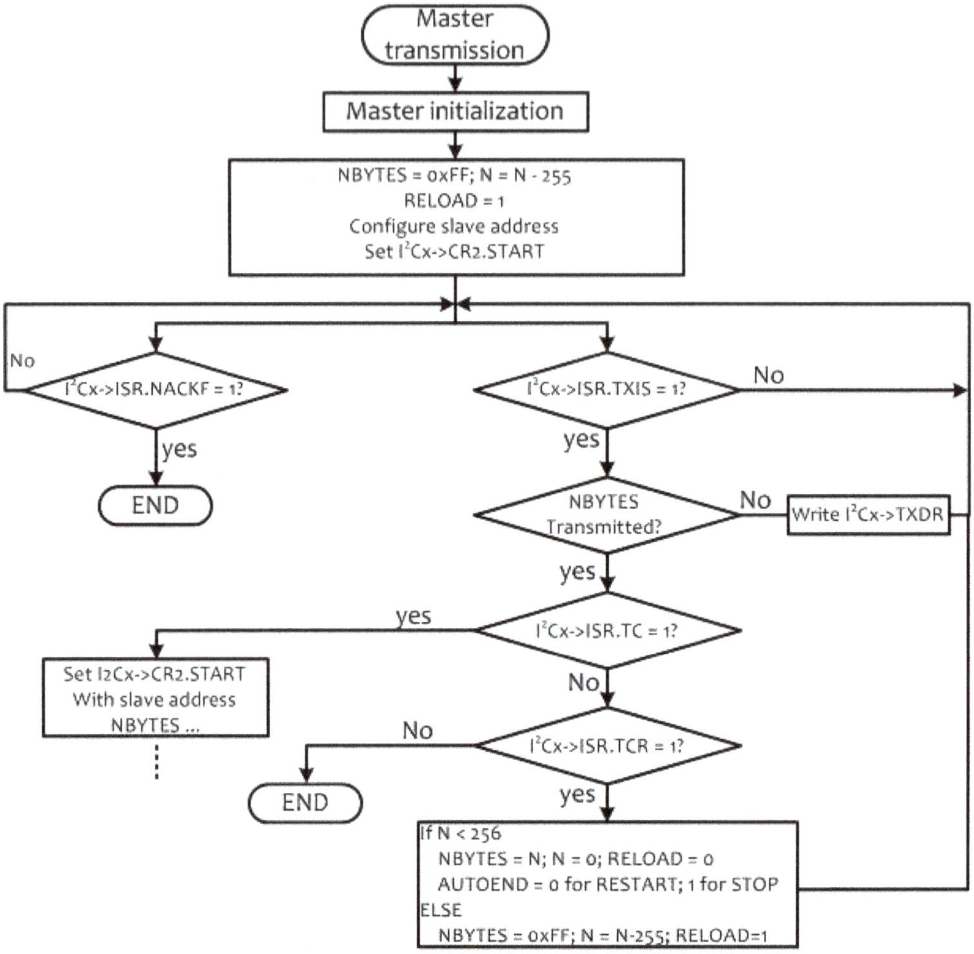

Figure 11.34 Transfer sequence for I²C master transmitter with N > 255 bytes

11.5.8 MASTER RECEIVER

The RXNE flag is set after the reception of each byte. An interrupt will be generated if the RXIE flag in the I2Cx->CR1 register is set. The RXNE flag is cleared when the I2Cx->RXDR register is read.

If the total number of bytes to be received is greater than 255, reload mode must be selected by setting the RELOAD bit in the I2Cx->CR2 register. In this case, when NBYTES[7:0] data bytes have been transferred, the TCR flag is set and the SCL line is stretched low until a nonzero value is written into the NBYTES[7:0] field.

When the RELOAD bit is 0 and NBYTES[7:0] bytes have been transferred, there are two possible situations:

- In automatic end mode (AUTOEND bit = 1), a NACK and a STOP condition are automatically sent after the last received byte. An example of the master receiving two bytes in automatic stop mode is illustrated in Figure 11.35.
- In software end mode (AUTOEND bit = 0), a NACK is automatically sent after the last received byte, the TC flag is set, and the SCL line is stretched low in order to allow the software to take one of the following two actions:

1) Generate a RESTART condition by setting the START bit in the I2Cx->CR2 register with the proper slave address configuration and the number of bytes to be transferred. Setting the START bit clears the TC flag. After that, the START condition and the slave address are sent on the I²C bus.
2) Generate a STOP condition by setting the STOP bit in the I2Cx->CR2 register. Setting the STOP bit clears the TC flag, and the STOP condition is sent on the I²C bus.

An example of the I²C master receiving two bytes in software end mode is illustrated in Figure 11.36.

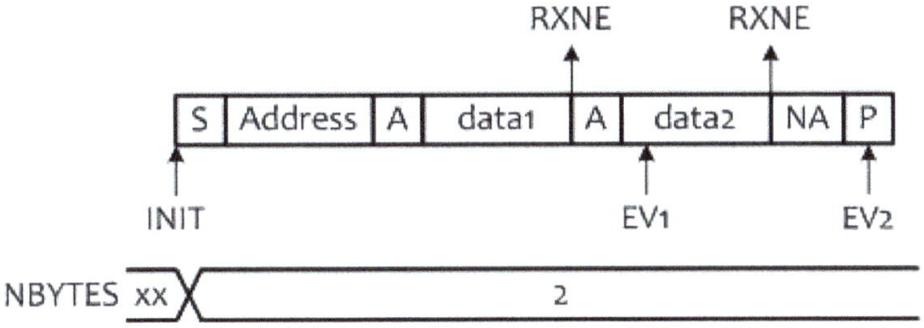

INIT: program slave address, program NBYTES to 2, AUTOEND to 1, set START bit
EV1: RXNE ISR (interrupt service routine): read data1
EV2: RXNE ISR: read data2

Figure 11.35 Example of I2C master receiving 2 bytes in automatic end mode

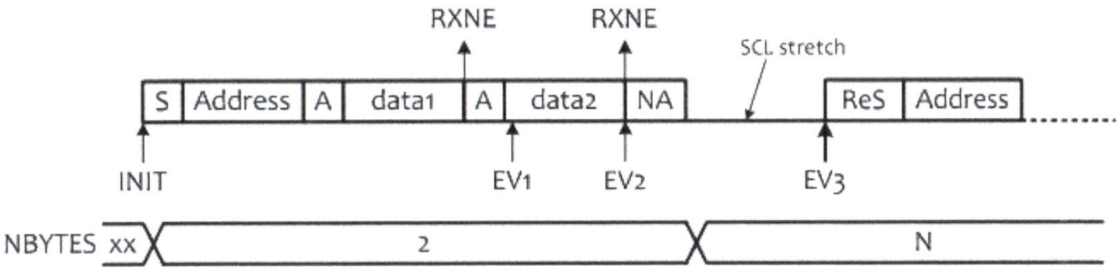

INIT: program slave address, program NBYTES to 2, AUTOEND to 1, set START bit
EV1: RXNE ISR (interrupt service routine): read data1
EV2: RXNE ISR: read data2
EV3: TC ISR: program slave address, program NBYTES to N, set START bit

Figure 11.36 Example of I²C master receiving 2 bytes in software end mode

The transfer sequence flowchart for I²C master receiver for receiving no more than 255 bytes and more than 255 bytes are shown in Figure 11.37 and Figure 11.38, respectively.

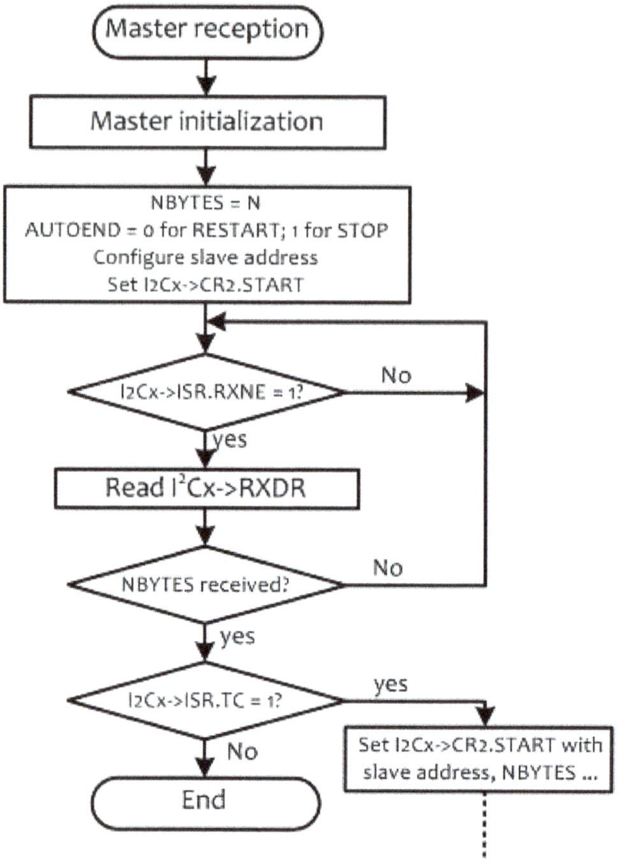

Figure 11.37 Transaction sequence for I²C master receiver with N ≤ 255 bytes

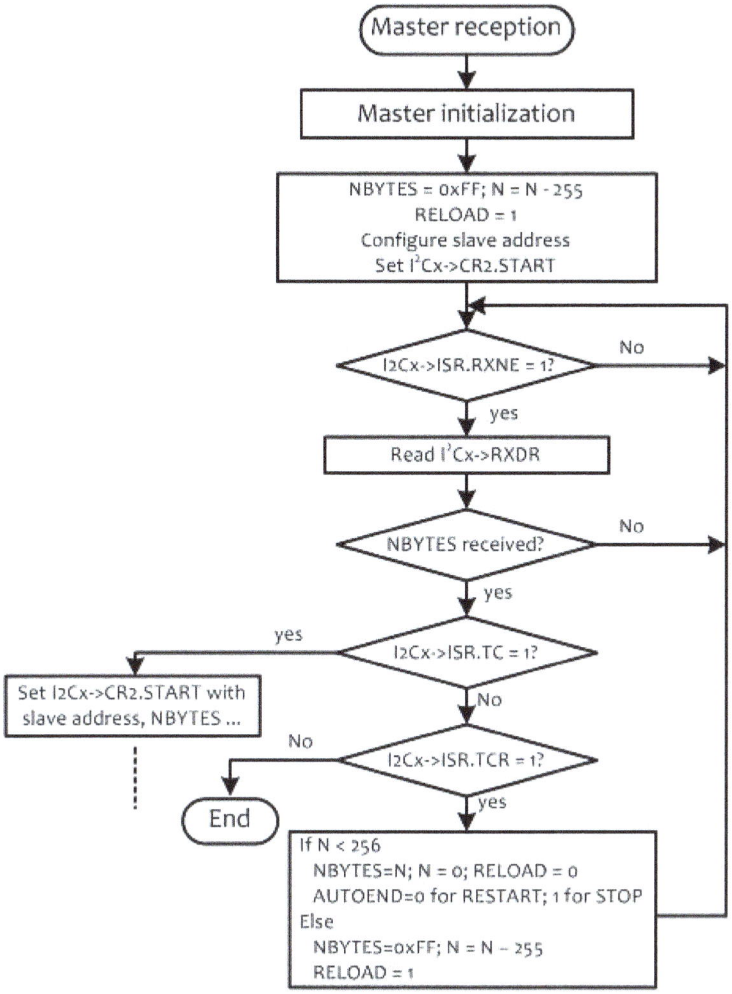

Figure 11.38 Transaction sequence for I²C master receiver with N > 255 bytes

11.6 I2C DMA Requests

Both transmission and reception can take advantage of the DMA capability.

11.6.1 TRANSMISSION USING DMA

The user must set the TXDMAEN bit in the I2Cx->CR1 register in order to use DMA for I²C transmission. Data are loaded from an SRAM area to the I2Cx->TXDR register whenever the TXIS bit is set.

Only data are transferred with DMA. In master mode, the slave address, direction, number of bytes, and the START bit are programmed by software. When all data are transferred using DMA, the DMA must be initialized before setting the START bit. The end of transfer is managed with NBYTES counter. If DMA is used for transmission, then the TXIE bit does not need to be set.

In slave mode, DMA must be initialized before the address match event disregarding the setting of the NOSTRETCH bit in the I2Cx->CR1 register.

11.6.2 RECEPTION USING DMA

I^2C reception is made possible by setting the RXDMAEN bit in the I2Cx->CR1 register. Data are transferred from the I2Cx->RXDR register to an SRAM area whenever the RXNE bit is set.

In master mode, the initialization, the slave address, direction, number of bytes, and START bit are programmed by software. When all data are transferred using DMA, the DMA must be initialized before setting the START bit. The end of transfer is managed with the NBYTES counter.

In slave mode with the NOSTRETCH bit cleared, the DMA must be initialized before the address match event or, in the ADDR interrupt service routine, before clearing the ADDR flag.

11.7 I2C Interrupts

Two interrupt vectors (I^2Cx_EV and I^2Cx_ER, x = 1, 2, or 3) are assigned to each I^2C module. The I^2Cx_EV vector is responsible for handling I^2C events, whereas the I^2Cx_ER vector is responsible for handling errors. All the I^2C interrupt requests are listed in Table 11.6. The I^2C interrupt handlers are:

- void I2C1_EV_IRQHandler (void);
- void I2C1_ER_IRQHandler (void);
- void I2C2_EV_IRQHandler (void);
- void I2C2_ER_IRQHandler (void);
- void I2C3_EV_IRQHandler (void);
- void I2C3_ER_IRQHandler (void);

Table 11.6 I^2C Interrupt requests

Type	Interrupt source	flag	Flag clearing method	Interrupt enable bit
Event	Receive buffer not empty	RXNE	Read I2Cx->RXDR register	RXIE
	Transmit buffer empty	TXIS	Write I2Cx->TXDR register	TXIE
	Stop detection interrupt flag	STOPF	Write 1 to STOPCF bit	STOPIE
	Transfer complete reload	TCR	Write I2Cx->CR2 with NBYTES[7:0] ≠ 0	TCIE
	Transfer complete	TC	Write START = 1 or STOP = 1	TCIE
	Address matched	ADDR	Write 1 to ADDRCF bit	ADDRIE
	NACK reception	NACKF	Write 1 to NACKCF bit	NACKIE
Error	Bus error	BERR	Write 1 to BERRCF bit	ERRIE
	Arbitration loss	ARLO	Write 1 to ARLOCF bit	
	Overrun/underrun	OVR	Write 1 to OVRCF bit	
	PEC error	PECERR	Write 1 to PECERRCF bit	
	Timeout/t_{LOW} error	TIMEOUT	Write 1 to TIMEOUTCF bit	
	SMBus Alert	ALERT	Write 1 to ALERTCF bit	

Example 11.5 Write a sequence of C statements to enable RXNE, TXIS, TCR, TC, and NACKF interrupts from the I2C module.

Solution:

```
I2C2->CR1 |= I2C_CR1_RXIE + I2C_CR1_TXIE + I2C_CR1_TCIE + I2C_CR1_NACKIE;
NVIC_EnableIRQ (I2C2_EV_IRQn);
NVIC_SetPriority (I2C2_EV_IRQn, 0);
__enable_irq ();
```

Example 11.6 Write a C function to configure the I²C2 module using PB10 and PB11 pins for SCL and SDA lines, setting f_{SCL} to 400 kHz assuming that f_{I2CCLk} may be either 80 MHz or 48 MHz. Many peripheral chips only support up to 400-kHz I²C frequency. Enable analog filter and set DNF to 3.

Solution: To choose the I²C clock source frequency, use the argument **fs**. When fs = 1, $f_{I2C2CLK}$ = 80MHz. Otherwise, $f_{I2C2CLK}$ = 48MHz.

```
void i2C2Init(uint32_t fs)
{
// configure PB10~PB11 for alternate function
    GPIOB->MODER  &= ~(GPIO_MODER_MODE10 + GPIO_MODER_MODE11);
    GPIOB->MODER  |=  GPIO_MODER_MODE10_1 + GPIO_MODER_MODE11_1;
// assign PB10~PB11 to AF4
    GPIOB->AFR[1]   &= ~(GPIO_AFRH_AFSEL10 + GPIO_AFRH_AFSEL11);
    GPIOB->AFR[1]   |=  GPIO_AFRH_AFSEL10_2 + GPIO_AFRH_AFSEL11_2;
// configure PB10~PB11 to open drain
    GPIOB->OTYPER |=  GPIO_OTYPER_OT10 + GPIO_OTYPER_OT11;
    if(fs == 0) // fI2CCLK = 48 MHz
        I2C2->TIMINGR = (5 << I2C_TIMINGR_PRESC_Pos) +
                (3 << I2C_TIMINGR_SCLDEL_Pos) + (3 << I2C_TIMINGR_SDADEL_Pos) +
                (3 << I2C_TIMINGR_SCLH_Pos) +
                (9 << I2C_TIMINGR_SCLL_Pos); // tSYNC1 + tSYNC2 = 250 ns
    else // fI2CCLK = 80 MHz
        I2C2->TIMINGR = (9 << I2C_TIMINGR_PRESC_Pos) +
```

```
                (3 << I2C_TIMINGR_SCLDEL_Pos) + (2 << I2C_TIMINGR_SDADEL_Pos) +
                (4 << I2C_TIMINGR_SCLH_Pos) +
                (10 << I2C_TIMINGR_SCLL_Pos); // tSYNC1 + tSYNC2 = 250 ns
// enable relevant interrupts and enable I2C2. Both TC and TCR interrupts are enabled by TCIE
    I2C2->CR1   = 0; // clear the CR1 register
    I2C2->CR1   |= I2C_CR1_ERRIE + I2C_CR1_TCIE + I2C_CR1_NACKIE + I2C_CR1_RXIE +
                   (3 << I2C_CR1_DNF_Pos) + I2C_CR1_TXIE + I2C_CR1_PE;
    NVIC_SetPriority(I2C2_EV_IRQn, 0);
    NVIC_EnableIRQ(I2C2_EV_IRQn);
}
```

11.8 Examples of Interfacing with Peripherals with I2C Interface

In the following sections, several peripheral chips will be used to illustrate how to utilize I²C bus to carry out data transfer.

11.9 Interfacing with 24FC256 Serial EEPROM

The 24FC256 is an EEPROM chip with I²C interface and 32-kB capacity. The pin assignment of this chip is shown in Figure 11.39. The control byte of the 24FC256 is shown in Figure 11.40.

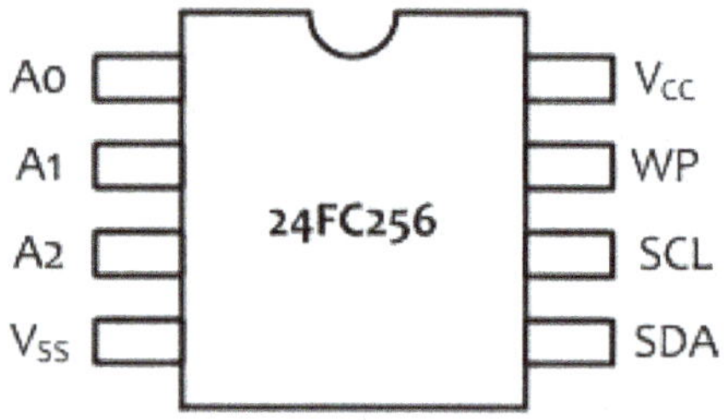

WP: write protection
A2~A0: Address inputs. Up to 8 24FC256 can be added to a system.
SDA & SCL: I²C signals

Figure 11.39 24FC256 pin assignment

1	0	1	0	A2	A1	A0	R/$\overline{W}$

Figure 11.40 24FC256 control byte

11.9.1 FEATURES OF 24FC256

The 24FC256 supports byte write, page write, current address read, random read, and sequential read operations and has the following features:

- A wide range of power supply: The power supply can be in the range of 2.5 V to 5.5 V.
- Supports standard-mode, fast-mode, and fast-mode-plus operations.
- Internal address pointer: This address pointer is automatically updated to next location after each access.
- Internal write buffer: The chip contains a 64-byte page write buffer.
- A long retention time: The chip has a retention time over 200 years.
- Short page-write time: The chip has an internal write time of 5 ms.

11.9.2 BYTE WRITE OPERATION

To write a byte into the 24FC256, the STM32L475 performs the following operations:

Step 1

Asserts the START condition.

Step 2

The STM32L475 sends a control byte to the 24FC256.

Step 3

The 24FC256 acknowledges the control byte.

Step 4

The STM32L475 sends a 16-bit address in two transfers to select a location inside the 24FC256.

Step 5

The 24FC256 acknowledges each address byte.

Step 6

The STM32L475 sends data to the 24FC256.

Step 7

The 24FC256 acknowledges the reception of the data byte.

Step 8

The STM32L475 generates a STOP condition to terminate the write byte operation.

The STOP condition initiates the internal write operation, which writes data into the EEPROM memory array.

11.9.3 PAGE WRITE OPERATION

The STM32L475 and any I²C master can write up to 64 bytes of data into the 24FC256 by sending a 16-bit address. A page write operation is started like a byte write operation. After performing the first seven steps in the **byte write operation**, the master continues to write up to 64 bytes of data into the 24FC256.

The 24FC256 has an internal 6-bit address pointer to keep track of the next byte to be written into. If the master writes more than 64 bytes, then the address pointer will roll over and the previously received data will be written over. When the master generates the STOP condition, the EEPROM starts the internal write operation.

11.9.4 ACKNOWLEDGE POLLING

When the 24FC256 is performing internal write operation, it does not acknowledge any other read or write access request. The I²C master can utilize this fact to find out whether the EEPROM internal operation has been completed. The polling procedure is illustrated in Figure 11.41.

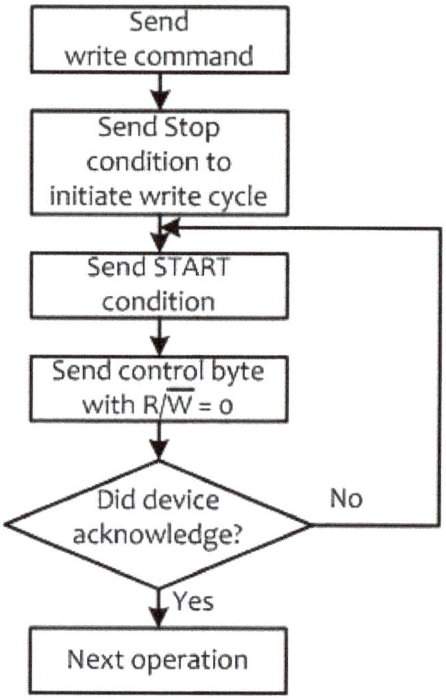

Figure 11.41 24FC256 acknowledge polling flow

11.9.5 CURRENT ADDRESS READ

The internal address pointer of the 24FC256 increments automatically after each read or write access. This mode allows the CPU to read the byte immediately following the location accessed by the previous read or write operation. The procedure is as follows:

Step 1

The I²C master generates a START condition.

Step 2

The I²C master sends out the control byte with R/bit set to 1.

Step 3

The 24FC256 sends back an ACK followed by a data byte.

Step 4

The I²C master sends back a NACK.

Step 5

The I²C master generates a STOP condition to terminate the operation.

11.9.6 RANDOM READ

This mode allows the I²C master to read the contents of any location in the EEPROM. The procedure is as follows:

Step 1

The I²C master generates a START condition.

Step 2

The I²C master sends a control byte with R/bit set to 0.

Step 3

The 24FC256 acknowledges the control byte.

Step 4

The I²C master sends the address of the byte to be read to the 24FC256 in two transfers.

Step 5

The 24FC256 acknowledges the address in two ACKs.

Step 6

The I²C master generates a RESTART condition.

Step 7

The I²C master sends the control byte with R/bit set to 1.

Step 8

The 24FC256 acknowledges the control byte and sends a data byte to the master.

Step 9

The I²C master asserts NACK to the 24FC256.

Step 10

The I²C master generates a STOP condition.

11.9.7 SEQUENTIAL READ

If the I²C master acknowledges the data byte returned by a read operation, the 24FC256 will transmit the next sequentially addressed byte as long as the I²C master provides the clock signals on the SCL bus.

Using the sequential read, the I²C master can read the entire chip or multiple bytes by sending a single address to the 24FC256. The user can implement a **block read** operation using this read mode.

11.9.8 CIRCUIT CONNECTION

An example of circuit connection between the STM32L475 and the 24FC256 is shown in Figure 11.42.

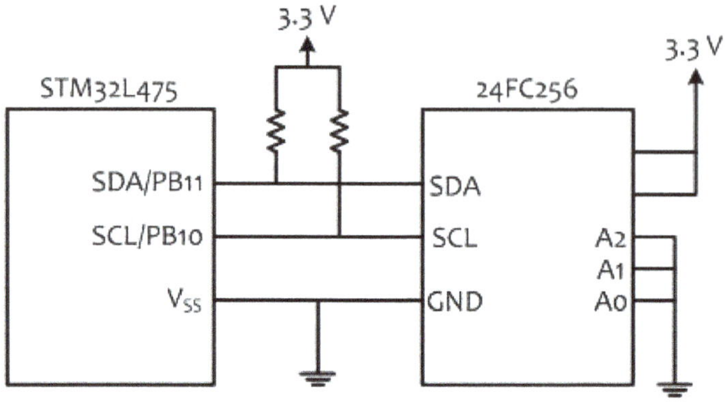

Figure 11.42 Circuit connection between the STM32L475 and the 24FC256

Example 11.7 Write a C function that can write k bytes into the 24FC256 ($1 \leq k \leq 64$) and also the interrupt service routine to handle appropriate I^2C interrupts during the data transfer phase.

Solution: Using the interrupt-driven data transfer approach, the I^2C interrupt service routine is responsible for writing data into the I2Cx->TXDR register or reading data from the

I2Cx->RXDR register. Any variables to be accessed by the interrupt service routine must be declared as global variables. For data transfer in EEPROM, the following global variables are defined:

- **blkSize**: number of bytes remained to be transmitted or received
- **wrBytes**: total number of bytes to be transferred
- **rdBytes**: total number of bytes to be received
- **wrNotDone**: internal EEPROM write operation not finished
- **inNACK**: in write polling operation (0: no; 1: yes)
- **inBuf[200]**: buffer to hold received data bytes (size depends on the application)
- **outBuf[100]**: buffer to hold data bytes to be sent (size depends on the application)
- **ix, jx**: indices to the inBuf[] and outBuf[] arrays.

These global variables are declared as follows:

```
uint32_t    blkSize, wrBytes, rdBytes, wrNotDone, inNACK;
uint8_t     inBuf[200]; outBuf[100];
uint16_t    ix, jx;
```

The I^2C event interrupt service routine is as follows:

```
void I2C2_EV_IRQHandler(void) // I2C event interrupt handler
{
    if(I2C2->ISR & I2C_ISR_TXIS) {
```

```
if(blkSize != 0){
        I2C2->TXDR = outBuf[jx++];
        wrBytes--;
        blkSize--;
} else {
        if((I2C2->ISR & I2C_ISR_TC) != 0){ // start the read process (write part is done)
                I2C2->CR2 &= ~(I2C_CR2_NBYTES + I2C_CR2_AUTOEND +
                                        I2C_CR2_RELOAD);
                if (rdBytes < 256) { // how many bytes to read?
                        I2C2->CR2 |= (rdBytes << I2C_CR2_NBYTES_Pos) +
                                        I2C_CR2_RD_WRN + I2C_CR2_AUTOEND;
                        blkSize = rdBytes;}
                else {
                        I2C2->CR2 |= (0xFF << I2C_CR2_NBYTES_Pos) +
                                        I2C_CR2_RD_WRN + I2C_CR2_RELOAD;
                        blkSize = 0xFF;
                }
                I2C2->CR2 |= I2C_CR2_START;
        }
        else if(I2C2->ISR & I2C_ISR_TCR) {
                if (wrBytes < 256) {
                        I2C2->CR2 &= ~I2C_CR2_NBYTES;
                        I2C2->CR2 |= (wrBytes << I2C_CR2_NBYTES_Pos) +
                                    I2C_CR2_AUTOEND;
                        blkSize = wrBytes;
                }
                else {
                        I2C2->CR2 |= (0xFF << I2C_CR2_NBYTES_Pos) +
                                    I2C_CR2_RELOAD;
                        blkSize = 0xFF;
```

```
                        }
                    }
                }
            }
            else if(I2C2->ISR & I2C_ISR_RXNE) {
                inBuf[ix++] = (uint8_t)I2C2->RXDR; // store the lowest byte
                rdBytes--;
                blkSize--;
                if(blkSize == 0) {
                    if((I2C2->ISR & I2C_ISR_TCR) != 0){
                        if (rdBytes < 256){
                            blkSize = rdBytes;
                            I2C2->CR2 |= (rdBytes << I2C_CR2_NBYTES_Pos) +
                                         I2C_CR2_AUTOEND;
                        }
                        else {
                            blkSize = 0xFF;
                            I2C2->CR2 |= (0xFF << I2C_CR2_NBYTES_Pos) +
                                         I2C_CR2_RELOAD;
                        }
                    }
                }
            }
            else if (I2C2->ISR & I2C_ISR_NACKF) { // enter write polling
                I2C2->ICR = I2C_ICR_NACKCF; // clear NACK flag
                inNACK = 1;  // STOP condition is automatically generated
                I2C2->CR2 |= I2C_CR2_START; // repoll the EEPROM
            }
}
```

The function that writes up to 64 bytes into the 24FC256 is as follows:

```
void writeBytesEE(uint8_t SLAddr, uint16_t addr, uint8_t byteCnt, uint8_t *ptr)
{
    wrBytes         = byteCnt + 2; // location address is two bytes long
    blkSize         = byteCnt + 2;
    rdBytes = 0;
    wrNotDone       = 0;
    outBuf[0]       = (uint8_t)(addr >> 8);
    outBuf[1]       = (uint8_t)(addr & 0x00FF); // low byte of EEPROM address
    for (jx = 2; jx < (byteCnt+2); jx++)
            outBuf[jx] = *ptr++; // copy data to output buffer
    jx      = 0;
    I2C2->CR2       = I2C_CR2_AUTOEND + (byteCnt << I2C_CR2_NBYTES_Pos) +
                      (SLAddr << 1);
    I2C2->CR2       |= I2C_CR2_START; // generate a START condition
    while(wrBytes);
    writePoll(SLAddr);
}
```

The write polling function is as follows:

```
void writePoll (uint8_t SLAddr)
{
    wrNotDone = 1;
    inNACK = 0;     // not has been NACK yet
    I2C2->CR2 |= I2C_CR2_START; // generate a START condition
    while(wrNotDone){ // test whether I²C2 has been NACK but now received ACK
            if (inNACK && ((I2C2->ISR & I2C_ISR_NACKF) == 0))
                    break;
    };
}
```

Example 11.8 Write a C function that can read a block of locations from the 24FC256 and stores them in a buffer pointed to by a pointer passed to this function.

Solution:

This function is also written as an interrupt-driven function and shares the use of the interrupt service routine written in the previous example. The read block function is as follows:

```
// -----------------------------------------------------------------------------------------------
// SLAddr: the slave ID of EEPROM,
// addr: the starting address of EEPROM from where data are to be read
// byteCnt: total number of bytes to read
// ptr: pointer to the buffer to hold data read back from EEPROM
// -----------------------------------------------------------------------------------------------
void readBytesEE (uint8_t SLAddr, uint16_t addr, uint16_t byteCnt, uint8_t *ptr)
{
    wrBytes         = 2;
    blkSize         = 2;
    rdBytes = byteCnt; // number of bytes to read
    outBuf[0]       = (uint8_t)(addr >> 8);
    outBuf[1]       = (uint8_t)(addr & 0x00FF); // low byte of EEPROM address
    jx = 0;
    ix = 0;
    I2C2->CR2       = (2 << I2C_CR2_NBYTES_Pos) + (SLAddr << 1);
    I2C2->CR2       |= I2C_CR2_START; // generate the START condition
    while (rdBytes); // wait until all bytes have been read
    for (ix = 0; ix < byteCnt; ix++)
            *ptr++ = inBuf[ix]; // copy the data to the buffer pointed to by ptr
}
```

11.10 Interfacing with the Relative Humidity and Temperature Sensor HTS221

The HTS221 consists of a sensing element and a mixed-signal ASIC to provide measurement information through the I²C and SPI interfaces. The sensing element consists of a polymer dielectric planar capacitor structure capable of detecting relative humidity (RH) variations.

The HTS221 can measure RH value ranging from 0% to 100% with very low power consumption. The RH measurement is accurate up to ±3.5% in the range from 20% to 80% RH. When measuring the temperature, the accuracy is ±0.5°C in the range from 15°C to 40°C. Both relative humidity and temperature measurement are represented in 16-bit values.

The block diagram of the HTS221 is shown in Figure 11.43.

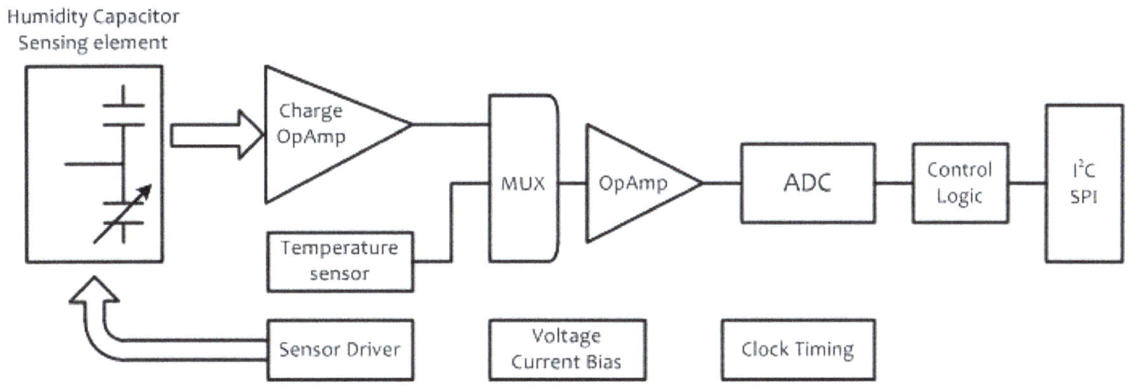

Figure 11.43 HTS221 RH and temperature sensor block diagram

11.10.1 HTS221 SIGNALS

The HTS has six signal pins:

- VDD: Power supply
- SCL/SPC: I²C serial clock (SCL) or SPI serial clock (SPC)
- DRDY: Data ready output signal
- SDA/SDI/SDO: I²C serial data (SDA)
- GND: Ground
- CS (SPI enable): I2C/SPI mode selection (0: SPI mode; 1: I²C enabled)

11.10.2 HTS221 I2C OPERATION

The HTS221 has a 7-bit **slave address** 1011111_2. All HTS221 operation parameters and temperature and humidity values are stored in registers. Each of these registers has a 7-bit address. The register names and addresses are summarized in Table 11.7.

Table 11.7 HTS221 register map

Register Name	Type	Register Address (hex)	Default (hex)
Reserved		0x00~0x0E	Do not modify
WHO_AM_I	R	0x0F	0xBC
AV_CONF	R/W	0x10	0x1B
Reserved		0x11~0x1C	Do not modify
CTRL_REG1	R/W	0x20	0
CTRL_REG2	R/W	0x21	0
CTRL_REG3	R/W	0x22	0
Reserved		0x23~0x26	Do not modify
STATUS_REG	R	0x27	0
HUMIDITY_OUT_L	R	0x28	output
HUMIDITY_OUT_H	R	0x29	output
TEMP_OUT_L	R	0x2A	output
TEMP_OUT_H	R	0x2B	output
Reserved		0x2C~0x2F	Do not modify
CALIB_0..F	R/W	0x30~0x3F	Do not modify

11.10.3 I2C WRITE TO HTS221 REGISTERS

The following steps must be followed to write to an HTS221 register:

Step 1

Generate a START condition.

Step 2

Send the HTS221 slave address with R/bit set to 0.

Step 3

Send out the register address.

Step 4

Send out write data.

Step 5

Generate a STOP condition.

To write data to multiple registers, the bit 7 of the register address must be set to 1 in Step 3. The MCU can send as many data bytes as needed in Step 4. Registers are written in the ascending address order.

11.10.4 I2C READ FROM HTS221 REGISTERS

To read a register, take the following steps:

Step 1

Generate a START condition.

Step 2

Send out the HTS221 slave address with the R/bit set to 0 (to be ACKed).

Step 3

Send out the register address (to be ACKed).

Step 4

Generate a RESTART condition.

Step 5

Send out HTS221 slave address with R/bit set to 1 (to be ACKed).

Step 6

Read back a data byte.

Step 7

The CPU sends back NACK.

Step 8

The CPU generates a STOP condition.

To read multiple registers with ascending addresses, the bit 7 of the register address sent out in Step 3 must be set to 1. The MCU can read back as many data bytes as appropriate in Step 6 by generating appropriate number of SCL pulses. The MCU must acknowledge all except the last byte from the HTS221.

11.10.5 HTS221 REGISTER CONTENTS

The contents of HTS221 registers are explained in the following:

WHO_AM_I (at 0x0F)

This register stores the HTS221 ID, which is 0xBC.

AV_CONF (at 0x10)

This register defines the humidity and temperature resolution mode. The contents of this register are shown in Figure 11.44.

7	6	5	4	3	2	1	0
--	--	AVGT2	AVGT1	AVGT0	AVGH2	AVGH1	AVGH0

AVGT2-0: Select the number of averaged temperature samples (2~256)
AVGH2-0: Select the number of averaged humidity samples (4~512)

AVGx2:0	Number of internal samples to be averaged		Noise (RMS)		I_{DD} 1 Hz
	Temperature (AVGT)	Humidity (AVGH)	Temp(°C)	RH%	μA
000	2	4	0.08	0.4	0.80
001	4	8	0.05	0.3	1.05
010	8	16	0.04	0.2	1.40
011(1)	16	32	0.03	0.15	2.10
100	32	64	0.02	0.1	3.43
101	64	128	0.015	0.07	6.15
110	128	256	0.01	0.05	11.60
111	256	512	0.007	0.03	22.50

1. x = H or T
2. Default configuration

Figure 11.44 Humidity and temperature average configuration

CTRL_REG1 (at 0x20)

This register controls the power-down mode and data-update mode and selects the output data rate. The contents of this register are shown in Figure 11.45. Setting the BDU bit to 1 prevents the register update unless both the upper and lower parts of the HUMIDITY_OUT and TEMP_OUT registers have been read. This feature prevents the reading of LSB and MSB related to two different samples. In Figure 11.45, the ODR[1:0] field specifies the number of conversions performed by the sensor. In the one-shot mode, the sensor performs one conversion and stops. When the ODR field is not 00, the sensor can perform 1 or 7 or 12.5 conversions per second.

7	6	5	4	3	2	1	0
PD	--	--	--	--	BDU	ODR1	ODR0

PD: Power-down control. 0: power down mode 1: active mode
BDU: block data update
0: continuous mode. The lower and upper register parts are updated continuously.
1: output registers not updated until both parts have been read.
ODR1, ODR0: output data rate selection

ODR1	ODR0	Humidity (Hz)	Temperature 1 Hz
0	0	One-shot	
0	1	1 Hz	1 Hz
1	0	7 Hz	7 Hz
1	1	12.5 Hz	12.5 Hz

Figure 11.45 Control register 1 (at 0x20)

CTRL_REG2 (at 0x21)

The contents of this register are shown in Figure 11.46. Setting the **One_Shot** bit starts a one-shot conversion on temperature and humidity. To start a one-shot conversion, the **ODR**[1:0] field of the **CTRL_REG1** register must be set to 00. Setting the **Heater** bit enables the heating element to quickly get rid of the environmental condensation.

7	6	5	4	3	2	1	0
BOOT	--	--	--	--	--	Heater	One_Shot

BOOT: reboot memory contents
0: normal mode 1: reboot memory contents
At device power-up, the contents of the flash memory block is transferred to internal registers related to trimming functions to permit good behavior of the device.
If, for any reason, the contents of the trimming registers are modified, it is sufficient to set this bit to restore the correct value (value stored in flash memory)
One_Shot:
0: waiting for start of conversion 1: start for a new dataset
Any time this bit is set, the chip performs a single acquisition of temperature and humidity.
At the end of conversion, new data are available in the output registers.
Heater: 0: heater disable 1: heater enable
This bit is used to control an internal heating element, that can be used to speed up the sensor recovery time in case of condensation. Temperature and humidity shouldn't be read during the heating cycle.

Figure 11.46 Control register 2 (at 0x21)

CTRL_REG3 (at 0x22)

The contents of this register are shown in Figure 11.47. This register allows the user to configure the property of the DRDY signal: disabled/enabled, active high/low, and open-drain/push-pull.

7	6	5	4	3	2	1	0
DRDY_H_L	PP_OD	--	--	--	DRDY_EN	--	--

DRDY_H_L: Data ready output signal active high, low
0: active high 1: active low (default)
PP_OD: Push-pull / open-drain selection on pin 3 (DRDY)
0: push-pull (default) 1: open-drain
DRDY_EN: Data ready enable
0: Data ready disabled (default) 1: Data ready signal available on pin 3
DRDY output is logical OR of STATUS_REG[1] and STATUS_REG[0] for humidity and temperature, respectively

Figure 11.47 Control register 3 (at 0x22)

STATUS_REG (at 0x27)

This register indicates whether new data for humidity and temperature are available. The contents of this register are shown in Figure 11.48.

7	6	5	4	3	2	1	0
--	--	--	--	--	--	H_DA	T_DA

H_DA: Humidity data available
0: new humidity data is not yet available.
1: new humidity data is available.
T_DA: Temperature data available
0: New temperature data is not yet available.
1: New temperature data is available.
Any time humidity or temperature data is read, then H_DA or T_DA bit will be cleared.

Figure 11.48 Status register (at 0x27)

Humidity Registers (HUMIDITY_OUT_H and HUMIDITY_OUT_L)

Humidity data stored in these two registers are represented in 2's complement format.

Temperature Registers (TEMP_OUT_H and TEMP_OUT_L)

Temperature data are stored in these two registers in 2's complement format.

11.10.6 DERIVING THE RH VALUE (%RH)

The relative humidity value RH is computed by linear interpolation of the current registers (HUMIDITY_OUT_H and HUMIDITY_OUT_L) with calibration registers. The contents of these registers are shown in Table 11.8.

Table 11.8 HTS221 calibration registers for computing RH% value

Addr	Variable	Format	b7	b6	b5	b4	b3	b2	b1	b0
0x28	H_OUT	s(16)	H7	H6	H5	H4	H3	H2	H1	H0
0x29			H15	H14	H13	H12	H11	H10	H9	H8
0x30	H0_RH_x2	u(16)	H0.7	H0.6	H0.5	H0.4	H0.3	H0.2	H0.1	H0.0
0x31	H1_RH_x2	u(16)	H1.7	H1.6	H1.5	H1.4	H1.3	H1.2	H1.1	H1.0
0x36	H0_T0_OUT	s(16)	7	6	5	4	3	2	1	0
0x37			15	14	13	12	11	10	9	0
0x3A	H1_T0_OUT	s(16)	7	6	5	4	3	2	1	0
0x3B			15	14	13	12	11	10	9	0

The procedure for obtaining the RH value is as follows:

Step 1

Read the values of coefficients H0_RH_x2 and H1_RH_x2 from registers 0x30 and 0x31.

Step 2

Divide the contents of H0_RH_x2 and H1_RH_x2 by 2 to obtain the value of coefficients H0_RH and H1_RH.

Step 3

Read the value of H0_T0_OUT from registers located at 0x36 and 0x37.

Step 4

Read the value of H1_T0_OUT from registers located at 0x3A and 0x3B.

Step 5

Read the humidity value in raw counts H_OUT from registers 0x28 and 0x29.

Step 6

Compute the RH% value by linear interpolation using the following formula:

$$RH\% = \frac{(H1\_RH - H0\_RH) \times (H\_T\_OUT - H0\_T0\_OUT)}{H1\_T0\_OUT - H0\_T0\_OUT} + H0\_RH \qquad \text{--- (11.8)}$$

where

H0_RH, H1_RH, H0_T0_OUT, and H1_T0_OUT coefficients are factory-calibrated at temperature T0 and stored in NVM memory, while the H_OUT value (registers 0x28 and 0x29) depends on temperature T measured from the sensor during the reading of RH%. It is possible to read the coefficients (Steps 1, 2, 3, and 4) only once and repeat cyclically only Steps 5 and 6.

RH% cannot be higher than 100%. In this case, force RH% to 100% (called **saturation**).

Example 11.9 Assume that H0_T0_OUT, H1_T0_OUT, H0_RH_x2, H1_RH_x2, and H_OUT are 4000, 6000, 40%, 80%, and 5000, respectively. What is RH%?

Solution:

H0_RH = H0_RH_x2 / 2 = 20%

H1_RH = H1_RH_x2 / 2 = 40%

Plug these values into Equation 11.8,

RH% = (40% - 20%) × (5000 – 4000) ÷ (6000 – 4000) + 20% = 30%

11.10.7 OBTAINING THE TEMPERATURE READING

The raw counts for temperature reading are stored in registers TEMP_OUT_H (0x2B) and TEMP_OUT_L (0x2A). The bit 7 of the TEMP_OUT_H indicates the sign of the temperature reading. The temperature value T is computed by linear interpolation of the current registers with calibration registers. The contents of these registers are shown in Table 11.9.

Table 11.13 HTS221 calibration registers for computing tempereature value

Addr	Variable	Format	b7	b6	b5	b4	b3	b2	b1	b0
0x2A	T_OUT	s(16)	T7	T6	T5	T4	T3	T2	T1	T0
0x2B			T15	T14	T13	T12	T11	T10	T9	T8
0x32	T0_degC_x8	u(16)	T0.7	T0.6	T0.5	T0.4	T0.3	T0.2	T0.1	T0.0
0x33	T1_degC_x8	u(16)	T1.7	T1.6	T1.5	T1.4	T1.3	T1.2	T1.1	T1.0
0x35	T1/T0 msb	(u2),(u2)	reserved				T1.9	T1.8	T0.9	T0.8
0x3C	T0_OUT	s(16)	7	6	5	4	3	2	1	0
0x3D			15	14	13	12	11	10	9	0
0x3E	T1_OUT	s(16)	7	6	5	4	3	2	1	0
0x3F			15	14	13	12	11	10	9	0

The procedure for obtaining temperature reading is as follows:

Step 1

Read the values of coefficients T0_degC_x8 and T1_degC_x8 from registers located at 0x32 and 0x33.

Step 2

Divide the contents of the previous two registers by 8 to obtain the coefficient values T0_degC and T1_degC.

Step 3

Read the two most significant bits (T1.9 and T1.8) of T1_degC and T0_degC from registers located at 0x35 to compute T1_degC and T0_degC.

Step 4

Read the value of T0_OUT from registers located at 0x3C and 0x3D.

Step 5

Read the value of T1_OUT from registers located at 0x3E and 0x3F.

Step 6

Read the value T_OUT from registers located at 0x2A and 0x2B.

Step 7

Compute the temperature by interpolation using the following equation:

$$T\,[\text{in}\ ^\circ C] = \frac{(T1\_degC - To\_degC) \times (T\_OUT - To\_OUT)}{T1\_OUT - To\_OUT} + To\_degC \quad \text{---}(11.9)$$

Example 11.10 Assume that T0_degC_x8, T1_degC_x8, T1/T0 msb, T0_OUT, T1_OUT, and T_OUT are 0x50°C, 0x40°C, 4, 300, 500, and 400, respectively. T0_degC_x8 and T1_degC_x8 are read from locations 0x32, 0x33, and 0x35. What is the actual temperature?

Solution:

T1/T0 msb = 01/00

T0_degC = (0 << 8 + T0_degC_x8) / 8 = 80°C / 8 = 10°C

T1_degC = (1 << 8 + T1_degC_x8) / 8 = 320°C / 8 = 40°C

The temperature is computed by using linear interpolation

T [in °C] = (40 – 10) × (400 - 300) ÷ (500 – 300) + 10°C = 25°C

11.10.8 CIRCUIT CONNECTION

The circuit connection between the I²C2 module and the HTS221 is shown in Figure 11.49.

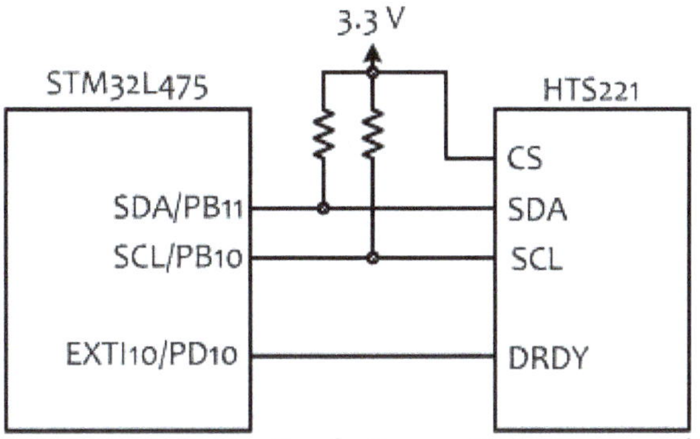

Figure 11.49 Circuit connection between STM32L475 and HTS221

Example 11.11 Assume that I²C2_EV interrupt has been enabled. Write a function to initialize the HTS221 in Figure 11.49 by configuring AV_CONF, CTRL_REG1, CTRL_REG2, and CTRL_REG3.

Solution:

This example will reuse the global variables and the interrupt service routine for I²C2.

Because the AV_CONF register is not contiguous with the other three registers. We need to perform two I²C transmissions in this example. The values to configure each register are passed to this function. The initialization function is as follows:

```
void initHTS221 (uint8_t avConf, uint8_t ctrl1, uint8_t ctrl2, uint8_t ctrl3)
{
    blkSize     =  wrBytes = 2;
    rdBytes     =  0;
    wrNotDone   =  0;
    jx          =  0;
    outBuf[0]   =  0x10; // address of AV_CONF register
    outBuf[1]   =  avConf;
    I2C2->CR2   =  I2C_CR2_AUTOEND + (2 << I2C_CR2_NBYTES_Pos) + 0xBE;
    I2C2->CR2   |= I2C_CR2_START; // generate a START condition
    while(wrBytes);
    outBuf[0]   =  0xA0; // address of CTRL_REG1 (0x20) + bit 7 set to 1
    outBuf[1]   =  ctrl1;
```

```
    outBuf[2]    =  ctrl2;
    outBuf[3]    =  ctrl3;
    blkSize      =  wrBytes = 4;
    jx           =  0;
    I2C2->CR2    =  I2C_CR2_AUTOEND + (4 << I2C_CR2_NBYTES_Pos) + 0xBE;
    I2C2->CR2   |=  I2C_CR2_START; // generate a START condition
    while(wrBytes);
}
```

Example 11.12 Write a C statement to call the **initHTS221** function to configure the HTS221 with the following parameters:

- AV_CONF: Select 16-bit and 32-bit samples for temperature and humidity measurement, respectively.
- CTRL_REG1: Set HTS221 to active mode, update registers when both high and low parts are ready, and use one-shot mode measurement.
- CTRL_REG2: Normal mode, disable heater, waiting for start of conversion.
- CTRL_REG3: Enable DRDY pin to active high and push-pull.

Solution:

The following statement will achieve the specified configuration:

```
initHTS221 (0x1B, 0x84, 0x00, 0x04);
```

Example 11.13 Write a general-purpose read function that can read multiple registers located at contiguous addresses.

Solution:

This function requires the following parameters:

1. Starting register address
2. Register count

This function will reuse the global variables declared in Example 11.6. The function is as follows:

```
void readHTS221Regs (uint16_t cnt, uint8_t addr)
{
    wrBytes         = 1;
```

```
    blkSize  = 1;
    rdBytes = cnt;
    wrNotDone       = 0;
    jx              = 0;
    ix              = 0;
    if (cnt > 1)
            outBuf[0]       = addr + 0x80; // prepare to read multiple registers
    else
            outBuf[0]       = addr;
    I2C2->CR2       = (1 << I2C_CR2_NBYTES_Pos) + 0xBE;
    I2C2->CR2       |= I2C_CR2_START;
    while(rdBytes);
}
```

Example 11.14 Write a function to perform a one-shot measurement of the relative humidity and temperature.

Solution:

The function is as follows:

```
void oneShotMeasure(void)
{
    wrBytes         = blkSize = 2;
    rdBytes = 0;
    wrNotDone       = 0;
    jx              = 0;
    outBuf[0]       = 0x21; // address of CTRL_REG2
    outBuf[1]       = 0x01; // command to start one-shot measurement
    I2C2->CR2       = I2C_CR2_AUTOEND + (2 << I2C_CR2_NBYTES_Pos) + 0xBE;
    I2C2->CR2       |= I2C_CR2_START;
    while(wrBytes);
}
```

Example 11.15 Write a function to wait until the humidity and temperature measurements are done.

Solution: This function needs to call the **readHTS221Regs()** function to read back the STATUS_REG register and check whether the conversion is done.

```
void waitforHTMeasurement (void)
{
    uint32_t notDone;
    notDone = 1;
    while(notDone) {
        readHTS221Regs(1, 0x27); // read back STATUS_REG
        if((inBuf[0] & 0x03) == 0x03) // are Humidity and Temperature data available?
            notDone = 0;
    }
}
```

Example 11.16 Write a sequence of C statements to

1. Read back H_OUT, H0_RH_x2, H1_RH_x2, H0_T0_OUT, and H1_T0_OUT.
2. Convert them into 16-bit values and store them in appropriate variables.
3. Compute the relative humidity.

Solution:

We need the following variables to hold temporary results:

```
uint16_t hTOut, h0RH, h1RH, h0t0OUT, h1t0OUT, humidity;
```

The following C statements will perform the specified operations:

```
readHTS221Regs(2, 0x28); // read HUMIDITY_OUT_L & HUMIDITY_OUT_H
hTOut     = (((uint16_t)inBuf[1]) << 8) + (uint16_t)inBuf[0];
readHTS221Regs(2, 0x30); // read H0_RH_x2 & H1_RH_x2
h0RH      = ((uint16_t)inBuf[0]) / 2;
h1RH      = ((uint16_t)inBuf[1]) / 2;
readHTS221Regs(2, 0x36); // read H0_T0_OUT (2 bytes)
h0toOUT   = (((uint16_t)inBuf[1]) << 8) + (uint16_t)inBuf[0];
readHTS221Regs(2, 0x3A); // read H1_T0_OUT (2 bytes)
h1toOUT   = (((uint16_t)inBuf[1]) << 8) + (uint16_t)inBuf[0];
```

```
humidity = ((h1RH - h0RH)*(hTOut - h0toOUT))/(h1toOUT - h0toOUT) + h0RH;
```

Example 11.17 Write a sequence of C statements to

1. Read back T_OUT, T0_degC_x8, T1_degC_x8, T1/T0 msb, T0_OUT, and T1_OUT.
2. Convert the read back values into 16-bit values.
3. Compute the temperature.

Solution:

We need to declare the following variables:

```
uint16_t  tOUT, t0DegC, t1DegC, t0OUT, t1OUT, t0, t1;
uint16_t  temperature;
```

The following C statements perform the specified operations:

```
readHTS221Regs(2, 0x2A); // read T_OUT
tOUT        = (((uint16_t)inBuf[1]) << 8) + (uint16_t)inBuf[0];
readHTS221Regs(2, 0x32); // read T0_degC_x8 & T1_degC_x8
t0          = inBuf[0];
t1          = inBuf[1];
readHTS221Regs(1, 0x35); // read the msbs of t0DegCx8 & t1DegCx8
t0DegC      = (t0 + ((inBuf[0] & 0x03) << 8)) / 8;
t1DegC      = (t1 + ((inBuf[0] & 0x0C) << 6)) / 8;
readHTS221Regs(4, 0x3C);
t0OUT       = (((uint16_t)inBuf[1]) << 8) + (uint16_t)inBuf[0];
t1OUT       = (((uint16_t)inBuf[3]) << 8) + (uint16_t)inBuf[2];
temperature = ((t1DegC - t0DegC)*(tOUT - t0OUT))/(t1OUT - t0OUT) + t0DegC;
```

11.11 Interfacing with the Barometric Sensor LPS22HB

The LPS22HB is a MEM-based digital barometric pressure and temperature sensor from ST Microelectronics. The LPS22HB can measure barometric pressure in the range from 260 to 1260 hPa (or mbar) and temperature from -40°C to 85°C.

Barometric pressure is measured as a 24-bit value, whereas temperature is measured as a 16-bit value. The output data rate for pressure measurement can be from 1 Hz to 75 Hz; that is, the LPS22HB can measure barometric pressure up to 75 times per second.

The LPS22HB provides both the SPI and I^2C interface for data transfer. This sensor may interrupt the MCU when converted data are ready, when FIFO flags are set, and when the pressure thresholds are exceeded. This sensor can operate with a power supply in the range from 1.7 V to 3.6 V. The **I^2C slave address** of this sensor is **101110x**b, where x is determined by the voltage of the SA0 pin. This pin allows two LPS22HBs to be used in a system.

The block diagram of the LPS22HB is shown in Figure 11.50. The block diagram of the digital logic block in Figure 11.50 is detailed in Figure 11.51.

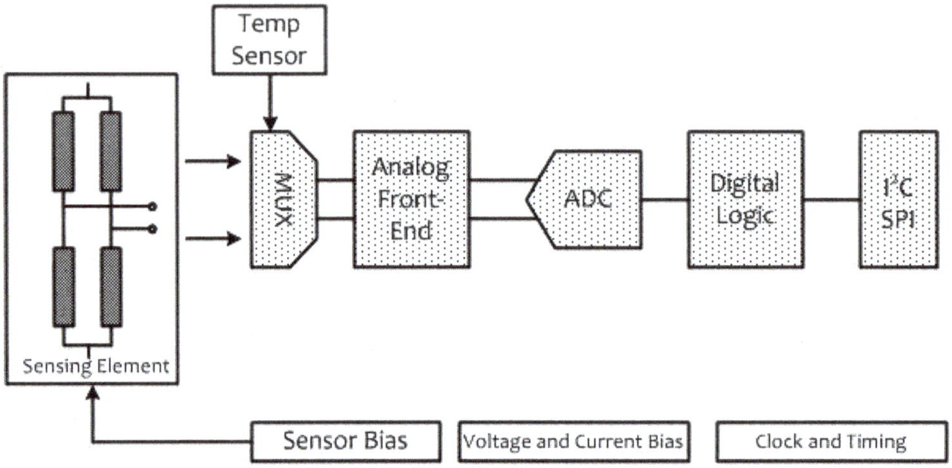

Figure 11.50 LPS22HB device architecture block diagram

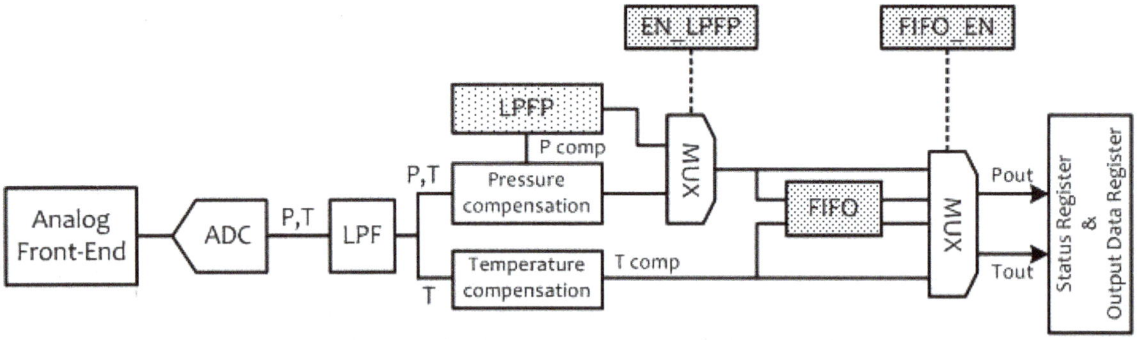

Figure 11.51 LPS22HB pressure sensor digital logic block diagram

11.11.1 LPS22HB SIGNAL PINS

The LPS22HB has 10 pins

- Pin 1: Vdd_IO. Power supply for I/O
- Pin 2: SCL/SPC. Clock signal for I^2C (SCL) or SPI (SPC)
- Pin 3: Reserved
- Pin 4: SDA/SDI/SDO. SDA signal for I^2C or the SDI/SDO pin for 3-wire SPI or SDI for 4-wire SPI
- Pin 5: SDO/SA0. Serial data output for 4-wire SPI or SA0 (serial address 0) input for I^2C
- Pin 6: CS (SPI enable). 0: SPI enabled; 1: I2C enabled (400 kHz)
- Pin 7: INT_DRDY. Interrupt or data ready

- Pin 8, 9: GND
- Pin 10: VDD

11.11.2 LPS22HB SENSING ELEMENT

The sensor in the LPS22HB is a silicon membrane. When a pressure is applied, the membrane deflection induces an imbalance in the Wheatstone bridge piezoresistances and produces a voltage output. The voltage output from the Wheatstone bridge is then amplified by a low noise amplifier, and then an ADC converts this voltage into a digital value. This chip uses a data ready (INT_DRDY) signal to indicate when a new set of measured pressure and temperature data are available so that the application can read the new pressure/temperature value.

11.11.3 CALIBRATION OF LPS22HB

Due to the manufacturing process variation, the LPS22HB devices will not have the same characteristics. Therefore, the measured pressure and temperature values must be calibrated to become accurate for use. The trimming values are calculated during the manufacturing process and stored inside the device in a non-volatile structure. When the device is powered up, the trimming (calibration) parameters are downloaded into registers to be employed during the normal operation, which allows the device to be used without any further calibration.

11.11.4 INTERPRETING PRESSURE READINGS

Pressure data are stored in three registers: PRESS_OUT_XL, PRESS_OUT_L, and PRESS_OUT_H. To derive the barometric pressure value, take the following two steps:

Step 1

Concatenate three registers into a 24-bit 2's complement value.

Step 2

Find the magnitude of the previous 24-bit value and divide it by 4096 in the unit of hPa (hector Pascal).

Example 11.18 Assume that the contents of PRESS_OUT_H, PRESS_OUT_L, and PRESS_OUT_XL are 0x3F, 0x80, 0x00, respectively. What is the corresponding pressure in hPa?

Solution:

Concatenate three values into a 24-bit value: 0x3F8000 = 4,161,536.

Divide the value by 4096:

$$\text{Barometric pressure} = 4161536 \div 4096 = 1016 \text{ hPa}$$

11.11.5 INTERPRETING TEMPERATURE IN OC

The temperature raw count is stored in registers TEMP_OUT_L (0x2B) and TEMP_OUT_H (0x2C). When the temperature is negative, the raw count is a 2's complement value. The temperature in °C can be determined by calculating the two's complement, if necessary, and by performing the following scaling:

Temperature in °C = #counts / scale = #counts ÷ (100 counts/°C)

Example 11.19 Assume that TEMP_OUT_L and TEMP_OUT_H hold 0x48 and 0x26, respectively. What is the corresponding temperature in °C?

Solution: Because the bit 7 of TEMP_OUT_H is 0, there is no need to compute the 2's complement. The 16-bit temperature count is 0x2648 = 9800 counts. The corresponding temperature in °C is

Temperature in °C = 9800 ÷ (100 counts/°C) = 98°C

11.11.6 LPS22HB FIFO DATA STRUCTURE

The LPS22HB embeds a FIFO data structure with 32 40-bit slots. This FIFO enables the MCU to be busy with other important operations instead of continuously polling data from the sensor to avoid losing pressure data. Each FIFO slot holds a 24-bit pressure and 16-bit temperature data.

The FIFO can operate in seven different modes:

- Bypass mode
- FIFO mode
- Stream mode
- Dynamic-stream mode
- Stream-to-FIFO mode
- Bypass-to-stream mode
- Bypass-to-FIFO mode

The FIFO mode is configured via the FIFO_CTRL register. The FIFO statuses, such as FIFO threshold status, FIFO overrun events, and number of unread samples, are available in the FIFO_STATUS register. The contents of FIFO_CTRL and FIFO_STATUS registers are shown in Figure 11.52 and 11.53, respectively. In Figure 11.52, the WTM[4:0] field specifies the depth (or number of entries, one entry has 5 bytes) of the FIFO to be used to hold data. The watermark is also called the threshold of the FIFO data structure.

7	6	5	4	3	2	1	0
F_MODE[2:0]			WTM[4:0]				

F_MODE[2:0]: FIFO mode selection

000: bypass mode   001: FIFO mode
010: Stream mode   011: Stream-to-FIFO mode
100: Bypass-to-stream mode   101: Reserved
110: Dynamic-stream mode   111: Bypass-to-FIFO mode

WTM[4:0]: FIFO watermark level selection

Figure 11.52 LPS22HB FIFO_CTRL register

7	6	5	4	3	2	1	0
FTH_FIFO	OVR	FSS[5:0]					

FTH_FIFO: FIFO watermark status
  0: FIFO filling is lower than threshold level
  1: FIFO filling is equal to or higher than the threshold level
OVR: FIFO overrun status
  0: FIFO is not completely full
  1: FIFO is full and at least one sample in the FIFO has been overwritten
FSS[5:0]: FIFO stored data level
  000000: FIFO empty
  000001: FIFO has one unread sample
  ....
  100000: FIFO is full and has 32 unread samples

Figure 11.53 LPS22HB FIFO_STATUS register

FIFO Bypass Mode

The FIFO is not operational in this mode and remains empty. Bypass mode is also used to reset the FIFO when in the FIFO mode. This mode is illustrated in Figure 11.54.

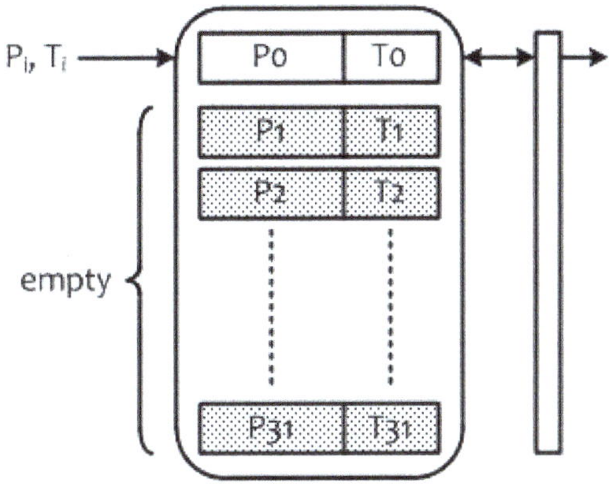

Figure 11.54 FIFO bypass mode

FIFO Mode

When the MCU writes into PRESS_OUT_XL, PRESS_OUT_L, PRESS_OUT_H, TEMP_OUT_L, and TEMP_OUT_H registers, all slots in the FIFO will be pushed down by one slot and the new set of value will be stored in the top slot (**P0:T0**), as shown in Figure 11.55. To read from the FIFO, the MCU reads from PRESS_OUT_XL, PRESS_OUT_L, PRESS_OUT_H, TEMP_OUT_L, and TEMP_OUT_H registers and the value in the bottom slot is returned.

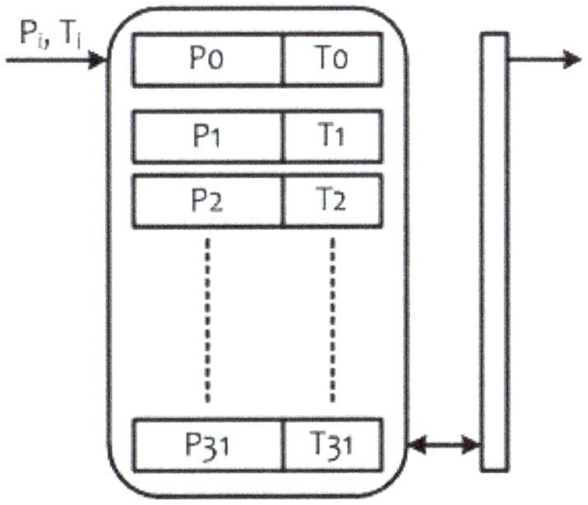

Figure 11.55 LPS22HB FIFO mode

By default, the FIFO has 32 slots. However, the depth of the FIFO can be resized by setting the CTRL_REG2 and FIFO_CTRL registers (by setting the **watermark**).

A FIFO interrupt can be enabled by setting the F_OVR bit in the CTRL_REG3 register. This interrupt is raised when FIFO is filled to the level specified by WTM[4:0] bits of the FIFO_CTRL register.

Stream Mode

This mode provides continuous FIFO update as new data arrive; the oldest one is discarded. If the MCU continues to read the FIFO until the entire FIFO has been read, the last data read remain in the FIFO and, hence, once a new sample is acquired, the FSS[5:0] value in the FIFO_STATUS register rises from 0 to 2. The user can enable the overrun interrupt to inform the MCU when the FIFO is full. If an overrun occurs, the oldest sample in FIFO is overwritten. So, if the FIFO was emptied, the lost sample has already been read (Figure 11.56).

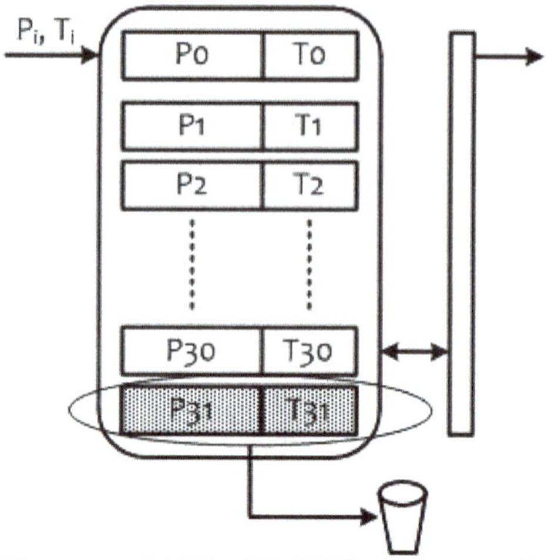

Figure 11.56 LPS22HB FIFO stream mode

Dynamic-Stream Mode

In this mode, after emptying the FIFO, the first new sample that arrives becomes the first to be read in a subsequent read burst. The number of new data available in FIFO does not depend on the previous reading. In this mode, the FSS[5:0] field in the FIFO_STATUS register represents the number of new pressure and temperature samples available in the FIFO buffer.

Stream mode is intended to be used to read all 32 samples of FIFO within the selected output data rate (ODR) after receiving an overrun signal. **Dynamic stream mode** is intended to be used to read FSS[5:0] samples when it is possible to guarantee reading data within an ODR (output data rate defined in the CTRL_REG1 register).

Stream-to-FIFO Mode

In this mode, the FIFO behavior changes according to the IA bit in the INT_SOURCE register. When the IA bit is 1, the FIFO operates in FIFO mode. When the IA bit is 0, the FIFO operates in stream mode. An interrupt generator can be set to the desired configuration through the INTERRUPT_CFG register. The **LIR** bit in **INTERRUPT_CFG** register should be set to 1 in order to have latched interrupt. The behavior of this mode is illustrated in Figure 11.57.

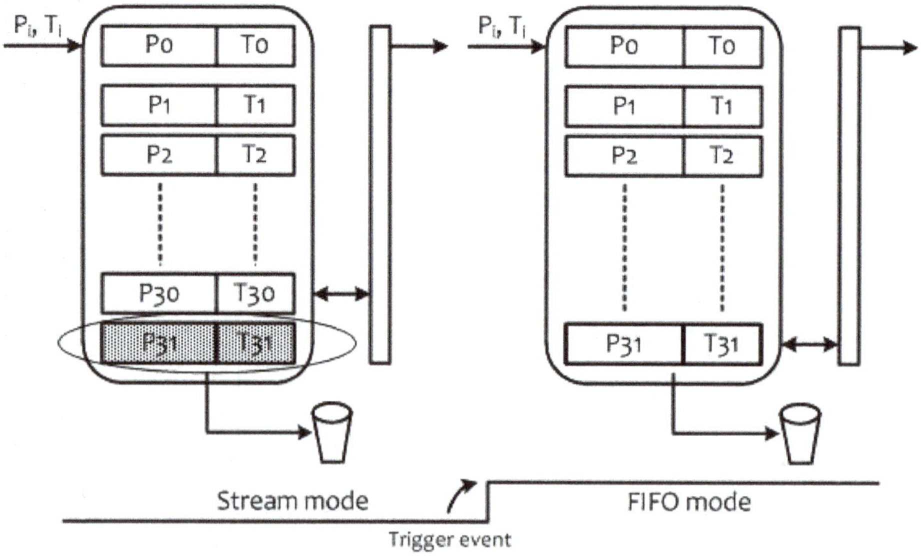

Figure 11.57 LPS22HB Stream-to-FIFO mode

Bypass-to-Stream Mode

In this mode, data management storage inside FIFO operates in stream mode when the IA bit in the INT_SOURCE register is 1. Otherwise, the FIFO operates in bypass mode. The operation of this mode is shown in Figure 11.58.

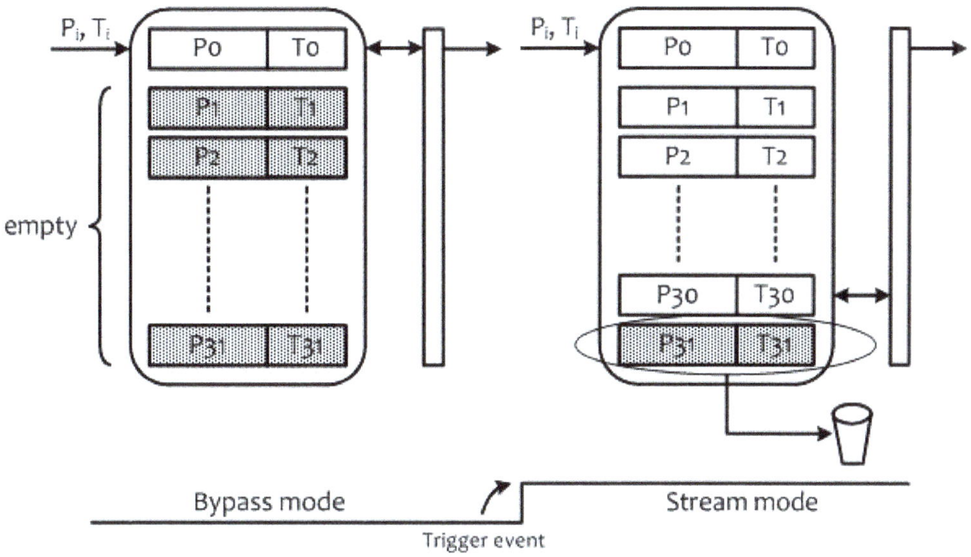

Figure 11.58 LPS22HB Bypass-to-Stream mode

11.11.7 RETRIEVING DATA FROM FIFO

FIFO data are read from PRESS_OUT and TEMP_OUT registers. Each time data are read from the FIFO, the oldest data are placed in the PRESS_OUT_XL, PRESS_OUT_L, PRESS_OUT_H, TEMP_OUT_L, and TEMP_OUT_H registers, and both single read and burst read operations can be used. The device automatically updates the reading address, and it rolls back to 0x28 when register 0x2C is reached. The LPS22HB registers are summarized in Table 11.10.

Table 11.10 LPS22HB register map

Register Name	Type	Register Address (hex)	Default (hex)	Function and comment
Reserved		0x00~0x0A	–	Reserved
INTERRUPT_CFG	R/W	0x0B	0x00	Interrupt register
THS_P_L	R/W	0x0C	0x00	Pressure threshold registers
THS_P_H	R/W	0x0D	0x00	
Reserved		0x0E	–	Reserved
WHO_AM_I	R	0x0F	0xB1	Who am I
CTRL_REG1	R/W	0x10	0x00	Control registers
CTRL_REG2	R/W	0x11	0x10	
CTRL_REG3	R/W	0x12	0x00	
Reserved	--	0x13	--	Reserved
FIFO_CTRL	R/W	0x14	0x00	FIFO configuration register
REF_P_XL	R/W	0x15	0x00	Reference pressure registers
REF_P_L	R/W	0x16	0x00	
REF_P_H	R/W	0x17	0x00	
RPDS_L	R/W	0x18	0x00	Pressure offset registers
RPDS_H	R/W	0x19	0x00	
RES_CONF	R/W	0x1A	0x00	Resolution register

Table 11.10a LPS22HB register map—(continued)

Register Name	Type	Register Address (hex)	Default (hex)	Function and comment
Reserved		0x1B~0x24	--	Reserved
INT_SOURCE	R	0x25	output	Interrupt register
FIFO_STATUS	R	0x26	output	FIFO status register
STATUS	R	0x27	output	Status register
PRESS_OUT_XL	R	0x28	output	
PRESS_OUT_L	R	0x29	output	Pressure output registers
PRESS_OUT_H	R	0x2A	output	
TEMP_OUT_L	R	0x2B	output	Temperature output registers
TEMP_OUT_H	R	0x2C	output	
Reserved	--	0x2D-0x32	--	Reserved
LPFP_RES	R	0x33	output	Filter reset register

INTERRUPT_CFG Register

This register lets the user to enable all possible interrupt sources from the LPS22HB. The contents of this register are shown in Figure 11.59.

7	6	5	4	3	2	1	0
AUTORIFP	RESET_ARP	AUTOREZO	RESET_AZ	DIFF_EN	LIR	PLE	PHE

AUTORIFP: AUTORIFP enable
0: normal mode (not enabled) 1: AutoRIFP enabled
RESET_ARP: reset AutoRIFP function
0: normal mode 1: reset AutoRIFP function
AUTOZERO: enable autozero function
0: normal mode 1: autozero enabled
RESET_AZ: Reset autozero function
0: normal mode 1: reset autozero function
DIFF_EN: Enable interrupt generation
0: interrupt generation disabled 1: interrupt generation enabled
LIR: Latch interrupt request to the INT_SOURCE register
0: interrupt request not latched 1: interrupt request latched
PLE: Enable interrupt generation on pressure low event
0: disable interrupt request
1: enable interrupt request on pressure lower than preset threshold
PHE: Enable interrupt generation on pressure high event
0: disable interrupt request
1: Enable interrupt request on pressure value higher than preset threshold

Figure 11.59 LPS22HB INTERRUP_CFG register (0x0B)

The LPS22HB allows the user to define a pressure threshold using the THS_P_L and THS_P_H registers and define a reference pressure using the REF_P_XL, REF_P_L, and REF_P_H registers. The user can choose to generate an interrupt when the difference between the measured pressure and the reference pressure is higher or lower than the threshold value. To do this, the DIFF_EN bit and one of the PLE and PHE bits (or both) in this register must be set.

When the **DIFF_EN** bit is set and the AUTOZERO or AUTORIFP is enabled, the defined **pressure threshold value** in THS_P (0x0C~0x0D) is compared with

P_DIFF_IN = measured pressure – REF_P

If the **AUTOZERO** bit is set to 1, the measured pressure is used as the reference in the register REF_P. From that point on, the output pressure register PRESS_OUT is updated, and the same value is also used for interrupt generation:

PRESS_OUT = measured pressure – REF_P

After the first conversion, the AUTOZERO bit is automatically cleared to 0. To return to normal mode, **RESET_AZ** bit has to be set to 1. This also resets the contents of the RES_P registers.

If the **AUTORIFP** bit is set to 1, the measured pressure is used as the reference in the register REF_P (0x15~0x17). From that point on, the value used for the interrupt generation is the following:

P_DIFF_IN = measured pressure – REF_P

The output registers PRESS_OUT (0x28~0x2A) show the difference between the measured pressure and the contents of the RPDS registers (**pressure offset**):

PRESS_OUT = measured pressure – RPDS

After the first conversion, AUTORIFP bit is automatically cleared to 0. To return to normal mode, the **RESET_ARP** bit must be set to 1.

THS_P_L and THS_P_H Registers

These two registers hold user-defined threshold value for pressure interrupt event. The **interrupt threshold (hPa)** is ±THS_P / 16. To enable the interrupt event based on this user-defined threshold, the DIFF_EN bit in the INTERRUPT_CFG register must be set to 1, and the PHE or PLE bit must be set.

CTRL_REG1 (0x10)

This register allows the user to

1. Select conversion rate.
2. Enable or disable low pass filter on pressure data when continuous mode is selected.
3. Select continuous or block output registers update until MSB and LSB have been read.
4. Select SPI mode (4-wire or 3-wire).

The contents of this register are shown in Figure 11.60.

7	6	5	4	3	2	1	0
0	ODR2	ODR1	ODR0	EN_LPFP	LPFP_CFG	BDU	SIM

ODR[2:0]: Output data rate selection (for both pressure and temperature)
000: one-shot mode enabled 001: 1 Hz 010: 10 Hz
011: 25 Hz 100: 50 Hz 101: 75 Hz
EN_LPFP: Enable low pass filter on pressure data when continuous mode is used
0: low pass filter disabled (default) 1: low pass filter enabled
LPFP_CFG: low-pass configuration register (see Table 11.15)
BDU: Block data update
0: continuous update
1: Output registers not updated until MSB and LSB have been read
SIM: SPI mode selection
0: 4-wire selection 1: 3-wire selection

Figure 11.60 LPS22HB CTRL_REG1 register (0x10)

Table 11.11 Low-pass filter configuration

EN_LPFP	LPFP_CFG	Additional low-pass filter status	Device bandwidth
0	x	Disabled	ODR/2
1	0	Enabled	ODR/9
1	1	Enabled	ODR/20

CTRL_REG2 Register

This register allows the user to control a few LPS22HB functions. The contents of this register are shown in Figure 11.61.

7	6	5	4	3	2	1	0
BOOT	FIFO_EN	STOP_ON_FTH	IF_ADD_INC	I2C_DIS	SWRESET	0	ONE_SHOT

BOOT: Reboot memory contents
0: normal mode 1: reboot memory content
FIFO_EN: FIFO enabled
0: disabled 1: enabled
STOP_ON_FTH: Stop on FIFO watermark
0: disable 1: enable FIFO watermark level use
IF_ADD_INC: Register address automatically incremented during a multiple byte access
0: disable 1: enable (default)
I2C_DIS: Disable I2C interface
0: I2C enabled 1: I2C disabled
SWRESET: Software reset
0: normal mode 1: perform a software reset
ONE_SHOT: one-shot enable
0: idle mode 1: perform a one-shot conversion

Figure 11.61 LPS22HB CTRL_REG2 register (0x11)

The **BOOT** bit is used to reload the calibration data from flash memory block into the internal registers related to trimming functions to allow correct behavior. The loading of calibration data is automatically performed at device power-up.

When the SWRESET bit is set to 1, the INTERRUPT_CFG, THS_P_L, THS_P_H, CTRL_REG1, CTRL_REG2, CTRL_REG3, FIFO_CTRL, REF_P_XL, REF_P_L, and REF_P_H registers are reset to their default values.

Setting the ONE_SHOT bit to 1 when the ODR[2:0] field in the CTRL_REG1 register is 000 triggers a single measurement of pressure and temperature.

7	6	5	4	3	2	1	0
INT_H_L	PP_OD	F_FSS5	F_FTH	F_OVR	DRDY	INT_S2	INT_S1

INT_H_L: Interrupt active-high/low
  0: active high 1: active low
PP_OD: Push-pull/open-drain selection on interrupt pads
  0: push-pull 1: open drain
F_FSS5: FIFO full flag on INT_DRDY pin
  0: disable 1: enable
F_FTH: FIFO watermark status on INT_DRDY pin
  0: disable 1: enable
F_OVR: FIFO overrun interrupt on INT_DRDY pin
  0: disable 1: enable
DRDY: Data ready signal on INT_DRDY pin
  0: disable 1: enable
INT_S[1:0]: data signal on INT_DRDY pin control bits
  See Table 11.16.

Figure 11.62 LPS22HB CTRL_REG3 register (0x12)

Table 11.12 Interrupt configurations

INT_S2	INT_S1	INT_DRDY pin configuration
0	0	Data signal (in order of priority: DRDY or F_FTH, F_OVR or F_FSS5)
0	1	Pressure high (P_high)
1	0	Pressure low (P_low)
1	1	Pressure low or high

CTRL_REG3 Register

This register provides additional control to the interrupt signal (**INT_DRDY**) for the LPS22HB. The contents of this register are shown in Figure 11.62. The overall control for the INT_DRDY pin is shown in Figure 11.63.

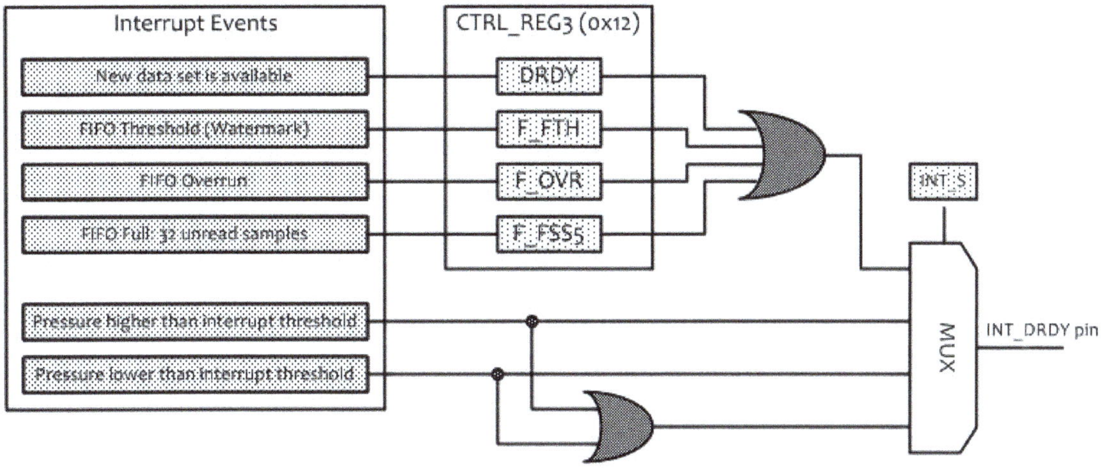

Figure 11.63 Interrupt events on INT_DRDY pin

REF_P_XL, REF_P_L, REF_P_H (0x15~0x17): Reference Pressure Registers

These registers are used when the AUTOZERO or AUTORIFP function is enabled.

RPDS_L, RPDS_H (0x18~0x19): Pressure Offset

The pressure offset is a 16-bit data that can be used to implement **one-point calibration** (OPC) after soldering the chip on the printed circuit board. The value is represented in 2's complement format.

RES_CONF (0x1A): Resolution Register

This register selects the current mode. The contents of this register are shown in Figure 11.64.

7	6	5	4	3	2	1	0
0	0	0	0	0	0	reserved	LC_EN

LC_EN: Low current (power) mode enable
0: normal mode (low noise mode)
1: low current mode

Figure 11.64 LPS22HB RES_CONF register (0x1A)

INT_SOURCE (0x25): Interrupt Source Register

This register records the LPS22HB interrupt sources. The contents of this register are shown in Figure 11.65.

7	6	5	4	3	2	1	0
BOOT_STATUS	0	0	0	0	IA	PL	PH

BOOT_STATUS:
0: normal mode 1: Boot phase is running
IA: Interrupt active
0: No interrupt has been generated 1: one or more interrupt events have been generated
PL: Differential pressure low
0: No interrupt has been generated 1: low differential pressure event has occurred
PH: Differential pressure high
0: No interrupt has been generated 1: high differential pressure event has occurred

Figure 11.65 LPS22HB INT_SOURCE register (0x1A)

STATUS Register (0x27)

The LPS22HB sensor operation status flags are recorded in this register. The contents of this register are shown in Figure 11.66.

7	6	5	4	3	2	1	0
--	--	T_OR	P_OR	--	--	T_DA	P_DA

T_OR: Temperature data overrun
  0: No overrun   1: A new data for temperature has overwritten the previous data
P_OR: Pressure data overrun
  0: No overrun   1: A new data for pressure has overwritten the previous data
T_DA: Temperature data available
  0: New data for temperature is not yet available
  1: New data for temperature is generated
P_DA: Pressure data available
  0: new data for pressure is not yet available
  1: a new pressure data is generated

Figure 11.66 LPS22HB STATUS register (0x27)

PRESS_OUT_XL, PRESS_OUT_L, PRESS_OUT_H (0x28~0x2A): Pressure Output Registers

The pressure output value is a 24-bit data that contain the measured pressure. It is composed of PRESS_OUT-_H, PRESS_OUT_L, and PRESS_OUT_XL. The value is expressed as 2's complement. The pressure output register PRESS_OUT is provided as the difference between the measured pressure and the contents of the offset register RPDS.

TEMP_OUT_L, TEMP_OUT_H: Temperature Output Register

This 16-bit register holds the measured temperature value.

11.11.8 CIRCUIT CONNECTION

Any STM32L475 I²C module can interface with the LPS22HB sensor. A circuit connection using the I²C2 to connect to the LPS22HB is shown in Figure 11.67.

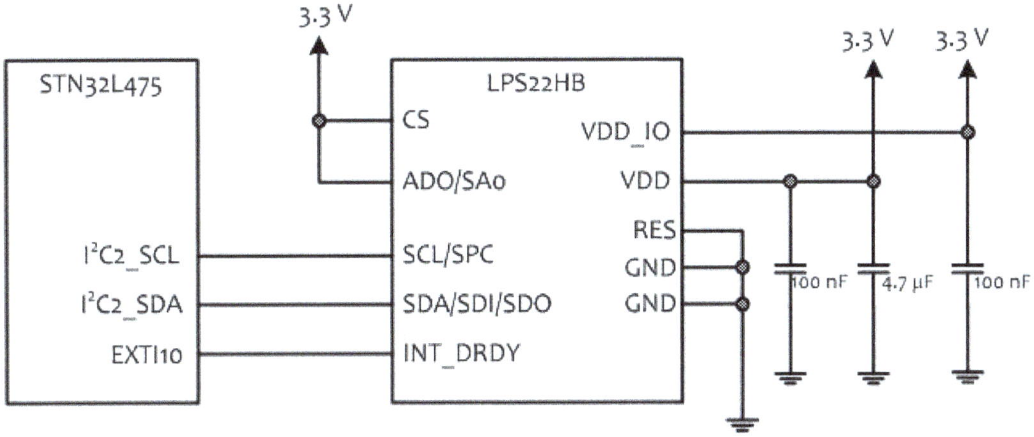

Figure 11.67 Circuit connection between the LPS22HB and STM32L475 IoT node

Example 11.20 Write a C function that writes values (stored in a buffer pointed to by **ptr**) into a group of **k** contiguous registers of the LPS22HB starting from address **regAdr** via the I²C interface assuming the circuit connection of the LPS22HB is shown in Figure 11.67.

Solution: Because the SA0 pin is pulled high in Figure 11.67, the slave address of the LPS22HB is 0xBA (including R/W bit, set to 0). The function is as follows:

```
void wrLPS22HBRegs(uint32_t k, uint8_t regAdr, uint8_t *ptr)
{
    uint32_t j;
    blkSize = wrBytes = k + 1;
    rdBytes    = 0;
    wrNotDone = 0;
    if (k > 1){
        outBuf[0]   = regAdr + 0x80; // address of first register to be written
    else
        outBuf[0] = regAdr;
    for(j = 1; j < k+1; j++)
        outBuf[j]   = *ptr++;
    ix    =    jx = 0;
    I2C2->CR2        = I2C_CR2_AUTOEND + (wrBytes << I2C_CR2_NBYTES_Pos) + 0xBA;
    I2C2->CR2        |= I2C_CR2_START; // generate a START condition
    while(wrBytes); // wait until all the bytes have been sent out
}
```

Example 11.21 Write a C function that reads back a group of **k** registers that have contiguous addresses and leaves the read back values in a buffer pointed to by **ptr**. Assume that the LPS2HB is connected to the STM32L475 via the I²C interface as shown in Figure 11.67.

Solution: The function is as follows:

```
void rdLPS22HBRegs(uint32_t k, uint8_t regAdr, uint8_t *ptr)
{
    uint32_t j;
    blkSize    = wrBytes = 1;
```

```
    rdBytes     = k;
    wrNotDone = 0;
    if (k > 1)
        outBuf[0] = regAdr + 0x80; // read back multiple registers
    else
        outBuf[0] = regAdr;
    jx    =    ix = 0;
    I2C2->CR2 = (1 << I2C_CR2_NBYTES_Pos) + 0xBA;
    I2C2->CR2 |= I2C_CR2_START;
    while(rdBytes);
    for (j = 0; j < k; j++)
        *ptr++ = inBuf[j]; // copy data to the buffer
}
```

Example 11.22 Write a sequence of C statements to configure the LPS22HB as follows:

- CTRL_REG1: Enable one-shot mode, disable low-pass filter, block data update.
- CTRL_REG2: Select normal mode, disable FIFO, enable register address increment after each access, enable I^2C.
- CTRL_REG3: Configure INT_EXTI10 (interrupt) to active high, push-pull, enable DRDY signal on INT_DRDY pin.

Solution:

The value to be written into CTRL_REG1 (register address is 0x10) is 0x02.

The value to be written into CTRL_REG2 is 0x10.

The value to be written into CTRL_REG3 is 0x04.

The following C statements perform the specified configuration:

```
uint8_t  regConf[10];
regConf[0] = 0x02;
regConf[1] = 0x10;
regConf[2] = 0x04;
wrLPS22HBRegs(3, 0x10, &regConf[0]);
```

Example 11.23 Write a sequence of C statements to perform the following operations:

- Configure PD10 pin for input and use it as the source of EXTI10.
- Configure EXTI10 to trigger on the rising edge.
- Enable EXTI10 interrupt and put it on highest priority (0).
- Enable interrupt globally.

Solution:

```
GPIOD->MODER        &= ~GPIO_MODER_MODE10; //configure PD10 for input
SYSCFG->EXTICR[2]   &= ~SYSCFG_EXTICR3_EXTI10;
SYSCFG->EXTICR[2]   |= SYSCFG_EXTICR3_EXTI10_PD; // select PD10 for EXTI10
EXTI->RTSR1         |= EXTI_RTSR1_RT10; // set EXTI10 for rising edge trigger
EXTI->IMR1          |= EXTI_IMR1_IM10; // unmask EXTI10
NVIC_EnableIRQ(EXTI15_10_IRQn);
NVIC_SetPriority(EXTI15_10, 0);
__enable_irq();
```

Example 11.24 Write a sequence of C statements to force LPS22HB to start a one-shot conversion.

Solution:

To start a one-shot measurement on the LHS22HB, set the bit 0 of the **CTRL_REG2** register to 1. The following statements perform the specified operation:

```
uint8_t  regConf[10];
...
regConf[0] = 0x01;
wrLPS22HBRegs(1, 0x11, &regConf[0]);
```

Example 11.25 Write an interrupt service routine for EXTI10 interrupt. This service routine will simply clear the PIF10 flag and set a global variable **pressNew** to 1 and return.

Solution: We need to declare pressNew as a global variable.

The interrupt service routine for EXTI10 is as follows:

```
uint32_t  pressNew;
```

```
void EXTI15_10_IRQHandler (void)
{
    if(EXTI->PR1 & EXTI_PR1_PIF10) { // is interrupt caused by EXTI10?
        EXTI->PR1 = EXTI_PR1_PIF10; // clear PIF10 flag
        pressNew = 1;
    }
}
```

Example 11.26 Write a sequence of C statements that start with waiting for the **pressNew** variable to be set to 1, read back the pressure data, convert that data to the value represented in **hPa,** and store the pressure and temperature readings in the variable newPressure and newTemp, respectively.

Solution:

We need to declare the following variables:

```
uint32_t    newPressure, pressNew;
uint16_t    newTemp;
```

The following statements perform the specified operations:

```
while(pressNew == 0);
rdLPS22HBRegs(5, 0x28, &presstemp[0]);
newPressure    =    (((uint32_t)presstemp[2])<<16) + (((uint32_t)presstemp[1]) << 8)+
               (uint32_t)presstemp[0]; // combine pressure high, middle, & low bytes
newPressure    = newpressure >> 12; // convert pressure to hPa unit
newTemp  = (((uint16_t)presstemp[4])<<8) + (((uint16_t)presstemp[3]));
newTemp  = newTemp / 100;
```

11.12 Summary

Compared with the SPI interface, the I²C bus offers the following advantages:

- There is no need to use chip-enable or chip-select signal to select slave devices.
- Multiple master devices can coexist in a system because I²C provides easy bus arbitration.
- Many more devices can coexist in the same I²C bus.
- Resources can be shared by multiple masters (microcontrollers).

However, the SPI has the following advantages over the I^2C bus:

- Higher data rate (no longer true for ultra-fast mode).
- Much lower software overhead to carry out data transmission.

Data transfer over the I^2C bus requires the generation of the following signal components:

- Start condition
- Stop condition
- ACK or NACK
- Restart condition
- Data

Whenever there are multiple master devices attempting to send data over the I^2C bus, bus arbitration is carried out automatically. The loser is decided whenever it attempts to drive the SDA line to high, whereas another master device drives the SDA line low.

To select the slave device without using the chip-select (or chip-enable) signal, address information is used. Both the 7-bit and 10-bit addresses are supported in the same I^2C bus. Ten-bit addressing will be used in a system that consists of many slave devices. The I^2C bus supports five speed rates:

- 100 kHz—standard mode
- 400 kHz—fast mode
- 1 MHz—fast-mode-plus
- 3.4 MHz—high-speed mode
- 5 MHz—ultra fast mode

The STM32L475 I^2C implementation supports three speed modes: standard mode, fast mode, and fast-mode-plus. Higher speed modes are not supported. The STM32L475 I^2C is also compatible to SMBus and PMBus.

Each data transfer starts with a START condition and ends with a STOP condition. One (7-bit addressing) or two control bytes (10-bit addressing) will follow the START condition, which specifies the slave device to receive or send data. For each data byte, the receiver must assert either ACK or NACK condition to acknowledge or un-acknowledge, respectively, the data transfer.

The 24FC256 is an EEPROM with I^2C interface. It has a 32-KB capacity. This chip has an internal address pointer that will increment automatically after each access. This feature can increase the access efficiency when the access patterns are sequential.

The HTS221 from ST Microelectronics is a device that can measure both the relative humidity and temperature. The MCU can use either the SPI or I^2C interface to access the HTS221.

The LPS22HB is a combined pressure and temperature digital sensor. Pressure output is 24 bits, whereas the temperature output is 16 bits. This chip can perform up to 75 conversions per second. Both the SPI and I^2C interfaces are supported.

11.13 Exercises

E11.1 Suppose that the 7-bit address of an I²C slave is B'1010A2A1A0' with A2, A1, and A0 tied to high, low, and high, respectively. What is the 8-bit hex write address for this device? What is the 8-bit hex read address?

E11.2 Refer to Table 11.2 and compute the $R_{P(max)}$ and $R_{P(min)}$ for standard mode.

E11.3 Find a value to be written into the I2Cx->TIMINGR register so that the I²C module can operate at fast mode, assuming that f_{I2CCLK} = 64 MHz. You can enable or disable analog and/or digital noise filter.

E11.4 Find a value to be written into the I2Cx->TIMINGR register so that the I²C module can operate at fast mode and fast-mode-plus assuming that f_{I2CCLK} = 50 MHz. You can enable or disable analog noise filter and digital noise filter.

E11.5 Assume that STM32L475 is running at 80 MHz. Write a test program to test the writeBytesEE () and readBytesEE() functions. The test program performs the following operations:

Step 1

Configure PORTA to drive 8 LEDs. Initialize I²C2 to operate in fast mode.

Step 2

Write one byte at a time and read it back and output the read back value to PORTA and wait for 200 ms. Perform this operation from address 0x0000 to 0x7FFF. For locations at even address, write 0x00. For locations at odd address, write 0xFF.

Step 3

Write one block of 64 bytes at a time and read back one block of 64 bytes at a time and store the read back data in a buffer. The values written into a block are from 1 to 64. After the read back data are stored, output the data one byte a time to PORTA and wait for 200 ms for each byte. Repeat this process until the whole EEPROM has been written into and read out.

E11.6 Write a few C statements to store the values 1, 2, 3, 4, 5, 6, 7, 8 at locations starting at 0x1024 to 0x1031 in the 24FC256.

E11.7 Write a sequence of C statements to read the contents of 16 bytes starting from 0x200 in the 24FC256 and save them in the array of bytes with the label of **xarr**.

E11.8 For the HTS221 humidity sensor, assume that T0_degC_x8, T1_degC_x8, T1/T0 msb, T0_OUT, T1_OUT, and T_OUT are 0x78°C, 0x20°C, 4, 300, 500, and 400, respectively. T0_degC_x8, T1_degC_x8, and T0/T1 msb are read from locations 0x32, 0x33, and 0x35, respectively. What is the actual temperature?

E11.9 For the HTS221 humidity sensor, assume that T0_degC_x8, T1_degC_x8, T1/T0 msb, T0_OUT, T1_OUT, and T_OUT are 0x78°C, 0x90°C, 4, 300, 500, and 400, respectively. T0_degC_x8 and T1_degC_x8, T0/T1 msb are read from locations 0x32, 0x33, and 0x35, respectively. What is the actual temperature?

E11.10 Assume that the values of H0_T0_OUT, H1_T0_OUT, H0_RH_x2, H1_RH_x2, and H_OUT read from the humidity sensor HTS221 are 4000, 7200, 30%, 90%, and 5600, respectively. What is RH%?

E11.11 Assume that the values of H0_T0_OUT, H1_T0_OUT, H0_RH_x2, H1_RH_x2, and H_OUT read from the humidity sensor HTS221 are 4000, 1600, 20%, 180%, and 13000, respectively. What is RH%?

E11.12 Assume that the values read out from registers PRESS_OUT_H, PRESS_OUT_L, and PRESS_OUT_XL of the pressure sensor LPS22HB are 0x4B, 0x00, and 0x00, respectively. What is the corresponding pressure?

E11.13 Assume that the values read out from registers PRESS_OUT_H, PRESS_OUT_L, and PRESS_OUT_XL of the pressure sensor LPS22HB are 0x48, 0x80, and 0x10, respectively. What is the corresponding pressure?

E11.14 Assume that the values read out from registers TEMP_OUT_L and TEMP_OUT_H of the pressure sensor LPS22HB are 0x42 and 0x16, respectively. What is the corresponding temperature in °C?

E11.15 Assume that the values read out from registers TEMP_OUT_L and TEMP_OUT_H of the pressure sensor LPS22HB are 0x32 and 0x10, respectively. What is the corresponding temperature in °C?

E11.16 Write a function that can write one or multiple registers into the ST MEM sensor. Assume the prototype of this function is as follows:

```
void wrSensorRegs (uint8_t slaveID, uint16_t regCnt, uint16_t regAdr, uint8_t *ptr);
```

where,

- slaveID: 7-bit sensor address (or called it sensor ID)
- regCnt : number of registers to be written into
- regAdr: the address of the first register to be written into
- *ptr: pointer to the buffer that holds the values to be written into MEM sensor registers

Assume that **blkSize**, **wrBytes**, **rdBytes**, and **wrNotDone** have been defined globally and the I^2C interrupt handling routines have been defined.

11.14 Laboratory Assignments

L11.1 Data Transfer with 24FC256. Use the I^2C3 module to interface with the 24FC256. Configure PC0 and PC1 to alternate function 4 (AF4) to be used as SCL and SDA pins. Configure PC0 and PC1 to open drain and connect them to appropriate pull-up resistors. Configure system clock to 80 MHz. Select APB1 clock as the source clock for I^2C3 (also 80 MHz). Configure the I^2C3 module to operate at fast-mode-plus. Write the values 10, 20, 30 to memory locations 0, 10, 20, respectively. Read them out and display these values in the terminal window of the PC.

L11.2 Humidity and Temperature Measurement. Use the I^2C2 module to interface with the HTS221 humidity sensor. Configure the I^2C2 module to operate at fast mode. Configure PB10 and PB11 for alternate function AF4 to be used as SCL and SDA. Configure PB10 and PB11 for open drain with pull-up. Measure both the humidity and temperature once per second and display them on the terminal window on the PC.

L11.3 Barometric Pressure Measurement. Use the I^2C2 module to interface with the LPS22HB pressure sensor. Configure PB10 and PB11 for alternate function AF4. Configure PB10 and PB11 for open drain with pull-up. Measure the barometric pressure once every second and display the pressure value on the terminal window of the PC.

A

Direct Memory Access (DMA)

A.1 Objectives

After completing this Appendix, you will be able to

- Describe the operation of DMA.
- Understand why DMA is more efficient than program-controlled transfer in transferring a large block of data.
- Understand the structure of the STM32L475 DMAs.
- Name the DMA registers.
- Configure a DMA channel for data transfer.
- Start a DMA transfer.

A.2 Introduction to DMA

When an embedded system is operating, there is always a need to transfer data from one place to another. The data transfer may occur between

- A peripheral and a memory location
- Two peripherals
- Two different memory locations

To perform a data transfer without the DMA, the processor is required to

1. Execute an instruction to fetch data from the source location and
2. Execute an instruction to store it in the destination.

When the application requires the processor to transfer a block of data, the processor is required to execute a program loop to carry out the transfer. In each iteration of the program loop, the processor is required to

Step 1

Test the termination condition of the program loop. If the loop is done, skip Steps 2 to 5.

Step 2

Execute an instruction to fetch data from the source location and update the source address pointer. This may take one to two clock cycles.

Step 3

Execute an instruction to write data to the destination location and update the destination pointer. This may take one to two clock cycles.

Step 4

Decrement the transfer count.

Step 5

Jump back to Step 1.

For each transfer, the processor is required to execute at least five instructions. For today's pipelined processor, one data transfer takes at least five clock cycles. This method is called **program-controlled transfer method**. During the block data transfer, the CPU cannot perform any other operation.

The **direct memory access (DMA)** is a data transfer method in which a special hardware performs the operations in Steps 2 and 3 while at the same time updates the source pointer, destination pointer, and the transfer count in each data transfer. The processor does not need to execute any instruction during the data transfer phase. For one data transfer, two clock cycles will be needed. Before the DMA transfer, the processor must set up the data source pointer, the destination pointer, transfer count, and the size (number of bytes) of each transfer. These are the overhead for setting up the DMA transfer. During the DMA data transfer phase, the processor is free to perform other operations including executing other instructions as long as there is no bus conflict with the DMA transfer.

When transferring a large block of data, DMA method is obviously much more efficient than the program-controlled method. When the number of transfers is not large, DMA may not be more efficient considering the overhead involved in setting up the DMA transfer.

A.3 The STM32L475 DMA Controller

The STM32L475 (and other STM32 Cortex-M4) processor accesses peripherals through the AHB1 and AHB2 buses. The peripherals are connected to the AHB1 bus via the APB1 and APB2 buses.

The STM32L475 has two DMA controllers: DMA1 and DMA2. Each DMA controller has seven channels and can perform peripheral-to-memory, memory-to-peripheral, memory-to-memory, and peripheral-to-peripheral data transfers.

Each DMA channel is associated either with a DMA request signal coming from a peripheral, or with a software trigger in memory-to-memory transfers. A DMA request from a peripheral can be programmed into four priority levels: **very high**, **high**, **medium**, and **low**. If two DMA requests are programmed to the same priority level, the request from the lower numbered channel has higher priority. For example, if a request from channel 1 and a request from channel 2 have been programmed to the same priority level, the request from channel 1 will be serviced before the request from channel 2.

The size of each DMA transfer can be a byte (8 bits), a half-word (16 bits), or a word (32 bits). The transfer sizes of the source and destination are independent. That is, the transfer sizes from the source and the destination can be different. Source and destination addresses must be aligned on the data size.

The circular buffer management is included in the DMA transfer between the peripheral and memory. That is, it is possible to use DMA to transfer the same block of data from memory to peripheral or from peripheral to memory repeatedly.

Interrupts can be generated from each DMA channel. The interrupt can be generated by three events: transfer complete, half transfer, or transfer error.

A.4 The STM32L475 DMA Implementation

A block diagram of the STM32L475 DMA controller is shown in Figure AppA.1. As shown in the diagram, the DMA controller performs direct memory transfer by sharing the AHB system bus with other system masters. The bus matrix implements the round-robin scheduling. DMA requests may stop the CPU access to the system bus for a number of bus cycles, when CPU and DMA target the same destination (memory or peripheral).

According to its configuration through the AHB slave interface, the DMA controller arbitrates between the DMA channels and their associated received requests. The DMA controller also schedules the DMA data transfer over the single AHB port master. The DMA controller generates an interrupt per channel to the interrupt controller.

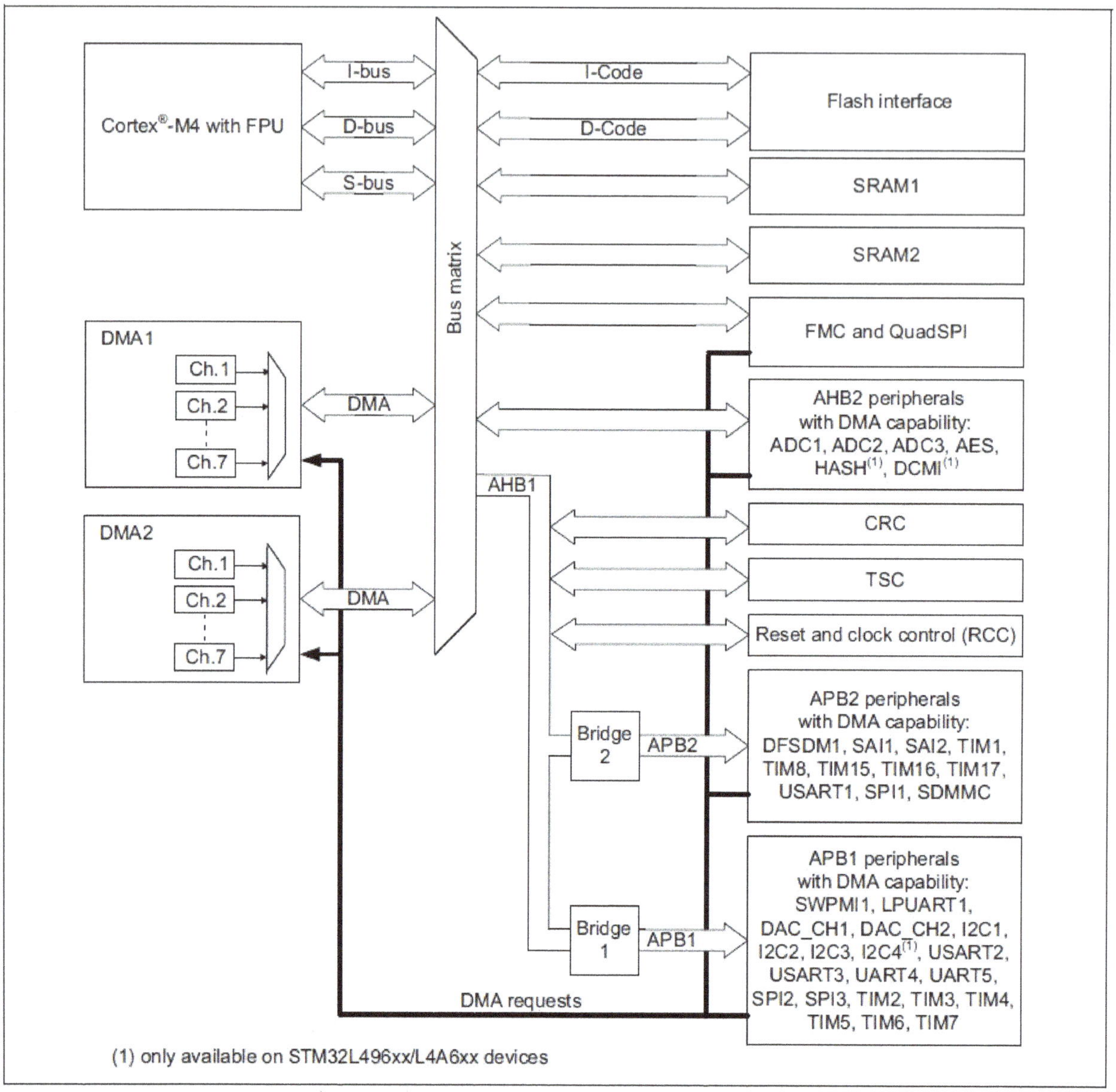

Figure AppA.1 STM32L475 DMA block diagram

A.4.1 REGISTER NAMING ISSUE

Each DMA channel has the following registers to support its operation:

- Channel controller register 1 (CCR)
- Number of data to transfer register (CNDTR)
- Channel peripheral address register (CPAR)
- Channel memory address register (CMAR)

The stm32L475xx.h header file provides the following struct data type definition to facilitate the access of these four registers:

```
typedef struct
{
    __IO uint32_t CCR;
    __IO uint32_t CNDTR;
    __IO uint32_t CPAR;
    __IO uint32_t CMAR;
} DMA_Channel_TypeDef;
```

Each DMA controller has two registers related to the interrupts of seven channels:

- DMA interrupt status register (ISR)
- DMA Interrupt flag clear register (IFCR)

The stm32L475xx.h header file provides the following struct data type definition to facilitate the access of these two registers:

```
typedef struct
{
    __IO uint32_t ISR;
    __IO uint32_t IFCR;
} DMA_TypeDef;
```

Each DMA controller also has a channel selection register

- DMA channel selection register (CSELR)

The stm32L475xx.h header file provides the following struct data type definition to facilitate the access of this register:

```
typedef struct
{
    __IO uint32_t CSELR;
} DMA_Request_TypeDef;
```

These registers are assigned to certain addresses and the stm32L475xx.h header file includes the following address assignment statements:

```
#define    PERIPH_BASE        ((uint32_t) 0x40000000U) // peripheral base address
#define    AHB1PERIPH_BASE    PERIPH_BASE
```

```
#define    DMA1_BASE              (AHB1PERIPH_BASE)
#define    DMA2_BASE              (AHB1PERIPH_BASE + 0x0400U)
#define    DMA1_Channel1_BASE     (DMA1_BASE + 0x0008U)
#define    DMA1_Channel2_BASE     (DMA1_BASE + 0x001CU)
#define    DMA1_Channel3_BASE     (DMA1_BASE + 0x0030U)
#define    DMA1_Channel4_BASE     (DMA1_BASE + 0x0044U)
#define    DMA1_Channel5_BASE     (DMA1_BASE + 0x0058U)
#define    DMA1_Channel6_BASE     (DMA1_BASE + 0x006CU)
#define    DMA1_Channel7_BASE     (DMA1_BASE + 0x0080U)
#define    DMA1_CSELR_BASE        (DMA1_BASE + 0x00A8U)
#define    DMA2_Channel1_BASE     (DMA2_BASE + 0x0008U)
#define    DMA2_Channel2_BASE     (DMA2_BASE + 0x001CU)
#define    DMA2_Channel3_BASE     (DMA2_BASE + 0x0030U)
#define    DMA2_Channel4_BASE     (DMA2_BASE + 0x0044U)
#define    DMA2_Channel5_BASE     (DMA2_BASE + 0x0058U)
#define    DMA2_Channel6_BASE     (DMA2_BASE + 0x006CU)
#define    DMA2_Channel7_BASE     (DMA2_BASE + 0x0080U)
#define    DMA2_CSELR_BASE        (DMA2_BASE + 0x00A8U)
```

With these address definitions, pointers to DMA1, DMA2, seven channels of each DMA, and the channel selection module of each DMA controller are defined:

```
#define    DMA1             ((DMA_TypeDef *) DMA1_BASE) // pointer to DMA1
#define    DMA2             ((DMA_TypeDef *) DMA2_BASE) // pointer to DMA2
#define    DMA1_Channel1    ((DMA_Channel_TypeDef *) DMA1_Channel1_BASE)
#define    DMA1_Channel2    ((DMA_Channel_TypeDef *) DMA1_Channel2_BASE)
#define    DMA1_Channel3    ((DMA_Channel_TypeDef *) DMA1_Channel3_BASE)
#define    DMA1_Channel4    ((DMA_Channel_TypeDef *) DMA1_Channel4_BASE)
#define    DMA1_Channel5    ((DMA_Channel_TypeDef *) DMA1_Channel5_BASE)
#define    DMA1_Channel6    ((DMA_Channel_TypeDef *) DMA1_Channel6_BASE)
#define    DMA1_Channel7    ((DMA_Channel_TypeDef *) DMA1_Channel7_BASE)
```

```
#define    DMA1_CSELR        ((DMA_Request_TypeDef *) DMA1_CSELR_BASE)
#define    DMA2_Channel1     ((DMA_Channel_TypeDef *) DMA2_Channel1_BASE)
#define    DMA2_Channel2     ((DMA_Channel_TypeDef *) DMA2_Channel2_BASE)
#define    DMA2_Channel3     ((DMA_Channel_TypeDef *) DMA2_Channel3_BASE)
#define    DMA2_Channel4     ((DMA_Channel_TypeDef *) DMA2_Channel4_BASE)
#define    DMA2_Channel5     ((DMA_Channel_TypeDef *) DMA2_Channel5_BASE)
#define    DMA2_Channel6     ((DMA_Channel_TypeDef *) DMA2_Channel6_BASE)
#define    DMA2_Channel7     ((DMA_Channel_TypeDef *) DMA2_Channel7_BASE)
#define    DMA2_CSELR        ((DMA_Request_TypeDef *) DMA2_CSELR_BASE)
```

With these pointers in place, registers within each struct can be accessed via these pointers. For example, the CCR, CNDTR, CPAR, and CMAR registers of channel 1 of the DMA1 are accessed (in a C program) using DMA1_Channel1->CCR, DMA1_Channel1->CNDTR, DMA1_Channel1->CPAR, and DMA1_Channel1->CMAR, respectively.

The CSELR register of DMA1 and DMA2 are accessed using DMA1_CSELR->CSELR and DMA2_CSELR->CSELR, respectively.

The ISR and IFCR registers of DMA1 and DMA2 are accessed using DMA1->ISR, DMA1->IFCR, DMA2->ISR, and DMA2->IFCR, respectively.

A.4.2 DMA REQUEST MAPPING

The peripherals of the STM32L475 are preassigned to the channels of each DMA controller. This assignment is fixed and cannot be changed. Because there are many more peripherals than the number of DMA channels, multiple peripherals must be assigned to each channel. Because only one peripheral's DMA request can be accepted to a channel at a time, the user is required to program the CnS[3:0] field of the DMA$_x$_CSELR->CSELR register to assign a peripheral to **channel n** (n = 1 to 7) of DMAx (x = 1 or 2). The contents of the DMA1_CSELR->CSELR and DMA2_CSELR->CSELR registers are shown in Figures AppA.1 and AppA.2, respectively. Another form of DMA channel assignment for peripherals is given in Tables A.1 and A.2.

31	30	29	28	27	26	25	24
				C7S[3:0]			
23	22	21	20	19	18	17	16
C6S[3:0]				C5S[3:0]			
15	14	13	12	11	10	9	8
C4S[3:0]				C3S[3:0]			
7	6	5	4	3	2	1	0
C2S[3:0]				C1S[3:0]			

Reset value = 0x0000 0000
Addr offset = 0xA8

C7S[3:0]: DMA channel 7 selection
- 0000: Channel 7 mapped on DFSDM3　　0001: Channel 7 mapped on SAI2_B
- 0010: Channel 7 mapped on USART2_TX　　0011: Channel 7 mapped on I2C1_RX
- 0100: Channel 7 mapped on TIM2_CH2/TIM2_CH4
- 0101: Channel 7 mapped on TIM17_CH1/TIM17_UP
- 0110: Channel 7 mapped on TIM4_UP　　0111: Channel 7 mapped on TIM1_CH3

C6S[3:0]: DMA channel 6 selection
- 0000: Channel 6 mapped on DFSDM2　　0001: Channel 6 mapped on SAI2_A
- 0010: Channel 6 mapped on USART2_RX　　0011: Channel 6 mapped on I2C1_TX
- 0100: Channel 6 mapped on TIM16_CH1/TIM16_UP
- 0101: Channel 6 mapped on TIM16_CH1/TIM3_TRIG
- 0110: Reserved　　0111: Channel 6 mapped on TIM1_UP

C5S[3:0]: DMA channel 5 selection
- 0000: Channel 5 mapped on DFSDM1　　0001: Channel 5 mapped on SPI2_TX
- 0010: Channel 5 mapped on USART1_RX　　0011: Channel 5 mapped on I2C2_RX
- 0100: Channel 5 mapped on TIM2_CH1　　0101: Channel 5 mapped on QUADSPI
- 0110: Channel 5 mapped on TIM4_CH3
- 0111: Channel 5 mapped on TIM15_CH1/TIM15_UP/TIM15_TRIG/TIM15_COM

C4S[3:0]: DMA channel 4 selection
- 0000: Channel 4 mapped on DFSDM0　　0001: Channel 4 mapped on SPI2_RX
- 0010: Channel 4 mapped on USART1_TX　　0011: Channel 4 mapped on I2C2_TX
- 0100: Reserved　　0101: Channel 5 mapped on TIM7_UP/DAC2
- 0110: Channel 4 mapped on TIM4_CH2
- 0111: Channel 4 mapped on TIM1_CH4/TIM1_TRIG/TIM1_COM

Figure AppA.2 DMA1 Channel selection register (DMA1_CSELR->CSELR)

31	30	29	28	27	26	25	24
				C7S[3:0]			

23	22	21	20	19	18	17	16
C6S[3:0]				C5S[3:0]			

15	14	13	12	11	10	9	8
C4S[3:0]				C3S[3:0]			

7	6	5	4	3	2	1	0
C2S[3:0]				C1S[3:0]			

Reset value = 0x0000 0000
Addr offset = 0xA8

C3S[3:0]: DMA channel 3 selection
- 0000: Channel 3 mapped on ADC3 — 0001: Channel 3 mapped on SPI1_TX
- 0010: Channel 3 mapped on USART3_RX — 0011: Channel 3 mapped on I2C3_RX
- 0100: Channel 3 mapped on TIM16_CH1/TIM16_CH4
- 0101: Channel 3 mapped on TIM3_CH4/TIM3_UP
- 0110: Channel 3 mapped on TIM6_UP/DAC1
- 0111: Channel 3 mapped on TIM1_CH2

C2S[3:0]: DMA channel 2 selection
- 0000: Channel 2 mapped on ADC2 — 0001: Channel 2 mapped on SPI1_RX
- 0010: Channel 2 mapped on USART3_TX — 0011: Channel 2 mapped on I2C3_TX
- 0100: Channel 2 mapped on TIM2_UP — 0101: Channel 2 mapped on TIM3_CH3
- 0110: Reserved — 0111: Channel 2 mapped on TIM1_CH1

C1S[3:0]: DMA channel 1 selection
- 0000: Channel 1 mapped on ADC1 — 0001~0011: Reserved
- 0100: Channel 1 mapped on TIM2_CH3
- 0101: Channel 1 mapped on TIM17_CH1/TIM17_UP
- 0110: Channel 1 mapped on TIM4_CH1 — 0111: Reserved

Figure AppA.2a DMA1 Channel selection register (DMA1_CSELR->CSELR)—(continued)

31	30	29	28	27	26	25	24
				C7S[3:0]			
23	**22**	**21**	**20**	**19**	**18**	**17**	**16**
C6S[3:0]				C5S[3:0]			
15	**14**	**13**	**12**	**11**	**10**	**9**	**8**
C4S[3:0]				C3S[3:0]			
7	**6**	**5**	**4**	**3**	**2**	**1**	**0**
C2S[3:0]				C1S[3:0]			

Reset value = 0x0000 0000
Addr offset = 0xA8

C7S[3:0]: DMA channel 7 selection
0000: Reserved
0001: Channel 7 mapped on SAI1_B
0010: Channel 7 mapped on USART1_RX
0011: Channel 7 mapped on QUADSPI
0100: Channel 7 mapped on LPUART_RX
0101: Channel 7 mapped on I2C1_TX
0110: Reserved
0111: Channel 7 mapped on TIM8_CH2

C6S[3:0]: DMA channel 6 selection
0000: Reserved
0001: Channel 6 mapped on SAI1_A
0010: Channel 6 mapped on USART1_TX
0011: Reserved
0100: Channel 6 mapped on LPUART_TX
0101: Channel 6 mapped on I2C1_RX
0110: Reserved
0111: Channel 6 mapped on TIM8_CH1

C5S[3:0]: DMA channel 5 selection
0000: Channel 5 mapped on ADC3
0001: Reserved
0010: Channel 5 mapped on UART4_RX
0011: Channel 5 mapped on TIM7_UP/DAC2
0100: Reserved
0101: Channel 5 mapped on TIM5_CH1
0110: Reserved
0111: Channel 5 mapped on SDMMC1

C4S[3:0]: DMA channel 4 selection
0000: Channel 4 mapped on ADC2
0001: Channel 4 mapped on SAI2_B
0010: Reserved
0011: Channel 4 mapped on TIM6_UP/DAC1
0100: Channel 4 mapped on SPI1_TX
0101: Channel 4 mapped on TIM5_CH2
0110: Reserved
0111: Channel 4 mapped on SDMMC1

Figure AppA.3 DMA2 Channel selection register (DMA2_CSELR->CSELR)

31	30	29	28	27	26	25	24
				C7S[3:0]			
23	**22**	**21**	**20**	**19**	**18**	**17**	**16**
C6S[3:0]				C5S[3:0]			
15	**14**	**13**	**12**	**11**	**10**	**9**	**8**
C4S[3:0]				C3S[3:0]			
7	**6**	**5**	**4**	**3**	**2**	**1**	**0**
C2S[3:0]				C1S[3:0]			

Reset value = 0x0000 0000
Addr offset = 0xA8

C3S[3:0]: DMA channel 3 selection
- 0000: Channel 3 mapped on ADC1
- 0001: Channel 3 mapped on SAI2_A
- 0010: Channel 3 mapped on UART4_TX
- 0011: Reserved
- 0100: Channel 3 mapped on SPI1_RX
- 0101~0111: Reserved

C2S[3:0]: DMA channel 2 selection
- 0000: Reserved
- 0001: Channel 2 mapped on SAI1_B
- 0010: Channel 2 mapped on UART5_RX
- 0011: Channel 2 mapped on SPI3_TX
- 0100: Channel 2 mapped on SWPMI1_TX
- 0101: Channel 2 mapped on TIM5_CH3/TIM5_UP
- 0110: Reserved
- 0111: Channel 2 mapped on TIM8_CH4/TIM8_TRIG/TIM8_COM

C1S[3:0]: DMA channel 1 selection
- 0000: Reserved
- 0001: Channel 1 mapped on SAI1_A
- 0010: Channel 1 mapped on UART5_TX
- 0011: Channel 1 mapped on SPI3_RX
- 0100: Channel 1 mapped on SWPMI1_RX
- 0101: Channel 1 mapped on TIM5_CH4/TIM5_TRIG/TIM5_COM
- 0110: reserved
- 0111: Channel 1 mapped on TIM8_CH3/TIM8_UP

Figure AppA.3a DMA2 Channel selection register (DMA2_CSELR->CSELR)—(continued)

Table A.1 DMA1 requests for each channel (n = 1 to 7)

$C_nS[3:0]$	Channel 1	Channel 2	Channel 3	Channel 4	Channel 5	Channel 6	Channel 7
0000	ADC1	ADC2	ADC3	DFSDM1_FLT0	DFSDM1_FLT1	DFSDM1_FLT2	DFSDM1_FLT3
0001	--	SPI1_RX	SPI1_TX	SPI2_RX	SPI2_TX	SAI2_A	SAI2_B
0010	--	USART3_TX	USART3_RX	USART1_TX	USART1_RX	USART2_RX	USART2_TX
0011	--	I2C3_TX	I2C3_RX	I2C2_TX	I2C2_RX	I2C1_TX	I2C1_RX
0100	TIM2_CH3	TIM2_UP	TIM16_CH1 TIM16_UP	--	TIM2_CH1	TIM16_CH1 TIM16_UP	TIM2_CH2 TIM2_CH4
0101	TIM17_CH1 TIM17_UP	TIM3_CH3	TIM3_CH4 TIM3_UP	TIM7_UP DAC_CH2	QUADSPI	TIM3_CH1 TIM3_TRIG	TIM17_CH1 TIM17_UP
0110	TIM4_CH1	--	TIM6_UP DAC_CH1	TIM4_CH2	TIM4_CH3	--	TIM4_UP
0111	--	TIM1_CH1	TIM1_CH2	TIM1_CH4 TIM1_TRIG TIM1_COM	TIM15_CH1 TIM15_UP TIM15_TRIG TIM15_COM	TIM1_UP	TIM1_CH3

Table A.2 DMA2 requests for each channel (n = 1 to 7)

$C_nS[3:0]$	Channel 1	Channel 2	Channel 3	Channel 4	Channel 5	Channel 6	Channel 7
0000	I2C4_RX(1)	I2C4_TX(1)	ADC1	ADC2	ADC3	DCMI	--
0001	SAI1_A	SAI1_B	SAI2_A	SAI2_B	--	SAI1_A	SAI1_B
0010	UART5_TX	UART5_RX	UART4_TX	--	UART4_RX	USART1_TX	USART1_RX
0011	SPI3_RX	SPI3_TX	--	TIM6_UP DAC_CH1	TIM7_UP DAC_CH2	--	QUADSPI
0100	SWPMI1_RX	SWPMI1_TX	SPI1_RX	SPI1_TX	DCMI(1)	LPUART1_TX	LPUART1_RX
0101	TIM5_CH4 TIM5_TRIG	TIM5_CH3 TIM5_UP	--	TIM5_CH2	TIM5_CH1	I2C1_RX	I2C1_TX
0110	AES_IN	AES_OUT	AES_OUT	--	AES_IN	--	HASH_IN(1)
0111	TIM8_CH3 TIM8_UP	TIM8_CH4 TIM8_TRIG TIM8_COM	--	SDMMC1	SDMMC1	TIM8_CH1	TIM8_CH2

Note 1. Only available on STM32L496xx/4A6xx
Note 2. Only available on STM32L48x/L4Ax devices

A.4.3 PARAMETERS OF DMA OPERATION

The DMA transfer parameters are configured channel by channel. The following parameters must be set up for a DMA transfer:

- Data size. A data transfer can be a byte, a half-word, or a word. The transfer size for the peripheral and memory need not be the same. The transfer size for peripheral and memory are set up by programming the PSIZE[1:0] and MSIZE[1:0] fields in the DMA_x_$Channel_n$->CCR register (x = 1 to 2, n = 1 to 7). The transfer size can be one byte, one half-word, or one word. The contents of the DMA_x_$Channel_n$->CCR register (x = 1 to 2, n = 1 to 7) are shown in Figure AppA.4.
- Pointers. The pointers to the peripheral register and the memory are set up by programming the DMA_x_$Channel_n$->CPAR and DMA_x_$Channel_n$ ->CMAR registers (x = 1 to 2, n = 1 to 7). These two registers are 32 bit in length. Each of these registers has a hidden internal buffer which is updated after each DMA transfer. The DMA_x_$Channel_n$->CPAR and DMA_x_$Channel_n$->CMAR registers do not change during the whole DMA transaction.
- Pointer incrementation. Peripheral or memory pointer can be incremented after each DMA transfer by setting the PINC or MINC bit in the DMA_x_$Channel_n$->CCR register. The amount of increment is defined by the PSIZE or MSIZE field.
- Number of transfers. The number of data items to be transferred is defined by the value contained in the DMA_x_$Channel_n$->CNDTR register (x = 1 to 2, n = 1 to 7). In a noncircular mode, no DMA request is served after the last data transfer.
- Channel priority. The channel priority is defined by the PL[1:0] field in the DMA_x_$Channel_n$->CCR register and can be programmed to be very high, high, medium, or low.
- Transfer direction. The transfer direction is defined by the DIR bit in the DMA_x_$Channel_n$->CCR register and can be **read-from-peripheral** (DIR bit = 0) and **read-from-memory** (DIR bit = 1). The read-from-peripheral direction can be configured to peripheral-to-memory and memory-to-memory versions. The read-from-memory direction can be configured to memory-to-peripheral and

memory-to-memory transfer. The result is that there are four possible transfer directions: peripheral-to-memory, memory-to-peripheral, memory-to-memory, and peripheral-to-peripheral.

- Circular mode. By enabling the circular mode, the DMA controller will transfer the same block of data repeatedly. The circular mode is enabled by setting the CIRC bit in the DMA_x_$Channel_n$->CCR register to 1.

31	30	29	28	27	26	25	24
--	--	--	--	--	--	--	--
23	**22**	**21**	**20**	**19**	**18**	**17**	**16**
--	--	--	--	--	--	--	--
15	**14**	**13**	**12**	**11**	**10**	**9**	**8**
--	MEM2MEM	PL[1:0]		MSIZE[1:0]		PSIZE[1:0]	
7	**6**	**5**	**4**	**3**	**2**	**1**	**0**
MINC	PINC	CIRC	DIR	TEIE	HTIE	TCIE	EN

Reset value = 0x0000 0000
Addr offset = 0x08+14 × (x − 1), x = 1–7

MEM2MEM: memory-to-memory mode
0: disabled 1: enabled
PL[1:0]: priority level
00: low 01: medium 10: high 11: very high
MSIZE[1:0]: memory size-- defines the data size of the identified memory.
00: 8 bits 01: 16 bits 10: 32 bits 11: reserved
In memory-to-memory mode, this field identifies the memory source if DIR = 1 and the memory destination if DIR = 0.
In peripheral-to-peripheral mode, this field identifies the peripheral source if DIR = 1 and the peripheral destination if DIR = 0.
PSIZE[1:0]: peripheral size—defines the data size of the identified peripheral
00: 8 bits 01: 16 bits 10: 32 bits 11: reserved
In memory-to-memory mode, this field identifies the memory destination if DIR = 1 and the memory source if DIR = 0.
In peripheral-to-peripheral mode, this field identifies the peripheral destination if DIR = 1 and the peripheral source if DIR = 0.
MINC: memory increment mode
0: disabled 1: enabled
In memory-to-memory mode, this field identifies the memory source if DIR = 1 and the memory destination if DIR = 0.
In peripheral-to-peripheral mode, this field identifies the peripheral source if DIR = 1 and the peripheral destination if DIR = 0.
PINC: peripheral increment mode
0: disabled 1: enabled
In memory-to-memory mode, this field identifies the memory destination if DIR = 1 and the memory source if DIR = 0.
In peripheral-to-peripheral mode, this field identifies the peripheral destination if DIR = 1 and the peripheral source if DIR = 0.

Figure AppA.4 DMA channel x configuration register (DMA_x_$Channel_n$->CCR)

31	30	29	28	27	26	25	24
--	--	--	--	--	--	--	--
23	**22**	**21**	**20**	**19**	**18**	**17**	**16**
--	--	--	--	--	--	--	--
15	**14**	**13**	**12**	**11**	**10**	**9**	**8**
--	MEM2MEM	PL[1:0]		MSIZE[1:0]		PSIZE[1:0]	
7	**6**	**5**	**4**	**3**	**2**	**1**	**0**
MINC	PINC	CIRC	DIR	TEIE	HTIE	TCIE	EN

Reset value = 0x0000 0000
Addr offset = 0x08+14 × (x − 1), x = 1–7

CIRC: circular mode
0: disabled 1: enabled
DIR: data transfer direction—must be set only in memory-to-peripheral and peripheral-to-memory modes
0: read from peripheral
(a) Source attributes are defined by PSIZE and PINC, plus the DMADMA$_x$_Channel$_n$->CPAR register. This is still valid in a memory-to-memory mode.
(b) Destination attributes are defined by MSIZE and MINC, plus the DMADMA$_x$_Channel$_n$->CMAR register. This is still valid in a memory-to-memory mode.
1: read from memory
(a) Destination attributes are defined by PSIZE and PINC, plus the DMA$_x$_Channel$_n$->CPAR register. This is still valid in a memory-to-memory mode.
(b) Source attributes are defined by MSIZE and MINC, plus DMA$_x$_Channel$_n$->CMAR register. This is still valid in a peripheral-to-peripheral mode.
TEIE: transfer error interrupt enable
0: disabled 1: enabled
HTIE: half transfer interrupt enable
0: disabled 1: enabled
TCIE: transfer complete interrupt enable
0: disabled 1: enabled
EN: channel enable
0: disabled 1: enabled
When a channel transfer error occurs, this bit is cleared by hardware. It cannot be set again until the TEIFx bit of the DMA$_x$->ISR register is cleared.
When this bit is set, all other bits in this register cannot be written.

Figure AppA.4a DMA channel x configuration register (DMA$_x$_Channel$_n$->CCR)—(continued)

A.4.4 ACCESSING BIT FIELDS OF DMA REGISTERS

Macros that define the DMA register bit fields are provided in the **STM32L475xx.h** header file. Three macros are provided for a bit field that has only 1 bit. For example, the DIR bit of the DMA1_Channel1->CCR register has the following macro definitions:

```
#define DMA_CCR_DIR_Pos   (4U)                       // bit position is 4
#define DMA_CCR_DIR_Msk   (0x1U<<DMA_CCR_DIR_Pos)    // shift right 4 places
#define DMA_CCR_DIR       DMA_CCR_DIR_Msk
```

With these macro definitions, the name DMA_CCR_DIR is equal to the value of 0x00000010.

A bit field with 2 bits has 5 macro definitions. For example, the 2-bit MSIZE field has the following macro definitions:

```
1  #define  DMA_CCR_MSIZE_Pos   (10U)                          // bit position 10
2  #define  DMA_CCR_MSIZE_Msk   (0x3U<<DMA_CCR_MSIZE_Pos)      // shift left 10 places
3  #define  DMA_CCR_MSIZE       DMA_CCR_MSIZE_Msk
4  #define  DMA_CCR_MSIZE_0     (0x1U<<DMA_CCR_MSIZE_Pos)
5  #define  DMA_CCR_MSIZE_1     (0x2U<<DMA_CCR_MSIZE_Pos)
```

With these macro definitions, the bit field values **01**$_2$ and **10**$_2$ have been provided by the 4th and the 5th macros. The bit field value **11**$_2$ can be obtained by adding DMA_CCR_MIZE_0 and DMA_CCR_MSIZE_1 together. For example, the following statement sets DIR field to 1 and the MSIZE field to **10**$_2$ for the channel1 of the DMA1:

```
DMA1_Channel1->CCR  &= ~DMA_CCR_MSIZE;       // clear the MSIZE field
DMA1_Channel1->CCR |= (DMA_CCR_DIR + DMA_CCR_MSIZE_1);
```

When the value of all bit fields are to be set in one assignment, then simply add the appropriate macro names of all bit fields and assign the sum to the corresponding DMA register.

A.4.5 CHANNEL CONFIGURATION PROCEDURE

To configure a DMA channel, follow this procedure:

Step 1

Set up the peripheral address in the DMA$_x$_Channel$_n$->CPAR register.

Step 2

Set up the memory address in the DMA$_x$_Channel$_n$->CMAR register.

Step 3

Configure the total number of data to transfer in the DMA$_x$_Channel$_n$->CNDTR register.

Step 4

Configure the parameters listed below in the DMA$_x$_Channel$_n$->CCR register:

- The channel priority
- The data transfer direction
- The circular mode
- The peripheral and memory increment mode
- The peripheral and memory data size
- The interrupt enable at half and/or full transfer and/or transfer error

Step 5

Activate the channel by setting the EN bit in the DMA_x_$Channel_n$->CCR register.

The last two steps may be merged into a single access to the DMA_x_$Channel_n$->CCR register, to configure and enable the channel.

Example A.1 Write a C function to initialize the channel 3 of DMA1 in the following manner:

- Configure DMA1 channel 3 so that the DMA requests from SPI1 are selected
- Transfer data from memory array DacArray[60] to the SPI1 data register
- Set transfer count to 60
- Enable circular mode
- Set DMA priority to the highest level
- Set transfer size to 16 bits
- Enable memory increment mode
- Fixed peripheral address

Solution: The following function performs the specified configuration:

```
void DMA1_Channe3_Init(void)
{
  DMA1_CSELR->CSELR         = 0x01 << 8; // assign SPI1 DMA request to DMA1 channel 3
  DMA1_Channel3->CPAR       = (uint32_t)(SPI1 + 0x0C);
  DMA1_Channel3->CMAR       = (uint32_t)DacArray;
  DMA1_Channel3->CNDTR      = 60;
  DMA1_Channel3->CCR        = DMA_CCR_PL_1 + DMA_CCR_MSIZE_0 +
                              DMA_CCR_PSIZE_0 + DMA_CCR_MINC + DMA_CCR_CIRC +
                              DMA_CCR_DIR + DMA_CCR_EN;
}
```

A.4.6 DMA ARBITRATION

The DMA arbiter manages the priority between the different channels. When an active channel n is granted by the arbiter, a single DMA transfer is issued (such as an AHB read followed by write transfer of a single data). Then, the arbiter considers the set of active channels and selects the one with the highest priority.

The channel priorities are managed in two stages:

- Software: The priority of each channel is configured in the DMA_x_$Channel_n$_CCR register to one of the four different levels: very high, high, medium, or low.
- Hardware: If two requests have the same software priority level, the channel with the lower index gets priority. For example, channel 2 gets priority over channel 4.

A.4.7 MEMORY-TO-MEMORY MODE

When a DMA channel operates without being triggered by a request from a peripheral, it is operating in memory-to-memory mode. This mode is initiated by software.

When a DMA channel is enabled, the memory-to-memory DMA transfer is started by setting the MEM2MEM bit in the DMA_x_$Channel_n$->CCR register to 1. The transfer stops once the DMA_x_$Channel_n$->CNDTR register is decremented to 0. The memory-to-memory mode should not be used in the circular mode.

The memory-to-memory mode can be entered from either memory-to-peripheral mode (DIR = 1) or from the peripheral-to-memory mode (DIR = 0).

When DIR = 1,

- Write the source (a memory block) attributes of the transfer into the DMAx_Channeln->CMAR register, the MSIZE[1:0] field, and the MINC bit in the DMAx_Channeln->CCR register.
- Write the destination (also a memory block) attributes into the DMA_x_$Channel_n$->CPAR register, the PSIZE[1:0] field, and the PINC bit of the DMA_x_$Channel_n$->CCR register.

When DIR = 0,

- Write the source (a memory block) attributes of the transfer into the DMA_x_$Channel_n$->PAR register, the PSIZE[1:0] field, and the PINC bit of the DMA_x_$Channel_n$->CCR register.
- Write the destination (also a memory block) attributes of the transfer into the DMA_x_$Channel_n$->CMAR register, the MSIZE[1:0] field, and the MINC bit in the DMA_x_$Channel_n$->CCR register.

Example A.2 Write a sequence of C statements to copy the array **array1** to **array2**. The array array1 is an array of 30 32-bit elements that has been initialized. The array array2 is declared to be an array of 30 32-bit elements but not initialized.

Solution: We will use DMA1, channel 1 to perform the transfer.

```
// use read from memory mode to transfer (set DIR bit to 1)
    DMA1_CSELR->CSELR = ~DMA_CSELR_C1S; // use DMA1 channel 1 to perform transfer
    DMA1_Channel1->CMAR = (uint32_t)array1;
    DMA1_Channel1->CPAR = (uint32_t)array2;
    DMA1_Channel1->CNDTR = 30;
    DMA1_Channel1->CCR = DMA_CCR_PL_1 + DMA_CCR_MSIZE_1 + DMA_CCR_PSIZE_1 +
                DMA_CCR_MINC + DMA_CCR_PINC + DMA_CCR_DIR + DMA_CCR_EN;
    DMA1_Channel1->CCR |= DMA_CCR_MEM2MEM; // start DMA transfer
```

In this example, we can also set DIR to 0. Using this DIR setting, the contents of CPAR and CMAR must be swapped. Memory-to-memory transfer can be performed in any channel of the DMA1 or DMA2 controller.

A.4.8 ENABLING PERIPHERAL TO PERFORM DMA TRANSFER

A peripheral can request DMA transfer if it is enabled. For example, the user can enable a USART peripheral to perform DMA transfer on transmission and reception and disable DMA transfer when there is a reception error by programming the DMAT and DMAR bit in the USARTx->CR3 register (x = 1 to 3). An ADC peripheral can be enabled to transfer the A/D conversion result stored in the ADC->DR register to a memory location or a data register of another peripheral by setting the DMAEN bit in the ADCx->CFGR register (x = 1 to 3). The channels 1 and 2 of the DAC peripheral can be configured to perform DMA transfer by setting the DMAEN1 and DMAEN2 bits in the DAC->CR register. Readers are encouraged to look up the reference manual of the STM32L475 to find out the appropriate DMA control bit for each peripheral that can utilize DMA to automate data transfer.

A.4.9 PERIPHERAL-TO-PERIPHERAL MODE

Any DMA channel can operate in peripheral-to-peripheral mode in two ways:

- Using the hardware request from a peripheral to trigger the DMA channel. This peripheral is the DMA initiator and paces the data transfer from/to this peripheral to/from a register belonging to another memory-mapped peripheral (this one being not configured in DMA mode).
- No peripheral request is selected and connected to the DMA channel. The software configures a register-to-register transfer by setting the MEM2MEM bit of the DMA_x_$Channel_n$->CCR register.

The source and destination attributes of the DMA transfer must be set up. The setting of the DIR bit in the DMA_x_$Channel_n$->CCR register determines how to set them up:

- When DIR = 1: the attributes of the source peripheral must be loaded into the DMA_x_$Channel_n$->CMAR register, the MSIZE[1:0] field, and the MINC bit in the DMA_x_$Channel_n$->CCR register. The attributes of the destination peripheral must be loaded into the DMA_x_$Channel_n$->CPAR register, the PSIZE[1:0] field, and the PINC bit in the DMA_x_$Channel_n$->CCR register.
- When DIR = 0: the attributes of the source peripheral must be loaded into the DMA_x_$Channel_n$->CPAR register, the PSIZE[1:0] field, and the PINC bit in the DMA_x_$Channel_n$->CCR register. The attributes of the destination peripheral must be loaded into the DMA_x_$Channel_n$->CMAR register, the MSIZE[1:0] field, and the MINC bit in the DMA_x_$Channel_n$->CCR register.

Example A.3 Write a sequence of C statements to set up the DMA transfer from ADC3 to DAC channel 1 using 12-bit resolution. Use DMA2.

Solution: When enabled, the A/D converter ADC1 can request a DMA transfer when A/D conversion result is available in the ADC1->DR register. The address of the ADC1->DR register is **ADC1 + 0x40**. The variable ADC1 is defined as a pointer to the first A/D converter in the stm32L475xx.h header file. To start a DAC conversion on channel 1, the processor writes the value to be converted to one of the following front-end holding register:

- DAC->DHR12R1: DAC channel 1, 12-bit, right-aligned holding register
- DAC->DHR12L1: DAC channel 1, 12-bit, left-aligned holding register
- DAC->DHR8R1: DAC channel 1, 8-bit, right-aligned holding register

In this example, we will use 12-bit resolution, right-aligned mode. The address of the DAC->DHR12R1 is **DAC + 0x08**.

The following sequence of C statements performs the specified configuration:

```
DMA2_CSELR->CSELR = 0x03; // use DMA2 channel 3 to carry out transfer

DMA2_Channel3->CMAR = (uint32_t)DAC + 0x08;

DMA2_Channel3->CPAR = (uint32_t)ADC1 + 0x40;

DMA2_Channel3->CNDTR = 1;

DMA2_Channel3->CCR = DMA_CCR_PL_1 + DMA_CCR_MSIZE_0 + DMA_CCR_PSIZE_0 +

                      DMA_CCR_EN;

ADC1->CFGR |= ADC_CFGR_DMAEN; // enable ADC DMA transfer
```

A.4.10 DMA DATA WIDTH, ALIGNMENT, AND ENDIANNESS

When the PSIZE[1:0] and MSIZE[1:0] fields in the DMA_x_$Channel_n$->CCR register are not equal, the DMA controller performs data alignment during the data transfer process. The data alignment among different data width is illustrated in Table A.3.

Table A.3 Programmable data width and endian behavior(when PINC = MINC = 1)

Source Port width	destination Port width	Number of data items to transfer	Source content: Address/data	DMA Transfer	Destination content: Address/data
8	8	4	@0x0 / B0 @0x1 / B1 @0x2 / B2 @0x3 /B3	1: read B0[7:0] @0x0 then write B0[7:0] @0x0 2: read B1[7:0] @0x1 then write B1[7:0] @0x1 3: read B2[7:0] @0x2 then write B2[7:0] @0x2 4: read B3[7:0] @0x3 then write B3[7:0] @0x3	@0x0 / B0 @0x1 / B1 @0x2 / B2 @0x3 / B3
8	16	4	@0x0 / B0 @0x1 / B1 @0x2 / B2 @0x3 /B3	1: read B0[7:0] @0x0 then write 00B0[15:0] @0x0 2: read B1[7:0] @0x1 then write 00B1[15:0] @0x2 3: read B2[7:0] @0x2 then write 00B2[15:0] @0x4 4: read B3[7:0] @0x3 then write 00B3[15:0] @0x6	@0x0 / 00B0 @0x2 / 00B1 @0x4 / 00B2 @0x6 / 00B3
8	32	4	@0x0 / B0 @0x1 / B1 @0x2 / B2 @0x3 /B3	1: read B0[7:0] @0x0 then write 000000B0[31:0] @0x0 2: read B1[7:0] @0x1 then write 000000B1[31:0] @0x4 3: read B2[7:0] @0x2 then write 000000B2[31:0] @0x8 4: read B3[7:0] @0x3 then write 000000B3[31:0] @0xC	@0x0 / 000000B0 @0x4 / 000000B1 @0x8 / 000000B2 @0xC / 000000B3
16	8	4	@0x0 / B1B0 @0x2 / B3B2 @0x4 / B5B4 @0x6 /B7B6	1: read B1B0[15:0] @0x0 then write B0[7:0] @0x0 2: read B3B2[15:0] @0x2 then write B2[7:0] @0x1 3: read B5B4[15:0] @0x4 then write B4[7:0] @0x2 4: read B7B6[15:0] @0x6 then write B6[7:0] @0x3	@0x0 / B0 @0x1 / B2 @0x2 / B4 @0x3 / B6
16	16	4	@0x0 / B1B0 @0x2 / B3B2 @0x4 / B5B4 @0x6 /B7B6	1: read B1B0[15:0] @0x0 then write B1B0[15:0] @0x0 2: read B3B2[15:0] @0x2 then write B3B2[15:0] @0x2 3: read B5B4[15:0] @0x4 then write B5B4[15:0] @0x4 4: read B7B6[15:0] @0x6 then write B7B6[15:0] @0x6	@0x0 / B1B0 @0x2 / B3B2 @0x4 / B5B4 @0x6 / B7B6
16	32	4	@0x0 / B1B0 @0x2 / B3B2 @0x4 / B5B4 @0x6 /B7B6	1: read B1B0[15:0] @0x0 then write 0000B1B0[31:0] @0x0 2: read B3B2[15:0] @0x2 then write 0000B3B2[31:0] @0x4 3: read B5B4[15:0] @0x4 then write 0000B5B4[31:0] @0x8 4: read B7B6[15:0] @0x6 then write 0000B7B6[31:0] @0xC	@0x0 / 0000B1B0 @0x4 / 0000B3B2 @0x8 / 0000B5B4 @0xC / 0000B7B6
32	8	4	@0x0 / B3B2B1B0 @0x4 / B7B6B5B4 @0x8 / BBBAB9B8 @0xC / BFBEBDBC	1: read B3B2B1B0[31:0] @0x0 then write B0[7:0] @0x0 2: read B7B6B5b4[31:0] @0x4 then write B4[7:0] @0x1 3: read BBBAB9B8[31:0] @0x8 then write B8[7:0] @0x2 4: read BFBEBDBC[31:0] @0xC then write BC[7:0] @0x3	@0x0 / B0 @0x1 / B4 @0x2 / B8 @0x3 / BC
32	16	4	@0x0 / B3B2B1B0 @0x4 / B7B6B5B4 @0x8 / BBBAB9B8 @0xC / BFBEBDBC	1: read B3B2B1B0[31:0] @0x0 then write B1B0[15:0] @0x0 2: read B7B6B5B4[31:0] @0x4 then write B5B4[15:0] @0x2 3: read BBBAB9B8[31:0] @0x8 then write B9B8[15:0] @0x4 4: read BFBEBDBC[31:0] @0xC then write BDBC[15:0] @0x6	@0x0 / B1B0 @0x2 / B5B4 @0x4 / B9B8 @0x6 / BDBC
32	32	4	@0x0 / B3B2B1B0 @0x4 / B7B6B5B4 @0x8 / BBBAB9B8 @0xC / BFBEBDBC	1: read B3B2B1B0[31:0] @0x0 then write B3B2B1B0[31:0] @0x0 2: read B7B6B5B4[31:0] @0x4 then write B7B6B5B4[31:0] @0x4 3: read BBBAB9B8[31:0] @0x8 then write BBBAB9B8[31:0] @0x8 4: read BFBEBDBC[31:0] @0xC then write BFBEBDBC[31:0] @0xC	@0x0 / B3B2B1B0 @0x4 / B7B6B5B4 @0x8 / BBBAB9B8 @0xC / BFBEBDBC

A.4.11 DMA INTERRUPTS

Each DMA channel has four interrupt flags:

- Transfer error flag (TEIF)
- Half-transfer flag (HTIF)
- Transfer complete flag (TCIF)
- Global interrupt flag (GIF)

The GIF flag is set whenever one of the other three flags is set. The first three interrupt flags may generate an interrupt to the CPU if they are enabled. All seven channel interrupt flags are recorded in the DMA_x->ISR register (x = 1 0r 2). These interrupts are enabled by programming the corresponding bits in the DMA_x_

Channel$_n$->CCR register. The DMA interrupt flags can be cleared by writing into the DMA interrupt flag clear (DMAx->IFCR) register. The contents of the DMAx->ISR and DMAx->IFCR register are shown in Figures A.5 and A.6, respectively.

31	30	29	28	27	26	25	24
--	--	--	--	TEIF7	HTIF7	TCIF7	GIF7
23	**22**	**21**	**20**	**19**	**18**	**17**	**16**
TEIF6	HTIF6	TCIF6	GIF6	TEIF5	HTIF5	TCIF5	GIF5
15	**14**	**13**	**12**	**11**	**10**	**9**	**8**
TEIF4	HTIF4	TCIF4	GIF4	TEIF3	HTIF3	TCIF3	GIF3
7	**6**	**5**	**4**	**3**	**2**	**1**	**0**
TEIF2	HTIF2	TCIF2	GIF2	TEIF1	HTIF1	TCIF1	GIF1

Reset value = 0x0000 0000
Addr offset = 0x00

TEIF$_n$: transfer error (TE) flag for channel n (n = 1~7)
A DMA transfer error is generated when reading from or writing to a reserved address space.
0: No TE event 1: a TE event occurred
HTIF$_n$: Half transfer (HT) flag for channel n (n = 1~7)
This flag is set when the DMA transfer count is decremented to half of its original value.
0: No HT event 1: a HT event occurred
TCIF$_n$: Transfer complete flag for channel n (n = 1~7)
This flag is set when the DMA transfer count is decremented to zero.
0: No TC event 1: a TC event occurred.
GIF$_n$: Global interrupt flag for channel n (n = 1~7)
This flag is set if at least of one the TEIFn, HTIFn, and TCIFn flags is set.
0: No TE, HT, or TC event 1: a TE, HT, or TC event occurred

Figure A.5 DMA interrupt status register (DMAx->ISR)

31	30	29	28	27	26	25	24
--	--	--	--	CTEIF7	CHTIF7	CTCIF7	CGIF7
23	**22**	**21**	**20**	**19**	**18**	**17**	**16**
CTEIF6	CHTIF6	CTCIF6	CGIF6	CTEIF5	CHTIF5	CTCIF5	CGIF5
15	**14**	**13**	**12**	**11**	**10**	**9**	**8**
CTEIF4	CHTIF4	CTCIF4	CGIF4	CTEIF3	CHTIF3	CTCIF3	CGIF3
7	**6**	**5**	**4**	**3**	**2**	**1**	**0**
CTEIF2	CHTIF2	CTCIF2	CGIF2	CTEIF1	CHTIF1	CTCIF1	CGIF1

Reset value = 0x0000 0000
Addr offset = 0x04

Setting the global clear bit CGIFn of the channel n in this DMAx->IFCR register, causes the DMA hardware to clear the corresponding GIFn bit and any individual flag among TEIFn, HTIFn, TCIFn, in the DMAx->ISR register.

Setting any individual clear bit among CTEIFn, CHTIFn, CTCIFn in this DMAx->IFCR register, causes the DMA hardware to clear the corresponding individual flag and the global flag GIFx in the DMAx->ISR register, provided that none of the two other individual flags is set. Writing 0 into any flag clear bit has no effect.
CTEIFn: transfer error flag clear for channel n (n = 1~7)
CHTIFn: half transfer flag clear for channel n (n = 1~7)
CTCIFn: transfer complete flag clear for channel n (n = 1~7)
CGIFn: global interrupt flag clear for channel n (n = 1~7)

Figure A.6 DMA interrupt flag clear register (DMAx->IFCR)

A.5 Exercises

EA.1 Write a sequence of C statements to associate the USART1_RX to DMA1 channel 4 and enable it to perform DMA transfer. The received data (from the USART1->RDR register) will be stored in the input buffer inBuf1[40]. When 25 bytes are received and saved in inBuf1, stop the DMA.

EA.2 Write a sequence of C statements to associate the USART1_TX to DMA1 channel 5 and enable it to perform DMA transfer. The data to be written into the USART1->TDR register are stored in the array outBuf1[50]. DMA stops when 40 characters have been transferred to the USART1->TDR register.

EA.3 Write a sequence of C statements to associate the USART2_RX to DMA1 channel 6 and enable it to perform DMA transfer. The received data (from the USART2->RDR register) will be stored in the input buffer inBuf2[40]. DMA stops when 25 bytes have been received and saved in inBuf2.

EA.4 Write a sequence of C statements to associate the USART2_TX to DMA1 channel 7 and enable it to perform DMA transfer. The data to be written into the USART2->TDR register are stored in the array outBuf2[50]. DMA stops when 40 characters have been transferred to the USART2->TDR register.

EA.5 Write a sequence of C statements to associate the I2C1_TX to DMA1 channel 6 and enable it to perform DMA transfer. The data to written into the I2C1->TXDR register are stored in the output buffer outBuf3[40]. When 40 bytes have been transferred, stop the DMA.

EA.6 Write a sequence of statements to associate the I2C1_RX to DMA1 channel 7 and enable it to perform DMA transfer. The received data (the I2C1->RXDR register) will be stored in the input buffer inBuf3[40]. DMA stops when 30 bytes have been received and stored in inBuf3.

B

Music Note Frequencies

A_4 = 440 Hz

Speed of sound = 345 m/s

(Middle C is C_4)

Table AppB_01 Complete list of frequencies of music notes (Page 1)

Note	Frequency (Hz)	Wavelength (cm)	Note	Frequency (Hz)	Wavelength (cm)
C_0	16.35	2100	$G^{\#}_1/A^b_1$	51.91	665
$C^{\#}_0/D^b_0$	17.32	1990	A_1	55.00	627
D_0	18.35	1870	$A^{\#}_1/B^b_1$	58.27	592
$D^{\#}_0/E^b_0$	19.45	1770	B_1	61.74	559
E_0	20.60	1670	C_2	65.41	527
F_0	21.83	1580	$C^{\#}_2/D^b_2$	69.30	498
$F^{\#}_0/G^b_0$	23.12	1490	D_2	73.42	470
G_0	24.50	1400	$D^{\#}_2/E^b_2$	77.78	444
$G^{\#}_0/A^b_0$	25.96	1320	E_2	82.41	419
A_0	27.50	1250	F_2	87.31	395
$A^{\#}_0/B^b_0$	29.14	1180	$F^{\#}_2/G^b_2$	92.50	373
B_0	30.87	1110	G_2	98.00	352
C_1	32.70	1050	$G^{\#}_2/A^b_2$	103.83	332
$C^{\#}_1/D^b_1$	34.65	996	A_2	110.00	314
D_1	36.71	940	$A^{\#}_2/B^b_2$	116.54	296
$D^{\#}_1/E^b_1$	38.89	887	B_2	123.47	279
E_1	41.20	837	C_3	130.81	264
F_1	43.65	790	$C^{\#}_3/D^b_3$	138.59	249
$F^{\#}_1/G^b_1$	46.25	746	D_3	146.83	235
G_1	49.00	704	$D^{\#}_3/E^b_3$	155.56	222

Table AppB.2 Complete list of frequencies of music notes (page 2)

Note	Frequency (Hz)	Wavelength (cm)	Note	Frequency (Hz)	Wavelength (cm)
E_3	164.81	209	C_5	523.25	65.9
F_3	174.61	198	$C^{\#}_5/D^b_5$	554.37	62.2
$F^{\#}_3/G^b_3$	185.00	186	D_5	587.33	58.7
G_3	196.00	176	$D^{\#}_5/E^b_5$	622.25	55.4
$G^{\#}_3/A^b_3$	207.65	166	E_5	659.26	52.3
A_3	220.00	157	F_5	698.46	49.4
$A^{\#}_3/B^b_3$	233.08	148	$F^{\#}_5/G^b_5$	739.99	46.6
B_3	246.94	140	G_5	783.99	44.0
C_4	261.63	132	$G^{\#}_5/A^b_5$	830.61	41.5
$C^{\#}_4/D^b_4$	277.18	124	A_5	880.00	39.2
D_4	293.66	117	$A^{\#}_5/B^b_5$	932.33	37.0
$D^{\#}_4/E^b_4$	311.13	111	B_5	987.77	34.9
E_4	329.63	105	C_6	1046.50	33.0
F_4	349.23	98.8	$C^{\#}_6/D^b_6$	1108.73	31.1
$F^{\#}_4/G^b_4$	369.99	93.2	D_6	1174.66	29.4
G_4	392.00	88.0	$D^{\#}_6/E^b_6$	1244.51	27.7
$G^{\#}_4/A^b_4$	415.30	83.1	E6	1318.51	26.2
A_4	440.00	78.4	F_6	1396.91	24.7
$A^{\#}_4/B^b_4$	466.16	74.0	$F^{\#}_6/G^b_6$	1479.98.98	23.3
B_4	493.88	69.9	G_6	1567.98	22.0

Table AppB.3 Complete list of frequencies of music notes (page3)

Note	Frequency (Hz)	Wavelength (cm)
$G^{\#}_6/A^b_6$	1661.22	20.8
A_6	1760.00	19.6
$A^{\#}_6/B^b_6$	1864.66	18.5
B_6	1975.53	17.5
C_7	2093.00	16.5
$C^{\#}_7/D^b_7$	2217.46	15.6
D_7	2349.32	14.7
$D^{\#}_7/E^b_7$	2489.02	13.9
E_7	2637.02	13.1
F_7	2793.83	12.3
$F^{\#}_7/G^b_7$	2959.96	11.7
G_7	3135.96	11.0
$G^{\#}_7/A^b_7$	3322.44	10.4
A_7	3520.00	9.8
$A^{\#}_7/B^b_7$	3729.31	9.3
B_7	3951.07	8.7
C_8	4186.01	8.2
$C^{\#}_8/D^b_8$	4434.92	7.8
D_8	4698.64	7.3
$D^{\#}_8/E^b_8$	4978.03	6.9

References

1. ARM Inc., "Arm_SB_Q4_2018_Roadshow_Slides_FINAL," March 2019.
2. Han-Way Huang, "PIC Microcontroller: An introduction to Software and Hardware Interfacing," 2005, Thomson Delmar Learning.
3. Wikipedia, "Serial peripheral interface." https://en.wikipedia.org/wiki/Serial_Peripheral_Interface#cite_note-W25Q16JV-17
4. ST Microelectronics, "RM0395 Reference Manual—STM32L4x5 advanced ARM-based 32-bit MCU," February 2016.
5. ST Microelectronics, "RM0351 Reference Manual—STM32L4x5 and STM32L4x6 advanced ARM-based 32-bit MCU," April 2018.
6. Texas Instrument, "TMS320F2837xS Delfino Microcontrollers Technical Reference Manual," September 2017.

www.ingramcontent.com/pod-product-compliance
Lightning Source LLC
LaVergne TN
LVHW062033101126
852251LV00025B/324
* 9 7 9 8 3 8 5 1 2 7 0 2 3 *